D0724189

THE
PEOPLE
OF ANCIENT
ISRAEL
AN INTRODUCTION
TO OLD TESTAMENT
LITERATURE, HISTORY,
AND THOUGHT

THE PEOPLE OF ANCIENT ISRAEL

AN INTRODUCTION TO OLD TESTAMENT LITERATURE, HISTORY, AND THOUGHT

J. KENNETH KUNTZ
The University of Iowa

Harper & Row, Publishers
New York, Evanston, San Francisco, London

To My Parents

Sponsoring Editor: Walter H. Lippincott, Jr.
Project Editor: Alice M. Solomon
Designer: Emily Harste
Production Supervisor: Bernice Krawczyk

Cover photograph courtesy of Georg Gerster, Rapho Guillumette

THE PEOPLE OF ANCIENT ISRAEL
An Introduction to Old Testament Literature, History, and Thought

Library of Congress Cataloging in Publication Data

Kuntz, John Kenneth.
    The people of ancient Israel.

    Bibliography: p.
    1. Bible. O. T.—Introductions.   2. Bible. O. T.
—History of Biblical events.   I. Title.
BS1140.2.K86   221.9'5   74-8042
ISBN 0-06-043822-3

CONTENTS

CHRONOLOGICAL CHARTS

MAPS

PHOTOGRAPHS

PREFACE

This book is an introduction to an ancient literature that has played a crucial role in the development of three great religions of the Western world—Judaism, Christianity, and Islam. It seeks especially to acquaint the reader, who more often than not will be an undergraduate college or university student, with the people who gave birth to that literature, and it portrays their origins, growth, demise, and renewal in some detail.

Whether these writings be collectively designated as the Old Testament (following the example of Christians) or the Hebrew Bible or Tanak (in accord with Jewish practice), even today they enjoy considerable status and authority. Nevertheless, respect for and understanding of religious literature are not necessarily one and the same. Some people who maintain that their faith is firmly anchored in the biblical tradition do not find the Bible easy to read. And others who are indifferent to ecclesiastical institutions yet genuinely interested in the Bible do not feel adequately skilled in the art of reading and comprehending ancient texts.

The need for secondary texts in the field of biblical studies is therefore authentic. Although it is largely answered by numerous Old Testament surveys that are presently available, the need for another is not a fiction. Certainly the accumulating findings based on contemporary scholarly research deserve to be passed on in an uncomplicated manner to the interested layman. But the question of how the biblical traditions are best communicated to inquiring nonspecialists has never been fully resolved. For example, the method of locating the Old Testament literature in a historical-chronological setting has often been embraced by authors of secondary texts. Yet some critics have recently protested that this splits up the large literary groupings of Law, Prophets, and Writings, which merit inspection in their canonical integrity.

In the light of the continuing debate and the realization that no method is truly flawless, the present text affirms the historical approach. It recognizes that religious literature time and again reflects a real, historical people who possessed certain strengths and weaknesses, and that it was informed by specific goals. Clearly, the ancient Israelites did not live in a cultural vacuum. As the accumulating archaeological evidence never ceases to remind us, they were but one segment among the heterogeneous human family that inhabited the ancient Near Eastern world. Therefore, knowledge about ancient Israel's historical, sociological, and intellectual context directly bears upon an understanding of her literature. To be sure, serious study of the literary traditions can be a very fascinating and worthwhile endeavor. But we dare not forget that the Old Testament message itself issues from the long history of a people made up of leaders, followers, and even deserters.

With rare exception, we shall affirm the widely accepted chronology of William F. Albright as it is embraced and somewhat modified by John Bright in his *History of Israel* (1972). Every book of the Hebrew Bible will be examined, although those that present the ancient Israelites most fully will be treated at greater length. Now and then we shall cite and comment on crucial extrabiblical texts that clarify one or more aspects of Israelite history, literature, and thought. Above all, we shall be concerned with the biblical text. Therefore, let it be clear from the outset that this introduction is never intended as a substitute for the Bible itself; it is to be read with the Bible at hand—and open!

Several words of acknowledgment are assuredly in order. The sound scholarship and outstanding teaching of my Old Testament professors at Union Theological Seminary, in New York City—James Muilenburg, Samuel L. Terrien, and George M. Landes—have remained a vital source of inspiration. My approach to the biblical traditions has been further informed and sharpened by a decade of teaching the Old Testament to many able undergraduates at Wellesley College and the University of Iowa. They have offered me much challenge and reward. I am grateful to Walter H. Lippincott, Jr., of the College Department at Harper & Row, for his encouragement and sound counsel, and to Alice M. Solomon, Project Editor of this book. The faithful help of my research assistants, Henry J. Postel, Gordon A. Folke, Gary S. Maxey, William A. Young, and Dale S. Wright is fondly acknowledged. Each of these graduate students in turn supported my work on the emerging manuscript. I am likewise indebted to James C. Spalding, director of the School of Religion at the University of Iowa, for his personal interest in this undertaking. The secretaries in the School of Religion also cheerfully answered my appeals for help.

To my wife, Ruth, goes my most enthusiastic expression of gratitude. Not only did she assist me in clarifying what was vague and in weeding out most of the jargon, but she also typed much of the initial draft of the manuscript and joined our children, David and Nancy, in helping a preoccupied author to maintain perspective. Finally, this book is dedicated to my parents, John F. and Zula Reed Kuntz, who through their informal teaching initiated my exposure to the Bible. They have always encouraged me in my quest to explore the world of the Bible and permitted me the freedom to reflect in my own idiom on what I have seen and heard.

J. Kenneth Kuntz

Part I

AN INTRODUCTION TO THE PEOPLE

1

THE OLD TESTAMENT TODAY: ANCIENT TRADITIONS INTERSECT WITH A MODERN WORLD

If you were to open a copy of the Old Testament[1] and turn its pages at random, your eyes might light on such assertions as the following:

> Then Yahweh said to Cain, "Where is Abel your brother?" He said, "I do not know; am I my brother's keeper?" (Gen. 4:9)

> You shall not revile God, nor curse a ruler of your people. (Exod. 22:28)

> Yahweh said to Joshua . . . "No man shall be able to stand before you all the days of your life; as I was with Moses, so I will be with you." (Josh. 1:5)

> Wise men lay up knowledge,
>   but the babbling of a fool brings ruin near. (Prov. 10:14)

> Let justice roll down like waters,
>   and righteousness like an ever-flowing stream. (Amos 5:24)[2]

Out of context such verses mean little. Yet collectively they might lead you to infer that the Old Testament presents diverse perspectives from a wide range of human experience and reflection. If you were to read several chapters of the Old Testament, you would conclude that in matters probably related to industry and technology the Hebrew Scriptures have little to offer. And if you were to sample the quite readable Joseph narrative in Genesis 37, 39–50, you might respond, "It's interesting, but Joseph's historical situation and my own have little in common." Still you might be willing to acknowledge, partly because so many people do, that the Bible has remarkable staying power. Modern men and women still read it, new translations of it continue to appear, and universities continue to offer introductory courses in the Old and New Testaments.

MAKING CONTACT

But may we reasonably claim in this rather late stage of the twentieth century that the ancient biblical traditions have an abiding value and significance? The answer to this question cannot be forced. Assuredly it invites the candid personal response of individual readers of the Bible. Moreover, undergraduates approach the text from many directions and bring to it quite diverse expectations. A few come to the material with abject piety, a few approach with an insatiable and contagious curiosity, and a few confidently appear with the knowledge that here is one way of fulfilling a distribution requirement for the degree. And by virtue of their presence in the course, all students attest to the sometimes mystifying intersection that involves an ancient text and present-day human existence.

Three goals will govern our deliberations in this chapter. We shall comment on both the relevance and essential stance of the Old Testament. We shall deal with various approaches to reading the biblical text. And we shall present three methods indispensable for a sound comprehension of the life and thought of ancient Israel.

THE RELEVANCE
OF THE OLD TESTAMENT

Generally speaking, the relevance of the Old Testament is upheld by its diligent readers and either challenged or ignored by others. This incredibly ancient document, which is not called the "Old" Testament without good reason, reveals a people who lived and died in antiquity. By the time ancient Rome was founded in the middle of the eighth century B.C., the Israelites of the Old Testament had experienced an appreciable block of history. David and Solomon, who stand at approximately the chronological center of the Old Testament, lived nearly three thousand years ago. Their hopes, actions, and death were unmistakably ancient realities. Yet something seems to have endured, and for want of a better term we call that something "tradition." Despite its ancient origins, that tradition has had a striking influence on contemporary Judaism and Christianity.

Western culture has been informed by the Bible in many ways. Old Testament persons and events abound in classical art, folk music, and the modern novel. We may call to mind Michelangelo's impressive marble statues of Moses and David created in the early 1500s. Of more recent vintage is the delightful ballad "Little Moses," emanating from the Cumberland Mountains and popularized by Mike Seeger. Biblical tradition is skillfully reflected in such classical oratorios as Haydn's *The Creation* (1798) and Mendelssohn's *Elijah* (1846), as well as in

Schoenberg's unfinished opera, *Moses and Aaron* (1932–1951). In Faulkner's *Absalom, Absalom!* (1936) we witness a heavy reliance on selected Davidic traditions in 2 Samuel. Similarly the Bible has informed the penetrating Joseph tetralogy of Thomas Mann (1933–1943) as well as MacLeish's verse drama *J.B.* (1958), which refracts the ancient Job story, and Chayefsky's play *Gideon* (1962), which mirrors the chaotic period of the Israelite judges. Despite its remoteness and diversity, the Old Testament lives on.

Thus, to know the literature of the Old Testament is to become better equipped to deal with today's artistic and intellectual currents. The Hebrew Bible need not be read solely with this purpose in view, yet a study of this ancient literature does yield benefits. We may resort to an analogy: Just as one who lacks knowledge of the Hellenic heritage cannot fully appreciate British literature of the Renaissance, one ignorant of the faiths of Judaism and Christianity cannot fully grasp contemporary Western culture.

The relevance of the Old Testament may be asserted in another way. When one reads this ancient document on its own terms, one transcends barriers of time and space. For example, modern man tends to take history seriously. He makes an effort to discern its basic outlines and movements. He is unwilling to dismiss his environment as illusion. Similarly, Old Testament man was constantly impressed by the realities of his tenuous existence. He lacked the disposition to evaluate his world with complete detachment, but he was impressed with his surroundings. Ordinarily he did not resort to abstractions, yet in his apprehension of time as a haunting, wholly significant aspect of human existence, biblical man has some affinity with modern man.

Finally, part of the relevance of the Old Testament lies in its capacity to reflect the human condition as it actually is experienced, not as one thinks it should be experienced. The main personalities of the Bible do not live without significant goals. First and foremost they impress the reader as real men and women. The fear that overtakes Abraham (Gen. 12:10–20) is paralleled in the uncertainty and distrust that modern man also experiences. Job's detachment from his God is not uncommon in our own time. Job does not understand the seemingly arbitrary ways of God and the world. Here biblical man is grossly alienated from the assumptions of traditional religion (for example, God is always good to the righteous) that assail him from every side. Such alienation is common to ancient and contemporary life alike—so too, is the buck passing in which Adam engages (Gen. 3) when he is called to account by the all-seeing deity. In Gen. 3:12 Adam makes the feeble statement, "The woman whom thou gavest to be with me, she gave me fruit of the tree, and I ate." At a number of turns the Old Testament may help contemporary man to find out who he is.

THE ESSENTIAL STANCE
OF THE OLD TESTAMENT

To summarize the essential stance of the Hebrew Bible in a few paragraphs borders on folly. Yet the reader who approaches this material for the first time has a right to ask what he can expect the Old Testament to say. Despite its vastness and diversity, the Hebrew Bible presents a unified position with respect to God, man, and the world. That position is set within the context of history. It is related to the ongoing sequence of remembered events, happenings that have been designated as the acts of God. The history recorded by the Old Testament spans nearly two millennia. The materials in the Old Testament were written over a period of 1,100 years (ca. 1200–100 B.C.), a period almost equivalent to the stretch of time between the literature of English-speaking peoples from Beowulf of the eighth century A.D. to Virginia Woolf of our century. Nevertheless, the various authors of the Bible generally share a single world view. And that view is most readily accessible to us when we inquire into the biblical perception of history.

Although its emphasis varies from book to book, the Bible is basically oriented along a historical axis. The ancient Israelites held that God continually functioned on the stage of human history. They never lost themselves in metaphysical speculation on historical questions, but they affirmed the importance and vitality of history. They did this primarily through historical credos or statements of faith (for example, Deut. 26:5–9) that witnessed to God's action in the world. There Israel confessed her relatedness to God. She likewise acknowledged her duty to worship the deity with a spirit of joy and thanksgiving. Time and again the ancient Israelites rehearsed God's deeds, which they believed had been accomplished in their behalf (see Deut. 6:20–24; Josh. 24:2–13). It was in this context that human experience took on its greatest significance for the community of faith.

Nowhere in the Hebrew Bible do we find a chapter devoted to a rational defense of God's existence. His active being is simply assumed. The major figures of the Bible (including Abraham, Moses, Samuel, Amos, and Jeremiah) were subject to momentary communion with deity when he intervened in human life and disclosed his name, nature, and will. They would have unanimously consented to the dictum that "God is what he does." Because the Bible consistently discloses a God who acts, biblical theology becomes in large measure a confessional recital of the deeds of God in history.[3]

This affirmation of divine impingement signified that for biblical man, history was essentially an ongoing engagement between man and God. In Exodus 3, for example, Moses is offered only a brief moment to inspect the burning bush. At once he finds himself a central participant in an engrossing I-Thou encounter. The confrontation between God and man recorded in the Hebrew Bible is immediate and personal. And that intrusion is acknowledged as the intervention of God's word. Setting in motion both judgment and salvation, the divine word called the people of God into being and steadily shaped its ongoing existence.

Biblical man persisted in proclaiming that God was at work in the world and that often in the unfolding of history it was God who took the initiative. He believed that in this way his existence acquired direction and meaning. This is obviously an articulation of faith. The discerning reader of the Old Testament may or may not be personally convinced by the confessional claims of this faith. But whatever the quality of his response, he will not doubt that ancient Israelite man was gripped by the notion that God continually intervened in mundane human life.

APPROACHES TO READING
THE BIBLE

Serious discussions about biblical personalities, events, and concepts depend to a great extent on how the Bible is read. And because the text may be read on more than one level, more than one interpretation is justified. Let us consider three approaches that are widely acknowledged as helpful.

First, we may justifiably examine the Bible as living literature. This approach assumes that the biblical text as a whole reveals literary genius. While not defending the esthetic merit of every chapter, it holds that the Bible should be enjoyed as living literature relevant to our sophisticated present. The typical procedure is to establish by some criterion a list of the passages that represent the best literature the Bible has to offer and to read those passages as authentic works of art. Stylistic studies of the Bible have their rightful place in the task of biblical interpretation. The Old Testament has its share of classical literary units. These include the engaging narratives about the patriarchs in Genesis, the realistic court history of David in 2 Samuel, and the expansive and optimistic poetry of Second Isaiah (Isa. 40–55).

The Bible reflects literary genius, yet the biblical writers did not engage in art for art's sake. In our efforts to appreciate its literary merits we should always bear in mind that the Bible is inseparable from the life that gave it birth. Particular occasions evoked this material, and on each occasion the community of faith had something to say. Biblical man did not take lightly how something was said. He was even more concerned, however, with the burden of a particular message. In sum, the careful Old Testament critic will recognize Hebraic artistic forms, but he will also acknowledge that these forms serve the content that they set forth.

A second helpful approach regards the Bible as historical and cultural accumulation open to critical inspection. It recognizes that the Hebrews of the Old Testament were at best a minority in the total population of the ancient Near East. And it contends that insofar as the evidence allows, both the Semitic and non-Semitic peoples may be studied objectively.

Such a method naturally raises questions concerning the reliability of conflicting and complementary biblical traditions. It is concerned with the development and editing of literary sources. Moreover, it is interested in identifying genuine contacts between the literature of the Bible and the literary corpus of the ancient Near East that preceded, and was contemporaneous with the literature of the Bible.

This approach is not preoccupied with matters of belief and disbelief. It seeks neither to prove biblical miracles nor to disprove legends. Instead, it attempts to evaluate as precisely as it can the nature, scope, and intent of various biblical traditions. It assumes that just as it is possible for modern man to study the ancient Egyptians through their literary remains, it is possible to study the ancient Israelites through their written traditions as revealed in Old Testament literature. To read the Bible in this manner is to familiarize oneself with both the events that ancient Israel witnessed and the reaction of the people to those events. When properly pursued, this approach can yield unusually fine results.

Finally, the Bible can be read as a religious—indeed, a theological —document. This approach begins by recognizing the obvious—namely, that the Bible is theocentric. God is persistently thought of as the subject and human life as the object. The writings that make up the Old Testament are permeated with unmistakably religious elements. The biblical writers and the transmitters of oral tradition who preceded them made numerous theological assumptions. These men did not invent a theology. They reflected the theology that was evolving in their own communities.

This theology is typically advanced through spontaneous poetry; it is rarely the prose product of disciplined reason. But this is not to suggest that the religious affirmations are peripheral. Plainly they are not. The Hebrew Scriptures describe many encounters between a God who was thought to be at work in history and a people who were part of that history. Surely if the biblical record is to be read on its own terms, it will be read with this consideration in mind.

LEADING METHODS EMPLOYED
IN BIBLICAL STUDY

In terms of method, the Old Testament is to be grasped along three lines—the literary, the historical, and the theological. Though this categorization coincides with the three approaches to reading the Bible we have just referred to, each methodology merits closer examination.

Literary Analysis

As a body of literature, the Old Testament is fair game for close literary analysis. Ever since the appearance of Eichhorn's three-volume Old Testament Introduction (1780–1783),[4] literary criticism of the Hebrew Scriptures has been refined along scientific lines.

Various concerns challenge the talents of the biblical literary critic. He may wish to establish the most suitable text of a given passage.[5] Or on the basis of certain clues, he may seek to make suggestions concerning its authorship, date, and place of writing. If so, he must relate the passage to the larger literary unit. Further, the literary critic may be interested in such rhetorical matters as meter, style, and diction, and in the formal elements of discourse within a given passage. Here he will pay special attention to the length, movement, and texture of the literary unit as well as its genre. This, in turn, will suggest possibilities about the intent and use of the text. Clearly, literary criticism of the Old Testament is a multifaceted discipline.

As we pursue the method of literary analysis in this book, we shall often become aware that ancient texts lack contemporary counterparts. Ordinarily when we come across a book in the library, we have no trouble in establishing its author, title, publisher, and date of publication. The book's table of contents and index also help us determine its nature and scope. We assume that the book is the product of the author's own mind and that he will acknowledge the influence of other sources in his footnotes. If our purpose in examining the book is to appreciate it as literature, we can focus immediately on matters of style, diction, and content.

What a contrast this is with our approach to the books that comprise the Old Testament. Typically, they embody a significant number of written and oral traditions. The written traditions have been modified, and the oral traditions are now cast in written form for the first time. Both the oral material and the written material are independent units that the biblical author has freely placed in his own work. The writer made the selection from the material available, drawing on that which suited his purposes.

The authors and editors of the books of the Old Testament were firmly rooted in the Israelite community. They were not concerned with literary recognition. As member Israelites they were intent on preserving traditions that they and their contemporaries valued highly. Yet the ways in which they transmitted these traditions invariably bring to contemporary interpreters of the Bible both frustrating and satisfying moments.

The War Scroll from Qumran. The Dead Sea Scrolls
consist of both biblical texts and sectarian writings. Among
the latter is the War Scroll. This military (and theological)
manual offers instructions for the waging of war between
"the sons of light" (the tribes of Levi, Judah, and Benjamin)
and "the sons of darkness" (the Edomites, Moabites,
Ammonites, Philistines, and Greeks). Column 8, which is
shown here, contains directives for the priests and Levites
in the proper trumpet signals for military advance and
retreat. The lower edge of the scroll has been badly damaged
by rodents. Even so, it is a good sample of Hebrew script
presumably dating to the second half of the first century B.C.
(Courtesy of the Consulate General of Israel, New York.)

In the disciplined literary criticism of any book in the Old Testament, such questions as the following are likely to be raised:

1. Does the book incorporate one or more previously existing literary
   sources, and if so what are they? What is the evidence for their
   prior existence and present use?
2. Are one or more oral traditions being set down in writing for the
   first time? What is the evidence?

3. With regard to the book as a whole, who may have been its author and with what degree of certainty may one attach his name to this written material? Should the possibility of multiple authorship be entertained?

4. How much editing has the book received subsequent to its initial writing, and how has this altered its fundamental character? What is the evidence?[6]

5. Where does the book seem to have been written? How secure is the evidence?

6. For what audience was the book intended, and which verses provide an elementary profile of that audience?

7. Have any known historical events stimulated the writing of the book? What is the evidence?

8. To what extent, if any, did the book draw on extrabiblical literature, and how was that literature put to use?

9. When was the book written? Are we to go on general stylistic and ideological impressions, or do specific clues suggest the earliest and latest possible date?

10. What are the book's chief stylistic and rhetorical features, to what extent have they been employed, and how have they assisted in communicating the book's message?

11. On the basis of its message, what seem to be the author's purposes in writing the book?

12. In light of the above questions, what appears to be the primary significance of this biblical book?

In sum, literary criticism devotes itself to a thorough reading of texts. It insists that such a reading will engage the text with penetrating questions. When it is well done, literary criticism paves the way for a cogent interpretation of the biblical message.

A comprehensive literary methodology in Old Testament studies must also take account of what is known as "form criticism." Whether we realize it or not, our lives are directly influenced by specific, easily identifiable forms of discourse. An advertising circular, a classified ad, a telegram, a Gospel hymn, a personal will, and a political address all use language differently. Various situations call for various types of language. And this distinction is the basis of form criticism.

Contemporary writing and ancient literature alike attest that communication has to do not only with what is said but with the form in which it is said. Hence, as Koch writes, "in anything that we read we habitually assimilate not only the sense of the individual sentences but also the particular style of language which is used."[7] This is especially true of ancient writings, in which the author's individuality was of relatively little consequence. Close study of the form of a given piece of writing therefore greatly assists our comprehension of its message and intention.

The pioneer and leading exponent of form criticism was Gunkel

(1862–1932), who outlined the various literary genres of the Old Testament. Gunkel identified the types closely, gathered many examples of each, and established their respective (and somewhat relative) chronological sequences. He hoped to produce a literary history that would take proper account of Israel's literature, her history, and even her spiritual experience.

As Gunkel saw it, form criticism involved three steps. The first was literary classification. Each Old Testament literary type (*Gattung*) was identified. Its formal characteristics were described, its style delineated, and its history traced back to a preliterary stage.

Next each literary type was related to a concrete life setting (*Sitz im Leben*) reflecting the communal existence of the ancient Israelites. Here Gunkel linked the formal literary unit to a living context. He held that instruction was offered by the priest before the sanctuary, terse aphorisms were spoken by the wise men to attentive pupils, verdicts were issued by judges at the city gate, and hymns intoning Yahweh's praise were sung by cultic choirs in the Jerusalem Temple. In this way Gunkel tried to demonstrate that the Old Testament was truly Israel's book and that its literature emerged from the concrete experiences of a real people.

There was also a third step: the comparison of Israelite forms with examples drawn from other literature of the ancient Near East. Thus, certain affinities were established between the Old Testament literature and related materials from Canaanite, Egyptian, and Mesopotamian literature.

Gunkel's approach to Old Testament literature has attracted many disciples, for it regards highly both the literature and the people who created it.[8] In its quest for the preliterary stage of a given literary type, form criticism recognizes the importance of the oral transmission of traditions in the life of the ancient Hebrews. The people of the Old Testament were much more adept at memorizing than we are today. They did not exalt the printed word. In preexilic Israelite culture (prior to 587 B.C.) writing played a rather circumscribed role. Moreover, form-critical studies emphasize that for the ancient Israelites, convention and form often dictated the shape of human discourse. Consequently, many of the hymns in the Psalter sound somewhat alike, and many of the prophets' oracles of woe resemble one another. While there is always room for variation, the mere selection of a given form determines to no small extent the scope of the message to be articulated.

Form criticism is to be commended for its readiness to view ancient Israel within her larger ethnic and cultural context. Israel did not exist in a vacuum. She inhabited a significant land bridge that connected the well-established and influential cultures of Egypt and Mesopotamia. By searching intently for formal parallels in the extrabiblical literature, form criticism acknowledges Israel's contact with the world. As useful as they may be, however, the techniques of form criticism should not be carried to extremes. For example, the charge has been raised that in the work of some form critics, "literary units have been reduced to mere snippets, strophes have been taken for independent poems, resort has been made to precarious emendations . . . and Near Eastern parallels have been exaggerated."[9] Moreover, sometimes so much attention is placed on the presence of conventional elements of discourse and on typical stylistic representations that the Bible's most distinctive qualities are eclipsed. On balance, however, the contributions of form criticism easily outweigh its limitations.

Historical Criticism

Even limited contact with the Old Testament is enough to convince the reader that this ancient document is much concerned with history. The vivid, relatively precise qualities of Israel's historical narrative may be sampled by reading such verses as Judg. 1:19–21 on the Hebrew conquest of Canaan, 1 Kings 12:13–17 on the collapse of the United Monarchy, and 2 Kings 25:1–7 on the Babylonian destruction of Jerusalem. Of course, not every historical text in the Hebrew Bible is equally expressive and readable. Historical narrative abounds, however, and it reflects a strong interest in events and their meaning. This interest was shared by many ancient Israelites who told, wrote, and transmitted ancient Hebrew tradition.

Historical criticism may be defined as the task of reconstructing the matrix of events, social groups, individual personalities, and concepts that were the source of both the literature and thought of ancient Israel. In the process, an intelligible chronology must be established and illumined by careful historical reconstruction. This chronology of biblical events is more easily arrived at for some phases of Israelite life than it is for others. The exilic and postexilic phases of Israelite history are reflected by few historically grounded biblical texts, and the earliest years of Israel's existence are cloaked in mystery. The period of Israel's monarchy, however, is covered rather well.

Approximately a half-century ago, Luckenbill claimed that "History begins with the vanity of kings."[10] It began with the desire of kings to record their military conquests, to put into written form treaties entered into with other nations, and to codify through writing the laws that would be binding on the citizens of a given land. This, of course, presupposed the invention of writing near 3300 B.C. Many centuries later (ca. 1020 B.C.) Israel instituted a monarchical form of government, and recorders and scribes were soon attached to the court so that her own kings could enjoy a little vanity.

It may be argued that the history of Israel should be reconstructed in a manner analogous to the reconstruction of the history of any ancient people. Therefore, contemporary scholars who focus on the history of Israel are called on to evaluate the credibility of the biblical witnesses, measure their theological bias, and move carefully from specific data to generalization. They must be prepared to defend their judgments that one set of biblical texts is historically credible and another is not. Further, extrabiblical documents should be drawn on whenever they assist in the critical assessment of the biblical material. The resulting history of Israel will therefore make its own contribution to our knowledge of ancient world history.

Nevertheless, such method must not lose sight of ancient Israel's uniqueness, which is rooted in her singular reading of historical events. Both ancient and contemporary Judaism have impressed the world with their distinctive grasp of history. Judaism knows perhaps better than any other religion that historical memory is a splendid human talent. In fact, the beginnings of Judaism's historical recollection trace back to formative events that bestowed on those who experienced them and their descendants a strong sense of identity. Israel's experiences of a deliverance from Egypt and a covenant at Sinai could hardly be expected to have accomplished less. Here Israel was profoundly touched by what she discerned to be divine activity on history's stage. She claimed that her God, Yahweh, revealed himself through his concrete dealings in human life. For Israel, history was sanctified by the intrusive divine presence. Her history was sacred history. And this makes Israelite history distinctive in its significant events and fundamental intent.

To be sure, ancient Israel's historical testimonies do not provide all the data of interest to historical criticism. Archaeological findings also feed directly into this discipline.[11] The archaeological discoveries made throughout this century in Syria-Palestine and elsewhere in the Near East have been extensive. Numerous excavations in biblical lands have probed the habitations of many centuries. They have come into close touch with physical remains that precede or are contemporaneous with those centuries witnessed by the Old Testament. And the biblical historian is, of course, interested in the nature and scope of the finds.

It must be said, however, that the chief function of Syro-Palestinian archaeology as it relates to biblical studies is not to prove that the Bible is true. A pointed remark against the position that seeks to present archaeological work as an effort to authenticate the Bible is offered in James A. Michener's novel *The Source* (New York: Random House, 1965), p. 4. There the leading character, John Cullinane, is about to depart from Chicago for archaeological work in Israel. When asked by a newspaper reporter whether he intends to prove the truth of the Bible, Cullinane retorts, "No, we're not out to help God steady the ark." Though such a statement is not intended to deify science, it does respect the objective methods and goals of competent archaeological work. The chief function of Syro-Palestinian archaeology as it relates to biblical studies is to illustrate and explain biblical narrative so that its various elements may be better understood. Because the historian tries to understand rather than to defend the biblical narrative, he must be cautious in his use of archaeological data. Yet when carefully advanced, archaeological insights can bring some historical factors into sharper focus. The archaeologist Nelson Glueck once claimed, "Archaeology becomes the handmaid of history. The ground in which entire civilizations have been buried can be made to reveal its secrets."[12]

Basically, archaeology supplements the Old Testament record. The biblical authors were often quite selective. They did not tell all. Archaeological study often fills in the gaps. For example, the Omri dynasty of Israel (876–842 B.C.) was far more important than the passages in 1 Kings lead us to believe. The Moabite Stone adds much to the scanty eight verses devoted to Omri in 1 Kings 16:21–28. Similarly, the sociological notations of the Nuzi tablets from Mesopotamia, which date from the fifteenth century B.C., facilitate our understanding of certain patriarchal customs attested in Genesis 12–50.

While most of the evidence archaeological field work brings to light is not written evidence, some noteworthy epigraphic specimens are uncovered in each modern decade. Such extrabiblical texts are becoming increasingly plenteous as anyone knows who is familiar with James B. Pritchard's *Ancient Near Eastern Texts Relating to the Old Testament*.[13] With its ample inclusion of ancient myths, epics, legends, legal texts, kings' lists, rituals, hymns, prayers, and historiographic reports, the Pritchard volume brings an alien, distant world closer to today's historian. A careful study of its contents draws the reader into the vibrant thought patterns of the ancient Near East. That mentality obviously relates to Israel's mentality. Though the parallels between this literature and Israel's should not be drawn too easily, such texts can assist the work of Old Testament historical criticism. Often a serious study of such material enables the biblical historian to reconstruct the larger intellectual, cultural, and religious context of which Israel was emphatically a part. In sum, historical criticism benefits greatly from the archaeological and extrabiblical data now available to us.

Theological Interpretation

What It Meant.[14] From first to last, the authors of the Hebrew Bible sought to advance a fundamentally theological view of reality.[15] Biblical literature constantly juxtaposes God and man. It attests that Hebrew man felt keenly the impact of God on his life and that the deity was himself strongly affected by the ways of this people, Israel, whom he had called. Thus, the Old Testament speaks of a continuous interaction involving a summoning God and a people who say yes to the invitation to live in an ongoing relationship with him.

Theological interpretation of the Old Testament examines the prevailing themes of the Hebrew canon, including creation, revelation, election, covenant, sin, judgment, and salvation. In its critical inspection of such themes, theological interpretation uncovers the breadth and depth of the ancient Israelite perspective on God, man, and the world.

Much of the Hebrew Bible meditates on God's creation and maintenance of the cosmos, and his initial and subsequent acts of self-revelation to historical Israel. Much is also said about the deity's infinite concern in electing Israel for the fulfillment of his own purposes, and his participation in a specific covenant or agreement. (The crucial Old Testament term $b^e r\hat{i} th$, rendered by the English noun "covenant," will be defined more precisely in Chapter 6. For the moment, let us accept "agreement" and "contract" as rough equivalents.) Through the covenant and its attendant law, the divine expectation could be clearly perceived. The Hebrew Bible discloses in detail ancient Israel's failure to respect and follow the law. In addition, much is said about the corrective judgment that is the consequence of that sin and about the divinely wrought salvation that will follow on the heels of judgment. These provocative themes are the golden threads of Old Testament theology.

If in our theological investigation of the Hebrew Bible we remain mindful of two basic considerations, our answer to the question, "What did it mean?" will probably treat the biblical material justly.

First, the theology inherent in the Old Testament is not presented systematically. The Hebrew Scriptures do not offer contemporary man one coherent theological system cast in an evenly written idiom. Legend, historical narrative, legislation, hymn, lament, prophetic oracles of both woe and promise, and wisdom sayings all disclose theological elements, but each genre has its own way of doing so. Moreover, the Hebrew Bible is a remarkably spontaneous and disorganized body of literature. The views it advances on God, man, the Israelite nation, and the world at one moment do not completely square with the views it expresses at another.

Second, the Old Testament rarely argues for or debates its position on theological issues. In its entirety, the Hebrew Bible offers a diverse record of a God in search of man. It presents an equally diverse account of the response of man who discovers, sometimes to his undoing, that he is being sought. But no classical proofs are offered in rational defense of God's existence. Nor are the biblical sources, which so freely witness to the mighty deeds of God, inclined to interpret these deeds according to the categories of contingency or necessity. Also divine actions are not explicitly presented as being either conditional or absolute in character. Psalm 14:1 simply states, "The fool says in his heart, 'There is no God.' " No attempt is made to explain why one who says such a thing is a fool. Then in such verses as the following, confession eclipses philosophical argumentation:

> The heavens are telling the glory of God;
>   and the firmament proclaims his handiwork. (Ps. 19:1)

> Sing to Yahweh, for he has triumphed gloriously;
>   the horse and his rider he has thrown into the sea. (Exod. 15:21)

> For thus said the Lord God, the Holy One of Israel,
>   "In returning and rest you shall be saved;
>   in quietness and in trust shall be your strength." (Isa. 30:15)

Similarly, man's own actions are never thoroughly analyzed as links in a chain of causation. It sufficed that their reality was acknowledged. Also the ancient Israelites did not always distinguish clearly between purpose and result.

Even so, we should not infer that the Hebrew Bible is incapable of pressing an argument to its logical conclusion. In particular, biblical wisdom traditions speak to the contrary. For example, the sheer meaninglessness of life that so impressed the author of Ecclesiastes is asserted at the beginning of the book and maintained throughout. Nevertheless, even he is not concerned solely with speculative matters. In sum, the theological components within the Old Testament are more devoted to declaring the "what" than they are to elaborating the "why" and the "how." They therefore ensure that the accepted religious truths within the ancient Israelite faith will be openly confessed and enthusiastically celebrated.

What It Means. The theological interpreter of the Old Testament has two responsibilities. In addition to comprehending the theological perspective of the ancient Hebrews and discovering "what it meant," he is expected to assess the relevance of the ancient biblical viewpoint for modern man. If the biblical themes are a living reality, the issue of "what it means" cannot be ignored. Questions of relevance and meaning belong to the task of biblical hermeneutics, that is, to the ongoing discussion of viable principles and methods of interpretation. That discussion involves the believer, nonbeliever, historian, and even casual reader. Hermeneutics is not a solely ecclesiastical enterprise, though much of the conversation thus far has focused on the challenge of comprehending the Old Testament in the light of the Christian church and its theology.[16] To engage in the Old Testament hermeneutical task is to engage in a dialogue with ancient Israel. As that dialogue unfolds, the interpreter will be required to place his own view of the world on trial. As he puts questions to the ancient biblical text, that text will question his own assessment of God, man, and the world.

In its attempt to highlight the relevance of Old Testament motifs and to suggest "what it means," theological interpretation becomes admittedly existential. Certainly the theological interpreter of the Bible has a right to press for the relevance of his area of scholarship and interest. The Old Testament world does entertain some forms of thought and self-understanding that are alien to our own. A text may have to be divested of its mythological overtones so that its thoughts are made more relevant to the intellect of the modern world. Even so, in reading the literature treasured by ancient Israel, modern man may yet be able to gain new perspectives that bear directly on his own existence. The tenacious faith of Isaiah, the scheming of Jacob, and the honest theological searching of Job just might have something to say about his own faith, scheming, and search.

All in all, a critical study of the ancient traditions resident in the Old Testament may help to tell us who we are and what our life within the human family is fundamentally about. If it fails to do so, it will still have succeeded in presenting the rich traditions of an historically significant people.

NOTES

1. Some readers will frown on the designation "Old Testament" for those books we are about to study. Instead, the books may be called "The Hebrew Scriptures," "The Hebrew Bible," or "Tanak." ("Tanak" is a Jewish designation derived from the initial consonants of the three large groupings of the biblical books—*Tôrāh* [the Law], *Nᵉbîʾîm* [the Prophets], and *Kᵉthûbhîm* [the Writings].)

2. *Revised Standard Version*, Copyrighted 1946, 1952, and 1971 by the Division of Christian Education, National Council of Churches. Unless otherwise indicated, all biblical quotations are drawn from this translation. "Yahweh" is our equivalent for the RSV, "the LORD."

3. See especially the monograph by G. Ernest Wright, *God Who Acts: Biblical History as Recital*, Studies in Biblical Theology, no. 8 (London: SCM Press, 1952); or the briefer and more recent treatment by Wright, "Theology as Recital," in Samuel Sandmel, ed., *Old Testament Issues* (New York: Harper & Row, Harper Forum Books, 1968), pp. 11–38.

4. Johann G. Eichhorn, *Einleitung in das Alte Testament*, 3 vols. (Leipzig: Weidmann, 1780–1783).

5. This is the work of textual criticism, which for want of space is not described in the present volume. The following, however, are recommended: "Methods of Textual Critical Work," in Martin Noth, *The Old Testament World*, trans. Victor I. Gruhn (Philadelphia: Fortress Press, 1966), pp. 349–363; Ernst Würthwein, *The Text of the Old Testament*, trans. Peter R. Ackroyd (Oxford: Basil Blackwell, 1957), pp. 70–82; and especially D. R. Ap-Thomas, *A Primer of Old Testament Text Criticism*, 2d ed. (Oxford: Basil Blackwell, 1964).

6. This question highlights the work of tradition criticism. That discipline asks how individual literary units were established in their present con-

text and offers informed judgments regarding the impact of the final redaction of these units on the edited literary product. For a sound introductory presentation of tradition criticism and its interaction with both literary and form criticism, see Walter E. Rast, *Tradition History and the Old Testament* (Philadelphia: Fortress Press, 1972).

7. Klaus Koch, *The Growth of the Biblical Tradition: The Form-Critical Method,* trans. S. M. Cupitt (New York: Charles Scribner's Sons, 1969), p. 4. This volume offers a useful introduction to form criticism. In addition, see James Muilenburg, "The Gains of Form Criticism in Old Testament Studies," *The Expository Times* 71 (1960): 229–233; and Gene M. Tucker, *Form Criticism of the Old Testament* (Philadelphia: Fortress Press, 1971).

8. See especially Artur Weiser, *The Old Testament: Its Formation and Development,* trans. Dorothea M. Barton (New York: Association Press, 1961); Georg Fohrer, *Introduction to the Old Testament,* trans. David E. Green (Nashville: Abingdon Press, 1968); Otto Eissfeldt, *The Old Testament: An Introduction,* trans. Peter R. Ackroyd (New York: Harper & Row, 1965). Moreover, *The Interpreter's Handbook of Old Testament Form Criticism* (Rolf P. Knierim and Gene M. Tucker, eds.) is now in progress. Nine Old Testament scholars well versed in the techniques of form criticism are at work on a significant two-volume study that is expected to appear in the late 1970s. The entire Hebrew Bible is under inspection. Special attention is being given to matters of structural analysis, genre, setting, and intention.

9. Muilenburg, *op. cit.,* p. 232.

10. Daniel D. Luckenbill, *The Annals of Sennacherib* (Chicago: University of Chicago Press, 1924), p. 1.

11. For a more detailed treatment of this area, see Paul W. Lapp, *Biblical Archaeology and History* (New York: World Publishing Co., 1969).

12. Nelson Glueck, *The Other Side of the Jordan* (Cambridge, Mass.: The American Schools of Oriental Research, 1970), p. 39.

13. 3d ed. (Princeton, N.J.: Princeton University Press, 1969).

14. The distinction between "what it meant" and "what it means," which we employ here, is drawn from Krister Stendahl, "Contemporary Biblical Theology," in George A. Buttrick et al., eds., *The Interpreter's Dictionary of the Bible* (Nashville: Abingdon Press, 1962), A–D, pp. 419–420.

15. For a clear presentation and evaluation of a variety of positions asserted in the context of Old Testament theology, see Gerhard F. Hasel, *Old Testament Theology: Basic Issues in the Current Debate* (Grand Rapids, Mich.: Wm. B. Eerdmans, 1972).

16. The following two collections of essays may be consulted for a much more thorough coverage of the hermeneutical issue: Bernhard W. Anderson, ed., *The Old Testament and Christian Faith* (New York: Harper & Row, 1963); Claus Westermann, ed., *Essays on Old Testament Hermeneutics,* English trans. ed. by James L. Mays (Richmond: John Knox Press, 1963).

2
THE LAY
OF THE LAND:
THE GEOGRAPHICAL
CONTEXT
OF THE
OLD TESTAMENT

Whenever a people is studied as a historical or cultural entity, the specific geographical space that it occupied becomes a matter of interest. The climate of that land area may also be expected to have an impact on the daily lives of its inhabitants.

The latter consideration applies directly to Palestine, the land area that figures most prominently in the Old Testament. During the biblical period and even today, those living near the Mediterranean coast experience much less temperature change than do their neighbors who inhabit the Jordan river valley some 30 miles to the east, where a midday temperature exceeding 100° may be followed by a night reading of 60°. Moreover, striking differences in rainfall exist as one moves from north to south. While Upper Galilee receives 45 inches of annual rainfall, in the Negev of southern Palestine the annual rainfall is a mere 8 inches.[1] Bedouin existence in the south was not and still is not at all congruent with agrarian life in the north. In Beer-sheba (the Negev) one may be able to obtain hotel accommodations on a par with those available in Haifa (Galilee), yet ancient life styles persist. To ride a bus a few miles beyond the outskirts of Beer-sheba is to enter a desert whose face has changed but slightly over the centuries. The modes of activity, speech, and thought found in fertile Galilee and in the arid Negev are by no means identical. Hence, if we are to know the diverse people of the Old Testament, we must become conversant with their geography. A rudimentary understanding of the geography of nearby lands will also prove useful.

Our reaction to ancient Israel's religious institutions, material culture, and literary output will all be influenced by our ability to grasp the people's geographical context. Israel occupied a land traversed by countless foreigners. Palestine was, with Syria to the north, the land

A Negev Spring at Ein Avdat. In about 300 B.C. the Nabateans, a tribal
people from Arabia, settled in Transjordan and in the Negev. They founded
the city of Avdat, which lies about 40 miles south of Beer-sheba. A few miles
further south is a magnificent crater and refreshing pool known as Ein Avdat.
It is one of the few major sources of water available amid the arid stretches
of the Negev Desert. Water sources such as the one pictured here are
extremely valuable to Israel in her present effort to irrigate barren soil.
(Courtesy of the Israel Government Tourist Office, Chicago.)

bridge that linked the two well-established cultures of Egypt and Mesopotamia located to the southwest and northeast, respectively.

Geographical realities militated that Israel could not live her life in
isolation. With its lack of good harbors, the western seacoast neither
threatened nor enriched Palestinian life. The remainder of Palestine's
perimeter, however, afforded no natural protective barriers. Nevertheless, the invasion of Palestine's borders was not a constant occurrence.
The land's natural resources and material culture were not impressive
enough to attract the leading ancient empires continuously. Palestine is
often referred to in the Hebrew Bible as "a land flowing with milk and
honey" (for example, Exod. 3:8, Num. 13:27, Deut. 26:9), but this
statement betrays the perspective of the desert nomad long accustomed
to a wilderness existence. Even so, various military and trade routes did

pass through Palestine, so that the land had undisputed strategic importance. The great powers of Egypt and Mesopotamia often tried to maintain some sort of supremacy in the land. Moreover, since the cultural foundations of Egypt and Mesopotamia were established centuries before Israel was to emerge as a nation, they frequently informed Israel's development. Where ancient Israel lived mattered considerably in terms of what she was to become.

But how is the geographical context of the Old Testament best grasped? Obviously, the careful reading of a thorough volume on the geography of Palestine and the spending of a junior year abroad in Israel would serve the cause quite nicely.[2] To gaze at the sharp rocks and impressive slopes in the central hill country of Palestine and realize that the Hebrew Bible does not exaggerate in its use of the term "mountain," to feel an uncomfortably penetrating warmth upon your tired body at noon and appreciate Abraham's need "as he sat at the door of his tent in the heat of the day" (Gen. 18:1), to notice Bedouin tents dotting a spacious but parched southern landscape and to recall the confessional words of Deut. 26:5, "A wandering Aramean was my father," and to ascend the hilly road that brings you into Jerusalem and visually comprehend the strategic location of that marvelous city,

The Sea of Galilee. Although this beautiful body of water in northern Palestine has long been known as "the Sea of Galilee," strictly speaking, it is a fresh-water lake. Its surface is 696 feet below sea level. The heart-shaped lake is approximately 13 miles from north to south and is 8 miles across at its widest point. (Courtesy of the Consulate General of Israel, New York.)

such impressions would help you to view the Hebrew Bible with an enviable freshness. But for those who have neither time nor money to visit the land of the Bible, the reading of this present chapter commends itself as an alternative.

You will no doubt wish to take note of the two maps provided in this chapter. The first treats Israel's wider geographical setting and the second focuses upon Palestine itself. In order to keep both maps clear and simple, very few geographical regions and features are mentioned beyond those actually discussed in the present chapter. More detailed maps appear elsewhere in the book.

ISRAEL'S WIDER
GEOGRAPHICAL SETTING

Here we are concerned with the geographical features of the ancient Near East that relate directly to our understanding of ancient Israel. Clearly, the Old Testament phrase "from Dan to Beer-sheba" (Judg. 20:1, 1 Sam. 3:20, 1 Kings 4:25), intended to designate the extremities of Palestine, fails to represent the extent of the biblical world. The countries that play a vital role in the Old Testament lie in several heterogeneous areas clustered around the points where Asia, Africa, and Europe meet. Israel knew Hittite neighbors to the northwest in Asia Minor, Babylonians and Assyrians to the east, and Egyptians to the southwest.

Israel and her neighbors inhabited a spacious curving sector of arable land stretching from Egypt to Mesopotamia. The Egyptologist James Henry Breasted called this region the "Fertile Crescent."[3] The adjective "fertile" is misleading, however. It implies a level of agricultural bounty that surpasses the actual Near Eastern situation. Nor does the rather narrow belt of territory covered by Breasted's noun "crescent" always serve our purposes. It is sometimes effective in suggesting where the action is, but it virtually excludes the mountainous areas and desert zones that contributed much to the history of the ancient Near East. The northern mountainous zone runs parallel to the Fertile Crescent and then protrudes westward to include Asia Minor. Famous among the mountain people were the Hittites of Asia Minor and, somewhat later, the Persians of Iran. The mountain ranges and plateaus contained a rugged, energetic people whose southern advance threatened the tranquillity yet enriched the existence of the Fertile Crescent itself.

Much the same thing can be said for the desert tribes who moved from southern Arabia to more arable northern regions. Palestine is flanked by desert on both its eastern and southern sides. Since no natural barriers protect the sown region from the unsown, the ancient

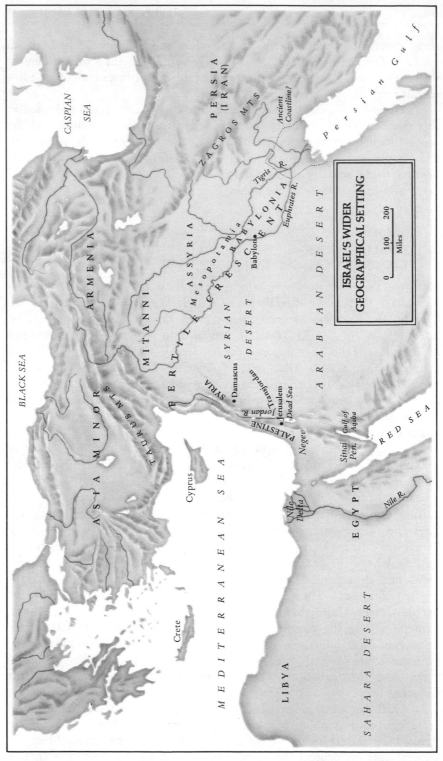

ISRAEL'S WIDER
GEOGRAPHICAL SETTING

0   100   200
Miles

CASPIAN
SEA

BLACK SEA

PERSIA
(IRAN)

ZAGROS MTS

Ancient
Coastline?

Persian Gulf

Tigris R.

Euphrates R.

ARMENIA

MITANNI

ASSYRIA

Mesopotamia

FERTILE CRESCENT

BABYLONIA

Babylon

SYRIAN DESERT

ARABIAN DESERT

ASIA MINOR

TAURUS MTS

Damascus

SYRIA

Transjordan

Jordan R.

PALESTINE

Jerusalem

Dead Sea

Negev

Sinai
Pen.

Gulf of
Aqaba

RED SEA

Cyprus

MEDITERRANEAN SEA

Nile
Delta

Nile R.

EGYPT

Crete

LIBYA

SAHARA DESERT

24

inhabitants of Palestine felt keenly the impact of the desert stretches. The sparse desert population migrated regularly, and these tribes impinged on the settled folk living in the Fertile Crescent. The Syro-Arabian Desert to the east of Palestine and the Sinai Desert to the south consist of a fine stratum of humus anchored in calcareous soil and thorny desert brush. Thanks to the winter rains, there is sufficient vegetation to encourage the nomad as he tends his flocks. Daily he migrates within the desert expanse, and when it is his good fortune to find an oasis that is watered, albeit temporarily, by a brook, he momentarily settles. Between Palestine itself and the desert proper is a thin strip of steppe with its grass, brush, and oases (such as Jericho). Within the steppe, very simple forms of agriculture could be pursued. Here a transition from tenuous desert life to a richer and more settled existence was within reach. To summarize, semifertile plains, mountainous regions, and desert expanses all contributed to the composition of the ancient Near East.

The 1,200-mile stretch of semifertile territory that comprises the Fertile Crescent is not homogeneous. The best agricultural areas lie near the tips of the Crescent and the least fertile regions are, for the most part, located at its center. Thus, northern Mesopotamia with its Hurrian-inhabited land of Mitanni is virtually a desert, whereas the

Mount Hermon. This rugged mountain, which is about 9,100 feet high, forms the southern spur of the Anti-Lebanon range. While it lies beyond the borders of Palestine, the crown of this snow-covered mountain is visible for miles. (Photo by the author.)

land adjacent to the Nile in Egypt and the alluvial plains north of the Persian Gulf are much more fertile.

The northern and eastern regions of the Crescent benefit from two major rivers, the Tigris and the Euphrates, and their tributaries. The courses of these rivers begin in the mountainous regions of Armenia. At first, the Tigris and Euphrates lie far apart, but further south near ancient Babylon they are but some 20 miles apart as they continue to move toward the Persian Gulf. They provided a ready means for irrigating the surrounding land and transporting its inhabitants.

The ancient Greeks termed a portion of the land between the Tigris and Euphrates "Mesopotamia," meaning the "land between the rivers." In time the proper noun came to apply to the entire area between the two great rivers. Gradually the construction and maintenance of dikes and canals, which ensured successful irrigation in the area, enabled the great kingdoms of Sumer, Babylonia, and Assyria to emerge. Nevertheless, the absence of good natural boundaries meant that disruptive invasions by the enemy were frequent, as we shall see in Chapter 4.

By contrast, at the other extremity of the Fertile Crescent we meet a geographically insular Egypt. The Red Sea and marshes in the northern part of the Nile Delta ordinarily protected ancient Egypt from invading Asian peoples. Moreover, the western desert and the southern cataracts of the Nile usually guarded Egypt from an onslaught by other African peoples. But Egypt's northeastern frontier was vulnerable to foreign infiltration. Thus, she was invaded by the Asian Hyksos in the seventeenth century B.C. and by the sea peoples in the twelfth century B.C. Such invasions occurred late in the development of Egyptian culture, however. In general, Egypt pursued an isolationist course.

The air of confidence, which Egypt's atmosphere of seclusion was bound to foster, was reinforced by the life-sustaining Nile River. The ancient Greeks were the first to describe Egypt as a gift of the Nile. Rising from its sources in equatorial East Africa, the Nile played a vital role in Egyptian commerce and agriculture. The Nile was, and remains, Egypt's natural commercial artery. It united the inhabitants of the relatively narrow stretches of "black land" that flanked the banks of the river. And the overflowing Nile provided the water necessary for good farming. In October, when the river reaches its high point, all agrarian territory in the valley of the Nile is covered. True, too high a Nile meant the destruction of canals and dams, and too little inundation was the harbinger of a year of famine. Yet generally the Nile treated the ancient Egyptians with benevolence. Its banks of rich soil were able to support a remarkable Egyptian civilization that produced the longest cultural period in history—one that endured for 3,000 years.

THE GEOGRAPHY
OF PALESTINE

Palestine itself is a vital land bridge; in antiquity it carried countless wandering citizens of the ancient Near East from one destination to another. It could not help but awaken the interest of major powers in the ancient world as they pursued their military and commercial interests. Yet as we have already said, the land was not rich. Palestine could satisfy reasonably well the pastoral and agrarian aspirations of its inhabitants, but it yielded few raw materials. Moreover, there was little land. If we consider a western border of Mediterranean coast, an eastern frontier of wilderness steppe in Transjordan, a northern border at Dan, and a southern border at Beer-sheba, then a land area approximately 10,000 square miles may be claimed for Palestine. This is but twice the size of the state of Connecticut or the rough equivalent of Vermont.

Topographically, Palestine is not of one piece. It consists of four longitudinal strips that extend from its southernmost extremities into northern Syria. Each is a self-contained zone. Thus, a political unity embracing all of ancient Palestine was most difficult to achieve. While the ancient Israelites took the land from the east and gradually moved westward in successful conquest, we shall follow the lead of most topographers and attack the land from the west.

The Coastal Plain

Fronting the Mediterranean Sea is Palestine's coastal plain. This basically fertile region varies in width. At Mount Carmel and at other northern points it is only a few hundred feet wide, yet in the south, where the Mediterranean coastline swings westward, it reaches a width of 30 miles. Since much of the seashore consists of sand dunes, the main coastal cities such as Ashdod and Gaza were located a few miles inland. Through them passed an important international highway known as "the way of the sea" (later called the *Via Maris*). A virtually unbroken coastline discouraged the inhabitants of Palestine from engaging in commercial ventures on the Mediterranean Sea. The coastal dweller in Palestine turned his back to the sea and his eyes toward the central hill country. Since he was working soil that yielded a respectable crop, he renounced the possibility of a seafaring existence. At Accho, Palestine did have a decent harbor facility, yet it was poorly protected from sea winds and was frequently claimed by the Phoenicians who pressed southward. There were other harbors at Dor, Joppa, and Ashkelon, but none was adequate. Moreover, during much of the history depicted in the Hebrew Bible, the Philistines rather than the Israelites commanded the Mediterranean coast.

The Mediterranean Coast at Caesarea. Across the miles, Palestine's Mediterranean seacoast assumes many faces. Here is a view of the seacoast from Caesarea, which is approximately 23 miles south of Mount Carmel. (Photo by the author.)

Nevertheless, the coastal plain figures in Old Testament history, and its several regions should be noted. The northernmost region is the Plain of Accho or Acre, a small but fertile area north of Mount Carmel. Its most important town was Accho, which Israel controlled only sporadically. Mount Carmel itself interrupts the fertile coastal plain, but directly south of it lies the marshy Plain of Sharon. This well-watered area had good forests, but its sluggish rivers did not provide adequate drainage. Its farmland was of only modest value to ancient Israel. South of the port of Dor lay the impressive fertile region of Philistia. This was controlled for several centuries by the Philistines, who gave Palestine its name. In "Palestine," the Latinized form of the noun "Philistia," we have the name that was eventually to apply to the land as a whole. Philistia is the most extensive land area in all of Palestine that is reasonably level. The rich soil in the Philistine plain and the smaller but fertile Plain of Accho gave the coastal plain a good name in agriculture. But this plain was not the axis of ancient Israelite life in Palestine.

The Central Hill Country

Between the coastal plain and the Jordan river valley lies the central hill country. This longitudinal strip is the geographical backbone of Palestine. Historically, it is the most important region for ancient

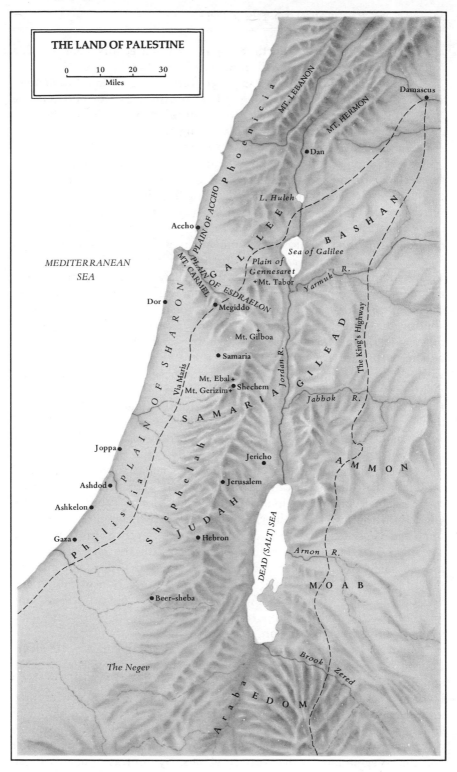

THE LAND OF PALESTINE

0   10   20   30
Miles

Damascus

MT. LEBANON

MT. HERMON

Dan

Phoenicia

L. Huleh

Accho

PLAIN OF ACCHO

BASHAN

GALILEE

Sea of Galilee

Plain of
Gennesaret
+ Mt. Tabor

MEDITERRANEAN
SEA

MT. CARMEL

PLAIN OF ESDRAELON

Yarmuk R.

Dor

PLAIN OF SHARON

Megiddo

Mt. Gilboa

Samaria

GILEAD

The King's Highway

Via Maris

Mt. Ebal +
Mt. Gerizim +

Shechem

Jordan R.

SAMARIA

Jabbok R.

Joppa

Shephelah

Jericho

AMMON

Ashdod

Jerusalem

Ashkelon

Philistia

Gaza

JUDAH

Hebron

DEAD (SALT) SEA

Beer-sheba

Arnon R.

MOAB

The Negev

Brook Zered

Arabah

EDOM

Israelite existence. From north to south, the three divisions of this rough, rocky territory are Galilee, Samaria, and Judah.

Galilee consists of the expansive foothills of Mount Lebanon, whose elevations decrease as one moves southward. Northern Galilee is quite hilly. Southern Galilee with its more friendly climate provides a reasonably good quantity of arable rolling land.

Functioning as the southern border of Galilee, the Valley of Jezreel cuts dramatically into the hill country in an east-west direction— its western portion is often called the Plain of Esdraelon. Mount Carmel to the extreme west comes within several hundred feet of the Mediterranean Sea. Thus, it was risky for ancient armies and caravans to move along the Mediterranean shore path. Enemies commanding the mountain might easily discern the movements of those below. A pass at Megiddo offered a safer and more direct route from the Plain of Sharon into the Plain of Esdraelon to the east. As early as the third millennium B.C., the strategic significance of Megiddo was recognized. It guarded the vital pass that allowed northern residents in Galilee to advance southward. Also it gave caravans coming from the south a chance to move into the plain, traverse the western shore of the Sea of Galilee, and press toward Damascus. Given its strategic importance, this east-west rift in the central hill country was the setting of several battles mentioned in the Old Testament. It witnessed Deborah as she inspired the Israelite troops in successful combat with the Canaanites (Judg. 4–5), Saul as he died warring against the Philistines (1 Sam. 31:1–5), and Josiah as he was killed fighting Pharaoh Necho and his Egyptian forces (2 Kings 23:29).

Due south of Jezreel is the region of Samaria, the geographical center of Palestine. Looking across the Valley of Jezreel, Samaria's northernmost landmark, Mount Gilboa, faces Mount Tabor in southern Galilee. In the midst of hilly Samaria are the twin mountain peaks of Ebal and Gerizim. They overlook the city of Shechem and command the main pass below, which links Shechem with the city of Samaria located some 10 miles to the northwest. Numerous valleys cut into the mountainous regions of Samaria enabling the cultivation of grains and vegetables. These crops, in addition to the fig and olive trees growing on the hills themselves, support the people living in the many small villages throughout the region.

Judah is the third main region in the central hill country. Its elevation decreases as one moves toward Jerusalem and increases once more south of the city. Its highest point (over 3,300 feet) is just north of Hebron. While not overly fertile, some of Judah's fields support farming, and in many stretches flocks are herded. The gentle western slopes of Judah lead to the Shephelah, a vital area of fertile foothills. The clouds that move in from the Mediterranean Sea provide enough rain to foster sufficient vegetation on the western slopes. By contrast, Judah's harsh

Judean Desert between Jerusalem and Jericho. The barren hills on Judah's west bank have a forbidding appearance. This photo was taken beside a modern paved road that runs between Jerusalem and Jericho. The lower portion of the photo is approximately at sea level. Jerusalem is about 2,500 feet above sea level, whereas Jericho is about 900 feet below sea level. Thus, the 20-mile stretch of road between these two sites is steep. The west bank of Judah, which descends sharply toward the River Jordan, is striking in its lack of vegetation. (Photo by the author.)

slopes east of the watershed receive only sparse rainfall. And its extremely steep terrain, which advances toward the Dead Sea, adds to its wasteland quality. The bleak cliffs of eastern Judah and its intersecting valleys leading to the Dead Sea may be seen as one travels by boat along the Dead Sea. The southernmost vicinity of Judah is the Negev wilderness.

The Jordan River Valley

Due east of the central hill country and west of the Transjordan highlands lies the Jordan river valley. It consists of a gigantic rift or geological fault that begins in northern Syria, extends to the Red Sea at the Gulf of Aqaba, and moves further south into easternmost Africa. The Palestinian portion of this lengthy fissure contains the Jordan valley and the Dead Sea. The sources of the River Jordan are located on the southern slopes of Mount Hermon. The Jordan, which means "the descender" in Hebrew, is well named. Where the Jordan flows into Lake Huleh in northern Galilee, it is 229 feet above sea level.[4] Ten miles due south,

Sources of the Jordan River in Upper Galilee. The Jordan
River originates in the union of four different sources.
These emerge in the parting of the watersheds to the south
of Mount Hermon in northern Galilee. The waters then
begin their serpentine descent through the Sea of Galilee to
the Dead Sea. (Courtesy of the Israel Government Tourist
Office, Chicago.)

the Jordan enters the Sea of Galilee at an elevation of 696 feet below
sea level. In Old Testament times, the Sea of Galilee was designated
the "Sea of Chinnereth" (Num. 34:11) or "Chinneroth" (Josh. 12:3).
South of this sea, the Jordan descends 594 feet in its serpentine journey
of approximately 195 miles (only 65 miles due south) to the point where
it empties into the Dead Sea. Here at 1,290 feet below sea level is the
lowest exposed portion of the earth's surface.[5] The Bible itself refers to
this highly saline body of water not as the "Dead Sea" but as the "Sea of
the Arabah" (Deut. 3:17), the "Eastern Sea" (Ezek. 47:18), or the more

The Jordan River. Palestine's longest river passes through the central portion of a great geological fissure that stretches all the way from northern Syria into Africa. This is how the Jordan appears a few miles south of the Sea of Galilee. While its meandering course can be forded in many places, the Jordan did serve as a useful natural border between ancient Israel and rival nations to the east. Below the Sea of Galilee the Jordan normally attains a width of approximately 100 feet. (Photo by the author.)

familiar "Salt Sea" (Gen. 14:3). The Jordan completes its course at this northern end of the sea. In the Araba, the region between the Dead Sea and the Gulf of Aqaba, the floor of the rift rises rapidly. Sixty miles due south of the Dead Sea, approximately midway between the Dead Sea and the Gulf of Aqaba, it is 656 feet above sea level. Closer to the Gulf of Aqaba the rift slopes downward again.

The Jordan river valley is quite varied. It offers to northern Palestine the small Sea of Galilee, whose fresh water yields some very good fish. On its northwestern shore is the fertile Plain of Gennesaret with its grains, fruits, and vegetables. Other sides of the lake are rather steep. By contrast, the Dead Sea in Judah was of no great value to biblical man. Exploitation of its saline content appears to be a modern enterprise. Moreover, the hot, oppressive climate frustrates the growth of vegetation near its shores. Another contrast is to be seen in the extent of cultivation along the Jordan rift. To the north and south of the Sea of Galilee, the valley is well plowed, but further south and closer to the northern extremity of the Dead Sea a lack of rainfall discourages agrarian pursuits. Finally, we might note that although there are several places where the Jordan gorge can be forded, it served well as a border between Israel and many of the rival nations to the east.

The Transjordan Highlands

East of the Jordan rift is Palestine's fourth longitudinal zone, known as the Transjordan highlands. It consists of a tableland that is rarely less than 1,500 feet in elevation. The Transjordan plateau is cut by four main east-west tributaries: the Yarmuk, Jabbok, and Arnon rivers, and the Zered brook. These bodies of water provide the boundaries for Transjordan's various geopolitical regions. Thus, Bashan lies north of the Yarmuk and Gilead lies south of it. Ammon is located between the Jabbok and Arnon rivers, Moab between the Arnon River and the Zered brook, and Edom is situated to the south of the Zered. Throughout eastern Transjordan, the plateau levels off into an expanse of desert. Of particular importance in antiquity was a north-south path of caravan trade that traversed the desert. This route, known as the "King's Highway" (Num. 20:17), provided a vital link between Damascus in Syria and the Gulf of Aqaba.

Northern portions of Transjordan are more fertile than its southern regions. Bashan produces large amounts of grain and Gilead has many streams and springs, which support numerous inhabitants. Yet southern Transjordan has other assets. The high plateau vicinity of Moab encourages the herding of sheep and at least some agriculture. Though ancient Edom had to cope with an arid climate, its hills contained impressive deposits of copper and iron ore. In ancient times, residents of Moab and Edom were related to the Israelites. The family relationship was not always harmonious, however. While Transjordan sometimes lay completely outside of Israel's domain, Numbers 32 reports that the

The Transjordan Plateau Facing the Sea of Galilee. This view of the Transjordan highlands is visible from the northwestern shore of the Sea of Galilee at a site traditionally designated "the Mount of Beatitudes" (see Matt. 5–7). (Photo by the author.)

tribes of Reuben, and Gad, as well as half the tribe of Manasseh took land in Transjordan.

Here we conclude our geography lesson. But continuing awareness of the geography of Israel and her Near Eastern context should enhance your ability to interpret many of the details of ancient Israel's history that will be examined in the chapters to follow. Having caught the lay of the land, you should now be in a better position to understand the ancient events that helped the biblical terrain acquire its historical significance.

NOTES

1. See the instructive article by R. B. Y. Scott, "Climate of Palestine," and its inclusion of a detailed rainfall map, in George A. Buttrick et al., eds., *The Interpreter's Dictionary of the Bible* (Nashville: Abingdon Press, 1962), K–Q, pp. 621–626.
2. Among the outstanding works available are Yohanan Aharoni, *The Land of the Bible: A Historical Geography*, trans. A. F. Rainey (Philadelphia: Westminster Press, 1967); Denis Baly, *The Geography of the Bible: A Study in Historical Geography*, rev. ed. (New York: Harper & Row, 1974); Martin Noth, "Geography of Palestine," in Noth's *The Old Testament World*, trans. Victor I. Gruhn (Philadelphia: Fortress Press, 1966), pp. 2–104; and G. Ernest Wright and Floyd V. Filson, *The Westminster Historical Atlas to the Bible*, rev. ed. (Philadelphia: Westminster Press, 1956).
3. James Henry Breasted, *Ancient Times: A History of the Early World* (Boston: Ginn, 1916), p. 100.
4. The small, swampy Lake Huleh has been drained by the modern state of Israel. In order to make more land available for farming, Lake Huleh's Jordan outlet was artificially deepened.
5. The elevation figures are taken from Wright and Filson, *op. cit.*, Plate I, opposite p. 20.

Part II

THE ORIGINS OF THE PEOPLE

3

THE TORAH: ITS ORIGIN AND STRUCTURE

In Part II we shall focus on ancient Israel's emergence as a people. In faith she claimed that her sovereign God, Yahweh, had chosen her as his special possession. She maintained that within time and space, she had been summoned by a God who continually sought to use her for his purposes. Accordingly, amid the business of addressing the incessant pressures of daily existence, ancient Israel cultivated a religious perspective that assigned profound meaning to what otherwise might have been an undistinguished existence.

In reflecting on their origins, the people of ancient Israel posed many questions. From what kind of a historical situation had Yahweh first summoned Israel? What motivated Yahweh to invite Israel to be his favored possession? What motivated Israel to accept that invitation? As the people of deity active in history, what form was Israelite life and thought supposed to take? How might Israel's historical continuity as Yahweh's special instrument be assured? What was the nature of Israel's relation to the other nations, how was she to deal with them, how might they deal with her, and what was Yahweh's plan for them?

Ancient Israel generated a substantial body of tradition as she reflected on her beginnings. At first that tradition was oral, but gradually it was committed to a written format. It consisted mainly of short poetic units, extended prose narrative, and several bodies of legislation of varying antiquity and length.

This simple yet rich tradition is found primarily in the Torah, the first five books of the Hebrew Bible. These books had an extraordinary impact on Israelite life and thought, presenting such compelling matters as the world's creation, Israel's Exodus, and the Ten Commandments. As a most influential portion of scripture, the Torah has become the object of both religious piety and biblical criticism. In the following section we shall examine its origin and structure.

INITIAL IMPRESSIONS OF THE FIRST FIVE BOOKS

Typically designated by their Graeco-Roman names—Genesis, Exodus, Leviticus, Numbers, and Deuteronomy—the books of the Torah address the many-sided question of Israelite origins. Genesis 1–11 discusses the origins of the world from the creation to the time of Abraham. Genesis 12–50 deals with Israel's patriarchs: Abraham, Isaac, Jacob, and Joseph. Exodus 1–18 recounts Israel's deliverance from Egypt. The stipulations and implementation of the Sinai covenant are the subject of Exodus 19–40, Leviticus 1–27, and Num. 1:1–10:10. In Num. 10:11–36:13 the sojourn in the Sinai Peninsula and in Transjordan, and the testing in the wilderness are described. And Deuteronomy 1–34 records the final address of Moses, which constitutes historical and legal recapitulation.

Certainly, the most crucial component of the six is the third, which reflects on Israel's deliverance from Egypt. Much of Exodus 1–18 is a stirring and detailed account of Israel's rescue from the throes of Egyptian bondage. There we read that Yahweh heard the cries of the people whom he had already chosen and that with the effective assistance of Moses, he proceeded to do something about Israel's plight. Exodus 1–18 brilliantly declares that Israel was divinely chosen and that this dramatic act of election occurred in history.

Yet these chapters do not stand alone. They are buttressed by previous chapters that refer to Yahweh's election of the patriarchs who predated Moses (Gen. 12–50) and even to his concern for the world at large (Gen. 1–11). The narrative about Israel's deliverance in Exodus 1–18 is likewise strengthened by successive chapters (Exod. 19–Num. 10:10) that account for the covenantal bond linking Yahweh and his people in continuing fellowship.

The sojourn in the Sinai Desert and in Transjordan (Num. 10:11–36:13) is a time of discontent and testing. It offers Israel further, sometimes painful insight into the character of the God who has impinged on her existence. Finally, as the Book of Deuteronomy opens, Israel is encamped in the western plains of Moab. She is ready to cross the Jordan and take the city of Jericho. Yet prior to that initial act of conquest in the Land of Promise, the people are invited to hear Moses' words of farewell. These meditate on the realities of Israelite history and law that have already given shape to the people's existence.

Despite its several components, the story of ancient Israel's origins has a strong sense of continuity. This first act of the biblical drama begins with the deity's decision to call the world into being and ends with a resounding chord of expectancy. The elderly Moses has just died, but Israel is not permitted to die in her infancy. With Joshua as the divinely appointed successor to Moses, Israel has reason to anticipate that she will soon inherit the Land of Promise.

If this is in broad outline the content of the first five books of the Hebrew Bible, how shall they be referred to in their entirety? Judaism has traditionally referred to them as the "Torah," and the Hebrew noun *tôrāh* is most often equated with the English word "law," but the equation of Torah and law is misleading. The noun *tôrāh* derives from a verb root whose consonants *y*, *r*, and *h* denote the act of teaching or directing. Thus, *tôrāh* is not confined to legislative facts; it is better equated with such English nouns as "instruction," "guidance," and "direction." As law, the Torah informed Israel about what God expects. Yet as narrative with an intrinsic capacity to instruct its readers in right living, the Torah disclosed Yahweh's relationship to mankind in general and to Israel in particular.

The first major division of the Hebrew Bible has also been designated "the books of Moses." In contrast with the noun *tôrāh*, which in essence declares what is contained, this label emphasizes the author. Some modern readers accept the genitive "of Moses" as clear-cut testimony that Moses himself wrote these books. Many discount their Mosaic authorship, although some grant that the person of Moses had a strong impact on the material.

The predications "Pentateuch," "Hexateuch," and "Tetrateuch" are often used by scholars. The noun "Pentateuch," which is of ancient Greek origin, simply affirms the existence of five scrolls or books. In the third century A.D., Origen applied this label to the first five books of the Old Testament, and it has been much used ever since. In "Pentateuch" we have a neutral term that merely reminds us that five elements make up the whole. Various scholars maintain, however, that the number "five" does not correspond with the basic composition and structure of the first books in the Bible. They prefer the nouns "Hexateuch" or "Tetrateuch," which accept the first six, or first four, books of the Old Testament, respectively, as a more intelligible entity.

Those who use "Hexateuch" insist that the Book of Joshua should be considered with the Pentateuch. They correctly observe that the conquest of Canaan is nowhere depicted in the Pentateuch. At the close of Deuteronomy, the Israelites are still in Transjordan. Certainly, Yahweh's promise of land to the patriarchs, which is asserted so positively in Genesis and reiterated in the succeeding books, remains unfulfilled unless one grafts the Book of Joshua onto the Pentateuch. The conquest of the land is amply reported in Joshua, and accordingly, the marvelous promise is realized. The unlikelihood that Israel produced a truncated epic and the reasonable demand for thematic resolution require that the first six books of the Hebrew Bible be grasped as a whole. In the nineteenth century Wellhausen accepted the Hexateuch as an indispensable category, and in our time von Rad has argued for the thematic unity of the Hexateuch, which offers its readers a sustained narrative of unusual proportions.[1]

The term "Tetrateuch" is favored by several contemporary scholars who accept the material from Genesis through Numbers as the first meaningful unit of the Old Testament. Though they do not imply that Israel sponsored the writing of a truncated epic, they insist that the Book of Deuteronomy marks the beginning of the second great epic of the Old Testament rather than the conclusion of the first. They maintain that a lengthy and integrated history of ancient Israel opens with Deuteronomy and extends through 2 Kings and was edited by Deuteronomic historians preoccupied with Israel's conquest of, and existence in, the Land of Promise. Since Deuteronomic traditions are rarely evident in the first four books and the land itself is a central motif in the Book of Deuteronomy, it follows that the break ordinarily assumed to exist between Deuteronomy and Joshua should be considered to fall between Numbers and Deuteronomy. In particular, Noth and Engnell have argued for the cogency of the Tetrateuch as a category.[2]

We shall side with the consensus of biblical scholarship by regarding the Pentateuch as the most ancient completed portion of the Hebrew Bible. We also favor the term "Torah" for denoting the fundamental content and purpose of the diverse materials in these books. In addition, however, we affirm the partial validity of the four-books position espoused by Noth and Engnell, and defer a thorough consideration of Deuteronomy until Chapter 14. As finally edited materials, Genesis through Numbers and Deuteronomy through Kings are in all likelihood the literary realities that must be grasped.

THE ACCEPTANCE AND REJECTION OF MOSAIC AUTHORSHIP

Through the centuries the claim of Mosaic authorship for the first five books of the Old Testament was successively met with apathy, affirmation, and denial. With copyright legislation an undreamed of reality, ancient man was largely indifferent to questions of authorship. The life of the individual was so taken up with his own community that the matter of who wrote what was of little consequence. The overriding assertion seems to have been, "This is our story," not, "This is his book."

Yet even in the postexilic era, the name of Moses was linked with the Torah. Such passages as Ezra 6:18 and Neh. 13:1 explicitly refer to "the book of Moses," and Dan. 9:11 indicates that the law of Moses was a written entity. Ezra 3:2 and 7:6 suggest that by about 400 B.C. there were Jewish scribes who credited Moses with having written the law that was binding on all Israel. In the Pentateuch itself, several verses (Exod. 17:14; 24:4; 34:27–28; Num. 33:2) claim that Moses knew how to write. In the New Testament, Acts 15:21 states, "For from early generations Moses has had in every city those who preach him, for he is read every sabbath in the synagogues." (In the New Testament, see also Mark 12:26, John 5:46, Rom. 10:5.) Finally, Philo and Josephus, who played an active role in the Jewish life of the first century of the Christian era, both accepted Moses as the actual author of the Torah.[8]

Then why did thinking people shift from affirming to doubting that Moses wrote Judaism's most ancient and sacred books? In the first place, a close reading of the Pentateuch discloses a duplication of narrative material. For example, both Gen. 16:4–14 and 21:9–21 report Hagar's expulsion from Abraham's household. The deity's three assurances to Abraham that one day Sarah would bear a son also seem repetitious. In Gen. 15:4 the deity as Yahweh makes the promise to Abraham, in Gen. 17:16 as Elohim he assures Abraham that a son will be born, and in Gen. 18:10 as Yahweh he voices this declaration anew to the patriarch. Other instances of duplication include the twice-told report that Jacob assigned the name "Bethel," meaning "house of God," to a Canaanite site formerly named "Luz" (cf. Gen. 28:19 and 35:6, 15), the two namings of Beer-sheba (cf. Gen. 21:22–34 and 26:26–33), and the twice-narrated story that the deity initially revealed his special name "Yahweh" to Moses (cf. Exod. 3:14–15 and 6:2–3). Such passages have led critics to ask why Moses would have persisted in repeating himself and whether in fact he wrote this material.

Second, careful readers of the Pentateuch have noticed discrepancies. According to Genesis 1, man was created after the animals, but in Genesis 2 he was the first of God's creatures to come into existence (cf. Gen. 1:24–27 and Gen. 2:4b–7, 18–20). In Gen. 6:19 God instructs Noah to bring a male and female member of each animal species into the ark, yet in Gen 7:2 he commands Noah to collect seven pairs of the clean animals in contrast to one pair of the unclean. In Exod. 20:24–26 legislation on the Israelite altar permits the existence of many Yahwistic worship centers, but the altar legislation in Deuteronomy 12 insists on one central sanctuary. We also meet a noteworthy inconsistency as to precisely when the divine name "Yahweh" was first revealed to Israel. Exodus 3:14–15 implies and Exod. 6:3 states explicitly that the name had not been disclosed to the Israelites prior to the time of Moses. Yet Gen. 4:26 suggests that men knew that special name of the deity by the time Adam had a grandson. Moreover, Gen. 12:8, 14:22, and 24:3 all attest Abraham's use of the name Yahweh. Such inconsistencies must have led many discerning readers to ask what accounted for his frequently confused state of mind if Moses wrote this material.

A third factor leading to the rejection of Mosaic authorship of the Pentateuch is inept chronology. According to Gen. 12:11, 14, Abraham was married to an attractive Bedouin woman. Yet the reader is at a loss when he tries to relate the comments on Sarah's beauty to indications of her age. Genesis 12:4 reports that Abraham was seventy-five when he migrated from Haran to Canaan. Soon the childless couple moved to Egypt. Since Gen. 17:17 discloses that Abraham and Sarah were a hundred and ninety years of age, respectively—a problem in itself—it may be inferred that Sarah was all of sixty-five when she impressed the Egyptians with her good looks.

Pentateuchal anachronisms are likewise troublesome. For example, eight verses in Genesis and two in Exodus refer to the Philistines (Gen. 10:14; 21:32, 34; 26:1, 8, 14, 15, 18; Exod. 13:17; 23:31). Prevailing historical judgment maintains that the Philistines did not inhabit the land of Canaan until the first half of the twelfth century B.C., when Rameses III was pharaoh in Egypt. The Philistines therefore came to the land shortly after the Israelites had arrived. Hence, their mention in the patriarchal traditions is anachronistic. It is highly improbable that the Philistines had direct dealings with either Abraham (Gen. 21) or Isaac (Gen. 26).[4] Such chronological inaccuracy has encouraged critical readers to assume that Moses was not the only Israelite who influenced how Pentateuchal tradition would eventually appear in its fixed literary form.

A fourth issue concerns matters of style. When the entire Pentateuch is examined, its diverse literary styles are apparent, and the chances of its having come from the hand of one writer are drastically reduced. True, Moses may have known how to write. If so, we have no grounds for asserting that his literary style was limited to one form. But because various passages devoted to a similar subject reveal a strikingly diverse style, the impression of multiple authorship is sharpened.

Some Pentateuchal narratives are fresh, fast-moving, and naïve in their appeal, whereas others are formal, slow-moving, and prolix. For example, the creation narrative in Gen. 2:4b–25 is crisp, lively, and delightfully simple. These qualities are lacking in the creation account provided by Gen. 1:1–2:4a, where a dignified and liturgical style conveys much formality and repetition. Yet each narrative reflects on the creation. Moreover, the divine dignity communicated in Genesis 1 is resolutely upheld in Genesis 17, where God's summons to Abraham is portrayed in formalistic, utterly explicit terms that climax with the establishment of the Hebrew ritual of circumcision. God's role is that of speaker; Abraham's that of listener. Clearly, Genesis 17 cannot be considered a convincing, three-dimensional narrative. By contrast, in Gen. 15:5 during another confrontation between the deity and Abraham,

God personally brings Abraham outside his tent to have a good look at the stars. Here the deity is anthropomorphically portrayed as Abraham's concerned friend. Theological assumptions and narrative styles in Genesis 15 and 17 are scarcely identical.

Moreover, when we compare larger units of the Pentateuch, differences in proper names emerge. Sometimes God is referred to as Yahweh, sometimes as Elohim. His special mountain is known by two different names—Sinai and Horeb. The pre-Israelite dwellers in Canaan are referred to both as Canaanites and as Amorites. Jethro, Hobab, and Reuel are all introduced as Moses' father-in-law. If such considerations fail to clinch the argument for multiple authorship, they do reinforce the doubt that the entire Pentateuch is attributable to Moses.

The sudden shifts and interruptions within the Pentateuchal narrative constitute a fifth consideration challenging any easy notion of Mosaic authorship. More than once the story breaks off abruptly to be continued only at a later point. Two examples will suffice. First, the detailed and well-organized narrative about the patriarch Joseph begins in Genesis 37. Even though the unity of this chapter is often questioned, it maintains an interest in Joseph throughout. The same is true of Genesis 39–50. The intervening chapter, Genesis 38, however, is an independent account of Judah and his daughter-in-law Tamar. Joseph is nowhere mentioned. Genesis 38 awkwardly imposes itself on the narrative.

Exodus 4:24–26 is equally intrusive. According to Exod. 3:1–4:17, the deity must summon much energy and patience in order to convince Moses that he should lead Yahweh's people out of Egypt. Moses finally submits to his divine calling, and in Exod. 4:18–20 he prepares to return to Egypt. In Exod. 4:24–26, however, we are jarred by a fragmentary and puzzling narrative about the circumcision of Moses that begins, "At a lodging place on the way Yahweh met him [Moses] and sought to kill him." Why would the deity now wish to annihilate the man he has just succeeded in summoning for a special task? This independent unit so disturbs the flow of biblical narrative that one is tempted to ask whether Moses was a poor organizer or whether several different hands contributed to the final version of the Pentateuch.

There are several miscellaneous considerations that throw into question Mosaic authorship of the entire Pentateuch. For example, a few verses in the Pentateuch report that Moses engaged in a writing task, but not one specifically states that he drafted the first five books of the Hebrew Bible in their entirety. And the third-person references to Moses are so constant in Exodus-Deuteronomy that it taxes the imagination to think that he is the author. Furthermore, a few Pentateuchal verses imply that the Pentateuch was written in an age later than Moses. Thus, the statement of Gen. 36:31, "These are the kings who reigned in the land of Edom, before any king reigned over the Israelites," reflects a date after monarchy had been established as an official institution in Israel. Perhaps this verse is contemporary with David's reign (ca. 1000–961 B.C.); if so, it could not have come from Moses. Then too, such passages as Num. 22:1 and Deut. 1:1 reflect the thinking of one who is living to the west of the Jordan river, yet Moses died before Israel entered the Land of Promise. The Book of Deuteronomy opens with the statement, "These are the words that Moses spoke to all Israel beyond the Jordan in the wilderness." It thereby implies that Israel's occupation of Canaan is an accomplished fact, and it squares poorly with the assumption of Mosaic authorship. Finally, the last chapter of Deuteronomy depicts the death of Moses and gives a generous assessment of his worth. Unless we are willing to call Moses a boastful clairvoyant, it is difficult to credit him with that chapter.

The dogma of Mosaic authorship of the Pentateuch has, therefore, been rejected by many critical readers. The profound impact of a historical Moses on his people is not necessarily denied. But once the Hebrew Bible is subjected to the kind of critical scrutiny brought to bear on other kinds of ancient literature we must confront such problems as those just enumerated. Having outlined the main problems, let us review the contributions of the scholars most responsible for the development of an informed criticism of the Pentateuch.

THE GRADUAL EMERGENCE AND TRIUMPH
OF PENTATEUCHAL CRITICISM

Even as far back as the early centuries of the Christian era, a few persons were unwilling to say that Moses wrote all of the Torah.[5] In the early fifth century, Jerome claimed Moses was the author and Ezra the editor of the Pentateuch. The first questioning within Judaism was expressed in a Talmudic text written in about 500: "Joshua wrote the book that bears his name and [the last] eight verses of the Pentateuch."[6] This would refer to the conclusion of Deuteronomy, 34:5–12, which gives an account of Moses' death and his obituary. To deny that even this small section was written by Moses was to imply that the Torah is composite. Yet in the centuries that followed, Mosaic authorship of the Torah was infrequently challenged.

By 1700, however, rationalist critics were maintaining that Moses was not responsible for certain segments of the Pentateuch. They suspected that it was a compilation of earlier documents, but they were not yet in a position to identify those documents. Then, in 1711, Pastor Witter of Hildesheim, Germany, asserted that the use of two names for deity in Genesis, Yahweh and Elohim, confirmed the already suspected presence of older documents in the Pentateuch. Witter concluded that Genesis 1–3 contains two distinct creation narratives. In 1753 Astruc, a French Catholic physician, argued that Genesis reflects two primary and ten secondary sources. The former were to be identified on the basis of their use of the divine names Yahweh and Elohim. But neither Witter nor Astruc was willing to scrap the tradition of Mosaic authorship for all portions of the Pentateuch. In fact, Astruc asserted that Genesis 1–3 preserves the work of Moses who drew upon two previously existing sources.

In the 1780s Eichhorn subjected the Book of Genesis to careful literary analysis. He concluded that the two main sources in Genesis, now identified as the Elohist and Yahwist after the divine names employed, each had a distinctive style. He further claimed that a redactor (editor) of the two sources, someone other than Moses, had edited Genesis into a meaningful whole.

The Documentary Hypothesis of Graf-Wellhausen

In the decades that followed, biblical scholars asserted variant opinions about the Pentateuch. In 1853 Hupfeld maintained that the Pentateuch attests two Elohist sources, one early and one late. These two sources along with the Yahwist source, said Hupfeld, were integrated by a redactor whose eccentricities are partly to blame for the present condition of the Pentateuch. In the following year, Riehm argued for the independence of Deuteronomy as a separate document.

With the views of Hupfeld and Riehm soon gaining ground, the next major task was dating the two Elohist sources (the original E and subsequent P), the Yahwist source (J), and Deuteronomy (D). Here a word should be said about the use of letters for sources. For more than a century, these letters have been used as the official designations for the sources of the Pentateuch. One Elohist source is labeled "E," for the divine name "Elohim." The other, which also attests "Elohim," is called "P" because it reflects strong priestly interests. "D" stands for the Book of Deuteronomy and other brief passages in the Tetrateuch that are thought to bear the mark of Deuteronomic influence. "J" denotes the Yahwist source and its preferred divine name, "Yahweh." In German, both the source and the divine name begin with the "J" consonant, which is pronounced like our English "Y."

Hupfeld maintained that the chronological order of the three sources with which he was concerned was P-E-J. In the late 1860s Graf spoke for the reverse order: J-E-P. Moreover, Graf adopted De Wette's earlier judgment (1806) that a seventh-century date may be assigned to Deuteronomy since the Deuteronomic Code in chapters 12–26 can be equated with the book of law found in the Jerusalem Temple in 622

B.C. This documentary hypothesis, with its affirmation of four sources whose chronological sequence is J-E-D-P, was most effectively articulated by Wellhausen.

In his brilliant *Prolegomena to the History of Ancient Israel*[7] (1885), first published in German in 1878, Wellhausen masterfully argued his case. There he accepted Graf's ordering and dating of the Pentateuchal documents—J (ninth century B.C.), E (eighth century), D (seventh century), and P (fifth century). Wellhausen's special interest, however, was to integrate the documentary hypothesis with a detailed reconstruction of the history of Old Testament religion.

Wellhausen, who was strongly influenced by the philosophy of Hegel, accepted the premise that all history—Israel's included—follows an evolutionary pattern. Within the Hebrew Bible, he found virtually every form of belief from animism to ethical monotheism. Wellhausen affirmed that "the nearer history is to its origin the more profane it is."[8] He therefore pointed to signs of sophistication and religious refinement in the latest Pentateuchal source (P) that were wanting in the earliest source (J). He accorded only minor historical significance to the Pentateuchal documents, for all were written many centuries after the events they purported to relate. Nevertheless, he did view each document as a remarkable index of the customs, beliefs, and conditions of the period in which it was composed.

Wellhausen commented extensively on each source. He regarded J as the earliest, since on the basis of style, theology, and implied social customs its depiction of Israelite beginnings was the simplest of the four. He observed that the early J document reflected an anthropomorphic portrait of the deity. He further noted that the tendency for J to assign numerous events to Beer-sheba and Hebron spoke for a southern Palestinian setting as its point of origin. Wellhausen also believed that the J document reflected a peaceful and confident situation within the religious community. He therefore posited that it had been written in Judah during the successful and tranquil reign of Jehoshaphat (873–849 B.C.).

In the E document Wellhausen saw a parallel narrative reflecting a sociological and theological advance over J. He noted that E offered a less anthropomorphic depiction of the deity by introducing the format of vision and the use of the angelic messenger as means of assuring that the confrontation between God and man would be less intimate. Since the E document, with its marked interest in Shechem and Bethel, was oriented further north and since it appeared to be one evolutionary step ahead of J, Wellhausen assigned it a northern origin and dated it to the reign of the Israelite king Jeroboam II (786–746 B.C.).

As for the D document, Wellhausen subscribed to the earlier view of De Wette, who had identified the book of the law discovered in Josiah's reign (622 B.C.) with the Deuteronomic Code (chaps. 12–26).

Wellhausen, who regarded the independent document of D as the key to establishing a relative chronology for all four Pentateuchal sources, stated that here was a work written in the middle of the seventh century B.C. that stemmed from the Jerusalem priesthood.

Wellhausen then maintained that the complicated style, preoccupation with priestly rubric, and ethical and religious refinement of the P source all betrayed its late emergence as a Pentateuchal element. Its marked interest in Sabbath, circumcision, and covenant formality encouraged Wellhausen to conclude that P was the written product of a priest-dominated Israelite theocracy of the fifth century B.C. far more concerned with religious matters than with political realities. Finally, on the issue of source redaction, Wellhausen claimed that the J and E documents were first combined, the D source was affixed to them, and the P document was amalgamated with an already redacted J-E-D literary entity. He dated the Pentateuch in its present format to about 400 B.C.

Beyond Wellhausen

Since Wellhausen, two events that have done much to shape the intellectual world as a whole have directly influenced Pentateuchal criticism. First, the experience of two world wars and other political disruptions has instilled in twentieth-century thinkers an uncertainty that man's history is marked by steady progression and improvement. Today Wellhausen's evolutionary assumption that the later stages of ancient Israel's history automatically reflect a society's maturation in social, intellectual, and religious matters is widely dismissed as erroneous.

Second, the interpretation of abundant archaeological evidence uncovered since Wellhausen challenges previously held notions about the meager capacity of the Pentateuchal documents to reflect conditions that existed during Israel's earliest years. Wellhausen charged that none of the four Pentateuchal sources adequately reflected Israelite life and thought of the second millennium B.C. Today that judgment must be revised. While it is not held that the Book of Genesis is everywhere historically trustworthy, it is believed that the customs and conditions described in Genesis 12–50 present data indigenous to the second millennium B.C.[9]

Two post-Wellhausian trends in Pentateuchal criticism are so significant that they must be noted here. The first freely accepts source analysis as a viable critical approach to the literary material, but argues that form criticism must also be allowed to have its say. Scholars who support this view emphasize both the short units of Israelite tradition and the larger complexes to which they belong.

A second trend rejects Wellhausen's approach as so inept that source criticism of the Pentateuch must be abandoned completely. In the remainder of this chapter, we shall characterize these two important trends in greater detail.[10]

Again Gunkel deserves mention. He was convinced that sound Pentateuchal analysis depends on both source criticism and form criticism. In his *Genesis* commentary (1901) and other works Gunkel attempted to grasp the separate preliterary traditions behind the literary sources.[11] He was especially interested in ascertaining the various forms of Hebrew discourse and the specific life situation that gave rise to each. By searching for the preliterary forms, drawing on widespread archaeological and literary data from the ancient Near East, and positing the function of particular forms within the context of Israelite life and worship, Gunkel freed Pentateuchal research from impending sterility. He readily appreciated how certain popular sagas could be sustained and kept perpetually fresh through a constant retelling within the ancient Israelite community. Even so, he showed little interest in relating the short individual units he had successfully isolated to the larger whole. The question of how these different sagas had been drawn together into one body of literature had yet to be satisfactorily answered.

More recently, von Rad and Noth have applied the techniques of form criticism to the entire sweep of Pentateuchal narrative.[12] Though they accept the traditional four sources, they move far beyond the written documents. Isolating the ancient credos preserved in Deut. 26:5–9, Deut. 6:20–24, and Josh. 24:2–13, von Rad claims that here were texts whose rhythm and alliteration ushered the reader into the era of the judges (the twelfth and eleventh centuries B.C.), when on specified occasions the great deeds of Yahweh were cultically recalled by the assembled tribes. Israel's Aramean origin, her Exodus from Egypt, and her conquest of the Land of Promise were the three great themes recited there. In developing his own story, which constitutes the backbone of the Pentateuch, the Yahwist (J) adopted and expanded on the ancient schema of the well-established Israelite credo. He accepted its three compelling themes. In addition, he incorporated the Sinai, patriarchal, and primeval traditions. Subsequently added E and P strata then provided supplementary data, but did virtually nothing to shape the Hexateuch, since that had already been achieved by the Yahwist.

In answering the question, "How were the brief and wholly separate units of tradition gradually assembled into one completely redacted Pentateuch?" Noth points to the existence of five great themes: Israel's Exodus from Egypt, her conquest of the land of Canaan, Yahweh's promise to the patriarchs, Israel's wilderness wandering, and the revelation of Yahweh to Israel at Sinai. Noth interprets these themes as the veritable rubrics under which the various Pentateuchal narratives were organized. Because he believed that all five themes were inherited by the Yahwist, the J strand reflects a less creative mind in Noth's analysis than it does in von Rad's. Noth traces these great themes from their present literary form back to what he takes to be their inception. In doing so, he has emphasized the constant reshaping of the original thematic traditions. Yet for all the gains made in tracing traditional blocks of material back to their preliterary form, von Rad and Noth have sometimes been charged with subjectivism.[13]

Hence, a second trend, which embraces what is called the "traditio-historical" approach, urges that the source-critical task be abandoned altogether. The terminology we are employing is admittedly problematic. We are applying the term "traditio-historical" to an approach that is manifestly impatient with source criticism. Yet the titles of Noth's works, *Überlieferungsgeschichtliche Studien* and *Überlieferungsgeschichte des Pentateuch*, reveal that he was an investigator of the "history of traditions." (The title of the latter in its English edition is *A History of Pentateuchal Traditions*.) In Noth's view, oral traditions and written sources both require consideration. The outright rejection of source criticism has been most evident among Scandinavian biblical scholars, and it is their position that we now seek to sketch.

To Scandinavian scholars, source criticism is a bookish anachronism. For example, Engnell argues that writing was relatively infrequent in ancient Israel; only within Israel's postexilic period, he says, was writing of any significance. Scandinavian scholarship assesses the written Pentateuch as a late accomplishment in ancient Israel's lifetime. Yet the oral narrative and legal traditions behind that writing are acknowledged to be ancient.[14]

This approach denounces the impulse to delineate parallel documents in the Pentateuch as a misguided desire informed by "western desk logic."[15] Instead, it is argued that small units, larger complexes, and comprehensive collections of oral tradition must all be grasped adequately. In this view, the living Israelite congregation, with its effective leaders and ongoing cult, had little need to commit ancient traditions to writing. Hence, discrepancies and duplications in the Pentateuch do not reflect parallel sources. Instead, they demonstrate that the epic "law of iteration" (repetition) is at work in the ongoing transmission of oral tradition. Though the tradition was passed on orally with far more reliability than is possible for most moderns to appreciate, variants did evolve. But only an utterly jarring historical experience would have stimulated Israel to change the age-old pattern of oral communication and that was not to occur until 587 B.C. with the destruction of Jerusalem. At that moment, with the disruption of an independent life in Judah, the abolishment of the Jerusalem cult, and the abrupt and humiliating exile in Babylon, Israel finally recognized that she must commit her oral traditions to a fixed literary form if they were to endure. Only then was she on her way to becoming the people of the book.

Although the Scandinavian contribution to the ongoing task of Pentateuchal criticism has been considerable, two valid objections may be raised. First, to say that writing was almost never practiced in ancient Israel until the postexilic period is to speak in extremes. How are we to know that no part of the Pentateuch was written prior to 587 B.C.? Israel's neighbors had acquired the art of writing prior to that date. It is also probable that the court history of David (2 Sam. 9–20, 1 Kings 1–2) was written down not long after the termination of his rule in 961 B.C. And surely in the Gezer Calendar (ca. 925) and the Siloam Inscription (ca. 705) we have two good examples of preexilic Israelite writing. Recent epigraphic discoveries have shown that the art of writing in monarchical Israel was far more widespread than the Scandinavian scholars have allowed.[16]

Second, although Engnell rejects source criticism, he has not moved beyond some of its basic concerns. Bright advances this consideration as a semantic criticism of Engnell in the following question: "If material corresponding to the symbols D and P (and, by subtraction, to JE) can be found, does not the task of separating it still remain, whether one calls it literary criticism or not?"[17]

The task of Pentateuchal criticism is still unfinished. Old positions continue to be reaffirmed and new ones advanced. Precisely what direction future studies will take is hard to say. Nevertheless, at present the following seems clear: (1) scholars respond in diverse ways to the composite and complex character of the Pentateuch; (2) source and form criticism are usually both considered valuable; (3) Wellhausen's chronological arrangement of the strata is generally accepted, although J is increasingly fixed to the tenth and E to the ninth century B.C.; (4) the importance and tenacity of oral tradition is acknowledged; (5) the significance, especially the creativity, of the Pentateuchal redactors is recognized today with increasing enthusiasm; and (6) the individual units of Pentateuchal tradition are being appraised as objects worthy of detailed study (today even the imaginative J stratum is only rarely celebrated as an independent masterpiece).

The Graf-Wellhausen documentary hypothesis is with us still. On occasion its doom has been proclaimed, just as the end of the world has been foretold. It seems, however, that in both instances we have a mistaken prophecy on our hands in which some rejoice and others lament.

NOTES

1. See Julius Wellhausen, *Prolegomena to the History of Ancient Israel,* trans. Allan Menzies and J. Sutherland Black (Edinburgh: A. & C. Black, 1885), pp. 297–362, also published by Meridian Books (New York, 1957); and "The Form-Critical Problem of the Hexateuch," in Gerhard von Rad, *The Problem of the Hexateuch and Other Essays,* trans. E. W. Trueman Dicken (London: Oliver & Boyd, 1966), pp. 1–78; and Gerhard von Rad,

Genesis: A Commentary, rev. ed., trans. John H. Marks, The Old Testament Library (Philadelphia: Westminster Press, 1972), pp. 13–43.

2. See "The Pentateuch," in Ivan Engnell, *A Rigid Scrutiny: Critical Essays on the Old Testament,* trans. John T. Willis (Nashville: Vanderbilt University Press, 1969), pp. 50–67, for a well-wrought defense of the Tetrateuchal ("P work") category. For a brief presentation of Noth's detachment of Deuteronomy from the Pentateuch, see Martin Noth, *The History of Israel,* 2d ed., rev. trans. Peter R. Ackroyd (New York: Harper & Row, 1960), pp. 42–49.

3. For the views of a representative conservative biblical scholar who defends Mosaic authorship, see Gleason L. Archer, Jr., *A Survey of Old Testament Introduction* (Chicago: Moody Press, 1964), pp. 96–109. He exposes what he feels are the fallacies of the documentary theory of Pentateuchal criticism and advances Moses' qualifications as a writer.

4. The frequent mention of the domesticated camel in Genesis (12:16; 30:43; 31:17; 32:7, 15; 37:25; and throughout chap. 24) is also commonly dismissed as an anachronism. Iron Age archaeological strata in Palestine disclose the bones of both asses and camels, but earlier Bronze Age strata have yielded no camel bones. This suggests that the camel was probably not domesticated in Palestine until late in the thirteenth century B.C. The camel comes off in Genesis as a literary intrusion and a historical embarrassment.

5. In the presentation of this section and the two following, the author is indebted to the competent historical surveys of Pentateuchal criticism by Robert H. Pfeiffer, *Introduction to the Old Testament,* rev. ed. (New York: Harper & Row, 1948), pp. 135–141; C. R. North, "Pentateuchal Criticism," in H. H. Rowley, ed., *The Old Testament and Modern Study* (New York: Oxford University Press, 1951), pp. 48–83; and Artur Weiser, *The Old Testament: Its Formation and Development,* trans. Dorothea M. Barton (New York: Association Press, 1961), pp. 74–81.

6. Maurice Simon and Israel W. Slotki, trans., *Baba Bathra Translated into English with Notes, Glossary and Indices* (London: Soncino Press, 1935), p. 71 (Baba Bathra 14b).

7. Wellhausen, *op. cit.*

8. *Ibid.,* p. 245.

9. For additional reflection on the prevailing changes in the academic climate that have affected Pentateuchal criticism since Wellhausen, see John Bright, "Modern Study of Old Testament Literature," in G. Ernest Wright, ed., *The Bible and the Ancient Near East* (Garden City, N.Y.: Doubleday, Anchor Books, 1965), pp. 5–18.

10. More comprehensive treatments are available in North, *op. cit.,* pp. 48–83, and R. J. Thompson, *Moses and the Law in a Century of Criticism since Graf,* Vetus Testamentum Supplement, vol. 19 (Leiden, Neth.: E. J. Brill, 1970), pp. 109–163.

11. For an English translation of the detailed introductory section in Gunkel's *Genesis* commentary, see Hermann Gunkel, *The Legends of Genesis: The Biblical Saga and History,* trans. W. H. Carruth (New York: Schocken Books, 1964).

12. See Gerhard von Rad, "The Form-Critical Problem," *op. cit.,* pp. 1–78;

and Martin Noth, *A History of Pentateuchal Traditions,* trans. Bernhard W. Anderson (Englewood Cliffs, N.J.: Prentice-Hall, 1972), pp. 5–41. For a helpful summary of the work of von Rad and Noth, see G. Ernest Wright, "Recent European Study in the Pentateuch," *The Journal of Bible and Religion* 18 (1950): 216–225.

13. See Wright, *op. cit.,* pp. 222–223, who doubts that the five Pentateuchal themes can be isolated as fully as Noth contends, and Bright, *op. cit.,* pp. 17–18, who respects Noth's erudition but denounces his historical negativism.

14. On the importance of oral tradition for biblical research, see Eduard Nielsen, "The Role of Oral Tradition in the Bible," in Samuel Sandmel, ed., *Old Testament Issues* (New York: Harper & Row, Harper Forum Books, 1968), pp. 68–93.

15. Engnell, *op. cit.,* p. 54.

16. For a useful presentation of the evidence, see A. R. Millard, "The Practice of Writing in Ancient Israel," *The Biblical Archaeologist* 35 (1972): 98–111.

17. Bright, *op. cit.,* p. 13.

4

ORIGINS ANTICIPATED: THE PATRIARCHAL TRADITIONS

One article of faith for ancient Israel was that her God, Yahweh, had entered into special dealings with her as his covenant people. She also believed that the process of selecting one historical people for the realization of his purposes began when Yahweh touched the lives of Abraham, Isaac, Jacob, and Joseph. In Israelite tradition these patriarchs were presented as the first to hear Yahweh's promises for the future.

This was, most assuredly, the reflection of a maturing faith. Only gradually did the ancient Hebrews affirm that the encounters with deity of Abraham, Isaac, Jacob, and Joseph were confrontations with the same God who had so decisively revealed himself during the Exodus. Yet slowly the various pieces fell into place, and one coherent, refined theological structure ultimately developed. We see the process beginning during the era of the judges in the ancient cultic credos in Deut. 6:20–24, Deut. 26:5–9, and Josh. 24:2–13, which exult in Yahweh's choice of a people. These confessions declare that Yahweh committed himself to a band of slaves and shaped them into a community, through his mighty acts of deliverance, with a meaningful present and a promising future. Thus, even in premonarchical Israel (the twelfth and eleventh centuries B.C.), the continuity of Yahweh's supportive dealings with one people was confidently upheld. While all three credos celebrate the Exodus above all else, each specifically alludes to what took place prior to Hebrew enslavement in Egypt. For example, Josh.

Biblical texts to be read prior to and in conjunction with the present chapter: Gen. 11:10–32 and all of Genesis 12–50. Pay particular attention to the following: (a) the Abraham cycle: Genesis 12, 14, 15, 17, 18, 22, 23; (b) the Jacob cycle: Genesis 24 and Gen. 25:21–34; 27:1–45; 28:10–22; 32:22–32; (c) the Joseph "cycle": Genesis 37, 39, 43, 45, 50.

24:3 declares through the speech of the deity, "I took your father Abraham from beyond the River and led him through all the land of Canaan, and made his offspring many."

As the traditions become more elaborate, this view of the story of the Genesis patriarchs as a vital prologue to the story of the Exodus itself became an increasingly fixed element in Israelite mentality. Hence, in the Old Testament as we now have it, the divine and human drama preserved in Genesis 12–50 is a crucial prelude. It looks forward to the deliverance of a group of Hebrew slaves from Egypt and their formation into a single people who viewed themselves as the committed followers of a triumphant God. Israel's origins are presented by way of anticipation. Then, in time, hope becomes reality.[1]

THE ANCIENT NEAR EAST
PRIOR TO THE PATRIARCHAL AGE

The ancient Israelites who gave substance and shape to Genesis 12–50 felt no compulsion to describe in comprehensive fashion the settled world powers and wandering tribes that blanketed the Fertile Crescent at the outset of the second millennium B.C. Nevertheless, the patriarchs of ancient Israel were highly mobile and did not live alone; they belonged to larger folk movements that were penetrating the Syro-Palestinian region. Throughout much of the Fertile Crescent such migrations disturbed previously settled cultures. Consequently, before we consider the patriarchal traditions in terms of their basic shape, historicity, and major themes, we shall allude to certain events in the ancient Near East that took place prior to and during the patriarchal age.[2] Not all the details are likely to be absorbed on a first reading. Yet even an initial encounter with this material should make clear that the founding fathers of ancient Israel did not live in a historical vacuum.

Mesopotamia

By the time that the Hebrew patriarchs sojourned in Palestine during the first half of the second millennium B.C., life in the Near East had already been in progress for over a thousand years since history's dawn. At the beginning of the third millennium B.C., the protoliterate culture of Mesopotamia, the predynastic culture of Egypt, and the proto-urban culture of Palestine were all in existence.

In the open alluvial plains of Mesopotamia, classical Sumerian culture flourished from about 2800 to 2360 B.C.[3] Rather than organizing themselves into a monolithic empire, the Sumerians formed several city-states. Each city-state took the worship of its own deity quite seriously. In size and splendor, the temple eclipsed all other buildings.

The local Sumerian ruler was chief servant of the city's patron god and had the special responsibility of meeting the interests of that deity. Sumerian literature and art were permeated by a religious perspective.

Yet despite their advances in religion, literature, and law, the Sumerians were overrun by outsiders. In the middle of the third millennium, bands of roving Semites from the Arabian Desert advanced into the Tigris-Euphrates plain with increasing force. And they came to stay. Speaking the Semitic language of Akkadian, these invaders adopted the Sumerian cuneiform, syllabic script for their own texts and even appropriated the Sumerian pantheon.

These peoples seem to have coexisted successfully for many decades. Then with the energetic Sargon, a powerful Semitic dynasty came into being and fashioned history's first great empire. Flourishing from about 2360 to 2180 B.C., the empire of Akkad drew all Mesopotamian civilization to itself.[4] Sargon's conquests swept across vast portions of the Near East. At home the palace replaced the temple as the principal edifice. Since the emperors of Akkad linked themselves with leading deities, already overlapping religious and political causes now coalesced. Akkadian became the dominant tongue and the language of court inscriptions.

In about 2180 B.C., however, the empire of Akkad succumbed to the Guti invasions. But these barbarians, who swarmed in from the northeast, were unable to reign with a firm hand. Consequently, under the Third Dynasty of Ur (ca. 2060–1950) Sumerian culture enjoyed a renaissance, especially in the spheres of jurisprudence and art. Once more the Mesopotamian city-states pursued a fundamentally self-contained course. Nevertheless, as the third millennium B.C. gave way to the second, the Sumerians experienced their last moments of independence. Invading forces from Elam, Asshur, and Mari, along with marauding Northwest-Semitic peoples known as "Amorites," made sure that with the collapse of the Third Dynasty of Ur, the Sumerians would no longer function as a distinct, albeit loosely structured political entity.

Egypt

Since Egypt had western Asia under its control during most of the third and second millennia B.C., the fate of this ancient world power is also of interest to those who study the patriarchal age.[5] With the emergence of the First Dynasty of Egypt in the twenty-ninth century B.C., Egypt's Old Kingdom period began. By the middle of the third millennium, Egyptian culture found creative expression in religion, literature, and architecture. The huge pyramids that emerged gave dramatic testimony to the technical know-how, organizational capacity, and energy of countless Egyptians who devoted themselves to satisfying the needs of the

I. THE ANCIENT NEAR EAST PRIOR TO THE ISRAELITE EXODUS (ca. 3200–1300 B.C.)

DATE (B.C.)	EGYPT	PALESTINE	MESOPOTAMIA
3200	Predynastic culture	Proto-urban culture	Protoliterate culture
2800	Old Kingdom (29–23 cents.)		Classical (early dynastic) Sumerian culture (ca. 2800–2360)
2400	1st Intermediate Period (ca. 22–21 cents.)	Seminomadic invasions	Empire of Akkad (ca. 2360–2180) Guti invasions (ca. 2180)
2000	Middle Kingdom (mid-20–mid-18 cents.) 12th Dynasty (ca. 1991–1786)		3d Dynasty of Ur and Sumerian renaissance (ca. 2060–1950) Rival Amorite Dynasties
1800	2d Intermediate Period, results in Hyksos incursions and rule of Egypt (ca. mid-18–mid-16 cents.)	The Patriarchal Era	Mari Age (ca. 1750–1697) Zimri-lim, king of Mari (ca. 1730–1697) 1st Dynasty of Babylon (ca. 1830–1530) Hammurabi (ca. 1728–1686)
1600	New Kingdom (mid-16–12 cents.) 18th Dynasty (ca. 1552–1306) Amosis' rule and Hyksos expulsion (ca. 1552–1527) Thutmosis III (ca. 1490–1436) Amenophis II (ca. 1438–1412)		Hittite invasions spell end of 1st Dynasty of Babylon; thrusts Mesopotamia into a dark age (ca. 1530)
1400	Amenophis III (ca. 1403–1364) Amenophis IV (Akhnaton) (ca. 1364–1347) Haremhab (ca. 1333–1306)	The Amarna Era (ca. 1400–1350)	Assyrian ascendance and dominion (ca. 1356–1197)

pharaoh for adequate burial. It was crucial that this one who was both god and king be ready for the life beyond.

The aggressive pharaohs of the Old Kingdom tried to rule their people justly and to extend the sphere of Egyptian influence far into western Asia. Their successful reigns assured that the land of the Nile would be blessed with a stable government whose continuity would benefit all men. Beyond the national frontier, Egyptian brawn worked the copper mines in the Sinai Peninsula, and military forces regularly accompanied the pharaohs to Palestine and Syria. Egypt succeeded in controlling important coastal routes of trade and exploiting a firm trade connection with Byblos in northern Phoenicia.

So far as Palestine is concerned, the Old Kingdom of Egypt dominated the thoroughfares that passed northward along the coastal plain, eastward through the Valley of Jezreel, and then northeastward to Damascus. Though Egypt could not manage tight control of all the city-states of Palestine that were then emerging, she set up strategic garrisons along her primary trade route. Elsewhere she secured the services of city-state heads who functioned as client-rulers.

During the third millennium B.C., Palestine itself witnessed extensive urban activity. It saw the establishment and rebuilding of such major cities as Jericho, Ai, Megiddo, Shechem, and Gezer, all of which were to play an important role in biblical history. These cities, which bear Semitic names, were occupied by a Canaanite-speaking population whose life style was no doubt similar to that of later Canaanites whose practices are depicted in the Hebrew Bible. In contrast with Egypt and Mesopotamia, these cities did not organize into a larger whole. As Egypt successfully pursued her commercial interests in western Asia, the indigenous inhabitants of Canaan tended to the needs of their independent urban centers and their related agrarian economy.

The Old Kingdom, however, became increasingly incapable of maintaining a united Egypt. Gigantic building programs, expensive military exploits, weak rulers, and encroaching Asians who infiltrated the Nile Delta all contributed to Egypt's plight. She passed therefore from her Old Kingdom phase into her First Intermediate period, which involved most of the twenty-second and twenty-first centuries B.C. Egypt's internal disunity, which prevented adequate surveillance of northern territories, and the dramatic swell of seminomadic incursions into western Asia at the end of the third millennium could not help but affect Palestine. Palestine was devastated on both sides of the Jordan as the invading Amorites overthrew the city-states. But once they had unleashed their fury, the Amorites settled and brought to the land a new vitality. Undoubtedly, among these folk were the near-ancestors of those Israelite patriarchs Abraham, Isaac, and Jacob, who receive the main attention of Genesis 12–50.

THE ANCIENT NEAR EAST
DURING THE PATRIARCHAL AGE

Now let us briefly consider several historical aspects of the ancient Near East datable to the first half of the second millennium B.C. (2000–1500), which is widely accepted as the age of the Hebrew patriarchs. Again, we shall focus on developments in Mesopotamia and then turn to Egypt and related territories in western Asia.

Mesopotamia

As a result of the collapse of the Sumerian Third Dynasty of Ur in about 1950 B.C., various Semitic elements tried to take the lead in Mesopotamia. Of particular significance were the "Westerners" now located in northwest Mesopotamia and northern Syria. They are designated "Amurru" in various cuneiform texts and "Amorites" in the Old Testament. Speaking dialects of Northwest-Semitic (to which biblical Hebrew belongs), these folk ruled the Mesopotamian landscape with increasing vigor. A few of their descendants appear in Genesis 12–50. For approximately two hundred years after the fall of the Third Dynasty of Ur, many unimpressive dynasties rivaled one another in Lower Mesopotamia.

Located on the middle Euphrates River, the city-state of Mari impressively held sway over Upper Mesopotamia during the second half of the eighteenth century B.C. Mari flourished under the leadership of Zimri-lim (ca. 1730–1697), who extended its influence and physical borders in several directions. Thanks to the excavations undertaken at Mari in the late 1930s, many details about the so-called Mari age have come to light.[6] Mari boasted an excellent army, and the monarch himself claimed as home a palace consisting of almost three hundred rooms. Business and administrative documents in remarkable abundance disclose that Mari was a center of extensive trading. Even so, Mari soon had to acknowledge the supremacy of Babylon to the south.

The First Dynasty of Babylon began its three hundred years of Amorite rule in about 1830. Clearly, the well-known Hammurabi (ca. 1728–1686) was its greatest monarch.[7] With his ascendancy to the throne, Hammurabi recognized that Mari, Assyria, and Elam all posed a serious threat to Babylonian existence. Hammurabi soon engaged in brilliant military conquests, and somewhat later in his reign he wielded Mari a fatal blow. Hammurabi, who is famous largely for his Babylonian legal code, diligently applied himself to empire consolidation and reorganization. Since Babylon lies beneath the water table, it cannot be excavated today. Nevertheless, it seems that Babylon was a rather unimportant ancient Near Eastern city that became an outstanding cultural and commercial center during Hammurabi's reign. This was a busy era of pseudoscience (magic and astrology, for example), literary output, and a well-defined religion that elevated Marduk to the top position in the Mesopotamian pantheon. Babylon was Marduk's city, and it was prospering.

But during his last years of rule, Hammurabi was involved in continuous warfare, and in the decades that followed all Mesopotamia languished. In the seventeenth and sixteenth centuries B.C., bands of Hurrians (called "Horites" in the Old Testament) swarmed southward from the mountains of Armenia and traversed the entire Fertile Crescent. Their center appears to have been Nuzi to the east of the Tigris, where several thousand texts dating to the fifteenth century B.C. have been

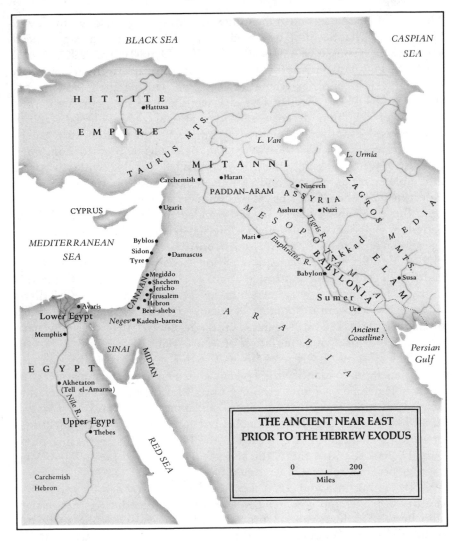

THE ANCIENT NEAR EAST
PRIOR TO THE HEBREW EXODUS

0   200
Miles

discovered. Some of these texts reveal predominantly Hurrian practices that bear directly on patriarchal customs attested in Genesis.

The remaining years of the First Dynasty of Babylon were insignificant. Finally, in about 1530 B.C., that dynasty succumbed to invading Hittite forces that penetrated from the west. Yet the Hittites, who had the means to travel from distant Asia Minor, lacked the talent to consolidate their military gains in Mesopotamia. For several decades prior to 1530 and for many after, Mesopotamia had fallen victim to a dark age.

Egypt

The advent of the second millennium B.C. brought good days to Egypt. She left her chaotic First Intermediate period behind and experienced far-reaching resurgence under the Twelfth Dynasty (ca. 1991–1786). With the new prosperity, the Middle Kingdom (mid-twentieth through mid-eighteenth centuries) came into its own. During their long reigns, the pharaohs of the Twelfth Dynasty were able to maintain a rigorous program of irrigation, defense, and international trade. Political stability and peaceful conditions prompted accomplishments in literature, medicine, and mathematics. Moreover, the pharaohs expressed continued interest in western Asia, which they controlled loosely. Byblos was still a reliable Egyptian colony, and various geographical points in Syria and Palestine were the sites of Egyptian commercial undertakings.

But when the Twelfth Dynasty ended in about 1786, the Middle Kingdom experienced hard times. Internal chaos within Egypt and the aggression of Syro-Palestinian Asians contributed significantly to Egypt's plight. Her Second Intermediate period began in the middle of the eighteenth century B.C. and lasted about two hundred years. During this interval, foreigners swept down into Egypt and eventually ruled there. These invaders were designated "Hyksos" by the ineffectual pharaohs of the Middle Kingdom. Meaning "foreign chiefs," the label may have carried the pejorative connotation of "barbarians."

The scarcity of written sources for this period frustrates contemporary attempts to identify the Hyksos and their accomplishments. They were not members of one ethnic group. We know, for example, that Semitic, Hittite, and Hurrian names all appeared on Hyksos scarabs. In all likelihood, Egypt had no choice but to accept the forthright thrust of Amorite elements that moved into the Nile Delta in increasing numbers. Having migrated there, the Hyksos first subdued Lower Egypt and then gained control of Upper Egypt.[8]

Beginning in about 1650 B.C., the Hyksos provided Egypt with a century of leadership when she was incapable of producing that leadership herself. If this situation proved politically embarrassing to Egypt, it did assist her economy. With their capital at Avaris (Tanis) near the northeastern Egyptian frontier, the Hyksos conquered some of Asia as well. Trading between Egypt and Asia became commonplace, and Egypt imported many luxury wares. As the Hyksos mingled with Hurrian and Indo-Aryan populations in Palestine itself, they acquired use of the composite bow and horse-drawn chariot. Consequently they became excellent warriors.

Despite their accomplishments, the Hyksos were scarcely admired by all of Egypt's native population. By the middle of the sixteenth century, Egypt found herself in the happy position of being strong enough to expel these intruders. The Hyksos expulsion was gradual and reached a climax under Pharaoh Amosis (ca. 1552–1527).[9] He founded the splendid Eighteenth Dynasty, which successfully ruled Egypt and exercised extensive control over Palestine from about 1552 to 1306 B.C. In addition to ridding Egypt of the Hyksos intruders, Amosis occupied the Hyksos fortress of Sharuhen in southwestern Palestine. Now Egypt had easy access to western Asia. Thus if the late sixteenth century B.C. found many people in Mesopotamia wishing for better and more stable days, it witnessed an Egyptian vigor both within and beyond the nation's borders.

In sum, the first half of the second millennium B.C. offered confusing, exciting, and sometimes turbulent moments. Somewhere within that broad time span lived ancient Israel's founding fathers, whose welfare and aspirations were of special interest to those who gave expression to the traditions recounted in Genesis 12–50.

THE SHAPE AND HISTORICITY
OF THE BIBLICAL MATERIAL

When individuals and communities have both the inclination and the means to record the events they have experienced, the trained historian of a later era can set forth a history of the people involved. By scrutinizing, sifting, and interpreting the evidence in its various forms, he engages in the work of historical reconstruction and out of this evolves his written history. Yet this is hardly possible when the evidence simply does not exist or when it is too rare or tangential. Such is the situation with respect to the Hebrew patriarchs.

Despite the considerable gains of Syro-Palestinian archaeology in the last hundred years, our knowledge of the lives of Abraham, Isaac, Jacob, and Joseph depends solely on the Hebrew Bible. We cannot confidently place Abraham in a particular century within the first half of the second millennium B.C. nor can we assign Jacob to his century. In both instances, direct extrabiblical confirmation is lacking. In short, we stand at some distance from the Abraham and Jacob of history.

Still, it is assumed by many biblical interpreters that the background of Genesis 12–50 correlates well with what is known about the Fertile Crescent during the first half of the second millennium B.C. Thanks to the discovery, decipherment, and interpretation of various ancient texts, contemporary biblical scholars have some understanding of matters of nomenclature, sociological and religious customs, and geographic settlement as these bear on Israel's earliest ancestors.

Nevertheless, we cannot link a single event recorded in Genesis 12–50 to a specific happening attested by extrabiblical texts. The testimony of archaeology, while helpful, is consistently indirect.[10] To be sure, Nuzi texts of the fifteenth century B.C. help us understand patriarchal dealings regarding adoption and birthright. Patriarchal names are more intelligible in the light of our present knowledge of the ancient nomenclature of northwest Mesopotamia. And the ease with which the patriarchs roam from Upper Mesopotamia to Palestine and back parallels the situation described in many of the Assyrian texts of the eighteenth century B.C. turned up at Mari. Such materials, however, bring us nowhere close to an actual biblical personality named Abraham.

Obviously, Genesis 12–50 and portions of Genesis 11 closely linked with this material cannot be defined as history. Rather, these chapters contain vital Israelite legend. While we dare not minimize the capacity of legend to reflect on the past in truly meaningful ways, such literature has certain limitations. For example, the Genesis legends center on a relatively small number of persons who, while not utterly self-concerned, have only fleeting contact with outsiders. Segments of remote time are portrayed in general terms. The number of details offered about any

Painted Pottery Juglet of the Middle Bronze Age. This juglet with its distinctive painted concentric circles was found in a tomb near Ginossar on the northwestern shore of the Sea of Galilee. It belongs to a phase of the Middle Bronze period (IIA, ca. 1950–1730) when potters expressed their inventiveness in a wide range of forms. Note the juglet's well-defined lip, substantial handle, virtually globular body, and small flat base. (Courtesy of the Israel Department of Antiquities, the Israel Museum, Jerusalem.)

single event may be appallingly few. Too often the events themselves have been telescoped, refracted, and chronologically rearranged. The carefully observed distinction of tenses that characterizes history writing is also of no special concern to legend.

Yet for all its imprecision, legend can reveal both the feelings and actions of real individuals. With delightful abandon, it tends to internalize history by informing us of how certain persons felt about the past, and that is the primary thrust of "oral history" today.[11] Legend can therefore be historically significant in its capacity to instruct us about how Israel experienced those events of which legends speak.

Moreover, the legends of Genesis have other assets. They relate to specific geographical settings. Shechem, Bethel, Ai, Hebron, and Beer-sheba are all mentioned as vicinities visited by Israel's founding fathers. Even the personal names employed in legend sometimes have historical interest. In the Shem genealogy presented in Gen. 11:10–26, Nahor, Peleg, Serug, and Terah are enumerated as Abraham's ancestors. These personal names turn out to be close equivalents of Nakhur, Paliga, Sarugi, and Til-turakhi, respectively, which are attested place names in the vicinity of Haran in northwest Mesopotamia. These names suggest something about the original home of the patriarchs. Nevertheless, Gen. 11:10–26 can scarcely be accepted as good historical narrative.

Finally, we must acknowledge that the stories set forth in Genesis 12–50 did not acquire a written form for many years. The Yahwist, for example, may have composed his material almost a millennium after Abraham existed. Certainly Genesis 12–50 cannot be regarded as a reliable contemporary witness. This is not to imply that the tales of Abraham, Isaac, and Jacob preserved over the centuries at the cultic centers of Hebron, Beer-sheba, and Shechem were incapable of recording authentic recollections of actual happenings. Despite the oversimplification of ancient Israel's legends, the essence of history is recorded there and the continuing impact of past events is skillfully preserved. Hence, the legends of Genesis are a useful index of Israelite history, even when they fail to tell us all we would like to know. They encourage us to believe that the patriarchs actually existed. And through the reading of such biblical legend, we are permitted a close look at how ancient Israel viewed her own calling and destiny. That, too, is part of the achievement of the Genesis legends.

THE ABRAHAM CYCLE OF TRADITIONS:
GENESIS 12–23

In Abraham (Gen. 12–23), Jacob (Gen. 24–36), and Joseph (Gen. 37–50) we can identify the three foci of ancient Israel's patriarchal traditions.

Only in Genesis 26 do we have a chapter that deals exclusively with Isaac, and not all of it is unique. In terms of genealogy, Isaac is the vital link through which the divine promise and blessing offered to Abraham is transmitted to Jacob. He is little more, although the Yahwist's portraits of Isaac's marriage (Gen. 24:62–67) and old age (Gen. 27:1–40) are admittedly vivid. The other founding fathers of ancient Israel are depicted in greater detail. On the basis of the Genesis legends, we shall try to sketch reasonable profiles of Abraham, Jacob, and Joseph.

The initial statements about Abraham in the Hebrew Bible appear at the end of Genesis 11. A priestly passage (vv. 31–32) referring to the first phase of patriarchal migration instructs us that Terah, Abraham's father, led his family from Ur of the Chaldeans to Haran, the city in northwest Mesopotamia in which he later died. No doubt this migration, which focuses on one family, is part of the sweeping movement of Amorites that took place throughout much of the Fertile Crescent early in the second millennium. Moreover, the journey of Abraham's family is the concern of the following J passage (Gen. 11:28–30).

The migration tradition reported in Genesis 11 and continued in Genesis 12 has two phases. The first brings Abraham many miles to the northwest of Ur, presumably in Lower Mesopotamia, to Haran. The second finds him moving southwestward from Haran to Canaan. The location of Ur is problematic. Ur's absence in the Septuagint (the Greek version of the Old Testament) in Gen. 11:28, 31 suggests that the name may have been added to the text at a later time. Southern Mesopotamia did not have a significant influence on the patriarchal tradition of Genesis. By contrast, points of contact with the Arameans of northwest Mesopotamia are rather convincing. Thus Haran may legitimately be regarded as the home of the Israelite patriarchs. It was the point of departure for Abraham's journey of faith into Canaan, and Genesis 24 discloses that Abraham kept in contact with the people of that region.

Of far greater theological interest is Genesis 12, in which the Yahwist offers a paradigm of Abraham's life with its convincing blend of unwavering faith and human assertion. The crucial call of Abraham narrated in 12:1–7 relates how God impinges on the patriarch's personal life. It also conveys Israel's understanding of how she was uniquely summoned to Yahweh's service.

The deity comes suddenly and unexpectedly. Nothing is said about the form of Yahweh's abrupt appearance. God simply says to Abraham, "Go from your country and your kindred and your father's house to the land that I will show you" (v. 1). Yahweh expects a great deal of the patriarch. He asks Abraham to leave his native Haran and move to a place as yet unidentified. Yahweh simply assures this man of his choice that he will ultimately point it out and that from Abraham a great nation will emerge. The prospects for Abraham must have been plainly unappealing. Yahweh was urging him to leave the clan and the comforting sense of belonging that it provided. Also, Sarah's barren condition (11:30) would hardly have encouraged Abraham to think himself capable of fathering a great nation. Yet Abraham moves faithfully and obediently.

In the environs of the Canaanite sanctuary of Shechem (12:6), Yahweh meets Abraham once more in a theophany and succinctly declares, "To your descendants I will give this land." Broadly defined, a theophany is a momentary manifestation of the deity during which he communicates to man something of his nature, name, and purpose.[12] Genesis 12:7 tersely states that Yahweh appeared and spoke briefly to Abraham, and that Abraham responded by erecting an altar in Yahweh's honor. Abraham is now instructed that the land on which he is sojourning will one day be owned by his heirs. In this chapter the two divine promises of progeny and land that dominate the Book of Genesis are stated. Once more Abraham readily accepts a vital promise simply given. He continues his journey of faith southward into the Negev.

Genesis 12:10 introduces a new episode in Abraham's life, one that finds him bankrupt in faith but well endowed with self-assertion. The tension that sometimes exists between a staunch faith and its complete absence is superbly presented. Despite God's promise to protect and bless, Abraham now faces the demands of a grim famine and takes matters into his own hands. He and Sarah will go to Egypt in quest of food. Once there, Sarah will comply with Abraham's scheme by telling the Egyptians that she is his sister.

Bedouins and Their Camels in the Negev. In the parched wilderness of the Negev, a sight such as this is quite typical. (Photo by the author.)

The Yahwist sees in Pharaoh a foreigner who is both gracious and moral. Pharaoh's efforts to be a good host and to show respect for the marriage bond are evident. It is Abraham's character, not Pharaoh's, that suffers. He resorts to a lie, and once the truth is known he is ordered to leave with his wife. In seeking foremost to preserve his own life, Abraham has blundered.

The wife-sister motif seems to have originated in a Hurrian practice described in the Nuzi texts of the fifteenth century B.C. The sanctity of the marriage bond was highlighted in a legal transaction that had the husband simultaneously accept his bride as wife and sister. In resorting to the wife-sister equation, Abraham was presumably placing himself under the strong arm of the law.[13] The Yahwist, who wrote some five centuries later, did not have a firm grasp of Hurrian law. This failing is unimportant in the text, however, for the emphasis is not on the details of Hurrian legislation but rather on the kind of man Abraham was and the kind of deity that Yahweh was. When faith had momentarily evaporated, God's concern for his people had not.

The Yahwist's work in Genesis 13 all but dominates, just as it did in Genesis 12. Here is an ethnological legend designed to explain the separation of the Moabites and Ammonites (Lot's descendants) from the Israelites (Abraham's descendants). The wealth of Abraham and Lot—evidence of Yahweh's abundant blessing—occasions the separation. The land of Canaan is represented as insufficient for the needs of these two great seminomads. Yet having parted, Abraham's interest in Lot's welfare does not vanish.

The unique text of Genesis 14 (neither J nor E nor P) depicts Abraham's dealings with four assertive eastern monarchs and his contact with Melchizedek, the priest-king of Salem.[14] Abraham, the peace-loving nomad of Genesis 13, is portrayed here as a shrewd, forthright warrior who enters the field of battle to rescue his nephew Lot, who has been captured. Moreover, the patriarch receives a blessing from Melchizedek and in a high-minded manner pays his tithe and refuses to keep any of the booty for himself.

Thus far, attempts to fix a date for this battle and to determine the kings involved have not led to a positive identification. It appears, however, that southern Transjordan had a settled population at the time of the invasion. The extensive surface exploration of Glueck, involving a careful analysis of remains presently visible on the earth's surface, has demonstrated that no settlements existed there between the nineteenth and thirteenth centuries B.C. Yet immediately prior to that era, southern Transjordan seems to have been heavily populated. Settled life was completely disrupted in about 1900, and Glueck relates Genesis 14 to that experience.[15] This would place Abraham early in the second millennium B.C. While no precise decade for the battle can be offered, such a date for Abraham is entirely plausible.

Attempts to identify the eastern protagonists have been largely frustrating. Amraphel is a Babylonian (Shinar) monarch as yet unidentified, although on linguistic grounds alone we may be sure that he cannot be equated with Hammurabi. The names "Arioch" and "Chedorlaomer" are Hurrian and Elamite, respectively, but they cannot be attached to historically known persons. Further, the notion that Tidal is identical with one of several Hittite kings who bore the name "Tudḫalias" is suggestive, but imprecise. The earliest of the Tudḫalias monarchs lived in the seventeenth century, and that fact does not mesh with the upheavals in southern Transjordan, which, given certain archaeological evidence, must be dated earlier.

Nevertheless, at least three elements in the narrative (Gen. 14) make sense. First, the rich mineral deposits near the southeastern shore of the Dead Sea might have looked attractive to a confederation of eastern monarchs. Second, in a surprise attack Abraham and his 318 trained men might have been able to harass the enemy sufficiently to win back a few prisoners and their possessions. And third, Chedorlaomer of Elam is here accepted as the head of the eastern coalition, which would have been entirely possible somewhat before and after the reign of Hammurabi, when Elamite expansion was an impressive reality.

To say this much, however, is not to argue that this unique narrative should be accepted at face value. Genesis 14 is an isolated tradition poorly integrated with other patriarchal legends in Genesis. Even so, the underlying intention of its climax is clear. Abraham is deliberately connected with David's throne. He pays a tithe to the priest-king of Salem (Jerusalem) who reigns at the site David will one day take over as his capital. Further, in a special sense Jerusalem is understood here as God's dwelling place. The centrality of Jerusalem for Israelite faith and history is affirmed, for Abraham himself is associated with this ancient city and its solemn leader.

Though on historical grounds Genesis 14 is not successful in relating Abraham to the world of men, on theological grounds Genesis 15 and 17 relate him to the design of God. In Genesis 15 (essentially E with some J elements) Abraham worries because he has no natural heir. His adopted son, Eliezer, is his only hope. He is to provide for Abraham and Sarah in their old age, bury and mourn for them at the time of their death, and receive the family inheritance as his due reward.

Tablets of sonship found at ancient Nuzi specify that it is legal for a couple incapable of having children to adopt an heir. They also state that if a natural heir is born to the couple afterward, he will receive the inheritance.[16] Abraham appears to rely on this Hurrian custom. But Yahweh has a different plan in mind and commits himself unreservedly to the patriarch. Promised by the deity that he will have a natural son, Abraham dares to believe (15:6). Even so, Abraham is still uncertain. When Yahweh declares that he will make Abraham a gift of land,

Abraham seeks assurance that the deity will carry out his radical promise (15:8). He is then given ritualistic instructions, and immediately a covenant ceremony is undertaken. As Abraham sleeps, a weirdly drawn deity passes between the animal parts Abraham had been instructed to lay out for that ceremony. Despite the deliberate imprecision of the narrative, the reader is led to conclude that through this event Yahweh voluntarily committed himself to this man of his choice.

The precise, ritualistic prose of Genesis 17 records the priestly understanding of Abraham's divine calling and high destiny. In Genesis 15, a baffling encounter between Yahweh and Abraham takes place, the numinous quality of deity is conveyed, and Abraham is allowed to express his incredulity. By contrast, the priestly version in Genesis 17 is devoted almost entirely to a long divine monologue addressed to the patient Abraham. Only in vv. 17–18 is Abraham portrayed forcefully, and then it seems to be for the purpose of inviting further divine speaking, which resumes immediately in v. 19.

In the opening words of the theophany, God discloses who he is: "I am God Almighty" (v. 1). Abraham's obedience is immediately enjoined, and the chapter is devoted to the implementation of the covenant with its physical sign of circumcision. Once more divine assurance of progeny and land is communicated. The priests, however, are equally preoccupied with covenant details and the formal institution of circumcision that will symbolize the covenant.

Circumcision appears to have originated in ancient times as a puberty rite that acknowledged the readiness of the male for marriage. It was observed by some of Israel's neighbors (for example, the Egyptians), and ignored by others (for example, the Philistines). One Egyptian text written at the end of the third millennium B.C. refers to the successful circumcision of 121 males, which must have been no minor operation.[17] Yet however common this practice may have been in the ancient Orient, in Israel it was associated with the essence of the people's religion. Circumcision became a confessional act whereby the community of faith accepted with profound seriousness God's claim on his chosen people. Moreover, it was a constant reminder that through this association with Abraham, the deity chose to relate himself to one of earth's families in a special sense. Israel was now foremost in the divine mind.

Our total impression of the man Abraham is naturally the result of reading about him in many different contexts. His humanity is emphasized by the Yahwist, who mentions that Abraham fathered a child by Hagar (Sarah's Egyptian maid) and then acceded to Sarah's wishes to expel Hagar from the household for having looked on her mistress with contempt (16:4–6). Abraham's hospitality, boldness, and ethical sensitivity are captured by the Yahwist in Genesis 18, which depicts

Yahweh's mysterious and unexpected visit at midday with Abraham and the latter's intercession in behalf of Sodom. The Elohist offers a superb glimpse of Abraham's piety by providing an account of Abraham's near-sacrifice of Isaac in Gen. 22:1–19. And while it now stands within a priestly setting, Genesis 23 appears to be fundamentally the Yahwist's account of Abraham's bargaining capacities and faith, as he sought a suitable burial place for his recently deceased wife.

Because of their literary excellence and theological insights, portions of Genesis 18, 22, and 23 merit closer inspection. In Gen. 18:20–21 Yahweh shares with Abraham his intention to destroy the depraved cities of Sodom and Gomorrah. Abraham openly intercedes with Yahweh on Sodom's behalf: "Shall not the Judge of all the earth do right?" (18:25). In early Israelite history, communal suffering was commonplace. A whole family might suffer extinction because of the misdeeds of one of its members (see Josh. 7:6–26). The tenth-century B.C. Yahwist, who is both a believer and a humanist, appears to be reversing the equation and asking, "If this is right, might it not be right that many should be delivered because of the virtue of a few?" Ultimately, however, Abraham does not object to the destruction of Sodom and Gomorrah, for he seems to recognize that the Judge has acted righteously (Gen. 19:28).

Nowhere are Abraham's piety and total obedience revealed more dramatically than in Gen. 22:1–19, which contains the E tradition of the near-sacrifice of Isaac. Here God seems to demand the absurd. Abraham is told to give up his only son, Isaac; in other words, to destroy the only evidence that he will truly be the father of a great multitude. Perhaps the deity is arbitrarily revoking his earlier promise. God's command, if it is only a test of Abraham's faith, seems extreme and Abraham's compliance cruel.

Understandably this narrative has offended many contemporary readers. Still, several considerations help to explain its inclusion in the Bible. It attests to the remarkable capacity of some within Israel's ranks to tell a truly gripping story. It defends a cultic point of view that God requires of man animal sacrifice, not human holocausts. And it speaks of the predicament of Abraham, who enjoys the privilege of a high calling and suffers its consequences.

The economy of style in Genesis 22 is impressive. There is no explanation of why God abruptly addresses Abraham at this moment in his life. Few adjectives describe the human destiny that temporarily stands in awful jeopardy. No mention is made of the emotions that must have gripped Abraham and his beloved son on their fateful journey. Yet the very absence of detail contributes to the excellence of the narrative.[18]

Abraham finds himself in an extremely tense situation. Neverthe-

Mosaic Floor at Beth Alpha Depicting the Near-sacrifice of Isaac. At the foot
of Mount Gilboa lies Beth Alpha. In 1928 a superbly preserved and most
elaborate mosaic floor from a synagogue of the sixth century of the Christian
era was discovered there. From left to right in its bottom panel can be seen
Abraham's two servants with the ass, the ram tied to a tree situated under
the hand of the deity, Abraham holding a sacrificial knife in his right hand and
Isaac in his left, and the flaming altar. Above the patriarch and his son are
their names, and below God's hand are the words, "Lay not"—the initial
element in the deity's command that Isaac be spared. The words "Behold the
ram" appear above the animal, which is to be the substitute sacrifice.
(Courtesy of the Israel Government Tourist Office, Chicago.)

less, at the eleventh hour as he steadies his hand to thrust the knife into
Isaac, he is told that the test is over. Abraham is again permitted to hear
the divine promise of abundant progeny. The chapter ends on a powerful note with Abraham the victor and God the provider. Clearly, Abraham's faith is of remarkable dimensions.

Before ending our discussion of the Abraham cycle, a few remarks
about the tradition of Abraham's purchase of the cave of Machpelah
(Gen. 23) are in order. Abraham is in full command of the situation as
he seeks a proper burial place for Sarah. Oriental courtesy and hard
bargaining all but dominate the narrative. Abraham covets full legal
ownership of the burial site. Only in this way may he give fitting
expression to his faith in God's promise that his heirs will one day
possess the land. In placing Sarah in the cave of Machpelah and in anticipating his own burial there, Abraham's intention is clear. The father
and mother of the Israelite nation that is to emerge and eventually take
over the land of Canaan are to be physically present within its precincts.
Abraham's determination to purchase a piece of property in Canaan is

one more demonstration of his faith in the deity who first summoned him and continued to dominate his personal life.

THE JACOB CYCLE OF TRADITIONS: GENESIS 24–36

The Jacob cycle of traditions begins with Genesis 24. Strictly speaking, Genesis 24 depicts an Abraham who is still alive and makes no mention of Jacob's birth, which is not reported until Gen. 25:21–26. Nevertheless, Genesis 24 anticipates what lies ahead. In a long, vivid chapter, the Yahwist demonstrates his capacity to tell a good story. It is devoted to a problem that weighs heavily on the aged Abraham: his son Isaac must find a suitable wife.

Here the Yahwist affirms, as he does elsewhere in the Jacob and Joseph cycles, that the sovereign deity often guides men even when they are insensitive to his leading. At one level, Rebekah is brought from northwest Mesopotamia to be Isaac's spouse because it just happened that Abraham's servant, who had been sent on this mission, met her and not someone else at the city well of Nahor. Yet at another level, the Yahwist lets us see that the deity himself has chosen this fair young woman to be Isaac's bride.

At the beginning of the chapter, Abraham is certain about several matters. It is time that Isaac acquire a wife, and she dare not be chosen from the neighboring Canaanite women. That would threaten the unity and the religious health of the clan. Also, Abraham is convinced that although Canaan is thus far only the promised land, Isaac, as heir to the promise, must not leave its soil. The patriarch therefore charges the senior servant of his household with the task of finding the bride. Events unfold according to divine plan. Laban can do no other than consent to the servant's request, and Rebekah herself is willing to leave. In time she is brought to Isaac and becomes his wife. While the Genesis legends are not silent about Isaac from this point on, he dominates the literature only once more, in Gen. 27:1–28:9, and then as an elderly man who in his blindness is tricked into giving Esau's superior blessing to the scheming Jacob.

The Jacob traditions are remarkably well told and require only brief comment. In Gen. 25:21–34 the Yahwist gives us two vivid glimpses of Jacob. His first act in life is to grab hold of his twin brother Esau's heel as he exits the womb. Then some years later this supplanter outwits the dull Esau, who is but moments older, by usurping his birthright.

As the younger son, Jacob had no legitimate claim to the family inheritance. Yet what is not Jacob's by virtue of chronology becomes his through clever manipulation. The hungry Esau is willing to trade his birthright for some bread and lentil soup. Although the Nuzi tablets attest that such bartering between brothers was permissible in this era, in Genesis the parties involved are allowed to have second thoughts on the matter.[19] Esau came to despise his birthright (25:34), and the way that Jacob had to scheme to obtain Isaac's blessing suggests that this struggle for the birthright was not entirely acceptable to Jacob himself. One partially effective scheme demanded another. Thus, the Yahwist informs us in Gen. 27:1–45 that Jacob, with his mother's help, snatched the family blessing from his father. Through the formal act of an orally delivered blessing, the power and status of the aged patriarch are transferred to the first-born. And that is precisely the problem. Jacob is not the first-born son of Isaac. Once Jacob's treachery becomes open knowledge, he has no choice; he must flee to his uncle Laban in Haran.

By the standards of an Oriental society, Jacob has deceived his father in one of the worst ways imaginable. Jacob is the cad, yet he is likewise the recipient of God's blessing. The deity deliberately chooses him to be the heir of the promise. Divine mystery is accepted as extraordinary. This legend reminds Israel who she is. Her own election was not earned. Yahweh was not handing out rewards in response to human accomplishments. Both J (32:28) and P (35:10) declare that Jacob is renamed "Israel." The man Jacob personifies the aspirations, struggles, self-assertion, and blessing that Israel knows to be her own. Jacob is Israel when Yahweh is least pleased with his people. He is Israel when life seems nothing more than the survival of the fittest. And Jacob is Israel when she is brought into theophanic contact with the deity and allowed to hear words of special promise.

The Genesis tradition boldly depicts Jacob's humanity. As his experiences with Laban show so clearly, Jacob confronts the world of men and succeeds. But Jacob is also met by the deity, who invades his life in a theophanic encounter. Here, too, struggle and victory dominate. If on one level Jacob manages his own affairs, on another the deity arranges the course of Jacob's life to fulfill his own purposes. At Bethel and at Peniel, Jacob is shown to be subject to theophanic disclosure, and he begins to comprehend the special nature of his calling.

The Bethel episode in 28:10–22 (JE) unfolds immediately after Jacob has fled from his father's home in Beer-sheba and struck out for Haran. Here Jacob has a nocturnal vision of Yahweh. The deity identifies himself as the God of the fathers and extends to Jacob the promise of land and progeny that he had previously set forth to Abraham and Isaac. Through those words and the related vision of a "ladder" linking heaven and earth, Jacob recognizes the awesome quality of the locale. He fittingly names it "Bethel" ("house of God"). And he binds himself to the deity in an extremely transparent oath: "If God will be with me, and will keep me in this way that I go, and will give me bread to eat and clothing to wear, so that I come again to my father's house in peace, then Yahweh shall be my God . . ." (vv. 20–21). Why not? There seem to be distinct advantages in such a relationship! Theologically, this episode legitimizes Yahweh worship at a place that formerly belonged to the Canaanite cult. It also confirms Jacob's honesty and God's design to deal directly with Jacob and shape his destiny.

In the confrontation with deity at Peniel (32:22–32 [J]), an anticipated night of rest is transformed into an intense physical struggle. Whatever the legend conveyed in its original form, as used by the Yahwist it suggests that Jacob met a man, wrestled with him all night, and by daybreak learned that his opponent was not man but God. Jacob's determination is evident everywhere in the narrative. His struggle for blessing is passionate. At times in his life it seems as if this is the only means by which blessing may be obtained. Even so, the blessing is given, and it is prized by its possessor.

THE JOSEPH CYCLE OF TRADITIONS:
GENESIS 37–50

Genesis 37–50 is devoted primarily to Joseph. Two chapters, however, stand apart from the otherwise well-integrated Joseph narrative: The singular story of Judah and Tamar in Genesis 38 interrupts the Joseph narrative shortly after it has begun;[20] and Gen. 49:1–28 relates the so-called Blessing of Jacob, which turns our attention to the twelve sons who hear a momentous disclosure from the dying Jacob.[21] Nevertheless, within the remaining literary material of nearly four hundred verses, the piety, wisdom, accomplishments, and fate of Joseph are richly depicted. Some P elements are present in this unified narrative, but most of the material can be traced to the J and E strata. In their having been brought together they have been so skillfully united that stylistic unevenness and factual discrepancies ordinarily remain in the woodwork.

The Joseph saga is narrated in a highly polished style and is thoroughly comprehensible. It is a detailed account of the successful adventures of Jacob's favorite son as he makes a life for himself in the Nile Delta. There are times when the theme of success seems to be patterned as much after the literature of the ancient world as it is after the interests of Israel's faith. Thus, the repeated and forthright proposal of adultery that Potiphar's wife extends to handsome Joseph, his clear-cut refusals, and the false charges against him on that matter (Gen. 39:6b–18) have a close parallel in "The Story of Two Brothers,"[22] an Egyptian myth. Nevertheless, the Israelite affirmation that Yahweh intervened in the life of Joseph is present in the narrative. In fact, the episode with Potiphar's wife concludes with the statement that although Joseph was now in prison, "Yahweh was with him; and whatever he did, Yahweh made it prosper" (39:23). Genesis 45:5–8 and 50:19–21 offer further testimony that Joseph's presence and work in Egypt are the result of Yahweh's will. Joseph is not simply the victim of fraternal treachery.

True, Joseph is not always portrayed as a particularly convincing or winsome character. With extraordinary consistency, he does the right thing at the right time. His hands remain clean. He does not participate in life to the extent that Abraham and Jacob did. Moreover, Joseph's final statement to his brothers is telling: "As for you, you meant evil against me; but God meant it for good, to bring it about that many people should be kept alive, as they are today" (50:20). He seems capable of forgiving, provided that he is granted the opportunity to utter this didactic, moralistic remark.

Yet if the eminently successful Joseph is not the favorite biblical character of most critical readers of the Hebrew Bible, the Joseph legend makes at least two significant contributions. It suggests a date for the patriarchs, and it also reveals important aspects of Israel's theology and self-awareness.

We have already stated that Egypt's Second Intermediate period began in the middle of the eighteenth century B.C. and that in the approximately two hundred years that followed, the land was regularly invaded by waves of Asian Hyksos. From about 1650 to 1550, Egypt was so plagued by internal discord that aggressive Asian princes were able to take over in ways that helped Egypt return to economic health; in fact, throughout the entire patriarchal period, various Asiatics penetrated into Egypt. Here was an era offering conditions most favorable for a Semite such as Joseph to be appointed to responsible public office and Joseph was someone who would make both his presence and influence felt. Thus, Joseph's status as reported in the biblical record would not have been improbable while the Hyksos were in control. Also, much of the Hyksos penetration of Egypt was gradual and nonviolent. This accords well with the way in which Genesis depicts the descent of Jacob's family into Egypt.

Even so, Joseph cannot be confidently related to any known pharaoh of the Second Intermediate period. Thus the Amarna age of the fourteenth century B.C. with its famous pharaoh, Akhnaton (ca. 1364–1347), has also been suggested as the historical setting for the Joseph saga. Akhnaton did employ some officials who were not Egyptian and on this count Joseph obviously qualifies. Nevertheless, this view is weakened by one major consideration. Egyptian records reveal that Akhnaton's concerns and innovations were mainly religious, but the portrait of Pharaoh in Genesis 40–50 has no religious cast. When we compare what is known about the Amarna age with the Hyksos period, the latter seems the more likely historical context of the Joseph narratives.[23]

How, then, are Israel's theology and self-awareness advanced by the Joseph saga? First, ancient Israel persisted in regarding herself as a covenant community existing under the sovereignty of God. She recognized that the ancient Israelites violated covenant fellowship all too often and ventured forth on their own. In the Joseph tradition, the brothers, not Joseph, constitute the problem. By getting rid of their brother, Jacob's faithless sons work at cross-purposes with the deity. Still, they are forgiven (50:20–21). In the telling and retelling of the Joseph narrative, Israel had ample opportunity to meditate on her own condition as a covenant people.

Second, the Joseph saga helped Israel understand that in the midst of human alienation and struggle, success might visit the divinely blessed. Within admittedly oversimplified legend, Joseph is seen as the wise deliverer responsible for feeding all mankind (41:57). Despite the exaggeration, such a passage instructed Israel that if it were the deity's design, one man might engage in amazing deeds directly related to salvation itself. The incredible Joseph was God's answer to a needy world. Perhaps in another time of need Yahweh might react similarly.

Finally, the Joseph episodes help Israel to understand herself in an international context. The geography suggests as much. The narrative does not portray wandering nomads in Canaan who hear God's assurance that their descendants will settle here. It focuses on Joseph's tenure in Egypt, on one who is later joined there by his family. The international aspect of the Joseph saga depends even more on conceptual than on geographical actualities. These didactic chapters are filled with wisdom motifs that are basically anthropological and universal in character.[24] Under the influence of Egyptian wisdom, the Joseph story presents a wise man able to interpret troubling dreams. He does the right thing at the right time. He is self-contained rather than passionate. He is enlightened in every respect. This dimension of the Joseph saga does not undermine Yahweh's cause with Israel. But just as the Book of Proverbs can in faith declare, "A man's steps are ordered by Yahweh" (20:24), the wisdom stance of the Joseph stories affirms that Yahweh was at work in Joseph's life. Thus, curiosity about the world and its ways reaches far beyond the confines of ancient Israel.

THE RELIGION ATTRIBUTED TO THE PATRIARCHS

Undoubtedly, the Genesis strata present an idealized portrait of patriarchal belief and worship. Nonetheless, we suspect that they offer a somewhat trustworthy witness, for the patriarchal religion depicted there is sufficiently distinct from later Yahwism. Variations in the type of deity worshiped, the name by which he is known, his covenant demands, and actual worship practices may all be discerned. Genesis therefore presents something more than an outright grafting of a tenth-(J), ninth-(E), or fifth-century B.C. (P) "present" onto a dimly remembered past. Still, the lack of cultic credos in Genesis 12–50 and its vague depiction of religious practices when they do occur indicate that we cannot discuss patriarchal religion with absolute confidence.[25]

The names of deity employed by Genesis 12–50 are most helpful. As an admittedly general designation for the deity, "Elohim" is the favorite within the E stratum, although that name is not confined to E. The root meaning of this comprehensive term seems to be "power." "El," which stems from the same Semitic root as "Elohim," frequently appears in the texts of Genesis as the divine name. Because it is accompanied by different epithets, it is variously employed. Three representative "El" predications in Genesis will illustrate what we mean.

"El Shaddai" is a common designation for deity in the P stratum (for example, 17:1; 28:3; 35:11; 48:3). That name is linked with God's action in initiating and maintaining the covenant between himself and the patriarchal line. The original meaning of the name, however, is difficult to establish. Like the Akkadian noun šadda'u ("mountaineer"), it may refer to a mountain deity, or metaphorically to the strength of such a god. In any case, this epithet typically appears in important covenant contexts.

"El Elyon," meaning "God Most High," is found only in Gen. 14:18–20 in the blessing Melchizedek bestows on Abraham. There El Elyon is viewed as the deity of pre-Israelite Jerusalem. His very name reflects a preoccupation with transcendence. "God Most High" would scarcely be regarded by his following as being a deity interested in promoting intimate God-man contact.

"El Roi," which means "God of seeing," appears in Gen. 16:13 (J) in the story of Hagar's eviction from Abraham's household. Hagar is amazed that she has seen God and lived. The account of Jacob's struggle at Peniel displays a similar fear of immediate divine presence (32:30). In patriarchal religion, the unpredictable appearance of God is cause for man's consternation. In general, the divine epithets make useful suggestions about the character of patriarchal belief.

The family pattern of patriarchal religion should also be noted. For example, God discloses himself to Jacob at Bethel in order to perpetuate the covenant promise of land and progeny that he has previously made to Abraham and Isaac. At that time he declares, "I am Yahweh, the God of Abraham your father and the God of Isaac" (28:13). Here and elsewhere (for example, 26:24; 32:9), the deity's connection with the patriarchal clan is made explicit. This companion deity may not have run stiff competition with the more remote El, whom the patriarchs also worshiped. The God of the fathers, however, did manifest himself in a more intimate and friendly manner. He addressed the patriarchs as persons. On balance, the patriarchal concep-

Early Bronze Age Canaanite Altar at Megiddo. This
open-air circular altar was erected by the Canaanite
residents of Megiddo in the middle of the third
millennium B.C. and was used until about 1800 B.C.
A great number of animal bones discovered at the
foot of the six steps leading up to the altar attest
that many animals were sacrificed as burnt offerings
here. Although this enormous altar was erected
and used several centuries prior to Abraham,
Canaanite religious practices at Megiddo may have
undergone little change down to Abraham's day.
(Courtesy of the Israel Colour Slide Company,
Jerusalem.)

tion of God was more dynamic than coherent, more synthetic than
single-minded, more practical than contemplative.

Presumably, patriarchal man related to God by simple forms of
sacrifice and prayer. His was a lay religion. It was more preoccupied
with establishing a meaningful sense of fellowship between God and

man than it was with removing human guilt through agreed on ceremonial procedures. Nevertheless, to facilitate such fellowship the
patriarchs did engage in specific tasks. In particular, they are depicted
as having founded simple sanctuaries at places where God had revealed
himself. There they made their offerings immediately after the theophany had concluded. Through the presentation of animals, liquid, and
vegetable substance, the patriarchs sought to strengthen the relationship
between God and man. Such offerings seem to have been made out of
simple faith that although God did not depend on such gifts for his own
maintenance, they were nevertheless pleasing to him. These offerings
were not intended to cajole the deity into providing favors. Unpretentious sacrifice was respected as an entirely appropriate way of approaching God.

Finally, the patriarchal religion presented in Genesis reflects a God
and people who are singularly mobile. The deity's primary attachment
was to a people who moved, not to a permanent site. Nowhere does the
Genesis text suggest that the wandering patriarchs used any one sanctuary continually. Moreover, apart from Israel's (Jacob's) return to
Beer-sheba (Gen. 46:1–2), the patriarchs do not frequent a given sanctuary in order to evoke a theophanic confrontation. God comes by his own
decision. And while patriarchal religion is not self-consciously monotheistic, it is profoundly personal. This notion of a personal God who initiates divine-human encounter, and in so doing draws man within the
orbit of his own will for the world, is not peculiar to Genesis. It is
central to the Old Testament as a whole.

NOTES

1. In this chapter and the three that follow, the first note will present a
   provisional delineation of the Pentateuchal strata involved. The strata in
   Genesis 11–50 will be outlined for the present chapter. Due to its distinctive qualities, the P stratum is easily isolated. The separation of E
   from J, however, is sometimes problematic. Moreover, Genesis 14 lies
   beyond the scope of J, E, and P. Genesis 23 should be labeled "PJ,"
   meaning that it is a Yahwistic narrative tradition set within a P framework. The poetic unit in Gen. 49:2–27, the so-called Blessing of Jacob,
   predates the three main strata in Genesis. We label it "J" because the
   Yahwist presumably incorporated it in his own work.

   To the distinctive and not overly extensive P stratum we provisionally assign the following: Gen. 11:10–27, 31–32; 12:4b–5; 13:6, 11b–12a;
   16:1a, 3, 15–16; 17:1–27; 19:29; 21:1b–6; 25:7–20, 26b; 26:34–35; 27:46–
   28:9; 31:18b; 33:18a; 35:9–13, 15; 35:22b–37:2a; 41:46a; 46:6–27;
   47:5–12, 27b–28; 48:3–7; 49:1, 29–33; 50:12–13.

   To the J stratum: Gen. 11:1–9, 28–30; 12:1–4a, 6–20; 13:1–5, 7–11a,
   12b–18; 16:1b–2, 4–14; 18:1–19:28, 30–38; 21:1a, 7; 22:20–24; 24:1–67;
   25:1–6, 21–26a, 27–34; 26:1–33; 27:1–45; 28:10, 13–16, 19; 29:1–30:43

(with E elements); 32:3–12, 22–32; 33:1–17; 34:1–31; 35:16–22a; 37:2b–20, 25–27, 28b; 38:1–39:23; 42:27–28; 43:1–44:34; 46:28–34; 47:1–4, 13–27a, 29–31; 49:2–28; 50:1–11, 14.

　　　To the E stratum: Gen. 15:1–21 (with J elements); 20:1–18; 21:8–22:19; 28:11–12, 17–18, 20–22; 31:1–18a (with J elements), 19–55 (with J elements); 32:1–2, 13–21; 33:18b–20; 35:1–8, 14; 37:21–24, 28a, 28c–36; 40:1–41:45, 46b–57; 42:1–26, 29–38; 45:1–46:5 (with J elements); 48:1–2, 8–22; 50:15–26.

2. For a more detailed treatment, to which the author is indebted, see John Bright, *A History of Israel*, 2d ed. (Philadelphia: Westminster Press, 1972), pp. 41–66.

3. For an informative presentation of classical Sumerian culture, see Samuel Noah Kramer, *The Sumerians: Their History, Culture, and Character* (Chicago: University of Chicago Press, Phoenix Books, 1971).

4. Although Akkad, Sargon's capital, lay in northern Babylonia, it has not as yet been discovered. For a competent survey of the Akkadians, see A. Leo Oppenheim, *Ancient Mesopotamia: Portrait of a Dead Civilization* (Chicago: University of Chicago Press, Phoenix Books, 1968).

5. For a helpful introduction to the Egyptians, see John A. Wilson, *The Culture of Ancient Egypt* (Chicago: University of Chicago Press, Phoenix Books, 1951).

6. See George E. Mendenhall, "Mari," in David N. Freedman and Edward F. Campbell, Jr., eds., *The Biblical Archaeologist Reader* (Garden City, N.Y.: Doubleday, Anchor Books, 1964), 2: 3–20.

7. Debates about the so-called low, middle, and high chronologies of the ancient Near East often center on the date of Hammurabi's reign. Here we are adopting the widely accepted low chronology of William F. Albright.

8. John van Seters, *The Hyksos: A New Investigation* (New Haven, Conn.: Yale University Press, 1966).

9. For a revealing source contemporaneous with the event, see "The Expulsion of the Hyksos," in James B. Pritchard, ed., *Ancient Near Eastern Texts Relating to the Old Testament*, 3d ed. (Princeton, N.J.: Princeton University Press, 1969), pp. 233–234.

10. The argument that archaeological interpreters should not claim too much and that many problems of historicity and chronology are still unsolved is resonantly voiced by Maurice L. Zigmond, "Archaeology and the 'Patriarchal Age' of the Old Testament," in Ward W. Goodenough, ed., *Explorations in Cultural Anthropology* (New York: McGraw-Hill, 1964), pp. 571–598. Zigmond responds to many scholars, including Albright. For a statement of Albright's position, see "The Story of Abraham in the Light of New Archaeological Data," in William F. Albright, *Archaeology, Historical Analogy, and Early Biblical Tradition* (Baton Rouge: Louisiana State University Press, 1966), pp. 22–41.

11. Writing on "saga," a term he prefers to "legend," Buber states, "Here history cannot be dissevered from the historical wonder . . ." (Martin Buber, *Moses: The Revelation and the Covenant* [New York: Harper & Row, Harper Torchbooks, 1958], p. 16.) On the matter of relating Old Testament legends to oral history, your author is supported by Wall, of Grinnell College, who has worked in American oral history: "This is a

most proper analogy, for this is what all history originally was—narrative within the oral tradition. This is what the late Allan Nevins had the genius to understand and to revive in our day." (Joseph F. Wall, personal correspondence, 12 March 1971.)

12. See J. Kenneth Kuntz, *The Self-revelation of God* (Philadelphia: Westminster Press, 1967), for a fuller definition of theophany (p. 45), an outline of its basic form (p. 59), and a more detailed presentation of the Genesis theophanies (pp. 134–168).

13. E. A. Speiser, *Genesis: Introduction, Translation, and Notes,* The Anchor Bible, vol. 1 (Garden City, N.Y.: Doubleday, 1964), pp. xl–xli, 91–94.

14. The isolated character of this tradition is widely acknowledged. See Speiser, *op. cit.,* p. xxxv, who accepts Genesis 14 as part of "the Residue."

15. Nelson Glueck, *Rivers in the Desert: A History of the Negev* (New York: Farrar, Straus, & Cudahy, 1959), pp. 68–74.

16. Cyrus H. Gordon, "Biblical Customs and the Nuzu Tablets," in Freedman and Campbell, *op. cit.,* p. 22.

17. "Circumcision in Egypt," in Pritchard, *op. cit.,* p. 326.

18. This is noted in Erich Auerbach, *Mimesis: The Representation of Reality in Western Literature,* trans. Willard Trask (Garden City, N.Y.: Doubleday, Anchor Books, 1953), pp. 5–9.

19. On the Hurrian custom at Nuzi, see Gordon, *op. cit.,* p. 23.

20. Genesis 38 reflects ancient tribal history and emphasizes the law of levirate marriage (cf. Deut. 25:5–10), which is here taken far more seriously by the widowed Tamar than it is by her father-in-law, Judah. That law requires that the brother of a man who had died without a male descendant marry his widowed sister-in-law to perpetuate the name of the deceased and his inheritance. The territorial enlargement of the impressive tribe of Judah and its loose but real connections with related Canaanite clans through intermarriage are also attested in Genesis 38, though admittedly in the form of a scandalous narrative.

21. Genesis 49:1–28 includes blessings, curses, and declarations of fact. It contains some ancient material that predates by several decades the inception of the United Monarchy in about 1020 B.C. Some references in the Judah and Joseph strophes (vv. 8–12 and 22–26, respectively), however, point to a later era postdating David's permanent victory over the Philistines shortly after 1000 B.C. Many of the historical allusions in this poem cannot be understood by the contemporary reader. Theologically, the poem declares that it is the deity's will that the loosely connected tribes of Israel show diversities in strength and purpose.

22. Pritchard, *op. cit.,* pp. 23–25. Here Bata, the younger brother, declines the invitation of the wife of his older brother, Anubis, to lie with her. Consequently, he is accused of having done so. That the brothers in this instance are gods does not cancel out the affinity between this narrative and Genesis 39. See also John D. Yohannan, ed., *Joseph and Potiphar's Wife in World Literature: An Anthology of the Story of the Chaste Youth and the Lustful Stepmother* (New York: New Directions Publishing Corp., 1968), where more than a dozen versions are examined.

23. See John M. Holt, *The Patriarchs of Israel* (Nashville: Vanderbilt University Press, 1964), pp. 189–196. Although Holt favors the Hyksos period,

he marshals sound evidence that both supports and questions the Amarna period as a cogent historical backdrop for the Joseph traditions.

24. See "The Joseph Narrative and Ancient Wisdom," in Gerhard von Rad, *The Problem of the Hexateuch and Other Essays*, trans. E. W. Trueman Dicken (London: Oliver & Boyd, 1966), pp. 292–300.

25. For more detailed studies on this topic, see "The God of the Fathers," in Albrecht Alt, *Essays on Old Testament History and Religion*, trans. R. A. Wilson (Garden City, N.Y.: Doubleday, Anchor Books, 1966), pp. 1–100; Helmer Ringgren, *Israelite Religion*, trans. David E. Green (Philadelphia: Fortress Press, 1966), pp. 17–27; and Holt, *op. cit.*, pp. 127–173.

5

ORIGINS ACTUALIZED: THE EXODUS EVENT

The main strata of the Pentateuch all declare that through her deliverance from Egyptian oppression and her covenant with the deity at Mount Sinai, Israel truly became Yahweh's people and Yahweh truly became her God. Although the details of these events are obscured by the present shape of the literary traditions, both gave significant definition to the people of the Old Testament. In the present chapter we shall examine key elements in Exodus 1–18.[1] This literature opens with mention of Israel's presence in Egypt, finds its climax in the Exodus, and concludes with a report of a crucial meeting in the wilderness between Moses and his father-in-law, Jethro. Here, indeed, were formative moments that contributed much to ancient Israel's self-understanding.

THE SHAPE AND FUNCTION OF THE BIBLICAL MATERIAL

The text in Exodus takes the form of legend. Accordingly, the past becomes the object of sustained meditation rather than the target of cold analysis. Some events are reported in alarmingly slight detail. While others are disclosed at greater length, they do not present the hard facts of history. This applies particularly to descriptions of the departure of the Israelites from Egypt. The Song of the Sea (Exod. 15:1–18) is rich in metaphor, yet almost nothing is asserted about the

---

Biblical texts to be read prior to and in conjunction with the present chapter: Exodus 1–18. Note in particular Exod. 1:1–6:9; 12:29–51; 13:17–15:25a; 16:1–17:7; 18:1–27.

manner of Israel's escape. Though the figures of speech facilitate our comprehension of what ancient Israel thought about this crucial deliverance, they do not expose the event itself. Nevertheless, the Exodus legend is skillful in portraying Moses, Aaron, and Jethro, and in emphasizing the plight of the ancient Hebrews in Egypt.

Since for the most part the Exodus event was expressed within the Israelite cult, needs for religious reflection had priority over those for historical accuracy. According to Pedersen, much of the first half of the Book of Exodus consists of a cultic legend that was intimately linked with Israel's Passover festival.[2] Moreover, Beyerlin isolates numerous cultic components in Exodus 19–24, 32–34 with its depiction of crucial happenings at Mount Sinai.[3] Both scholars contend that the recurring context of ancient Israelite worship provided the occasion for the reenactment of earlier historical events. Therefore, subsequent Israelite generations could share the pain of Egyptian oppression as well as the joy of divine deliverance.

From the standpoint of form criticism, the Exodus text is to be viewed as cultic legend created and continually reshaped by ongoing corporate worship. Thus, it is a story designed to meet the confessional needs of the Israelite congregations that regularly assembled to celebrate Yahweh's mighty deeds. Source criticism reminds us, however, that as a final literary product, the Exodus text is the redaction of three different strata (J, E, and P) with mutual as well as separate interests to uphold.

The J stratum in the Book of Exodus is simple, bold, and incisive. It presupposes an earth-centered cosmos in which credible activity is undertaken by well-drawn personalities. It also accepts the possibilities of natural causation. In Exod. 10:13 an east wind drives the plague of locusts into Egypt; in 14:21 the same wind turns the sea into dry land that offers an unexpected escape route for the fleeing Hebrews.

In comparison with J, the E stratum contains only partially convincing human characterizations and attests a less immediate contact between God and man. In particular, the Elohist shows special interest in Moses. He reports that the deity first disclosed his special name, "Yahweh," to Moses; that he provided Moses with a rod to wield in order that divine wonders might come into being; and that at Sinai he was the unique covenant and theophanic mediator on whom God and Israel both depended.

Finally, in the P stratum, rather pallid personalities function within a heaven-centered cosmos. Regulations governing various cultic rituals are set forth in an elaborate manner. P also shows a greater concern for Moses' brother Aaron than J and E do: Aaron wields the rod of God.

Despite the variations, however, all three strata confirm Israel's presence in Egypt and the deity's concern for his special people. Moreover, all three contain provocative legend that meditates intently on the very essence of the events being celebrated.

THE HISTORICAL SETTING
FOR THE EXODUS

Egyptian documents have nothing to say about the Exodus. This Israelite flight might easily have been dismissed by the Egyptian authorities as a minor clash involving the escape of only a small number of assertive slaves near the nation's border. Certainly, a slave population still remained in Egypt. Thus, for better or worse, the biblical witness stands in isolation. Yet let us step back from the Exodus event and consider the situation faced by the ancient Hebrews in Egypt.

Historically we now enter the Late Bronze Age (ca. 1550–1200 B.C.), which witnessed signs of appreciable strength in Egypt. This was Egypt's New Kingdom, or Empire, period. It commenced in about 1552 with the emergence of the Eighteenth Dynasty, which successfully expelled much of the Hyksos element from Egyptian soil.[4] This prestigious dynasty remained in power for nearly 250 years (until ca. 1306). As one of its most effective pharaohs, Thutmosis III (ca. 1490–1436) conducted sixteen Asian campaigns. Troublesome Hyksos and Canaanite elements were the main targets of his raids. The graphic report of Thutmosis' first (and highly successful) campaign against a league of Canaanite kings at Megiddo in about 1468 is a classic.[5] As a result of his campaigns, Egypt enjoyed a position of unusual strength in Syria and Palestine.

The last fifty years of the Eighteenth Dynasty were far from auspicious, however. The chief figure here was Amenophis IV (ca. 1364–1347), who changed his name to Akhnaton meaning "the Splendor of Aton." He is credited with enthusiastic sponsorship of Egypt's Aton heresy. Clashing with a well-established priestly class that defended the superiority of the Egyptian god Amon, Akhnaton decreed that the Aton, the solar disk, was now to be accepted as Egypt's only deity. The Aton cult prohibited the use of any images save that of the solar disk with its rays pointed toward earth. It desecrated the name and claim of Amon in every way possible and affirmed that the Aton was known to no one save Akhnaton. The god-king Akhnaton and his family venerated the Aton, and his courtiers (along with other Egyptians) venerated Akhnaton as the one who bestowed blessings on them. Among the Egyptian masses, however, many may have been unaware of this new religious doctrine.

Because the Aton Hymn, which was written by Akhnaton himself or a member of his court, contains some interesting approximations to

Cast Head of Akhnaton from Amarna.
This cast head depicts the famous
pharaoh of the Eighteenth Dynasty. The
head is about 10 inches high. Pupils,
eyelids, and eyebrows have been
emphasized by means of a black dye.
(Courtesy of the Ägyptisches Museum,
Berlin.)

monotheism and several parallels with Psalm 104, we cite a few of its
lines:

> Thou appearest beautifully on the horizon of heaven,
> Thou living Aton, the beginning of life!
> When thou art risen on the eastern horizon,
> Thou hast filled every land with thy beauty.
> Thou art gracious, great, glistening, and high over
>   every land;
> Thy rays encompass the lands to the limit of all that
>   thou hast made:
> As thou art Re, thou reachest to the end of them;
> (Thou) subduest them (for) thy beloved son [Akhnaton].
> .   .   .   .
> How manifold it is, what thou hast made!
> They are hidden from the face (of man).
> O sole god, like whom there is no other!
> Thou didst create the world according to thy desire,
> Whilst thou wert alone:
> All men, cattle, and wild beasts,
> Whatever is on earth, going upon (its) feet,
> And what is on high, flying with its wings.[6]

Both the Aton Hymn and Psalm 104 show a clear shift from day
to night and back to day, both focus on the daytime activities of the
animal kingdom, and both marvel at the infinite wisdom of the creator.
Note, however, that since in the hymn Aton is equated with Re, the

Egyptian sun deity of Heliopolis, a pure form of monotheism is not espoused. Moreover, the reference "O sole god" may be a literary convention rather than a theological assertion. In earlier Egyptian eras, such deities as Amon, Re, and Atum were each praised as "the sole god."

While Akhnaton's incipient monotheism just decades prior to the age of Moses may have exerted some positive influence on the formation of Mosaic religion, the Aton innovation was ill suited to the Egyptian masses. It forced a monotheistic faith on them prematurely and lacked any genuine interest in promoting social justice. The Aton religion was short-lived. After Akhnaton's death the cult of Amon again held a strong position, and Akhnaton, as Atonism's chief proponent, was remembered with scorn.

If Akhnaton advanced a religious cause of limited popularity and duration, his statesmanship also failed to win him honors. The Amarna letters disclose that Egypt's hold in western Asia became quite tenuous at this time. These ancient texts were first discovered by Egyptian farmers in 1887 at Tell el-Amarna, the modern equivalent of ancient Akhetaton (Akhnaton's capital). They were written by apparently loyal Egyptian vassals stationed in western Asia who fervently sought military reinforcements. Although Amenophis III (ca. 1403–1364) thought the situation in Canaan was stable, gradually and imperceptibly it worsened.

By the time that Akhnaton began his reign, large portions of Phoenicia and Canaan were in the throes of internal discord. The Amarna correspondence vividly documents the strife current in Syria-Palestine not long before the main thrust of Israelite penetration. It also reveals Akhnaton's unwillingness to appear with an army and stabilize conditions. The insecure vassal princes were left to look after their own interests as best they could.[7] During Akhnaton's rule, Egypt suffered a steady decline.

Only the vigorous efforts of Haremhab (ca. 1333–1306) a few years later managed to keep the Egyptian empire intact. This Egyptian general crushed the Aton heresy, brought within Egypt's borders a new sense of security and confidence, and helped Egypt reassert herself in western Asia.

Haremhab was followed by Rameses I, who initiated the Nineteenth Dynasty. That strong, notorious power was responsible, among other things, for oppressing the Hebrews who resided in the Nile Delta. Rameses I reigned for only a few months (ca. 1306–1305). He was followed by his son, Seti I (ca. 1305–1290), who transferred the Egyptian capital northward to Avaris, the site of the earlier Hyksos capital. Seti I and his son, Rameses II (ca. 1290–1224), who renamed Avaris "the House of Rameses," conducted an ambitious building program there with the help of slave labor. Raamses and Pithom became store cities for housing Egyptian military provisions.[8] In this way, the Nineteenth Dynasty pharaohs could claim adequate

The Amon Temple at Karnak. During his long reign
Rameses II engaged in an extensive, somewhat
impulsive building program. Although this
Nineteenth Dynasty pharaoh did not initiate the
Amon Temple at Karnak, he completed its great
Hypostyle Hall. With its 134 spectacular columns,
this hall was the most outstanding part of the
temple. In this photo a few of the 80-foot columns
can be seen. (Photo by George W. E. Nickelsburg.)

control of the Nile Delta. Hebrew males who were to undergo the
Exodus experience were presumably members of the compulsory work
teams that fortified those cities.

At least three considerations help explain the presence of Israelite
ancestors in Egypt at this time. First, Egyptian documents indicate that
in times of famine Asiatic Bedouins often made their way to Egypt. As
necessity required, a shifting population would be on the move. Second,

some Hebrews in Egypt were no doubt direct descendants of the Hyksos who had previously overtaken the land. Though many of the Hyksos had been expelled from Egypt in the middle of the sixteenth century, a remnant surely remained. Third, as Egyptian pharaohs returned from successful exploits in western Asia, they often brought back prisoners of war. For example, Amenophis II (ca. 1438–1412) once recorded that he returned from Asia with 3,600 Habiru captives.[9]

But of what significance is the name "Habiru"? While they are not equivalent, the words "Hebrew" and "Habiru" appear to be related. The Habiru were landless aliens who moved as need and opportunity dictated. Lacking citizenship and national purpose, they grasped what they could. The Habiru were willing to hire themselves out as mercenaries. In desperate times they would even sell themselves into slavery. Among their ranks were displaced persons, social outcasts, and various landless individuals in search of a rich territory in which to settle. Throughout the better part of the second millennium, their presence in the ancient Near East is widely attested in a host of texts from many different places. Therefore, we cannot state categorically that all Habiru were Hebrews and vice versa. On the whole, however, the Habiru appear to be a nonethnic, nonprofessional body, which meshes with an expression in Exod. 12:38 that refers to the escaping Israelites as a "mixed multitude." Presumably among the Habiru enslaved in the Nile Delta during the thirteenth century were elements that would eventually become part of the people of Israel.[10]

The opening chapter of Exodus declares that whereas Israelite tenure in Egypt had at first been an agreeable experience, a sudden reversal took place. There was a new Egyptian monarch now who "did not know Joseph" (1:8). In his harsh treatment of Joseph's descendants, the new pharaoh apparently discounted Joseph's earlier contributions to the Egyptian economy. He taxed these Asiatics whom he did not trust with hard work. Despite such adversity, however, they reproduced with greater rigor (1:12). Though such conventionalized legend has no parallel in any extant Egyptian document, we are not left entirely in the dark. Such Palestinian sites as Hazor, Bethel, Debir, and Lachish were destroyed in the latter part of the thirteenth century. It is entirely possible that this was the work of the Israelite tribes as they penetrated the Land of Promise. Indeed, these sites are listed in the biblical record as cities that Israel took for herself. (On Hazor, see Josh. 11:10–11; on Bethel, Judg. 1:22–26; on Debir, Josh. 10:38–39; and on Lachish, Josh. 10:31–32.) If so, we may work backward and assign Israel's Exodus from Egypt to an earlier time in the same century.

Accordingly, Seti I (ca. 1305–1290) may be considered the pharaoh of the oppression who thought too lightly of Joseph. Then to his successor, Rameses II (ca. 1290–1224), goes the designation "pharaoh of the Exodus." This accords with what we know of Marniptah (ca. 1224–

1211), who was Rameses' son and successor. An account of Marniptah's campaign in western Asia conducted in the fifth year of his reign (ca. 1220) is inscribed on a huge black granite stela that he placed in his mortuary temple at Thebes. Among the opponents listed are the Israelites now located in the land of Canaan.[11] Hence, when Exod. 1:8 mentions the emergence of a new king and 2:23 recounts his death, we may assume that both notations refer to Seti I. In subsequent portions of the Exodus narrative allusions to an unnamed pharaoh apparently refer to Rameses II.

Nevertheless, this identification of the pharaohs mentioned in the Book of Exodus does not mean that we must necessarily take all that is said there at face value. For example, it is difficult to understand why Seti I would try to exterminate his labor force by killing all male infants born to the Hebrews (1:16). If he really did not want the Hebrews around, he could have expelled them. And if these Hebrew males made good slaves, why would he prevent them from propagating? Clearly, the historical events were more complex than the Bible would lead us to believe.

Nor can we confidently determine which Israelite tribes existed in thirteenth-century Egypt. Surely not all Israel's tribes suffered under Egyptian bondage. Indeed, in the militant books of Joshua and Judges, Shechem hosts a peaceful settlement. Fellow Israelites had probably established their home there in an earlier era. It has sometimes been thought that surely the tribe of Levi once existed in Egypt, for several of its members have Egyptian personal names—Moses, Phinehas, Hophni, Passhur, Merari. Even so, the early history of this tribe is enigmatic. We may be confident of two matters, however. First, Egyptian documents indicate that subject Habiru folk did live in Egypt throughout her Empire period, and it is improbable that ancient Israel would have invented a tradition of ignominious slavery unless to some degree that tradition squared with historical fact. Second, through repeated cultic reenactment during the years that followed, the experience of a few Hebrews became an experience appropriated by many. All later Israelite generations could therefore join in affirming their faith that "Our fathers were in Egypt, and Yahweh brought them out." Indeed, in the same breath they were to say, "Yahweh brought us out."

THE FIGURE OF MOSES

The liberation of this enslaved people required that one among them be divinely selected and equipped to function as leader. Beginning with Exodus 2, Moses becomes a figure of special interest. His background, education, and call to the prophetic office are all described in the Exodus traditions.

II. THE ERA OF EXODUS, CONQUEST, AND SETTLEMENT (ca. 1300–1020 B.C.)

DATE (B.C.)	EGYPT	PALESTINE	MESOPOTAMIA
1300	19th Dynasty (ca. 1306–1200) Rameses I (ca. 1306–1305) Seti I, pharaoh of the Hebrew oppression (ca. 1305–1290) Rameses II, pharaoh of the Exodus (ca. 1290–1224) Marniptah (ca. 1224–1211) Defeat of the sea peoples (ca. 1220)	Israelite Exodus (ca. 1280) The wilderness trek (ca. 1280–1250) Israelite conquest of Palestine (ca. 1250–1200)	Ascendance and dominion (ca. 1356–1197)
1200	20th Dynasty (ca. 1185–1069) Rameses III (ca. 1183–1152) Defeat of the sea peoples (ca. 1175) Decline	Era of the judges (ca. 1200–1020) Philistines settle in Palestine (ca. 1200–1150) Israelite victory over Canaanite forces as noted in the Song of Deborah (Judg. 5 [ca. 1125])	Decline (ca. 1197–935); brief resurgence under Tiglath-pileser I (ca. 1116–1078)
1100	21st Dynasty (ca. 1069–935) Decline (ca. 1060)	Battle of Aphek: Philistine victory and fall of Shiloh (shortly after 1050) Philistine pressure on Israel intensifies (ca. 1045–1020)	

Moses' birth and early years are treated in Exod. 2:1–10. This passage affirms that the frightful slaughter of Hebrew male infants becomes the means by which the deity's human agent is equipped for leadership. This son of Levite parents is set afloat on the Nile. Maternal instincts overtake Pharaoh's daughter, who is bathing in the river. Unknowingly, she returns the child to the care of his own mother. At a later time, the boy is presented by his mother to the Egyptian princess for adoption, and the princess confers on him the Egyptian name "Moses." In the years that followed, a sound Egyptian upbringing and education were presumably offered to the one who would someday turn against his benefactors in his brave attempt to deliver his people from their dismal condition.

Again, significant Israelite tradition is transmitted through legend, but this legend is not entirely unique; similar folk motifs exist in birth stories about other ancient heroes. The fifth century B.C. historian Herodotus preserved a popular legend about the birth of the Persian Cyrus.[12] The infant is fortuitously delivered from a ruler who seeks his life, and later overcomes that ruler to become king himself. Similarly, in the birth legend of Sargon of Akkad his mother protects him by carefully putting him in a reed basket that she places in the Euphrates River.[13] The baby is found by a peasant, and ultimately the goddess Ishtar endows him with the power of kingship. Divine providence is affirmed in all three cases. Yet in contrast with the Cyrus and Sargon legends, the Mosaic birth account has a more rigorous historical grounding. As a result of decisions made by Pharaoh's daughter, Moses is reared in close proximity to his antagonist, Seti I.

In the remainder of Exodus 2, we view the adult Moses. We learn that although his attachment to the court of Pharaoh may have isolated him from his own people and their problems, Moses did not forget his Hebraic identity. By killing the Egyptian aggressor who was brutalizing a Hebrew slave, Moses assumed a grave risk. Since the pharaoh soon learned of the deed, Moses had no choice but to flee. He moved eastward into Midianite territory and soon made contact with the family of Jethro, a Midianite priest, whose daughter Zipporah he married. (Here we accept the commonly held notion that Exod. 2:18 should begin, "And they [the daughters of the priest of Midian] came to their father, Jethro, the son of Reuel.")

Even a first reading of Exodus 2 suggests that in the Israelite tradition Moses was revered as a towering figure. Scarcely a single episode in his life could be recounted without recalling his extraordinary contribution to Israelite life, faith, and thought. Here was a unique man who rallied a despondent, heterogeneous mass into a people that would one day exit Egypt and penetrate the uncertain wilderness. Moses conferred on his following a strong sense of purpose. As the singular mediator between the celestial and earthly realms, he brought Yahweh and the people of Israel into creative juxtaposition. In sum, the origins and accomplishments of Moses are scarcely presented in the biblical narrative with a note of detachment.

The Book of Exodus shows much interest in Yahweh's initial summons of Moses. In the earth-centered JE account (3:1–4:17), Yahweh's self-disclosure unfolds spontaneously. Moses is occupied with his father-in-law's livestock when suddenly he is surrounded by the divine presence. He is first confronted by the spectacular (a bush that burns in strange fashion), and he reacts as a curious spectator. But subtly the visual element of the theophany gives way to the audible. Moses the spectator is suddenly called by name (3:4).

The remainder of the story offers Yahweh's declaration that he has beheld the misery of his people and now, through his selection of the human Moses, he intends to deliver them. The refreshingly honest tradition highlights the insecurity and stubbornness of the man Moses. By offering four different excuses he tries to evade the formidable prospect of encountering Pharaoh to remove the yoke from his people (3:11, 13; 4:1, 10). In each instance, however, the deity responds with assurances of his own (3:12, 14; 4:2–9, 11, 14–16). Yahweh is patient and persistent. It is he, not Moses, who has the last word: Moses finally accepts the appointment and leaves Jethro.

The P tradition of the call of Moses (6:2–9) moves along substantially different lines. In the span of eight verses the deity has quite specific lessons to teach. First, he is the same God who has previously manifested himself to the patriarchs of Genesis, yet they knew him by the name "God Almighty" ("El Shaddai"). Second, the time is now ripe for the fulfillment of the promises Yahweh previously made to the fathers. And third, Israel's deliverance from bondage will be spectacular; Yahweh will redeem his people with "outstretched arm" and "great acts of judgment." Moreover, the new divine name is disclosed. In maintaining that the name "Yahweh" had not been revealed until Mosaic times, P sides with the E rather than the J tradition. Although J has the antediluvian patriarchs call Yahweh's name (Gen. 4:26), the testimony of E and P is probably more accurate.

There are several significant differences between Exod. 6:2–9 and Exod. 3:1–4:17. The JE call account takes place on Midianite soil, but the P tradition implies an Egyptian site. While visual elements are significant at the beginning of the JE tradition and then recede completely, they are not mentioned at all in P. In contrast to JE, the P account is silent about Moses' reaction to the call. He simply listens, then obeys. Moreover, while the JE and P accounts are both concerned with establishing a connection between the era of Moses and that of the patriarchs, P is far more explicit than JE. We cannot read Exod. 6:2–9 without being reminded of the prior covenant with Abraham (Gen. 17), who responded obediently to the divine summons. Finally, the JE tradition reveals the people's capacity to believe in Moses (Exod.

4:31), but in P their "broken spirit" and "cruel bondage" have jeopardized their chances of responding positively to Moses (6:9).

Despite such differences, the two narratives do not work entirely at cross-purposes. Both emphasize that the deity intervened in history to claim the man of his choice, that he declared to this attending mortal his design for Israel's immediate future, and that within this context he disclosed the name "Yahweh." According to Exod. 3:14, the name "Yahweh" is directly linked with the Hebrew verb *hwh*, meaning "to be." It is commonly, though not unanimously, believed that "Yahweh" is a causative form of that verb and therefore means, "He causes to be." More than anything else, this name of Israel's God denotes active, dynamic being. Clearly, these call accounts suggest that significant encounter between the oppressor and the oppressed is in the offing.

Before we take up the various stages of that encounter, let us ponder the Yahwist's mystifying narration of the circumcision of Moses (4:24–26). A first reading of the text may easily lead the reader to infer that after having worked at length to obtain the services of Moses, Yahweh now wishes him dead.

The effect is jarring. Is the Yahwist asserting that Israel's God is an entirely arbitrary deity? Closer inspection of the narrative reveals that this is not precisely his intent. The Yahwist seems to have at least two goals in mind. First, he may be giving ironic expression to his conviction that the deity, who draws near at one moment to reveal his purpose in support of his own, functions at another moment in a strikingly unfathomable manner (cf. Gen. 22). Second, the Yahwist is simply trying to account for the origin of circumcision in ancient Israel. In contrast to the priestly view that circumcision was initiated in the time of Abraham (Gen. 17), this obscure, reworked story declares that the custom was of Midianite origin (Zipporah conducts the rite) and was first observed by Israel in Mosaic times. The role that must have originally been played by a local demon is assumed by Yahweh himself. Zipporah rescues her husband from attack by circumcising their son and simulating Moses' circumcision by touching Gershom's foreskin to Moses' genitals; the euphemism in v. 25 is "feet." Perhaps a more ancient version had Zipporah circumcising Moses just prior to their marriage as a means of warding off harassment on the wedding night by a local demon who sought to establish his claim on the bride. The later Israelite practice of child circumcision doubtlessly inspired the insertion about Moses' son.[14]

NEGOTIATIONS, PLAGUES, AND FESTIVALS

The Exodus narrative is deliberately slow yet steady in pace. Israel's folk memory fostered a legend that spelled out in virtually endless detail the difficulties that the Hebrews, and especially Moses, encountered. Presumably that legend was heard each spring by the Israelites who gathered to observe Passover. Early in its existence, the twelve-tribe Israelite confederation seems to have appropriated a Canaanite nature festival and thoroughly historicized it by placing at its center favorite episodes about the Exodus. Although these legends do not constitute an objective historical transcript, they reflect an undeniably crucial assumption that Yahweh acted in history to deliver his people Israel.

The Passover legend focuses at length on Moses' contest with Pharaoh, who has no intention of letting the Hebrews go. According to Exodus 5 (J), the first audience with Pharaoh is a colossal failure. Moses informs Pharaoh of Yahweh's desire that his people go into the wilderness for a few days for a religious celebration. The unimpressed Pharaoh retorts that he can scarcely be expected to allow his slaves time off to worship an unrecognized deity (5:2). Instead he takes measures to intensify their labors. The general condition of the Hebrew slaves worsens. Moreover, Moses and Aaron experience a frustration of their own in having to sustain the anger of the Hebrew foreman (5:21). They are accused of having foolishly provided Pharaoh with an excuse to increase the suffering of the Hebrews. Moses turns to Yahweh and protests (5:22–23). Yahweh's short response (6:1) is a request that Moses have faith in the irony that momentary defeat, however bitter, is the initial link in a chain of events that will ultimately ensure victory for God and people.

As slaves in Pharaoh's service, the Hebrews must secure royal permission if they are to depart. In the context of the plague episodes, that permission is persistently given and withdrawn. Though a precise literary delineation cannot be established, these chapters on the plagues appear to contain three different types of narrative, though no single stratum in Exod. 7:8–11:10 attests all ten plagues. In J, the prophet Moses regularly encounters Pharaoh and announces an impending plague, which then unfolds. In E, the rod that Moses wields is instrumental in bringing on the plague in question. In P, Aaron accompanies Moses and acts as his spokesman before Pharaoh.

All three strata maintain the same stylized format. The plague narrative opens with Yahweh's instruction to Moses about what Pharaoh is to be told. Pharaoh is thus informed, whereupon the plague begins. Its effects are depicted, and then Pharaoh promises that he will let Israel go and requests that the plague abate. The plague is halted, which induces in Pharaoh a hardening of heart that forbids Israel's exit.

In these chapters, nature and theology commingle. On the natural level it may be argued that each plague is correlated with a seasonal or random Egyptian catastrophe. Colored pieces of earth redden the Nile in the summer. Frogs breed in the mud of the Nile after it overflows each year, and gnats can be a nuisance in autumn. Skin infections among human beings and cattle are not unlikely. Egypt is sometimes

The Rock Temple of Rameses II at Abu Simbel. Rameses II also sponsored the building of a great cliff temple in Nubia at Abu Simbel. Four mammoth statues of the pharaoh face the Nile as they guard the temple entrance. Each of the three that are still well preserved is 65 feet high. The facade of this rock temple, however, is more impressive than its interior. (Photo by George W. E. Nickelsburg.)

victimized by hailstorms. Locusts frequent its regions, and the plague of darkness may refer to the remarkable quantity of sand and dust brought in from the desert by the spring winds.[15] But whatever natural phenomena are present, they are theologically interpreted. The Exodus legend affirms that the plagues are wrought by Yahweh so that its victims may witness that Yahweh is the sovereign deity determined that his elect will be delivered from cruel oppression. His will that the Hebrews leave Egypt, however, is never seen as an open invitation to unlimited freedom. In 7:16; 9:13; and 10:3 we find the recurring statement, "Let my people go, that they may serve me." Israel's departure is to be motivated by her transfer of service from Pharaoh to Yahweh.

But what of Pharaoh? Sometimes the narrative contains the matter-of-fact statement that "Pharaoh's heart was hardened," presumably by his own design (see 7:13; 8:19; 9:35). In other instances we are told that "Yahweh hardened Pharaoh's heart" (see 9:12; 10:20, 27). The latter easily suggests to the contemporary reader that Pharaoh was merely Yahweh's puppet. Thus the perplexing issue of divine and human freedom is raised. Probably ancient man was less prone to differentiate between purpose and result than are we today. In all these verses the narrators simply affirm that Yahweh lifts up instances of human rebellion to actualize his own purpose.

Although the final plague—namely, the killing of the Egyptian first-born—is publicly announced in Exodus 11, it does not take place until 12:29–32. The intervening verses (12:1–28) and those immediately following (12:33–13:16), relate to cultic matters that demonstrate Yahweh's formal possession of Israel. The emphasis falls on instituting three rites: the feast of Passover, the feast of unleavened bread, and the dedication of the first-born. All three rituals surely had a pre-Exodus history during which time they afforded men an opportunity to honor the mysterious powers of nature. Israel reshaped these rituals by insisting that history takes precedence over nature. All three rites, which are described in both J and P material, were cultically celebrated by Israel in commemoration of the Exodus.

In the feast of Passover, the Israelites are blessed under the protection of the covenant. Their first-born escape slaughter. The sprinkling of blood on the doorposts ensures a safe distance between Hebrews and Egyptians; Yahweh does not plan to deal similarly with each group. The feast of unleavened bread, which early merged with that of Passover, symbolically reveals that the preparations for the departure had to be made in haste. The ritual of the dedication of the first-born affirms that Israel and her possessions belong to Yahweh and to him alone.

The final plague is announced in 11:1–9 and carried through in 12:29–32. On the grim night ahead, the first-born of Egypt will be smitten, but Yahweh will spare his elect. This graphic account portrays the punitive miracle that the deity works against Egypt in smiting the first-born and the urgent appeals of the Egyptians that the Hebrews leave at once. The slaughter of the first-born has produced in the Egyptians cries of anguish and a complete dread of Yahweh. Israel now complies with what has ironically become Egypt's request. That same night Israel departs, though, as we shall see, she has not heard the last of Egypt.

PROSE AND POETIC WITNESSES
TO ACTUAL DELIVERANCE

The Issue

The flight of the Hebrews from Egypt is variously depicted in Exod. 13:17–15:21. Toward the end of Exodus 13 the J stratum reports that Yahweh was present in pillars of cloud and fire located at the head of the marching Israelite ranks for daytime and nocturnal direction. These pillars anticipate the imagery in Exodus 19 used to present Yahweh's self-revelation at Sinai. Exodus 14 preserves two thoroughly interwoven prose accounts (J and P) of the rescue at sea. Then in Exod. 15:1–21 J

transmits two different poetic witnesses of the event: the Song of the
Sea (vv. 1–18) given by Moses and the Song of Miriam (v. 21) given by
Moses' sister. While these four versions describe what was surely a
historical event, Noth admits that "the incident itself ... remains
veiled from our sight."[16]

However, a few intelligent judgments can be made. The first is that
we cannot plot the precise route of the Hebrews as they moved from
the Nile Delta to Canaan. Rarely can we be confident in equating biblical
and contemporary place names.

We do know that at some point along the Egyptian frontier the
Hebrews were presumably trapped: water lay directly ahead and
Egyptians were advancing behind them; and in an unexpected moment
they somehow managed to escape. But this marvelous happening did not

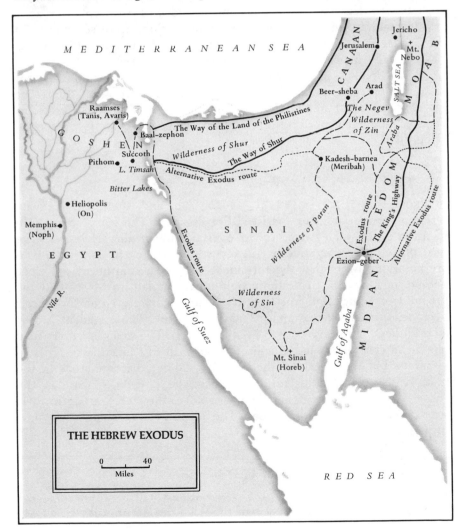

THE HEBREW EXODUS

0   40
Miles

unfold at the Red Sea. While this is what the Septuagint (Greek Old Testament) first erroneously attested and what many other translations have also claimed, the Hebrew original reads *yam-sûph,* meaning "sea of reeds." That designation would apply to any lake or marshy region along the northeastern Egyptian frontier. The site of the event probably lies in the vicinity of what is now the Suez Canal. Lake Timsah, not far from Succoth (13:20), is a likely possibility.

Furthermore, rationalistic explanations of the encounter between the Hebrews and Egyptians are at base problematic. Hay highlights the inadequacy of most rationalizations by saying, "Whereas the water must be assumed to have been *shallow* enough to account in a credible way for the wind's removal of it, it must then be assumed to have been *deep* enough upon its return to sweep away the entire Egyptian force."[17] Perhaps the Hebrews originally understood this confrontation as a striking military victory whose theistic dimensions were secondary. In the final analysis, however, Israel showed virtually no interest in asking, "What really happened?"

And finally, each biblical version of the deliverance confesses that in a moment of supreme human need, Yahweh intervened to rescue his elect. It is not innate Hebrew superiority but Yahweh's gracious, decisive impingement on the terrestrial scene that invites recurring celebration.

The Yahwist's Prose Version of Deliverance

In Exod. 14:5–7, 10–14, 19–21, 24–25, 27b, and 30–31 the Yahwist offers a prose account of the Reed Sea escape.[18] The story opens with mention of Pharaoh's decision to overtake the fleeing Hebrews. The next phase of the narrative (v. 10) focuses on the fearful Israelites, who are painfully aware that the formidable Egyptian charioteers are close behind. In a state of panic the people now complain to Moses that the prospect of being dead but free in the desert hardly commends itself over being enslaved but at least alive in Egypt. The confident Moses admonishes, "You have only to be still" (v. 14). The sovereign deity now has an intense east wind change the sea into dry land. Israel crosses in safety, but the wheels of the Egyptian chariots become stuck in the mud (v. 25). Having lost all confidence, the Egyptians abandon the chase. With the pressure momentarily abated, the Hebrews affirm their fear of God and trust in Moses. The posture of complaint has now turned to one of faith.

The Priestly Prose Version of Deliverance

The P account in Exod. 14:1–4, 8–9, 15–18, 22–23, 26–27a, and 28–29 intensifies the miraculous aspects of the Reed Sea event. Yahweh directs

Moses to wave his rod. The waters separate so that the Hebrews may pass without so much as getting their feet wet. At the appropriate moment the sea is restored to its original state, and with this the pursuing Egyptian host is engulfed in the tide. The priestly version is the one emphasized in Cecil B. De Mille's film *The Ten Commandments*. It focuses on Israel's defiance in leaving Egypt (v. 8), the safe position the people enjoy as a result of the deity's intervention (v. 29), and Yahweh's concern to glorify himself through a decisive event (vv. 4, 17). This crucial moment will, it is hoped, teach the enemy a needed lesson: "the Egyptians shall know that I am Yahweh" (vv. 4, 18).

The Song of Miriam

In Exod. 15:1–18 and 15:21 Israel's deliverance at sea is celebrated in song. The terse, more ancient poem is sung by the prophetess Miriam, who leads the women in their victory dance. The more recent composition, which is far longer, is attributed to Moses.

Miriam's hymn is Israel's most ancient witness to Yahweh's intervention at the Sea of Reeds. This cultic song focuses on the essence of the Exodus event—rescue at sea. It has two brief components: an invitation to praise Yahweh followed by a statement of what he has done to merit man's praise. It is likely that from the middle of the thirteenth century B.C. on, this hymn was regularly used in Israel's worship. Of course, its brevity as a cultic confession would have necessitated the use of a narrator who told the story of the sea miracle and related Exodus happenings in more detail. Therefore, it is not surprising that the Song of Miriam soon gave rise to the more elaborate Song of the Sea, whose oral composition may date back to the era of the judges.[19]

The Song of the Sea

Although Exod. 15:1–18 is not brief, it makes few allusions to the battle itself. The song reports that the Egyptians were annihilated and that the Israelites crossed in safety, but how these things happened is of only minor interest. Rather, one hymnic line is piled on another to form a stirring song of victory.

The dramatic tenor and hymnic majesty of the poem are obvious. The composition deftly reflects Israel's experience of victory as made possible by a triumphant deity who in v. 3 is referred to as "a man of war."[20] The rhetorical question, "Who is like thee, O Yahweh?" (v. 11) and the concluding declaration, "Yahweh will reign for ever and ever" (v. 18) are typical of good hymnic style. The person of Yahweh dominates throughout, yet colorful metaphors and direct discourse reflect on human action and destiny. Exodus 15:5, 10 instruct that the Egyptians sank into and were covered by the sea. This is presented as Yahweh's doing, not Israel's. References to Philistia, Moab, Edom, and Canaan in vv. 14–15 invite the conclusion that the poem was written after the Israelite conquest of Canaan. Nonetheless, Exod. 15:1–18 offers a very early witness to the Exodus event. Since it is commonly recognized that poetic forms are transmitted with greater exactitude than their prose counterparts, many scholars hold early biblical poetry in high esteem. The rich, spontaneous language of this composition stirs the imagination. While it may not bring us close to the Exodus event as history, it does lay before us something of its essence.

THE THREATENING WILDERNESS

The remaining portions of the Book of Exodus meditate on the question, "For what purpose was Israel delivered?" The answer given points to a covenantal fellowship with the deity that was to define Israelite existence. Having been saved from extreme hardship, Israel is now invited to continue a journey of both physical and spiritual dimensions.

In Exod. 15:22–18:27 we follow the Israelites from the Sea of Reeds to Mount Sinai, the mountain of Yahweh. The traditions preserved in this section imply that Yahweh, the husband, has chosen Israel for his bride. While Israel is sometimes obedient, during this wilderness period, essentially we see a people who are long on complaint and short on faith. Of course, the predicament of the Hebrews should not be minimized. Insecurity, hunger, and thirst may have surrounded them often, and such misfortune naturally led to complaint. Ready murmuring sometimes grew into outright rebellion that was repeatedly overcome by Yahweh's patience and forgiveness.[21] The fervent desire of the people for a structured life was fully comprehensible to the deity. Fromm helpfully remarks, "It seems that God understands that slaves, even after they have freed themselves, remain slaves at heart, and therefore there is no reason to be angry."[22] With these general observations in mind, let us turn to three of the wilderness crises depicted here: the incident at Marah, the hunger problem in the wilderness of Sin, and the episode at Kadesh.

The Marah incident is reported in Exod. 15:22b–26, with its core Yahwistic element in vv. 22b–25a. Disturbed by the bitter water, the people murmur against their leader. Moses is not especially angered by the complaint and does not rebuke the people for their present lack of faith. In his mediating role between God and people, Moses simply appeals to Yahweh, who immediately points to a satisfactory solution. Then in the Deuteronomic expansion of vv. 25b–26, Yahweh himself is referred to as Israel's healer, for it is he who has provided an answer to the problem.

The priestly narrative of Exodus 16, which contains a few earlier

Yahwistic elements, presents the crisis as one caused by hunger. The people express both their physical discomfort and lack of faith in Yahweh's leadership. By supplying his people with daily provisions of manna and quail, Yahweh amply demonstrates his providential concern. Moses and Aaron respond to the grumbling about hunger, which they interpret as a complaint against the deity, by arguing for God's nearness and resourcefulness (vv. 6–8).

This tradition can be interpreted in naturalistic terms. As flocks of quail migrate to a European summer, they pass over Sinai. When overcome by exhaustion, they move at a low altitude or touch ground, where they can easily be caught. Manna is a secretion of two species of scale insect that feed on tamarisk bushes. This sweet, sticky secretion, which tastes like honeydew, soon solidifies so that it can be gathered up, though scarcely at the biblical rate of over two quarts daily.[23] But such explanations fail to address the psychological and religious aspects of the quail and manna tradition. Israel's capacity to complain and Yahweh's capacity to provide are writ large in this priestly narrative. As far as the Sabbath dimension in the text is concerned, the antiquity of that institution is plausible indeed. But it is doubtful that the nomadic Hebrews observed the Sabbath as scrupulously as this story suggests.

Israel's faithlessness is also expressed at Kadesh in northern Sinai. In the composite account of Exod. 17:1–7, the people experience thirst once more. Clearly, Israel's rebellion has now intensified, as have the tensions between the contending parties. Two place names are mentioned in v. 7—"Massah," from the Hebrew verb "to test," and "Meribah," from the verb "to find fault." Lacking water, the people complain to Moses and even accuse him of trying to kill them (v. 3). Yahweh advises Moses to strike a rock to obtain water. It is a geological fact that beneath the hard outer surface of the limestone indigenous to the Sinai region lies soft porous rock with deposits of drinkable water. Theologically, however, the tradition again presents the people as rebellious and skeptical of divine leadership. Such was the tenor of Israel's wilderness experience, and she was honest enough to admit it.

MOSES, JETHRO, AND THE KENITE HYPOTHESIS

In Exodus 18 the Elohist has produced an engaging narrative that focuses on Jethro, the father-in-law of Moses. His response to Moses' good news about Yahweh's deeds in Israel's behalf is to conduct an on-the-spot ritual. He reacts to Moses' customary procedure in dispensing justice among his people by advising him in the ways of sound administration (vv. 13–27). Jethro proposes that the appointment of honest, God-fearing associates to solve minor problems will free Moses so that he can tackle weighty problems that may necessitate a knowledge of legal precedent. Hence, the Elohist is declaring that at one time such a division of labor was an innovation for ancient Israel and that it was instituted at the recommendation of a non-Israelite priest.

Exodus 18:1–12 is of even greater significance. There Moses' disclosure of all that Yahweh has accomplished in Israel's behalf induces Jethro to speak solemnly and to engage in a ritualistic act. He confesses Yahweh's superiority over all other deities (v. 11) and does so as a priest who immediately prepares sacrifices (v. 12).

More than any other passage in the Hebrew Bible, Exod. 18:1–12 has inspired the formulation of the Kenite hypothesis, which traces the origins of the Yahwistic faith to the Kenite clan of Midian. It declares that Jethro responded formally to new truth about a deity with whom he was already familiar and also accepted the Mosaic segment of Yahwism. This hypothesis, which was first set forth by Ghillany in the 1860s,[24] argues that Moses first heard about Yahweh from Jethro, who was a Midianite priest of Yahweh. From the Kenite clan the Israelites learned Yahweh's name. They also adopted certain cultic and social practices from the Kenites. The Kenite hypothesis emphasizes that it is the priest Jethro who prepares a sacrifice for the deity and then permits Aaron and the Israelite elders to participate with him in solemn ritual.

The Kenite hypothesis has several strong points. First, the hypothesis acknowledges that the connection of God's self-revelation to Moses in Midianite territory is attested by the most ancient layers of Israelite tradition and that *where* Moses received a theophany from Yahweh is a matter of some consequence. The hypothesis also accepts the reasonable premise that the faith of a people is conditioned by the geographical and social context in which it exists. Furthermore, the Kenite hypothesis fosters a sensible and appealing reading of Jethro's words in 18:11, "Now I know that Yahweh is greater than all gods." It is more likely that the affirmation "Now I know" is the utterance of one who is well established in the faith than the spontaneous declaration of a recently converted proselyte.

Yet opponents of the Kenite hypothesis are eager to point out its weaknesses.[25] In particular, they call attention to the reference in Exod. 18:12 declaring that Jethro offered the sacrifice "to God." Rather than mentioning the more specific name of deity, "Yahweh," the text uses the general designation "Elohim." Furthermore, the text is said to call into question the witness of Gen. 4:26 (J) that even prior to the great flood, men addressed the deity as Yahweh. Defenders of the Kenite hypothesis respond that the text of Exod. 18:12 has been corrupted and that the P and E strata both oppose the assumption of J that the name "Yahweh" had been offered to man in pre-Mosaic times.

On balance, the Kenite hypothesis, which we believe to be cogent, neither enjoys decisive proofs nor suffers from annihilating denial. To some extent, Moses may have been impressed by Kenite religion, and to a far lesser degree he may have been influenced by the incipient mono- theism of Akhnaton. But if ancient Israel borrowed from her Midianite kin, she significantly reshaped the product. For the Kenites, Yahweh was a nature deity who was fixed to an important mountain in Midianite territory. For Israel, Yahweh was a God who transcended nature's perimeter and decisively influenced historical events. The content of Kenite Yahwism and Mosaic Yahwism were not identical.

With its spontaneity, formalism, charm, and confusion, Exodus 1–18 testifies to the actualization of the origins of the people of Yahweh. The humanity and singular appointment of Moses are vividly presented. The adverse conditions facing the ancestors of Israel, their penchant for complaint, and their capacity to endure are likewise attested in a cult narrative that sometimes achieves magnificent dimensions. Yet at this stage in the salvation drama, ancient Israel does not fully know who she is or what she is to become. Her origins are to be clarified at Mount Sinai through a theophany and covenant ceremony, which we shall examine in Chapter 6.

NOTES

1. The strata in Exodus 1–18: Again it is easier to separate P from JE than to disentangle J and E from one another. What follows depends largely on Martin Noth, *Exodus: A Commentary*, trans. J. S. Bowden, The Old Testa- ment Library (Philadelphia: Westminster Press, 1962). To the P stratum we provisionally assign the following: 1:1–7, 13–14; 2:23–25; 6:2–30; 7:1–13, 19–20a, 21b–22; 8:5–7, 16–19; 9:8–12; 11:9–10; 12:1–20, 28, 40–51; 13:1–2; 14:1–4, 8–9, 15–18, 22–23, 26–27a, 28–29; 15:22a, 27; 16:1–36 (with earlier J elements); 17:1a.

    To the J stratum: 1:8–12; 2:15–22; 3:1–4a, 5, 7–8, 16–18; 4:1–31 (with E elements); 5:1–23; 6:1; 7:14–18, 20b–21a, 23–25; 8:1–4, 8–15, 20–32; 9:1–7, 13–35 (with E elements); 10:1–29 (with E elements); 11:4–8; 12:21–23, 29–39; 13:20–22; 14:5–7, 10–14, 19–21, 24–25, 27b, 30–31; 15:1–21, 22b–25a; 17:1b–2, 7.

    To the E stratum: 1:15–22; 2:1–14; 3:4b, 6, 9–15, 19–22; 11:1–3; 13:17–19; 17:3–6, 8–16; 18:1–27. The following appear to be the work of Deuteronomic editing: 12:24–27; 13:3–16; 15:25b–26.

2. Johannes Pedersen, *Israel: Its Life and Culture, III–IV* (New York: Oxford University Press, 1940), "The Crossing of the Reed Sea and the Paschal Legend," pp. 728–737.

3. Walter Beyerlin, *Origins and History of the Oldest Sinaitic Traditions*, trans. S. Rudman (Oxford: Basil Blackwell, 1965).

4. On Egypt's Empire period, see George Steindorff and Keith C. Seele, *When Egypt Ruled the East*, rev. ed. (Chicago: University of Chicago Press, Phoenix Books, 1963).

5. See "The Asiatic Campaigns of Thut-mose III," in James B. Pritchard, ed., *Ancient Near Eastern Texts Relating to the Old Testament*, 3d ed. (Princeton, N.J.: Princeton University Press, 1969), pp. 234–238.

6. The entire hymn appears in Pritchard, *op. cit.*, pp. 369–371. Words in parentheses are the translator's interpolations to facilitate comprehension of the text, and the name in brackets has been added by your author.

7. Should you wish to sample these texts firsthand, read Letters 287 and 290 in Pritchard, *op. cit.*, pp. 488–489.

8. For helpful remarks on the identification and function of the store cities of Pithom and Raamses, see G. Ernest Wright, *Biblical Archaeology*, rev. ed. (Philadelphia: Westminster Press, 1962), pp. 58–60.

9. "The Asiatic Campaigning of Amen-hotep II," Pritchard, *op. cit.*, p. 247. (Amen-hotep II = Amenophis II.)

10. For further data about the Habiru, see the definitive study of Moshe Greenberg, *The Ḫab/piru* (New Haven, Conn.: American Oriental Society, 1955). For more concise treatments, see John Bright, *A History of Israel*, 2d ed. (Philadelphia: Westminster Press, 1972), pp. 92–95, 131–135; and Kathleen M. Kenyon, *Archaeology in the Holy Land*, 3d ed. (New York: Frederick A. Praeger, 1970), pp. 183–185.

11. See Pritchard, *op. cit.*, p. 378. Marniptah's victory stela is of special interest to the biblical historian because it discloses that by about 1220 B.C., Israel was directly associating with various Canaanite elements. This text, however, lists Israel as a landless people; her permanent settlement in Canaan is not attested here. This is the earliest mention of ancient Israel outside the Bible.

12. Herodotus, *Histories*, I. 108–113.

13. See "The Legend of Sargon," in Pritchard, *op. cit.*, p. 119.

14. We are in agreement with Noth, *op. cit.*, p. 50.

15. For a more detailed consideration of the individual plagues as they relate to natural phenomena, see Jack Finegan, *Let My People Go: A Journey Through Exodus* (New York: Harper & Row, 1963), pp. 47–57.

16. Martin Noth, *The History of Israel*, 2d ed., rev. trans. Peter R. Ackroyd (New York: Harper & Row, 1960), p. 117.

17. Lewis S. Hay, "What Really Happened at the Sea of Reeds?" *Journal of Biblical Literature* 83 (1964): 398.

18. Although some Elohistic traces may be found in vv. 5–6 and 19, this conflated narrative is basically the product of the Yahwist.

19. Frank M. Cross, Jr., *Studies in Ancient Yahwistic Poetry* (Baltimore, Md.: Johns Hopkins University, 1950), p. 90.

20. For a thoughtful interpretation of the Old Testament portrayal of God as warrior, see Patrick D. Miller, Jr., "God the Warrior," *Interpretation* 19 (1965): 39–46.

21. See the thorough study of George W. Coats, *Rebellion in the Wilderness: The Murmuring Motif in the Wilderness Traditions of the Old Testament* (Nashville: Abingdon Press, 1968).

22. Erich Fromm, *You Shall Be As Gods: A Radical Interpretation of the Old Testament and Its Tradition* (New York: Holt, Rinehart and Winston, 1966), p. 109.

23. See F. S. Bodenheimer, "The Manna of Sinai," in G. Ernest Wright and

David N. Freedman, eds., *The Biblical Archaeologist Reader* (Garden City, N.Y.: Doubleday, Anchor Books, 1961), 1: 76–80.

24. It was later refined by Hugo Gressmann, *Die Anfänge Israels* (Göttingen, Ger.: Vandenhoeck & Ruprecht, 1922), pp. 86–94.

25. See Theophile H. Meek, *Hebrew Origins*, rev. ed. (New York: Harper & Row, Harper Torchbooks, 1960), pp. 93–99.

6

ORIGINS CLARIFIED: THE THEOPHANY AND COVENANT AT SINAI

As it is remembered in her traditions, no events in ancient Israel's years of wilderness wandering were more telling than the theophany and covenant at Mount Sinai. It is these events that are narrated in the second half of the Book of Exodus.[1] It was at Sinai that Israel obtained a clearer comprehension of the expectation of her God and the nature of her own mission. Through Yahweh's self-disclosure there, which involved the promulgation of divine law and ritualistic steps of covenant ratification, ancient Israel's origins were significantly clarified.

THE STRUCTURE, CHARACTER, AND INTENTION OF THE LITERARY TRADITION

The basic structure of Exodus 19–40 is relatively easy to discern. A priestly notation in 19:1–2a mentions Israel's arrival at Sinai, and in 19:2b the Elohist specifies that "Israel encamped before the mountain." The remainder of Exodus 19 contains the integrated E and J accounts of the theophany of God before the awestruck people. There the divine will is set forth in two legislative codes: the Decalogue (Ten Commandments) in 20:1–17 and the Covenant Code in 20:22–23:33. Ratification of the covenant dominates chapter 24. Loosely attached to the J (24:1–2, 9–11) and E (24:3–8) accounts of the sealing of the covenant is the brief

---

Biblical texts to be read prior to and in conjunction with the present chapter: Exodus 19–40. Pay particular attention to the following: Exod. 19:1–20:20; 24:1–18; 32:1–34:35.

priestly notation on the Sinaitic theophany (24:15b–18a). These verses preface the extensive cultic legislation in 25:1–31:17, which is presented by P as the disclosure of Yahweh to Moses atop the holy mountain. That legislation is repeated in Exodus 35–40, where it is said to have been executed by the obedient Moses. (Legislation on the ordination of priests [Exod. 29], however, is not implemented until Lev. 8.) The Israelite cult thereby comes into existence; religious experience can therefore assume concrete forms of expression that will significantly influence the corporate life of the people. Sandwiched between the issuing of the Sinaitic priestly ordinances and their implementation are chapters 32–34, which deal with the breaking and renewal of the covenant. This thoroughly redacted section gives a vivid description of Israel's apostasy (which lavishes itself on a golden calf), the intervention of Moses, and divine reassurance. Exodus 19–40 relates the Israelites to the mountain of God in the wilderness of Sinai and links them with divine expectation and grace.

Exodus 19–40 weds narrative legend and legislation. Once more we confront a tradition shaped and maintained by the cultic community. As such, it has several important characteristics. First, this narrative about the theophany and covenant at Mount Sinai both respects and transcends the limits of time and space. That the original event actually took place is highly plausible. Its continuing impact on the existence of the people of the Old Testament discourages us from saying that the Sinai story was merely the invention of a later era.[2] Nevertheless, the traditional, composite portrait of Yahweh's self-revelation at Sinai masks the actual event. Thus, the narrative elements in Exodus 19–40 inform the biblical reader about how Israel herself remembered and interpreted the Sinaitic theophany and covenant. The language of that narrative legend was largely conventionalized for cultic utilization so that the reality of a former event might be experienced by the present community of faith.[3] Mention of a purification ritual that prefaces the moment of divine disclosure (19:10–11a, 14–15), the blast of the horn as an indication of the divine voice (19:16, 19), and the sacrificial rites involved in the ratification of the covenant (24:1–11) all appear as ritualistic narrative dimensions that significantly kept alive the original experience of the Sinaitic theophany. As sheer historical happening the Sinai event was refracted in the cult into something other than what it had been originally. Even so, the essence of the historical event was made all the more prominent: In that moment, Yahweh became the God of Israel and Israel became Yahweh's people.

Second, these chapters in Exodus emphasize the centrality of the law for biblical man. Through the law, the will of Yahweh was made clear and concrete. Of course, the historical circumstances involved in the giving of the law at Sinai cannot be ascertained in detail. We cannot assume that every law in the Decalogue (20:1–17), the Elohistic

Covenant Code (20:22–23:33), the priestly legislative corpus (25:1–31:17), and the Yahwistic Covenant Code (34:10–26) is of Mosaic origin. On the contrary, many of these laws presuppose the existence of a settled people. For example, the law that the sojourner within Israel's gates should join the native Israelite in Sabbath observance (20:10) assumes that Israel in fact has gates. However, the tradition of Moses as the covenant mediator between God and his people does not appear to be fictional. A portion of the Sinaitic legislation may connect directly with the historical Moses who confronted the deity in a special way at Sinai. At subsequent times, the remaining bulk of this legislation was imputed to the Sinai setting. It was within that context that the portraits of Yahweh as the lawgiver and Moses as the covenant mediator were so thoroughly drawn. The theological potential of Mount Sinai, then, outdistanced its historical actuality. Though the Israelite clans who originally assembled surely were not indifferent to the theophany and covenant ratification, the full impact of Sinai on Israelite religion was to assert itself only gradually.

Third, much of Exodus 19–40 draws the distinct elements of divine grace and expectation into a unified theological whole. The Sinai narrative reminds Israel that the God who had acted graciously in history to redeem her from the throes of Egyptian bondage also made certain demands. Yahweh invited the people to enter an ongoing covenant fellowship that required strict obedience to covenant legislation. Such law shaped the relationship between Yahweh and the people. This mutuality between unmerited deliverance and covenant expectation is asserted dramatically in 19:4–5 at the head of the E narrative of the Sinaitic theophany. Yahweh's request for covenant fidelity (v. 5) is prefaced by direct allusion to the recent rescue (v. 4): "You have seen what I did to the Egyptians, and how I bore you on eagles' wings and brought you to myself." Witness to Yahweh's mighty deed in Israel's behalf prefaces the invitation that Israel join Yahweh in covenant fellowship. The Elohist therefore assumes that the people who beheld the theophany at Sinai were the ones who had previously been delivered during the Exodus.

But were the Exodus and Sinai traditions joined from the beginning? Bright would answer yes.[4] Von Rad, however, has argued that these traditions were independent for a long time prior to their literary juxtaposition.[5] The issue is not easily settled. While ancient legend tends to oversimplify, we doubt that a Pentateuchal separation of themes for liturgical utilization is sufficient reason for claiming that the people involved in the Exodus and Sinai events were not essentially one and the same.[6] We hold, therefore, that Exodus 19–40 affirms the dual realities of unmerited divine grace, which has unfolded in history, and covenant loyalty, which is expected of Israel as she lives out her existence maintaining a special relationship with the deity.

THEOPHANIC CONFRONTATION
AT MOUNT SINAI

The Witness of E

The E, J, and P strata all recount the theophany on Sinai, but the Elohist's account is more elaborate than the other two. It has six crucial components. First is the divine invitation to the people and their positive response (19:2b–8). Yahweh tells Moses what he should say to the people by way of theophanic invitation. Reflecting on their marvelous deliverance from the Egyptians, the Israelites are invited to answer yes or no to Yahweh's covenant summons. As the unique mediator of the covenant, Moses proposes this to the people. He then conveys the people's readiness to the deity, which leads immediately to the second part of this account, the sanctification of the participants (19:10–11a, 14–15). The people are to indicate their readiness for the theophany by washing their garments. Only those who are ritually clean will be permitted to behold the divine presence. Abstention from sexual intercourse, which is demanded by the last phrase in 19:15, may be a later addition.

The third part of the account attempts to portray the ineffable theophany itself (19:16–17, 19). Here the trembling people witness divine nearness through their perception of audible and visual phenomena; thunder and blast of the horn, lightning and thick cloud. Except for the horn, these elements project the image of a storm associated with the deity. Indeed, the thunder is equated with Yahweh's voice (v. 19). And as the theophany on Sinai was cultically reenacted, it was the horn that signaled divine speaking.

The fourth part of the account is the fear of the people as they witness the theophany and their entreaty that Moses draw near God in their place (20:18–21). (In the original sequence of the E narrative, Exod. 20:18–21 probably preceded 20:1–17.) Moses tries to allay their fear by explaining that God has come near so that they may have a direct experience of his terrible presence. This will arouse in them a positive fear of God, which should assist them in adhering to the divine will soon to be communicated.[7] Then, as the unique representative of his people, Moses approaches the darkness that encompasses the deity, who is enthroned on the holy mountain.

God's giving of his name ("I am Yahweh") and the specific disclosure of his will through the Ten Commandments constitute the fifth component of the theophany (20:1–17). Finally, the covenant is formally established and sealed (24:3–8). The requisite ritualistic undertakings include the construction of an altar and erection of twelve pillars, the sacrifice of offerings, and the distribution of the blood that seals the covenant between God and people. Moses also conveys to the people "all the words of Yahweh," and they freely pledge their obedience to the divine will.

The E witness to the Sinaitic theophany leaves us with several clear impressions. First, it portrays the deity as the one who *continually* resides on this his sacred mountain. He does not descend from the heavens to confront Moses; he calls him to the top of the mountain, which is his regular dwelling place. Second, this theophany is attended by all the people who respond positively to the deity's covenantal invitation. Although Moses fulfills a mediating function between God and people, the entire congregation is involved. And third, the narrative offers a dual reflection of the gracious and demanding aspects of deity. Exodus 19:4 and 20:2 proclaim that Yahweh brought Israel out of Egypt simply because it was his inexplicable nature to be gracious in her moment of need. Yet the divine imperatives in the Ten Commandments poignantly remind Israel that the God who has approached her in theophanic meeting is holy and righteous. He expects unswerving obedience from those whom he has graciously chosen.

The Witness of J

The Yahwist's narrative of the Sinaitic theophany encompasses Exod. 19:9, 11b–13, 18, 20–25; 24:1–2, 9–11. We suspect that only a portion of the original has been preserved. According to J, Sinai was host to three distinct, yet related theophanic happenings. The first is Yahweh's self-disclosure to all people as a way of authenticating Moses as their covenant mediator (Exod. 19). The second is witnessed by Moses, Aaron, Nadab, Abihu, and seventy elders (Exod. 24). The third is a special theophany to Moses, who doubts that the offended deity will continue with his people (Exod. 33–34).

The first two happenings, which concern us now, are noteworthy in several ways. With its many references to time and space, J shows a cultic preoccupation with proper preparation for and conduct during theophanic encounter. In 19:11b the moment of theophanic meeting is established ("on the third day"). Then 19:12–13a specifies that mortal man must not intrude on the divine presence. The people are to show appropriate respect toward a previously profane locale which is to become holy by virtue of Yahweh's impending visitation. Then too, the J narrative specifies the manner of divine approach (19:9, 18). Yahweh intends to move earthward in a "thick cloud" that will conceal him from the gaze of mortals and function as his vehicle of descent. Yahweh is equipped to meet man on his terrestrial level. The visual aspects of the theophany are also of special interest to J. According to 19:11, Yahweh will descend "in the sight of all the people," and 19:18 emphasizes the smoke. Moreover, in 24:9–11 the covenant is sealed through a ritualistic meal involving seventy-four people who "saw the God of Israel" (24:10).

The Witness of P

The brief unit of Exod. 24:15b–18a (P) shows only modest interest in the "how" of the Sinaitic theophany. It is concerned mainly with the extensive body of cultic legislation in Exodus 25–31. Nevertheless, P declares that the sacred mountain was covered by a cloud that enveloped Yahweh's glory. That was the manifestation of divine nearness that was of special concern to Israel's priests. The crucial theophanic encounter must first be anticipated. Only on the seventh day does Yahweh invite Moses to come up the mountain. The direct confrontation will involve solely the deity and Moses. Since the covenant had already been established with Abraham (Gen. 17) and reaffirmed in the call of Moses (Exod. 6), P does not attest any covenant rituals as J and E do. And yet the Sinaitic theophany is affirmed as the context for Yahweh's authoritative disclosure of the legislation that was the basis of ongoing Israelite worship.

In sum, the E, J, and P strata agree that the Sinaitic theophany was decisive for Israelite faith. That disclosure affirmed the demanding nature of the God who had drawn near the people of his choice. As the theophany was repeated in the Israelite cult, the memory of this crucial event, which involved Yahweh, Moses, and the people, was constantly renewed.[8]

THE DECALOGUE

Israelite tradition claimed that at Sinai, Yahweh (who had already shown himself to be sovereign over history) now set forth certain stipulations in several codes of law. Appropriately the Ten Commandments (Exod. 20:1–17) head the sequence. Surely in its present form the Decalogue does not trace back to Moses, for two incompatible styles are evident here. For example, the terse commandment "You shall not kill" (Exod. 20:13), merely two words in the Hebrew, may indeed reflect ancient origins. By contrast, the involved commandment on the Sabbath (Exod. 20:8–11) appears to be the product of several generations, although a succinctly stated Decalogue may have existed in Mosaic times.[9] In any case, all legislative codes in the Book of Exodus appear to have undergone a complex evolution.

The profound initial statement of the deity in 20:2 ensures that the Ten Commandments will be viewed within the larger context of God's redemptive design: "I am Yahweh your God, who brought you out of the land of Egypt, out of the house of bondage." Each stipulation that follows is to be read with full recognition that Yahweh delivered Israel from the cruelties of Egyptian servitude.

The first four commandments (20:3–11) concern man's relationship with God; the remaining six (20:12–17) concern his relationship with his neighbor. Originally these laws were probably all expressed in terse negative form. Behind such a formulation may lie a series of curses (resembling those in Deut. 27:15–26) directed at those whose conduct threatened the welfare of the covenant community.

The Decalogue has often been unjustly attacked for its negativism. To say that only two of the ten laws, as we now have them, are positive in expression is to miss the point that this fundamentally negative code has a remarkable capacity to establish policy. Although it cannot anticipate every kind of deviant behavior, it offers useful guidelines to the people of God for conducting their daily affairs. It defines human life within the covenant by specifying what is objectionable. By indicating what is not permitted, a wide range of ethical options remains open.

The first three commandments invite brief comment. The first (v. 3) prohibits the veneration of other gods, and the second (vv. 4–6), forbids any bowing down before idols. Together they uphold the priority of Yahweh, who will endure no rival. If worship remains imageless, there is less chance that Yahweh will be manipulated by thoughtless devotees. The servant status of the congregation is suggested by the third commandment (v. 7), which speaks against an irreverent use of the divine name for magical and selfish ends. We see here the ancient notion that knowledge of a name, which represents the very essence of that which is named, means control over what is named. Yahweh's name is to be praised, not abused for second-rate purposes. The remaining commandments are clear enough to preclude comment. All ten exemplify the life style that Israel's covenant Lord expects of her.

THE COVENANT CODE

The Covenant Code, sometimes designated "The Book of the Covenant" (see Exod. 24:7), encompasses diverse legislation that was eventually linked with the Sinai tradition. The latest legislation in these chapters seems to stem from the eighth century B.C., for the code itself does not press for cultic centralization as the seventh-century Code of Deuteronomy does. Since some of the legislation presupposes a settled agrarian people, it is unlikely that the complete code issued from Mosaic times. Nevertheless, it undoubtedly contains some ancient elements.

This legislation reminds us of Israel's belief that all life came under the scrutiny and providential care of the deity. Diverse situations therefore invite Israel's attention. The regulations, which generally are more humane than comparable regulations in other ancient Near Eastern codes, fall into two categories—casuistic law and apodictic law.[10]

Casuistic, or case, legislation, which is commonplace in the ancient

"Moses Shows the Tablets of Law" by Rembrandt. This canvas by the Dutch master Rembrandt van Rijn (1606–1669) was completed in 1659. (Courtesy of the Gemäldegalerie of the Dahlem Museum, Berlin.)

Near East, is cast in an "if-then" format. A specific situation is expressed in the introductory "if clause." In the following clause or clauses, the penalty or outcome is set forth. In Exod. 22:14, for example, the "if clause" is "If a man borrows anything of his neighbor, and it is hurt or dies, the owner not being with it"; the remainder of the verse, the clause of consequence, is "he [the borrower] shall make full restitution." During their settlement in Palestine, the Israelite tribes doubtlessly appropriated the if-then formulation from their Canaanite neighbors.

The other legislative form, apodictic law, is uniquely Israelite in origin. This succinct, authoritative law is expressed in three different ways, all of which are seen in the relatively brief compass of Exod. 22:18–31. Most succinct is the "You shall not" formulation so typical of the Ten Commandments. Completely lacking in qualifying phrases, the law in 22:18 reads, "You shall not permit a sorceress to live." On occasion, apodictic law opens with the words "He who" or "Whoever," and once more the law is set forth with resounding clarity. Exodus 22:20 states, "Whoever sacrifices to any god, save to Yahweh only, shall be utterly destroyed." Certain kinds of human conduct are therefore banned through terse prohibitions. Less frequently, apodictic law is expressed positively. What is expected is declared. Thus, Exod. 22:31a reads, "You shall be men consecrated to me." In all three forms, apodictic law is unconditional. It is divinely promulgated, and as the covenant people of Yahweh, Israel is expected to obey.

The appeal of the Covenant Code for our own time is admittedly limited. Most of us are not accustomed to stealing animals, burning an opponent's field, or boiling a goat. Moreover, some of the legislation seems unusually severe. At first the lex talionis decree of 21:22–25 may strike us as barbaric. There striving men are permitted to render "life for life, eye for eye, tooth for tooth," and so forth. Yet this well-known law did place limits on human retaliation. It sensitized ancient man and gave him a new level of social responsibility. Clearly, ancient Israel accepted the Covenant Code as a thoughtful, highly useful guide for daily conduct.

THE SINAITIC
PRIESTLY LEGISLATION

The systematic P code in Exodus 25–31 is concerned with various cultic equipment and procedures. In Exod. 25:2–9 Moses is to take on the function of fund raiser, obtaining an offering so that the cultic paraphernalia about to be legislated may in fact be manufactured. In Exod. 25:10–40 the ark, table, and lampstand are emphasized as significant furnishings for the priestly tabernacle. Construction of the tabernacle and its outer court is the concern of Exodus 26–27. Then instructions pertaining to the priesthood and to miscellaneous cultic matters take up chapters 28–31. Such legislation shows an admittedly indiscriminate enthusiasm for the tabernacle. The assumption that this edifice could have been built in the wilderness is incredible. It has also been said of the P writer that "the impossibility of transporting such a monstrous structure without the aid of a freight train never occurred to him."[11] Of course a much less elaborate tent-shrine may have played an important role in Israel's wilderness experience.

A few particulars in this priestly legislation require brief comment. First, Yahweh declares in 25:8 that he wants a sanctuary in order that he may dwell with his people. He wants to be available to them, and he has a specific plan for tabernacle building. This motif reflects the ancient assumption that celestial models directly influenced the design of earthly temples and their furnishings.

Second, the ark of the covenant is thoroughly described in 25:10–22. A little over 2 feet wide and high and a little under 4 feet long, it was to contain the tablets of law and support a gold-covered mercy seat on which the deity would be invisibly enthroned. Of particular importance were the poles attached to the ark, which ensured its portability. As an implement intimately related to a deity who himself was not confined to one region, it could hardly have been otherwise.

Finally, we should observe that the main legislation on the priestly tabernacle closes with a vital passage (29:43–46) that deftly sets forth an assurance about Yahweh's gracious presence. It likewise recollects the crucial Exodus event that has made possible the continuing cultic service of Yahweh.

COVENANT BREAKING
AND RENEWAL

Exodus 32–34 offers an important composite of J, E, and P materials, which taken together project a profoundly vital theological concern: How are divine law and divine grace related? Having rescued her through gracious intervention, Yahweh made a legal covenant with Israel. If the obedience that the deity had a right to expect of those who had responded positively to his covenantal invitation did not come, what then?

These chapters declare that the deity neither openly rejects his elect for neglect of covenant stipulation nor indulges them at the expense of the needs of justice. Though his people are inclined to be undependable, Yahweh will maintain his covenant relation with them by working through its noteworthy leaders—in this case, Moses—whose faithfulness is apparent.

Exodus 32 recounts the incident of the golden calf.[12] The people are waiting at the foot of Mount Sinai. Impatient with Moses' long delay at the top of the mountain, they demand that Aaron fashion visible tokens of deity to whom they may express their trust. Aaron produces a calf, the fundamental symbol of fertility throughout much of the ancient Near East. This worship object, so alien to authentic Yahwistic religion, is then legitimized through the people's spontaneous and excessive celebration (v. 6).

Yahweh can only view such action as a deliberate rejection of the newly instituted covenant, but he does not annihilate the people. Instead, he defers to the logic of Moses' intercession (vv. 11–13). For Yahweh to exterminate Israel would be to thwart the intention of the Exodus. Yahweh had already extended himself in rescuing this people;

for him to reject them now would be fatal to his own design. Moreover, in ridicule the Egyptians would say that Yahweh was a sinister god who had deliberately brought the Hebrews out of Egypt in order to kill them in cold blood. Moses further reminds the deity that slaying the people would nullify the promises which he had previously made to the patriarchs. Even so, Moses' own dealings with the people are by no means gentle (vv. 19, 20, 28). (Note also Aaron's ludicrous disclaimer [v. 24], "I threw it [the people's gold] into the fire, and there came out this calf.")

In Exodus 33 we confront a series of originally unrelated passages that have been drawn together under the rubric of divine presence and absence. Yahweh's command that Moses guide his people to the Land of Promise (v. 1) leads him to ponder whether the deity will continue with his people once they leave Mount Sinai. That question, of course, is complicated by the people's recent apostasy. The holy Yahweh informs Moses that he chooses not to dwell with defiant calf-worshiping Israel lest in wrath he consume them (v. 3). He will send a messenger instead. But the dissatisfied Moses needs more assurance. Boldly he voices his desire for a glimpse of Yahweh's majesty: "Show me thy glory" (v. 18). While Yahweh is willing to honor this unusual request, he alone will specify the ground rules for theophanic meeting. Moses is placed in the cleft of an available rock and covered by Yahweh's anthropomorphic hand during the fatal moment when the divine glory moves by. Then the hand is removed so that Moses may have a view of God's back. The chapter testifies to Israel's belief that the fundamental distinction between deity and mortal cannot be circumvented.

Yahweh's renewal of his covenant with Israel unfolds in Exodus 34. Now Moses etches the commandments in new tablets of stone. The legislation in vv. 10–26 had a history of its own prior to being incorporated into the present context. It is frequently referred to as the "Ritual Decalogue," but the designation "Yahwistic Covenant Code" is preferable. It is not clear that we are here confronting a decalogue (ten commandments), and the cultic contents of these verses more closely parallel the Elohist's Covenant Code (20:22–23:33) than they do his Decalogue (20:1–17). Here Israel's unswerving allegiance to Yahweh is pressed to the virtual exclusion of everything else. Pagan forms of worship are absolutely prohibited, which is itself an admission of idolatry's intrinsic appeal. It is hoped that by realizing that Yahweh's name is "Jealous" (34:14), Israel will be stirred to new levels of loyalty.

THE THRUST
OF COVENANTAL RELIGION

Mosaic Yahwism was essentially a covenantal religion. Nevertheless, the clarity of that religion, with its own legislation and unambiguous expectations involving Yahweh and his people, did not emerge suddenly and completely in the lifetime of Moses. Nor did the concept of covenant originate with ancient Israel. Although she applied the idea to her religion in a unique way, she borrowed from what was already available.

In the last two decades, biblical scholars have often claimed that Israel's formulation and comprehension of covenant were influenced by Hittite suzerainty treaties of the Late Bronze Age (ca. 1550–1200 B.C.).[13] Such formal agreements were not entered into by equals. They involved the sovereignty and initiative of the Hittite suzerain and the willing response of the lesser vassal. The treaty had a definite form. It opened with a statement by the suzerain in which he identified himself and then reviewed the history of the relationship between the two parties of the covenant. The sovereign's benevolent acts in behalf of the vassal's well-being were emphasized. Next, the stipulations of the treaty were enumerated. These clarified the sovereign's interests in a manner that permitted the vassal some measure of freedom. Nevertheless, he was required to obey no one other than the Hittite sovereign who initiated the treaty. Divine and cosmic witnesses, blessings and curses, and provisions for the deposit and preservation of the treaty document were also matters of concern. At first glance, the affinities of the Hittite suzerainty treaty with the Sinaitic covenant seem striking. In Exod. 20:2, in the preamble to the Decalogue, Yahweh first identifies himself and then openly alludes to his gracious rescue of the Israelite clans from Egyptian captivity. In the legislation that follows (20:3–17), the deity's concerns are equally explicit. He expects unswerving fidelity of Israel yet he does not bind the people at every turn. He provides structure without forcing an absolute determinism on her daily existence.

Recently, however, ancient Israel's presumed reliance on available Hittite models has been questioned. Some scholars hold that the form-critical parallel between the Hittite suzerainty treaties and the covenant forms of the Old Testament is unconvincing. Yet it seems that there did exist in ancient Israel a covenant ritual whose steps closely paralleled the sequence attested in the Hittite treaties.[14] In any case, debate on this matter continues in academic circles.[15]

Certainly, we cannot ignore the unique dimensions of Israel's covenant faith. At the very center of that faith was her recollection that Yahweh had intervened in history to deliver a people who were precious in his sight. This was the mysterious and wonderful reality of grace. Lacking intrinsic merit, Israel had been rescued from a meaningless existence of enslavement and promised a purposive life as Yahweh's special possession. Though covenantal stipulations demanded much of ancient Israel, such stipulations were firmly rooted in the divine favor. Hence, the covenant concept helped ancient Israel significantly in her quest for self-understanding. Covenant law made possible the pursuit of an orderly life in Israelite society. It illumined the daily existence of each member of the covenant community.[16]

If the covenant law frequently evoked rejoicing in biblical man (see Ps. 119:97, 105), it could likewise lead him to moments of deeply felt consternation. When he corrupted the covenant and took its stipulations too lightly, divine judgment lay on the immediate horizon. In a word, the covenant and its legislation served as a transcendent criticism of the entire range of ancient Israelite existence.

Whenever Israel broke the law, she could expect to reap the consequences. As the prophets of ancient Israel knew so well, the covenant and its law constituted a permanent source of Israel's correction and hope. Within the context of a covenantal religion, Yahweh dynamically related to his people in ways that truly mattered.

NOTES

1. The strata in Exodus 19–40: We assign the following passages to (a) the P stratum: Exod. 19:1–2a; 24:15b–18a; 25:1–31:18a; 34:29–40:38; (b) the J stratum: Exod. 19:9, 11b–13, 18, 20–25; 24:1–2, 9–11; 32:9–14, 25–34; 33:1–6; 33:12–34:28; (c) the E stratum: Exod. 19:2b–8, 10–11a, 14–17, 19; 20:1–23:33; 24:3–8, 12–15a, 18b; 31:18b–32:8; 32:15–24, 35; 33:7–11. P is more extensive than E, and E more extensive than J.
2. See Martin Noth, *The History of Israel*, 2d ed., rev. trans. Peter R. Ackroyd (New York: Harper & Row, 1960), p. 128; and John Bright, *A History of Israel*, 2d ed. (Philadelphia: Westminster Press, 1972), p. 124.
3. This is convincingly emphasized by Gerhard von Rad, *The Problem of the Hexateuch and Other Essays*, trans. E. W. Trueman Dicken (London: Oliver & Boyd, 1966), p. 29.
4. Bright, *op. cit.*, p. 124.
5. Von Rad, *op cit.*, pp. 18–19.
6. See also G. Ernest Wright, "Book of Exodus," in George A. Buttrick et al., eds., *The Interpreter's Dictionary of the Bible* (Nashville: Abingdon Press, 1962), E–J, p. 195.
7. See Moshe Greenberg, "*Nsh* in Exodus 20:20 and the Purpose of the Sinaitic Theophany," *Journal of Biblical Literature* 79 (1960): 273–276.
8. For a more detailed analysis of the theophanic confrontation, see J. Kenneth Kuntz, *The Self-revelation of God* (Philadelphia: Westminster Press, 1967), pp. 72–103.
9. See also H. H. Rowley, "Moses and the Decalogue," *Bulletin of the John Rylands Library* 34 (1951–1952): 81–118.
10. See "The Origins of Israelite Law," in Albrecht Alt, *Essays on Old Testament History and Religion*, trans. R. A. Wilson (Garden City, N.Y.: Doubleday, Anchor Books, 1966), pp. 101–171.
11. Harry M. Buck, *People of the Lord: The History, Scriptures, and Faith of Ancient Israel* (New York: Macmillan, 1966), p. 149. A detailed and instructive article on "The Priestly Tabernacle," by Frank M. Cross, Jr., appears in G. Ernest Wright and David N. Freedman, eds., *The Biblical Archaeologist Reader* (Garden City, N.Y.: Doubleday, Anchor Books, 1961), 1: 201–228.
12. For a statement of the reasonable hypothesis that the narrative of the

golden calf of Aaron (Exod. 32) and that of the golden calves of Jeroboam (1 Kings 12:28–29) are interdependent, see Moses Aberbach and Leivy Smolar, "Aaron, Jeroboam, and the Golden Calves," *Journal of Biblical Literature* 86 (1967): 129–140.

13. See especially George E. Mendenhall, *Law and Covenant in Israel and the Ancient Near East* (Pittsburgh: The Biblical Colloquium, 1955), pp. 26–34. For specific Hittite texts, see James B. Pritchard, ed., *Ancient Near Eastern Texts Relating to the Old Testament*, 3d ed. (Princeton, N.J.: Princeton University Press, 1969), pp. 201–205, 529–530. Although the Hittites may not have been the innovators of the suzerainty treaty, it is only through the discovery of Hittite literature that such a form has come to light.

14. Here we follow Johann J. Stamm and Maurice E. Andrew, *The Ten Commandments in Recent Research*, Studies in Biblical Theology, 2d series, no. 2 (London: SCM Press, 1967), pp. 42–43.

15. A good idea of the controversy may be obtained from reading Dennis J. McCarthy, *Old Testament Covenant: A Survey of Current Opinions* (Richmond: John Knox Press, 1972).

16. For a more comprehensive treatment of covenantal religion, see Delbert R. Hillers, *Covenant: The History of a Biblical Idea* (Baltimore, Md.: Johns Hopkins Press, 1969).

Part III

THE GROWTH OF THE PEOPLE

7

WILDERNESS WANDERING AND THE CONQUEST OF THE LAND

Ancient Israel's traditions about the patriarchs of Genesis, the deliverance of the clans from Egypt, and the theophany and covenant at Mount Sinai reflect on the origins of the people of Yahweh. In this next series of chapters (7–11), we shall examine the growth of the people. This will involve an inspection of the traditions that portray further wandering in the wilderness, entrance and settlement in Canaan, the emergence and first phases of the Hebrew monarchy, and the work of Israel's earlier prophets. Such an examination will bring us to the end of the ninth century B.C.

The biblical literature of this period primarily falls into four categories: the prose narrative of legend, the prose narrative of history, the early poetry of hymnic celebration or lament, and the poetry of prophetic oracle. The portions of Numbers, Joshua, and Judges to be studied are primarily the prose product of legend. Frequently they offer a provocative meditation on the significance of Israel's past. Many of the prose passages in the books of Samuel and Kings that we shall study merit the label "historical." The detail in a given episode may still be slight, and the causal relationships may be vaguely sketched. Even so, the sources in Samuel and Kings allude to events that occurred not that long before the time of writing. And they emphasize national concerns rather than domestic happenings. Accordingly, they satisfy the interests of history rather than those of legend.

Poetry also plays a vital role in distilling the essence of Israel's past. Israel's (and Yahweh's) victory over Canaanite troops in the Esdra-

---

Biblical texts to be read prior to and in conjunction with the present chapter: Num. 10:29–14:45; 16:1–50; 20:1–24:19; 27:12–23; Deuteronomy 34; Joshua 1–11, 24; Judg. 1:1–2:5.

elon plain in the late twelfth century is celebrated in the Song of Deborah (Judg. 5). Moreover, Israel's loss of Saul and Jonathan at the end of the eleventh century is movingly expressed in a poetic lamentation attributed by tradition to David (2 Sam. 1:19–27). In both instances, the poetic cadences aptly portray the essence of undeniably critical moments of ancient Israelite history. Visionary and prophetic individuals likewise resorted to poetic utterances. Although the words and actions of such prophets as the tenth-century Nathan and the ninth-century Elijah are found primarily in prose contexts, we meet poetic oracle in their predecessor Balaam and, to a lesser extent, in the prophet Samuel. In sum, the texts we are about to study utilize many literary forms as they seek to preserve crucial Israelite experience.

CRITICAL MOMENTS
IN THE WILDERNESS TREK

Our last inspection of the people of the Old Testament found them at the foot of Mount Sinai, and this is where we meet them as the Book of Numbers begins. In the present chapter we shall omit any formal consideration of the Book of Leviticus and shall inspect only one chapter of Deuteronomy (34), which tells of the death of Moses. Deuteronomy is best examined within the context of events relating to the last quarter of the seventh century B.C. (see Chapter 14). And since Leviticus is throughout the vehicle of priestly legislation, it is most appropriately studied as material with direct bearing on the worship life of the post-exilic Jewish community (see Chapter 19). But we cannot take leave of the Pentateuch immediately.[1] Indeed, important phases in Israel's wilderness wandering are depicted in the Book of Numbers. This crucial work, which preserves early as well as late traditions, connects the epic of Israel's deliverance from Egypt with the epic of her appropriation of the Land of Promise. As we shall see, the dominant theological themes of divine leadership and human rebellion are thoroughly expressed in the Book of Numbers.

The Historical Situation

A precise historical reconstruction of this era lies beyond the reach of biblical scholarship. Neither the list of forty places where Israel encamped (Num. 33:1–49) nor the assertion that the people were condemned to forty years in the desert (Num. 14:33–34) can be taken at face value. The temporal reference may be simply a conventional way of declaring that the clans lived in the desert for many years, or possibly for one full generation. As far as the forty stations of wilderness encampment are concerned, the late, secondary tradition of Numbers 33

(P) does not mesh satisfactorily with the data submitted by preceding chapters in Exodus and Numbers. Nor is it congruent with the résumé offered in Deuteronomy. Similarly, the attempt to equate the biblical place names with modern Arabic place names has met with only modest success. Finally, the notations that the male population alone that followed the lead of Moses reached 603,550 (Num. 1:46; 2:32) tax our credulity.[2]

Nevertheless, a few positive remarks are in order. Several different groups of Hebrews probably spent years wandering in the desert steppe prior to taking up residence in Canaan. At the head of one group was Moses, and eventually the tradition about life in the wilderness under Mosaic direction gained ascendancy over other traditions.[3] Ultimately, Moses is credited with having led all Israel through the wilderness.

Moreover, the basic projection of the Numbers narrative sounds entirely credible. It instructs that some of the nomadic Hebrew clans spent most of their time in the wilderness at the oasis of Kadesh, which is located some 50 miles south of Beer-sheba. These clans could not overtake Canaan from the south. Their journey through southern Transjordan was likewise troublesome owing to the assertiveness of settled peoples in Edom and Moab who were eager to defend themselves against foreign incursions.

Finally, the hunger, thirst, and struggles for leadership depicted in the wilderness tradition imply that harmony, discipline, and faith were in short supply. This is entirely understandable given the mixed multitude ("rabble" in Num. 11:4) that often had to struggle for its own existence. Although the post-Sinai phase of the wilderness trek cannot be reconstructed in detail, the biblical tradition seems in large measure to be geographically and historically plausible.

The Intention and Structure of the Book of Numbers

This fourth book of the Pentateuch is commonly called "Numbers." The name is derived from the Vulgate (Latin) designation *Numeri*, which in turn came from the Septuagint (Greek) title *Arithmoi*. Such nomenclature is inspired by the opening chapter of the book, which tells of a census of the Israelite tribes that Moses undertook. The Hebrew designation *B^emidbār* ("in the wilderness") is preferable, since the census narration takes up but a small fraction of the book. Numbers, which is dominantly the work of P, is a book of striking contrasts. On the one hand, its heavy postexilic editing of earlier traditions as well as marked concern for ritualistic legislation and arithmetic precision are readily evident. On the other hand, this book offers a humorous account of Balaam and his talented ass, absorbing episodes centering on real tensions in the desert trek, and, sometimes, honest and intense conversation among the personages in the narrative.

As the Book of Numbers opens, Israel is still in the wilderness of Sinai, supposedly near Yahweh's sacred mountain. Moses is divinely commanded to take a census of all Israelite males twenty years of age or older (chap. 1). He is also briefed about the arrangement of the encamped and marching tribes (chap. 2). Much of what Yahweh says after that bears on Levitical responsibilities and cultic conduct. With the Sinai sojourn completed in Num. 10:10, the people move northward into the wilderness of Paran. The main site of encampment, however, lies even further north at the oasis of Kadesh, where the tribes spend most of their time. Here the people regularly demonstrate a lack of faith. So wanting is their confidence in the leadership of Moses and Aaron, and by implication, in Yahweh's guidance, that the deity resolves that none of the Exodus generation shall enter Canaan except Caleb and Joshua, whose loyalty has been exceptional (14:30). Yet when the clans fail to enter the Land of Promise from the south (chaps. 13–14), they do not abandon hope. After their departure from Kadesh (chap. 20), the people undertake a difficult yet successful detour through Transjordan. Finally, they station themselves in the plains of Moab ready to attack Canaan from the east (chaps. 22–36).

The Book of Numbers is a selective narrative edited by the post-exilic priests who provided the dominant religious leadership in the restoration community. The book reveals that Israel's sojourn in the wilderness constituted a period of supreme trial. Yahweh, Moses, and the people themselves were all put to the test. The people's faith was frequently challenged, but so was Yahweh's patience. The people might trust in Yahweh's ability to provide for them, or they might fret over the lively possibilities of imminent annihilation. They might endure the adversities of desert existence and thereby acquire new strength, or they might lapse into despondency. Numbers is less a record of sequential wilderness history than it is a work that advances significant theological questions. In particular, it attests to the extraordinary vitality of that ongoing relation between God and people.

Further Stages in Journey and Rebellion

Though the rebellious spirit of the wandering Hebrews is convincingly disclosed in the Book of Exodus, several new elements appear in Numbers 10–20. For example, most of Numbers 11 conveys two originally independent wilderness complaints: the people complain that they lack meat and other good things to eat, and Moses tells the deity that he cannot shoulder the awesome responsibilities of leadership alone. The cry of hunger reminds us of the manna tradition in Exodus 16, and the burden of Mosaic leadership recalls the meeting of Moses and Jethro in Exodus 18. Yahweh responds directly to both complaints. If the people crave meat, then they shall have it, but in such excessive portions that it will come out of their nostrils (Num. 11:20). The meat will be a miraculously wrought gift and an odious reminder to the clans that in their rebellious complaint over their diet, they were rejecting the deity. In order that Moses' burden might be eased, Yahweh instructs that seventy of the elders be given a portion of the Mosaic spirit. This will equip them to share the heavy task of overseeing the people.

Although the narrative is somewhat tedious, it offers a choice remark by Moses. The people's displeasure over diet and Yahweh's anger over Israel's infidelity lead Moses to ask God in desperation, "Did I conceive all this people? Did I bring them forth, that thou shouldst say to me, 'Carry them in your bosom . . .?' " (11:12). Tension in the wilderness is real indeed. There is irony as well. When the complaint reaches Moses that Eldad and Medad are excessive in displaying their charismatic talent, Moses retorts, "Are you jealous for my sake? Would that all Yahweh's people were prophets, that Yahweh would put his spirit upon them!" (11:29). This episode may reflect a later age when competing prophetic groups in Israel had to struggle for recognition.[4] Even so, its inclusion in the present narrative is entirely fitting.

In Numbers 12, Moses' marriage and charismatic abilities are the targets of an assault from those closest to him. Because Miriam alone is punished, it would appear that originally it was she who objected to Moses' marriage to a "Cushite" woman—the noun would apply to various Arabic peoples including Midianites. As punishment, Miriam must endure a week of leprosy with its attendant ostracism. In her other attack against Moses she is joined by Aaron. They question the singularity of Moses' function as the covenant mediator and chief leader of the people. These offenders are divinely informed that whereas prophets ordinarily perceive the divine will indirectly through visions and dreams, Moses alone benefits from Yahweh's direct communication (12:6–8). The incomparability of the meek man Moses is forcefully defended in the face of gross human insubordination.

Israel's unsuccessful southern offensive against Canaan is depicted in Numbers 13–14. Somewhat complex source analysis reveals that the later P material has the spies inspecting the entire land and shows favoritism to Joshua. The more ancient verses report that the Israelite scouts did not penetrate further north than Hebron and that it was Caleb who pressed on his contemporaries the desirability of taking the land. Our concern, however, is to grasp the major emphases in this material. Moses sends twelve spies from Kadesh to press northward into the Negev and inspect the hill country near Hebron. The land impresses them, but the size of its inhabitants and its cities intimidates the people. Their deep-seated fear of Canaan's citizens outdistances their capacity to believe that Yahweh's presence will ensure victorious conquest.

In Num. 14:39–45 we read the Yahwist's account of Israel's abortive attempt to take Canaan from the south. The men feel adventurous. They declare that they might as well attack the hill country near Hebron. Moses reads this as misguided zeal, for Yahweh's beneficent presence is not to be found among those who have thwarted his will. Moses remains at Kadesh. Without divine endorsement, the men are defeated by the Amalekites in the Negev and the Canaanites in the southern hill country. Also present in Numbers 14 is a lengthy P passage (vv. 26–38) that regards the forty years of wilderness existence as a direct manifestation of divine judgment. Yahweh will no longer tolerate the persistent murmurings of a "wicked congregation" (v. 27). Only the very young, along with Joshua and Caleb, may expect to enter the Land of Promise. Even when we read Numbers 13–14 closely, we cannot determine what actually took place. Nevertheless, among the historically plausible memories preserved here are rebellious assertions by the Israelite contingents, conflicting proposals on appropriate courses of action, strong statements of faith from Joshua and Caleb, intercessions of Moses with an angry deity, and an unsuccessful attempt to conquer Canaan from the south.

The unhappy sojourn at Kadesh is further depicted in Numbers 16, which presents three versions of overt rebellion against authoritative leadership. First, the JE account in vv. 1b–2a, 12–15, 25–34 attests to a secular insurrection by the Reubenites Dathan and Abiram against Moses' civil authority. Since the ground miraculously swallows up the rebels, the position of Moses is obviously upheld. Second, the basic priestly version deals not with the outburst of dissatisfied laymen but with a rebellion of 250 Israelite leaders headed by Korah. They resent the privileged position of Moses and Aaron (v. 3). Yahweh determines who is holy by having fire consume Korah and his companions. Third, the final priestly redactor assumed that the rebellion of Korah had its roots in a controversy among priestly professionals. Presently Korah, who is of Levitical descent, leads 250 Levites in objecting to the privileges of the Aaronite priesthood of Jerusalem. Again Korah fails, and the prerogatives of the priests of Aaron are defended (v. 40). In each version certain individuals voice their disapproval of some manifestation of established authority. Protest is expressed passionately, and it is consistently met with decisive action.

One remaining Kadesh controversy that summons our attention centers on a lack of water. This is the Meribah incident of Num. 20:2–13 (P), which has close affinities with the people's thirst at Meribah portrayed in Exod. 17:1–7 (JE). What is outstanding in the Numbers tradition, however, is the divine declaration that Moses and Aaron will not be permitted to set foot in the Land of Promise. Yahweh instructs Moses to command a rock to yield water. In anger and disbelief, Moses and Aaron address their people: "Hear now, you rebels; shall we bring forth water for you out of this rock?" (Num. 20:10). Whatever such a comment might be expected to accomplish, it assuredly does not sanctify Yahweh before the people who are assembled. The offended deity now resolves that neither Moses nor Aaron will bring the people into Canaan.

The Detour Through Transjordan

In Num. 20:14 a new note is struck in the wilderness narrative. The time seems ripe for the Israelites to leave Kadesh and make an eastern detour through Transjordan. Although the actual itinerary of the people cannot be established, it appears that by journeying within the rift of the Araba, they are able to pass along the western edge of Edom. (Permission to travel on the King's Highway, a thoroughfare that passed through the middle of Edom, is emphatically denied [20:14–21]). Near the Zered brook located on Edom's northern border, the Israelites advance eastward to a position that permits them to edge northward in the desert along the border of Moab.

Numbers also attests that the Israelites are poorly received by the Moabites and Amorites. As monarch of the small kingdom of the Amorites, Sihon refuses to allow these sojourners to traverse his land (21:23).

Tell Heshbon in Moab. This site in Transjordan is approximately 50 miles due east of Jerusalem in the northern part of Moab. The Moabites lost Heshbon to the Amorite king Sihon, who made it his capital. But Sihon, in turn, lost the city to the Israelites as they penetrated northward in Transjordan during the thirteenth century B.C. Subsequently, members of the tribes of Reuben and Gad settled there. (Photo by George W. E. Nickelsburg.)

Instead, he openly attacks the Israelites and loses. As the ancient taunt in 21:27–30 reveals, Israel's successful defeat of the Amorites involves overtaking the capital city of Heshbon, which the Amorites had snatched from the Moabites. Success induces the Israelites to move northward and attack Og's kingdom of Bashan, which is to the north of the Jabbok River.

One of the most memorable traditions about Israel's triumphs in Transjordan tells of Balak, the king of Moab. So perturbed is he by Israel's presence that he secures the services of Balaam, a renowned Babylonian seer. The latter is remembered both for his four poetic oracles, which bless rather than curse Israel, and for his talented ass, whose perception outdistances that of its insensitive rider. The humorous story of Balaam in Numbers 22–24 makes for delightful reading. Balak's fear and frustration, the assertiveness of Balaam's talking ass, and the clear-cut triumph of Yahweh's will over Balak's all contribute to its fundamental appeal. Balak is hopeful that with the help of Balaam's powers of divination, the Israelites can be overcome. Balak assumes that curses can be bought for the going fee (Num. 22:7). The biblical tradition declares, however, that while Balak promised Balaam money and honor for applying his talent in Moab's behalf, Balaam had no choice but to fall in line with Yahweh's will. The divination within reach of this visionary had no opportunity to dominate the triumphant will of Yahweh, who had already brought Israel out of Egypt and was determined that his people would inherit the Land of Promise.

In the first divination (23:7–10), Balaam is unwilling to pronounce a curse. Recognizing Israel's peculiar calling, Balaam simply prays that at the end of his lifetime he will experience the death of a righteous man. Balak selects another site in the hope that if Balaam inspects the encamped Israelites from another direction, a new omen in support of Balak will issue forth. In this second oracle (23:18–24), Balaam declares that he has no choice but to bless Israel: "Behold, I received a command to bless: he has blessed, and I cannot revoke it" (v. 20). At still a third site another oracle is given (24:3–9). Balaam now abandons divination in favor of a prophecy emphasizing Israelite safety and prosperity. A fourth oracle (24:15–19) comments on the time when Israel will enjoy an impressive monarchy at Moab's expense. Yahweh's people are therefore blessed by splendid lyrics, and Balak is betrayed by a Babylonian diviner who is constrained to utter the efficacious word that Yahweh wishes him to speak.

The Commissioning of Joshua and the Death of Moses

Numbers 27:12–23 (P) speaks of Joshua's commissioning as the successor to Moses. Yahweh commands Moses to go up the mountain of Abarim so that he may inspect the promised land, which he himself cannot enter because of his faithless conduct at Meribah. Moses voices no protest against this punishment or his impending death. He requests, however, that Yahweh appoint his successor lest the people be condemned to live without the benefit of a leader. Yahweh designates Joshua, who is installed in the office by Moses himself. Presumably Joshua's native talent (27:18) and freshly conferred authority will equip him to follow in the steps of Moses.

Moses' death is solemnly related in Deuteronomy 34. The mention of two different Transjordan sites in v. 1 as the setting (Mount Nebo and Mount Pisgah) reveals that more than one tradition about this event was in circulation. Yahweh is responsible for giving Moses a decent burial at an unknown location (v. 6). On the whole, Deuteronomy 34 unfolds with a simplicity and dignity that suit its content quite well. The closing verses respectfully attest to the incomparability of the man Moses, whose office and undertakings had dramatically set him apart from his contemporaries.

CONQUEST OF THE LAND
OF PROMISE

The Problem of Historical Reconstruction

Israel's conquest of Canaan is portrayed primarily in Joshua 1–11 and Judg. 1:1–2:5. The pervasively religious tone of this material, its frequent omission of important historical details, and its discrepancies frustrate any objective historical reconstruction. Therefore, Old Testament historians do not agree as to which theory makes the best use of the available biblical and extrabiblical data.

We shall refer to three different interpretations that have gained recognition in our time. According to Noth, the Hebrew "conquest" of Canaan was not accomplished through decisive military assault as the Book of Joshua implies.[5] The tribes that were eventually to make up the Israelite twelve-tribe confederation penetrated peaceably into Canaan. The primary task of the Israelite invaders was clearing the forests in the sparsely inhabited hill country so that a modest but effective program of agriculture might sustain continuous settlement. Undoubtedly the seminomadic Israelites needed land. They first arrived in Canaan in a so-called change of pasture, and there they settled permanently. It took some years for each tribe to occupy its Palestinian territory. Indeed, not all the tribes took up residence in the Land of Promise in the same decade.

Noth claims that the historical experience that was to involve the twelve settled tribes of Israel gave rise to the assumption that from the beginning all the tribes had overtaken the land in a united front. For example, in the tradition Benjamin's victories over Jericho, Bethel, and

Gibeon were transformed into victories involving all Israel. Moreover, all tribal energies were misunderstood as being motivated by a belief in Yahweh. Because the conquest of virtually all Palestine was not a reality until the tenth century during David's reign, Joshua 1–11 is of minimal historical value. The tribes did not function as a single force under Joshua. Noth argues that historically speaking, Joshua was not even Moses' successor. The Joshua of history was simply a local tribal hero. But after "the house of Joseph" (Ephraim and Manasseh) gained ascendancy, Joshua's image changed significantly. The highly embellished stories of his success turned Joshua into a national hero who led all Israel in its successful attempt to take the Land of Promise.

Another interpretation of the data is provided by Bright, who finds less cause to discredit the Joshua text.[6] He admits that the nation Israel that developed in Canaan consisted of various groups that had penetrated the land at different times and from different directions. Nevertheless, he finds the portrait of the conquest provided in Joshua historically useful. In contrast to Noth, Bright argues that some of the Israelite tribes banded together and adopted the Yahwistic faith in the wilderness era prior to their assault on Canaan. For them not to have done so until after their settlement in Canaan would leave too short a time interval for independent tribes to come closely together as "all Israel." Moreover, the archaeological witness to the violent eruptions experienced by Canaan in the late thirteenth century must not be ignored. Indeed, they may be attributed to the concerted efforts of several tribes that had joined forces in a common quest of land: "There is no reason to doubt that it was, as the Bible depicts it, a bloody and brutal business. It was the Holy War of Yahweh by which he would give his people the Land of Promise."[7]

Hence, Bright avers that in her conquest of Canaan, Israel often engaged in military conflict. Some of the conquest may have involved gradual and peaceful infiltration, but that is only part of the story. Canaanite sites as far apart as Bethel, Lachish, and Debir were thoroughly destroyed during the second half of the thirteenth century, and this just might have been Israel's doing. To be sure, the Deuteronomic historian has ordered the disparate traditions in Joshua 1–11 to make Joshua the prime actor. Yet this does not vitiate the strong possibility that on occasion certain Israelite tribes did cooperate in an attack against many established towns and even settle in them. Therefore, the conquest narratives in Joshua are not historically irrelevant.

Let us consider a third interpretation of the data, which is offered by Mendenhall.[8] He associates the arrival of the Hebrews from Egypt with the Habiru revolt that plagued Canaan in the Amarna period. He claims that even then many Hebrews had settled in various Canaanite cities, but that most of them were so dissatisfied with existing political regimes that they migrated to fringe areas. There they organized as

Habiru who knew that they must live beyond the realm of established society. These Habiru were successful in subduing some of the petty kings of Canaan and in taking over portions of their land. Mendenhall maintains that the Hebrews who arrived in the fringe areas of Palestine in the thirteenth century came with the stirring message that their deity, Yahweh, had delivered them from political oppression in Egypt. This word was highly supportive for the peasants, who for some time had been in revolt against the Canaanite city-states. Many disenchanted Canaanites, holds Mendenhall, converted to the Yahwistic faith. Indeed, the missionary power of this new religion was already apparent, and this was much of what the Hebrew "conquest" of Canaan was about.

Each of these interpretations has merits and limitations. The slow penetration of separate tribes into Palestine, so vital to Noth's analysis, urges on us the necessity of reading the biblical texts with as much objectivity as we can muster. Yet Noth's jaundiced view of the reliability of the Joshua legend induces him to reject many verses that may be historically useful. Bright's determination to relate archaeological evidence of the thirteenth century B.C. to the biblical material is instructive. Even so, we have no way of verifying that such sites as Bethel, Lachish, and Debir were leveled by the invading Israelites. Perhaps there were other invaders in Canaan at this time. Sometimes Bright is too facile in attributing site devastation to Israel. And though Mendenhall's insightful analysis explains some aspects of the conquest, it gives insufficient credit to the military achievements of the Hebrews who had escaped Egypt under Mosaic direction and made their way to Canaan. Like his predecessors, Mendenhall advances a hypothesis that accounts for some, but not all, facets of ancient Israel's conquest of the land. Our own understanding may best be presented in several remarks that bear on the problem of historical reconstruction.

Surely by the time the traditions in Joshua 1–11 had been fixed in written form, historical circumstances that had originally affected single tribes were perceived as relating to all Israel. We can no more reasonably assume that all Israel under Joshua's guidance took any given site in the Land of Promise than we can suppose that the entire nation of twelve well-defined tribes left Egypt in one decisive moment during the lifetime of Moses. The biblical narratives about the conquest of Hebron and Debir illustrate this tendency to broaden the base of participation in earlier events.[9] Ancient tradition (Josh. 15:13–19; Judg. 1:12–15) credits Caleb and Kenaz with the conquest of these two cities. A subsequent tradition (Judg. 1:10–11) ascribes the success to the tribe of Judah. Still later (Josh. 10:36–39) the victory is claimed for the entire nation under the inspired leadership of Joshua.

The witness of Joshua 1–11 and that of Judg. 1:1–2:5 should be examined with care. Neither is a homogenous unit. Though the composite quality of Joshua 1–11 is acknowledged, the lack of uniformity in

Judg. 1:1–2:5 has not always been recognized. In the Judges account, the mainly successful southern conquests of the tribe of Judah (1:1–21) are contrasted with the less impressive experience of the tribes to the north, which periodically meet strong resistance in central and northern Canaan (1:22–2:5). Although the antiquity and the historical credibility of the Judges account may evoke our appreciation, they ought not be overrated. Neither the traditions contained in Judg. 1:1–2:5 nor those preserved in Joshua 1–11 warrant an uncritical reading.

Relevant findings of Palestinian archaeology should be considered significant data. The Hebrew Bible mentions that Israel destroyed several Canaanite sites. Where any finding gives clear archaeological evidence that severe destruction (datable by pottery analysis) took place in the late thirteenth century B.C., that evidence should be regarded as possibly testifying to Israel's military activity in Canaan. This activity is all the more likely when the data point to the emergence of a different, materially inferior culture following such a conflagration. The archaeological evidence at such sites as Bethel, Debir, Lachish, and Hazor may thus be accepted as supportive of the biblical traditions. If they do not offer conclusive proof of those traditions, they do make them more intelligible.

The Hebrew conquest of Canaan should be regarded as a complex phenomenon involving times of both bloodshed and relative calm. The biblical record admits that lives were lost. Regardless of how contemporary readers may react, in ancient Israel's eyes of faith, Yahweh had chosen one of earth's peoples for a special purpose; in the course of its fulfillment, the brutal wrenching of land was inevitable. The admonition from the Decalogue, "You shall not kill" (Exod. 20:13) was not applicable to the Israelite takeover of Palestine, for at the head of the troops was Yahweh himself leading his people in holy war.[10] Nevertheless, not all Canaan seems to have been caught up in the turmoil of war. For example, military action in the central hill country, which was sparsely settled, was probably infrequent. And many of the battles in Canaan must have been conducted on a relatively small scale. The city-states of Canaan were not inclined to meet the Israelite invaders as a solid, well-organized front. Nor would the seminomadic invaders have been unusually skilled in the art of war. While impressive, the military achievements of Yahweh's people should not be exaggerated.

Literary and Theological Dimensions of the Book of Joshua

The Book of Joshua is an integral part of the Deuteronomic work that spans Deuteronomy through 2 Kings. Largely the product of a Hebrew historian living in Judah after the fall of the southern kingdom (587 B.C.), this Deuteronomic history has incorporated disparate oral and written sources. Repetitions and inconsistencies appear in the biblical text. Israel crosses the Jordan in Josh. 3:17 only to do so again in 4:10–11. According to 4:8, twelve commemorative stones are removed from the Jordan and erected at Gilgal; in 4:9 they are set up in the middle of the river. Joshua 6 preserves two different versions of the siege of Jericho. According to one, the Israelite army marches silently around the city seven times, raises a war cry, and attacks. According to the other, trumpet-blowing priests lead the Israelite host and during the seventh trip around the city, Jericho's famous walls collapse. Then in 8:3 Joshua dispatches 30,000 men to lie in ambush to the west of Ai; in 8:12 he sends 5,000 men for the same purpose. The presence of such variants, however, is insufficient evidence to warrant the conclusion that the Book of Joshua incorporates continuous narrative strata. A so-called J or E source does not seem to be present, though a few passages (4:15–18; 5:10–12; 9:15–21) appear to be priestly in character.

Yet theologically the Book of Joshua has an intimate connection with the Pentateuch, for the latter anticipates the realization of Yahweh's promise to Abraham that his descendants will acquire the land of Canaan. The Book of Joshua therefore makes possible a Hexateuch that allows the resolution of significant Pentateuchal motifs. To be sure, authentic historical traditions in this book have been pressed into the service of cultic reenactment. Statements of faith articulated in the context of ancient Israelite worship claimed that Yahweh had given the land to his people and that continuity in human leadership was realized when Joshua succeeded Moses.

Such cultic confession is not preoccupied with establishing accurate historical sequences. Nor does it hesitate to draw the figure of Joshua in superhuman proportions. His task is to assure that the Hebrews follow Yahweh's lead in waging holy war. Should they fail to destroy certain Canaanite cities, Canaanite life styles would inevitably ensnare them. The Deuteronomist realized that Yahweh's chosen people had not always fared well in maintaining a unique faith and way of life. Overcome by a strong sense of nostalgia, the Deuteronomist was shaping his massive work in Judah at a time when his people clearly did not possess, let alone control, the Land of Promise. Many of his compatriots were exiles in a foreign land. The great city of Jerusalem had been thoroughly destroyed, and Jehoiachin, the king of Judah, was imprisoned in Babylon. These circumstances probably did much to shape the conquest narrative in Joshua. The zealous tenor of the story militates against frequent qualifying comment. (Even so, Josh. 13:3; 16:10; 17:11–13; and 17:16–18 do refer to a limited Israelite conquest of Canaan.) If that narrative is overwritten, so are the details about the anarchy that followed during the period of the judges, when faith in Yahweh became alarmingly weak (see Judg. 2:6–3:6). However, the

Deuteronomic historian seems to have looked forward to the day when Yahweh's purged people would again take possession of the land and demonstrate their allegiance to the divine will.

A Foothold in the Central Hill Country

The Deuteronomist has ordered his materials so that Israel's campaign under Joshua has three phases. First comes the task of securing a foothold in the sparsely populated central hill country (Josh. 1–9). Next is Joshua's campaign against southern Canaan, which involves a vast segment of territory eventually occupied by the tribe of Judah (Josh. 10). Finally, there is the campaign against the inhabitants of northern Canaan, which results in the Israelite destruction of the fortified city of Hazor (Josh. 11). A summary of Israelite victories is provided in Joshua 12, and the assignment of the tribes to their respective territories is the main concern of Joshua 13–22. This is followed by Joshua's farewell admonition (Josh. 23) and a crucial ceremony of covenant renewal conducted at Shechem (Josh. 24).

The greater part of the Joshua account of the conquest is devoted to the takeover of Canaan's central hill country. On the eastern banks of the Jordan the Israelites stand ready to attack. Yet they are not to ford the river until Yahweh utters his (Deuteronomic) address to Joshua (1:2–9), and Joshua in turn speaks to the people about the impending conquest (1:11–18). Joshua 2 narrates the dispatching of the spies to Jericho, their visit with Rahab, and their successful return. Convinced that Yahweh is truly with his people and that the hour for attack is at hand, the Israelites cross the Jordan and set up camp at Gilgal (Josh. 3–5). Then come the conquest of Jericho (Josh. 6), the unsuccessful and then successful attack on Ai (Josh. 7–8), and the establishment of a treaty with the sly Gibeonites (Josh. 9). Joshua's charisma and the war-like enthusiasm of his following are evident throughout these chapters. And the same must be said of the fear that grips the remaining inhabitants of the land once they learn of the sweeping success of the Israelites.

Several elements in these chapters merit closer examination. Joshua 2 is a remarkably well-told narrative; it opens with Joshua's command that two spies leave the present Israelite encampment of Shittim in Transjordan and take a good look at Jericho and its environs. In secret, the two men stay at the home of Rahab. Harlotry is Rahab's profession, and her dwelling atop the city wall of Jericho is understandably frequented by strangers. The narrative declares that she is able to exact a promise from the spies concerning her own safety and that of her immediate family. Eventually the two men return to the Israelite camp and make their encouraging report to Joshua (2:24).

Jericho, "the City of Palms." In Deut. 34:3 and 2 Chron.
28:15 Jericho is designated "the city of palm trees," and in
Judg. 3:13 Jericho's name is implied by the mention of
palms. This oasis with its tall palm trees is near Jericho; it
offers a welcome contrast to the arid stretches of the nearby
Judean Desert. (Courtesy of the Israel Government Tourist
Office, Chicago.)

The historicity of this account has been questioned by those who
define the story of the spies as an etiological legend—that is, as a legend
that attempts to explain an existing phenomenon. To view Joshua 2
etiologically is to say that this legend answers the question, "Why did
this house at Jericho withstand an onslaught when the rest of the town
went under?" Presumably the tale about the spies and Rahab's willingness to offer them asylum was framed as the appropriate answer.
Although the etiological approach is not unreasonable, it may have been
the case that in actuality one house in Jericho was left undisturbed.
True, Joshua 2 offers us embellished legend. Nevertheless, it is doubtful
that the legend was solely inspired by the curious sight of a house spared
destruction within a ruined city.

Joshua 3–4 reflects on the miraculous crossing of the River Jordan
and its commemoration. As the priests who bear the ark of the covenant

stand on dry ground in the middle of the Jordan, the people pass safely across. Just as the waters of the Reed Sea separated under Mosaic leadership, the waters of the Jordan do so in Joshua's presence. As a memorial to this spectacular event, twelve stones are erected. In 4:6–7 the etiological emphasis is especially prominent. The child's question, "What do these stones mean to you?" is regarded as inevitable. In his answer, the parent is to tell his child about the time that the normal flow of the Jordan was miraculously interrupted to facilitate Israelite passage to the western side.

The people are then associated with Gilgal. While the location of this site is uncertain, it cannot have been far from Jericho. At Gilgal a new generation of Israelites was circumcised, since those who had borne the sign of the Yahwistic covenant proved faithless and died along the way (Josh. 5). According to one interpretation, the etiological name "Gilgal" is connected with the Hebrew root *gll*, meaning "to roll away." This would apply to the reproach of the past, which Yahweh has now removed. But the noun "Gilgal" means "circle." So perhaps the original connection rested with the circle of twelve stones that symbolized Israel's success in fording the Jordan, not with the ritualistic act of circumcision. In any case, the presence of an etiological feature in the narrative does not itself warrant the conclusion that ancient Israel in Joshua's day never camped at Gilgal. This site could have been the locus from which Joshua and his men launched several attacks against central Canaan.

The Hebrew conquest of Jericho is sketched in Joshua 6. The priestly leadership, daily procession, blowing of horns, and shouting of the people all speak for the cultic tenor of this narrative. At the opportune moment, the walls of Jericho simply collapse, and the Israelite host moves into the city. According to the sacrificial ban of holy war, all life in the city is to be destroyed. Technically known as the *ḥerem*, this requirement specified total annihilation of the enemy. Nevertheless, for her generous hospitality, Rahab is to be spared along with her family. Valued objects of silver, gold, bronze, and iron are also to be brought to Yahweh's treasury—an obvious anachronism since in Joshua's day the Jerusalem Temple had not been planned, let alone built. Everything else is to be completely destroyed as a holocaust to the deity. Though this attitude is alarming to present-day sensibilities, in biblical times the prospect of culture contact between Israel and Canaan was regarded as irrevocably damaging. Total allegiance to Yahweh's cause was a must.

In whatever manner the city of Jericho was taken by ancient Israel, its destruction is not substantiated by the findings of Palestinian archaeology. Late Bronze Age (ca. 1550–1200 B.C.) remains at Jericho are negligible, for which extensive erosion is partly to blame. As Kenyon asserts, "The excavation of Jericho, therefore, has thrown no light on the walls of Jericho of which the destruction is so vividly described in the Book of Joshua."[11] A few pieces of pottery, the foundations of one wall, and a small clay oven scarcely authenticate the biblical record. Jericho may have been only a Canaanite garrison in Joshua's time. And yet the continuing reputation of Jericho's past greatness and the fact that this was the first site in western Palestine taken by the

Pre-Pottery Neolithic Tower at Jericho. The earliest evidence of human life at Jericho traces back to about 8000 B.C. Still standing at ancient Jericho is a magnificent 30-foot tower erected by its Pre-Pottery Neolithic inhabitants in the sixth millennium B.C. This solid stone tower was used for purposes of defense. Inside it are twenty-two steep steps reaching from the foundation to the top, which is now covered by a steel grate (top right). (Photo by William R. Watters, Jr.)

Hebrew invaders dictate that the victory should be narrated in grandiose terms.[12] Yahweh's promise of land to his people was beginning to be realized.

Having triumphed in their attempt to overtake Jericho, the Israelites are said to have moved under Joshua's leadership in a northwestern direction to the city of Ai. According to Joshua 7–8, Ai was the first Canaanite city in the central hill country to be captured by Israel. Because the covetous Achan had violated the *herem* regulation at Jericho and kept some of the precious booty for himself (7:21), Israel's initial campaign against Ai was abortive. Military tactics had to be suspended until a solemn act of expiation was undertaken. Achan and his entire family had to be exterminated. Achan's crime was a matter of grave concern. He had "broken faith" (7:1) and offended Yahweh's holiness. Moreover, society in Achan's day was sufficiently corporate that one member could easily jeopardize the well-being of all others. Again we confront an etiological reference. Joshua 7 concludes with the notation that over the dead Achan was raised a pile of stones "that remains to this day." Did the presence of an impressive heap of stones inspire the Achan legend, or did a real man named Achan exist who violated a crucial regulation of holy war? Although no definitive proof is available, we favor the latter alternative.

In any case, the second siege against Ai, which in its realistic portrayal in Joshua 8 involves a clever ambush, was completely effective. The legend declares that as "evidence" of Israel's success one has only to look at the monument existing "to this day" (8:29) erected over the body of the king of Ai, who was publicly executed. Because the

Early Bronze Age Acropolis at Ai. Archaeological excavations at Ai, under the direction of Joseph A. Callaway, have uncovered an Early Bronze Age city of 27.5 acres. In the photo above we see the foundations and walls of the Early Bronze III temple, the eastern part of a temple-palace complex with its own system of fortifications within the city. Located at the highest point of the tell, the temple-palace citadel dominated the city. (Photo by the author.)

noun "Ai" means "ruin" in Hebrew, it could not have been the original name of the city. Archaeological investigations have shown that for almost a millennium, Ai flourished as a city of the Early Bronze Age. It was destroyed in about 2400 B.C. and only reoccupied after 1200 B.C. Because it lay in ruins for so long, its rubble might well have inspired this narrative. The Book of Judges does not mention Israel's conquest of Ai. But in Judg. 1:22–26 we are told that the "house of Joseph" overtook Bethel, a city less than 2 miles west of Ai. Thorough destruction in the thirteenth century is attested at Bethel, yet the Book of Joshua makes no mention of Israel's victory at that site. Thus, Albright has cogently proposed that the narrative of the Israelite conquest of Bethel was later transferred to Ai as a way of interpreting the existence of that conspicuous ruin.[13] Moreover, prior to its destruction in the thirteenth century, Bethel was a well-built Canaanite city. Yet on its wreckage emerged a set of far less impressive buildings. It is tempting to speculate that this was, in fact, the work of ancient Israel.

Approximately 7 miles southwest of Ai lay Gibeon. In self-defense, the inhabitants of Gibeon settled on a ruse that would link them with the winning Israelites (Josh. 9). Looking the worse for wear from an allegedly long journey (9:4–5), the Gibeonite imposters told Joshua that out of respect for Yahweh's reputation, they had come from a distant place to enter into a covenant with his elect. After a hastily made treaty between the two parties (9:15), the Israelites learned to their surprise that these rascals were actually neighboring Canaanites. Because of the binding nature of the recently established covenant, Israel had to permit the tricksters to exist within their own city. Whereas the Gibeonites acted with fear and cunning, Israel acted rashly and without the benefit of divine direction. This candid narrative reveals that certain Canaanites easily sustained the Israelite conquest of their land.

The Southern Campaign

Joshua 10 narrates the southern, or Judean, campaign of Joshua, who came to the assistance of the Gibeonites. The latter were being harassed by a coalition of five Amorite kings headed by Adonizek, king of Jerusalem. Among the southern cities in this league were Lachish and Debir, whose archaeological remains confirm that they were destroyed in the thirteenth century.[14] Such an alliance of Canaanite cities and their kings is historically possible. But the stopping of the sun so that more fighting time might be gained (10:12–14) can only be viewed as figurative. There is also the etiological reference in the cave of Makkedah tradition that stones exist "to this very day" (10:27) at its mouth and that the bodies of the five dead kings lie there.[15] Yahweh's action in the holy war is freely confessed. The coalition that fled before Joshua is

The Valley of Aijalon. According to the tradition preserved in Joshua 10, five Canaanite kings were defeated by Joshua and his troops in this vicinity. The valley of Aijalon, which is directly east of Gezer, is a vital pass into the mountains of Judah, which appear here in the background. (Photo by the author.)

said to have suffered more from Yahweh's hailstones than from the Israelite swords (v. 11). Here the Deuteronomist advances his conviction that in the Hebrew conquest of Canaan, the victory truly belonged to Yahweh.

The Northern Campaign

Approximately two-thirds of Joshua 11 is given to a report of Joshua's northern campaign (vv. 1–15); the remainder (vv. 16–23) is devoted to a typically rash Deuteronomic summary claiming that "Joshua took the whole land, according to all that Yahweh had spoken to Moses" (v. 23). Under the leadership of Jabin, king of Hazor, a group of northern Canaanite kings united against Israel. Hazor is specifically mentioned as "the head of all those kingdoms" (11:10). This allusion to Hazor's supremacy has been supported by archaeological investigation.[16] Located some 10 miles north of the Sea of Galilee, Tell el-Qedah (ancient Hazor) is a large mound of 25 acres that boasts a huge rectangular plateau approximately 3,000 feet long and 2,000 feet wide. Protected by a gigantic wall of earth, that plateau functioned as a compound for Hyksos horses and chariots. Once demolished by invaders in the thirteenth century, this enclosure remained for centuries in virtual abandonment. An impressive Canaanite city with an excellent temple and abundant houses existed on the tell itself. After its destruction, Hazor hosted a significantly poorer settlement. While Hazor was the only walled city reported to have been taken by Joshua in his northern campaign (11:13), word of Hazor's downfall may have made the Israelites appear all the more formidable to the Canaanites of the north. Again the biblical text interprets military success as the joint accomplishment of Joshua and Yahweh (11:8). The sweeping summary toward the end of the chapter implies that all of Canaan had now fallen under Israelite control.

The Witness of Judges 1:1–2:5

This opening segment of the Book of Judges offers relevant and relatively ancient information about the Hebrew conquest of Canaan. Though this passage has some affinities with Joshua 1–11, it does not refer to the exploits of the man Joshua. Rather, it states in its opening verse that Joshua had died. Battles for both southern and northern territories are reported, but the exploits are the efforts of individual

Middle Bronze Age Gateway at Shechem. Here is a portion of the sturdy fortification system characteristic of Shechem at the end of the Middle Bronze Age. This eastern gateway was first erected in about 1650–1550 B.C., and its steps form a short descent into the city itself. On the whole, this was a prosperous period for Shechem's citizens. (Photo by the author.)

tribes. The most significant southern city to be taken is Hebron (Judg. 1:10; cf. Josh. 10:36–37). While Judg. 1:8 erroneously mentions Judah's conquest of Jerusalem, Judg. 1:21 is a contradictory and undoubtedly more honest notation that its original Jebusite inhabitants were not dislodged. Only in the tenth century under David did the Israelites capture that city (2 Sam. 5:6–9). This portion of the Book of Judges confers most of the honors on the tribe of Judah. Many of the exploits of the Joseph tribes (Ephraim and Manasseh) in the north are unimpressive. Since we are at the mercy of a southern (Judean) editing, it is difficult to determine what actually took place. Moreover, this Judges passage is a collection of miscellaneous fragments of tradition that vary in date and historical credibility.

Despite these complexities, careful reading of both Judg. 1:1–2:5 and Joshua 1–11 encourages the following conclusions: (1) the Israelite conquest of Canaan was accomplished under the leadership of several persons, not one charismatic man; (2) individual tribal effort was the rule rather than the exception; (3) the Israelite invasion was gradual; and (4) because the land was not completely taken by Israel until the time of David, many of its natives coexisted with the infiltrating Israelite population.

Covenant Renewal at Shechem

In much of central Palestine, Israel had no need to engage in warfare against the Canaanites. Rather, infiltrating Hebrews were meeting relatives and associates in an entirely friendly manner. The Old Testament therefore presents no narrative about the Israelite conquest of Shechem. Instead, it offers in Joshua 24 an account of a crucial covenant renewal ceremony that took place there. The tribes had already been assigned to their respective territories, so that perhaps only certain Israelite leaders attended the ceremony. Because they came "before God" (24:1), we might infer that they stood in the presence of the sacred ark of the covenant. In any case, it was at Shechem that Joshua recited in an extraordinarily well-articulated credo (24:2–13) the mighty acts of Yahweh that had unfolded between the call of Abraham and the recent conquest of the Land of Promise.

In Josh. 24:14 historical recollection blends into straightforward exhortation. Joshua challenges his listeners to put away other gods whom they have previously honored and give themselves to Yahweh without reservation. After the people offer their allegiance, the ceremony concludes with the sealing of the covenant and the erection of a stone witness (24:25–27).

This event at Shechem was of supreme importance in the drama of ancient Israel's faith, for it meant that a covenant now existed between Yahweh and a united Israelite people. Mosaic Yahwism was extended to tribes that had not been parties to the Exodus from Egypt

Late Bronze Age Masseba at Shechem. This sacred stone pillar, or *masseba*, consists of a white limestone socket and a broken slab. It was used at Shechem during the Late Bronze Age in what was presumably the sanctuary of Baʿal Berith. In function it may partially resemble the freestanding stones at Gezer, which its Canaanite inhabitants regarded as sacred. The original height of this large slab cannot be determined. Nevertheless, the excavators hoisted it into its socket and returned it to what they suspected was its original location. (Photo by the author.)

and the covenant at Mount Sinai. Fellow Israelites who had been living amicably with their Canaanite neighbors now accepted the conditions of the Sinai covenant and pledged to serve the God of that covenant. This cultic occasion was marked by clarity. Yahweh's mighty acts were rehearsed. His power and grace were attested. And in the light of these awesome realities, the people were confronted with a choice. Either they would serve Yahweh or they would not. Their decision and their willingness to abide by it could not help but influence the life of ancient Israel in the days that lay ahead. Joshua 24 testifies to the missionary character of ancient Israelite religion and to its magnetic power to attract new adherents, which extended Mosaic Yahwism dramatically.

NOTES

1. The strata in the remaining books of the Pentateuch: while it contains much ancient legislation, all of Leviticus may be assigned to P. For the special character of Leviticus 17–26, which is commonly labeled the "Holiness Code," see Chapter 19.

    Numbers contains two strata, P and a thoroughly redacted JE

stratum, which cannot be further differentiated with any confidence. The following appear to be the priestly sequences in Numbers: 1:1–10:28; 13:1–17a, 21, 25–26a; 14:1a, 2–3, 5–10, 26–38; 15:1–41; 16:1a, 2b–11, 16–24, 35–50; 17:1–19:22; 20:1–13, 22–29; 21:4a, 10–11; 22:1; 25:6–36:13. Hence, to JE belong 10:29–12:16; 13:17b–20, 22–24, 26b–33; 14:1b, 4, 11–25, 39–45; 16:1b–2a, 12–15, 25–34; 20:14–21; 21:1–3, 4b–9, 12–35; 22:2–25:5.

As for Deuteronomy, apart from the priestly interpolations in 1:3; 4:41–43; 32:48–52; 34:1a, 7–9, and the Elohist's witness in 31:14–15, 23, the remainder of the book may be assigned to D.

2. The male population figure given in Num. 26:51 (also P) is somewhat lower: 601,730. George E. Mendenhall, in "The Census Lists of Numbers 1 and 26," *Journal of Biblical Literature* 77 (1958): 52–66, holds that the Numbers census lists contain tribal quotas for military purposes and offer reliable data from an ancient Israelite period. But the Hebrew word *'eleph*, which originally referred to a section of a tribe, was misunderstood by postexilic Israel as meaning "thousand." Therefore, the numbers that follow the word "thousand" in each of the tribal listings (500 for Reuben in 1:21; 300 for Simeon in 1:23, and so on) may be historically accurate. This would fix the male total in Numbers 1 at 5,550 men.

3. For further details, see Ivan Engnell, *A Rigid Scrutiny: Critical Essays on the Old Testament*, trans. John T. Willis (Nashville: Vanderbilt University Press, 1969), p. 213; and John Bright, *A History of Israel*, 2d ed. (Philadelphia: Westminster Press, 1972), pp. 125–126.

4. See Martin Noth, *Numbers: A Commentary*, trans. James D. Martin, The Old Testament Library (Philadelphia: Westminster Press, 1968), p. 90.

5. Martin Noth, *The History of Israel*, 2d ed., rev. trans. Peter R. Ackroyd (New York: Harper & Row, 1960), pp. 53–84.

6. John Bright, *Early Israel in Recent History Writing*, Studies in Biblical Theology, no. 19 (London: SCM Press, 1956), pp. 79–110.

7. Bright, *A History of Israel*, op. cit., p. 138.

8. George E. Mendenhall, "The Hebrew Conquest of Palestine," in Edward F. Campbell, Jr., and David N. Freedman, eds., *The Biblical Archaeologist Reader* (Garden City, N.Y.: Doubleday, Anchor Books, 1970), 3: 100–120.

9. As pointed out by Yohanan Aharoni and Michael Avi-Yonah, *The Macmillan Bible Atlas* (New York: Macmillan, 1968), p. 44.

10. In premonarchical Israel, Yahweh was regarded as the one true leader and victor in Israel's military efforts. Hence, Israel's assault on Canaan was interpreted by the clans as holy war. As such, it placed specific demands on the people with respect to preparation, personnel, and conduct. For a fuller explanation, see L. E. Toombs, "Ideas of War," in George A. Buttrick et al., eds., *The Interpreter's Dictionary of the Bible* (Nashville: Abingdon Press, 1962), R–Z, pp. 796–801. Toombs' treatment is based on Gerhard von Rad's classic monograph, *Der Heilige Krieg im alten Israel*; its most recent (5th) ed. was published in 1969 by Vandenhoeck & Ruprecht, Göttingen, Ger. Some of von Rad's comments on the subject are available in English translation in his chapter, "Deuteronomy and the Holy War," in *Studies in Deuteronomy*, trans. David Stalker, Studies in Biblical Theology, no. 9 (London: SCM Press, 1953), pp. 45–59.

11. Kathleen M. Kenyon, *Digging Up Jericho* (New York: Frederick A. Praeger, 1957), p. 262.
12. The author is in agreement with G. Ernest Wright, *Biblical Archaeology,* rev. ed. (Philadelphia: Westminster Press, 1962), p. 80.
13. William F. Albright, *The Biblical Period from Abraham to Ezra* (New York: Harper & Row, Harper Torchbooks, 1963), pp. 29–30.
14. Since Eglon is a suitable personal name and Debir is not, Josh. 10:3 should probably read, "Eglon king of Debir." See William F. Albright, "A Revision of Early Hebrew Chronology," *Journal of the Palestine Oriental Society* 1 (1921): 70.
15. Joshua 10:33 provides a seemingly reliable notation that Horam, king of Gezer, came to help the inhabitants of Lachish. Presumably, Horam did not recognize the seriousness of the situation soon enough. His troops arrived too late to prevent Joshua's attack.
16. Yigael Yadin, *Hazor,* 4 vols. (Jerusalem: Hebrew University Press, 1958–1966).

8

ISRAEL'S SETTLEMENT IN CANAAN

Ancient Israel's entry into the Land of Promise did not exempt her from having to confront an uncertain future within its borders. During the two centuries that followed, the people of Yahweh were caught up in seemingly endless problems of physical and religious survival. The anarchy and faithlessness that often characterized this era of Israelite settlement are richly portrayed in the Book of Judges (2:6–16:31). But before we examine the exploits of Israel's judges recorded there, we must first reflect on the character, background, and purpose of the Book of Judges. Then we shall consider Israel's social organization during the era of the judges.

THE CHARACTER, BACKGROUND, AND PURPOSE OF THE BOOK OF JUDGES

The Literary Question

Again the biblical material comes to us from the Deuteronomist, whose editorial hand is not always subtle. We do not know how he received the traditions he has included. He may have had access to several dif-

---

Biblical texts to be read prior to and in conjunction with the present chapter: Judg. 2:6–16:31. As a way of limiting our task, we shall not formally investigate Judges 17–21, which is an appended account of the migration of the Danites and the outrageous conduct of the Benjaminites. While the Judges appendix contains stories that relate chronologically to the era of the judges, it does not treat Israel's celebrated judges as such. It also fails to sustain the chronological scheme and religious assessment for which Judg. 2:6–16:31 is famous.

ferent cycles and independent units of tradition. Perhaps a pre-Deutero-
nomic scroll depicting the heroic deeds of certain Israelite deliverers had
already been compiled. If so, it would probably have contained a loose
collection of hero stories such as we have in Judg. 2:6–16:31. Nevertheless, brief summary statements about the "minor" judges (such as that
offered on Tola in 10:1–2), an overarching chronological scheme, and
certain moralistic evaluations (such as that given in 2:6–3:6) would
surely have been lacking. These elements appear to have been the work
of the Deuteronomist, who may also have had a say in determining the
sequence of the narratives.

We may, or may not, wish to posit the existence of a pre-Deuter-
onomic Judges scroll. In either case, however, we may be certain that
the various tales that came to the Deuteronomist portrayed local crises
of limited scope that were successfully overcome by military tactics.
At the center of each deliverance stood an Israelite "judge" whose military prowess, wisdom, and charisma placed him well ahead of his contemporaries. In fact, the judge was thought to possess some portion of
Yahweh's "spirit." He was Yahweh's answer to a people in need. Yet
the Deuteronomist's interpretation was that each local judge was a
national hero who saved all Israel from enemy harassment.

The Political and Social Climate

The twelfth and eleventh centuries did not offer an era of confidence
and stability to Canaan's inhabitants. The Israelite clans were hardly
able to establish a strong united government that might firmly control
the land. The presence of Moabites and Ammonites in Transjordan,
as well as Canaanites and recently arrived Philistines to the west of the
River Jordan, meant that ancient Israel was in no position to relax in the
land she had recently infiltrated. Nor could the Canaanites feel at ease,
for they were now required to coexist with the Israelite intruders. Moreover, no major world power dominated Canaan at this time. Egypt's
influence was nominal. The Hittites were ill equipped to govern Canaan;
not long before, the sea peoples had swept through their land in Asia
Minor and left it a shambles. Nor was any nation in Mesopotamia sufficiently enterprising to penetrate as far west as Canaan.

That Canaan lay in a political power vacuum was both a hindrance
and a help to Israel. With no one nation capable of policing the whole
land, chaos must have been widespread. This is certainly suggested by
the archaeological evidence. Bethel experienced four destructions by
fire in the twelfth and eleventh centuries, and the anarchy in that area
must have been considerable. Moreover, the presence of deep storage
bins for grain at Debir, which would have provided a sufficient amount
of food while the inhabitants sustained a surprise attack, symbolizes
the insecurity of this era. It is remarkable that ancient Israel persisted

0   10   20   30
Miles

Sidon

MT. LEBANON

MT. HERMON

Tyre

Dan

A S H E R

N A P H T A L I

D A N

Kedesh

Hazor

Accho

Sea of
Chinnereth

B A S H A N

Mt. Carmel

Kishon R.

Z E B U L U N

I S S A C H A R

Mt. Tabor

Megiddo

VALLEY OF
JEZREEL

Taanach

Beth-shan

Ramoth-gilead

THE GREAT SEA

Mt. Gilboa

Jabesh-
gilead

M A N A S S E H

M A N A S S E H

G I L E A D

+ Mt. Ebal

Schechem

Penuel

Mt. Gerizim

G A D

Jabbok R.

Aphek

E P H R A I M

Shiloh

Jordan R.

Bethel

Ai

D A N

Gibeon

Gilgal

Rabbah

A M M O N

Gezer

Jericho

BENJAMIN

Gibeah

Ashdod

Ekron

Jerusalem

Shittim

Mt.
Pisgah

Heshbon

Beth-shemesh

Bethlehem

Ashkelon

Gath

J U D A H

Mt. Nebo

R E U B E N

P H I L I S T I N E S

Lachish

Gaza

Hebron

Debir

Arnon R.

Sharuhen

S I M E O N

Beer-sheba

Arad

SALT SEA

M O A B

Brook Zered

The Negev

E D O M

in the land at all. Yet had one of the great powers of the Fertile Crescent now imposed its will and a little order on Canaan, a permanent Israelite settlement might have been virtually impossible. In short, "Israel settled in Canaan when Canaan was ready to receive it."[1]

But how did Israel, a new and loosely structured people, maintain its hold? The biblical record affirms that the Israelites rallied around certain charismatic figures who, with conspicuous divine support, led them to victory. In the eleventh hour "Yahweh raised up judges" (2:16). The chief function of the judges was to deliver the Israelites from those nations and leaders who sought to overcome them (2:16–18).

Here we would do well to recognize how the term "judge" was understood by ancient Israel. Though the Hebrew root *špṭ* conveys the notion of judging, it does not relate solely to jurisprudence. True, the one who judges might well be the vindicator who upholds the cause of the righteous. Presumably he sought to set right what was wrong. The major judges, however, are not remembered for the justice they dispensed in routine circumstances. Rather, they are appreciated for their heroic deeds—particularly their military exploits, which delivered Israel from harassment and oppression. The Israelite tribes lived mainly unto themselves. In periods of uncomfortable pressure, however, two or more tribes might join forces and follow the leadership of one judge who presented himself as the man of the hour (Judg. 4:10; 6:35). He was so identified because in him the spirit of the deity could be easily detected. Therefore, the Book of Judges asserts, in effect, that decisive rescue is really Yahweh's doing.

A Theology of History

An overarching theology of history that unifies the separate Judges episodes is expressed most directly in the Deuteronomic editorial introduction in Judg. 2:6–3:6. This passage states that during Joshua's lifetime, the people adhered to the covenant faith. But subsequently a new generation of Israelites arose that "did not know Yahweh or the work which he had done for Israel" (2:10). Indifference to the covenant became a matter of course. Consequently, an entire historical cycle was set in motion.

That cycle has four stages. (1) The Israelites depart from Yahweh and his covenant. Not knowing or wanting to know Yahweh and his accomplishments, the people succumb to the enticements of Canaanite religion. (2) His wrath aroused, Yahweh responds by turning his people over to their enemies, who harass and subjugate them. (3) The people cry out in their affliction and express their penitence. (4) Moved by pity, Yahweh raises up a judge who delivers Israel from the oppressor. Because the deity is truly present in the judge, Israel is freed from the grip of the enemy. The charismatic judge restores order, and in the ensuing years of his rule the land enjoys peace. But with the death of the judge, the cycle begins anew. The people again turn from Yahweh to the gods of Canaan and must once more suffer the consequences of religious defection.

This theology of history is the creation of the Deuteronomic historian, who affirms that throughout the era of the judges one round of apostasy-oppression-repentance-deliverance was followed by another. Sometimes this pattern is summarized at the beginning and end of the narratives about Israel's major judges. Obviously such a schematic interpretation is incapable of treating history objectively. Nevertheless, it casts a penetrating glance at the inner fiber of the Israelite nation.

As man's history has often demonstrated, the collapse of a people may be as much a matter of internal decay as it is an assertion of foreign aggression. Moral erosion can begin years before campaigns are lost on the battlefield. In this instance, the Deuteronomist is saying that as the ancient Israelites experienced spiritual degeneration, they were sold into the hands of the enemy. That was Yahweh's doing. Yet it was also a divine act that the oppressed people were delivered from the enemy at the opportune moment. By dispatching the charismatic judge, Yahweh was still willing to say, "Nevertheless." That divine qualification meant that Israel was not condemned to live beyond the sphere of redemption.

The Lure of Canaanite Culture

A people whose religious literature discredits an envious farmer named Cain (Gen. 4) and a drunken gardener named Noah (Gen. 9) may rightly be expected to regard with a jaundiced eye the agrarian norms that were widely accepted in the ancient Near East. Actually quite a few Israelite arrivals may have become enthusiastic about the agricultural practices of Canaan. Why should they not accommodate themselves to a new vocational and economic pattern? That farming and sex were closely linked and existed at the very center of Canaanite culture were realities to be accepted. After all, the Canaanites seemed adroit in aligning themselves with the mysterious principles of nature and harnessing the powers of fertility for their material gain. Perhaps the time was ripe for Israel to share in the physical blessings that were coming to her Canaanite neighbors.

Nevertheless, there remained in the corporate memory of ancient Israel a nomadic ideal rooted in the belief that Yahweh was fundamentally a desert deity. Although he was not thought to be confined to one locale, the desert was nonetheless his home. The nomad's sufferings and hopes were his special concern. Moreover, it had been Yahweh's choice to reveal himself within the context of crucial historical events. He was not a deity to be locked in by the rhythms of nature. Thus, the Israelites did not enter Palestine without certain religious preconceptions. On the contrary, the memory of formative moments at Sinai had begun to confer on Israelite religion its distinctive shape. Its devout adherents therefore had reason to be alarmed by prevailing Canaanite religious practice, which looked attractive to the presumably weaker members of the faith.

What, then, was the essential character of the Canaanite religious witness?[2] The Old Testament itself has several negative comments to make about the Baᶜalim and Ashtaroth (gods representing the male and female principles, respectively) which the Israelites began to worship (Judg. 2:12–13; 10:6). Our leading source of information, however, is the tablets of Canaanite epic literature first discovered in 1928 at Ras Shamra (ancient Ugarit) on the coast of northern Syria. These texts were written in Ugaritic, a Semitic language with a cuneiform alphabet. While they fail to provide a complete portrait of ancient Canaanite religion, they offer us some vivid flashes. The longest of these epic cycles,[3] which focuses on the god Baᶜal and his sister-consort Anath, has made Canaanite religion much more intelligible to contemporary minds. This cycle tells of how Baᶜal, the fertility and storm deity of Canaan, acquired sovereign status among the other gods of the Canaanite pantheon as well as a palace atop a mountain. Moreover, it is possible, though not certain, that the seasonal cycles of nature are implied by these texts.[4]

Let us take note of the leading divine figures and the fundamental intention of the ritualistic enactment of this epic within the Canaanite cult. El was the head of the divine family of Canaanite deities. He was a somewhat shadowy character who had little direct contact with the doings and destiny of mankind. A good-natured figure, he consistently acceded to requests made of him, but it was important that he be consulted. This mature and inactive deity was the final arbiter in controversies among the gods, and at one time he had been supreme in the Canaanite pantheon. Yet by the fourteenth century B.C., the general date of the Ras Shamra texts, his son Baᶜal was well along in the process of obtaining supremacy. Asherah was El's wife and divine consort who bore him a family of seventy gods and goddesses. The presence of this mother goddess in the cult was signaled by a pole or sacred tree that stood beside the altar. Asherah's most important offspring was Baᶜal, who married his sister Anath. Apparently Asherah was successful in maintaining her position as head goddess in the pantheon, though at times she had to compete with Anath.

Baᶜal himself, whose name means "lord" or "owner," controlled the rain, which directly affected earth's vegetation. Whenever Baᶜal fertilized mother earth with his rain-sperm, a worthwhile production of crops was expected. As a god of the storm that accompanied the rain,

"Ba^cal of the Lightning." This limestone stela, which was discovered in a sanctuary at Ras Shamra, portrays Canaan's famous deity of storm and fertility. Presumably Ba^cal is standing on top of the mountains. He holds a club in his right hand and a lance in his left. The lance seems to be either a stylized tree or a lightning symbol. (Courtesy of the Louvre Museum.)

Ba^cal possessed a sonorous voice that was heard in the thunder. He ruled the other Canaanite deities so that they and men alike might "become fat," for only he could supply rain.

Ba^cal had to earn his enviable position in the pantheon by overcoming a sea-god, Yamm, and the god of death, Mot. Many interpreters of the Ras Shamra texts have held that each year, Ba^cal had to restrain Yamm, who sought to lay claim to the earth through severe floods and strong winds. And once each year Ba^cal also had to confront Mot. That physical encounter brought on Ba^cal's temporary death, at which time earth's vegetation and powers of fertility languished. The dry summer months (May through September) symbolized that the powers of destruction and death held sway. But thanks to the assistance of his militant consort, Anath, who was a goddess of war as well as love, death was overcome and Ba^cal revived. Vegetation and animal life experienced dramatic renewal. Ba^cal mated with the female principle, the rains came, and once more nature yielded its riches.

Here, then, was a nature mythology chiefly devoted to affirming that the force of fertility (Ba^cal), the primordial sea (Yamm), and death itself (Mot) were engaged in a three-way struggle for mastery over the world. It recognized that natural forces existed in a state of continual conflict.

Canaanite mythology and religious practices went hand in hand. If Ba'al was to reign supreme and if the ground he owned was to be fertile, then it was essential that he and his consort engage in sexual intercourse. In order that nature's powers of fertility might be fully realized, the Canaanites themselves practiced sacred prostitution at various sanctuaries that dotted the land. Men identified with Ba'al and women with Anath as they lost themselves in an admittedly erotic religion. Moreover, suggestive fertility plaques were common in Canaanite homes.[5] Presumably if they were properly handled, they might confer fertility on the one who was in need.

The mythology and ritualistic acts of the Canaanites must have evoked varied reactions from Israelite settlers. Deuteronomy's emphatic legislation against cultic prostitution (23:17–18) conveys a disgust that at least some Israelites may have felt toward Canaanite religion from the beginning. They were ready to dismiss Canaanite religion as a dirty, licentious, and rather simple-minded affair.

Nevertheless, in Israelite society "all shades are represented, from the people who unreservedly adopted Canaanite civilization to those who condemned it completely."[6] Some Israelites must have thought it very useful to worship Yahweh and Ba'al. Yahweh's reputation for decisive historical intervention, especially in military combat, made him a good candidate for religious allegiance. In addition, Ba'al's way with the soil was not to be taken lightly. A dual loyalty in things religious might lead to a profitable outcome.

Israel's accommodation to Canaanite culture was sometimes subtle and unintentional. When a former Canaanite sanctuary such as Bethel and Shechem was taken over by Israel, its history was likely to exert some influence on its present use. The Canaanite agricultural calendar was acceptable to the Israelites, who, after all, did become a nation of farmers. Some Israelite parents also named their children after Canaanite deities without any conscious intention of showing disloyalty to Yahweh. Most of Israel's moves toward adopting Canaanite culture were not malicious. It is as if the people were saying to Yahweh, "Thanks for bringing us here, but now go away." We must recognize, therefore, that "what influential groups at a later date considered to be irreconcilable with what they understood by 'pure Yahwism' cannot be accepted as the norm for earlier epochs in the religious history of Israel."[7] The judgment of the Deuteronomist that all Israel deliberately abandoned the covenant faith is inordinately harsh.

In the final analysis, the religious disposition of Canaan and that of Israel remained distinct. Israel continued to affirm that Yahweh alone was sovereign and that it was his nature to be jealous. If some Israelites

Canaanite Fertility Figurines. Many figurines of nude females
and goddesses, such as those depicted here from the
Palestine Archaeological Museum, have been discovered
throughout Palestine. They date from the Middle Bronze to
the Iron II period (ca. 2100–600 B.C.) and confirm the vital
role of female deities in Canaanite religion and culture.
(Photo by James B. Pritchard.)

paid homage to select Canaanite deities, others held firm to an austere
form of Mosaic Yahwism. Israelite religion remained imageless, and
therein lay part of its uniqueness. Israel also refused to incorporate into
her own faith one premise that was basic to Canaanite religion—
namely, that the deity who matters most to human existence dies and
is reborn. We have no indication that the death of Yahweh became
part of any Israelite rite as did the death of Baʿal in Canaanite religion.
In their race toward accommodation in the land of Canaan, Israelite
settlers never bought the Canaanite religious package outright.

MAJOR EXPLOITS
AND ACCOMPLISHMENTS

Othniel and Ehud

The first episode involving a major judge centers on the exploit of Othniel (Judg. 3:7–11), who delivered his people from the oppressive hand of Cushan-rishathaim, king of Mesopotamia. The personality of Othniel is all but lost in this manifestly Deuteronomic passage. We are simply informed that Yahweh chose him to rescue his penitent people and that he was endowed with the divine spirit. This episode seems to have reduced the clan of Othniel to an obscure heroic individual (see Judg. 1:12–13). The name of the foreign oppressor and his nationality are suspect. The raids in southern Canaan that the Othniel clan brought to an end may actually have involved invading Edomites who had pressed westward into Judean territory. Whatever the form of the original encounter, it is virtually eclipsed in the present narrative.

The story of Ehud (3:12–30) is an earthy, uninhibited account of Benjaminite treachery that put an end to Moabite harassment. The narrative opens in typical Deuteronomic idiom. After Othniel's death (3:11), the people abandon the Yahwistic faith. Hence, with Yahweh's help, the Moabites advance into Jericho, the city of palms. Having heard the cry of his oppressed people (3:15), Yahweh raises up Ehud. Deliverance of the oppressed is possible now through the payment of tribute and a surprise murder in the outhouse. The graphic prose exults in a decisive Israelite victory over the people of Moab and their obese monarch Eglon.

The record of six of Israel's judges is scant indeed. Only one verse (3:31) is devoted to Shamgar, and only two or three verses each are given to Tola (10:1–2), Jair (10:3–5), Ibzan (12:8–10), Elon (12:11–12), and Abdon (12:13–15). Although Shamgar triumphs over the Philistines, the other five figures are not represented as participating in war. Noth holds that the Israelite tribal confederation formally designated these minor judges the custodians and interpreters of the covenant law.[8] Accordingly their main task would be to promulgate and apply a body of legislation that was binding on their people. Nevertheless, in discerning two different kinds of leadership in the Book of Judges, Noth seems to make an unnecessary distinction between legal and military functions, which on occasion may have been united in a single individual during this era.

Deborah and Barak

The most impressive mutual effort of the Hebrew tribes during the period of the judges is related in the story of Deborah and Barak. The tradition has been preserved in both prose and poetry. The victory ode of Judges 5 and the prose narrative of Judges 4 present complementary, occasionally conflicting witnesses to a critical moment in the life of premonarchical Israel. Both describe a battle between Israelites and Canaanites in northern Canaan. They agree that Deborah inspired her people to engage in military conflict; that Sisera and his forces threatened the Israelites; that Yahweh himself brought victory to his people; and that Jael, the wife of Heber the Kenite, assassinated Sisera in her tent.

Even so, there are several important discrepancies between the two versions. First, in the prose account Sisera is the commander of the army of Jabin, king of Hazor, who is Israel's chief oppressor; in the poem Sisera is regarded as the villain who is commander-in-chief of his own armies. Second, in the prose version only two tribes, Zebulun and Naphtali, oppose the Canaanites; in the poetic version ten tribes are invited to participate and six actually enter the field of battle. And finally, according to the prose narrative, Sisera is murdered by Jael as he sleeps within the tent; in the poem Jael kills Sisera while he takes refreshment at the tent door.

Although the later prose account is not to be discredited, it is the vibrant poem of Judges 5 that attracts our attention. Known as the Song of Deborah, it is a poem addressed to Deborah rather than one actually sung by her (see 5:12, which is undoubtedly more reliable than the prose introduction in 5:1). This archaic poem is historically significant for two reasons. First, it is the only literary piece in Judges that offers a relatively fixed date for a historical event. Megiddo and Taanach were neighboring towns that ordinarily did not flourish simultaneously.[9] The armed conflict unfolded at Taanach (5:19). Stratum VII of Megiddo was destroyed in about 1150 B.C., and for a time lay in ruins. Since the occupants of Stratum VI laid out their town on entirely new lines, they were probably Israelites. They would not have been free to settle there, however, until after they had defeated Sisera and his Canaanite forces. That Israelite victory probably occurred between the Stratum VII and VI (ca. 1125 B.C.) occupations at Megiddo, and if so, shortly before 1125. Judges 5 is also of historical value because it shows how the loosely organized Israelites acted in an environment dominated by small, yet sometimes well-organized Canaanite states.

At this moment Israel's situation in Canaan was precarious. With the Plain of Esdraelon beyond her control, Yahweh's people were in no position to organize effectively against any formidable opponent. This wedge of land virtually cut her into two independent geographical units. Israelites from the hill country north of the plain would be unable to unite with their covenant partners who struggled in the hill country stretching to the south. The Plain of Esdraelon hosted a Canaanite confederacy that enjoyed the benefits of walled cities and a well-equipped standing army. Normal trade relations were a fiction, and at any time an Israelite village might be raided and its people sold into slavery. But spurred on by Deborah's leadership, Yahweh's virtually weaponless peasantry took action. Overlooking whatever differences of manner and opinion existed between them, the tribes of Ephraim, Benjamin, Manasseh (Machir), Zebulun, Issachar, and Naphtali joined the cause of Deborah and Barak. However, the Song of Deborah criticizes four tribes for having ignored the call to arms. Due to their geographically distant location in Transjordan, Reuben and Gilead declined. If the tribe of Dan had already migrated into northern Canaan, then Dan shared with neighboring Asher one motive for turning down Deborah's summons.[10] The maintenance of an existing lucrative sea trade depended on cooperative relations with Canaanite chiefs. If certain Israelite tribes to the south were suffering from Canaanite subjugation, that was their problem.

But what about the battle itself? Although military details are scant, the wording of 5:21 implies that the Canaanite chariotry were bogged down in a rainstorm of unusual proportions. This permitted the light-footed Israelite forces to turn quickly against the enemy. That Yahweh's people were successful in reducing Sisera's forces, however, did not mean they could freely assert themselves throughout the Plain of Esdraelon. Nevertheless, they could now move about with greater safety.

As a literary composition, the Song of Deborah is best described as impressionistic. For example, the poem progresses from galloping horses in battle (5:22) to the curse of Meroz (presumably an Israelite town that refused to participate in the battle, 5:23) to the blessing of Jael (5:24). A series of eyewitness impressions is conveyed in a highly episodic manner. It appears that "the events have been strung together like pearls on a necklace, with no regard for their logical causes and consequences."[11] What reason might consider of peripheral interest is here given special attention. More is said about Sisera's death than about the battle itself. And the impressionistic art of the poet conveys the deep feelings of the moment through stark contrasts. We shall mention but a few. A poetic affirmation of the strength of Yahweh—whose coming causes the earth to tremble, the mountains to quake, and the rains to descend—is followed by a vivid word picture of Israel's weakness (5:4–7). The faithful tribes who respond to Deborah's summons bring to mind their opposites, who are cursed for standing still (5:14–18). The brave deed of Jael is played off against the ironic waiting of Sisera's mother, who looks for the return of her heroic son (5:25–30). In short, Judges 5 is an unmistakably brilliant and passionate composition.

Finally, the Song of Deborah gives us a glimpse of the religious and military fervor of this era. The piety of the composition is assertive. Indeed, it is militant: "The struggle against the enemies of Yahweh is carried on in the very name of God; indeed, is God's own struggle.

Two Dye Vats from Tell Beit Mirsim. A number of cylindrical stone dye vats were uncovered in the eighth century B.C. level of Tell Beit Mirsim (presumably, biblical Debir). Each vat consisted of a single chunk of carved limestone. The opening in the center permitted thread or cloth to be dyed. A chiseled grove around the rim directed excess dye, which passed through a small hole back into the vat. A verse in the Song of Deborah (Judg. 5:30) implies that dyed cloth was a precious commodity. The discovery of many dye vats and loom weights at Tell Beit Mirsim encourages the hypothesis that it was the site of a town guild of dyers and weavers. (Photo by the author.)

The Song of Deborah glorifies the warlike propaganda of religion, religious fanaticism, heroic piety."[12] In effect, Yahweh is once more celebrated as a "man of war" (see Exod. 15:3), one who is alone capable of dispersing and defeating the enemy. It is he who sends the torrential rain that results in Canaanite undoing. And with the battle now past, Yahweh is appropriately thanked and glorified.

Gideon and Abimelech

Judges 6–8 narrates the adventures of Gideon, who assumed leadership over the tribe of Manasseh. These chapters contain disparate heroic tales that honor two different kinds of accomplishment. Through cultic reform, Gideon delivers his people from apostasy, and through courageous acts on the field of battle he saves them from the oppressors. As a younger son in his father's house it is important that Gideon be divinely summoned (6:11–24). The angel of Yahweh appears while

Gideon is threshing grain. Gideon's lack of confidence and the reassuring divine word are both emphasized. The call climaxes with Gideon erecting a Yahwistic altar and naming it, "Yahweh is peace" (v. 24).

What, then, was the manner of Gideon's cultic reform? His initial adventures find him cleaning up the home front in Ophrah, an undetermined site that seems to be near Shechem (see Judg. 9:5-6). Decisively Gideon encounters the apostasy of his immediate neighbors. His own father is a devotee of Ba°al and Asherah, and presumably some other clan members worship deities other than Yahweh. In 8:27 we are told that Gideon himself made an "ephod," presumably an image of the deity, which "all Israel" in her harlotry revered. For the moment, however, Gideon is the inspired Yahwistic reformer. Working at night, he demolishes the Canaanite altar and in its place raises an altar to Yahweh. Distressed townsmen confront Joash, Gideon's father, with his son's outrageous deeds and recommend the death penalty. Joash retorts, "Let Ba°al contend against him" (6:32), which is intended to explain the name "Jerubba°al" that is accorded to Gideon. Ba°al's claims are negated, and Yahweh's are affirmed.

Most of the Gideon narrative centers on its hero's military endeavors, however. Transjordan peoples, including the Midianites and Amalekites, are victimizing Yahweh's apostate people (Judg. 6:1-6). Having once assumed the role of encroaching nomads, Israel must now withstand attack herself. The land rocks with confusion.[18] In the face of this new, terrifying threat, Yahweh's people experience acute defeatism (6:6), and well they should since the invading Midianites enjoy the services of the domesticated camel. Without advance notice, the Midianites could plunder the countryside at harvest time and terrorize its inhabitants. Yahweh's people stood in need of immediate help. Fortunately the spirit of Yahweh fell upon Gideon (6:34), and thus equipped he led his people to victory. But the troops from Asher, Zebulun, Naphtali, and Manasseh itself, who rallied to Gideon's cause (6:35), first had to be reduced to a mere three hundred men (7:2-7). This ensured that if victory came, the credit would mainly be Yahweh's. Israel was not to boast about her own deeds.

Having openly displayed his leadership talent by helping his people to taste victory, Gideon is invited to be their king (8:22). A dynastic monarchy is even envisaged, for the people suggest that in time Gideon's son and grandson should in turn take the throne. Gideon's response becomes the classical motto of those within ancient Israel who harbor strong reservations about the monarchy: "I will not rule over you, and my son will not rule over you; Yahweh will rule over you" (8:23). But while Gideon was not king in name, his numerous wives and his possession of a concubine as well imitate the way of kingship in the ancient Near East (8:30-31). Moreover, Gideon's son Abimelech wanted to be king and figured the only way to secure the prize was to assassinate his brothers. Perhaps Gideon's antimonarchical statement in 8:23 was put into his mouth by a later narrator. Surely Gideon's exploits in defense of his vulnerable people elicited their profound respect. They may have relied on his spirited leadership for some time. At the very least, Gideon's tribesmen conferred on him a casual kind of sovereignty, and presumably he accepted that gift.

The lengthy narrative of Judges 9 then reports how Abimelech, who was half Canaanite, grasped at kingship of his mother's town of Shechem. Through his own unprincipled efforts, Abimelech reigned there for three years. Initially the vivid narrative may have been shaped by a spectator or by someone who lived shortly after the events depicted. The Deuteronomist must have relished the moral thrust of the narrative. It claimed that this unscrupulous murderer, the son of Gideon's Canaanite concubine, got his just deserts in the political hostilities that brought his brief reign to an abrupt halt.

Abimelech did not share his father's reputed attitude toward Israelite monarchy. In due course he must hear a pointed fable from Jotham, his youngest brother. That fable about the trees (9:8–15) may have distilled an attitude toward Abimelech's ruthless ambition that several of Shechem's citizens now shared. In Jotham's fable, the bramble eagerly accepted an office that the olive, fig, and vine tree rejected as unsuitable for themselves. In an era when the Israelite tribal confederacy was purposely loose and unstructured, when individual decisions were to be encouraged, one who ought to be pursuing the livelihood of farmer should not push himself into the objectionable role of overlord. Ultimately, Abimelech sustained a mortal blow inflicted by a millstone let loose by a nameless woman. The fact that his crime did not pay is didactically asserted in 9:56. "Thus God requited the crime of Abimelech, which he committed against his father in killing his seventy brothers."

Jephthah and Samson

The Judges narrative moves on to tell of Jephthah's accomplishments in delivering Gilead from the Ammonites (10:6–12:7). The character of Jephthah is convincingly drawn. This son of a harlot is expelled from his father's family lest he assert any claim on the family inheritance. In Transjordan Jephthah now gathers together some tough compatriots who apparently sustained themselves physically by raiding caravans and defenseless villages. When the elders of Gilead find it necessary to take action against the intruding Ammonites, they obtain the services of Jephthah, whose reputation for winning in a rough-and-tumble world must have been considerable. Note, however, that Jephthah's fee is extremely high. He will lead the troops only if he is formally declared head of the tribe (11:9–11).

Here we encounter one of the most moving narratives in the Bible. Jephthah's fervent concern for Yahweh's support in the impending battle makes him utter a desperate oath. Upon his triumphant return, he will offer as a human holocaust to the deity whoever comes out of his tent to meet him. Presumably it would have been a member of his family. Since he was the father of only one child (11:34), there would have been decidedly few candidates for the sacrifice. To undertake such a vow was to act rashly, but the pressure on the tribe of Gilead was intense. Regrettably it is Jephthah's only daughter who meets her victorious father. The distraught hero must inform his daughter of his oath. Instinctively she realizes that the choice of breaking the vow is not his to make, and she requests a two-month interim during which she and those closest to her may depart and lament her virginity.[14]

Four chapters (Judg. 13–16) are devoted to the exploits of Samson, that legendary Danite hero who has frequent contact with the Philistines. The Samson narrative scarcely testified to a life of fervent piety, generosity, and heroism. Samson's exploits seem to be the result of his desire to build up his own reputation. He does not devote all his energy

Philistine Installation at Tell Gezer. Ancient Semites, Egyptians, Canaanites, Philistines, and Hebrews all occupied this important site in the Shephelah at one time or another. Above is a Philistine installation of the Iron I era (ca. 1200–900 B.C.) under examination in 1968. Note the stone-lined bin for grain storage (left) and the oven for domestic use (center). Near the oven (at bottom of picture) is a large, isolated flat stone that may have functioned as a counter top during meal preparation. (Photo by the author.)

to rescuing his people from existing Philistine pressure. Of course, it may be argued that at this point in time, the clashes between the Israelites and the Philistines were informal and sporadic. Perhaps the religious message in these chapters lies in their portrayal of someone whose gifts were wasted. The Deuteronomist may well have regarded Samson as a negative example.

In any event, the religious impact of the Samson tales is not especially pointed. Samson himself appears more as an Israelite Hercules than as an authentic judge. Whenever the biblical Samson is compared with the Samson of Milton's *Samson Agonistes* (1671), the former invariably comes off second best. The exploits of the biblical Samson are personal. Despite this rogue's inability to triumph over women, he can give the Philistines a hard time. Yet ultimately Samson succumbs to the Philistines, who blind and imprison him. The gift of superhuman strength remains, however, and in the final scene, Samson heroically pulls down the pillars of the Philistine temple of Dagon, causing the edifice to crash down on both the Philistines and himself.

These entertaining chapters have some historical import, for they "authentically reflect the situation on the Philistine frontier before open war broke out."[15] Perhaps Samson's aggressive acts symbolize similar but historically unknown deeds undertaken by other Israelites against the Philistines. Certainly in the opening chapters of 1 Samuel, Israelite-Philistine relations are under great strain. It is fitting that the crucial midsection of the Book of Judges (2:6–16:31) concludes with some consideration of the Philistines. It was their assertive presence more than anything else that provoked Yahweh's people to institute a monarchical form of government.

ISRAEL'S SOCIAL ORGANIZATION DURING THE ERA OF THE JUDGES

As we complete our study of the Book of Judges and the various phases of Israelite settlement in Canaan, we should briefly consider the social organization that appears to have dominated Israelite life during the era of the judges. For several decades, biblical scholarship has shown much interest in the possible existence of a so-called Israelite amphictyony. As reflected in the records of ancient Greece and Italy, the amphictyony was a religious league of states which took part in the cult of a common deity. Applied to the corporate life of ancient Israel, the noun "amphictyony" has been made to refer to the league of Israelite tribes who committed themselves to the worship of Yahweh at such crucial sanctuaries as Shechem and Shiloh.

The best-known interpreter and defender of the Israelite amphictyony is Noth, whose monograph on the subject appeared in 1930.[16]

Noth worked closely with the various Old Testament lists of the sons of Jacob (Israel) who are accepted as the name-giving ancestors of the Israelite tribes, and drew comparisons with the amphictyonic organizations in the ancient Greco-Roman world. This led him to posit that in the era of the judges, the Israelite tribes were members in a sacred league. That confederation worshiped a common deity at a central sanctuary and accepted the stipulations of a sacred law that was binding on all its members. An Israelite amphictyony was earliest manifested in the six Leah tribes (Reuben, Simeon, Levi, Judah, Zebulun, Issachar) and existed at the time Joshua led "the house of Joseph" into central Palestine. The arrival of the latter group resulted in the establishment of the twelve-tribe system. While local Israelite shrines were common enough in Canaan at this time, the true basis of the spiritual community of Israel was the amphictyonic center. Although that center shifted now and then as Israel's circumstances and needs shifted, the central shrine was sanctified by the presence of the ark of the covenant.

Noth held that at the amphictyonic shrine, Israelite worship assumed its most formal expression. The tribes gathered there regularly to hear the reading of the divine law. Accordingly, Yahweh's claim on

The Gezer High Place. This installation, which dates to about 1600 B.C., consists of ten large monoliths and a rectangular stone block or laver. Although the significance of these stones is not fully known, they seem to have been erected simultaneously. These limestone monoliths, which assume a north-south alignment, vary considerably in size and dressing—two are more than ten feet in height. In all likelihood they commemorated an important covenant-making event in which the Canaanite inhabitants of Gezer participated. (Photo by the author.)

the league members was deeply felt. The assembled people would enter into a ritual of covenant renewal whereby the proclamation of Yahweh's deeds and will was followed by a formal act of commitment (see, for example, Josh. 24 with its account of the proceedings at Shechem). And especially with the hearing of the law, the assembled Israelites might acquire fresh insights into their own identity.

The amphictyonic hypothesis as advanced by Noth has been embraced by several scholars as a valuable explanation of the structure and life of premonarchical Israel.[17] It has sustained a heavy assault, however, from Orlinsky, who claims that the concept of amphictyony does not really assist us in understanding the world of the judges.[18] Orlinsky believes that genuine tribal cooperation was stimulated solely in the case of a common enemy. The Israelite tribes were autonomous, and their actions were largely influenced by geographical conditions: "In those days there was no king in Israel; every man did what was right in his own eyes" (Judg. 17:6 and 21:25).

In support of his position, Orlinsky summons such evidence as the following: (1) The separate major judges such as Ehud and Jephthah carry out impressive military achievements, but these heroes do not associate with either domestic Israelite needs or a specific shrine. (2) The Book of Judges mentions no occasion when any amphictyonic confederation convened for the purpose of choosing a judge or consenting to a particular plan of action. (3) The Song of Deborah (Judg. 5) does not directly attest any central religious shrine nor does its prose counterpart (Judg. 4), and yet the historical moment was critical. (4) The existence of numerous Israelite shrines in ancient Palestine meant that Yahweh was worshiped in many places and that a centralized cult was scarcely necessary. (5) Since there was no centralized authority among the Ammonites, Midianites, and Moabites, who followed the lead of local chieftains, it is unlikely that the situation was any different among the Israelites.

Though it is refreshing, Orlinsky's essay is open to several legitimate criticisms. First, it is so absorbed with the Book of Judges that it ignores Joshua 24, in which the elders of the tribes assemble in significant and solemn encounter. We believe that Joshua 24 presupposes a confederation of Israelite tribes which in its corporate worship and organizational structure achieved some degree of integration. Nor is it altogether clear that the Song of Deborah (Judg. 5) rules out the possibility of a central shrine. Many of the Israelite tribes are mentioned, and the league obligation is emphasized. The ten tribes are summoned to participate in the military confrontation with the Canaanite enemy. In fact, this religious composition, which is both textually corrupt and remarkably intact, may have been preserved at the central sanctuary itself. Its failure to mention that sanctuary by name is at best an argument from silence. Orlinsky also minimizes the fact that supporters of

Noth's hypothesis often admit that the tribal structure was loose. Finally, the existence of a tribal confederation makes more plausible the rapid emergence of the Israelite monarchy soon to follow. A loosely but meaningfully organized people were requesting a tighter, more elaborate governmental structure. In this tribal league we may detect the theocratic Israelite monarchy in embryonic form.

It is true that by its very nature the amphictyonic thesis presupposes a degree of stability that may never have existed in Syro-Palestinian society during the era of the judges.[19] Still, that era seems to have been something other than a meaningless sequence of chaotic events. The tribes did sometimes unite in a concerted attempt to overthrow the enemy. And if it is impossible to set forth in a definitive sequence the central sanctuaries of the tribal confederation, it stands to reason that any center that currently served as custodian of the ark of the covenant might claim prominence. The annual trip that Samuel's parents made to Shiloh where Yahweh's ark was once located (1 Sam. 1:3) may have been undertaken then, and in the years immediately preceding, by many devout Israelites. Hence, we would argue for a creative balance which (1) takes seriously those texts which imply that the forces of centralization are sometimes at work here, and (2) embraces those passages wherein tribal and personal individuality are pronounced. The present trend of discrediting the term "amphictyony" as being truly appropriate for ancient Israel's tribal league is well taken. Loyalty to the entire tribal confederation was probably not nearly so intense as this noun presupposes. Nevertheless, a partially common history, faith, and need to survive all ensured that precarious existence in the Land of Promise would now and then be ameliorated by integrated tribal effort.[20]

NOTES

1. John L. McKenzie, *The World of the Judges* (Englewood Cliffs, N.J.: Prentice-Hall, 1966), p. 21.
2. Among many available studies on Canaanite religious literature and its relation to the Hebrew Bible, two deserve special mention: William F. Albright, *Yahweh and the Gods of Canaan: A Historical Analysis of Two Contrasting Faiths* (Garden City, N.Y.: Doubleday, Anchor Books, 1969); and John Gray, *The Legacy of Canaan*, 2d ed., Vetus Testamentum Supplement, vol. 5 (Leiden, Neth.: E. J. Brill, 1965).
3. Strictly speaking, in the Ba^cal and Anath material we have a cycle of mythological poems, not an epic per se. Nevertheless, the term "epic" may be applied to this material in an informal manner.
4. The Ba^cal cycle may be read in James B. Pritchard, ed., *Ancient Near Eastern Texts Relating to the Old Testament*, 3d ed. (Princeton, N.J.: Princeton University Press, 1969), pp. 129–142.

5. G. Ernest Wright, *Biblical Archaeology*, rev. ed. (Philadelphia: Westminster Press, 1962), p. 113.
6. Johannes Pedersen, "Canaanite and Israelite Cultus," *Acta Orientalia* 18 (1940): 1.
7. G. W. Ahlström, *Aspects of Syncretism in Israelite Religion*, trans. Eric J. Sharpe (Lund, Swed.: C. W. K. Gleerup, 1963), p. 12.
8. Martin Noth, *The History of Israel*, 2d ed., rev. trans. Peter R. Ackroyd (New York: Harper & Row, 1960), pp. 101–103.
9. We follow the view of William F. Albright, *The Archaeology of Palestine*, rev. ed. (Baltimore, Md.: Penguin Books, 1961), pp. 117–118. For a date between 1100 and 1050, see A. D. H. Mayes, "The Historical Context of the Battle Against Sisera," *Vetus Testamentum* 19 (1969): 353–360.
10. Judges 18 preserves the tradition that the tribe of Dan, which first settled in the Shephelah, later moved north in search of more promising territory. That migration probably took place prior to 1150 B.C.
11. Gillis Gerleman, "The Song of Deborah in the Light of Stylistics," *Vetus Testamentum* 1 (1951): 171.
12. *Ibid.*, p. 174.
13. This is masterfully expressed in Paddy Chayefsky, *Gideon* (New York: Random House, 1962).
14. The ritualistic mourning for the deceased god of fertility (for example, Tammuz in Babylonia and Baʿal in Canaan), a rite that was quite central to the nature-oriented religions of the ancient Near East, may have something to do with this episode.
15. John Bright, *A History of Israel*, 2d ed. (Philadelphia: Westminster Press, 1972), p. 174.
16. Martin Noth, *Das System der zwölf Stämme Israels*, Beiträge zur Wissenschaft vom Alten und Neuen Testament, IV–1 (Stuttgart: Kohlhammer, 1930). See also Noth, *The History of Israel, op. cit.*, pp. 85–109.
17. For example, Noth's reconstruction is accepted by Bright, *op. cit.*, pp. 156–166 and *passim*, who makes rather few modifications, and was earlier affirmed by William F. Albright, *From the Stone Age to Christianity: Monotheism and the Historical Process*, 2d ed. (Garden City, N.Y.: Doubleday, Anchor Books, 1957), p. 281. Bright dislikes the term "amphictyony," however, because "the parallels, while illuminating, are not exact" (p. 159, n. 48).
18. Harry M. Orlinsky, "The Tribal System of Israel and Related Groups in the Period of the Judges," in Meir Ben-Horin et al., eds., *Studies and Essays in Honor of Abraham A. Neuman* (Leiden, Neth.: E. J. Brill, 1962), pp. 375–387.
19. The author is in partial agreement with McCarthy, who maintains, "Tribal affinities can be very strong! However, frankly such passionate loyalty to the whole does not seem to me particularly characteristic of the world of the judges." (Dennis J. McCarthy, *Old Testament Covenant: A Survey of Current Opinions* [Richmond: John Knox Press, 1972], p. 65.)
20. For further discussion about ancient Israel's tribal confederation, see George W. Anderson, "Israel: Amphictyony," in H. T. Frank and W. L. Reed, eds., *Translating and Understanding the Old Testament* (Nashville: Abingdon Press, 1970), pp. 135–151.

9

THE
UNITED MONARCHY
UNDER SAUL
AND DAVID

Ancient Israel entered her period of monarchy in about 1020 B.C. Within two generations, the components of a loose tribal organization were welded into a strong unified state. The impressive accomplishments of three kings—Saul (ca. 1020–1000), David (ca. 1000–961), and Solomon (ca. 961–922)—have led some interpreters to refer to this era as "Israel's Golden Age." The people of Yahweh were obviously coming of age. Yet though the Israelite monarchy was to exist for more than four hundred years (until 587), the United Monarchy lasted barely a century (until the schism of 922). The Divided Monarchy was in effect from 922 to 722, with Israel in the north and Judah in the south. The northern kingdom succumbed to Assyrian aggression in 722. From that year to 587, which marks the fall of Jerusalem, the monarchy of Judah was to live out the remainder of its time.

In this chapter we shall consider the factors that influenced Israel to settle on a course of monarchy, and we shall examine the rule of Saul and David. It will soon become apparent that despite its potential, an appreciable number of Israelites did not accept the monarchy as either politically expedient or theologically legitimate. Who really was king—Yahweh or David? But lest we get ahead of the story, we turn to a consideration of the relevant literary material.

Biblical texts to be read prior to and in conjunction with the present chapter: 1–2 Samuel. Pay particular attention to 1 Samuel 1–5, 7–11, 13–16, 18, 28, 31; 2 Samuel 1–7, 9–12.

THE CHARACTER
OF THE LITERARY WITNESS

The books of 1–2 Samuel offer fascinating narrative and a corrupt Hebrew text. Fortunately the textual critic can depend on the Septuagint and the Hebrew books of 1–2 Chronicles for some assistance. Though no broad outline of 1–2 Samuel is entirely satisfactory, a summary might prove useful.

In 1 Samuel 1–7 episodes relating to Samuel, Eli, and the ark of the covenant are set forth. Narratives depicting Samuel's earlier approval and later rejection of Saul are covered in 1 Samuel 8–15. In 1 Samuel 16–31 the narratives about Saul and David extend to Saul's death in battle against the Philistines. Events relating mainly to the public life of King David are the subject of 2 Samuel 1–8. 2 Samuel 9–20 and 1 Kings 1–2 constitute the court history, focusing on David's domestic life. Then in 2 Samuel 21–24 we have an appendix of prose and poetry containing a Davidic psalm (2 Sam. 22 = Psalm 18), the last words of David (2 Sam. 23:1–7), and an account of David's census (2 Sam. 24).

This is historical narrative of a high order. While legendary elements are sometimes present—notably, in the narratives about the ark of the covenant—much of the text is concerned with the fortunes of such public figures as Samuel, Saul, and David. We are informed of Israel's military engagement with the Philistines, the Davidic takeover of Jerusalem, and the transfer of the ark to Jerusalem in order that even an implied separation of "church and state" might be discouraged. Chronological exactitude and sufficient detail are sometimes lacking, yet the significance of historical events is superbly grasped in a sequence of engaging narratives. These reflect on the individual and corporate life of Israelite man considered in the light of the sovereignty, concern, and action of God. In 1–2 Samuel, Israel's historians are still not asking, "What really happened?" at every turn. Nevertheless, in its persistent attempt to assess public events and national personalities, most of 1–2 Samuel merits the designation "history."[1]

Once more we confront the composite product of the Deuteronomist, who was undoubtedly responsible for the final shaping and sequence of the Samuel material. The books of 1–2 Samuel depend on a wide range of ancient oral and written traditions. They are also indebted to an extraordinary historical source commonly known as the Davidic court history (2 Sam. 9–20, 1 Kings 1–2). This narrative of David's court is superbly written; it has a literary grandeur, historical honesty, and psychological depth unexcelled in the Hebrew Bible. A well-integrated document, it is extremely candid in its presentation of David's strengths and weaknesses. While we know nothing about its author, he probably lived during the time of the events he so ably depicts.[2] In vivid contrast with the unified court history, the appendix of 2 Samuel 21–24 contains disparate material meant to satisfy a variety of concerns.

The literary witness in 1 Samuel 1–2 Samuel 8 does not lend itself to easy analysis. Numerous source critics have held that these chapters contain two major strands: an A (early) source supporting the Israelite monarchy and a B (late) source opposing it. In order that these two sources might come out of hiding, it is suggested that you set this text-book aside for the moment and read 1 Sam. 9:1–10:16, 11:1–15 as an A (early, promonarchical) selection, and 1 Sam. 8:1–22, 10:17–27 as a B (late, antimonarchical) selection. In the former, the institution of monarchy is depicted as Yahweh's answer to the Philistine threat; Samuel is a visionary figure of only local stature; and the monarchy formally comes into being at Gilgal. In the latter, the people's obsession to imitate the other nations by designating a king is condemned as faithless and rebellious. The request is granted as Yahweh's and Samuel's concession, but only after unambiguous warnings are issued. In this source, Samuel's reputation and influence are obviously significant, and the monarchy is instituted at Mizpah.

The A source plainly regards the new monarchical structure in Israel as the gift of a God who took pity on his oppressed people. Yahweh prompts Samuel to anoint Saul as king in order that Israel may free herself from Philistine harassment. This source appears to have been narrated by an eyewitness to the action. The contrasting B source, which is thought to have been composed some two centuries later, looks at the Israelite monarchy as an affront to Yahweh. The demand for a king comes from an ungracious people who are now defecting from the covenant faith. Indeed, the presence of a human Israelite king is liable to eclipse Yahweh, who truly is king.

Not all the duplicate narratives in 1 Samuel cluster around the inception of the Israelite monarchy, however. For example, the collapse of the priestly house of Eli is anticipated twice (2:31–36; 3:11–14). Samuel emphatically rejects Saul in 13:7b–14 only to do so again in 15:17–31. After David has been introduced to Saul in 16:15–23, he is brought into Saul's personal entourage as one whom the king does not know (17:55–58). As someone who dislikes Saul and respects the ideology that no malcontent may kill Yahweh's anointed, David spares Saul's life in 1 Samuel 24 only to act honorably in like manner in 1 Samuel 26. The two locations, En-gedi and the wilderness of Ziph, point to the same general vicinity. Such conflicting representations have sometimes encouraged the speculation that two distinct sources are present here.

Nevertheless, a two-source theory for 1 Samuel 1–2 Samuel 8 has its failings. It cannot explain the fact that Saul is declared king on three different occasions (10:1; 10:24; 11:15), and it ignores the episodic quality of 1 Samuel. Connected epic narrative is more a property of the Pentateuch than it is of 1 Samuel.

The question of focus has also to be raised. For example, various traditions in 1 Samuel 1–3 are grouped around the figure of Samuel. Another set of traditions in 1 Samuel 4–6 focuses on the ark of the covenant. A strong public personality such as the prophet Samuel and a significant piece of cultic equipment such as the ark were crucial enough in Israelite history to attract a body of oral and perhaps written tradition. Such observations invite the judgment that a two-source hypothesis for 1 Samuel 1–2 Samuel 8 is too simplistic to be useful.

In any event, the Deuteronomist offers us neither a fully connected narrative nor a totally unbiased account. His own religious perspective finds room for expression—for example, in Samuel's farewell address (1 Sam. 12). Even so, the books of Samuel instruct us about the existence of Yahweh's people during a critical period of their history, and often the telling reflects the ability of the Israelite historians both to fashion engaging narrative and to assess the events and people involved in a truly responsible manner.

THE PREVAILING RELIGIOUS AND POLITICAL CRISIS

The emergence of the Israelite monarchy must be viewed in the light of Egyptian weakness and increasing Philistine pressure. Egypt's impressive period of empire had come to an end. The Egyptian tale of Wen-Amon, which dates to about 1060 B.C., furnishes a vivid, humorous, and ironic account of Egypt's rapidly waning influence in western Asia.[8] It speaks of a functionary of Amon-Re's temple who undertook a journey from Thebes to Byblos in Phoenicia to purchase cedar for the ceremonial boat of Amon-Re. For this high official mission, Wen-Amon was given little money and no protection save his portable idol, "Amon of the Road." In the course of his adventures, Wen-Amon's money was stolen, and he was insulted by various Asian princes. The conversations in this short story present a situation in Asia that contrasts sharply with an earlier era when Egypt's influence there was pronounced. And Egypt was not the only nation experiencing weakness at this time. Assyria was facing internal problems, and a united Hittite empire was no longer a reality.

With the major powers at bay, we might expect Israel to have assumed a position of significance with relative ease. But the Israelites were not Canaan's only newcomers. The Philistines had recently entered the land and were establishing themselves on the southern coastal plain in a pentapolis (a confederacy of five cities) consisting of Ashdod, Ashkelon, Ekron, Gath, and Gaza. Their warriors were of considerable stature. As far as we know, the Philistines were the first people to bring iron with them into Palestine. The presence of an energetic people who lived in the land's most fertile stretches and held a monopoly of iron could not help but jar Israelite existence.

The informal hostilities between the Philistines and the Israelites suggested by the Samson narrative were merely the prelude to more pronounced forms of tension between Israelites and Philistines. If Israel were to persist in the land, she had to answer the Philistine threat and answer it more forthrightly than she could by merely utilizing the resources available within the loose twelve-tribe confederation. The extreme seriousness of the political situation came to Israel's attention through the battle of Aphek, fought in Ephraimite territory not long after 1050 B.C. (1 Sam. 4). The Israelite army was badly beaten. Eli's priestly sons, Hophni and Phinehas, were killed, and the cherished ark of the covenant was taken by the Philistines as a war trophy. The

Anthropoidal Coffin from Tell Fara. This clay sarcophagus was discovered in an Early Iron Age (presumably Philistine) tomb at Tell Fara (Sharuhen) in southwestern Judah. A highly stylized human face and arms appear on its distinctive lid. Such coffins are not native to Palestine, and Egyptian influence is suspected. Egyptian coffins often depicted the deceased. (Photo by William R. Watters, Jr., taken in the Palestine Archaeological Museum, Jerusalem. Used with permission of the Israel Department of Antiquities and Museums.)

Israelites were now forced to organize more tightly and continuously in a common cause.

Israel stood in need of effective leadership, and this was to come in the person of Samuel. His portrait, which emerges in the composite tradition of 1 Samuel, is multifaceted. In 1 Samuel 9 Samuel is depicted as a seer, a man of God, who is consulted in connection with the loss of the asses owned by Saul's father, Kish. In 1 Sam. 7:15–17 Samuel is portrayed as a judge whose circuit is the limited area of Ramah, Bethel, Gilgal, and Mizpah. Samuel is sketched in 1 Sam. 7:3–14 as a judge over all Israel, and by analogy with the courageous and talented judges he is viewed as one able to deliver Israel from impending enemy threat. Moreover, in 1 Samuel 9–11, Samuel is the anointer of Israel's first king. On two occasions (1 Sam. 10:5–7 and 19:18–24), Samuel is linked with a group phenomenon that might be labeled "ecstatic prophetism." With its marked interest in evoking contagious seizures of the divine spirit in which all the assembled participants might share, ecstatic prophetism appears for the first time in Israel's history. Although Samuel may have had more than one function to fulfill, his portrait in 1 Samuel is not the product of a unified tradition.

The materials in 1 Samuel 1–3 are thought to be relatively late traditions designed to explain how Samuel's remarkable role in Israelite history could be attributed to his miraculous birth, to the consecration of his life to Yahweh's service, and to the deity's own summoning and commissioning. At the outset we are introduced to a familiar motif. Elkanah has two wives. Peninnah is capable of bearing children, but Hannah is not so blessed. The Jacob-Leah-Rachel trio comes to mind. Hannah, who is rightly concerned about her problem, accompanies her husband (and his other wife) on his annual journey to the central sanctuary at Shiloh. On one occasion Hannah makes an all-important vow to Yahweh (1:11). After an initially awkward incident with Eli, the presiding priest, Hannah returns home and in due course bears a son.

The opening verses of 1 Samuel 2 present Hannah's prayer of thanksgiving. Read out of context, one would hardly take this song to be a mother's joyous poetic recounting of the birth of her child. Rather, this composition appears to be a psalm of thanksgiving celebrating national deliverance. Its theme, the humiliation of the lofty and the exaltation of the lowly, is not elaborated with specific reference to Hannah's situation. Still, the belief that Yahweh invests human events with strength and compassion is expressed. And of course the faith in Yahweh advanced here may have been akin to Hannah's own faith. In the regal declaration in 2:10 the monarchy appears to be a fact. Like many of the poems in the Old Testament, its exact age cannot be readily ascertained. If the Deuteronomist chose to include this poem for its artistic and religious merits, it is unlikely that he regarded it as pertinent historical commentary.

The Samuel call narrative (1 Sam. 3:1–14) attests that Yahweh addressed the boy Samuel as he was sleeping before the cherished ark of the covenant in the Shiloh sanctuary. Here Yahweh declares his intention to destroy the offensive house of Eli. Once Samuel reveals Yahweh's plan to Eli, the old priest accepts the divine will as good (3:18) and all Israel acknowledges Samuel as Yahweh's prophet (3:20). That the prophet was destined for success and recognition is hinted at in 2:26: "Now the boy Samuel continued to grow both in stature and in favor with Yahweh and with men."

Except for its opening phrase (4:1a), 1 Samuel 4–6 makes no mention of Samuel. Instead, the ark of the covenant is its unifying motif. The Philistine triumph over Israel near Aphek, the loss of the ark to the enemy, its presence as a critical Philistine problem, and its return to Israelite territory are all depicted. The pressure that the Philistines were now applying against Israel had intensified. As part of the sea peoples who had arrived on the coastal plain early in the twelfth century, the Philistines were acquiring what territory they could. Their monopoly of iron and the effectiveness of their pentapolis along the coastal plain made them a formidable opponent. Apparently at this time (ca. 1050 B.C.), the Philistines confidently embarked on a program to subdue their Israelite rivals once and for all. At the edge of the plain the Hebrew hosts organized at Ebenezer, and the Philistines assembled nearby at Aphek. The Israelites experienced defeat both before and after their ark had been brought into the battle. Among the many Israelites who were killed were Eli's two unfaithful sons. Upon hearing the news, Eli died and Phinehas' wife bore a son. In the short time between the son's birth and her own death, she named the child "Ichabod," meaning, it seems, "Where is the glory?" Then, as if intent on answering her own question, her final words were, "The glory has departed from Israel, for the ark of God has been captured" (4:22). Doom and judgment are unmistakable in the vivid narrative of 1 Samuel 4.

The two relatively short chapters that follow portray the vicissitudes of the captured ark. This trophy arouses considerable curiosity and becomes an embarrassment to the Philistines who seize it in triumph (1 Sam. 5:4, 6, 9–10). Soon the Philistines express their eagerness to rid themselves of this highly unpredictable item. The ark of the covenant is sent with magic and ceremony to Beth-shemesh (6:9, 12). At that site, seventy men show their contempt for Yahweh by looking into the ark, and as a result are immediately slain by the deity (6:19). It is fatal to meddle with the Holy One of Israel. God and ark are closely related (see Num. 10:35–36), and neither is susceptible to indiscriminate probing. This singular narrative affirms that the requisite distance between the holy deity and mortal man must not be taken lightly.

Having most recently been exposed to ancient ark traditions, we are ushered back into later material that again bears directly on the figure of Samuel (7:3). An idealized report in 7:3–14 discloses that with Yahweh's help, the Israelites regained lost cities and generally subdued the Philistine contingents. In fact, the record states that throughout Samuel's lifetime, Yahweh's hand kept the Philistines in check (v. 13). But we have no means of knowing the actual historical situation. Undoubtedly, various encounters between Israelites and Philistines occurred at this time, with victory going first to one side and then to the other. Nevertheless, it must have become apparent that the tribal league could not hold the Philistines in check. The answer lay in the monarchy that was now to emerge.

THE KINGSHIP OF SAUL

Samuel and the Implementation of the Monarchy

Although the Israelite hosts triumphed temporarily over the Philistines, the future of Yahweh's people in the Land of Promise looked bleak indeed. Out of pressing political need, a monarchy was born in ancient Israel, and it was the prophet Samuel who selected and anointed Saul as Israel's first king.[4] In the composite chapters of 1 Samuel 8–11, Samuel's attitude toward monarchy is ambivalent. But regardless of his initial feelings, he could not endorse Saul indefinitely.

According to ancient tradition preserved in 1 Samuel 11, the clear-cut victory of Saul against the Ammonites led to his being chosen king. Israelite territory in Transjordan was coveted by Nahash and his Ammonite men, who lay siege to the city of Jabesh-gilead. Having received Yahweh's spirit (11:6), Saul set to work at once. Dramatically he secured the services of the men of Israel who assembled "as one man" to conquer the Ammonite enemy. The Israelite troops won a striking victory. Saul was appropriately celebrated as the man who was wholly capable of meeting Israelite needs. At Gilgal he was declared king.

But 1 Samuel also espouses an antimonarchical viewpoint that claims that in her willful selection of a king, ancient Israel consciously and ungratefully defected from Yahweh. In serving as judge over Israel, Samuel had affirmed the practice of earlier decades. But now there were those who preferred to slough off signs of Israelite distinctiveness and to follow the example of neighboring monarchies. However, the thought that Israel should turn her back on an earlier social structure that had been authenticated by existing covenant law appalled Yahweh loyalists who increasingly assumed an antimonarchical stance.

The situation is vividly portrayed in 1 Samuel 8. Samuel's sons, who are judges at Beer-sheba, pervert the cause of justice. The dissatisfied people ask Samuel to appoint a king for them. In no uncertain terms Samuel expresses concern about his people's lack of faith in Yahweh and their insensitivity to the disadvantages Israel will assuredly experience under royalty. Samuel's denunciation of kingship has been thought to be a late source interpretation, one that reacts against the oppressive days of Solomon and successive monarchs when the free spirit of Israel was severely threatened. The words put in Samuel's mouth on this occasion would not have been his. Nevertheless, Samuel might have been pointing to practices that predated and were current in his own day. Mendelsohn has argued persuasively that prevailing modes of semifeudal Canaanite society are reflected in Samuel's denunciation of the monarchy.[5] He alludes to extrabiblical Akkadian texts from the eighteenth to the thirteenth century B.C. that have been discovered at Alalakh and Ugarit in Syria. Thus either the prophet himself or an unknown contemporary may be credited with the antimonarchical attitude there expressed. References to professional warriors in the standing army of the king (v. 11), the king's confiscation of lands containing vineyards and olive orchards (v. 14), the levying of a tithe (v. 15), and forced labor (v. 16) all have parallels in these Akkadian texts, which existed prior to Samuel's time. Hence, we cannot dismiss 1 Samuel 8 as a historical "rewrite" by a later opponent of the monarchy.

Theologically the chapter insists that if God, even grudgingly, sanctions the institution of monarchy, the people must recognize that further apostasy from the traditional Yahwistic faith is now a threat. To borrow from the political and social structures of the ancient Near East comes close to appropriating their underlying religious ideology. The welfare of Mosaic Yahwism was in jeopardy.

Saul as a Man of Valor

Samuel anointed Saul and thereby conferred a special status on this inspired, courageous Benjaminite. A man of seemingly limitless valor, Saul had the honor of being Israel's first king. Nevertheless, the edited books of Samuel convey a more sympathetic portrayal of David than they do of Saul. The instances of courage, brilliance, and selflessness in David's life are amply celebrated, and sometimes this is achieved at Saul's expense.

This was no easy time to be king. Saul had little in the way of a standing army (14:52), yet his rule seems to have been devoted to the cause of war. Saul had to work hard simply to keep the nation together. Thus, to regard Saul as Israel's first king is not entirely accurate. It is perhaps better to accept him as a transitional figure standing somewhere between the Israelite judge and the Israelite king to follow. Saul never enjoyed the full support of his people. In fact, they were not shy about voicing their disapproval (10:27). Nor did he really succeed with

III. THE UNITED MONARCHY AND EARLIEST PHASE OF THE DIVIDED MONARCHY (ca. 1020–900 B.C.)

DATE (B.C.)	EGYPT	PALESTINE		ASSYRIA
1020	21st Dynasty (ca. 1069–935)	The United Monarchy (ca. 1020–922) Saul (ca. 1020–1000) Samuel		Decline continues (ca. 1020–935)
1000	Period of weakness	David (ca. 1000–961) Nathan Solomon (ca. 961–922)		
950	22d Dynasty (ca. 935–725) Shishak (ca. 935–914) Shishak's invasion of Palestine (ca. 918)	Disruption of the United Monarchy (922)		Gradual resurgence (ca. 935–)
		Southern Kingdom (Judah, 922–587)	Northern Kingdom (Israel, 922–721)	
		Rehoboam (922–915) Abijah (915–913) Asa (913–873)	*Jeroboam I (922–901) Nadab (901–900)	

*Founder of new dynasty in the northern kingdom (Israel).

the religious elements in Israel. Although he was a demonstrably religious person, in his role as king Saul inevitably competed with previously established religious offices and functions. The antimonarchical motto attributed to Gideon (Judg. 8:23) must have impressed devout Yahwists who were convinced that the times were clearly out of joint.

The statement that "there was hard fighting against the Philistines all the days of Saul" (1 Sam. 14:52) may be taken at face value, and herein lay Saul's greatest contribution. This charismatic warrior, who had triumphed over the Ammonites, was no less successful in combat against the Philistines. His first deed as king of Israel was to defeat the Philistines near Gibeah (13:2–4), his hometown, which he now chose as the base of his own rustic government. Angered by Saul's aggression, the Philistines assembled at Michmash to the northeast and from there raided Israel on several sides (13:16b–18). Through his own valor and that of his son Jonathan, Saul defeated the enemy. Undoubtedly, Yahweh's people now experienced a welcome freedom of movement within the central hill country.

Although he was an effectively militant monarch, Saul made no attempt to subvert tribal loyalties, to establish an intricate governmental bureaucracy, or to spend impressive sums and human effort in building a splendid capital. Excavations at Tell el-Ful (ancient Gibeah) have brought to light the ruins of a large building (169 by 114 feet), which is thought to have been Saul's residence. The edifice was a well-fortified building that looked more like a citadel than it did a palace. Its simple interior lacked the gold, silver, and ivory objects that were to decorate the courts of later Israelite monarchs. Certainly the storage jars, grinding stones, arrowheads, and stones for slingshots found in the debris reveal the plain life of its monarch. The rustic simplicity of his people was good enough for Saul.

Even though the narration of the Israelite war against the Philistines bogs down somewhat in 1 Samuel 14, this chapter of admittedly ancient traditions reveals both the temper of the times and the behavior of Israel's first monarch. In v. 24 we encounter Saul's injunction against eating as a way of pleasing Yahweh. If the men fast, they are more likely to triumph. In v. 27 we read of Jonathan's unwitting violation of the prohibition, and later we witness the vivid protestation of his innocence. Saul's concern that appropriate sacrificial measures are carried out is apparent in vv. 31–35, and in v. 41 we note the king's willingness to use the sacred lots, the Urim and Thummim, to ascertain Yahweh's will. Further, Saul's decree that Jonathan shall die for having eaten honey during the ban (v. 44) shows that he was far more concerned with honoring the requirements of holy war than he was with supporting the principle of dynastic kingship, wherein the son follows his father to the throne. Saul's willingness to accede to the people's request that Jonathan be spared demonstrates that his monarchy was by no means absolute.

Saul was frequently successful on the battlefield. He was able to subdue the Amalekites who had conducted raids into the Negev (1 Sam. 15). Then, ignoring the existing Israelite-Gibeonite treaty (Josh. 9), he moved in against the Gibeonites (2 Sam. 21:1–2). And finally, as we have already noted, this man of valor secured several triumphs over the Philistines.

Saul as a Man of Troubles

Biblical tradition recalls another aspect of Saul's character: his emotional instability. The wound he suffered when Samuel pulled out the props of prophetic support from under him never healed. Moreover, Saul's contacts with the highly promising David made difficult matters worse.

The severe tension between Saul and Samuel, who had first installed him in his kingly office, is skillfully depicted in 1 Samuel 13, 15, and 28. In 1 Samuel 13, a terrible rupture between the "man of God" and the king takes place as Saul prepares to fight against the Philistines at Michmash. This is holy war, and Saul is expected to wait for Samuel to arrive and offer the appropriate sacrifice to Yahweh prior to the battle. When Samuel fails to appear at the appointed time, Saul makes the sacrifice himself. Samuel arrives immediately thereafter and condemns the monarch (13:13–14). It is the prerogative of prophet-priests, not warrior kings, to deliver burnt offerings to the deity. Obviously, the king's sacral and secular functions are yet to be defined. Perhaps Samuel was disturbed by the thought that Saul, who had recently been invested with political power, now claimed religious authority as well. By placing this ancient tradition where he does, the Deuteronomist is implying that Saul's kingship was tainted from its earliest days. In a practical sense, Saul had no choice but to act immediately, for his volunteer army was already dispersing. Yet to offer the sacrifice himself meant that he would offend the old guard, which in every way possible supported the norms of the sacred Israelite league of the recent past. (While Saul is here informed that he has absolutely no right to take the lead in ritualistic matters, 1 Sam. 14:35 reports that Saul set up an altar to Yahweh, and neither Samuel nor the Deuteronomist appears distraught.)

Another instance of tension between the monarch and the prophet is reported in 1 Samuel 15. Saul and his army subdue the marauding Amalekites, but Saul violates the canons of holy war. He deliberately ignores the requirements of the herem. By sparing Agag, the king of Amalek, and the best of the Amalekite livestock, Saul violates the Israelite practice of total annihilation of the enemy. Viewed pragmatically, in sparing the king and the animals Saul made available to himself splendid spoils of war that might aptly symbolize the king's victory.

Yet from the religious perspective Samuel entertained, the *herem* was mandatory. In not fulfilling it, Saul showed his indifference toward Yahweh's will as it had been revealed in ancient legislation. Again Saul is rebuked for exercising his own initiative. Then comes the prophetic sermon with its pointed declaration: "Behold, to obey is better than sacrifice, and to hearken than the fat of rams" (15:22). Saul is roundly rejected by Samuel. The king's entreaties are abortive. The undoing of Saul seems inevitable.

Also in 1 Samuel 28, Saul experiences in Samuel's presence the shattering withdrawal of prophetic support. Through the medium of Endor, Saul confers with the spirit of the now deceased Samuel. Another battle with the Philistines is pending, and the pathetic Saul seeks some guidance from the deity whose spirit no longer rests upon him. The dead Samuel is summoned, but his attitude toward the monarch has not changed. He reminds the king that it is really Yahweh who has rejected him (v. 17). Samuel's word about Saul's impending battle with the Philistines is ominous indeed (v. 19). Once more the prophet triumphs over the monarch.

These three episodes reveal tragic aspects of Saul's life. The old tribal order as upheld by Samuel is not ready to yield graciously to the new monarchy. And Saul is the first target of those intent on keeping the political realm subservient to the religious. His success as king is contingent on Samuel's continuing support, which does not come.

We must also examine the dynamics of the relationship between Saul and David, which further contributed to Saul's disintegration. But before doing so, some attention should be given to David's emergence and his new career, with its frequent blessings and successes. David is first mentioned in 1 Samuel 16 just after Samuel rebukes Saul for his conduct in the Amalekite affair. Samuel is now divinely dispatched to Bethlehem for the purpose of anointing David, the youngest of Jesse's sons. Once anointed in the context of a private ceremony, "the Spirit of Yahweh came mightily upon David from that day forward" (16:13). Saul's negative condition is then described (16:14). He is now the victim of a divinely sent "evil spirit." His future has nothing to commend it. If such declarations frustrate the possibility of narrative suspense, at least they indicate that in successive episodes, David's rapid ascent to popularity and power will be accompanied by a further breakdown in Saul. At once David is introduced to the court as an accomplished musician who may soothe Saul's disturbed mind (16:15–23). Ironically, it is David who will one day take over Saul's kingdom.

In 1 Samuel 17 David's initial contact with Saul is depicted along quite different lines. Here David is introduced to Saul as the fiercely courageous lad who was able to pelt the Philistine Goliath in the forehead (17:58). In the Samuel appendix (2 Sam. 21:19) the slaughter of Goliath is attributed to Elhanan. The Chronicler lamely tries to har-

The Valley of Elah. According to tradition, Saul's Israelite troops and those of the Philistines were stationed in this valley at the time young David killed Goliath (1 Sam. 17). The site is approximately 15 miles west of Bethlehem. (Photo by the author.)

monize the two witnesses by writing that Elhanan slew Lahmi, Goliath's brother (1 Chron. 20:5). David's capacity to kill Goliath is in keeping with the Old Testament portrait of the younger David. Perhaps the name "Goliath" is erroneous in the witness of 1 Samuel 17. This possibility would permit David to have slain some unknown Philistine giant, and Elhanan might be credited with having done in Goliath. Or if "David" should be a throne name, then Elhanan might have been David's name prior to kingship. The legendary tenor of 1 Samuel 17 at least encourages the thesis that someone other than David killed Goliath, but that in later years the magnificent deed was attributed to David himself.

Many things appeared to be going for David from the outset. He was physically attractive (16:12), and he was a skilled musician (16:16). His speech was prudent, and he enjoyed the support of Yahweh's presence (16:18). Also he benefited from Jonathan's close and lasting friendship (18:1). The women sang about David's victories (18:7), and Saul, who distrusted David, happily removed him from the court proper and designated him a military commander (18:13). Steadily David was growing into a prominent hero. Indeed, Saul must have realized that David's popularity would have a deadly effect on his own rule. David would have to be expelled at all costs. The outlandish Philistine foreskin incident of 18:20–29 simply symbolizes the extreme measures Saul undertook to have David exterminated.

Before long, David was forced to flee from the king and live the precarious life of an outlaw. Nevertheless, David grasped at whatever opportunities were available. Feeling insecure before Achish, the Philistine king of Gath, David feigned madness and thus was permitted to exit freely (22:1). Indeed, the outlaw David was able to attract some four hundred men to his own side (22:2). Here was a motley collection of distressed, indebted, and discontented citizens drawn from David's native Judah. As their captain, David led them in raids against Negev Bedouins (1 Sam. 30:1). Later this group would form the nucleus of his standing royal army. Also David married the recently widowed Abigail and acquired many sheep and goats as the dowry (1 Sam. 25). Even the Philistines were sometimes pleased with David. Achish came to accept David's signs of loyalty as genuine and gave him the town of Ziklag in the Negev as a place of residence (27:5–6). On the surface it appeared that David was joining the Philistines in their continuing fight against Saul. Thus David coped with the precarious present and laid plans for a more promising future.

In the last dozen chapters of 1 Samuel, the paranoid Saul fervently directs his attention to chasing David over miles of Judean desert. In

Mount Gilboa. Strategically positioned near one of the two valleys that connect the Jordan valley with the valley of Jezreel, Mount Gilboa is best remembered in ancient Israelite history as the site where Saul and his three sons met their tragic deaths in battle against the Philistines (I Sam. 31). Mount Gilboa consists of a chain of hills that reach a height of 1,737 feet. (Courtesy of the Consulate General of Israel, New York.)

time this led to Saul's ultimate undoing. The Philistines had undoubtedly benefited from Saul's intense concentration on David. Eventually Saul had to face the Philistines at Mount Gilboa. While it is not a comprehensive account, 1 Sam. 31:1–5 reports that the Israelite hosts suffered a stunning defeat, that three of Saul's sons were slain, and that Saul himself was severely wounded by Philistine archers. As a desperate final deed, Saul fell upon his own sword.

Assessing the Reign of Saul

Both positive and negative forces were at work during Saul's reign. His public life began on a promising note. His physical well-being, personal initiative, and courage must have won the respect of many. Popular demand as well as prophetic designation had thrust him into kingship. Saul's campaign in Transjordan against the Ammonites, his punitive expedition against the Amalekites, and his assertiveness toward the Philistines all contributed to Israel's welfare.

Certainly Saul had to work against tremendous odds. Apathy was now manifesting itself within Israel. This meant that Saul had to struggle simply to secure an army and a following. Recurring raids from neighboring peoples must have proved costly. In this age Israelite wealth (what there was of it) was constantly depleted. Saul never had the satisfaction of leading a truly united Israel. Imaginative efforts toward unification were resisted by tribal loyalties, which were still very much alive. Though Saul may have been successful in breaking the Philistine monopoly on iron, within a relatively small Israelite army weaponry probably remained scarce.

Saul suffered as much personally as he did from his historical situation. His feelings of rejection, his constant exposure to prophetic rebuke, and his consuming envy of David all made for a wretched existence. Yet at the very least, Saul should be remembered as an unsung hero of Israelite history. As a diligent warrior and as a humble, honest practitioner of Israelite statecraft, he paved the way for David.

THE KINGSHIP OF DAVID
National and International Accomplishments

David is no stranger in this chapter. Yet before we take note of his accomplishments as king of Judah (2 Sam. 2–4) and then as king of a united Israel and Judah (2 Sam. 5–8), let us ponder the historical situation in about 1000 B.C. We agree fully with the assertion that at this time "few observers would have predicted such brilliance for a people that had just been decisively defeated in battle, that had lost its first king, and that was now scattered over the land without effective leadership."[6] Yet despite these complications, this brilliance was realized during the rule of David.

Upon the death of Saul, two contenders immediately sought his throne. One was Saul's surviving son, Ishbaᶜal, often written as "Ishbosheth" to rid the name of its theophoric Baᶜalistic element; the other was David. Though Ishbaᶜal may have been better equipped for the task than the pro-Davidic narrative of 2 Samuel would have us believe, David did not have to compete with him for long. Israelite factions were poorly united at the time of Saul's death, but Davidic genius was successful in bringing the nation together. It was during David's rule that Israel fully realized the promise of land that Yahweh had already made to Abraham (Gen. 15:18–21). As one who could be both religiously sensitive and politically crafty, David proved worthy of the office that accorded him moments of challenge, satisfaction, and worry.

As 2 Samuel begins, the thread of history is carried forward without interruption. Informed of the death of Saul and his sons, David utters his moving lament over Israel's tragic loss (1:19–27): "How are the mighty fallen!" David's lament is a superb example of Hebrew lyric. While David displays what must have been an authentic note of affection for Saul, he is even more moved—and understandably so—over Jonathan's death. The two had been close friends. As Saul's eldest son, Jonathan had never competed with David for the throne. Rather, he consistently offered David the protection that he needed.

The Mound of Beth-shan. This impressive mound is located at the intersection of the fertile valleys of Jezreel and the Jordan. It contains the ancient ruins of a powerful Canaanite city first settled in the late fourth millennium B.C., long controlled by the Egyptians as an important garrison, and eventually taken by the Israelites—probably in the tenth century B.C. during David's reign. (Photo by the author.)

The establishment of Davidic rule over Judah is the subject of 2 Samuel 2. This crucial event unfolds at Hebron, where unspecified men of Judah anoint David as their king (2:4). Since David had already been so designated by Samuel earlier, perhaps no further prophetic endorsement was thought necessary. With the acumen of a seasoned politician, David dispatches a message of appreciation to the men of Jabesh-gilead who had courageously given the exposed bodies of Saul and his sons a decent burial (2:5–6; cf. 1 Sam. 31:11–13). A word of political self-interest, however, is also evident: "Now therefore let your hands be strong, and be valiant; for Saul your lord is dead, and the house of Judah has anointed me king over them" (2:7). But immediately we learn that Israel has her own monarch in Ishbaᶜal, who was made king by Abner, the commander of Saul's army. The dynasty of Saul was thus established in Gilead east of the River Jordan. These were turbulent days, partly because of the rivalry between Abner's Saulide troops and the Davidic troops under Joab's command. Abner's murder of Joab's brother, Asahel, (2:23) only intensified the hostility. A blood feud now emerged between Joab and Abner, which 2 Sam. 3:1 summarizes succinctly: "There was a long war between the house of Saul and the house of David; and David grew stronger . . ."

Three further happenings in 2 Samuel 3–4 steady David's position. First, Abner and Ishbaᶜal have a falling out. Abner had become friendly with Ishbaᶜal's concubine Rizpah, and he understandably took Ishbaᶜal's accusation very hard (3:8–10). Being charged with visiting a monarch's concubine was tantamount to being accused of aspiring to the throne. Looking after his own interests, Abner appeals to David in the hope that they will enter into a mutually helpful covenant (3:12). David has good reason to respond positively and draw Abner to his side, and it is David who writes the conditions (3:13).

Second, David's position is enhanced when Abner meets death at Joab's hand (3:27). The blood feud is fulfilled, but not without David's well-timed lament over Abner (3:33–34). Once more David expresses loyalty to Saul's house. It is well that he should. As a military commander, Abner held a highly respected position in Israel. He had been assassinated by David's own military commander, though David was unaware of Joab's doings. Desiring to unite the Hebrew kingdom under his own person, David knows that his innocence in the death of Abner must be accepted. He further recognizes that if he is to reach his goal he must win the support of Saul's followers, who are presently supporting the ineffectual Ishbaᶜal. That David was successful in this matter is indicated by the sweeping remark in 3:36, "everything that the king did pleased all the people."

Finally, Ishbaᶜal is mercilessly killed during his noon break (4:5–8). His executioners exercise appallingly poor judgment; they bring Ishbaᶜal's head before David. But David is unimpressed by their reasoning

The Pool of Gibeon. According to the somewhat obscure narrative in 2 Sam. 2:12–17, the forces of David crossed swords with those of Ish-ba°al beside the pool of Gibeon. Pictured here is the cylindrical upper part of the pool, which is 37 feet wide and 35 feet deep. This rock-hewn installation, which belonged to the city's water system, was constructed by energetic inhabitants, who removed 3,000 tons of limestone to obtain safe access to the rich supply of fresh water that lay 80 feet below their homes. (Photo by the author.)

that in this murder they have carried out Yahweh's vengeance against Saul. He pronounces a death sentence against the scoundrels (4:12). With Abner's defection from Ishba°al, Abner's assassination, and Ishba°al's murder in cold blood, it was now possible for David to realize his fondest dreams and become monarch of a united Israel and Judah.

A portrait of David's public life as king of all Palestine is offered in 2 Samuel 5–8. Each chapter has its distinctive data to impart. In 2 Samuel 5 we learn of the anointing of David as monarch of "all Israel and Judah," his brilliant conquest of Jerusalem, and his successful exploits against the Philistines. In 2 Samuel 6 we read of how David brought the ark of the covenant to Jerusalem so that religious and political factors might coalesce. The oracle of the court prophet Nathan to the king, which legitimizes the Davidic dynasty, is rendered in 2 Samuel 7, and the Deuteronomist's summary of David's reign appears in 2 Samuel 8. All but the last-mentioned chapter require closer inspection.

THE UNITED MONARCHY

0   10   20   30
Miles

Sidon •

Damascus •

MT. LEBANON

MT. HERMON

SYRIA (ARAM)

Tyre •

Dan •

SIDONIANS

Hazor ■

Accho •

Sea of
Chinnereth

BASHAN

Mt. Carmel

THE GREAT SEA

En-dor •

Megiddo ■

Ramoth-gilead •

Beth-shan •

Mt. Gilboa +

ISRAEL

Jabesh-gilead •

GILEAD

Jordan R.

+ Mt. Ebal
Mt. Gerizim + • Shechem

Mahanaim •

Aphek •

• Shiloh

Bethel •
• Mizpah
• Michmash

Rabbath-ammon •

Beth-horon •

Gezer ■
Gibeon •
• Gibeah
• Anathoth

AMMON

Baalath ■

Ashdod •
Ekron •
Beth-shemesh •

■ Jerusalem

Ashkelon •

Gath •

• Bethlehem

JUDAH

Gaza •

• Hebron

SALT
SEA

PHILISTINES

En-gedi •

• Ziklag

• Beer-sheba

MOAB

The Negev

AMALEKITES

Tamar ■

EDOM

At the beginning of 2 Samuel 5 we are informed that the Israelite elders traveled south to Hebron to anoint David as king of Israel. David could now formally exert his influence over a far wider territory. Hebron proved an unsatisfactory site for the capital, however. It was too far from the center of the kingdom, and David sought another site. He resolved to conquer the Jebusite city of Jerusalem, which enjoyed a central location and a strategic setting in the hills, and had no previously existing Israelite tradition that might offend the south.[7] (The Jebusite clan dominated Jerusalem prior to David's conquest.) On both religious and political grounds, Jerusalem stood in a basically neutral position.

With the assistance of his own army, David took the city (2 Sam. 5:6–9).[8] In the process, he seems neither to have displaced nor killed off its Jebusite inhabitants. Presumably they were allowed to remain while David organized his court at this newly acquired site. By ruling from a city that had previously existed beyond the realm of Israel's internal history, David was able to conduct himself without the restrictions of earlier tradition. This city was truly David's, and it was well on its way to becoming the most crucial city in all Palestine.

Even earlier than this time, it must have dawned on the Philistines that David was no longer their ally. In 5:17–25 we have an account of David's successful combat against the Philistine forces. No longer would they exist as a united front to threaten the welfare of Yahweh's people.

Soon after David had consolidated his position in Jerusalem (2 Sam. 6), he decided to bring the ark of the covenant to his capital. In this way Jerusalem would acquire religious as well as civic and military significance. Saul's error in ignoring the ark and thus alienating the priesthood (see 1 Sam. 22) would not be repeated by David. Instead, he would unite religious and political forces to his own advantage. Above all, Yahweh would be invisibly but truly present in David's city, for it was commonly understood that where the ark was, so was Yahweh. Disaster and celebration both accompany the ark's transfer to Jerusalem. For his inadvertent physical contact with this sacred object, Uzzah suffered death (2 Sam. 6:7; cf. Num. 4:15). The uncertain David had the ark placed for a season in the home of Obededom. On learning that the ark had been of benefit to its custodian, David transferred it to Jerusalem with spontaneous ceremony and dance.

A careful reading of 2 Samuel 7 reveals the extraordinary esteem in which David was held during his lifetime and long after death. The central figures in the narrative are David and his court prophet, Nathan. David tells Nathan of his desire to construct a temple for Yahweh in which the ark of the covenant might be permanently housed. Initially Nathan approves David's plan, but an oracular experience soon leads him to change his mind. Yahweh reminds Nathan of his divine determination to remain mobile. He gives Nathan a prophetic message that he is expected to convey to the monarch. That message centers on a

Jerusalem: The Old City. This photo, which was taken from the roof of the Convent of the Sisters of Zion, Jerusalem, offers some idea of how the walled Old City, with its ancient buildings and narrow medieval streets, appears today. (Photo by the author.)

play on the word "house" (*bayith*). The Hebrew noun means both "dwelling place" and "family." David is not to create a house, a dwelling place, for Yahweh. Rather, Yahweh will create a house, a family, for David, and it will be eternal.

Therefore, 2 Samuel 7 dares to legitimize the family of David as Yahweh's permanent choice for Jerusalem. While specific kings might be disciplined for their errors, the Davidic dynasty was never to end. The king is portrayed in extremely close relationship with Yahweh, who declares, "I will be his father, and he shall be my son" (v. 14). Kingship is accepted here as a sacred institution, as it is elsewhere in the ancient Near East. The king—be he David or one of his perpetual descendants—is understood as the divine representative.

Certain passages in the Psalms, which are steeped in a royal theology, express a similar view. Thus, in Ps. 2:7 Yahweh tells the newly installed king, "You are my son, today I have begotten you," and in Ps. 89:27 the king is declared Yahweh's first-born. In fact, the royal psalms (for example, Ps. 2, 18, 20, 21, 45, 110, 132) contain a rather well-developed theology of Davidic kingship. That theology highlights Yahweh's eternal choice of the house of David and his desire to dwell permanently in Zion. Accordingly, David's dynasty and his city are both celebrated as inviolable realities. For further remarks about the royal psalms, see Chapter 19.

In 2 Samuel 7 a new interpretation of the covenant departs significantly from the memory of Sinai. The covenant implemented at Mount Sinai (Exod. 19–24) and renewed at Shechem (Josh. 24) clearly obligated Israel to Yahweh. Stipulations governing human life within the covenantal framework demanded dutiful obedience. By contrast, the covenant notion advanced in 2 Samuel 7 emphasizes Yahweh's obligation to the king rather than the king's obligation to Yahweh. As with the Abrahamic covenant, it is Yahweh who primarily commits himself. To be sure, the view of Israelite kingship espoused in 2 Samuel 7 had a profound effect on monarchical stability. With thoughts like these circulating in Jerusalem, the threat of a palace revolt would be minimized.

The Domestic Plight of David

David's domestic plight is brought to light in the superbly written court history (2 Sam. 9–20, 1 Kings 1–2). Here we have an utterly candid photograph of King David. Like Saul, David has to suffer in the later years of his reign when he grasps for what is not truly his. Saul usurped priestly functions (1 Sam. 13) and attempted to rewrite the rules of holy war by sparing Agag (1 Sam. 15). These actions set in motion the forces that led to Saul's undoing. Similarly, when David, who by virtue of his kingship was expected to set an example of righteous conduct, went after Bathsheba, the wife of Uriah the Hittite, the personal tragedies of his later years were spawned. In both instances, it is not blind fate but the divine will that intervenes. Therefore, the court history of David meditates on the Israelite covenant community as it exists under the will and scrutiny of Yahweh. Yet in establishing its theological perspective, the interests of good narrative prose are never sacrificed.

As this remarkable composition opens, David is linked with his predecessor Saul (2 Sam. 9). David invites Saul's surviving son, Mephibosheth, to join his court. Because it was a common practice in the ancient Near East for a new dynasty to exterminate all possible claimants remaining from the old one, Mephibosheth had good reason to distrust the new king. But David assures Mephibosheth of his strong intention to honor the covenant loyalty that had existed between Jonathan and himself. Here David acts shrewdly. This crippled son of Saul is unlikely to cause David harm. But by granting him special consideration, David dutifully honors the memory of Saul and Jonathan. The scene shifts in 2 Samuel 10 with its account of Israel's successful struggle against the Ammonites and their Aramean or Syrian allies. Although the military history that unfolds is significant, its primary function is to set the stage for the serious domestic problems that begin to unfold in the Davidic court.

It all began late one afternoon (11:2). David remained in Jerusalem while his valiant men continued their contest with the Ammonites. Israel besieged Rabbah, the capital of the Ammonites. But David went after Bathsheba. He lay with her and later groped unsuccessfully for a way of attributing Bathsheba's pregnancy to her husband, Uriah. Subsequently, in an act of gross deception, David implemented Uriah's death.

But the wrong did not go unnoticed. Yahweh summoned Nathan to point out to David the seriousness of his behavior (12:1). David's violence would be met and judged by further violence. In David's presence, Nathan resorted to a powerful parable. Ordinarily the biblical parable has the special capacity to tease the conscience of the listener to whom it is addressed. Under optimum conditions, it may induce a change of mind, if not outright repentance. The succinct prophetic indictment comes speedily in 12:7—"You are the man." David acknowledged his sin, and accepted his punishment. Even so, mercy had its way. Though the child that Bathsheba had conceived would die, Yahweh would spare his anointed the same fate. Nevertheless, David would be led to recognize that moral sanctions apply as much to the monarch as they do to any other member of the Israelite community.

Presently, tragic events begin to unfold that center on David's son Absalom (2 Sam. 13–18). As the Absalom narrative begins, our attention is directed to Amnon, another son of David. By feigning sickness, Amnon manages to be alone with his virgin half-sister, Tamar, whom he rapes. By implementing Amnon's death (13:28–29), Absalom avenges this crime against his sister and also disposes of a leading contender to the throne. David, who has participated in adultery and murder, must now witness the same behavior in his own sons. And the abused woman is David's own daughter. Clearly, David accepts the death of Amnon more readily than he does the absence of Absalom, who has now fled into Transjordan for protection (13:39). Knowing that David's heart grieves for Absalom so deeply that the effectiveness of his rule is threatened, Joab instigates Absalom's return to Jerusalem.

But David's household is still in turmoil. Absalom now begins his rebellion against his distraught father (2 Sam. 15). Absalom is well endowed with personal charm and sorely lacking in scruple. Eagerly he embarks on a treacherous course to overthrow David and seize his throne. Selecting Hebron, David's former capital, as his base of operation, Absalom has himself declared king. He advances northward to Jerusalem with a large following, and David must leave his own capital.

As the account of David's flight unfolds (15:13–17:29), Ittai, a leading Philistine from Gath, joins David's cause (15:21). The priests Zadok and Abiathar assist David by stationing themselves in Jerusalem and dispatching word to the refugee monarch (15:29). David's court advisor, Hushai, confounds the wisdom of Ahithophel, who is an ally of Absalom (17:7). Nevertheless, David must hear the curses uttered against him by Shimei, a member of the family of Saul, who delights in David's moment of extreme need (16:7–8).

In the moving prose of 2 Samuel 18 the tragedy is compounded. Because of the poor judgment of a mule and its rider, Joab chances to see Absalom "hanging in an oak" (18:10). Ignoring David's advice to deal gently with Absalom, Joab thrusts three darts into Absalom's heart. David's grief on hearing of Absalom's end is moving indeed: "O my son Absalom, my son, my son Absalom! Would I had died instead of you, O Absalom, my son, my son!" (18:33).

It is a time for mourning, yet in Joab's judgment, the king has paid too little attention to the duties of state (another parallel with Saul's later days). The forceful Joab jolts David back into reality (19:6). The remainder of the court history in 2 Samuel depicts David's attempt to pick up the pieces of his kingdom. As David returns to Jerusalem, a heated debate emerges between the men of Israel and Judah over who should escort the king into his city (19:41–43). The union of Israel and Judah under David was fragile at best, which explains Sheba's revolt against David (20:1–2). Although this assertive Benjaminite was soon arrested, his action was disconcerting. Since Sheba was assassinated by his own people, we cannot take seriously the statement that "all the men of Israel withdrew from David, and followed Sheba" (20:2). Yet we may perceive here a valid expression of northern discontent over David's unwarranted generosity to Absalom's southern supporters. By favoring Judah, the king was ignoring the demands of justice.

The Davidic court history offers a truly provocative theological commentary on human life as it unfolds under the scrutiny of a sovereign deity. Divine will and genuine human freedom are both evident in these chapters, and the two interact mysteriously. Although we have no way of determining the identity of the historian who gave shape to this material, it is clear that he was keenly aware of what took place in David's court. And he refused to accept those events as the products of historical accident. Nor did he interpret the fulfillment of David's destiny—and Absalom's—as an arbitrary affair, unrelated to the personal decisions that constitute a vital part of every human life. In his masterful narrative, the court historian points to the existence of that "tightly drawn chain of causality which links sin with suffering. The insidious allurement of ambition, honour, and achievement enmeshes men in their own guilt and brings them to destruction."[9] The drama involves the thoughts, words, and actions of real human beings. At the same time, there is no point within that drama where one can declare that the deity is absent.

To be sure, the court historian does not believe Yahweh to be present in the court of David in the same sense that Yahweh was present when the Israelite clans encountered him at Sinai. Nevertheless, he believes that all facets of this predominantly domestic history connect with the providential will of God. In no small way, this intriguing blend of divine will and human freedom is responsible for the marked appeal that the court narrative has had for centuries.

Assessing the Reign of David

Perhaps freshest in our minds is the impression that David was an indulgent, indecisive person whose competence as a family patriarch was limited. Not always the master of his emotions, this monarch was almost broken by a turbulent family life. Yet even if David's domestic unhappiness undercut his generally judicious rule over his people, there was much more to the man than that.

The portrait the Hebrew Bible offers of David is multifaceted. David stands at the center of a crucial royal theology in monarchical Israel; later he appears as a key figure in an exilic and postexilic Jewish messianism. And by making no mention whatever of the Bathsheba affair, 1 Chronicles presents David as a virtually faultless monarch. The Chronicler's depiction is more than compensated for, however, by the candid court history of 2 Samuel.

On balance, David's numerous accomplishments were impressive. During his reign, Philistine power was successfully and conclusively suppressed. With his establishment of Jerusalem as the new capital, he astutely settled on neutral territory that enjoyed a commanding position. This move served the cause of monarchy. Under David's rule, such a mingling of Hebrew and Canaanite populations took place that the Israelites must have no longer felt themselves to be strangers in the Land of Promise.

In no small way, the valiant David and Joab, his energetic military commander, gave Palestine to Israel. David's son Solomon inherited a larger kingdom than any king who would later mount the Jerusalem throne. David had the ability to win friends and organize them effectively for the realization of his regal dreams. Impressed by Egypt's example, he set up some longstanding administrative machinery. Men appointed to his court left behind any strong ties with the tribes from which they came. David did not openly oppose the venerable traditions of Israel's earlier tribal confederation; rather, he embraced these traditions for his own ends. This is at no time more evident than when he transferred the ark of the covenant to Jerusalem. Finally, David established sound relationships with foreign powers. In particular, he opened lines of communication with mercantile Phoenicia and thereby laid the groundwork for his son Solomon, who would one day replace him on the throne. Clearly, the ancient and still current opinion that David was Israel's greatest king is not lacking in substance.

NOTES

1. B. Davie Napier, *From Faith to Faith: Essays on Old Testament Literature* (New York: Harper & Row, 1955), pp. 108–109, draws an analogy in terms of function between the Israelite historian and the Greek poet as understood by Aristotle. Both are in search of the essential meaning of specific events.

2. This is the prevailing assessment of 2 Samuel 9–20 and 1 Kings 1–2 among biblical critics. For an alternative analysis that has some following, see R. N. Whybray, *The Succession Narrative: A Study of II Samuel 9–20; I Kings 1 and 2*, Studies in Biblical Theology, 2d series, no. 9 (London: SCM Press, 1968). Whybray holds that these chapters attest more to the working of the human imagination than they do to the assembling of historical facts. He believes that although the "public events" mentioned are basically historical, the work should be classified as a historical novel that attempts to justify Solomon's claim to the throne and that essentially it is political propaganda. Whybray regards its author as a wisdom teacher who was writing at the outset of Solomon's reign.

3. "The Journey of Wen-Amon to Phoenicia," in James B. Pritchard, ed., *Ancient Near Eastern Texts Relating to the Old Testament*, 3d ed. (Princeton, N.J.: Princeton University Press, 1969), pp. 25–29.

4. For a useful introduction to the character and multiple functions of the man Samuel, see William F. Albright, *Samuel and the Beginnings of the Prophetic Movement* (Cincinnati: Hebrew Union College Press, 1961).

5. Isaac Mendelsohn, "Samuel's Denunciation of Kingship in the Light of the Akkadian Documents from Ugarit," *Bulletin of the American Schools of Oriental Research*, no. 143 (October 1956): pp. 17–22.

6. Eugene H. Maly, *The World of David and Solomon* (Englewood Cliffs, N.J.: Prentice-Hall, 1966), p. 50.

7. We agree with John Bright, *A History of Israel*, 2d ed. (Philadelphia: Westminster Press, 1972), p. 194, n. 33, that the events in 2 Samuel 5 are not in chronological order and that David's war against the Philistines must have taken place prior to his seizure of Jerusalem. Even so, we have arranged our remarks to accord with the sequence of 2 Samuel 5.

8. This brief, obscure narrative offers few details concerning how David and his men actually captured Jerusalem. The slightly different report in 1 Chron. 11:4–9 scarcely solves the problem. Several cogent remarks are provided by Hans W. Hertzberg, *I & II Samuel: A Commentary*, trans. J. S. Bowden, The Old Testament Library (Philadelphia: Westminster Press, 1964), pp. 268–269.

9. "The Beginnings of Historical Writing in Ancient Israel," in Gerhard von Rad, *The Problem of the Hexateuch and Other Essays*, trans. E. W. Trueman Dicken (London: Oliver & Boyd, 1966), p. 196. Von Rad's analysis of the Davidic history (pp. 176–204) is packed with illuminating comment.

10

SOLOMONIC RULE AND THE ENSUING SCHISM

In Solomon (ca. 961–922) we meet the third and last monarch to rule a united Israel and Judah. Blessed by a favorable international climate, Solomon sponsored a golden age that brought much attention to himself yet imposed heavy burdens on his subjects. Although he was to maintain and stabilize various administrative policies that David had innovated, his personality contrasted sharply with his father's. In fact, it is fair to say that Saul was a charismatic man; David was a charismatic man with a talent for organization; and Solomon was an organization man, virtually devoid of charismatic potential. Solomon's departure from the Yahwistic norms of the earlier tribal league and his insatiable ambition to enhance his own court were less than subtle.

The international scene was good to Solomon. Egypt was in no position to assert herself in western Asia, and Assyria would thrust no serious problems into Israel's lap for nearly a century. Through commercial alliances and military surveillance, Solomon was usually successful in dominating those lesser nations, which were Israel's more immediate neighbors. He effected his own political and commercial advantage with Egypt through a nameless pharaoh of the Twenty-first Dynasty (1 Kings 3:1). Moreover, he enjoyed useful contacts with the Phoenicians through formal agreements with Hiram I, king of Tyre (5:1, 10–11), and with the Sabeans of Arabia through the queen of Sheba (10:1–13).

Biblical texts to be read prior to and in conjunction with the present chapter: 1 Kings 1:1–12:20. In addition, read the following passages from the Book of Genesis, which (with one exception) are all attributed to the J (Yahwist) stratum: 2:4b–3:24 on man's creation and fall; 4:1–16 on Cain and Abel; 4:17–26, which features Lamech; 6:1–9:29, which preserves a conflated J and P flood tradition; 11:1–9 on the Tower of Babel.

While Solomon may have put things ahead of people, he worked diligently at affairs of state. As an assertive merchant prince, an intent sponsor of ambitious building operations, and an astute leader in Israel's national defense program, Solomon helped Israel to gain international esteem. An unprecedented Israelite intellectual and cultural flowering was also realized under his rule.

This was Israel's golden age. But it proved very costly. At the close of Solomon's oppressive rule, many freedom-loving Israelites were fed up with monarchy. In fact, statements in 1 Kings betray that throughout Solomon's lifetime all did not run smoothly. For example, the sweeping declaration that "Judah and Israel were as many as the sand by the sea; they ate and drank and were happy" (4:20) leads us to suspect that some of Solomon's subjects were disgruntled at his excessive expectation of labor and material goods; it simply protests too much in Solomon's behalf. It is likewise difficult to accept the statement in 9:22 that "of the people of Israel Solomon made no slaves; they were the soldiers, they were his officials, his commanders, his captains, his chariot commanders and his horsemen." This is directly refuted by the witness of 5:13 that "Solomon raised a levy of forced labor out of all Israel" (cf. 12:4). Further, the claim that "King Solomon excelled all the kings of the earth in riches and in wisdom" (10:23) sounds like boastful rhetoric. Solomon's rule may have been long on dazzle and splendor. But if the king had been truly discerning, he would have been aware of the seeds of political destruction that he himself was sowing. In sum, the Solomonic tradition preserved in 1 Kings 1–11 requires careful reading.

THE LITERARY SOURCES
AND EDITING OF 1–2 KINGS

While not all of its material is of concern to us at present, this is perhaps the best occasion for taking note of the sources and Deuteronomic editing of 1–2 Kings. Some sources are explicitly named, whereas others must be inferred. To the first category belong the Book of the Acts of Solomon (1 Kings 11:41), the Book of the Chronicles of the Kings of Israel (1 Kings 14:19),[1] and the Book of the Chronicles of the Kings of Judah (1 Kings 14:29).[2] Among the inferred sources are the Davidic court history, which concludes in 1 Kings 1–2; a cycle of Elijah traditions encompassing 1 Kings 17–19, 21, and 2 Kings 1; the Elisha cycle in 2 Kings 2–13; a document that might aptly be titled "The Acts of Ahab," in 1 Kings 20:1–43 and 22:1–38; and an Isaiah source appearing in the bulk of 2 Kings 18–20 that closely resembles Isaiah 36–39.

The specifically titled sources in 1–2 Kings purport to be annals and archives that were available to the Deuteronomist. Presumably, the Book of the Acts of Solomon was a legendary biographical work designed to celebrate Solomon's wisdom, wealth, and splendor. It was itself a compilation of court annals, temple records, and folk stories that focused on Solomon's ostentatious reign. Typical of this source is the folk tale reported in 1 Kings 3:16–28 in which two harlots dispute ownership of a child. Solomon is presented as exceptionally able in discerning the motives of the contenders. Mention of Solomon's alliance with the reigning Egyptian pharaoh through marriage to his daughter (3:1) and of his dream at Gibeon, where Solomon fervently prayed for the gift of wisdom (3:3–15), are other representative instances of this source. We doubt that the Deuteronomist copied the Book of the Acts of Solomon verbatim, because the idiom and content of 1 Kings 3–11 are rather diffuse. In fact, the Deuteronomist provides his own running commentary (for example, 1 Kings 3:3, 6, 14; 5:3–5; 6:11–13). But most of 1 Kings 3–11 is dependent on this earlier biographical creation with its flattering portrayal of Solomon's building enterprises.

The Book of the Chronicles of the Kings of Israel and its Judean counterpart are now lost folk histories. The Deuteronomist sometimes drew from them to construct his own narrative. Their style and emphases suggest that they were not official palace documents. Both works probably contained various notations on military, building, and commercial undertakings that were attempted by the kings in question. These were popularly written sources to which the ancient reader might refer for more information.

The nameless sources on which 1–2 Kings is dependent require little comment at the moment. In 1 Kings 1–2 we see the final segment of the Davidic court history, whose style and intention we have already studied. The Elijah and Elisha cycles consist of prophetic traditions that had gathered about their respective heroes. The separate historical and legendary components originated and circulated within the prophetic communities founded by these two prophets of the ninth century B.C. We shall examine these traditions more closely in the next chapter. The Ahab source in 1 Kings 20:1–43 and 22:1–38 is a historical document devoted to King Ahab's political and military achievements. This source disrupts the smooth flow of the Elijah cycle. It is preoccupied with Israel's wars with Syria and the heroism of this Israelite king, who died on the battlefield. Finally, an independently conceived body of Isaiah legends occupies much of 2 Kings 18–20. This source concentrates on the last known phases of Isaiah's prophetic activity, which found him at work in a beleaguered Jerusalem that nearly succumbed to Assyrian assault in 701 B.C.

The admittedly varied components in 1–2 Kings are not, however, chaotic. Recurring chronological formulas succeed in arranging them in a sensible historical sequence. They are also integrated by a comprehensive theological perspective. Having no recourse to an absolute chronology, the Deuteronomist linked the kings of Israel and Judah together in synchronistic fashion. As a given king takes the throne in Jerusalem, he is related chronologically to his counterpart in Israel. For example, 1 Kings 15:9 declares that King Asa of Judah began his reign in Jeroboam's twentieth year as king of Israel. Also Israelite monarchs are synchronistically related to their Judean contemporaries (for example, 1 Kings 15:33).

The Deuteronomic edition of 1–2 Kings is likewise the product of stark theological bias. It insists that from among all the existing nations Yahweh chose Israel for purposes of covenantal fellowship, and at the nucleus of this fellowship was the exclusive, zealous worship of Yahweh. Even a quiet toleration of foreign gods is dismissed as loathsome. And since Yahweh is one, so is the legitimate locus of corporate Yahweh worship. Only in the Jerusalem Temple is Israel to come together with the deity in cultic meeting.

Accordingly, Solomon's tragic flaw is assumed to be his willingness to accede to the religious interests of his foreign wives (1 Kings 11). He was unimpressed with the mandate that Israel must worship one God within the precincts of one Jerusalem Temple. Difficulties during the reign of the broad-minded Solomon are directly linked with his syncretic behavior. Other kings are also viewed adversely because they either permitted or encouraged the worship of Yahweh in places other than Jerusalem. By definition, in the era of the Divided Monarchy, no Israelite king could be accepted as virtuous because each sponsored the worship of Yahweh in his capital, which obviously was not in Jerusalem. Only two Judean kings, Hezekiah (2 Kings 18:3–7) and Josiah (2 Kings 22:2), are given an unqualified Deuteronomic endorsement. They are fondly remembered for having closed the doors of second-rate sanctuaries. Five Judean kings receive a modest acclamation that would have been more enthusiastic had they abolished the sacrifices at the high places.[3]

The Deuteronomic doctrine of retribution is also conspicuous in 1–2 Kings. Solomon is a case in point. His far-flung commercial enterprises, concrete manifestations of wisdom, and interest in the Jerusalem Temple are all viewed favorably. But the deplorable aspects of his reign are summed up in 1 Kings 11, as if to suggest that they all blossomed in Solomon's last years. Solomon's tolerant attitude toward his wives' foreign deities evokes Yahweh's wrath. Consequently, Solomon must lose the outermost fringes of his land to rival monarchs. Hadad the Edomite and Rezon of Damascus are cited as adversaries whom Yahweh raised up against Solomon (11:14, 23). Actually, Hadad began to assert himself as soon as he had heard that David and Joab were dead, and thus at an early stage in Solomon's rule (11:21). Nevertheless, this historical fact in no way moved the Deuteronomist from his firm theological position that during the dark later phase in his reign, Solomon rebelled against the deity and was given his just deserts. Moreover, through the crucial disclosure of the prophet Ahijah, Jeroboam's impending opposition against Solomon and his son is legitimized (11:31–39). Yet as rulers of the northern kingdom of Israel, Jeroboam and his successors are all upbraided for having permitted the worship of Yahweh in cities other than Jerusalem. Despite his crass reductionism, which we are liable to find offensive, the Deuteronomist insists that Yahweh alone is sovereign and worthy of the thoughtful allegiance of his covenant people and their kings.

As a final literary consideration, what date should be assigned to the editing of 1–2 Kings? The Deuteronomist probably completed his interpretive editing shortly before the death of the righteous Josiah in 609 B.C. Since the Deuteronomist firmly endorses the notion of a single sanctuary, it is likely that he worked after 622, the time at which Josiah intensified his religious reform that culminated in restricting cultic meeting to Jerusalem. The prediction that Josiah would one day be gathered to his grave in peace (2 Kings 22:20) suggests that a first Deuteronomic edition of Kings emerged in Josiah's lifetime. Actually, Josiah met a violent death in battle against Pharaoh Necho at Megiddo. The pragmatic Deuteronomist was convinced that national prosperity was contingent on an unwavering obedience to Yahweh's covenant expectations. And he wished his readers to learn that lesson well. This first edition of 1–2 Kings probably terminated at 2 Kings 23:25a, where Josiah is lavishly praised as a model of piety but not yet reported deceased. Because the last dated event in the book (2 Kings 25:27) relates to the year 561, we may infer that a second edition, which extended the history by approximately half a century, emerged in about 550. This editing of Kings by another member of the Deuteronomic school took place after Jerusalem's destruction in 587 and prior to its renewal, which was set in motion by Cyrus' edict in 538 (Ezra 1:2–4). The second edition of Kings therefore alludes to the harsh reality of Babylonian exile (for example, see 1 Kings 8:46–53; 9:6–9; 2 Kings 22:16–17). It also regards the fall of Jerusalem as theologically justifiable, and expresses the faint hope that God's people will witness a brighter future.

SOLOMON'S CONQUEST
OF THE THRONE

With the Davidic court history renewed in 1 Kings 1–2, it is evident that several years have intervened. David has aged and literally cooled off. Hence, the ravishing Abishag was brought in as David's nurse. David's physical weakness in his old age provided the occasion for court intrigue. The problem of who should reign was compounded by the fact that David had seventeen sons (2 Sam. 3:2–5; 5:14–16).

Chronologically, Solomon stood in an unimpressive tenth position. Adonijah, David's fourth son, coveted the throne. Born next after the now deceased Absalom, Adonijah may have once been the king's choice. Adonijah was supported by the military commander Joab and the priest Abiathar, who had both been loyal to David. But Solomon was the pampered favorite of an active party at court consisting of his mother, Bathsheba; a royal guard named Benaiah; the priest Zadok; and the prophet Nathan. Upon learning that Adonijah had had himself declared king at the sacred spring of En-rogel southeast of Jerusalem, Bathsheba and Nathan moved quickly to David's bedside. They pressed that Solomon be formally acclaimed his successor. David complied, and soon Solomon was publicly anointed by Zadok at the Gihon spring.

Following David's death, Solomon worked swiftly to strengthen his position as king. First, Adonijah put himself into a most vulnerable position by petitioning Solomon to let him marry Abishag, David's nurse. Here indeed was evidence that Adonijah had not yet abandoned his claim to the throne. Solomon recognized the implications of this request and took decisive action. He ordered that Adonijah be executed (1 Kings 2:25). Another enemy of Solomon, the priest Abiathar, was spared because of his previous support of David. Even so, he was sent home to Anathoth (2:26). Joab now rushed to seek asylum at the altar. At Solomon's command, he was struck down in sacred territory. According to 1 Kings 2:5–6, 32–33, the aged David had actually commanded Joab's assassination as a way of avenging Joab's murder of Abner and Amasa. Since these killings inevitably cast their shadow on David's innocence, perhaps this notation is not entirely fictional.[4] Shimei, the Saulide who had cursed David during his flight from Absalom (2 Sam. 16:5–8), was confined to Jerusalem, apparently so that he could be carefully watched. Shimei had little choice but to agree to these terms. But three years later Solomon ordered his execution after learning that Shimei had taken it upon himself to leave and return to Jerusalem at will (1 Kings 2:46).

It is remarkable that Solomon could kill so many of his opponents without inciting rebellion from the Israelite rank and file. Perhaps he moved so quickly that such formidable opposition as might emerge lacked sufficient time to organize. The court history ends with the matter-of-fact statement, "So the kingdom was established in the hand of Solomon" (2:46b). Solomon had indeed taken over.

SOLOMON'S ADMINISTRATION OF THE EMPIRE

As the energetic chief administrator of a large kingdom that had come of age, Solomon was able to demonstrate his unusual capacities as an organization man. Each aspect of his administration merits some consideration.

Provincial Reorganization

To exert tighter control over his kingdom, Solomon engaged in a provincial reorganization that increased the taxation as well as the discontent of his subjects. He reorganized the nation into twelve administrative districts and placed one officer in charge of each (1 Kings 4:7–19). In general, this redistricting played havoc with previously established tribal boundaries; it meant that personal loyalty to the Jerusalem court would become more likely than loyalty to tribal history. Such gerrymandering helped Solomon to exercise greater authority over his subjects. Each of the districts was to supply the provisions of the Jerusalem court for an entire month. The excessive quota set by 4:22–23 would easily

Early Iron Age Storage Jar at Tell Gezer. Shown in its original position is a large storage jar of the tenth century B.C. It was discovered at Gezer in the Solomonic gateway complex during the 1968 season of excavation. Such jars are often over 2 feet in height. (Photo by the author.)

have fed some five thousand persons. If this enhanced the status of the Jerusalem court, it also imposed much work on native Israelites.

Solomon's reorganization affected manpower as well as material provisions. Enormous building projects required much brawn. David exacted compulsory labor from the peoples whom he conquered (2 Sam. 12:31), and so did Solomon. When this source proved insufficient in supporting his extravagance, Solomon instituted the corvée. He levied labor gangs that were dispatched northward into Lebanon to obtain the wood that his building program demanded (1 Kings 5:13–14). In addition, slaves tended the copper mines along the Jordan valley and the Araba. We cannot be sure of the extent to which the labor gangs included freeborn Israelite draftees. Although native Israelites were probably not forced into the copper mines, they may have been ordered into Lebanon or assigned specific building tasks in Jerusalem. The thesis that Solomon exploited some Israelites in this manner is best supported by the Israelite lynching of Adoram (Adoniram), who was in charge of Solomon's forced labor (1 Kings 12:18). The corvée would have given ample motive; indeed, it was "Israel's chief complaint against Solomon."[5]

Military Affairs

Solomon's chief attempts at military intensification were the reinforcement of strategic cities in his kingdom and the exploitation of the war chariot. In addition to strengthening Jerusalem, Solomon established a band of military centers along the nation's perimeter (1 Kings 9:15–19). Having fortified Hazor, Megiddo, Gezer, Beth-horon, Baalath, and Tamar, Solomon was equipped with a war machine that might promptly repel military attacks from the north, west, and south. Moreover, he recognized that now was the time to appropriate the chariot for use in Israel's military. Though Solomon is said to have acquired 1,400 chariots and 12,000 horsemen (10:26), archaeological efforts have not as yet been able to uncover his chariot installations (9:19).[6] Of course, this does not mean that some did not once exist. While Solomon himself did not take to the battlefield, he seems to have known how to handle the hardware of war.

Foreign Affairs

Solomon pursued a reasonably friendly course with foreign powers who were potential competitors. Frequently he entered into international alliances. That these were typically confirmed by marriage might explain the reputed extensiveness of Solomon's harem (1 Kings 11:1–3). Of special interest is his marriage to the daughter of an unknown pharaoh of the Twenty-first Dynasty (3:1; 7:8).[7] As the dowry Solomon received the Canaanite city of Gezer, which was currently in Egypt's possession (9:16–17). His most useful alliance was with Tyre and its Phoenician king, Hiram I. Phoenicia's maritime trade and building techniques were of great help to Israel.

Commerce and Industry

Solomon's numerous commercial and industrial activities are alluded to in 1 Kings 10. Influenced by the example of Phoenicia, Solomon sought to conquer the seas with a trade program of his own. With the help of Phoenician shipbuilders and sailors, he established an important seaport at Ezion-geber on the Gulf of Aqaba (10:22; 9:26–28). Solomon also engaged in caravan trade with the Sabeans of Arabia. Because Solomon's kingdom stood at the northern terminus of the Sabean trade routes, simple self-interest may have led the queen of Sheba to visit Solomon (10:1–13). The king also became an effective middleman in the horse and chariot business (10:28–29). He imported horses from the northern breeding center of Cilicia (biblical Kue) and wooden chariots from Egypt. To Solomon's distinct advantage, the northern Syrians depended on Israel for chariots, and the southern Egyptians looked to Israel for horses. His was a highly effective monopoly. Solomon also exploited the copper resources in the Jordan river valley and in the Araba to the south (7:45–46).

The Building Program

Archaeological evidence at Beth-shan, Beth-shemesh, Gezer, Hazor, and Megiddo reveals that Solomon sponsored a rigorous building program.[8] Gezer, Hazor, and Megiddo all had grandiose four-entry-way gate systems that were virtually identical. Many of Solomon's building operations were in Jerusalem. There he sponsored the construction of a palace that took thirteen years to complete (1 Kings 7:1). Solomon's "House of the Forest of Lebanon" (7:2) was presumably built as an armory (see Isa. 22:8). His own residence was in another portion of the court complex, as was the private house for Pharaoh's daughter (1 Kings 7:8). But the most important edifice built under Solomon's sponsorship was the Jerusalem Temple.

The Temple was of such significance to the continuing life and religion of ancient Israel that it is not surprising that the Deuteronomist devoted all of 1 Kings 5–8 to an account of its construction and dedication. Today it is not possible for a trained archaeologist to uncover the tenth-century Solomonic Temple, because above it lies the Moslem sanctuary of Haram esh-Sherif, with its famed and ornate Dome of the Rock. Nevertheless, the biblical account instructs us that Solomon's temple was thoroughly Phoenician in construction. While Israel fur-

Solomonic Gateway at Tell Gezer. Ancient cities were insecure without walls, and the most vulnerable part of a city wall was understandably its entrance. The excavated Solomonic gate system at Gezer, whose entrance is shown above, brought to light two guard rooms and four pairs of piers. These piers were once part of massive stone walls behind which soldiers defended the city in times of enemy attack. (Photo by the author.)

nished a substantial labor force, King Hiram of Tyre supplied the architects, contractors, carpenters, and masons who planned and directed the work (1 Kings 5).

Most helpful in facilitating an understanding of Solomon's temple is the eighth-century temple uncovered at Tell Tainat in northern Syria. Though this temple is smaller than Solomon's (as described in 1 Kings 6), it is of Phoenician design and is rectangular in shape. It has three rooms arranged similarly to those of the Jerusalem Temple. There is the outer court with its two exterior columns, a large main hall, and a flight of steps entering into the innermost holy of holies. Like the windows in Solomon's temple, those at the Tell Tainat temple were located just beneath the ceiling.

Solomon's temple boasted considerable equipment inside and out. Two skillfully constructed free-standing pillars, named Jachin and Boaz, flanked the main entrance (7:21). They seem to have had either a mystical or a symbolic significance. They were over 37 feet high and may have represented the cosmos or twin mountains between which the sun rose in the morning. Or they may have served as fire altars. Another conspicuous object was the Molten Sea, a huge copper bowl

The Dome of the Rock. Situated in the Old City of Jerusalem, the Dome of the Rock marks the site where tradition says that Abraham bound Isaac for sacrifice to the deity (Gen. 22) and Mohammed ascended to heaven. This mosque was built by the Caliph Marwan in the seventh century of the Christian era. The sacred rock sheltered by the golden dome lies at the center of Mount Moriah, which, according to 2 Chron. 3:1, was also the site of the Solomonic temple. (Courtesy of the Israel Government Tourist Office, Chicago.)

15 feet in diameter and more than 7 feet high. It was located at one side of the Temple courtyard and rested on the backs of 12 oxen (7:23–26). The Chronicler understood that this was where the priests washed (2 Chron. 4:6). But since its rim stood 10 feet above the pavement, we may wonder just how the priests performed their ablutions. Perhaps the Molten Sea had some mythological connection with the Mesopotamian *apsû* (subterranean fresh water), from which all life and fertility were thought to originate.

Obviously the construction of the Temple and its furnishings was not directly informed by the concerns of traditional Israelite religion. Those who planned and directed the work of temple building were not followers of Yahweh. A temple designed by non-Israelites might indeed influence the developing religion of the Israelites who worshiped there. Of course, the popularity of Doric and Ionic pillars in American church architecture in times past cannot be interpreted as an indication that Christianity was selling out to certain Greek deities. Some art forms

The Molten Sea Outside Solomon's Temple. This photo and
the two that follow show portions of a careful scale model
reconstruction (1950). Pictured here is the Molten Sea.
Although the purpose of this gigantic copper bowl is not
precisely known, its cosmic significance is indeed probable.
(The Howland-Garber Model Reconstruction of Solomon's
Temple.)

simply give pleasure to the eye. Even so, the Israelites who worshiped
in Solomon's temple might easily have been susceptible to certain influences of Canaanite religion transmitted by this Phoenician edifice. Fertility motifs on the Temple walls, which were covered with gold leaf,
would scarcely have recalled to the Israelite mind the austere God of
Sinai who had brought the Hebrews into Canaan. To the extent that the
Jerusalem Temple existed as Solomon's dynastic chapel, indigenous
Israelite religion might not have been radically threatened. But that is
not the whole story. From the outset, Solomon's temple was the resting
place of the sacred ark of the covenant and a locus of formalistic Yahweh worship that touched the lives of many. Consequently, Yahweh's
own attachment to this Phoenician building must have been a serious
concern to more than one loyal Yahwist.[9]

With its account of the Temple's dedication, 1 Kings 8 attempts to
bring the comforting assertion, "The Lord is in his holy Temple," into
sharp focus. Solomon first had the ark placed in the Temple under the
protective wings of the cherubim. Thereupon the cloud and glory of
Yahweh filled the sacred space of the Temple (v. 11). Solomon then
addressed the people who had assembled for this momentous occasion
(vv. 12–21). Heavy Deuteronomic editing frustrates our knowledge of

The Paneling Inside Solomon's Temple. This scene was repeatedly depicted in gilded wood carving throughout the Temple interior (see 1 Kings 6:29). A palm tree stands between a pair of cherubim who are facing one another. In the ancient Near East cherubim were viewed as guardians of sacral precincts. Due to its longevity and large yield of fruit, the palm tree was regarded as the tree of life. (The Howland-Garber Model Reconstruction of Solomon's Temple.)

the extent to which these were Solomon's sentiments. In any case, the religious perspective set forth in 1 Kings 8 had come into being by about 600 B.C. and may even trace back to Solomon's time. Most crucial here is v. 12, which insists that although Yahweh has prominently fixed the sun in the heavens, he himself elects to dwell in darkness. The inner room of the Temple had no windows. Therefore, it offered a suitable environment for the ark, which had consistently been quite closely associated with Yahweh himself.

With formal installation of the ark in Solomon's temple, it appears that Yahweh would be understood as less active and more intimately identified with one place. Nevertheless, the sovereignty of Israel's deity was not subverted. A sharp distinction is drawn between Yahweh and the sun (8:12). Whereas other nations reverently adore the sun, Israel worships the maker of the sun. Moreover, Solomon's prayer stoutly defends Yahweh's omnipresence: "Behold, heaven and the highest heaven cannot contain thee; how much less this house which I have built!" (8:27). Even the entire celestial sphere is considered inadequate as a dwelling place for the incomparable Yahweh. Hence, the Temple

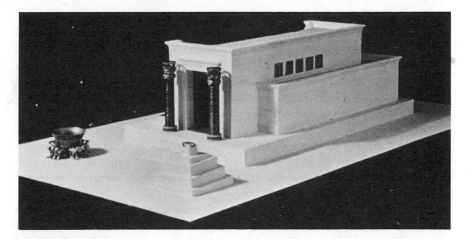

King Solomon's Temple. Here is a view of the Temple from the northeast. Note the Molten Sea, the altar for burnt offerings, and the two freestanding pillars flanking the Temple entrance. (The Howland-Garber Model Reconstruction of Solomon's Temple.)

becomes the place where Yahweh's name resides. This edifice is Yahweh's concession to human need. It gives the Israelite assurance that God will hear his fervent prayer. Since to the ancient Hebrew an essential component of the deity was his name, to say that Yahweh's name was in the Temple was to declare that Yahweh was more than incidentally present. But the Temple was not to be interpreted as Yahweh's tomb. Therefore, if the Temple construction flirted with paganism, the dedication ceremonies (as conveyed by the Deuteronomist) respected the authentic need of a pure Yahwistic religion to affirm God's nearness and uniqueness.

ISRAEL'S CULTURAL ACHIEVEMENT UNDER SOLOMON

Israel's golden age proved a most auspicious era for the development of intellectual and cultural talent, especially in the realm of literature. Historical writing, with its marked interest in the court, now began to dominate earlier legendary materials. David and Solomon became the focal points of historical exposition. For example, the manifestly honest account of David's rise to power (2 Sam. 1–8) and the candid court history of David (2 Sam. 9–20, 1 Kings 1–2) were most likely written in the environs of the Jerusalem court during the reign of Solomon.

It is also likely that during this vibrant age the Yahwist was at work selecting from various well-established traditions in order to shape his masterful literary epic (J). We have already reviewed representative portions of the Yahwist's epic that portray Yahweh's promises to and his dealings with Israel. Later in this chapter we shall examine the universal backdrop (portions of Gen. 2–11) of the give and take between God and man that so profoundly concerned the Yahwist. A deft literary architect and sensitive theologian, the Yahwist symbolizes the intellectual capacity of the Solomonic era at its best.

During Solomon's rule, Israel pursued friendly contacts with other cultures. Citizens of the United Monarchy who were so inclined seized the moment to compose music, formulate sagacious proverbs, and, to a lesser extent, participate in the graphic arts. Their achievements reflected a certain sophistication.

Israel was to become aware of her cultural potential, especially within the Solomonic wisdom movement. Ancient Hebrew tradition has generously credited Solomon with great learning and insight. He is said to have been the author of three canonical wisdom books—Proverbs, Ecclesiastes, and the Song of Songs. Actually, he may have authored only a small fraction of Proverbs. Ecclesiastes and the Song of Songs certainly postdate the Solomonic era. Even so, Solomon seems to have been an early supporter of an Israelite wisdom movement, which maintained that man with his powers of observation and reason could learn much from the diverse realms of nature and human experience. (On the question of Solomonic authorship and for a fuller definition of Israel's wisdom movement, see Chapter 20.) Frequent contact with Egypt, where sapiential activity was especially pronounced, stimulated Solomon's wisdom interests. In 1 Kings 4:31 we find the immodest claim that Solomon "was wiser than all other men." He is said to have uttered 3,000 proverbs and composed 1,005 songs, and to have offered his views on such natural subjects as trees, beasts, birds, reptiles, and fish (4:32–33).

Perhaps Solomon did formulate his own views of life. Yet there is in 1 Kings too much talk about Solomon's great wisdom for us to accept it all as fact. The narrative about the dispute of the two harlots over a child (1 Kings 3:16–28) and Solomon's brilliance in rising to the occasion has all the markings of a popular Oriental tale that might have been appropriated for the greater glory of Solomon. The monarch's humble prayer that Yahweh grant him wisdom (1 Kings 3:7–9) meshes poorly with the portrayal in 1 Kings 2 of the ruthless Solomon who sets in motion the purges that enable him to rule Israel without interference. Though Solomon may have sponsored an internationally inspired wisdom movement, we suspect that he did not lead the professional sages by personal example. It is impossible to say to what extent the rank and file were influenced by sapiential concerns. It appears, however, that both courtly and commercial needs stimulated an enthusiasm for writing.

Several writing schools may have existed in Solomon's day. One aspect of their work is attested in the Gezer Calendar, which was discovered in 1908 at Gezer in the Shephelah. This soft limestone plaque is 4 1/4 inches long, 2 3/4 inches wide, and 5/8 inches thick. Its subject is an agricultural ditty. Because repeated letters assume different forms and the calendar shows signs that it was constantly scraped to clear the surface for new inscriptions, it is thought to have been a schoolboy's exercise tablet.

The calendar reads as follows:

> His two months are (olive) harvest,
>   His two months are planting (grain),
>   His two months are late planting;
> His month is hoeing up of flax,
>   His month is harvest of barley,
>   His month is harvest and *feasting;*
> His two months are vine-tending,
>   His month is summer fruit.[10]

By opening with mention of the olive harvest, the Gezer Calendar affirms a year that begins with a two-month season (mid-September to mid-November). It ends with the year's final month (mid-August to mid-September), when figs, grapes, and pomegranates could all be gathered. The Gezer Calendar has a threefold significance. It provides a good description of the agricultural year in ancient Israel. Various farming activities are arranged according to the year's twelve months. The principal agricultural tasks rather than the names of the months are listed. It is also an example of the Hebrew language, which was in vogue during the Solomonic era. On paleographic grounds, it is ordinarily dated to ca. 925 B.C. And this is the oldest significant Israelite inscription available. In its modest way, this tablet is one more token of the Israelite culture that flourished under Solomon.

THE YAHWIST AND HIS
REFLECTIVE UNIVERSALISM

That Israelite genius whom we refer to as the Yahwist shared with many of his contemporaries a strong interest in reflecting at length on the ways of God, man, and society.[11] In contrast to her position in earlier decades, Israel's position in the Land of Promise seemed remarkably secure. The crucial divine word to Abraham had been gloriously fulfilled. His offspring were many, and truly they possessed the land that Abraham had earlier traversed. It was unthinkable that the deity would abandon his chosen people in the days ahead. Yahweh's experiment with Israel had succeeded, and surely things would continue to prosper.

But was it enough for Israel to rest in the thought that she had come of age? While the Yahwist did not wish to undermine the confidence of his peers, he was convinced that life's greatest problems and blessings were not likely to be grasped by those who pursued a course of easy optimism. True, Yahweh had done great things for Israel. But the larger dimensions of his redemptive design also demanded serious reflection. The question, "What is God's way with the world at large?" had to be raised. The Yahwist therefore believed that the deity's dealings with Israel were all the more apparent when viewed in the light of universal human origins. In much of Genesis 2–11 we encounter the Yahwist's reflections on these matters.[12] This universal thinker affirmed that at the beginning of time, the nation Israel was neither a historical reality nor a part of the divine purpose. Rather, God was intimately involved in the creation of the world and in the establishment of the human family, which would (so to speak) live on his estate. Life itself was a precious gift shaped by God's compelling word as it interacted with the world. At base the Yahwist was a creative theologian who maintained that what had originally been created as beautiful and good had in time become corrupt. He held that because man's assertiveness repeatedly disrupted his relationship with God as well as with his neighbor, man stood in dire need of God's saving action. And that action was to be realized when Yahweh summoned Abraham (Gen. 12:1–7). That call had the dual function of interpreting the total primeval narrative of Genesis 2–11 and introducing the patriarchal traditions in Genesis 12–50.

The Yahwist chose myth as the vehicle for communicating the truth he felt compelled to convey. But to label his work in Genesis 2–11 "myth" is not to imply that it is inferior. Let us be clear as to what we mean by myth.[13] Certainly myth is not the creation of a man who is incapable of formulating abstract ideas. Rather, myth is a highly figurative way of speaking that usually offers profound commentary on reality. The myths of ancient Near Eastern man were not geared to the purely imaginary. In his mythology he voiced serious convictions about his immediate environment. The myths of ancient man centered around life's most important moments—procreation, birth, and death. In his mythology, ancient man tried to interpret the real in terms of the ideal, to view isolated happenings as continuous situations. Thus, no sharp distinction is made between dreams, hallucinations, and ordinary vision. Moreover, space and time are not viewed abstractly; they are experienced.

The monotheistic and historical inclinations of ancient Israel prevented her from duplicating uncritically the myths of her neighbors. Though ancient Mesopotamian mythology consisted of elaborate stories involving many scheming deities, Israel could not accept this as a definitive myth pattern for herself. Yet, as we shall see, she could appropriate certain elements from the mythology of her neighbors and apply them in her own way.

The Yahwist's Narrative of the Creation and the Fall

With its primary focus on human origins, Gen. 2:4b–3:24 conveys the Yahwist's understanding of man's creaturehood and his tendency to act as God's number one rebel. It is not a self-contained creation account, because man's creation and his "fall" are regarded as closely linked. Nor is the Yahwist concerned with telling his readers precisely how creation took place. To the Yahwist and to the community of faith of which he was a member, it was obvious that the world had been created by the deity. Therefore, the analytical question, "How did it happen?" is upstaged by the proclamation of faith that it happened. The real issue, then, is to find out what it means to belong to creation.[14]

Although the Yahwist wastes little energy in establishing a precise creation sequence and is unconcerned about the amount of time involved, his narrative of the deity at work in the act of creation alludes to five different happenings: primeval irrigation, the creation of man, the establishment of plant life, the creation of animal life, and the creation of woman.

Primeval irrigation refers to the mist that emerges from the earth and waters "the whole face of the ground" (2:6). No plant may appear until fresh water falls on the land of paradise. Earth's crusty soil is the given element. The Yahwist does not assert that creation originated out of nothing. Rather, he understands that some raw material was in existence prior to the act of creation. This assumption was advanced earlier in the magnificent creation story *Enūma elish*, which is a product of ancient Babylonian reflection. There the body of Tiamat, the monster goddess of chaotic depths, is split by the triumphant god Marduk to form the earth below and the firmament above.[15] The earliest Hebraic witness to creation out of nothing appears in the Book of 2 Maccabees, which is from the first century B.C. There a widow instructs the youngest of her seven sons, who is about to join his six brothers in death at the hand of executioners, "Look at the heaven and the earth and see everything that is in them, and recognize that God did not make them out of things that existed" (7:28).[16]

Man is created from dust (Gen. 2:7). The ground is the raw material that will go into the making of man, and the deity gives the dust a definite shape. For man to exist at all, he must also receive breath from God. The resulting selfhood of man consists of the remarkable union of earthly body and divine breath. Here the text does not lead us to say, "Now man has a soul," but rather, "Now man is a soul." In Israelite thought, any decrease in vitality, be it momentary despondency or actual death, was expressed as a loss of breath. Man is therefore viewed here and elsewhere in the Old Testament as an integrated "living being," a psychophysical whole.[17]

The Yahwist also shows great interest in the creation of plant life in the garden. Two trees are mentioned in 2:9. One is the source of immortality; the other the source of wisdom. Presumably the original form of the Yahwist's story made special mention of a single tree— namely, the tree of the knowledge of good and evil from which man was not permitted to eat. The tree of life is not mentioned again until Gen. 3:22, after the temptation event has been narrated. Possibly it reflects another tradition that has been linked to the original.

The divine prohibition is absolutely central to the story. An obvious tension now enters human life. The prohibition is not intended to deprive man of the fulfillment of basic needs. Rather, through this limitation, God holds out to man the possibility of obedience, a possibility that places eternity within his reach. In this command, God shows his willingness to take man seriously as his partner. Man is placed in the garden as a servant (2:15). The garden belongs to God, not to man. The human condition prior to the fall involves meaningful work. The curse of Yahweh in Gen. 3:17–19 simply makes it more difficult for man to discharge his tasks.

A fourth concern is the creation of animal life, which again involves a physical engagement of the deity. Adam names the animals (2:19). Presumably, the Yahwist held the naïve belief that man named something an elephant when he decided that the animal in question looked more like an elephant than anything else that had previously passed his way. Nevertheless, the naming is taken seriously, for it is assumed that the name renders the essence of what is being named. By permitting man to name the animals, Yahweh assigns him a vital role in the creation process.

And finally, God creates woman out of man, because of man's great loneliness. Recognizing that companionship with the animals cannot answer man's deepest need, the deity resolves to improve a less than perfect situation. He has "deep sleep" overtake man (2:21). The Yahwist holds that "man cannot perceive God 'in the act,' cannot observe his miracles in their genesis; he can revere God's creativity only as an actually accomplished fact."[18] When Yahweh brings the woman to him, man's spontaneous celebration of her is splendidly expressed in poetry (2:23).

The Yahwist offers us a charming creation story, told in concrete, earthy language. The God-man-nature relationship affirmed here is remarkably direct. Yahweh and man move with ease on Eden's soil. Neither Yahweh's immediate contact with physical life nor man's encounter with Yahweh is viewed with alarm. What happens seems entirely natural. Nevertheless, man's existence in the garden is viewed quite soberly. He lives there under the divine order that certain fruit is not to be eaten. Yet even the allusion to the death sentence (2:17) is not intended to stifle human existence. The Yahwist is assuming that human potential and authentic freedom are best realized within the structure of finite mortal existence. Man is most fully himself, says the Yahwist, when he accepts his servant status and acknowledges the sovereignty of his creator.

The Yahwist's meditation on creation also has an etiological function (2:24). It explains the origin of human sexual drive. The Yahwist believes that a person's strong attraction to the opposite sex has existed from time immemorial. Sexual desire is presented without embarrassment as a divinely given impulse.

But the Yahwist tries to speak jointly of the creation and the fall, for the human condition itself is of greatest interest to him. He freely acknowledges that from the first, man tried to move beyond the limitations that the creator deity placed on human life. Here the Yahwist is far more concerned with the rebellious aspect of contemporary human existence than he is with original sin. Even so, he looks upon the history of man as the history of disobedience. Genesis 3 focuses on the rebellion of the first couple, who had made light of the divine command. Having pushed themselves beyond the divinely prescribed limits, they must soon be judged and expelled.

The Yahwist's penetrating account of the fall shows the radical change of circumstance experienced by the first couple as harmony and innocence give way to condemnation and alienation. The narrative opens with mention of the serpent. Less diabolical than clever, this animal lures the woman toward new avenues of experience in order to undermine her confidence in God's goodness (3:1). The serpent induces the woman to renounce her human condition, which was given so that she might grasp for divinity. In doing so, the radical distinction between creature and creator can be overcome, and dependence on self can swiftly usurp the place once held by childlike faith. The knowledge of "good and evil" sought here (3:5) is the colorful Hebrew counterpart to our saying, "knowing all things." But when the couple bite into the fruit, divine status is not what they gain (3:6–7).

Between this report of human misconduct and the divine pronouncement of various curses is 3:8–13. Here man feels his alienation from God and from woman. In a vividly anthropomorphic manner, Yahweh walks through the garden in fervent search of man. When discovered and called to account by the deity, he tries to justify his action. Disharmony, however, is all too evident. Adam blames the woman and even indirectly criticizes Yahweh for having created her as his gift to man (3:12). Whereupon she blames the serpent. Misguided human conduct is pawned off as an apparent good. In this instance, the self-justification is fervent and abortive. Here Thomas Mann's assessment of myth seems highly appropriate: "For it *is*, always *is*, however much we may say It was."[19]

Penalties are now issued through Yahweh's curse. The serpent is to experience hopeless enmity with mankind. Moreover, he is condemned to crawl on his belly—an etiological explanation of why serpents crawl rather than walk as other beasts. Because of her transgression, woman will suffer extraordinary pain during childbirth—the Yahwist's answer to another etiological question. Strictly speaking, it is the ground, not man himself, that is cursed, yet the distinction between the ground and man is not clear-cut. Hence, the Yahwist addresses himself to why man must labor for a living. The answer suggested is that it has always been that way since man first tried unsuccessfully to play God.

Toward the end of the narrative, Adam and Eve are banished from the garden (3:22–24) lest the fruit of "the tree of life" be tasted next. Presumably man will continue to transcend the limitations of his humanity unless Yahweh takes decisive action by placing the cherubim and flaming sword at the edge of the garden. In ancient Near Eastern practice cherubim functioned as guardians of sacred temples. The flaming sword was further assurance that the couple would not reenter paradise. Man now has no choice but to confront the hostile world, and in the uncertain time ahead his communion with the deity will become less intimate. However, divine grace as well as divine judgment are present. The concerned deity clothes the couple with animal skins, which prove vastly superior to fig leaves (3:21). The primordial pair is the object of Yahweh's care as well as his judgment. In effect, Yahweh is saying "Nevertheless!" The sobered couple is not abandoned.

This account of human rebellion is superbly drawn. In it, the Yahwist expresses his understanding that from the beginning of time, man reached out for what was prohibited and thereby lost his innocence and acquired feelings of shame. This shame induced in the first man an insecurity about his naked state, yet the shame is not related to sex. It is the direct outcome of the bitter realization that he has transgressed that prohibition, "Thou shalt not," whereby God had first taken him with profound seriousness. The Yahwist is reflecting on the assertiveness within man that finds him continually overstepping the limits prescribed for him by God. Therefore, he goes on record to say that a proper understanding of man's origins and innately problematic behavior must of necessity take into account his creation and fall.

The Cain and Abel Tradition

In meditating on the human condition, the Yahwist concludes that the outrageous act of the couple in the garden was only the beginning of man's rebellion against his Maker. As his story progresses, the Yahwist reveals the steady decline of the human family. In his judgment, the primordial era, which began with Adam and terminated with Yahweh's decisive summons of Abraham, was marked by man's open defiance of the deity. Primordial men were repeatedly caught in the act of trying to become minor gods. As this universalistic thinker traces the decline of the human family through several mythological episodes, he provides answers to a variety of searching questions: Why was God more eager to receive the shepherd's offering than the farmer's? Who was the world's first murderer? Why and how did the ancient destructive flood come about? Why are the Canaanites morally degenerate? Why do men speak many different languages? With great skill the Yahwist subordinated such considerations to his theological design of portraying the gradual deterioration of mankind and the determination of the offended deity to dispense justice and mercy.

The worsening human condition is first portrayed by the Yahwist through his story of Cain and Abel (Gen. 4:1–16). In contrast to the disobedience of Adam and Eve, rebellion now takes the form of fraternal discord. The spontaneous worship practices of two brothers leads to resentment and envy in one of the brothers and ultimately to the world's first murder. Though this is a meditation on the age-old conflict between a seminomadic and an agrarian life style, the Yahwist personalizes the problem in two characters, Cain and Abel, the sons of the first couple.[20]

Without invitation from the deity, both brothers bring their offerings. Cain's vegetables are found unacceptable, whereas Abel's flocks win Yahweh's favor. Is the narrator indicating that the occupation of shepherd is superior to that of farmer? Since the Yahwist accepts Adam as a legitimate gardener (2:15), such an interpretation is unlikely. Perhaps in analogy with Exod. 33:19, Yahweh arbitrarily extends grace to one person and not to another. This, however, does not accord with the impact of the Yahwist's work in Genesis 2–11, which affirms the deity's concern for all mankind. Hence, Abel's success with the deity may have resulted from having drawn on "the firstlings of his flock and of their fat portions" (4:4). He selected the sacrifice with care. Cain tended to his cultic affairs in a more perfunctory way, bringing undifferentiated "fruit of the ground" (4:3).

Yahweh tells the disappointed Cain that he will accept sacrifices offered with the proper motive. Sin is objectified as a predatory animal eagerly awaiting its prey. Although the deity has not accepted Cain's sacrifice, out of fatherly concern he shows Cain a way out of the dilemma. Cain takes the situation into his own hands, however. Very soon innocent blood is shed, and judgment is rendered. Yet Cain the murderer, who must be expelled from society, is offered a protective mark to ensure that as a fugitive he will not meet an untimely end (4:15). Once more divine judgment and mercy are wed. This, however, is not cheap grace. In the days ahead Cain will exist beyond Yahweh's presence. Though not fatal, the judgment is severe. And no doubt the Yahwist is implying that the judgment cannot possibly be light, for his whole story focuses on two grim contemporary realities that are inter-related—the painful rupture of harmonious communal life on earth and man's unwillingness to act responsibly for the sake of his brother.

The Kenite Genealogy

In the remainder of Genesis 4, the Yahwist provides brief notations that focus on the Cainite (Kenite) line. These verses contain ancient material that may have originated south of Judah, where Kenite clans are known to have roamed. Cain builds a city and thereby lays the foundations for a more permanent form of human existence (4:17).

While the cultural achievements (notably in music and the crafts) recorded in 4:19–22 are of interest, the Song of Lamech (4:23–24) is unquestionably the most significant element in the passage. By incorporating this defiant ancient composition, the Yahwist declares that the human condition is worsening. Adam and Eve asserted themselves against the divine will. Cain engaged in fratricide. Now Lamech boasts "Vengeance is mine!" In Lamech we detect an overweening arrogance that demands that no wrong, however slight, go unavenged. Man has once more moved beyond all established bounds, and he even boasts about it.

The Flood Narrative

Genesis 6:1–9:17 preserves ancient Israel's traditions about a universal flood. Contemporary geologists are convinced that the earth's surface was never completely covered by water after the appearance of human life. Nevertheless, many peoples in different locales and eras have transmitted stories that transformed local flood disasters into universal inundations. The disruptive aspects of even a small-scale flood could easily be interpreted by religious man as a sure indication that the gods, offended by degenerate human behavior, were now striking back.

In the alluvial plains of Mesopotamia flooding was frequent and sometimes intense. Flood deposits of clay have been uncovered at several excavated sites in the lower Tigris-Euphrates valley. The thickness of these deposits differs from site to site, and a cultural break is not always evident. Hence, it is conjectured that local floods in Lower Mesopotamia stimulated the emergence of a Babylonian flood tradition that reached its climax in Tablet XI of the *Epic of Gilgamesh*.[21] Since the Hebrew patriarchs hailed from Mesopotamia and lived in Canaan when such flooding was unlikely, we may infer that Israel's flood traditions were shaped by Babylonian flood experience. Nonetheless, Gen. 6:1–9:17 does not mindlessly ape the Babylonian prototype.

The Israelite flood stories of J and P have been thoroughly interwoven. The use of the two divine names "Yahweh" and "Elohim," irreconcilable references to time, and conflicting data about the animals to be taken into the ark have helped literary critics disentangle the strata. Genesis appears to contain the P flood tradition in its entirety and most of the J version. Nevertheless, there is a break at one important point in the narrative: between the witness that Yahweh was pleased with Noah (Gen. 6:8) and his command that Noah enter the ark (7:1) there must have been a passage containing Yahweh's command that Noah construct a suitable craft and a report that Noah complied.

In Gen. 6:1–4 the Yahwist deliberately opens his account by mentioning the contact between the sons of God and the daughters of men. This results in the birth of a race of giants (Nephilim) and the escalation of human depravity. The presence of a few unusually tall men among a people might easily foster the tradition that in antiquity giants walked the earth. The Yahwist has incorporated this traditional element, which originally had no bearing on the story of a primordial flood throughout the world. In Gen. 6:5–7 he offers an exquisite portrait of the intensity of human wickedness and the unfathomable depth of divine sorrow. The human heart, regarded by Hebrew man as the locus of conscious decision making, has become "only evil continually." Yahweh's own heart recoils from this deplorable situation. His decision to destroy all life is not made lightly. Yet the flood, which is an act of divine judgment marking the end of one epoch, is likewise a work of divine grace signaling the beginning of another. Man is to have a fresh start.

The details in the narrative—the seven pairs of clean animals and one pair of unclean animals that Noah takes into the ark, the forty days of rain, and the raven and dove sent out to determine how much the waters had receded—require no special consideration here. Note, however, that the deity is so pleased with the odor of Noah's burnt offerings that he resolves never again to curse the ground (8:20–22). Through the recurring cycles of nature, in "seedtime and harvest," Yahweh will continue to show mercy, even though man remains the rebel propelled by an evil inclination ("heart"). Yahweh does not acquiesce in human assertiveness, but once more he is saying, "Nevertheless!" How he is to keep wrath and mercy in delicate balance is Yahweh's business, not the narrator's. The Yahwist simply affirms that God's mercy is real and his patience deliberate.

In Gen. 9:18–27 the Yahwist also presents Noah as a tiller of the soil—the second Adam, as it were. These curious verses denote the transition of ancient man from a nomadic to an agricultural life style. As a tent dweller and a cultivator of vines, Noah is prone to drunkenness and nudity. Presumably the composite J passage fuses two conflicting traditions.[22] In the prose tradition of 9:18–24, Noah's sons are Shem, Ham,

"Noah in the Ark" by Hans Acker. Within the majestic Gothic Cathedral in Ulm, Germany, lies the small, inviting Besserer Chapel. Its five stained-glass windows, which date from the fifteenth century, present various scenes from the Bible. Their coloring and figuration were masterfully executed by Hans Acker of Ulm. One of the scenes depicts Noah. (Courtesy of the Evang. Dekanatamt Ulm, Ulm, Germany.)

and Japheth; in the more ancient poetry of 9:25–27, they are Shem, Canaan, and Japheth. The passage is far more concerned with Canaan than it is with Ham. The immodesty of Ham (Canaan) is stated overtly, although not in detail. The Canaanites are stigmatized here as an immoral people who gravitate toward that which, in Hebrew eyes, is odious and depraved. In their modesty, the other two brothers, Shem and Japheth, offer a striking contrast. Noah's powerful blessing and curse ensure that while Shem and Japheth are to be free and equal, Canaan is to be their social and political inferior. Through these words Noah expresses his will, and history is expected to bear it out.

The Tower of Babel

In his last mythological episode on the primeval condition of the human family (Gen. 11:1–9), the Yahwist deals with two etiological questions and expresses once more his theological position, which places man, the rebel, under divine judgment. The first question is, "Why do so many languages exist?" In v. 6 the naïve assumption is made that at one time all men conversed in one language. Then in vv. 7 and 9a we are informed that in order to arrest man's increasing assertiveness, Yahweh descended to earth and confused human communication. The second question, "How is the wide geographical distribution of people to be explained?" is answered in vv. 8 and 9b: Yahweh frustrated the efforts of men, who preferred to live self-sufficiently in one city, and he deliberately scattered them over the entire earth.

Since the Yahwist himself was probably a tenth-century urbanite, we doubt that he was using this myth to express a personal disdain for city life. Rather, the city and tower symbolize man's inclination to structure corporate human existence without thought of deity and to develop every resource that might ensure self-sufficiency. Therefore, in a swiftly executed act of judgment, Yahweh confuses the tongues of men and scatters mankind across the earth.

That the Yahwist fell heir once more to Mesopotamian influence is reflected in many details. For example, "Shinar" (11:2) is the biblical equivalent of "Babylonia." The making of bricks and the use of bitumen (11:3) reflects Mesopotamian building practices. The mention of a tower (11:4-5) may recall the tall temple towers or ziggurats constructed by the ancient Sumerians and Babylonians. And the name "Babel" (11:9) is close to the Akkadian term *Bâb-ilu* (Babylon), meaning "the gate of God."

Nevertheless, the Yahwist pursued his own theological course. In Mesopotamian religion the ziggurats, which stretched toward the heavens, were intended to facilitate a meaningful union between the gods above and the people below. They had been built in cooperation with the divine will. In the Yahwist's account, however, the tower's presence reveals that human will was once more colliding with the divine will. Hence, Yahweh's judgment against mankind is inevitable.

But on this occasion the divine word "Nevertheless" is not uttered. The Yahwist's story of the garden speaks of the deity's gift of skins to the ousted couple (3:21). His account of the brothers mentions the protective mark that Yahweh placed on Cain (4:15). The flood story preserves Yahweh's promise that he will never again curse the ground on man's account (8:21). But in Genesis 11 mercy does not qualify divine judgment. Instead, the Yahwist deliberately prepares his readers for the call of Abraham (Gen. 12:1-7), the next vital episode in the deity's continuing engagement with his creation. Momentarily, judgment reigns supreme.

But as the Yahwist moves on, the deity's determination to have meaningful contact with man persists. Abraham is summoned to be the father of a great people. This is the "Nevertheless" of the deity that follows man's defiance at Babel. By relating in a special way to Abraham's descendants, the sovereign deity reveals his determination not to give up on the world. This people Israel would be charged with a special mission as the deity works out his continuing agenda with mankind. By sharing his views with his Israelite contemporaries through the engaging medium of myth, the Yahwist must have given them cause to feel both humble and reverent—humble about the human condition and reverent as they approached the deity who had rallied them to his cause.

Each reader must form his own opinion about the Yahwist's message in Genesis 2–11. Is this a provocative mythology? Has it, even in our own time, the power to address the individual reader head-on? Or does this overrate the Yahwist's achievement? We can at least say that the Yahwist expresses the conviction that the origin and purpose of this world lie beyond the realm of known, tangible reality. His mythology declares that man is not the master of his own being and that a transcendent power sustains the world and guides its inhabitants. Because of their candor and immediacy, the Yahwist's reflections have fascinated men and women through the ages, and many have claimed that the mythology of the Yahwist has more relevance for our own time than does anything else that the Bible has to offer.

ASSESSING THE REIGN OF SOLOMON

Having given our attention to the Yahwist who may well have written during the Solomonic era, we now return to the monarch himself. If it was under David that Israel took her prominent place in the contemporary world, it was under Solomon that she continued to show obvious signs of strength. This king engaged in a host of enterprises that were possible, at least in part, because he did not have to spend his energy waging war. Edom and Damascus rebelled against Solomon, but did not trouble the Solomonic peace to any serious extent. Undoubtedly the king made an impact on the world of his day. In fact, tradition has it that when the queen of Sheba dropped in on him, she was momentarily overcome by the ostentatious splendor that engulfed her (1 Kings 10:5).

Solomon inherited much from Saul and David, and he worked hard to keep the machinery going. He seemed to know instinctively that his chief political task was to hold the Israelite state together, and for a time he managed that rather well. But as his building program progressed the Israelite populace, who had to bear the awful financial burden, grew more and more discontent. Though Israel's ancient tribal structure experienced a mortal blow as the result of extensive Solomonic reorganization, its spirit lived on in the many individuals who were not ready to relinquish past tradition.

In Solomon's concerted attempt to mold Israel into a typical Oriental state, he was divesting the nation of some things that loyal Yah-

The Israelite Temple at Arad. In the eastern Negev,
16 miles south of Hebron, lies the site of Arad. It
consists of both a large Canaanite city of the Early
Bronze Age and a more compact Israelite citadel
founded in Solomonic times. Recent excavations in
the citadel have brought to light a large royal
sanctuary. Patterned after the Solomonic temple in
Jerusalem, it was built in the tenth century B.C.
and used for at least 200 years. The "Holy of
Holies" is pictured above. Three steps lead from the
main hall to its entrance, which is flanked by two
nicely dressed stone incense altars. (Courtesy of
the Consulate General of Israel, New York.)

wists regarded as distinctive and precious. This organization man turned
monarch refused to acknowledge that the Mosaic covenant affirmed
freedom and equality for all Israelites. The observation with which the
Book of Judges concludes (21:25) must have been voiced frequently by
those who reflected on a not too distant past: "In those days there was
no king in Israel; every man did what was right in his own eyes."

Solomon inspired a class consciousness and social inequality that must have displeased the Israelite masses. And his formality in public worship surely induced in many individuals a longing for the more spontaneous leadership of David.

Some Israelites did benefit from the gifts of this reputedly golden age. Indeed, the Yahwist recognized that he was living at an extremely important time in the nation's history. Israel had arrived. But what was to come next? In due course, Solomonic splendor appeared to be Solomonic oppression in disguise. While Solomon did not commit blunder after blunder, he might have done better.

THE DISRUPTION OF THE UNITED MONARCHY

When Solomon died in 922, the United Monarchy suffered an irreparable disruption. As the royal son and potential successor of Solomon, Rehoboam traveled to Shechem to secure formal confirmation as monarch from the elders of the northern tribes (1 Kings 12:1). The situation was now ripe for making demands. When the north was unsuccessful in getting its way with Rehoboam, it seceded.

There were several general causes of the schism. First was the fundamental difference between the north and south. The agrarian population of the north had little sympathy for the Bedouin population of the south. The northern tribes believed that they were the true Israel. They came to resent the increasing domination of Judah. They opposed any move that might legitimize dynastic rule. Indeed, Sheba's revolt (2 Sam. 20:1–2) indicates that the north might at any time withdraw its support of the Jerusalem-based royal establishment.

Second, the sweeping excesses of Solomon's government contributed greatly to the ensuing schism. Solomon's rule had been harsh. He had not pacified the northern tribes with sound public relations nor had he convinced them that the southern dynasty was legitimate. In particular, his building projects and day-to-day needs placed a heavy burden on the populace. It was obvious that costs were exceeding income. The grandiose buildings in Jerusalem were expensive to construct and maintain. And Solomon's lavish support of the Jerusalem Temple further drained the people.

The provincialism of the north may be mentioned as a third general cause of schism. In Shechem and Bethel, the north had its own revered shrines, and in Jacob it had its special patriarchal figure around whom it could focus its loyalties. Now the Solomonic temple had been constructed with the assistance of a vast resource of northern labor in a place that had no meaningful connection with the religious traditions of the northern tribes. Toward the end of Solomon's rule, the feelings of discontent must have been considerable.

More specific causes of the schism are enumerated in 1 Kings 12;

each centers on a different person. First, there was Rehoboam. At Shechem the north asked for tolerance, but Rehoboam, acting on the advice of his younger men, refused to make any concessions. His public retort preserved in v. 14 is a classic example of ineptitude at the conference table: "My father made your yoke heavy, but I will add to your yoke; my father chastised you with whips, but I will chastise you with scorpions." At once the north voiced its cry of rebellion, "What portion have we in David? . . . To your tents, O Israel! Look now to your own house, David" (v. 16). The breach had been made.

Second, there was Adoram (Adoniram), who was stoned by Israelite rebels (12:18). Why had Rehoboam called Adoram to the scene? Was it to pacify the mob? If so, he was a poor choice. As taskmaster of the forced labor, his presence would only fan northern hatred. Or did Rehoboam summon Adoram in order to subject the rebels to the corvée? If so, the plan failed miserably. The north was both defiant and successful.

Third, there was Jeroboam. At the most propitious moment he returned from Egypt (12:20). This talented native of Ephraim had served under Solomon as a construction worker on certain Jerusalem fortifications. Solomon then placed him in charge of the forced labor of his native territory (11:28). However, Yahwistic prophecy now boldly interfered in the person of Ahijah, who symbolically informed Jeroboam that he would soon rule the north (11:29–39). So outraged was Solomon on hearing of this clandestine encounter between Jeroboam and Ahijah that he tried to kill Jeroboam. In Egypt, Jeroboam obtained political asylum. Now in 922 he returned and ruled over the north until his death in 901 (12:20). The division of the monarchy was not simply a political fact. It had prophetic support as well.

Thus, the north rallied around Jeroboam while southern Judah submitted to Rehoboam's rule. Israel and Judah now entered a period of civil strife, territorial loss, and economic hardship. Although no full-scale war broke out, both sides spent much energy attending to the tensions that the schism had created. After 922 B.C. a united Israel flourishing under the aegis of a golden age was quite unthinkable.

NOTES

1. First mentioned here and referred to on 16 other occasions in 1–2 Kings.
2. First mentioned here and referred to on 14 other occasions in 1–2 Kings.
3. Asa (1 Kings 15:11–15), Jehoshaphat (1 Kings 22:43), Jehoash (2 Kings 12:2–3), Azariah (Uzziah) (2 Kings 15:3–4), and Jotham (2 Kings 15:34–35).
4. We are in agreement with John Bright, *A History of Israel*, 2d ed. (Philadelphia: Westminster Press, 1972), p. 207.
5. *Ibid.*, p. 218, n. 92.
6. The pottery evidence relating to the elaborate stable complex of Stratum IV of Megiddo speaks for a date in the ninth rather than the tenth

century B.C. This casts light not on the rule of Solomon but on that of Ahab (869–850). See Kathleen M. Kenyon, *Archaeology in the Holy Land*, 3d ed. (New York: Frederick A. Praeger, 1970), pp. 248–249, 269.

7. See especially Siegfried H. Horn, "Who was Solomon's Egyptian Father-in-Law?" *Biblical Research: Papers of the Chicago Society of Biblical Research* 12 (1967): 3–17.

8. For succinct data on these Solomonic sites and several others, see Kenyon, *op. cit.*, pp. 248–258.

9. For further remarks on the architectural features and religious significance of the Solomonic temple, see G. Ernest Wright, *Biblical Archaeology*, rev. ed. (Philadelphia: Westminster Press, 1962), pp. 137–146.

10. James B. Pritchard, ed., *Ancient Near Eastern Texts Relating to the Old Testament*, 3d ed. (Princeton, N.J.: Princeton University Press, 1969), p. 320; the translation is by William F. Albright, whose article, "The Gezer Calendar," in the *Bulletin of the American Schools of Oriental Research*, no. 92 (December 1943): 16–26, may be consulted. The two words in parentheses are the translator's interpolations and the one italicized word is a conjectured reading.

11. We provisionally accept the following passages within Genesis 1–11 as belonging to the J stratum: Gen. 2:4b–4:26; 5:29; 6:1–8; 7:1–5, 7–10, 12, 16b, 17b, 22–23; 8:2b–3a, 6–12, 13b, 20–22; 9:18–27; 10:8–19, 21, 24–30; 11:1–9, 28–30.

12. For a first-rate existential interpretation of Genesis 2–12 in poetic garb, see B. Davie Napier, *Come Sweet Death: A Quintet from Genesis* (Philadelphia: United Church Press, 1967). Adam, Cain, and Noah are freshly seen, and the dynamics of the Yahwist's mythology are fully appreciated.

13. For a more detailed discussion, see the helpful monograph by Brevard S. Childs, *Myth and Reality in the Old Testament*, Studies in Biblical Theology, no. 27 (London: SCM Press, 1960), and Henri and H. A. Frankfort, "Myth and Reality," in Henri and H. A. Frankfort, eds., *Before Philosophy* (Baltimore, Md.: Penguin Books, 1949), pp. 11–36.

14. Here the remarks of Claus Westermann, "God and His Creation," *Union Seminary Quarterly Review* 18 (1963): 197–198, are most helpful.

15. See Pritchard, *op. cit.*, p. 67, on this critical moment in the Babylonian creation story, or its citation on p. 426 in this book.

16. The Yahwist's assumption of preexistent matter and his identification of the spilling forth of fresh water with the initial creative act are both reminiscent of an ancient Sumerian paradise myth, "Enki and Ninhursag," which speaks of the paradise of Dilmun. *Ibid.*, pp. 37–41.

17. For a more detailed treatment of this issue, see Aubrey R. Johnson, *The Vitality of the Individual in the Thought of Ancient Israel* (Cardiff: University of Wales Press, 1949), pp. 11–12.

18. Gerhard von Rad, *Genesis: A Commentary*, rev. ed., trans. John H. Marks, The Old Testament Library (Philadelphia: Westminster Press, 1972), p. 84.

19. Thomas Mann, *Joseph and His Brothers*, trans. H. T. Lowe-Porter (New York: Alfred A. Knopf, 1948), p. 33.

20. Insofar as the Yahwist was reflecting on the ancient conflict that sometimes existed between shepherds and farmers, he was not dealing with a unique literary theme. Centuries earlier a Sumerian story, "Dumuzi and

Enkimdu," depicted that rivalry. In this instance, however, the leading contenders are deities, and it is not the shepherd-god, Dumuzi, but rather the farmer-god, Enkimdu, who feels accepted. The poetic text appears in Pritchard, *op. cit.*, pp. 41–42.

21. The text of Tablet XI appears in *ibid.*, pp. 93–97.
22. We are in agreement with von Rad, *op. cit.*, p. 137, and E. A. Speiser, *Genesis: Introduction, Translation, and Notes*, The Anchor Bible, vol. 1 (Garden City, N.Y.: Doubleday, 1964), p. 62.

11

THE DIALOGUE
BETWEEN
ESTABLISHED
MONARCHY
AND EMERGING
PROPHETISM

The independent kingdoms of Israel and Judah, which were formed as a result of the ill-fated schism of 922 B.C., faced a series of dreary decades. Still, it was in the ninth century B.C. that prophetism grew into a vital Israelite institution. This was the age of Elijah, Micaiah, and Elisha. Yahweh's people had already witnessed the formative effects of prophetism in such figures as Samuel and Nathan. Now the singular role of the prophet assumed more definitive shape. The prophet as the representative of the nation's conscience and the monarch as the leading exponent of its political ambitions sometimes clashed in heated debate. If such confrontations alienated the parties involved, they also reminded the Hebrew kingdoms that no one less than Yahweh was directing the course of history.

In the present chapter we shall be concerned with the last two decades of the tenth century and much of the ninth century. In particular, we shall come to terms with a working definition of ancient Israelite prophetism and attempt to examine prophetism as it is reflected in the actions and proclamations of Elijah, Micaiah, and Elisha.

THE REIGNS OF JEROBOAM
AND REHOBOAM

The first half-century of the Divided Monarchy was uniformly grim. Rehoboam of Judah (922–915) recognized that he could not force the

---

Biblical texts to be read prior to and in conjunction with the present chapter: 1 Kings 12:25–14:31; 15:9–24; 16:8–34; 20:1–43; *17:1–19:21;* 21:1–29; 2 *Kings 1:2–2:12a; 1 Kings 22:1–40; 2 Kings 2:12b–25; 4:1–6:7; 8:7–15; 9:1–10:36.* Greater care should be taken in reading the italicized passages.

The Shishak Inscription. On the south wall of the temple of Amon at Karnak, Pharaoh Shishak had listed the Palestinian and Syrian towns captured during his dramatic invasion of western Asia in about 918 B.C. A large figure of the god Amon stands in the center of this monument. His right hand holds a sickle, and his left hand grips the cords that bind the captives. This list suggests the extent of Shishak's penetration of Syria-Palestine. (Photo by George W. E. Nickelsburg.)

northern tribes back into his own realm, and presumably he did not try. The northern garrisons of Solomon were now in the hands of Jeroboam I (922–901), and Judah's citizens showed little enthusiasm for a major confrontation with the north. Though Rehoboam extended his northern frontier by annexing Benjaminite territory to Judah, he suffered extensive losses in about 918 when Pharaoh Shishak (ca. 935–914) and his armies visited Palestine.

   This founder of Egypt's Twenty-second Dynasty sought once more to subject western Asia to Egyptian control. Three texts confirm Shishak's sweeping invasion. We learn in 1 Kings 14:25–28 that he advanced against Jerusalem and was bought off by substantial tribute, which Rehoboam raised for him. According to 2 Chron. 12:2–4, Shishak enjoyed the support of extensive troops and took fortified Judean cities. Shishak himself offers no narrative of his campaign, but he lists on the south wall of his temple at Karnak more than 150 places in Palestine and Syria that he claims to have conquered.[1] No mention is made of cities taken in the heart of Judah. But the Negev, northern Judah, Transjordan, and Israel all felt the brunt of his attack. This invasion placed both Hebrew kingdoms at a considerable disadvantage. In the few years that remained, Rehoboam was ill equipped to attack the northern kingdom. Happily, Shishak was unable to manage more than a hit-and-run campaign, and since Egypt was internally weak in the years ahead a repeat performance was out of the question for Shishak's successors.

During his two decades of rule, Jeroboam had to assemble a kingdom from scratch. While he could lay claim to such fortified Solomonic cities as Megiddo and Hazor at the outset of his rule, the northern kingdom lacked a capital, an administrative system, and a national shrine. Jeroboam first selected Shechem as his capital (1 Kings 12:25), although later he moved to nearby Tirzah, a site that might have been easier to defend. Jeroboam's initial choice was astute, for Shechem was centrally located. And since its rather extensive Canaanite population had only been partly assimilated into the ancient Israelite confederation, tribal jealousies would be minimal.

Of greatest concern to the Deuteronomic historian, however, were the cultic centers established by Jeroboam at the extremities of his kingdom. Northern and southern Israelites were encouraged to worship at Dan and Bethel, respectively. Both sites were an abomination to the Deuteronomist, who insisted that only in the Jerusalem Temple was the public worship of Yahweh legitimate. Nevertheless, the pragmatic Jeroboam pursued a wise course. He was cognizant of the attendant political dangers in allowing his subjects to participate in the Jerusalem cult. Likewise he acknowledged the need to unite his people around something other than military and political aspirations. Undoubtedly, Jeroboam was also aware that Dan and Bethel had figured in ancient patriarchal tradition.

In describing the cultic measures of Jeroboam, the Deuteronomist overemphasized the idolatry and polytheism fostered by this northern monarch. Upon having the two golden calves constructed, Jeroboam is represented as saying to the people, "Behold your gods, O Israel, who brought you up out of the land of Egypt" (1 Kings 12:28). While Jeroboam may have tried to establish a strong link between ongoing worship at these centers and the Exodus experience that was so formative in Israelite religion, we doubt that he deliberately forced his people into polytheistic modes of expression. Yet in selecting golden calves or bulls as the official cultic symbol of the religion, Jeroboam did open the way for a dissipation of Mosaic Yahwism. The bulls were not worshiped as such, but were rather the pedestals upon which Yahweh was invisibly enthroned. Even so, such a contraption could confuse nominal wor-

THE DUAL MONARCHY
OF ISRAEL AND JUDAH

0   10   20   30
Miles

Sidon

Damascus

MT. LEBANON

Zarephath

MT. HERMON

SYRIA
(ARAM)

Tyre

Dan

S
I
D
O
N
I
A
N
S

Hazor

BASHAN

Accho

GALILEE

Sea of
Chinnereth

Mt. Carmel

THE GREAT SEA

Megiddo

VALLEY OF
IFZREEL

Jezreel

Ramoth-gilead

I   S   R   A   E   L

G
I
L
E
A
D

Samaria

Tirzah

Jordan R.

Mt. Ebal

Shechem

Penuel

Mahanaim

Mt. Gerizim

Shiloh

Joppa

Rabbah

AMMON

Bethel

Mizpah

Ramah

Geba

Gilgal

Anathoth

Jerusalem

Ashdod

Ekron

Beth-shemesh

Ashkelon

Azekah

P
H
I
L
I
S
T
I
A

Gath

Tekoa

SALT SEA

Gaza

Mareshah

Lachish

Hebron

Gerar

Debir

Dibon

J
U
D
A
H

M
O
A
B

Beer-sheba

E   D   O   M

The Negev

shipers of Yahweh who were less than eager to keep Yahweh and Ba'al wholly separate. In any event, the Deuteronomist briskly wrote off Jeroboam as an evil monarch. And as long as the cultic centers of Dan and Bethel continued to exist, Jeroboam's successors were judged similarly.

The Deuteronomist, however, was not Jeroboam's only critic. According to 1 Kings 14, Ahijah, the prophet who had first supported Jeroboam as king, now openly rejected him. Presumably this tradition sought to account for the short life span of this dynasty, which extended merely two years beyond Jeroboam's lifetime to his son Nadab's reign (901–900). Although 1 Kings 14 does not impress us as objective historiography, Ahijah may in fact have become as disillusioned with Jeroboam as Samuel had with Saul. Perhaps Ahijah was disappointed that Jeroboam had failed to restore Israel to a premonarchical society. In sum, the resourceful Jeroboam took steps to strengthen the northern kingdom, but in the process he set an example that was loathsome to at least a few defenders of the faith.

NINTH-CENTURY SUCCESSORS
OF JEROBOAM AND REHOBOAM

We feel no compulsion to comment extensively on all the monarchs, sixteen in number, who were the ninth-century successors of the first kings of a divided Israel and Judah. Nevertheless, several royal personages and historical events deserve mention.

In Judah, Rehoboam's tenure of seven years (922–915) was followed by the even shorter rule of his son Abijah (915–913) and subsequently by the forty-year reign of his grandson Asa (913–873). Abijah made no lasting contributions to his kingdom, and Asa frequently found himself in adverse situations. Northern hostility troubled Asa. Having assassinated Nadab, Baasha (900–877) ruled Israel for nearly a quarter of a century, and during that time he and Asa were active rivals. According to 1 Kings 15:17–22, Baasha extended the Israelite border further south and blocked northern traffic into Jerusalem. Asa, however, was resourceful in checking Baasha's aggression. Though Baasha of Israel and Ben-hadad I of Syria (ca. 880–842) had already entered into a political alliance, on the receipt of appropriate gifts, Ben-hadad willingly broke with Baasha and sided with Asa. The disillusioned Baasha had to retreat from his southern position at Ramah, which was but 6 miles north of Jerusalem, and return to Tirzah, his capital. Ben-hadad no doubt relished this opportunity to demonstrate his military capacity and perhaps gain further territory in Transjordan. As for Asa, he wrecked the fortifications at Ramah and reused them in constructing his own defense systems at Geba and Mizpah.

Asa also achieved some religious reform (1 Kings 15:11–15). The syncretic policies of Solomon, Rehoboam, and Abijah were partially rescinded by the zealous Asa, who waged a successful campaign against cultic prostitution and the manufacture of idols. Gradually Judah's citizens came to enjoy a more tranquil existence and greater freedom to worship Yahweh without extensive Canaanite trappings. Intermittent warfare with the north had run its course, and when the upright Jehoshaphat (873–849) took the Jerusalem throne at the death of his father, he was able to benefit from Asa's gains.

We know little else about Baasha's reign over Israel. Nevertheless, allusion to "his might" in the Deuteronomic summary of 1 Kings 16:5 suggests that he was not unsuited to the office. At Baasha's death, his son Elah (877–876) took over, but he in turn was assassinated by Zimri, an army commander who was for one week a dynasty unto himself (1 King 16:15). When a general named Omri led the Israelite armed forces against Tirzah, Zimri recognized his defenseless condition and committed suicide. Omri (876–869) then inaugurated the northern kingdom's fourth dynasty, which was highly effective. Yet some time lapsed before Omri was able to win over the opposition, which had looked to a certain Tibni as its leader (1 Kings 16:21–22). Lacking a dynastic principle, the north enjoyed the advantages of charismatic leadership and suffered the disadvantages of sheer chaos. The last two Omrides to rule, Ahaziah (850–849) and Jehoram (849–842), were not very able. But certainly Omri and his son Ahab (869–850) were competent leaders who successfully guided a nation that had suffered greatly from a half-century of indecisive warfare and a steady depletion of goods and spirit.

Part of Israel's plight was rooted in the unfriendly international climate that she was forced to recognize. Although Egypt posed no threat, the Syrians with their headquarters in Damascus were eating away at Israelite holdings in Transjordan. Moreover, under Asshur-naṣir-pal II (884–860), distant Assyria awakened from her deep sleep. Western Asia would increasingly be required to recognize this uncomfortable reality.

For a time, however, Israel would benefit from the rule of Omri. While the Deuteronomist devotes a scant eight verses to Omri's reign (1 Kings 16:21–28), it is only his strong religious bias that prevents us from learning more. The Deuteronomist preferred to move quickly to the reign of Omri's son, Ahab, with its serious religious and social problems. An important Moabite inscription and the Harvard University excavations at Samaria both attest to Omri's greatness.

The Moabite Stone speaks of Omri's effectiveness in about 875 B.C. and of King Mesha's success at Israel's expense several decades later. This inscription was discovered in 1868 by an Arab sheik at Dhiban (biblical Dibon), which is 13 miles east of the Dead Sea.[2] It was soon brought to the attention of a Prussian missionary, F. A. Klein, and a French Orientalist, Charles Clermont-Ganneau. After a series of fasci-

IV. THE NINTH-CENTURY DIVIDED MONARCHY (ca. 900–800 B.C.)

DATE (B.C.)	EGYPT	PALESTINE		SYRIA	ASSYRIA
		Southern Kingdom (Judah)	Northern Kingdom (Israel)		
900		Asa (913–873)	*Baasha (900–877) Elah (877–876) *Zimri (876) *Omri (876–869) Ahab (869–850) Elijah Micaiah	Ben-hadad I (ca. 880–842)	Period of resurgence Asshur-naṣir-pal II (884–860)
		Jehoshaphat (873–849)			
850	Period of weakness	Jehoram (849–842) Ahaziah (842) Athaliah (842–837) Joash (837–800)	Ahaziah (850–849) Jehoram (849–842) *Jehu (842–815) Elisha Jehoahaz (815–801) Jehoash (801–786)	Battle of Qarqar (853) Israelite-Syrian coalition vs. Assyria Hazael (ca. 842–806)	Shalmaneser III (859–825) receives tribute from Jehu (841)

*Founder of new dynasty in the northern kingdom (Israel).

The Moabite Stone. On this black basalt monument, which is over 3 feet high, Mesha, king of Moab, celebrates his military accomplishments. As Mesha himself explains, these followed an era when the Moabites had been forced to recognize the supremacy of the Israelite king Omri. (Courtesy of the Louvre Museum.)

nating episodes, the reconstructed stone—now about two-thirds intact—was acquired by Paris' Louvre Museum in 1873. This monument to Mesha's firm rule over Moab appears to date from the end of Mesha's reign (ca. 830). Even so, its opening lines give an honest description of Israel's dominion over the Moabites in the generation preceding Omri's reign:

> I (am) Mesha, son of Chemosh- [. . .], king of Moab, the Dibonite—my father (had) reigned over Moab thirty years, and I reigned after my father,—(who) made this high place for Chemosh in Qarhoh [. . .] because he saved me from all the kings and caused me to triumph over all my adversaries. As for Omri, king of Israel, he humbled Moab many years (lit., days), for Chemosh was angry at his land.[3]

This reference to Omri's domination of northern Moab confirms the notation of 2 Kings 3:4 that Mesha had to pay substantial tribute to the king of Israel. Also Moab's defeat at the hands of Omri is interpreted in the Moabite Stone as evidence that the Moabite god Chemosh was angry with his people. This parallels the Deuteronomic notion so prominent in the Book of Judges that Israel's defeat is a sure sign of Yahweh's wrath. Of course, most of the Moabite inscription celebrates Mesha's victories over Israel after the reigns of Omri and Ahab. Nevertheless, biblical historians justly prize the opening sentences of this inscription, which broaden our understanding of Ahab and his rule.

Omri's occupation of Samaria is further evidence of his success as an Israelite king. Having first ruled at Tirzah, Omri sought a larger site that would be hospitable to his grandiose building plans. Thus Omri purchased an imposing hill from a certain Shemer and named it "Samaria" (1 Kings 16:24). Since Samaria was located on a principal north-south trade route, Omri could view any advance that Judah might initiate from the south and strengthen mutually satisfying relationships with Phoenicia to the north. Construction of this capital began under Omri's rule and continued in Ahab's. The entire summit was designed as a royal quarter reserved for the autocratic king and his court. Samaria's lesser citizens lived lower down on the mound. Samaria's sturdy fortifications, fine Phoenician architecture, and luxurious inlaid furniture all reveal that Omri and Ahab sponsored an extensive building program and nourished keen economic ambitions.[4]

In playing the game of international politics, Omri entered into a formal agreement with Ittoba῾al, king of Tyre. The latter's daughter, Jezebel, was given in marriage to Omri's son, Ahab (1 Kings 16:31). Whatever havoc this caused Israelite religion, it did symbolize the reciprocity that then existed between Israel and Phoenicia. This arrangement enhanced Phoenicia's position in dealing with Damascus and afforded Israel a good opportunity to export its agricultural surpluses. Then either late in Omri's reign or early in Ahab's, Athaliah, who appears to have been Ahab's half-sister, was dispatched to Judah, where she married King Jehoshaphat's son Jehoram.[5]

Since Ahab carried on many of the policies established by his father, Israel experienced further prosperity. Ahab's encounter with his Damascus opponent, Ben-hadad, is portrayed in 1 Kings 20. Penetrating southward into Transjordan and advancing toward the city of Samaria, Ben-hadad hoped to frustrate Israel's steady recovery. Although Ahab was first intimidated by Ben-hadad's aggression, ultimately he triumphed over the Aramean king in a battle staged in Transjordan. Ahab captured Ben-hadad and then magnanimously released him upon the conclusion of a treaty. Later Ben-hadad and Ahab had to join forces against their common foe, Assyria.

Shalmaneser III (859–825) had succeeded Asshur-naṣir-pal II as Assyrian monarch. Because Shalmaneser showed a marked interest in penetrating westward, a coalition of lesser states, including Israel and Damascus, quickly came into being. In 853 at the Syrian site of Qarqar, some 130 miles north of Damascus, this coalition confronted the Assy-

Remains of the Omri-Ahab Palace at Samaria. After ruling at Tirzah for six years, Omri purchased the spacious hill of Shemer (1 Kings 16:24), and on its bedrock he initiated the careful building of the palace of Samaria. At Omri's death the construction continued under Ahab's direction. While the remains of Israelite Samaria are not extensive, this photo offers a glimpse of some of the beautifully dressed stones that were part of the palace's Ashlar (Phoenician) masonry. (Photo by the author.)

rian monarch. While the battle of Qarqar is nowhere mentioned in the Hebrew Bible, it is referred to in Shalmaneser's annals, where he indicates that Ahab provided 2,000 chariots and 10,000 infantrymen.[6]

Momentarily, Shalmaneser was held in check, but with this mutual threat now set aside, the western states were more inclined to continue their petty rivalry than to support one another. It was within the context of such political give and take that the great ninth-century prophets emerged.

THE WAY OF OLD TESTAMENT PROPHETISM

We have already examined the activities of such prophetic personalities as Samuel and Nathan, but as yet we have not settled on a general definition of an Old Testament prophet.[7] In the Hebrew Bible the fundamental word for "prophet" is *nābî'*. This noun, which appears some 306 times, is applied to a variety of individuals. It is applied to the patriarch Abraham to point out his capacity to intercede with Yahweh in behalf of a misbehaving Philistine king (Gen. 20:7); it is used of the priestly, ordinarily self-contained Aaron (Exod. 7:1); it is employed in the narration of exciting engagements that involve Elijah (1 Kings 18:36); it is applied to the morally sensitive Nathan (2 Sam. 12:25), the politically active Isaiah (Isa. 37:2), and the mystical Ezekiel (Ezek. 2:5). Even those with antithetical viewpoints, let alone divergent personalities, were designated prophets—for example, the preexilic Jeremiah, who deplored the people's excessive reliance on the Jerusalem Temple, and the postexilic Haggai, who urged his people to finish rebuilding that edifice (cf. Jer. 1:5 and Hag. 1:1).

Despite the variations, at its core the Hebrew noun *nābî'* refers to one who has a message to proclaim. In Exod. 7:1 this is precisely the sense conveyed. When Moses complains that he is a miserable orator, Yahweh replies, "See, I make you as God to Pharaoh; and Aaron your brother shall be your prophet." The prophet is here understood to be a person who voices the will of the deity intelligibly. He is God's spokesman. Aaron is to proclaim the words that Moses will give him, and here the term *nābî'* is used in a functional sense. In this passage and elsewhere in the Hebrew Bible, the prophet must have a voice.

Although we cannot be certain about the root of the noun *nābî'*, it may have a cognate in a verb that appears in two Semitic languages, Arabic and Akkadian, meaning "to call, or announce." This verb has crucial active and passive connotations. Actively it implies that the prophet is a superb communicator of the intrusive divine word. Passively it suggests that the prophet, who is the caller, is also the one who *is* called. Waiting expectantly, he receives the announcement from Yahweh. The prophet speaks out of the conviction that he has been divinely summoned.

Old Testament prophetism involves an inspiration that is intense and an ecstatic feeling that is genuine. It acknowledges Yahweh's decisive impingement on history—in particular, his interaction with specific human beings:

> The special gift of a prophet is his ability to experience the divine
> in an original way and to receive revelations from the divine world.
> The prophet belongs entirely to his God; his paramount task is to listen
> to and obey his God. In every respect he has given himself up to his
> God and stands unreservedly at His disposal.[8]

Having lost the freedom of ordinary men, the prophet must shape his life in accord with the will of the deity who invades his existence.

In moments of religious ecstasy, the prophet is filled with the divine presence. His power of religious concentration may be so intense that he loses touch with his senses. This is what Lindblom refers to as "concentration ecstasy" as opposed to "absorption ecstasy," the loss of self through fusion with an undifferentiated universal power.[9] The prophet's rapture may take the form of fasting or dancing, or on a different level it may lead him to extended moments of prayer and meditation. But typically the Israelite prophet is open to recurring disclosures of the deity who is active in his life. It is revelation, not reason, that matters most. Having received the divine word with all its transcendent candor, the prophet recognizes that his primary mission is to impart it to Yahweh's people.

Depending on his disposition and his understanding of the deity, the prophet works apart from, within, or against the national cult. Sometimes the prophet himself is a participant in the Israelite cult. Yet he certainly has the capacity to criticize the apparatus of public worship when he is convinced that it is deficient. In countless situations the prophet declares boldly, "Thus says Yahweh!" The content of his message often alienates him from his public. But that is the price of the office he feels called upon to fulfill. Again, depending on his make-up, he might take solace in recognizing that in his daily activity as Yahweh's prophet, he is truly helping to communicate the will of Yahweh and, indeed, to bring it to fulfillment. The words of Amos 3:8 epitomize biblical prophetism: "The Lord God has spoken; who can but prophesy?"

ELIJAH THE TISHBITE

An Introduction to the Prophet

We turn now to the prophet Elijah, whose very name meant, "My God is Yahweh." Elijah's lasting impact is illustrated by the fact that his name is mentioned twenty-nine times in the New Testament. By contrast, Jeremiah's name appears there only three times. Elijah must have been an extraordinary person to have created such an impression on a later era. In the postexilic writing of Malachi, Elijah is taken to be the visible forerunner of the deity himself: "Behold, I will send you Elijah the prophet before the great and terrible day of Yahweh comes" (4:5). Indeed, Elijah dominated much of the speculative thought of later Judaism, in which he was regularly acclaimed the harbinger of the end-time.

No doubt Elijah was held in awe partly because of his reputed ability to perform miracles and his ready talent to appear and disappear when least expected. Nevertheless, the articulate word imparted by Elijah to his contemporaries as Yahweh's designated messenger was even more responsible for shaping the prophet's reputation. In the Elijah traditions, wonder is not cherished for its own sake. Rather, it accompanies the transcendent word of the deity, which the prophet communicates to his audience. Though Elijah is associated with the miraculous fire that came down from heaven in the thick of his contest with the prophet-priests of Baᶜal (1 Kings 18:38), he is linked even more closely with the burning word of the deity, which drove him on from one crisis to another.

Israelite Society in Elijah's Time

Ahab ruled Israel when Elijah functioned as Yahweh's prophet. Despite an Israelite resurgence during the years when Omri and Ahab reigned, all was not well. To be sure, these Omrides secured friendly ties with their neighbors to the immediate north and south. Yet internally Israel was the victim of social and religious crises that greatly distressed Elijah. While material prosperity was in evidence in Samaria's royal quarter, the narrative in 1 Kings suggests that northern farmers found themselves in a precarious position. Often the poor were victimized by the wealthy. In difficult times they were forced to pay exorbitant interest rates, and when they could not make the expected payments, they were required to sell themselves into slavery. The situation grew worse over the years so that in Amos' day (the middle of the eighth century),

Israelite Public Building at Hazor. This important ancient Palestinian city, which is 10 miles due north of the Sea of Galilee, has been the locus of extensive archaeological activity since 1955. Pictured above are two rows of monolithic pillars that once supported the roof of what must have been a large public building (perhaps a royal storehouse) dating to Ahab's reign (869–850 B.C.). A few of the excavators are resting in its shade. Although Hazor was a prospering metropolis in the ninth century B.C., it was destroyed by the Assyrians under Tiglath-pileser III in 732. (Photo by the author.)

the contrast between rich and poor had become scandalous. If it was still considered as a good thing for Hebrew man to look out for his covenant brother, Ahab and Jezebel were setting a dubious example.

Religion under Omride rule was equally bankrupt. Ahab's wife, Jezebel, was allowed to continue her religious practices on Israelite soil. In 1 Kings 16:32–33 we read that Ahab had a temple and an altar built for Jezebel's Tyrian gods, Ba°al (Melqart) and Asherah. Moreover, 1 Kings 18:19, with its exaggerated reference to the 850 prophets of Ba°al and Asherah who sat at Jezebel's table, indicates that the queen was permitted to support a massive cultic enterprise. Unimpressed by the cultural achievements and religious practices of the Israelite rank and file, this strong-minded daughter of Tyre tried to make Ba°alism the official religion of the land.

Though Ahab remained a nominal Yahwist, widespread apostasy now plagued the Israelites. Loyal Yahwists who were vocal in their objection to the religious policy of the court were victimized. Samuel with Saul, Nathan with David, and Ahijah with Solomon could criticize the ruling monarch without fear of retaliation. Now this no longer seemed possible. Some professional prophets submitted to court pressure and uttered only those oracles favorable to royal policy. Such prophets as Elijah and Micaiah, however, stood firm and suffered the consequences. The austere covenantal religion that Israel had brought into the Land of Promise from the desert was now severely threatened—so much so that Elijah once complained in a despondent moment (1 Kings 19:14) that he was its sole supporter.

The Elijah Tradition as Literature

The chapters in the Hebrew Bible devoted to Elijah (1 Kings 17–19, 21, and 2 Kings 1) are the stuff of legend. Infused with the miraculous, they offer only a partial glimpse of the prophet. Precisely when his interest in Elijah the man is highest, the narrative thrusts upon the reader the person of Yahweh himself and eclipses the prophet. Even so, the biblical narrative is exciting. It originates in the prophetic circle of Elijah, which during the first half of the eighth century gave shape to the oral tradition about their mentor. In the stories they told and retold, they glorified their inspired leader. Although such adulation frustrates our study of the Elijah of history, we are scarcely in a position to deny his existence. Indeed, as von Rad writes, these stories reveal "a man of enormous powers. Such a figure cannot simply have been invented, and can only be explained by saying that the stories reflect a historical figure of well-nigh superhuman stature."[10]

An element of mystery also surrounds the historical Elijah. In 1 Kings 17:1 the prophet simply appears. We know nothing of his family. The identity of his hometown, Tishbe, is also unknown, though Elijah appears to have hailed from Gilead in Transjordan. In the Elijah cycle of legends, it is difficult to isolate fact from legend. Still, we suspect that the episode of Naboth's vineyard (1 Kings 21) describing Elijah's righteous indignation can be defended as sober history, whereas the report about Elijah's miraculous feeding on his journey to the Sinai Peninsula (1 Kings 17:4–7) cannot. The various traditions about Elijah were originally self-contained testimonies to this ninth-century prophetic giant. In their present form these traditions offer a rather consistent portrait of the prophet, but it seems likely that they stem from more than one group of Elijah admirers.

The Early Career of Elijah

Although the popular legend of 1 Kings 17 that recounts Elijah's first confrontation with Ahab and his northward flight into Phoenician territory cannot be taken literally, it is a dramatic introduction to the prophet and his religion. At the outset we are informed that Elijah was a native of Gilead, a Transjordan territory that had had only partial exposure to the religion of Baʿal. While the northern kingdom of Israel had made extensive accommodations to Canaanite culture and religion, the tribes that had settled on the east side of the Jordan were colonizing virgin territory. Their brand of Yahwism could be far more demanding. This explains, at least in part, Elijah's austere and uncompromising character. Here the forbidding man of God personally instructs Ahab that rain, or the awful lack of it, depends solely on the will of the prophet and, in turn, of Yahweh, whom he represents (17:1). This announcement of a divinely sent drought sets the stage for the impending struggle between those who declare Baʿal responsible for rain and fertility, and those who make the identical claim for Yahweh.

Following the divine command (17:2–4), Elijah moves beyond Ahab's reach into a time of solitude during which he is both tested and sustained. Instructed by Yahweh to move to Zarephath (17:9), Elijah enters this Phoenician territory. What lies beyond Ahab's jurisdiction is still well within Yahweh's influence. Elijah can function as Yahweh's prophet even in the remote north. His contact with the world follows immediately upon his brush with solitude. Presently the prophet develops a gentle association with the Syro-Phoenician widow. The story that Elijah blessed the widow's jar of meal and oil container and revived her (nearly) dead son is the stuff of cherished legend. It defends both the humanitarian behavior of the prophet and the power of the God with whom he stood in immediate fellowship.

The Contest on Mount Carmel

One of the best-known traditions of the Hebrew Bible concerns Elijah's action on Mount Carmel (1 Kings 18). With the three-year period of drought now over, Ahab and Elijah experience another painful confrontation. A contest between prophet and monarch is staged on Mount Carmel. In the presence of "all the people of Israel" (18:20) Elijah takes on all the prophets of Jezebel's Baᶜalistic cult. Elijah does not entertain the assembled people with magic; instead, he confronts them with the words, "How long will you go limping with two different opinions? If Yahweh is God, follow him; but if Baᶜal, then follow him" (18:21). In the use of the verb "to limp" we have a provocative allusion to the double-mindedness of the contemporary Israelite population, who were not yet convinced that honoring both Yahweh and Baᶜal was such a bad idea. Elijah insists that there is but one God in Israel. Men must choose.

On Mount Carmel the prophet stands alone against the world, challenging his audience to reexamine their religious loyalty. He confronts the people with the claims of two competing religious systems. His sober approach is a magnificent contrast to that of the prophet-priests of Baᶜal. The latter cry aloud to their god. When they get no response, they limp about the altar and mutilate themselves. These theatrics lead nowhere. Yet in his prayers and actions, Elijah confers dignity on the occasion. The legend also suggests that he must have enjoyed the contest, for he mocks the tactics of Baᶜal's worshipers and Baᶜal's inability to respond to them (18:27). Of course, Elijah's purpose is to convert the Israelite populace back to Mosaic Yahwism. Having seen the wet sacrifice burst into flames, the people are now convinced that Yahweh has answered Elijah's plea with a fire from heaven. Joyously they proclaim, "Yahweh, he is God; Yahweh, he is God" (18:39).

We now witness a dark moment in Israel's history as Elijah slaughters the Baᶜal prophets (18:40). But this was not some demagogue at work, for Elijah was honoring the requirements of the ancient sacrificial ban. Still, this horrendous killing did not eradicate Baᶜalism from Canaan. The heart of Jezebel was in no sense drawn away from her Tyrian gods.

The Mount Carmel tradition attests to Elijah's stature and uncompromising dedication. Like Joshua (Josh. 24:15), Elijah challenged the religious allegiance of his contemporaries with a clear-cut choice. Yet despite whatever power of persuasion he may have had over the people, the environment in which Elijah had to work remained hostile. Having killed off Jezebel's prophets, he incurred her wrath and had no choice but to flee.

The Theophany on Mount Horeb

According to the legend preserved in 1 Kings 19, Elijah moved to another mountain, Mount Horeb (Sinai). Informed that the determined Jezebel was in hot pursuit, the despondent prophet traveled first to Beer-sheba and then into the desert. A new portrait of the prophet is offered. Whereas 1 Kings 18 depicts Elijah as a colossus, he is presented here as a defeated hero overcome by fear and a gnawing sense of failure (19:4). This zealous proponent of the faith had been no more successful than his ancestors in ridding the land of Ba‘al worship. Elijah passes from the bright day of firm belief into the dark night of the soul. Whatever problems the miraculous episode of 19:5–8 may hold for the contemporary reader, it proclaims that during life's lowest moments Yahweh does not abandon his faithful. The nourishment with which Elijah was provided equipped him to undertake the arduous pilgrimage to Mount Horeb (Sinai). There he tried to relate both to the geographical point of origin of the covenant faith and to Moses, who had implemented that faith.

The theophany of Yahweh that Elijah experienced at Sinai (19:9–18) was crucial not only to his personal growth but to the development of Israelite religion as a whole. The question Yahweh thrusts before Elijah is disarming: "What are you doing here, Elijah?" (19:13). Having expressed his loyalty to the covenant and his complaint (19:14), Elijah must hear words of divine rebuke. In fleeing from the queen, in displaying fear in the face of oppression, Elijah has discredited the prophetic office.

The prophet is expected to assume risks. Therefore, Elijah is thrust back into the world. But before we consider Elijah's commission, let us examine the manner of God's self-revelation.

The actuality of divine presence is stated in precise and provocative terms. Wind, earthquake, and fire, those natural phenomena that attended Yahweh's self-revelation at Sinai in the days of Moses, do not disclose the deity to Elijah. It is only after these potentially catastrophic forces have faded that Elijah is certain of Yahweh's presence. Divine nearness is perceived in the lull of eerie silence. This stillness is not the voice of Elijah's conscience; rather, it is "a silence that could be heard, as it is sometimes said that a darkness is so great that one can feel it."[11] Moreover, Elijah reacts to the divine presence in a decisive manner by wrapping his face in his mantle (19:13). This guarantees that too close an association between God and man will not take place. Yahweh's face and shape are not available to man.

In 1 Kings 19 it is asserted that Yahweh's self-disclosure is no longer to be conceived in traditional terms. The measured phrases of 19:11b–12 argue that the more ancient representation of Yahweh is now to be set aside. God is not apparent in the deafening outbursts of the storm; his presence is perceived in the stillness that follows. Theophany is now connected with "intelligible communication."[12] Through the theophanic message itself we discern that the God Elijah sought was not the God Elijah met. The prophet quested for rational certitude. He may also have coveted for himself the experience of Moses. But this theophanic encounter is shaped by divine sovereignty, not misguided human piety.

Elijah is now ushered back into the world with specific tasks to fulfill. He is commissioned to anoint Hazael king of Damascus; Jehu king of Israel; and Elisha, his disciple, a prophet in his place. The first command reveals Yahweh's concern for foreign nations. The second points to the prophetic support of the revolt led by Jehu against the Omri dynasty in 842. By such anointing, Elijah is to take part in revolutions against the existing regimes of Syria and Israel. Curiously, he fulfills neither commission, although his successor Elisha does (2 Kings 8:7–15 and 9:1–13). The third command then speaks for continuity within the prophetic movement. Elisha is to follow in the footsteps of his mentor, Elijah.

The remnant motif is another vital element within the text. Though this theme neither originates nor climaxes with the figure of Elijah, the existence of a righteous few is emphasized in 1 Kings 19:18. There Yahweh claims that 7,000 persons have remained loyal to the covenant faith. They are disassociated from the rest of Israel, and through them the hope abides that the covenant relationship between God and people will endure. In ancient Near Eastern politics, a remnant was usually fortunate enough to be spared death and unfortunate enough to have to endure physical hardship and international insignificance. Yet within the remnant existed the nucleus for that people's regeneration. Hence, the tradition of 1 Kings 19 joins other texts of the Hebrew Bible in affirming that whereas apostate Israel must suffer ruin, the righteous remnant, as Yahweh's elect, would experience a new day.

Naboth and His Vineyard

We turn now to the Naboth episode (1 Kings 21), which seems to have taken place some years later. Naboth was a small landowner in Jezreel who suffered the fate of having a home near Ahab's summer residence. Though Ahab offered him a good price for his vineyard, Naboth refused to sell because this land was the inheritance of his fathers. He respected the Levitical law that frowned on speculative bartering over property that was an integral part of Yahweh's gift of land to his people (see Lev. 25:23). That land was intended for the good of the whole community of faith, and corporate welfare was to remain a concern among those who inherited and later passed the land on to their offspring.

The sulking Ahab seems to have respected Naboth's conviction that a private commercial transaction would constitute a breach of covenant loyalty. The queen, however, had no intention of letting the matter rest, and she engineered Naboth's execution. Thereupon, Ahab had to hear Elijah's ominous judgment that Yahweh had now rejected him completely (21:21). Ahab confessed his remorse over the sordid Naboth affair (21:27). Jezebel undoubtedly regarded her husband Ahab's symbols of repentance, sackcloth and fasting, with utter con-

Horned Limestone Altar from Megiddo.
This cultic object was discovered in an
Iron Age level excavation at Megiddo.
It is about 30 inches tall and has four
horns on the top—one at each corner.
Such altars were used for burning
incense and for "sin" offerings, which
involved smearing blood on the four
horns. According to 1 Kings 1:51 and
2:28, the horns were also understood
as a place of refuge that might or might
not be honored by all the parties
concerned. (Photo by the author, taken
in the Palestine Archaeological Museum,
Jerusalem. Used with permission of the
Israel Department of Antiquities and
Museums.)

tempt. The judgment, however, was to be deferred to the era of Ahab's
son, and thus the record speaks moderately well of Ahab. The Elijah
cycle is largely free of Deuteronomic idiom, yet in 21:25–26 we meet
an undeniably harsh editorial criticism of the deceased Ahab.

This episode skillfully portrays Elijah's preoccupation with social
justice. He held that covenantal righteousness has two dimensions:
man's relation with his God and man's association with his neighbor.
Both were important to Elijah. This champion of Yahweh also defended
the poor, who were forced to live at the mercy of their wealthy
contemporaries.

Elijah's Last Days

The bloodthirsty opening chapter of 2 Kings speaks of Elijah's last
days, when Ahaziah (850–849) reigned over Israel. Ahaziah demonstrates his woeful lack of faith when after a severe fall he turns not to
Yahweh but to Ba'al-zebub, god of the flies, for help (1:2).[13] Elijah's
function is to pronounce a curse of death on the king. Again monarch
and prophet stand in a dialectical relationship.

This legend reports that Elijah called down fire from heaven
against the first two contingents of the king who attempted to arrest
him. Indeed, it was only due to the highly diplomatic captain of the
third contingent and Yahweh's merciful word to the prophet that the
third group was spared (1:13–16). In such a legendary witness, "the
greatness of the prophet is compromised by the adulation of much
smaller minds."[14] Yet significantly, in this third confrontation the

judgment of death against Ahaziah is not rescinded. Moreover, that transcendent word mediated through the prophet is fulfilled (1:17). With his prophetic task now completed, Elijah mysteriously ascends into the heavens (2:11).

At least four factors have contributed to the prophet's lasting significance: First, Elijah was zealous for Yahweh, who alone was to be worshiped in Israel. As Yahweh's special representative, Elijah was a singular match for Jezebel. While the prophet failed to convert Jezebel or undercut her zeal for Ba'alism, his enthusiasm for Yahweh impressed both his own and subsequent generations. Next, Elijah held that worship and ethics are intimately related. Even though the specific functions of the cult were conducted in Yahweh's name, this was not the limit of covenant responsibility. Elijah insisted that each loyal Israelite take to heart the aspects of the Torah that concerned the welfare of his covenant brothers. Furthermore, Elijah spoke in the name of a deity whose power was universal. He recognized that Israel's God was not bound by geography. Any loyal Yahwist who acted in his name within Israel's borders might act similarly beyond those borders.

Limestone Manger at Megiddo. The University of Chicago expedition (1925–1939) that worked at this ancient site found two stable complexes. Once thought to belong to Solomon, they are now regarded by scholars as the property of Ahab. The stables were large enough to house 450 horses. In front of the stalls were upright limestone pillars (hitching posts) with mangers between. Today's visitors can still see numerous mangers and hitching posts. (Photo by the author.)

Elijah's religion was neither tribal nor parochial. Finally, Elijah was linked with the biblical notion of the righteous few. His crucial encounter with the deity at Mount Horeb forced him to grasp the concept of election in a new way. In the light of these and other factors, Elijah has taken his rightful place among the Bible's most influential prophets.

ELIJAH'S PROPHETIC CONTEMPORARIES

Micaiah

Micaiah is another energetic and courageous prophet who pursued the role of lone dissenter while Ahab held the throne. Our knowledge of Micaiah is wholly dependent on the tradition in 1 Kings 22. There we learn that the winds between Israel and Syria had shifted. The days when Ahab of Israel and Ben-hadad of Syria had been allies were now past. At the moment, Ahab sought to reclaim Ramoth-gilead, a city in Transjordan now occupied by Syria but previously held by Israel. King Ahab requested that his lesser partner, King Jehoshaphat of Judah, visit him at his court in Samaria and support him in the impending endeavor.

Jehoshaphat must have known that Ahab regarded him as his vassal. Nevertheless, he did not wish to commit himself to any military strategy until prophetic opinion on the matter could be solicited. How did Yahweh view Ahab's plans? After Ahab's 400 court prophets had approved (22:6), Jehoshaphat pressed the inquiry further and Micaiah was called in. Ahab's contempt for this prophetic loner is masterfully expressed: "I hate him, for he never prophesies good concerning me, but evil" (22:8). While the imprisoned Micaiah was being summoned, a prophet named Zedekiah simulated Ahab's impending victory by putting on horned headgear. Like the prophetic word itself, that symbolic act was intended to give Ahab maximum encouragement.

Micaiah's initially favorable oracle only aroused Ahab's suspicion that Micaiah was mocking the easy optimism of existing court prophecy (22:15–16), which indeed he was. Then Micaiah communicated his true oracle, and Ahab's doom was resolutely predicted. Micaiah claimed that in a special vision he had learned of Yahweh's desire to oppose Ahab. Though he would not deceive Ahab directly, he would entice him through a heavenly volunteer. One of the members of Yahweh's celestial court had expressed his willingness to be a lying spirit who would enter the mouth of all the false court prophets of Samaria (22:21–23). While Micaiah was returned to prison for having spoken so candidly, the compelling prophetic word had nevertheless been disclosed.

This brief episode in the life of an enthusiastic Israelite prophet is significant for several reasons. It attests that by the ninth century B.C. Yahweh was conceived as a heavenly king surrounded by a court of

ministering spirits. This pluralism was a part of Israel's brand of monotheism, which embraced both the one and the many.

The account discloses the commonly held prophetic view that
Yahweh is responsible for all events in the world, whether they be
pleasant or terrifying. Ahab's end on the battlefield is decreed by Yahweh
and the "lying spirit." To be sure, Ahab had developed a strategy of
his own (22:30). Yet ultimately Ahab was killed, Jehoshaphat survived,
and Micaiah's prophecy was confirmed.

Furthermore, this vignette upholds the transcendent origins of
Hebrew prophecy. The differentiation made between the "lying spirit"
and the "spirit of Yahweh" affirms the radical difference between true
and false prophecy. Micaiah attributed his own knowledge not to his
intellect but to his receptivity to a singular vision of Yahweh and his
will. He had indeed felt a compulsion to speak. If such speech robbed
him of personal comfort and courtly praise, it remained true to the
course that had previously been charted by Mosaic Yahwism.

Elisha

Broadly speaking, the prophet Elisha was likewise a contemporary of
Elijah, though 2 Kings 13:14–19 reveals that his activity extended to the
beginning of Jehoash's reign (801–786). Pressed into service by Elijah
(1 Kings 19:16, 19–21), Elisha outlived Elijah and the Omri dynasty
by several decades. Biblical tradition relates Elisha to the last years of
the house of Omri. After his death in battle against the Syrians (1 Kings
22:34–35), Ahab was succeeded by two sons, Ahaziah (850–849) and
Jehoram (849–842). The former, who fell through the lattice in his room
and died (2 Kings 1:2, 17), occupied the throne for too short a time to
accomplish anything of significance. The latter did not conduct the kind
of religious reform that might have prompted praise from the Deuteronomist. Although 2 Kings 3:1–3 indicates that Jehoram removed "the
pillar of Baʿal," the presence of queen mother Jezebel must have made
authentic reform next to impossible. Israel's war with Damascus
lingered on, and Mesha, king of Moab, asserted himself against Jehoram.
Also the narrative in 2 Kings 9–10 suggests that Jehoram's leadership
was questioned by both prophetic and military elements within Israel.

Thus, in 842 B.C. Jehu and his soldiers advanced against Samaria
and conducted a bloody purge that promptly brought the Omri dynasty
to an ignoble end. Elisha himself set the revolt in motion (2 Kings
9:1–13). The ultimate success of Jehu, however, was circumscribed. His
reign was long (842–815), but unhappy. This usurper's relations with
Phoenicia and Judah were strained. The citizens of Tyre were scarcely
pleased by the news that Jehu had had Jezebel thrown out of the
palace window (9:30–33). And the citizens of Judah were incensed that
their king, Ahaziah (842), who was supporting Jehoram, had been

struck down at Jehu's orders (9:27). The indiscriminate Jehu therefore alienated the very allies Omri had taken pains to cultivate. Further, the best of Israel's leadership was hacked down by Jehu (2 Kings 10). There must have been a wave of resentment against Jehu's excessive coup d'état. While Jehu brought about the end of the cult of Ba'al Melqart, he conducted no reform program to honor the religious and social requirements of ancient Yahwism (10:28–31). Inequities within Israelite society persisted.

With Hazael (ca. 842–806) usurping the throne of Damascus in the same year that Jehu overtook Samaria, the Aramean kingdom achieved political and military prominence. The Aramean forces proved troublesome to Jehu, who was unable to defend Israel's borders. He and his son Jehoahaz (815–801) both lost out to this northern power. Fortunately by the time that Jehoash (801–786) ascendèd the Israelite throne, Damascus had been humbled by the Assyrians, who again charged westward. With Damascus now in check, Israel experienced some resurgence under Jehoash. In sum, Elisha lived at a time when Israel was weak politically and consistently meager in her demonstration of loyalty toward Yahweh.

The Elisha traditions are permeated with the miraculous. By tossing salt from a new bowl into the spring of Jericho, Elisha restores its waters to wholeness (2 Kings 2:19–22). By creating a continuous supply of oil that can be sold, Elisha assists the widow of a disciple when she is harassed by a persistent creditor (4:1–7). After the son of a well-to-do woman of Shunem dies of sunstroke, Elisha brings him back to life through oral resuscitation (4:18–37). During a famine, Elisha satisfies the hunger of 100 men with a very small quantity of food (4:42–44). Naaman, the commander of the Syrian army, finds that Elisha can cure his leprosy (5:1–19a). When a son of one of the prophets loses an iron ax head, Elisha makes it float on the water (6:1–7).

Despite their bizarre quality, these fanciful stories suggest that Elisha was held in great esteem by his following. Undoubtedly, after his death, their respect for their highly gifted and magnanimous leader increased. In fact, the cycle of traditions centering around Elisha attempts to assert the superiority of Elisha over Elijah, who had commissioned him. The effect on the contemporary reader, however, is less than satisfactory, for the historicity of Elisha is consistently obscured. We might even be tempted to question Elisha's existence were it not for 2 Kings 9:1–13, which links the prophet to Jehu's coup d'état.

Nevertheless, when we peel away the layers of wonder-working, some evidence remains that Elisha was an effective prophet who furthered the tenuous course of Yahwism in ninth-century Israel. His work may be viewed along three different lines.

First, Elisha was active in public life. Notably, he was responsible for anointing Jehu as king of Israel. The impact of this act on the sequence of events leading up to Jehu's coup d'état in 842 must not be underestimated.

Second, Elisha kept close company with the sons of the prophets, who were mainly drawn from low-class Israelite society. These roving charismatic bands were devoted to Elisha, and he worried about their comfort and daily undertakings. He addressed himself to their need for food (2 Kings 4:42) and shelter (6:1), as well as fair treatment (4:1). And as Elisha served this segment of humanity, he must have influenced the manner in which they conceived of the covenant deity.

Finally, as the narrative of 2 Kings 5:1–19a discloses with excitement and charm, Elisha associated with non-Israelites. When the Syrian Naaman came before Elisha to be healed, he anticipated a flashy miracle that would cure his leprosy. Elisha did not even come out of his house to greet him. He simply sent out instructions that Naaman should wash in the River Jordan. In contrast with much of the popular Elisha material, the healing is subtle and is not the climax of the story. Having cured Naaman, Elisha expected no gifts. Even so, Naaman offered them, and in addition, a confession of faith: "I know that there is no God in all the earth but in Israel" (5:15). With stateliness, calm, and compassion, Elisha had brought a non-Israelite into the faith.

In such ways as these, the prophet more than proved his worth to his contemporaries. To be sure, in our judgment Elisha's deeds may fail to measure up to those of Elijah, the ninth-century Israelite prophet par excellence. Nevertheless, Elisha should not be cavalierly dismissed.

NOTES

1. Several helpful notations on this list are presented in James B. Pritchard, ed., *Ancient Near Eastern Texts Relating to the Old Testament*, 3d ed. (Princeton, N.J.: Princeton University Press, 1969), pp. 263–264. Shishak's inscription has had some support from archaeological evidence.
2. For a well-written account of the discovery of the stone, see G. Frederick Owen, *Archaeology and the Bible* (Westwood, N.J.: Fleming H. Revell, 1961), pp. 261–262.
3. Pritchard, *op. cit.*, p. 320. Brackets with ellipses indicate lacunae; words in parentheses are the translator's interpolations to facilitate comprehension of the text. For additional remarks on the historical significance of this inscription, see R. J. Williams, "Moabite Stone," in George A. Buttrick et al., eds., *The Interpreter's Dictionary of the Bible* (Nashville: Abingdon Press, 1962), K–Q, pp. 419–420.
4. For further details on the archaeological finds of Samaria, see Kathleen M. Kenyon, *Archaeology in the Holy Land*, 3d ed. (New York: Frederick A. Praeger, 1970), pp. 262–269; and G. Ernest Wright, *Biblical Archaeology*, rev. ed. (Philadelphia: Westminster Press, 1962), pp. 152–155.
5. On the question of Athaliah's identity, see John Bright, *A History of Israel*, 2d ed. (Philadelphia: Westminster Press, 1972), p. 238, n. 41. In

any event, Athaliah was an Omride gift to the court of Judah intended to formalize an alliance of friendship between Israel and Judah.

6. Pritchard, *op. cit.*, pp. 278–279.

7. For a fuller treatment of the subject, see B. Davie Napier, "Prophet, Prophetism," in Buttrick et al., eds., *op. cit.*, K–Q, pp. 896–919, or the subsequent revision in book form, B. Davie Napier, *Prophets in Perspective* (Nashville: Abingdon Press, 1963).

8. Johannes Lindblom, *Prophecy in Ancient Israel* (Philadelphia: Fortress Press, 1962), p. 1.

9. *Ibid.*, pp. 4–6 and *passim*.

10. Gerhard von Rad, *Old Testament Theology*, trans. D. M. G. Stalker (New York: Harper & Row, 1965), 2: 14–15.

11. R. B. Y. Scott, *The Relevance of the Prophets*, rev. ed. (New York: Macmillan, 1968), p. 74.

12. John Gray, *I & II Kings: A Commentary*, rev. ed., The Old Testament Library (Philadelphia: Westminster Press, 1970), p. 410.

13. That name may well have been a derogatory form of an original "Ba'alzebul," god of the lofty dwelling, who, as the god of life, held sway in Syria to the north.

14. John Mauchline, "I and II Kings," in Matthew Black and H. H. Rowley, eds., *Peake's Commentary on the Bible*, rev. ed. (New York: Thomas Nelson & Sons, 1962), pp. 347–348.

Part IV

THE DEMISE OF THE PEOPLE

12

AMOS, HOSEA, AND THE END OF THE NORTHERN KINGDOM

The basic tenor of ancient Israel's existence from the thirteenth through the ninth centuries B.C. contrasted with much that was to take place from the eighth through the sixth centuries B.C. Of course, not all the years in the former category were marked by political, social, and religious advances. Nevertheless, to study the life and literature of eighth-century Israel and Judah is to confront a period when the health of Yahweh's people unquestionably took a turn for the worse. To be sure, during the first half of that century, Israel and Judah experienced resurgence under the leadership of Jeroboam II (786–746) and Uzziah (783–742). But by 745 western Asia was forced to cope with widespread Assyrian aggression, and in 722 the independent life of the northern kingdom came to an end. Merely two decades later (701), Judah suffered severely as Assyria menaced the land and almost overran Jerusalem.

As one decade followed another, the contrasts between rich and poor became even more pronounced in Israel. In the ninth century, the social abuses and sharp economic distinctions of an increasingly stratified society had been of little concern to the monarchy, and by the middle of the eighth century such problems were met with complete indifference. Even so, the eighth century produced an age of classical Israelite prophetism during which Amos, Hosea, Micah, and Isaiah voiced their sharp protests. Their fervent invitations to return to Yahweh evoked little positive response, however. And the dismal situation did not improve during the last century of Judah's existence, when the nation was often required to function as an obliging Assyrian vassal.

Biblical texts to be read prior to and in conjunction with the present chapter: 2 Kings 11:1–14:29; Amos; 2 Kings 15:8–31; Hosea; 2 Kings 17:1–41. The first-mentioned Kings passage may be given a quick reading.

The cause of Yahwism met with overwhelming frustration when Manasseh (687–642) was forced to impress on his people the necessity of paying homage to Assyrian deities. Then in 587, when Jerusalem fell to the Babylonians, who had now become the leading power in Mesopotamia, the nation of Judah came to an end. Hence, during the historical period that we shall examine in this chapter and the four that follow, the demise of the covenant people was apparent in many circles.

ISRAELITE HISTORY, SOCIETY, AND RELIGION PRIOR TO THE PUBLIC APPEARANCE OF AMOS

The proclamations of Amos, which date to the middle of the eighth century, are more intelligible in the light of the historical, sociological, and religious background of this era. You will remember that Jehu's coup d'état in 842 spelled political disaster. By doing away with Jezebel and the devotees of Baʿal, Jehu had alienated Phoenicia. Now he was required to face the threat of Syria alone. Momentary relief came in 841 when he paid Shalmaneser III of Assyria a handsome tribute to secure his services as an ally against Syria. Although this episode is nowhere mentioned in the Old Testament, it is depicted on the Assyrian monarch's famous Black Obelisk.[1] Within a few years, however, local problems absorbed Assyrian energy. For several decades westward expansion was clearly out of the question for Assyria. Thus, Jehu was once more left alone to withstand Syrian assertion. Territories in Transjordan and along the Mediterranean coast were lost to Syria. Jehu's Israel was substantially smaller than Omri's.

Late in the ninth century, however, Syrian harassment of Israel suddenly halted. In 802 the Assyrian forces moved westward and snuffed out the power of Damascus. Internal chaos and weak rulers both determined that Assyria would not move very far into western Asia during the next half-century. While this provided Damascus with some relief, there were many distractions that kept her from turning her military machinery on Israel. Consequently, during the first half of the eighth century Israel's citizenry was to benefit from a period of political resurgence. Relatively friendly neighbors and two effective monarchs— Jehoash (801–786) and Jeroboam II (786–746)—helped Israel's cause considerably.

But how did Judah fare at this time? After a brief and unimpressive rule, Jehoram (849–842) died and was followed by his son Ahaziah. The latter reigned for less than a year when he was assassinated on Jehu's orders. Thereupon, Athaliah, his mother, usurped the throne of Judah, and in the next six years the southern kingdom had to cope with her illegitimate rule. It was, of course, most disturbing that she was

Jehu Kneels Before Shalmaneser III. Three of the five panels appearing on the same side of Shalmaneser's Black Obelisk are shown here. In the top panel Jehu is depicted as the losing Israelite king who must prostrate himself before the triumphant Assyrian monarch. Each panel runs around all four sides of the obelisk and is described by the cuneiform inscription above it. Other faces of the Jehu panel depict Israelite porters who carry the tribute. (Courtesy of the Trustees of the British Museum.)

not a descendant of David. In addition, her sex and devotion to the Ba'al cult must have made her unpopular with many Judean inhabitants who persisted in their simple fidelity to Yahwism. To buttress her position on the throne, the queen tried to assassinate all male contenders within the Davidic house.

But little Joash, the son of Ahaziah, was whisked away and cared for by the temple priests. In 2 Kings 11 we read that at the tender age of seven (837) Joash was acclaimed king of Judah by the priest Jehoiada who led a limited but successful revolt against Athaliah. The queen and her Baʿalistic cult were both exterminated. Joash, who was in his mid-forties when he was assassinated in 800, suffered from too much counsel from Jehoiada in his youth and from too little enthusiasm for the royal office later on.

The first years of Judah's eighth-century existence were directed by Amaziah (800–783). Although Amaziah was able to dominate the Edomites to the southeast, he was beaten by Jehoash of Israel (2 Kings 14). Thereafter, Amaziah pursued an undistinguished career that ended in assassination. But under the leadership of Amaziah's son Uzziah (783–742) Judah experienced genuine resurgence. According to 2 Chronicles 26, Uzziah repaired the Jerusalem walls, refurbished Judah's army, and asserted himself in Edom and the Negev, as well as along the Philistine plain.

Israel's political and military awakening under Jehoash and Jeroboam II paralleled Judah's restoration. Jehoash reclaimed Israelite cities that the Syrian Ben-hadad II had grasped from his father, Jehoahaz (2 Kings 13:25). Yet it was Jeroboam II who was especially gifted in latching on to new territory. According to 2 Kings 14:25, Jeroboam "restored the border of Israel from the entrance of Hamath as far as the Sea of the Arabah." With Hamath located far north of Damascus, we assume that Jeroboam established his northern border where Solomon had previously. And since the "Sea of Arabah" is a synonym for the Dead Sea, Jeroboam must have penetrated far south as well. This verse in 2 Kings, coupled with two veiled references in Amos 6:13 to Jeroboam's triumphs in Transjordan, suggests that during most of the first half of the eighth century, Israel benefited from a remarkably strong military ruler whose forty-year reign brought great material prosperity to the court.

Nevertheless, Jeroboam's reign was woefully deficient in sociological and religious matters. The daily life of most poor Israelite citizens was burdensome. Once Israel had been a cohesive and classless society, but social stratification was building up at an ever-increasing pace. Dishonesty in business transactions was commonplace. Allusions in Amos 2:6 and 8:6 that the needy were being sold for a pair of shoes imply that creditors were allowed to sell debtors into slavery, even when indebtedness was minor. Israel's merchants falsified their weights and measures; they resented the Sabbath because it interrupted the sale of their goods (Amos 8:5). Established channels for the legal defense of the poor simply did not exist: "They hate him who reproves in the gate, and they abhor him who speaks the truth" (Amos 5:10). In sum, the common good was all too frequently eclipsed.

Though large numbers of people may have turned out for worship, their religious exercises were severely criticized by the classical prophets

V. THE EIGHTH-CENTURY DIVIDED MONARCHY (ca. 800–722 B.C.)

DATE (B.C.)	EGYPT	PALESTINE		SYRIA	ASSYRIA
		Southern Kingdom (Judah)	Northern Kingdom (Israel)		
800	Period of weakness	Amaziah (800–783) Uzziah (783–742)	Jehoash (801–786) Jeroboam II (786–746)		Period of weakness (ca. 800–750)
750	Period of weakness	Jotham as regent (ca. 750–742) Jotham as king (742–735) Isaiah (ca. 742–695) Ahaz (735–715) Syro-Israelite alliance harasses Ahaz (735) Micah (ca. 730–701)	Amos (ca. 750) Hosea (ca. 748–730) Zechariah (746–745) *Shallum (745) *Menahem (745–738) Pekahiah (738–737) *Pekah (737–732) *Hoshea (732–724) Fall of Samaria (722)	Rezin (ca. 740–732) Syro-Israelite alliance (735) Fall of Syria (732)	Tiglath-pileser III (745–727) overtakes Damascus (732) Shalmaneser V (727–722) Sargon II (722–705) crushes Samaria (722)

*Founder of new dynasty in the northern kingdom (Israel).

Public Silo at Megiddo. This massive circular granary was excavated at Megiddo. It was constructed during the prosperous reign of Jeroboam II (786–746 B.C.). Its shape resembles an inverted cone with a blunt base. Over 21 feet deep, 35 feet across the top, and about 21 feet across the bottom, this grain-storage pit has an estimated capacity of 12,800 bushels. Though with its stable complexes it had been a chariot city of the king in the preceding century, Megiddo now hosted a number of houses and shops. (Photo by the author.)

(Amos 4:4; 5:21–23; Hos. 8:11–13). Undoubtedly many local high places were encumbered by pagan trappings, and the quest for fertility may have dominated nearly all corporate Israelite worship (Amos 2:7–8; Hos. 4:13–14). Israel's impoverished religious leadership appears to have operated primarily out of a profit motive (Amos 7:12). Also many native Israelites interpreted their covenant with God too mechanistically. For them covenant fidelity was essentially cultic. It focused on elaborate ritual that induced in its participants a mighty surge of confidence (Amos 4:5; 6:1).

These were the conditions that confronted the eighth-century prophets who now appeared on the scene. Amos and Hosea may be roughly paired as contemporaries who addressed the northern kingdom. Micah and Isaiah may be similarly linked as essentially contemporary prophets who spoke to the needs of the southern kingdom. Thanks to their loyal disciples, scrolls bearing their names were to emerge and eventually assume a central position in the Hebrew Scriptures. As we shall see, the eighth-century prophets made a distinct contribution to their age. Indeed, they were responsible for "the golden age of prophecy."[2]

AMOS OF TEKOA

Literary Considerations

Amos and his eighth-century prophetic associates have sometimes been referred to as "writing prophets." Because we have no way of knowing to what degree they were involved in the actual writing down of their own utterances, or whether they knew how to write, we cannot accept this label as adequate. It is doubtful that in Amos' lifetime the writing of a polished book that mirrored the prophet's doings and sayings was considered a worthwhile undertaking. Yet once Amos had died, if not slightly earlier, the importance of recording the prophet's sayings would have been more fully acknowledged.

But regardless of when the spoken word of the prophet was committed to writing, the fact is that it was. The nature of the material is such that three literary questions require brief attention: What was the manner of the prophet's speech? How did the book that bears his name emerge? And what elements in the book cannot be accepted as the authentic work of Amos?

In answer to the first question, it is clear that Amos masterfully employed a variety of speech forms. For example, from wisdom circles he appropriated the graduated-numbers saying:

> For three transgressions of Damascus,
>   and for four, I will not revoke the punishment. (1:3)

He also used the proverb, which was a favorite way of speaking among the wise:

> Do two walk together,
>   unless they have made an appointment?
> Does a lion roar in the forest,
>   when he has no prey? (3:3–4a)

> Does evil befall a city,
>   unless Yahweh has done it? (3:6b)

Moreover, because of his ability to frame riddles, Amos was a good match for the wise man:

> Do horses run upon rocks?
>   Does one plow the sea with oxen?
> But you have turned justice into poison
>   and the fruit of righteousness into wormwood. (6:12)

This prophet could be vivid in his descriptions and denunciations. Speaking as the divine messenger he said:

> I gave you cleanness of teeth in all your cities. (4:6)

A more poignant expression of severe famine is scarcely imaginable. Against the covetous, heavily adorned women of Samaria he thundered:

Hear this word, you cows of Bashan,
  who are in the mountain of Samaria,
who oppress the poor, who crush the needy,
  who say to their husbands, "Bring, that we may drink!" (4:1)

Amos was a keen observer of the contemporary scene and a speaker who recognized the value of precision and variation. But he never spoke solely for art's sake. He felt strongly the urgency to communicate what he understood to be Yahweh's present will and concern. Typically he prefaced his oracles with those authoritative words, "Thus says Yahweh!" In sum, Amos spoke very well on things that in his view truly mattered.

How, then, are we to account for the emergence of the Book of Amos? Though scholars are not in full agreement on the details, several sound observations may be made. First came the spoken word of the prophet himself. The typical utterance of Amos did not take the form of lengthy, sustained discourse; instead it came forth as a terse oracle pregnant with meaning. Thus, in Amos 4:4 the prophet speaks crisply: "Come to Bethel, and transgress; to Gilgal, and multiply transgression; bring your sacrifices every morning, your tithes every three days." Whenever the occasion required, the prophet spoke briefly and to the point. It seems that only before the exuberant throng gathered at Bethel was Amos likely to have indulged in any prolonged speaking (1:3–2:16), and he himself may have played a role in compiling that material.[3]

A second step in the book's emergence involved collecting and arranging Amos' oracles. This work no doubt fell to Amos' disciples shortly after their mentor's death. Several of the separate collections can still be identified. Presumably the injunction "Hear this word" that begins Amos 3:1; 4:1; and 5:1 points in each case to another unit of collected prophetic utterances. The same thing is true of the word "Woe," which begins Amos 5:18; 6:1; and 6:4. Also the accounts of Amos' four visions in 7:1–9 and 8:1–3 may have been combined at one time as a separate literary collection; on stylistic grounds, a fifth vision narrated in 9:1–4 appears to be independent of the others.

Though it is difficult to determine precisely when most of the Book of Amos was written, a date shortly after 722 is often suggested.[4] Indeed, some consider the fall of Samaria (722) historical confirmation of Amos' admonitions and warnings. The Book of Amos was therefore brought together in the south after the northern kingdom had ceased to exist. This southern editing is especially evident in the superscription (1:1) that places Uzziah, king of Judah, ahead of his northern contemporary Jeroboam II. The Book of Amos, however, continued to develop. Where Judah's existence is implied, as in 1:2 ("Yahweh roars from Zion, and utters his voice from Jerusalem"), we may infer that the message of the now deceased Amos was reconstructed for the edification of the south. The work of collecting and ordering the sayings and narratives of Amos also generated new statements that did not come from the prophet himself.

This brings us to our third consideration: isolating the portions of the book that were not the work of Amos. Because the editorial superscription of a prophetic book is unlikely to be the work of the prophet in question, we suspect that 1:1 does not belong to Amos. And we have just voiced our reservations about accepting 1:2, with its strong Jerusalem orientation, as the work of the prophet. Moreover, the striking doxologies in 4:13; 5:8–9; and 9:5–6 probably did not originate with Amos. They interrupt the flow of personal, disarmingly simple speech so characteristic of Amos. These creation-centered doxologies use a participial form of introduction typical of the style of Second Isaiah (see Isa. 41:2–4; 42:5; 44:24–28). Although we cannot prove that these three passages are not the work of Amos, it seems likely that the doxologies were added to the Amos scroll during the Babylonian exile, when it was read liturgically in the synagogue.

Finally, the appendix in Amos 9:11–15 is probably not the work of Amos. There are several reasons. First, a distinct reference in 9:11 to the renewal of "the booth of David that is fallen" (that is, to the Davidic dynasty) presumes that Jerusalem and its royal family have already succumbed to the invading Babylonian forces that demolished the city in 587. Second, the Amos appendix, with its depiction of the luxuriant blossoming of nature (9:13), has a quality very much like the dream idiom of postexilic Jewish eschatology. And finally, the restoration of Israel's fortunes referred to in 9:14–15 contradicts Amos' belief that not all the people would participate in this experience. On balance, however, most of the Book of Amos appears to be a faithful representation of the prophet who bore that name.

Amos' Background

Amos hailed from Tekoa, an eastern Judean village. Presumably he spent much of his time with other shepherds in the desert stretches to the east of Tekoa that permitted the grazing of sheep and goats (Amos 1:1; 7:14–15). Amos was also a dresser of sycamore trees, who apparently punctured the fig-like fruit to improve its taste (7:14). Living outdoors as he did must have provided Amos with a range of symbols and metaphors to be used in formulating his prophetic utterances. And presumably it was in the wilderness that Amos had certain visions. Having perceived the divine summons, Amos left his rural southern environment to proclaim the prophetic word in regions of the northern kingdom that he believed were in dire need of Yahweh's transcendent criticism.

The tense encounter between the prophet and Amaziah, the priest of Bethel (Amos 7:10–17), is especially relevant to the issue of Amos' background. When the outraged Amaziah demands that Amos leave Bethel and prophesy in Judah, Amos retorts, "I am no prophet, nor a prophet's son" (v. 14). In some manner, Amos is declaring that the term "prophet" did not, or does not, apply to himself. Because the verb "to be" is only implied in Amos' rejoinder, more than one interpretation is possible. If the Hebrew is to be rendered, "I am no prophet, nor a prophet's son," then Amos is saying that he does not wish to be associated with Israel's run-of-the-mill prophets and that he is simply a perceptive layman claimed by Yahweh for a special purpose. Yet it is perhaps preferable to translate Amos' remark in the past tense: "I was no prophet." In that case, Amos would be saying that whereas he had once been a shepherd and dresser of sycamores, he had changed his vocation in the light of the deity's summons to prophetic office. Therefore, he would not be denying the appropriateness of the term "prophet" to his present condition.[5]

Then when did Amos function as Yahweh's prophet? In Amos 1:1 and 7:9–11 the prophet is linked with the rule of Jeroboam (786–746). Two considerations would argue for placing the prophecy of Amos rather late in Jeroboam's reign: First, this would allow adequate time for the warfare between Israel and Syria to cease and Israel to experience significant material resurgence. Certainly Israel's great wealth implied in several verses in the Book of Amos would have taken a few years to accumulate. Second, Amos seems to discern the rise of a nation that will in the near future be the instrument of Yahweh's judgment against his people. Presumably Amos had Assyria in mind (3:9). While Syria and Palestine were free from Assyrian aggression throughout the first half of the eighth century, in the late 750s Amos might well have had the insight to anticipate that Assyria would one day inflict itself on the west. A third consideration connects Amos with Jeroboam. The superscription (1:1) claims that the prophecy of Amos took place "two years before the earthquake." Although the earthquake cannot be assigned a fixed date, it must have been unusually severe. It was alluded to several centuries later in Zech. 14:5, where it was linked with the reign of Uzziah (783–742). Presumably Amos engaged in his prophetic work at the approximate midpoint of the eighth century B.C.

Major Sections of the Book of Amos

The Book of Amos has three major sections. The first (Amos 1–2) contains the prophet's oracles that are directed against neighboring nations and culminates in a shrill denunciation of Israel herself. The second section (Amos 3–6) consists of several collections of oracles that thunder against Israel's social and religious decay. A third section (Amos 7–9) preserves the narrative account of the prophet's five visions (7:1–3, 4–6,

7–9; 8:1–3; 9:1–4), the story of his encounter with Amaziah (7:10–17), and additional pronouncements (8:4–14; 9:5–15).

Amos 1:3–2:16 begins with a series of forceful indictments of Israel and her immediate neighbors. These denunciations take the form of graduated-numbers sayings, which are common to Hebrew wisdom literature.[6] These utterances are addressed by Amos to a festive crowd that swarms into the sanctuary at Bethel expecting the invocation of divine power for the nation's benefit. Surely God's name will be intoned in a manner that will put the enemy off guard. But what Amos has to say at Bethel is not intended to implement national triumph.

What does Amos say at Bethel, and how does he say it? As for the content of his denunciations, the citizens of Damascus and Ammon are accused of treachery in war (1:3–5, 13–15). Those of Philistia and Tyre are denounced for having exiled entire populations (1:6–8, 9–10). Edom is charged with having warred against Israel, thereby playing havoc with the harmony that should have existed, for Israel and Edom were descended from the brothers Jacob and Esau, respectively (1:11–12). Moab is berated for desecrating the dead (2:1–3) and Judah for disrespecting Yahweh's law (2:4–5). Finally, Israel is accused of a host of ethical and religious offenses (2:6–16).

Assuming that all these pronouncements belong to the prophet, Amos' masterful strategy as visiting speaker at the Bethel sanctuary should not go unnoticed. Amos first denounces the areas furthest from Bethel—Damascus to the northeast, Philistia to the southwest, Tyre to the northwest, and Edom to the southeast. He then draws a little nearer to his audience by reproaching the Transjordanian kingdoms of Ammon and Moab. Then he moves still closer by denouncing the ways of Judah, the rival southern kingdom, and this places him in a superb position to thunder in 2:6, "For three transgressions of *Israel*, and for four. . . ."[7]

Having carried his listeners along for the remarkable span of seven oracles of reproach and threat, Amos suddenly turns to their own social and religious depravity. Israel is judged for exploitation of the poor (2:6), immorality (2:7), senseless forms of worship (2:8), and silencing Yahweh's prophets (2:12). Amos insists that God's judgment against such offenses is inevitable (2:13–16). Israel's apparent strength under Jeroboam II will therefore fade away.

Despite their diversity, the oracles in the second major section of the book (Amos 3–6) emphasize Yahweh's imminent judgment against his people and claim that such judgment is justified. The wrath of an outraged deity has been provoked by the people's dereliction of social and religious obligations. Speaking for Yahweh, Amos proclaims: "You only have I known of all the families of the earth; therefore I will punish you for all your iniquities" (3:2).

Israel had been singled out for a particular relationship with deity.

The crucial events of the Exodus and the giving of the law at Sinai are recalled. Therefore, Israel is to be held accountable for wrongdoing. In her defection from a noble calling, Israel has stirred up Yahweh's wrath, which bursts forth in the stunning chastisement that will follow.

The prophet also complains that many festivals and sacrifices are supported by a false sense of values. The national shrines of Bethel and Gilgal are sites of Israelite transgression (4:4). Meaningless sacrifices abound (5:21–23). Amos satirizes these ostentatious public rituals and also criticizes the wanton behavior of the wealthy, who enjoy their idleness and beds of inlaid ivory (6:4).

Further, Amos attacks the people's smugness. Since they believed that they were Yahweh's favorites, they eagerly anticipated the day of Yahweh. That day, thought the Israelite populace, would surely be one of light. But Amos protests that it will be a day of terrifying darkness (5:18). Not to be confused with the Sabbath, the day of Yahweh was thought of as the decisive moment when Yahweh would intervene in history once more in Israel's behalf. In her worship Israel recalled those remarkable moments when Yahweh had impinged on historical events for the benefit of his chosen people. Surely what had happened in the past would happen again. But how could the deity be expected to work in behalf of a rebellious people? Amos sees that the faith in Yahweh formally espoused in the cult is repudiated by day-to-day human conduct. Therefore, the future looks exceedingly grim.

Amos argues that the people's attitude toward God has indicted them. In Amos 4:6–11 Israel's outrageous callousness is laid bare. The pattern is liturgical. Each of the five brief units in this section begins with the "I" of the deity and mentions one of his punitive acts against his people; each concludes with the "you" of Israel ("You did not return to me"). These declarations affirm that Israel has repeatedly ignored Yahweh's warnings and admonitions. Therefore, Amos exhorts, "Prepare to meet your God, O Israel!" (4:12). Here the prophet seems to be urging the people to enter into a serious act of covenant renewal with Yahweh.[8] At least a speedy and sincere amendment of ways might go part way in mending the broken relationship between Yahweh and his people.

Inescapable judgment is communicated in Amos 3–6. The future offers no grandiose moment of national vindication, because God's interests are not those of his insensitive people. Judgment is sure to come, and it will be divinely wrought by the hand of the enemy. Israel's defenses will be brought down by an unnamed adversary, presumably Assyria (3:11). That nation will invade both the northern and southern extremities of the land (6:14). In speaking of the horrendous divine judgment, Amos recalls the deity of Israel's desert days who was in effect "a man of war" (see Exod. 15:3). Yahweh himself will initiate the offensive measures of the enemy.

Then, is Amos completely lacking in hope? Everywhere in his proclamations, he contends that Yahweh is about to set in motion an awful
purge that the northern kingdom roundly deserves. This nation, which
is incapable of repentance, must suffer the consequences of its dereliction. Given Yahweh's righteous character and Israel's shameful conduct,
it could not be otherwise. Even so, Amos is fully aware that it is the
deity's love for Israel that dictates the severe course he must now take
with his people.

Perhaps a few individuals would repent and return to Yahweh.
While it is only a subordinate theme in his pronouncements, Amos does
refer to the remnant. Just as the shepherd salvages a small part of the
sheep from the mouth of the lion (3:12) and 10 percent of a city's
population remains after the enemy destroys the metropolis (5:3), so a
bit of Israel will be spared annihilation. In 5:15 Amos refers to "the
remnant of Joseph" that will perhaps be visited by Yahweh's grace. He
courageously believes that a small element within the nation is even
now precious in the divine sight. Indeed, if all Israel were doomed to
destruction, would Amos have risked life and limb to admonish the
people? Nevertheless, the images of a piece of a sheep's ear and a
remaining tenth of a city are not very encouraging. Deliverance in the
days ahead would be limited. If the impending judgment was not to be
a brutal finality for all concerned, it would nonetheless be horrible.

Amos' autobiographical visions in the third major portion of the
book (Amos 7–9) offer a revealing glimpse of the prophet. In the first
vision (7:1–3), Amos sees a brood of locusts attacking the pastures just
prior to the onset of summer drought. Should these insects fiercely
overtake the "latter growth" (v. 1), many small farmers would undoubtedly starve before obtaining new provisions from the next harvest. In
this vision, Amos sees the countryside stripped bare. He refuses to
accept this judgment. He intercedes and God "repents" (that is, changes
his mind), saying, "It shall not be" (7:3). The second vision (7:4–6)
emphasizes the fire that consumed "the great deep," the source of important springs and fountains (see Gen. 1:2). That fire was now at the
point of "eating up the land." Again Amos intercedes for Israel, and
again Yahweh reconsiders. It is hoped that the broken covenant relationship between God and people can still be restored.

But the third vision (7:7–9) is radically different. Amos is shown
a plumb line held by Yahweh as he stands beside a wall. Straightaway
Yahweh will discern the defects of its construction. This vision convinces
the prophet that the terrible hour of Israel's testing and judgment cannot
be postponed. A change of mind on God's part is now impossible (7:8).
So sensitive is Amos to the certainty of Israel's doom that he does not
attempt to talk Yahweh out of his plan. He realizes that he must simply
accept this ominous symbol of Israel's future and permit it to shape the
word of doom that the deity will require him to proclaim.

In the fourth vision (8:1–3) Amos sees a basket of summer fruit (qāyiṣ). That word for fruit somewhat resembles the word for "end" (qēṣ). With this pun—qāyiṣ-qēṣ—Amos becomes even more convinced of the certainty of divine judgment. Yahweh declares, "The end has come upon my people Israel" (8:2), and once more the deity reveals that his mind is fixed. Finally, in the fifth vision (9:1–4), Amos sees Yahweh standing beside the altar. If this were the royal sanctuary of Bethel, the vision would have come later in Amos' prophetic ministry. Again a decisive word is communicated. Yahweh commands a thorough destruction; none will be exempted (9:1). This vision authenticates the other four and speaks strongly for the inexorable character of divine judgment.

Such visions offered Amos a direct experience of the deity. They constituted his credentials as a prophet. They impressed Amos with the grim realities that the future held in store and reminded him that Yahweh might very soon make an end of his recalcitrant people.

The Message of Amos

Before complacent contemporaries Amos spoke about the impending wrath of a righteous universal deity who was supremely displeased by his people's attitude and performance. They would be held accountable for their flagrant violations of the Mosaic covenant. This covenant, which had first been presented to them as a divine gift intended to strengthen the community of faith, had now become the instrument of Israel's indictment. Through prophets whom he had already dispatched, Yahweh had favored Israel with a clear sign of his will (2:11). He had also directed a series of famines, plagues, and droughts against his people in the hope that they would once more take seriously their covenant relationship with him (4:6–11). To all but the most insensitive, these disasters would have been interpreted as warnings that Israel should repent and return to her Maker. Since the nation had not responded positively to such "exhortations," the deity had no choice but to let loose his wrath on the cataclysmic day of Yahweh.

In articulating such a message, Amos was rejecting many of the cherished notions of the northern kingdom. The people assumed that Yahweh was bound to serve Israel by previous legal arrangement. But Amos rigorously denied that Yahweh was the junior partner of the covenant, who existed for no loftier purpose than to meet Israelite need. Amos contended that the Israelites were no better and had no more claim on the deity than the Ethiopians, Philistines, or Syrians (9:7).

Though Israel experienced a special election by Yahweh, this did not give her license to pervert the covenant. Yahweh's past deeds in Israel's behalf had been misinterpreted in the urban sanctuaries, where a complacent population made extravagant claims on the deity. Because Amos thought that the corrupt cult was a delusion, he mocked what his listeners took seriously (2:7–8; 4:4–5; 5:21–23). Like Samuel, Amos failed to discover in sacrificial regulations and customs the essence of the relationship between God and Israel (5:25). Moreover, Amos' final vision (9:1–4), with its view of Yahweh standing beside an altar that the deity is about to tear down, emphasizes that for Amos the cultic enterprise was far from sacrosanct. He maintained that as long as the wealthy were oppressing the poor, Yahweh would not rush in with a brilliant display of his mercy in Israel's behalf.

As a fierce opponent of inflated nationalism, Amos sounded the call for immediate covenant renewal. At the final hour his God had directed him to say to the people, "Seek me and live" (5:4). If the people would immediately initiate genuine acts of repentance, assume a low profile, and quietly return to Yahweh, he might even yet be gracious to "the remnant of Joseph" (5:15). Though Amos did not anticipate a radical renewal of faith by the entire Israelite population, he was unwilling to insist that Yahweh would make a final end of the covenant people. Even Amos' deity was capable of saying, "Nevertheless!" In the final analysis, however, this stern prophet had little time for rhapsodic intimations of hope. The people's pride, their callousness to human need, and their perverse use of the cult did not allow Amos the luxury of optimism at this moment in Israelite history.

HOSEA

Literary Considerations

We turn now to Hosea, who was a contemporary of Amos. The words "Text corrupt, wife also," which a student once gave as his assessment of Hosea, are a fitting introduction to the prophet's chaotic book and faithless spouse, Gomer. Fortunately the many versions of the Book of Hosea, especially the Septuagint, restore some order and clarity to the poorly preserved text.

Two types of material in the Book of Hosea appear to be of secondary origin. If an oracle sternly condemning Israel is followed by one that deals favorably with Judah, we may suspect that the second is a later addition. Though Yahweh declares that he will not forgive the house of Israel (1:6), he adds, "But I will have pity on the house of Judah, and I will deliver them by Yahweh their God" (1:7). After 6:10 states that the northern kingdom has been defiled, 6:11 declares that Judah will be blessed by harvest. And the contrast between the two kingdoms in 4:15 centers on direct admonition: "Though you play the harlot, O Israel, let not Judah become guilty." Such Judean glosses were undoubtedly imputed to the text after the fall of the northern kingdom in 722.

We may also argue that statements anticipating a splendid future, which immediately follow pronouncements of doom, probably do not represent Hosea's original thought. In Hos. 1:10–11, for example, the reunion of the two Hebrew kingdoms is predicted, and the symbolic names of two of Gomer's children, "Not my people" and "Jezreel," which hitherto denoted awful divine judgment, are reinterpreted. It has also been proposed that the portrayal of Israel as luxuriant vegetation in 14:5–7 is a later addition. Since Hosea preached promise as well as doom, we must not be too quick to declare that the thoughts reflected in certain verses are emphatically not his. Even so, the Judean editors of his book did mitigate the sting of impending doom by entering into the record happy thoughts about the future. They created a tone that was not intended by the prophet. Finally, neither the book's superscription (1:1) nor its concluding editorial gloss (14:9) is the work of the prophet. Presumably the latter was affixed by a wisdom writer as a way of stressing the relevance of Hosea's teaching for subsequent Israelite generations.

Threats, invectives, exhortations, historical allusions, and promises have all made their way into the Book of Hosea.[9] While this book does not lend itself to a broad outline, the clear break between 3:5 and 4:1 marks a significant shift in content. Hosea 1–3 is grounded in the prophet's marriage experience, whereas Hosea 4–14 presents a series of oracles on Israel's social, political, and religious illnesses. Moreover, the oracles in Hosea 4–14 may be divided into three units: 4:1–9:9 meditates on the present malaise of the people with special reference to cultic and political misdoings; 9:10–13:16 conveys the prophet's understanding of the nation's sin in terms of its history, thereby maintaining that the present predicament is the natural outgrowth of Israel's dubious past; and 14:1–8 offers an invitation to Israel to return to Yahweh and a promise of the salvation that lies in store.

The first two oracular sections convey the uneven, abrupt quality of Hosea's speech. However, the prophet consistently employed two techniques that are extremely effective. First, he was masterful in his use of the imperative. With unmistakable directness he addressed his audience: "Plead with your mother" (2:2); "Rejoice not, O Israel! Exult not like the peoples" (9:1); "Return, O Israel, to Yahweh your God" (14:1); and so on. Second, Hosea knew how to raise significant rhetorical questions. Communicating Yahweh's criticism of prevailing cultic practices he inquired, "O Ephraim, what have I to do with idols?" (14:8). Articulating in first-person idiom Yahweh's dual need to love and punish his people, he asked, "How can I give you up, O Ephraim! How can I hand you over, O Israel!" (11:8). In addition, the oracles of Hosea are rich in metaphor. Thus, the relationship between God and Israel is poignantly viewed in terms of the dynamics between husband and bride, and between father and son. In sum, Hosea was capable of rising to the rhetorical occasion. Nonetheless, his jarring shifts from second- to third-person discourse and his own passionate, distraught frame of mind have not made his prophetic message easy to grasp.

Historical Background

Hosea embarked on his prophetic career in about 750 B.C. Therefore, the political, social, and religious elements that bore on the functioning of Amos relate no less to the work of Hosea. Not only is Hosea linked with the rule of Jeroboam (1:1), but Yahweh declares to the prophet, "For yet a little while, and I will punish the house of Jehu for the blood of Jezreel" (1:4). The Jehu dynasty ended in 745, when Jeroboam's reigning son, Zechariah (746–745), was struck down by Shallum (2 Kings 15:10), who then ascended the throne. Since the end of the Jehu dynasty is anticipated in 1:4, Hosea's earliest utterances presumably belong to the last years of Jeroboam.

Hosea's career as a prophet encompassed a far greater span of time than that of Amos. The Book of Hosea is forceful in informing us that the prophet anticipated the collapse of the northern kingdom in 722. Yet nowhere does the book suggest that Hosea actually witnessed the fall of Samaria. Probably his career spanned most of the third quarter of the eighth century. His oracles reflect the political uncertainty that the northern kingdom was experiencing at that time. For example, Hos. 5:8–6:6 seems to portray Israel's difficult situation in 733. Two years earlier an Aramean-Israelite coalition came into being, and in the ensuing months it unsuccessfully asserted itself against the Assyrian giant. (The way in which this coalition forced itself upon Judah in the hope that she too would take part in anti-Assyrian maneuvers will be discussed in Chapter 13.) In retaliation, Tiglath-pileser III (745–727) swept down the coast of Palestine and raked over much of Israel.

The rapid turnover of Israelite monarchs and the attendant political chaos that marked these years is at least implied by the Book of Hosea. King Shallum, who had killed Zechariah, ruled for merely a month when he was assassinated by Menahem (2 Kings 15:14). Though the docile Assyrian vassal Menahem (745–738) ruled Israel for the better part of a decade and died in peace, his own son Pekahiah (738–737) reigned only two years when he was murdered by his anti-Assyrian military commander, Pekah (2 Kings 15:25). But Pekah's relatively short reign was terminated in 732 by another conspirator, Hoshea (2 Kings 15:30), who became the last king (and ninth dynasty) to rule the waning northern kingdom. In barely more than a dozen years, four Israelite monarchs had been assassinated.

Political anarchy existed in Israel, and Hosea knew it. Seemingly the best that she could do was to grope for whatever alliances were available:

> Ephraim herds the wind,
>   and pursues the east wind all day long;
> they multiply falsehood and violence;
>   they make a bargain with Assyria,
>   and oil is carried to Egypt. (Hos. 12:1)

The nation's treaty with Assyria alluded to here was presumably effected when Hoshea took the throne (732), dispatched tribute to Tiglath-pileser, and thereby acknowledged Assyrian supremacy. Yet Hoshea's duplicity is also represented in this verse; at a later moment in his insecure reign, the king turned against Assyria and sought support from Egypt. Thus, the northern kingdom walked a long, disastrous path to her death in 722, and Hosea witnessed the greater part of that sad procession.

If Israel suffered because its political leaders could not agree on a well-defined foreign policy, she also languished in the light of Assyrian resurgence. When the ruthless Tiglath-pileser III took the throne in 745, he held Israel's death warrant in his hand. As early as 743 he was leading his contingents westward to expand Assyria's territorial holdings. Only Menahem's willingness to pay him a large amount of tribute induced Tiglath-pileser to stay away from Samaria for a time (2 Kings 15:20). Though Menahem's pro-Assyrian policy was no vote of confidence for Yahwism, it did buy time for Israel. For having continued his father's foreign policy, Pekahiah was soon knifed by Pekah, who openly resisted the Assyrian menace. In 732 Tiglath-pileser destroyed Damascus; executed its king, Rezin (ca. 740–732), who had rebelled against him; and restructured the city and its environs into several Assyrian provinces. The Assyrian monarch would have also ravaged Samaria had not Hoshea conspired against Pekah and extended to Tiglath-pileser a pledge of loyalty and tribute. In the Assyrian annals, Tiglath-pileser claimed that Hoshea was his own appointment to the Israelite throne.[10] While her territorial holdings were much reduced by steady Assyrian advance, Israel did persist for a few more years. Yet it must have been obvious to more discerning Israelites, Hosea among them, that Assyria might overtake the northern kingdom at any time.

Though we have some knowledge of the historical period in which Hosea lived, biographical details about him are scant. Most important was his infamous marriage experience, which we shall discuss in some detail. We know nothing of Hosea's family background and can only assume that he grew up in the northern kingdom. Close study of Hosea's discourse reveals that he spoke the dialect of his fellow Ephraimites. Recurring mention of Bethel, Gilgal, and Samaria also suggests that these were the northern cities that Hosea frequented most as Yahweh's prophet.

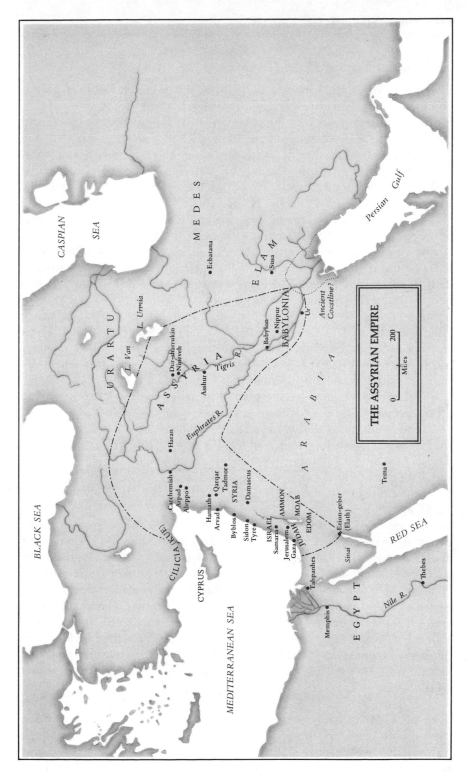

THE ASSYRIAN EMPIRE

CASPIAN SEA

M E D E S

• Ecbatana

E L A M

• Susa

Persian Gulf

U R A R T U

L. Van

L. Urmia

• Dur-sharrukin
• Nineveh

A S S Y R I A

• Asshur

Tigris R.

• Babylon
• Nippur

BABYLONIA

• Ur

Ancient Coastline?

200

0

Miles

Euphrates R.

• Haran

A R A B I A

• Tema

BLACK SEA

• Carchemish

• Arpad
• Aleppo

• Qarqar
• Tadmor

• Hamath

• Arvad

SYRIA

• Damascus

• Byblos

• Sidon

• Tyre

ISRAEL

• Samaria

AMMON

MOAB

EDOM

• Ezion-geber
(Elath)

CILICIA (KUE)

• Jerusalem

• Gaza

JUDAH

• Sinai

RED SEA

CYPRUS

MEDITERRANEAN SEA

• Tahpanhes

E G Y P T

Nile R.

• Thebes

• Memphis

Hosea's Reading of the Covenant

The noun "covenant" appears only three times in the Book of Hosea (2:18; 6:7; 8:1). Nevertheless, the prophet was most intent on clarifying the meaning and quality of the covenant relationship between God and people. He was well aware that Yahweh had formally initiated the covenant at Sinai and that he had issued directives on Israelite existence. Hosea also claimed that the relationship between Yahweh and his people had its informal beginnings in the era of the Exodus (9:10; 11:1; 13:4). In the covenant offered at Sinai (Exod. 19–24) and renewed at Shechem (Josh. 24), the crucial element was the relationship between Israel and her God. In Hos. 9:10–13:16 and elsewhere the prophet shows that he is knowledgeable about Israel's history, which reflects continual violations of the covenant. The cherished association between the transcendent deity and his people had been repeatedly defiled. Certainly Hosea had no interest whatever in thinking of the Yahwistic covenant as a bargain between equals. Yet in the cultic exercises practiced at Bethel, Gilgal, and Samaria, this is what the covenant had become. Hosea knew as fully as Amos had that the callous people were inclined to consider Yahweh a subservient partner who might readily be pressed into supporting their thoughtless aspirations.

In an effort to counter the prevailing religious trends, Hosea called on his people to see the covenant for what it truly was. In his proclamations, he emphasized the word *ḥesed*, "covenant love," and imputed to that Hebrew noun a new and vital significance (2:19; 4:1; 6:4, 6; 10:12; 12:6). Any single English equivalent fails to render it full justice. In translating *ḥesed* in its six appearances in Hosea, the RSV employs three different equivalents—"steadfast love" (2:19; 6:6; 10:12), "love" (6:4; 12:6), and "kindness" (4:1). A word relevant to Israel's understanding of her covenant relationship with deity, the noun *ḥesed* represents confidence in the covenant partner as well as devotion to him. As the narrative about David and Jonathan in 1 Samuel 20 reveals so well, such fidelity was important to covenants entered into by two human beings. In the Hebrew Bible, however, *ḥesed* also applied to the covenant devotion between God and people. For instance, Nathan informed David that Yahweh would show endless *ḥesed* to the king (2 Sam. 7:15). In this way, Yahweh's special support of David was dramatically pledged. *Ḥesed* denotes the responsibility and loyalty to each other that two partners in a solemn pact are expected to assume. In sum, it maintains the covenant relationship.

In Hos. 4:1 and 6:6, *ḥesed* has to do with good behavior in the light of what Yahweh expects of Israel. In both passages, the noun "knowledge" also appears. Together these verses affirm that although Yahweh desires "covenant love" and "knowledge" on Israel's part, these two cardinal virtues are sorely lacking. "Knowledge" relates directly to the confession that Israel was expected to give to the God of Sinai, who had already revealed to her his name, nature, and will. Presently the people, who had perverted their dealings with one another and defiled their relationship with deity, were betrayed by an ignorance that was everywhere apparent. Hebrew man's relationship with God and neighbor had been severely ruptured. And with her breach of faith, Israel had offended the deity. Israel's talent for corrupting the covenant relationship is summed up in Hosea's disclosure that

> There is no faithfulness or kindness [ḥesed],
>   and no knowledge of God in the land;
> there is swearing, lying, killing,
>   stealing, and committing adultery;
> they break all bounds and murder follows murder. (4:1b–2)

Here we have an implied comparison with the Decalogue itself. Israel's concrete behavior is antithetical to what Yahweh has enjoined within the context of her most basic ethical code. Hosea 4:1–3 reveals that "what Yahweh required was not the mindless practice of ceremonial religion, but a genuine understanding of who, and what kind of God, Yahweh was, and an intelligent grasp of the ethical implications of worshiping him."[11] Israel's bankruptcy thus occasioned Yahweh's negative assessment of his people: "Your love [ḥesed] is like a morning cloud, like the dew that goes early away" (6:4). Israel's ḥesed was remarkably undependable.

Hosea was convinced that the northern kingdom had been woefully delinquent in fulfilling the terms of the previously established covenant between God and people. Accordingly, Hosea let loose harsh threats and judgments that were on a par with those of Amos. Nevertheless, Hosea also spoke of Yahweh's pathos in having to bring a historical catastrophe on Israel and his determination to maintain a highly personal relationship with the people of his choice. Though Hosea was no exponent of easy salvation, the reality of Israel's heedlessness to divine expectation was set against the reality of Yahweh's extraordinary faithfulness.

Here the prophet made use of a uniquely human experience. He spoke of the covenant as a marriage bond. He symbolized Israel's period in the wilderness as an entirely harmonious matrimony involving Yahweh, the husband, and Israel, the bride. During the period of settlement that followed, however, wife Israel had become enticed by Canaanite Baʿalism. Nevertheless, her conduct did not result in automatic extinction. Hosea portrays the deity as the compassionate husband who takes back his wayward wife (especially in 2:16–23). In such a manner, the original relationship between God and people was thought to be restored.

Hosea also held that Yahweh had guided Israel as a concerned father guides his young son. Yahweh had instructed Israel in how to walk (11:3). It was he who had brought his son out of Egypt and into the land of Canaan with "cords of compassion" and "bands of love" (11:4). In the intervening years, however, defection had been gross. Here the deity speaks in a highly personal manner, "My people are bent on turning away from me; so they are appointed to the yoke" (11:7). However, Yahweh cannot dispense with this nation, which he still loves. The covenant relationship between God and people has been broken by only one side. Yahweh has yet to say no on the matter. He is thus understood to be the tortured father and husband (11:8) who still grasps Israel with his *ḥesed*.

While Hosea entertained no false hope that judgment may summarily be bought off by a scheming populace, he looked out on the landscape that existed on the other side of judgment. Hosea anticipated a fresh beginning for his people. Of course, the tension, pain, and promise that inform his work were primarily shaped by his own marriage to Gomer, as we shall see.

Hosea's Marriage

The most significant chapters in the book, Hosea 1–3, may be accepted as Hosea's call to the prophetic office. They describe Hosea's marriage, which had everything to do with how he conceived of his mission and comprehended the deity in whose name he spoke. So many interpretations of that marriage have been offered that one is tempted to think that these now exceed the number of men whom Gomer knew out of wedlock. But whatever the outcome of our own analysis, it depends on close examination of the text.

In Hosea 1 Yahweh instructs the prophet to secure "a wife of harlotry and have children of harlotry" (1:2). Thus, Hosea weds Gomer, who gives birth to two sons and a daughter. All the children are given symbolic names. Hosea calls the first "Jezreel," symbolizing that Yahweh will act in judgment against the bloodbath of Jehu (842 B.C.), which saw this usurper driving hard through the vicinity of Jezreel (2 Kings 9:16, 20). For its inhumanity, the house of Jehu will be severely punished. The deity's rejection of Israel is even more sharply signified in the names that Yahweh commands Hosea to give the other two children: "Not pitied" and "Not my people." In the naming of the last-born child (Hos. 1:9), the crucial words once delivered at Sinai, "I will be your God," are emphatically denied.

Hosea 3 offers a brief first-person account of the prophet's marriage. Yahweh summoned Hosea to "love a woman who is beloved of a paramour and is an adulteress" (3:1). She was purchased and kept under surveillance in order that she might not commit further deeds of harlotry.

Between these two chapters stands Hosea 2, which is less a reflection on the prophet's wife and children than a meditation on Israel's defection from the deity. Here we meet the language of the court. The passage begins in the form of a legal proceeding: the husband brings charges against his adulterous wife. The case is conducted in the hope that a reconciliation between partners will be effected. The cast includes a husband, his wife, their children, and the wife's lovers. Yahweh is the concerned husband; the wife stands for the people of Israel. In v. 2 the children seem to represent individual Israelites who are to be distinguished from the guilty nation, but in v. 4 they are said to share in the nation's transgression. In 2:14–15 Yahweh declares that he will take steps to reconcile his wife, Israel, to himself. Following this bewildering unit is a new passage (2:16–23) that reflects on the day of Israel's eventual restoration. This passage conveys Hosea's confidence that a new covenant and bond of marriage will be actualized. Such will follow on the removal of the Baʿalim from the land and an indication from Israel that she is ready to accept Yahweh's invitation to return to him in wifely piety.

If this is how we read the text, how is the marriage itself to be understood? In the following pages, we shall review several interpretations.

The Two-Women Interpretation. Pfeiffer holds that Hosea 1 and 3 are unrelated and that Gomer has been treated unjustly by biblical critics.[12] In Hos. 1:2 she is called "a wife of harlotry," but this is simply the figurative way of referring to the religious apostasy and whoredom that had swept across the northern kingdom. Theologically speaking, Gomer was a harlot because as an eighth-century northern Israelite she held membership in a community of whoredom. Hosea 3 then presents a different woman, a prostitute to whom Hosea showed compassion as a symbol of God's enduring love for his people who had defected.

This view has its drawbacks. First, there are too many women. How could Yahweh's love for Israel be at all well depicted by a married prophet who then extended himself to another woman? Second, Hosea was a northern Israelite and thus he should also have spoken of himself in abusive terms.[13] If the entire population was engaged in whoredom, he was part of the pack.

The Backward Literal Interpretation. This view sees Hosea 1 and 3 as the reflection of one continuous narrative, but it chooses to read Hosea 3 prior to Hosea 1. Thus, Robinson claims that Hosea consciously obeyed Yahweh's instruction to marry a prostitute at the time he was summoned to the prophetic office.[14] This gave him an excellent opportunity to confront Israel with her own whoredom, which involved sexual license at cultic places. In this view Hosea 3 precedes Hosea 1 and refers to the situation before marriage. Because Gomer was a sacred prostitute of the cult, she had to undergo a period of seclusion in order that her supernatural aura might fade away. Once married to the prophet, Gomer may or may not have remained loyal to her husband.

This interpretation is likewise plagued by certain problems. First, we do not know for sure that Gomer was temple property. Second, the word "again" in 3:1 has to be taken as redactional, but we have no concrete proof that it was not a part of the original text. Third, Yahweh's problem with adulterous Israel is better paralleled if the apostasy follows a period of marital fidelity.

The Proleptic Interpretation. This interpretation insists that when Hosea employed the term "harlotry" in 1:2, and did so with reference to Gomer, he was speaking by way of anticipation.[15] Actually, Hosea did not know at the time of his marriage that Gomer was a loose woman. He fell deeply in love with her, and presumably she expressed her love for him. The first child, Jezreel, was their own (see 1:3, "she conceived and bore him a son"). Hosea was the father. But soon Hosea discovered Gomer's unfaithfulness. In reflecting on this domestic crisis, Hosea was initially convinced that he had married Gomer under divine guidance. The second and third children were not his. Hosea became the humiliated husband. Although he realized that according to Hebrew law he could divorce Gomer, he knew that he still loved her. Hosea had that kind of patient love for Gomer that survives injury, and in this he perceived Yahweh's own humiliation and obstinate love to save and transform his people.

The proleptic interpretation has been dismissed as overly clever and modern. We cannot categorically deny that Hosea chose to address the problem of Israel's cult prostitution head-on by deliberately marrying a harlot in the hope that he would succeed in reforming her.[16] Even so, the proleptic view has much psychological potential. Hosea's grief and struggle, so evident in his broken oracles, may be an authentic reflection of his own conflicts about his tumultuous marriage.

The Straightforward Literal Interpretation. Lucidly advanced by Rowley,[17] this approach regards Hosea's marriage to a harlot as an actual event, declares that both Hosea 1 and 3 are historical chapters, claims that the same woman is portrayed in both, and holds that Hosea 1 should be read prior to Hosea 3. Thus Hosea complied with Yahweh's instruction to marry the woman, although he knew of her sordid past. She bore him children to whom he gave symbolic names. While these names gave Hosea an opportunity to expound on Israel's troublesome covenant situation, it is not until Hosea 2 that we learn that Hosea did not sire two of Gomer's offspring. Since Gomer felt unfulfilled in her quest for other lovers, in time she longed again for Hosea. But Gomer had fallen into slavery (Hos. 3:1–2), and it was in this ignoble condition that the prophet discovered her and restored her to himself.

This interpretation has a close parallel in Israel's relationship with Yahweh as Hosea understood it. Hosea deliberately married a bad girl to symbolize the fact that even in her childhood, Israel had not been responsive to the deity. Though Gomer no longer deserved Hosea's love after she left him, she continued to receive it. Hosea could do no other. In 3:2 he was not simply making a purchase. He was trying to win the woman back, and in this Hosea learned afresh the mystery and power of Yahweh's love for his own people.

Rowley's interpretation and the proleptic view appear to us the most attractive possibilities. The proleptic approach holds that in the call tradition of an Israelite prophet, a personal experience may be reassessed at a later time. Hosea's marital experience is subsequently reevaluated as having been divinely instigated. It was, in fact, the occasion of his calling to the prophetic office. Nevertheless, the appeal of the straightforward literal approach, which is rooted in solid scholarship, must also be acknowledged.[18]

Hosea's Message

While we have thus far given limited attention to Hosea 4–14, we shall proceed with several summary comments on Hosea's prophetic proclamation. First of all, when Hosea reflected on Yahweh's way with history, he achieved more depth than breadth. Hosea did not entertain thoughts about Yahweh's providential care of the nations at large. The universalism of Amos 9:7 has no parallel in Hosea's disclosures. The God of Hosea is essentially Lord of Israel and the land that Israel momentarily occupies. As her Lord, Yahweh first knew Israel in the desert, but the subsequent farming population had too often followed the gods of Canaan. Hosea stoutly maintained that Yahweh was Israel's Lord and that the nation's pastoral, agricultural, and commercial pursuits were under his sway. Because Yahweh was provider and master, Hosea denied the validity of the prevailing nature-oriented Canaanite syncretism.

For Hosea, it was history that gave meaning and direction to human existence. No preexilic Old Testament prophet was more concerned with the historical traditions of Exodus, wilderness wandering, and settlement than Hosea was. History, more than nature, was in Hosea's view the crucial arena of Yahweh's activity. Hosea also referred to the patriarchal traditions of Genesis (Hos. 12:2–6, 12), but there he suggested that Jacob's religion was not in harmony with the chief interests of Mosaic Yahwism. Thus, the former had no right to compete with the latter in its quest for the people's fidelity.[19]

On the issue of Israel's election and covenant relationship with the deity, Hosea claimed that Israel's election was actualized as she was called forth from enslavement to the Egyptian pharaoh. In his pronouncements, Hosea reviewed Israel's wilderness experience. Speaking for the deity in the first person he declared, "Like grapes in the wilderness, I found Israel" (9:10). Yet as the prophet surveyed Israel's past, he saw that chosen Israel, who was once Yahweh's bride, had become a miserable harlot (Hos. 2). Moreover, he portrayed elect Israel as Yahweh's problem child who remains the object of his loving concern. Nowhere is the prophet's expression of election and covenant more tender than in the masterful poetry of Hos. 11:1–9.

The present sickness of the nation also concerned Hosea. Essentially that sickness related to a lack of knowledge. The land did not know Yahweh (4:1). The people had rejected knowledge and the law that was an integral part of that knowledge (4:6). Instead, Israel persisted in a smug course that was especially reflected in a rigorous fertility cult and an over-confident monarchy. Hosea criticized both the cult and the state. He insisted that Israel's participation in Canaanite fertility religion was counter to the interests of a fundamentally austere Mosaic Yahwism. The cult also erred in offering sacrifices to gain opportunities and material goods (4:13; 5:6). Genuine expressions of thanksgiving had all but vanished.

Hosea linked part of the nation's sin directly with the monarchy. Having turned their backs on Yahweh, Israel's kings trusted only in themselves, and the people were too quick to rely on the judgments of these consistently weak monarchs. Hosea even asserted that Israel became a monarchy without Yahweh's consent. Through its ineffective alliances, the monarchy had become a wedge between Yahweh and his people. The evidence is not clear-cut (contrast 8:4 with 3:5), but the prophet may have hoped for the permanent overthrow of this questionable institution, which had no place in the internal structure and life style of Yahweh's covenant people. In any case, Hosea believed that Yahweh was Israel's true king.

Although he claimed that Yahweh would punish Israel in the days ahead, Hosea was not specific about what political form the punishment would take or when it would occur. Such passages as 8:3 and 10:10 affirm that judgment would be carried out through the invasion of an enemy nation. Yet he sometimes contended that Israel was already ensnared by her own deplorable activity. "Their deeds do not permit them to return to their God" (5:4). The wrathful judgment was really self-inflicted; it was Yahweh's response to Israel's misbehavior. Nevertheless, Hosea did not regard Israel's chastisement as absolutely final. The purifying discomforts would continue until Israel was acutely aware of her guilt and once more responded positively to the deity. This prophet heard Yahweh saying: "O Ephraim, what have I to do with idols? It is I who answer and look after you. I am like an evergreen cypress, from me comes your fruit" (14:8).

Paradoxically, the God who is consumed by wrath remains the God who is propelled by love for his people. As the concerned husband and father, Yahweh must somehow resolve the dual realities of wrath and love. As for Hebrew man, Hosea hoped that his affections would finally turn toward Yahweh, his Lord.[20]

THE END OF THE NORTHERN KINGDOM

We do not know in what year Hosea's prophetic career terminated, but presumably the date 725 B.C. would not be wide of the mark. As the third quarter of the eighth century unfolded, Israel's political future looked especially dismal. When Hoshea (732–724) came to the throne of Samaria, he ruled a territory considerably smaller than that which Jeroboam II had ruled. The Assyrian giant Tiglath-pileser died in 727. He was succeeded by his son Shalmaneser V (727–722), who at first won Hoshea's pledge of loyalty. Then foolishly trusting in Egyptian support, which proved worthless, Hoshea rebelled against Assyria by withholding payment of tribute (2 Kings 17:3–4). When confronted by Shalmaneser in 724, Hoshea apparently attempted peace overtures that failed. Shalmaneser took Hoshea prisoner and then began to lay siege to the Israelite capital.

The city of Samaria stoutly withstood the Assyrian attack for more than two years, but in the summer or fall of 722 it was brought to its knees. Shalmaneser died in that year, shortly before or after Samaria's citizens were forced to surrender. He was succeeded by his brother, Sargon II (722–705), who himself celebrated the conquest of Samaria as the outstanding event of his first year of rule. In his so-called cuneiform annals, the Assyrian victory is described.

> At the begi[nning of my royal rule, I . . . the town of the Sama]rians [I besieged, conquered] (2 lines destroyed) [for the god . . . who le]t me achieve (this) my triumph.[21] . . . I led away as prisoners [27,290] inhabitants of it (and) [equipped] from among [them (soldiers to man)] 50 chariots for my royal corps. . . . [The town I] re[built] better than (it was) before and [settled] therein people from the countries which [I] myself [had con]quered.[22] I placed an officer of mine as governor over them and imposed upon them tribute as (is customary) for Assyrian citizens.[23]

The Deuteronomist's version of the fall of the northern kingdom (2 Kings 17) mentions that the Assyrian monarch successfully took the city, had many Israelites deported, and brought some of his own people to live in Samaria. In contrast with Sargon's report, the biblical account is more concerned with interpreting that event than with describing it. It sets forth the reason for Israel's tragic experience:

> The people of Israel had sinned against Yahweh their God, who had brought them up out of the land of Egypt from under the hand of Pharaoh. . . . And the people of Israel did secretly against Yahweh their God things that were not right. (17:7, 9)

Hence, the Deuteronomist has more to say about the lamentable end of the northern kingdom than he does about the specifics of how it happened. In any event, we may be sure that the tragic moment had arrived.

NOTES

1. See James B. Pritchard, ed., *Ancient Near Eastern Texts Relating to the Old Testament*, 3d ed. (Princeton, N.J.: Princeton University Press, 1969), p. 280.

2. R. B. Y. Scott, *The Relevance of the Prophets*, rev. ed. (New York: Macmillan, 1968), p. 76.

3. We are in agreement with James L. Mays, *Amos: A Commentary*, The Old Testament Library (Philadelphia: Westminster Press, 1969), p. 13.

4. So Hughell E. W. Fosbroke, "Introduction and Exegesis to Amos," in George A. Buttrick et al., eds., *The Interpreter's Bible* (Nashville: Abingdon Press, 1956), vol. 6, p. 772.

5. Mays, *op. cit.*, pp. 137–138, argues that since in another oracle (2:11) prophets are accepted as having been raised up by Yahweh, surely "Amos knew of prophets with whom he would not deny identification."

6. See Prov. 30:18 and Job 33:14 for representative examples, and Samuel L. Terrien, "Amos and Wisdom," in Bernhard W. Anderson and Walter Harrelson, eds., *Israel's Prophetic Heritage* (New York: Harper & Row, 1962), p. 110, for helpful comment.

7. Questions about the authenticity of Amos' pronouncements against Tyre, Edom, and Judah have been raised, but the arguments are not always compelling. If there are any late additions here, they might be the replacements of earlier originals. It is unlikely that Amos would have exempted his own kingdom, Judah. Even if the Tyre and Edom oracles are discounted, Amos' strategy is still apparent.

8. We concur with Walter Brueggemann, "Amos 4:4–13 and Israel's Covenant Worship," *Vetus Testamentum* 15 (1965): 2.

9. For a detailed list, see Georg Fohrer, *Introduction to the Old Testament*, trans. David E. Green (Nashville: Abingdon Press, 1968), p. 422.

10. See Pritchard, *op. cit.*, p. 284.

11. Robert C. Dentan, *The Knowledge of God in Ancient Israel* (New York: Seabury Press, 1968), p. 36.

12. Robert H. Pfeiffer, *Introduction to the Old Testament*, rev. ed. (New York: Harper & Row, 1948), pp. 568–570.

13. We follow H. H. Rowley, "The Marriage of Hosea," *Bulletin of the John Rylands Library* 39 (1956–1957): 209.

14. Theodore H. Robinson, *Die zwölf kleinen Propheten: Hosea bis Micha*, Handbuch zum Alten Testament (Tübingen: J. C. B. Mohr, 1936), pp. 16–17.

15. This approach is taken by G. A. Smith, *The Book of the Twelve Prophets*, rev. ed. (New York: Harper & Row, 1928), 1: 250–252.

16. So Norman K. Gottwald, *A Light to the Nations: An Introduction to the Old Testament* (New York: Harper & Row, 1959), p. 297.

17. Rowley, *op. cit.*, pp. 224–226.

18. For a more comprehensive study of the entire subject, see *ibid.*, pp. 200–233.

19. Edwin M. Good, "Hosea and the Jacob Tradition," *Vetus Testamentum* 16 (1966): 137–151.

20. For a more thorough presentation of Hosea's prophetic proclamation,

see James M. Ward, "The Message of the Prophet Hosea," *Interpretation* 23 (1969): 387–407.

21. Sargon was a religious man who claimed support from the gods of Assyria.
22. The new population contained many Babylonians and Syrian folk from Hamath who had recently been captured. The Assyrian policy of making outsiders take up residence in Samaria hastened the process whereby the city would lose its former Israelite identity and become a subservient Assyrian province.
23. Pritchard, *op. cit.*, p. 284. Brackets show where the text has been restored; words in parentheses are the translator's interpolations to facilitate comprehension of the text.

13

MICAH, ISAIAH, AND THE STRUGGLE OF THE SOUTHERN KINGDOM

After Samaria fell to Assyria in 722, the southern kingdom managed to sustain itself for 135 more years. Nevertheless, Judah could not ignore the international life about her. Swept into the mainstream of political events, the Judean monarchy was called on to make important decisions. Since the northern kingdom had been turned into an Assyrian province, Judah was now considered a significant member of the family of lesser nations in western Asia. Hence, it was virtually impossible for the southern kingdom to assume an isolationist course.

In Isaiah, the court had the services of a discerning, active prophet who directed his insights to Judean royalty. Isaiah was an urbanite who appears to have been born and reared in Jerusalem. As such, he kept abreast of current events. In Micah, however, Isaiah had a rural counterpart who conceived of his task as that of confidently declaring "to Jacob his transgression and to Israel his sin" (Mic. 3:8). Presumably Micah pronounced most of his oracles during the reign of two Judean kings, Ahaz (735–715) and Hezekiah (715–687). Micah cannot compete with Amos, Hosea, and Isaiah, the great men of Hebrew prophetism's golden age. Still, the depth of Micah's sensitivity to social and religious abuse and the sting of his rhetoric convince us that he had a crucial role to play in the prophetic movement. Indeed, as Jer. 26:18–19 discloses, a century after Micah had offered his devastating prognosis of Judah's condition, he was recalled as one whose message bore the markings of authentic prophecy.

Biblical texts to be read prior to and in conjunction with the present chapter: 2 Kings 15:1–7, 32–38; 16:1–20; 18:1–20:21; Micah 1–3, 6:1–8; Isaiah 1–11, 20, 28–32. You may also wish to glance at Isaiah 36–39, which is based mainly on 2 Kings 18:13–20:19.

MICAH OF MORESHETH-GATH

Literary and Historical Considerations

Alternating oracles of threat and promise, rather than chronological considerations, determine the overall sequence of the Book of Micah. Micah 1:2–3:12 contains various oracles directed against Israel and Judah. They are especially sharp in their criticism of existing social oppression. This section is then followed by Mic. 4:1–5:15, which is frequently optimistic about Judah's impending restoration. Micah 6:1–7:7 maintains the idiom of the earlier prophecy; once more invective and threat predominate. Finally, in Mic. 7:8–20 further promises about Judah's renewal and the enemy's undoing are advanced in the well-balanced, confessional style of a psalmic composition.

Not all of the Book of Micah belongs to the eighth-century prophet. Except for 2:12–13, which depicts the people's return from exile, all of the first section (1:2–3:12) may be attributed to Micah. By contrast, Micah 4 does not seem to reflect the Micah of history. In Mic. 4:1–3 we have a duplicate rendering of the oracle about Zion's exaltation contained in Isa. 2:2–4. The rebuilding of Jerusalem, the return of the scattered people from their captivity, and the destruction of enemy nations are the main themes of 4:4–13. These expressions of encouragement seem to contradict the somber tones of Micah 1–3. While the concept of a coalition of princes in 5:5–9 does not accord with the notion of a solitary deliverer articulated in 5:2–4, other portions of Micah may bear the authentic imprint of the prophet.

Since Amos and Hosea are allowed some optimism, we cannot arbitrarily rule out the same possibility for Micah. The threats and exhortations of Mic. 6:1–7:7 probably contain both the words of Micah and those who continued his work. Most famous is the utterance of 6:6–8, which ends, "He has showed you, O man, what is good; and what does Yahweh require of you but to do justice, and to love kindness, and to walk humbly with your God?" (6:8).

Here is a prophecy of unquestionably high order that may have been uttered by Micah himself. But we do not really know. Although Mic. 6:6–8 does not resemble the oracles of Micah 1–3, it may present a vignette of a prophet who mellowed in his autumn years. On the other hand, Mic. 6:6–8 may be a superb example of the excellent kind of anonymous prophetic oracle attracted by the continuing Micah tradition. If it is not Micah's, it may nevertheless affirm the fundamental stance of his teaching. (Of course, it also reinforces what all the great eighth-century prophets stood for; Mic. 6:8 may be compared with Amos 5:24, Hos. 12:6, and Isa. 7:9.) Finally, with its developed psalmic style and liturgical phrases of assurance, Mic. 7:8–20 seems to reflect a postexilic cultic setting.

Since Micah had such devastating words for Jerusalem and its holy

Temple, it is only natural that many oracles that were not genuinely his were subsequently connected with his name. For example, the Micah of history presumably said, "Therefore because of you Zion shall be plowed as a field; Jerusalem shall become a heap of ruins, and the mountain of the house a wooded height" (3:12).

To tone down such an unconditional pronunciation of doom, many assuring words were added in chapters 4 and 5. These promise that Jerusalem will ultimately experience a brilliant restoration. The completed Book of Micah therefore becomes a source book that permits us a glimpse of the ongoing expansion and modification of Hebrew thought.

As for Micah's immediate background and person, we have appallingly little data to draw on. The various place names offered in Mic. 1:1, 14, and 15 all appear to be variant designations of present-day Tell el-Menshiyeh. The inhabitants of this insignificant frontier village in the southern Shephelah were humble rural folk who won Micah's confidence and concern. Feelings of insecurity were widespread in Moresheth-gath. Prior to Micah's day the region had been subjected to Philistine and Egyptian invasions. In Micah's own time the Assyrian armies of Sargon II and Sennacherib paraded through the Shephelah. Small wonder that Micah was preoccupied with thoughts about impending foreign invasion. Though this simple, rustic prophet traveled within a very limited area, he was capable of expressing himself in a highly intelligent and poignant manner.

He seems to have innately distrusted city life. He believed that the common citizenry of Palestine was being betrayed by the urban inhabitants of Samaria and Jerusalem. Through rhetorical questions he claimed to know where to lay the burden of guilt: "What is the transgression of Jacob? Is it not Samaria? And what is the sin of the house of Judah? Is it not Jerusalem?" (1:5).

His attack on sophisticated Samaria and Jerusalem is scathing. Micah 1:6 indicates that the prophet took up his calling prior to Samaria's collapse. Just how long Micah functioned we do not know. The most precisely dated statement is that of Mic. 3:12, which when cited in Jer. 26:18 is linked with the reign of Hezekiah (715–687). Thus, Micah appears to have witnessed Samaria's destruction from a distance and persisted in his conviction that Jerusalem would fare no better.

Micah's Message

Since the first section of the Book of Micah most accurately reflects the prophet's thought, we would do well to inspect more closely Micah's forbidding sense of doom (chap. 1), his denunciation of the wealthy (chap. 2), and his indictment of bankrupt leadership (chap. 3).

The initial oracle in Mic. 1:2–9 takes the form of a covenant lawsuit in which the earth and its inhabitants are invited to hear Yahweh's case against his people. The deity announces that he will leave his heavenly dwelling to subject Israel and Judah to annihilating judgment. With the help of the advancing Assyrians, Yahweh proposes to "make Samaria a heap in the open country" (1:6). Unfortunately, Samaria's gross misconduct is duplicated in Jerusalem itself. Thus, the prophet laments that Samaria's fate will also be Jerusalem's (1:8–9). Micah then anticipates Assyria's rape of the land of Judah (1:10–16). Mentioning numerous place names, the prophet skillfully communicates his conviction that Yahweh's people, be they northerners or southerners, are doomed to disaster.

The prophet's censure of the rich is especially pronounced in Micah 2. He claims that the well-to-do remain awake at night devising schemes of wickedness (2:1). He even outlines their illegal real-estate transactions (2:2). Then comes the awful disclosure of divine intention: "Behold, against this family I am devising evil, from which you cannot remove your necks; and you shall not walk haughtily, for it will be an evil time" (2:3).

But who precisely is the target of divine rebuke? Perhaps the term "this family" applies to Jerusalem's irresponsible upper classes.[1] Another view, however, holds that this term is a later gloss inserted by an unknown individual who wished to limit the disaster.[2] Neither alternative has to be accepted, however. Amos 3:1–2 and Jer. 8:3 illustrate that the noun "family" can denote the entire covenant people. If this is how Micah used the term, then he would be predicting the destruction of the entire country and the attendant suffering of rich and poor alike. Because the southern nation as a whole has become corrupt, it must suffer ruin. In 2:6–11 other examples of outrageous social behavior are mentioned. The affluent seem to have employed robber gangs to victimize their unsuspecting neighbors (2:8). The people have also silenced those who speak the truth. The one who says, "I will preach to you of wine and strong drink" (2:11) attracts an enthusiastic crowd, whereas the popular response to Micah's candor is, "Do not preach!" (2:6). In Micah's estimation, Judah's urban culture is plagued by rank corruption.

The leadership of Israel and Judah is sharply addressed in Micah 3. Though the various heads and rulers have a responsibility to guide their people in justice, they are the very ones who have turned against the commoner. Consequently, they will no longer have the benefit of Yahweh's answer (3:4). Judah's judges, priests, and prophets are all berated for their concern with accumulating personal wealth and their indifference toward their covenant brothers (3:9–11). A judgment of horrendous proportions lies in store for Jerusalem and Zion (3:12).

Although Micah's words are shrill, he appears to have been genuinely moved by the suffering of his fellow peasants. Assuredly Micah refused to support a Zion-centered theology that spoke lavishly of Jerusalem's continuity. Instead, he insisted that Judah's social and religious sickness had assumed tremendous proportions and that nowhere was that sickness in a more advanced state than in Jerusalem. In response to the urban leaders who had the unmitigated nerve to say, "Is not Yahweh in the midst of us? No evil shall come upon us" (3:11), Micah must have thought, "Wait and see! Wait and see!"

ISAIAH OF JERUSALEM

The Man and His Book

According to the superscription of Isa. 1:1, Isaiah prophesied during the reigns of Uzziah (783–742), Jotham (742–735), Ahaz (735–715), and Hezekiah (715–687). Presumably Isaiah was born in the 760s; he received his call to the prophetic office in 742, the year of Uzziah's death (6:1). Since we have no evidence of his efforts after 701 B.C., perhaps he died not many years later.

This prophet associated himself with the crises that threatened the reigns of Ahaz and Hezekiah. Throughout, he attempted to speak words of wisdom that were respectful of good faith and good politics alike. While Isaiah did not fall victim to the impracticalities of political isolationism, he did refuse to support monarchy in its quest for the expedient way out of whatever international dilemma it was facing. The sophistication of his thinking and the imagery of his prophetic pronouncements suggest that he spent his lifetime in Jerusalem, devoting himself to the instruction and welfare of its inhabitants. And from Isa. 7:3 and 8:3 we learn that Isaiah was married and had two sons.

Isaiah's career as Yahweh's prophet was long and varied. Like Amos and Hosea with their abrasive threats against the citizenry in the north, Isaiah was capable of harsh criticism of his southern contemporaries. In his earlier years, he felt compelled to speak against a complacent people who had recently prospered under the rule of Uzziah. Yet in the later phase of his prophetic ministry, Isaiah changed and so did the times. Toward the end of the eighth century, Jerusalem was feeling Assyrian pressure very keenly. Sister cities in Judah were being raked over by the ravaging army of Sennacherib (704–681). King Hezekiah was suffering a humiliating defeat as the Assyrians laid siege to Jerusalem. In this context, Isaiah dared to pronounce oracles of promise. He insisted that the capital with its holy hill of Zion would not be overtaken by the haughty Assyrians.

Of course, the biblical legend on Sennacherib's attack in Isaiah 36–39 and 2 Kings 18:13–20:19 has oversimplified the situation. Surely the Isaiah of history did not wave the nation's flag as fervently as these passages would lead us to believe.[3] Yet Isaiah may have mellowed in his last years. The biblical record is such that Isaiah's "function as court prophet, his relation to the cultic traditions of Zion, his use of wisdom materials, remain problematic."[4]

It seems, however, that when Jerusalem's situation was most outrageous, Isaiah confronted its harassed citizenry with a reassuring message. What mattered most was holding to the ancient faith that the sovereign Yahweh stood at the helm. It was he, not the arrogant Sennacherib, who would have the last say. It is likewise clear that Isaiah did not declare war on the Israelite institutions of kingship and cult. Unlike Micah, Isaiah did not impute to Yahweh a hatred of urban existence and culture. Still, Isaiah joined the other reforming prophets of eighth-century Hebrew society in demanding radical social and religious transformation. He knew as thoroughly as Amos, Hosea, and Micah did the illness of his people, and he had no less aptitude than they to disturb the complacent.

Yet before we may turn to specific texts that disclose the prophetic work of Isaiah we must come to terms with certain literary issues. A hard look at the text reveals that not all of the Book of Isaiah bears the imprint of the eighth-century prophet named Isaiah. Though our reasons for saying so will be given later on, we believe that Isaiah 40–55 and 56–66 may be labeled Second and Third Isaiah, respectively. (See the discussion in Chapter 17.) Moreover, as the following description of the six main blocks of Isaiah 1–39 will indicate, not all the material in the first thirty-nine chapters can be ascribed to Isaiah of Jerusalem. As you read each of the six sections that follow, try to think of a few adjectives that might characterize its content.

Isaiah 1–12. Isaiah 1–12, which is primarily the authentic work of the eighth-century Isaiah, reflects the early phase of the prophet's ministry. Isaiah 6 recounts his prophetic call, which occurred in 742 (the year of Uzziah's death). With rare exceptions, the rest of the material consists of prophetic oracles spoken both against and for Yahweh's people. The Isaiah preface (chap. 1) is a classical summary of the prophetic perspective, which is primarily Isaian. The discourse in 2:2–4 and 4:2–6 is concerned with Zion's restoration and the inauguration of a new age. Though it may not be confidently considered Isaiah's utterance, it maintains the posture and spirit of the prophet. Between these two sections on "Jerusalem the ideal" stand judgmental oracles (2:5–4:1) aimed at the wrongs of "Jerusalem the real." All of Isaiah 5 along with Isa. 9:8–10:4 may be designated authentic oracular material concerned with Yahweh's vineyard (Judah) and its woes. Isaiah 7:1–9:7 contains the prophet's disclosures about Immanuel and the Messiah, which presumably are linked with the crisis that Ahaz faced in 735 when the Aramean-Israelite coalition pressured him to join the cause of the western states against Assyria. In Isa. 10:5–34 the prophet regards Assyria as the proud instrument of Yahweh's anger.

With its marked eschatological quality, Isa. 11:1–9 also speaks of the Messiah, but it is probably a later extension of Isaiah's thought. Isaiah 11:10–16, with its emphasis on the Messiah's era rather than his person, appears to be a postexilic expression of hope in the return of Yahweh's scattered people. Two presumably non-Isaian songs of thanksgiving in 12:1–3 and 12:4–6 bring the variegated section of Isaiah 1–12 to a close.

Isaiah 13–23. Isaiah 13–23 offers a miscellany of pronouncements against foreign peoples analogous to the oracular sequences in Jeremiah 46–51 and Ezekiel 25–32. Stylistically, the most distinctive passage is the biographical Isaiah 20. It reveals the prophet's activity and proclamation prior to 712 when Ashdod succumbed to Assyrian brutality. While non-Isaian materials predominate in Isaiah 13–23, we believe that the eighth-century prophet is represented in the following oracles: 14:24–27 (on Assyria); 14:28–32 (on Phoenicia); 17:1–11 (on Damascus and Ephraim); 18:1–19:15 (on Egypt); 22:1–14 (on Jerusalem); and 22:15–25 (on Shebna, an officer of Hezekiah).[5]

Isaiah 24–27. This section of Isaiah consists of a group of poems commonly referred to as the "Isaiah Apocalypse." It offers great variety: poetic depictions of the present, eschatological prophecies anticipating an imminent catastrophe of worldwide dimensions, as well as highly lyrical units of praise and thanksgiving. Logical progression of thought and allusions to history are lacking, however. Although the age of this material is currently in dispute, it seems to postdate Isaiah of Jerusalem.

Isaiah 28–33. Isaiah 28–33 preserves a series of oracles connected with the late phase of Isaiah's ministry, when Jerusalem was laid under the terrible siege of Sennacherib. This predominantly Isaian material consistently advances the prophet's criticism of those who trust in fragile alliances with Egypt as a response to the threat of the Assyrians. Here especially we see Isaiah's preoccupation with faith in Yahweh, which he regards as the one requirement in approaching political affairs. The prophetic liturgy of Isaiah 33 probably stems from the postexilic era, though it may have been framed under the continuing influence of Isaiah. Certainly Isaiah 1–12 and Isaiah 28–33 are the two sections that offer the greatest amount of authentically Isaian utterance.

Isaiah 34–35. In Isaiah 34–35 we find two anonymous prophecies dating to the sixth century or later. The horrible doom predicted in Isaiah 34 for Yahweh's enemies (especially Edom) contrasts sharply with the eloquent oracle of salvation in Isaiah 35, which celebrates Zion's expected restoration. The message and style of Isaiah 35 recall Second Isaiah: the desert stretches are to be transformed into a thoroughfare on which the exiled and dispersed people of Yahweh will travel as they joyously return to Zion.

Isaiah 36–39. Isaiah 36–39 preserves a historical narrative that has been lifted with some change from the Deuteronomic history (2 Kings 18:13–20:19). These chapters meditate on those events attending Sennacherib's siege of Jerusalem in 701 and his departure. Fixing Isaiah's message in the context of dramatic narrative, these chapters may have entered the Isaiah collection many decades after the prophet's death.

An examination of the authentically Isaian sections will reveal that the prophet was a talented communicator. He spoke with dignity and power, and drew upon his own set of images. He offers a portrait of the defenseless Jerusalem as one who from head to toe is smitten with sores and wounds (1:5–6). He likens Yahweh's people to an inferior garden whose disappointing results incur the wrath of the one who had been so diligent in planting and tending it (5:1–7). He interprets encroaching Assyria as Yahweh's "rod of anger" and "staff of fury" (10:5). Like Hosea, Isaiah of Jerusalem knew the potency of symbolic names (Isa. 7:3; 8:1), and like Amos he knew how to make the most of a vivid play on words. Thus, in 5:7 Isaiah declares that Yahweh looked for "justice" (*mishpāṭ*) but instead found "bloodshed" (*miśpāḥ*), that he sought "righteousness" (*ṣᵉdhāqāh*) but only encountered a "cry" (*ṣᵉᶜāqāh*).

A matter of current academic interest concerns Isaiah's relationship to the wisdom movement of his time.[6] Such parables as the one about the ass and ox in Isa. 1:2–3 and the farmer in 28:23–29 reflect Isaiah's association with the wisdom movement of the ancient Near East, which held parables about daily life in high esteem. Isaiah likewise employed proverbial speech to point out the folly of Assyrian pride: "Shall the axe vaunt itself over him who hews with it, or the saw magnify itself against him who wields it? As if a rod should wield him who lifts it, or as if a staff should lift him who is not wood!" (10:15). The terms "counsel" and "counselor," which play an important part in Isaiah's proclamations, appear to have been taken from the Jerusalem court, where wise men made their recommendations. Clearly, this sophisticated urban prophet made effective use of a wide range of speech patterns.

Isaiah's Historical Context

At this point the historical context in which Isaiah prophesied requires further examination. Thanks to the aggressive program of Uzziah (783–742), which involved repairing Jerusalem's defenses, restructuring the Judean army, and obtaining a commanding position in Edom, Judah arrived at a level of self-sufficiency that she had never known in the ninth century.

Yet if Judah met good days, Uzziah fell upon bad. In about 750 he contracted leprosy. Since this affliction made him ritually impure, he could no longer enter the Jerusalem Temple. Nor was he now qualified to reign over the Judean citizenry. He was put into a rest home, and his son Jotham ruled as regent in his stead (2 Kings 15:5).

Our knowledge of Jotham's reign (742–735) is fragmentary. A reference in 2 Kings 15:35 states that "He built the upper gate of the house of Yahweh," and 2 Chron. 27:3 implies that Jotham continued the policy of his father in buttressing Jerusalem's defenses. The Chronicler also discloses that the Ammonites were required to pay Jotham heavy tribute over a three-year period (27:5). Indeed, the signet ring bearing the letters l-y-t-m, "belonging to Jotham," that was discovered at Ezion-geber suggests the range of Jotham's influence.[7] He appears to have inherited and maintained a respectable kingdom.

The rule of Jotham's son and successor, Ahaz (735–715), is reported in a most unfavorable light in 2 Kings 16:2b–4. Not only is Ahaz assessed as an ardent syncretist, but he seems to have revived the barbaric rite of human sacrifice, which faithful Yahwists regarded as the worst abomination of the Canaanites.

When and for what reasons did Ahaz make a burnt offering of his own son? Though we do not know for certain, two political crises suggest possible provocations for such extreme behavior.

Shortly before his death in 735, Jotham had been subjected to pressure from kings Rezin and Pekah, who unsuccessfully sought to draft Judah into their coalition against Assyria (2 Kings 15:37). When Jotham died, Ahaz came to the Judean throne. His inexperience encouraged the Aramean-Israelite coalition to try again to inflict its will on Judah. Though it failed, the coalition sought to oust Ahaz and make someone of its own choosing king—namely, ben Tabeel (Isa. 7:6). At about this time, Edom and Philistia apparently joined the northerners in their harassment of Judah.[8]

Faced by such political adversity, Ahaz may very well have appealed rashly for both human and divine assistance. In 2 Kings 16:7 we learn that he sought the services of Tiglath-pileser through an ill-advised note and the payment of tribute. Since Tiglath-pileser, who was undoubtedly aware of what Rezin and Pekah were up to, would have reacted on his own, Ahaz obligated himself unnecessarily. Moving westward, the Assyrian monarch reduced Israel's territorial holdings, devastated Damascus, and summoned Ahaz there to exact from him a pledge of allegiance to Assyria's cause (2 Kings 16:10–18). Ahaz was now required to venerate the gods of Assyria. A model of the Assyrian altar in Damascus was immediately erected in the Jerusalem Temple for the king's worship. Moreover, the Temple had to be stripped of some of its original furnishings to provide the substantial tribute Assyria now expected from its vassal Judah. Perhaps under the pressures of these moments Ahaz did in fact offer his son as a holocaust to deity in the hope that he might secure divine assistance.

A second trying moment that might have led Ahaz to give up his son was the Assyrian siege against the city of Samaria, which began in 724. After holding out for more than two years, Samaria capitulated to the Assyrian forces in 722. This would have given Ahaz ample cause to worry about the state of his own kingdom. Although he had not been party to the foolish anti-Assyrian coalition, Ahaz had little reason to suppose that Assyria would show any consideration for the wishes of Judah. In either case, the Deuteronomist despised Ahaz for his woeful lack of faith and indiscriminate conduct. He made no allowance whatever for the fact that Ahaz was required to rule Judah at a time when international relations were quite strained.

Hezekiah (715–687) ascended the throne at the death of Ahaz. As yet another son of Ahaz, he reversed his father's syncretic policies. Hezekiah first acted with caution and then, as the international situation permitted, he grew more bold (2 Kings 18:3–7). To some extent he was successful in returning his people to Mosaic Yahwism. Though his personal courage should not be discounted, he was blessed by favorable international circumstances whereas Ahaz was not. The Assyrian monarch, Sargon II, was busy quelling Babylonian rebellion in the east. Moreover, under its newly established Twenty-fifth (Ethiopian) Dynasty, Egypt experienced enough resurgence to encourage in the petty states in western Asia the hope that she might offer some support against Assyria.

In time, however, Hezekiah was also threatened by a political crisis. History took a critical turn after 705, when Sargon died and his son Sennacherib (704–681) assumed the lead in Assyria. Soon Sennacherib had to cope with a sweeping rebellion involving Babylon and Elam in the east, and Syria, Palestine, and Egypt in the west. The fact that the nationalistic Hezekiah had taken sides in the international turmoil is clear from the friendly reception he gave the envoys of Merodach-baladan, the Babylonian ruler who was now challenging Sennacherib (2 Kings 20:12–19). Although Hezekiah senselessly supported the anti-Assyrian coalition, he was wise enough to recognize that he had better tend quickly to Jerusalem's defenses and make provisions for an ample supply of water for the city just in case Sennacherib should come charging westward. The king had a new reservoir, the pool of Siloam, built within the city's fortifications. Then he had the Gihon spring, which was outside the city, covered up so that it would not be seen by the enemy and ordered that a tunnel be constructed under the hill of Ophel. This would bring the water from the Gihon spring into the city itself.

VI. THE SOUTHERN KINGDOM ON ITS OWN (722–587 B.C.)

DATE (B.C.)	EGYPT	SOUTHERN KINGDOM (JUDAH)	BABYLONIA	ASSYRIA
721	25th (Ethiopian) Dynasty (ca. 716–663)	Ahaz (735–715) Hezekiah (715–687)		Sargon II (722–705) overtakes Ashdod (712) Sennacherib (704–681) invades Judah (701)
700	Tirhakah (ca. 685–664) Thebes sacked by the Assyrians (663)	Invasion of Sennacherib (701) Manasseh (687–642)		Esarhaddon (680–669) Asshurbanapal (668–627)
650	26th Dynasty (ca. 664–525) Necho II (610–594)	Amon (642–640) Josiah (640–609) Zephaniah (ca. 630–622) Jeremiah (ca. 627–580) Deuteronomic reform (622) Nahum (ca. 615) Jehoahaz (609) Jehoiakim (609–598) Habakkuk (ca. 605)	Resurgence Neo-Babylonian empire established (626) Nabopolassar (626–605) Victory at Carchemish (605) Nebuchadnezzar (605–562)	Fall of Nineveh to Medes and Babylonians (612) Death of Assyrian empire (609)
600	Psammetichus II (594–589) Apries (589–570)	Jehoiachin (598–597) 1st deportation of Jews to Babylon (597) Zedekiah (597–587) Ezekiel (ca. 593–570) Fall of Jerusalem (587) 2d deportation of Jews to Babylon (587)		

Pool of Siloam in Jerusalem. This pool, located at the southern end of Hezekiah's tunnel, is only a fraction of the total construction effort undertaken by the king's engineers to provide Jerusalem's citizens with an ample interior source of water. A source within the city would be absolutely essential for Jerusalem's existence should the city have to sustain an enemy attack. Even today nearby inhabitants make use of this water supply. (Photo by the author.)

In 1880 an inscription was found some 20 feet from the Siloam pool. Its excellent classical Hebrew suggests that it was written by an educated workman who had been involved in the project. Despite the fact that it is incomplete, the Siloam Inscription provides a vivid account of how the conduit was constructed:

[... when] (the tunnel) was driven through. And this was the way in which it was cut through:—While [...] (were) still [...] axe(s), each man toward his fellow, and while there were still three cubits to be cut through, [there was heard] the voice of a man calling to his fellow, for there was *an overlap* in the rock on the right [and on the left].[9] And when the tunnel was driven through, the quarrymen hewed (the rock), each man toward his fellow, axe against axe; and the water flowed from the spring toward the reservoir for 1,200 cubits, and the height of the rock above the head(s) of the quarrymen was 100 cubits.[10]

This inscription is important for several reasons. It supplements biblical texts that mention the waterworks of Hezekiah (2 Kings 20:20, 2 Chron. 32:30, Isa. 22:11). It testifies to the technical effectiveness of Hezekiah's engineers who, with only primitive surveying equipment, achieved quite satisfactory results. It demonstrates the kind of alphabetic script that was in vogue in Judah at the end of the eighth century B.C. The opening lines of the inscription, which might have revealed the name and year of Jerusalem's reigning king, are missing. Nevertheless, the content and paleography of the inscription relate to Hezekiah's time.

It was not long before Babylon had to submit once more to Assyria. Both the Bible and the annals of Sennacherib reveal that by 701 the situation for Jerusalem and Hezekiah had become grim indeed. It is remarkable that this city and its king survived the pressures of Assyrian aggression. We have examined the lives and times of several eighth-century Judean monarchs in some detail. Let us turn now to three phases of Isaiah's lengthy and significant ministry.

Texts Reflecting the Early Phase of Isaiah's Ministry

We are concerned with a relatively brief period that extends from 742, when Isaiah received his call to the prophetic office, to 735, when Ahaz refused to comply with Isaiah's suggestions regarding his behavior in the face of increasing pressure from the Aramean-Israelite coalition.

The superbly written account of Isaiah's summons to the prophetic office is preserved in Isaiah 6. The text may be summarized by three simple words—"woe," "lo," and "go." Yahweh's holiness, which was to impress Isaiah throughout his career, must have been singularly real to the prophet on this occasion. His vision of the deity seems to have come during a moment of corporate worship in the Jerusalem Temple.

The theophany in Isaiah 6 consists of encounter (vv. 1–4), sanctification (vv. 5–7), and commission (vv. 8–11, with the addition of threatening words in vv. 12–13). Speaking is a dominant element. The opening speech of the seraphim (6:3) emphasizes the deity's holiness. The second speech—which begins with the telling phrase, "woe is me!"—is Isaiah's; in it he conveys his strong feeling of fear (6:5). The third speech (6:7)

is by one of the seraphim who takes the lead in the prophet's sanctification. The fourth speech consists of a question posed by the deity, "whom
shall I send?" and Isaiah's spontaneous and affirmative answer (6:8).
The final speech (6:9–13) offers Yahweh's special disclosure, which confers on Isaiah's commissioning its peculiar stamp.

The deity's regal nature is thoroughly affirmed. Yahweh's throne is
mentioned in 6:1, and he is referred to as "the King" in 6:5. In Judean
theology, the ark of the covenant was regarded as a replica of the
heavenly throne and the Temple that housed it was thought to be a copy
of Yahweh's celestial abode. Since Isaiah sees with the eyes of flesh and
faith, familiar elements in the cult are transformed by his inner experience. Affinities between Isaiah 6 and the royal enthronement alluded
to in Psalm 24 suggest that Isaiah may have participated in the Temple
services at the time of Jotham's coronation.

Of special interest are the seraphim, which are depicted as having
six wings, standing beside the divine throne of Yahweh, intoning his
praise, and participating in Isaiah's cleansing. The noun "seraphim"
derives from the Hebrew root śrp meaning "to burn." Certainly something is being transfigured in this passage, but what is it? The Temple
priests, the winged celestial creatures that decorated the Temple walls,
and the cherubim themselves have all been suggested. Perhaps the cherubim are the most plausible:

> At the annual enthronement ceremony, the innermost chamber of the
> Temple containing the ark and the cherubim would be open to the
> view of those standing in the Temple, as Isaiah was. When the
> bright sun lighted on the images, they could appear to be on fire, and
> hence the meaning of seraphim would be "the burning ones," in this
> case the burning cherubim.[11]

Yet if Isaiah were momentarily taken with the peculiar appearance
of the cherubim, in the long run they were not what mattered most.
They were present to celebrate the transcendent grandeur of the one
who was now summoning Isaiah to participate in the concrete fulfillment
of divine purpose. The antiphonal singing of the seraphim also attests to
Yahweh's resplendence: "Holy, holy, holy is Yahweh of hosts; the
whole earth is full of his glory" (6:3). Again the familiar is transfigured.
The seraphim utterance echoes "in the very shortest wording" the congregation's hymn of praise.[12] Hence, the familiar cultic anthem was now
heard by the entranced prophet as if chanted by the seraphim themselves.

Isaiah is simultaneously aware of God's splendor and his own
worthlessness. He reacts in fear. Brought to nothingness in the face of
deity, Isaiah becomes painfully aware that he is unclean (6:5). In this
theophanic experience he is given a new, dreadful insight concerning the
distance that exists between God and man. The prophet recognizes that

no matter what man does, he is bound to feel impure before his maker. Therefore, it is important that at Yahweh's initiation Isaiah be cleansed by one of the seraphim.

The narrative then moves to Isaiah's acceptance of his call. He embraces the challenge (6:8) before he is informed of its terrible nature (6:9–13). In contrast with the JE call of Moses in Exodus 3–4, Isaiah impulsively says, "Here am I" and trusts that God will approve. The prophet is sent to proclaim a message of death. Although he is to appeal to the people's hearts, they will not respond. From its inception, Isaiah's mission is destined to fail. Daring to hope that such a commission will be temporary, Isaiah inquires, "How long, O Yahweh?" (6:11). While the deity affirms that a purged remnant will remain (6:13), easy optimism is ruled out. The emphasis falls on the impending doom that Judah so richly deserves.

The oracles against Judah and Jerusalem preserved in Isaiah 1–5 reflect certain pronouncements that Isaiah made during Jotham's reign (742–735). Condemnation and threat dominate these chapters, and the tone has already been established in the exordium of 1:2–3. Here the heavenly and earthly populations are summoned to bear witness to Yahweh's people, who have reacted to him with ingratitude and defiance. Yahweh's fatherly character and the distant, almost inanimate manner of this senseless people are a striking contrast.

According to 1:10–17, the concerns of the people are completely out of harmony with those of Yahweh. (The oracle in Isa. 1:4–9 implies Jerusalem's predicament in 701 and thus relates to a much later phase in Isaiah's career.) Here Isaiah protests against the worthless practices of empty ritual. Without righteous conduct, lavish sacrifices and formal prayers only insult the deity. It is the fragmented quality of human relationships that draws Yahweh's attention, not the vain offerings thrust before him on festival days.

The brief oracle that follows in 1:18–20 offers a vivid depiction of Yahweh as judge and his own people as the accused. The guilty party is given a second chance to engage in covenant pursuits pleasing to the deity: "If you are willing and obedient, you shall eat the good of the land; but if you refuse and rebel, you shall be devoured by the sword" (1:19–20).

Judgment and promise are forcefully communicated in the oracle of 1:24–26. The purifying aspect of Yahweh's judgment depicted here is frequently alluded to in Isaiah's preaching. The refinement of silver demands that the dross be removed (1:25). Even so, the impending judgment is not final, for Isaiah expresses his certainty that an era of authentic righteousness will follow Jerusalem's doom.

In Isa. 2:5–3:15 the fruits of Judah's folly are portrayed at some length. Human pride and idolatry are thoroughly condemned in 2:6–22. Isaiah contends that the numerous idols in the land are powerless to deliver those who pay them homage (2:7–8). They only symbolize man's proclivity for self-exaltation. Judgment is inevitable: "And the haughtiness of man shall be humbled, and the pride of men shall be brought low; and Yahweh alone will be exalted in that day. And the idols shall utterly pass away" (2:17–18). In that judgment Judah's "stay and staff" (3:1, that is, its leadership) will be taken away from the people. Offices and functions regarded as essential to the smooth functioning of the state will collapse, and civil unrest will escalate into violence (3:5).

The outstanding passage in Isaiah 1–5 is the Song of the Vineyard (5:1–7), which artfully advances the familiar themes of divine reproach and threat by means of a parable that is sung. Functioning in the capacity of a wisdom teacher, "Isaiah draws an incident from the experience of man and nature in order to get across a forceful and foreboding message to his hearers."[13] The prophet may have sung this captivating ballad at a vintage festival attended by a joyous throng. Isaiah tells of his friend or "beloved" (5:1) who planted and tended an unproductive vineyard. The disappointed friend (Yahweh) takes over in 5:3 with his own jarring words. The unprotected vineyard will be devoured and trampled on by animals.

The sentence of doom is sounded, and lest there be someone around who does not understand the point of the parable, Isaiah offers his own lucid interpretation (5:7). The "men of Judah" comprise Yahweh's vineyard. Through the use of puns, which we have already noted, Isaiah declares that Israel has perverted the good and met Yahweh's outgoing love with ungrateful disobedience. With considerable talent, this prophet-strategist first entertains the people with a parable on the theme of tragic love and then suddenly forces them to recognize that the parable is the story of their own sordid situation. The oracles in Isaiah 1–5 must have jolted the well-to-do population. Political conditions under Jotham were not disastrous. Still, Judah's religious and social existence was falling far below the standards of the covenant, and the prophet labored to keep this matter before the attention of his people.

Some of the most fascinating biblical material on the early phase of Isaiah's ministry is found in Isaiah 7–8, which recounts the prophet's relationship with Ahaz just after the latter had assumed the throne. We have already observed that at the outset of his reign, Ahaz was threatened by the Aramean-Israelite coalition. As Isaiah 7 opens, the siege of Jerusalem is under way. The prophet is divinely instructed to go with his son Shear-jashub and address Ahaz who is, at the moment, inspecting Jerusalem's water supply and defenses (7:3). Through Isaiah's words and the presence of his son, whose name means "a remnant shall return," Ahaz will be confronted with a lucid disclosure of Yahweh's will. Ahaz is called on to make a momentous choice: Either he will continue his military operations or he will develop faith in Yahweh, faith that the deity will in his own way deliver Judah. Isaiah informs Ahaz that he need not worry about the assertiveness of Rezin and Pekah ("the son of Remaliah," 7:4), who are merely the heads of two unimpressive western states. Yahweh will not permit these intruders to overthrow Ahaz and alter Judah's fate. Isaiah's confrontation with Ahaz reaches its climax in 7:9, where the prophet states, "If you will not believe, surely you shall not be established." The monarch is asked to commit himself to Yahweh's cause.

In the second part of the encounter (7:10–17), the prophet offers a sign to Ahaz, who sanctimoniously announces that he will not put Yahweh to the test. Isaiah replies, "Behold, a young woman shall conceive and bear a son, and shall call his name Immanuel" (7:14). This name, which means "God with us," denotes solidarity. Isaiah then dates his prediction with respect to the present crisis of 735. Once Immanuel is weaned, becomes accustomed to a simple diet of curds and honey, and knows something about practical good and evil, the two troublesome northern powers will succumb to the ravages of the Assyrian army. The discernment of good and evil expected of the child will have to do with simple behavior (not touching a hot stove, not falling into an open cistern, and so on); it will not involve the sophisticated ethical distinctions that might be expected of an adult. Isaiah's eschatological reflection therefore relates to an immediate future. And sure enough, by 732 Tiglath-pileser had devastated Damascus and reduced Israel to the state of a vassal dependency. Nevertheless, as it is presently preserved, the promising word of 7:15–16 is checked by 7:17 with its declaration that in the course of her history, Judah will experience truly unpleasant days. Isaiah 7:17 is much like Isa. 8:6–8, which ominously predicts that the mighty Euphrates river (Assyria) will overtake the gently flowing Jerusalem canal of Shiloah (Judah). Both passages were no doubt inspired by Ahaz' unwillingness to take Isaiah seriously.

Biblical scholars have given many answers to the question, "What child is this?" The prophet may have been speaking of his own child. His name accords well with the fact that the prophet assigned meaningful names to his other children (7:3; 8:3). Perhaps Isaiah's wife was pregnant again. Or perhaps the child referred to was the son of Ahaz.[14] Without any change of Hebrew consonants, "She will call" in 7:14 might be rendered, "You will call." But if the son belonged to Ahaz, it was not Hezekiah; he could not have been born later than 740 (2 Kings 18:2). If Hezekiah had a younger brother, the Hebrew Bible says nothing about him. In any event, consensus about the identity of the child has not yet been reached. Two things are certain, however. First, the child is to be born and mature in Ahaz's lifetime as a sign of Judah's historical deliverance and momentary relief, and second, the child is not presented as the deliverer himself.[15]

Then what may we infer about the child's mother? By employing the noun ʿalmāh, the Hebrew of 7:14 discloses that she is a young woman of marriageable age. We have no way of knowing whether she was a virgin. Had the prophet desired to make clear that a miraculous birth was in the offing, he would surely have used the Hebrew noun bᵉthûlāh, meaning "virgin"; when emphasis is placed on virginity, as in Gen. 24:16, the noun bᵉthûlāh is ordinarily used. Since the Septuagint version of Isa. 7:14 reads parthenos ("virgin"), we suspect that an early Jewish tradition that regarded the birth as miraculous did emerge. The theological issue is admittedly complicated by the fact that in Matt. 1:23 the Evangelist quotes Isa. 7:14 and uses the Greek noun parthenos. Of course, if the woman in question were either Isaiah's or Ahaz's wife, one would scarcely wish to defend her virginity. The meaning of the child's name is much easier to determine than the status of his mother.

In Isa. 8:3–4 still another prophetic testimony is given in the hope that Ahaz will acquire confidence and act wisely. And this, too, is connected with the same international crisis. Isaiah's wife bears a son, and the prophet is divinely instructed to call him "Maher-shalal-hash-baz," meaning "the spoil speeds, the prey hastes." That name assures Ahaz that both Damascus and Syria will soon fall to Assyria. Before the child is old enough to address his parents by name, the northern trouble-makers will have been laid low by Assyrian pressure. All Ahaz has to do is to trust in divine power.

Despite Isaiah's assurances, the intimidated Ahaz appealed to Tig-lath-pileser for assistance. Although the Assyrian monarch complied, he fully expected financial and other forms of support from Ahaz. Isaiah was sorely provoked by the king's lack of faith (8:16–22). Having made contact with Tiglath-pileser, Ahaz had determined that Judah would be Assyria's vassal rather than Yahweh's. Hence, Isaiah now isolated himself from the Judean political scene. His words in Isa. 8:16, "Bind up the testimony, seal the teaching among my disciples," indicate that by this time (735) Isaiah had already acquired a loyal following. He would now focus his attention on them. After withdrawing from public life, Isaiah had a good opportunity to oversee the recording of the first collection of his prophetic proclamations. They would be written and sealed with the full expectation that as history unfolded, they would be verified.

A Text Reflecting the Middle Phase of Isaiah's Ministry

A short prose biography in Isaiah 20 relates to the so-called middle phase of Isaiah's ministry. When the Twenty-fifth Dynasty of Egypt was strong enough to become involved once more in the affairs of western Asia, some Palestinian inhabitants thought that the time was ripe for a rebellion against Sargon II. In about 714 the city of Ashdod openly defied Assyrian wishes. Its monarch, Azuri, withheld tribute from Assyria. Sargon then deposed Azuri and placed Ahimiti, his younger brother, on the throne. The latter, however, was soon driven out by the zealous native population. According to Sargon's account, Judah, Edom, and Moab were all summoned to join a coalition of Philistine villages that would plot against the Assyrians.[16]

While Hezekiah, who was rather new to the throne of Judah, was weighing the invitation, Isaiah felt inspired to enter public life once more. The prophet was divinely instructed to walk the streets of Jerusalem barefoot and nearly naked for a three-year period (Isa. 20:2–3). (Presumably Isaiah wore only a loincloth.) Assuming the humiliating posture of a prisoner of war, Isaiah was to be living testimony of the folly of joining Egypt and other western parties in open defiance of Assyria. He maintained his pro-Assyrian stance, for he remained convinced that Yahweh was actually implementing his will through the Assyrian menace. Isaiah therefore tried to counter the mounting conspiracy. Egyptian help was not forthcoming, and the Ashdod rebels were severely beaten. Since Ashdod, rather than Egypt, received the brunt of the Assyrian attack in 712, Isaiah probably delivered his oracle about the fate of Egypt and Ethiopia (20:3–6) before the Assyrian troops arrived. In any case, the prophet was intent on pointing out Judah's stupidity in trusting Egypt. Hezekiah seems to have accepted Isaiah's urging that Judah not involve herself in anti-Assyrian rebellion. When Sargon vented his rage on the western states in 712, he spared Judah. Clearly, her decision to remain on the sidelines turned out to be the wiser course.

Texts Reflecting the Late Phase of Isaiah's Ministry

Within a few years, however, Isaiah had to cope with a monarchy that was in quest of Egyptian support, a monarchy that made firmer commitments to human allies than to its saving Lord of history. The witness of biographical prose (2 Kings 18–20; Isa. 36–39) and poetic oracle (Isa. 28–33) are both relevant to our present concern. The former witness discloses Isaiah's willingness to involve himself again in the public issues of his time. The prophet's interaction with the monarch is especially vivid in Isaiah 39. There Isaiah is suspicious; he protests against the cordial reception Hezekiah had already extended to the Babylonian envoys of Merodach-baladan. Now that the inexperienced Sennacherib (704–681) had taken the throne, that Babylonian rebel sought to disturb the Assyrian equilibrium in every way possible. In Isaiah's view, too much cooperation with Merodach-baladan and readiness to enter into anti-Assyrian intrigue would spell political disaster for Judah (39:6–7). Meanwhile Hezekiah was negotiating with Egypt. Isaiah assessed such an ill-founded alliance as "a covenant with death" (28:15). Precise agreements with Babylonian and Egyptian cohorts would not buttress Judah's position.   ·

Actually Isaiah's political and theological counsel was sound. As a realist, he recognized that in these last years of the eighth century B.C., the small state of Judah could not hope to assert herself against the towering Assyrian empire. Even more, Isaiah spoke from a theological perspective that confidently declared that it was Yahweh's intention to use Assyria for his own purposes. For the moment, Assyria was Yahweh's rod of anger (10:5). Isaiah knew that on occasion man may feel entirely justified in saying of Yahweh, "Strange is his deed!" (28:21). Nevertheless, he was convinced that Yahweh would govern history as he saw fit. Judah would be held accountable for her social indifference and religious laxity. If Yahweh willed that Assyria should serve as the instrument of his wrath and chastisement, then Hezekiah should not take measures that oppose the divine will. Moreover, as recently won Judean allies, the Egyptians would be incapable of frustrating Yahweh's purpose: "When Yahweh stretches out his hand, the helper will stumble, and he who is helped will fall, and they will all perish together" (31:3b). Isaiah therefore urged that the present pro-Egyptian and pro-Babylonian course be abandoned.

This time Hezekiah did not agree. He voted for open revolt against the Assyrians. When part of Philistia refused to join the anti-Assyrian cause, Hezekiah dispatched his own armies to induce the people to reconsider (2 Kings 18:8). From Sennacherib's account we learn that the pro-Assyrian king of Ekron, Padi, was with Hezekiah's consent taken to Jerusalem and imprisoned there.[17] The monarch of Judah had irrevocably committed himself to political rebellion. By contrast, Isaiah offered Hezekiah counsel that pressed for political noninvolvement and unswerving faith in the deity: "In returning and rest you shall be saved; in quietness and in trust shall be your strength" (30:15). Hezekiah was in no better a position than his father, Ahaz, to accept Isaiah's recommendation. Swift stallions were a far more attractive option to him than patient faith (30:16). Again the prophet had reason to feel personally frustrated by monarchy.

In due course Sennacherib and his Assyrian army moved westward and overtook numerous Judean cities.[18] Before long, Jerusalem was completely isolated. While Sennacherib was besieging Lachish, he dispatched a delegation headed by his Rabshakeh, an Assyrian title meaning "chief steward" and not a proper name, to Jerusalem in order to urge its inhabitants to surrender.

The vivid and embellished account in Isaiah 36–37 offers a superb speech of propaganda designed to provoke great fear in its listeners. The Rabshakeh positions himself outside Jerusalem's walls. Sharply he admonishes the citizenry to guard against deception from Hezekiah by surrendering unconditionally to the Assyrians. The Jerusalem leaders politely ask that he speak in Aramaic, the current language of foreign diplomacy (36:11). In that way they will be able to hear the Assyrian deputy without running the grave risk of lowering the morale of the

Sennacherib Receiving the Surrender of Lachish. Seated high on a throne, with his feet resting on a footstool, Sennacherib receives the prisoners and booty from Lachish after its capitulation to the Assyrian forces near the end of the eighth century B.C. He is surrounded by soldiers and attendants. (Courtesy of the Trustees of the British Museum.)

city's defenders, who do not speak Aramaic. But instead of honoring that request, the Rabshakeh intensifies his message in the people's vernacular.

Very soon Sennacherib came up to Jerusalem, and his visitation must have profoundly humbled Hezekiah and the Jerusalem populace (Isa. 37:1). In Sennacherib's colorful annals, which report the critical events of 701, three features stand out.[19] First, Sennacherib rescued Padi, the pro-Assyrian king of Ekron, who had been imprisoned with Hezekiah's consent in Jerusalem. Second, the Assyrian king took forty-six of Hezekiah's fortified cities. And third, he forced Hezekiah into the submissive role of royal prisoner "like a bird in a cage." Jerusalem's situation looked utterly dismal.

Nevertheless, prior to and during the siege of Jerusalem, Isaiah refused to be intimidated. Although at first the prophet had believed that Assyria was the rod of Yahweh's anger, he became convinced that the arrogant tool was about to be cast aside. Isaiah now assured his people that the Assyrians would soon depart and Zion would be spared.

Isaiah shared with other inhabitants of Jerusalem the view that Yahweh had pledged himself to the dynasty of David and to its home base. Consequently, he gave the troubled Hezekiah certain assurances. First, Sennacherib would get wind of troubles back home, which would provoke his immediate departure from Jerusalem (Isa. 37:7). Second, within three years the ravaged land of Judah would be fertile once more (37:30-32). And third, the deity would intervene: "I will defend this city to save it, for my own sake and for the sake of my servant David" (37:35).

Sennacherib did in fact leave without overtaking Jerusalem.[20] Although he had not lifted the siege from Lachish until the city had been leveled, he left Jerusalem while it was still intact. Several explanations have been offered for this sudden turn of events. Perhaps Sennacherib and his forces were content with what they had already accomplished. They had broken the anti-Assyrian coalition in western Asia, taken forty-six of Hezekiah's fortified cities, and humbled the entire Jerusalem populace including the king himself. Little would be gained by spending more manpower and equipment on an already impoverished Jerusalem.

According to Isa. 37:36, the angel of Yahweh ravished the Assyrian camp one grim night and slew 185,000 soldiers. This legendary witness may be based on the vague suggestion in Isa. 31:8 that "the Assyrian shall fall by a sword, not of man." If such a legend is not to be interpreted literally, it might reflect the inroads that some unchecked disease was making within the Assyrian camp. We simply do not know.

A third possibility is that Sennacherib received word about difficulties back home that convinced him he should move his army eastward. Isaiah 37:7 reports Yahweh's intention of causing Sennacherib to hear a rumor that will induce him to lift the siege and hurry home. Certainly Sennacherib had been in the west long enough for the Babylonian forces to have regrouped. News about a fresh Babylonian uprising was therefore accepted by the biblical witness as evidence of Yahweh's direct intervention. This explanation of Sennacherib's sudden departure appears to be the most plausible.

Those who endured the siege understandably believed that Yahweh was responsible for the unexpected end to Assyrian harassment. Isaiah also interpreted this sparing of Jerusalem to be in full accord with the divine will. The unwarranted pride of the Assyrian host had reaped its just reward.

There must have been much rejoicing among Jerusalem's citizens, and undoubtedly Yahweh's beneficent presence was celebrated with unprecedented enthusiasm. The tragedy, however, was that through the events of 701, the dogma of Jerusalem's inviolability was inflated beyond all reasonable limits. Indeed, Isaiah himself feared that the people might misread the significance of the recent past by assuming that in any future crisis Yahweh would save Jerusalem. Of course, Jerusalem's destruction in 587 proved them wrong. With the abatement of historical crisis, Isaiah probably returned to the quiet, intimate circle of his followers. Presumably he died only a few years after Sennacherib had hurried back to his native Assyria.

Isaiah's Message in Retrospect

In summarizing Isaiah's message we shall focus on three issues: his conception of the deity, his understanding of man and the human predicament, and his view of the relationship between God and man.[21]

The Nature of the Deity. How did the prophet conceive of God? Often Isaiah conveyed his conception of the deity through divine epithets. For example, he referred to the deity as "the Holy One of Israel" (1:4; 5:19, 24; 10:20; 30:11, 15; 31:1). As one who is holy, Yahweh is without peer, and he expects the sustained loyalty of those who have entered into covenant relationship with him. His people are not to contaminate that relationship by running after other deities and manufacturing idols. Isaiah believed that "holiness *is* Yahweh. It is that without which Yahweh would be not Yahweh—without which Yahweh would not *be.*"[22] Israel's God is also "Yahweh of hosts" (1:9, 24; 2:12; 3:1, 15; 5:7, 9, 16, 24; 6:3). He alone controls all sources and powers in heaven and on earth. The noun "hosts" implies God's sovereignty, which is openly expressed in Isa. 6:5 where the deity is called "the King." Moreover, as "the Mighty One of Israel" (1:24), it is evident that Yahweh has no rival.

At the time of his call, Isaiah was struck by Yahweh's otherness and moved to an awareness of how his glory was manifested: "Holy, holy, holy is Yahweh of hosts; the whole earth is full of his glory" (6:3). Though Yahweh did not indulge mankind in immediate disclosures of himself, men could discover his work and presence within history. The transcendent deity was not indifferent to the world below. Indeed, in Isaiah's conception of Yahweh grandeur and concern were both affirmed.

Man and the Human Predicament. At the time he was summoned to the prophetic office, Isaiah regarded himself and his fellow Judeans as lost, sinful creatures. The prophet felt a profound sense of guilt and recognized that he lacked the resources to make proper expiation. In the Song of the Vineyard (Isa. 5:1–7) he is much concerned with human pride and rebellion. Man's disrespect for the Torah is evident everywhere. Though Isaiah was no iconoclast concerning the Jerusalem Temple, he did criticize cultic sacrifices and observances, which mask wrongdoing without transforming the human condition. In sum, the prophet knew something about human affections and insisted that man's fundamental flaw was his failure to believe in the divine will and to take God seriously.

The Relationship Between God and Man. Isaiah insisted that only by moving beyond self-reliance would man become what the deity had intended him to be. In proclaiming the necessity of faith to Ahaz (7:9) and to Hezekiah (30:15), Isaiah held that man is incapable of delivering himself and that he stands in need of divine wisdom and power. Therefore, he is called on to be a receptive instrument, to come to the deity in a willing posture of expectation. Certainly not all whom the prophet addressed would respond in this way to the deity, for human stubbornness is not easily overcome. Therefore, Isaiah never lost sight of the impending reality of divine judgment.

Yet despite the nation's obdurate delinquency, Isaiah did not abandon hope (1:18). In this connection, Isaiah made a bold distinction within the collective body of Israel. Rebuffed by monarch and commoner alike, the prophet realized that if his ministry and message were to endure, they would have to receive the support of those most sympathetic toward it. Isaiah resolutely believed that such a remnant would constitute the leaven through which God would work. Historical purging and judgment would not spell the end of Yahweh's people. Purposive chastisement would open the door to eventual deliverance.

Isaiah's belief in the inevitability of divine judgment, his preoccupation with the impending day of Yahweh, his belief in the remnant, and his confidence that the deity would not destroy his people completely all remind us of the proclamations of Amos. Nevertheless, Isaiah's comments on the relationship between God and man show the uniqueness of his own position. For example, with the exception of 10:26, Isaiah does not meditate on Israel's Exodus from Egypt. While there are a few allusions to Israel's past in the oracles of Isaiah (for example, 1:9; 9:3; 29:1), the prophet does not enter into the sustained examination of Israelite history so characteristic of Amos and Hosea. Moreover, reflecting on the relationship between Yahweh and Israel, Isaiah repeatedly focuses on Zion. This is where the holy deity truly dwells (8:18) and reveals himself (2:3). Though Isaiah refuses to argue for the inviolability of the Jerusalem cult, he insists that the living God is present in Zion. Such emphasis on Zion is not intended as a celebration of Judah's political power, which is also centered in Jerusalem. It is a way of reminding the people of Jerusalem that Yahweh of hosts is present in their own time and place. Of necessity, the actions of the living God were to be reflected in history. This would encourage greater confidence in Yahweh. It would likewise remind the people to act responsibly.

It is difficult to know precisely where the historical Isaiah stood on the subject of messianism. (Part of the problem centers on whether Isa. 9:2–7 and 11:1–9 truly reflect the thinking of the eighth-century Isaiah. In recent years, many scholars have taken a conservative position on this issue.) His faith in a messianic figure was influenced by his current dissatisfaction with the royal personages of Ahaz and Hezekiah as well as by his fundamental endorsement of monarchy as a divinely ordained institution. Isaiah was led to project into the future when a truly righteous and just king would amply manifest the gifts of Israel's best leaders. He also insisted that this presumably sacral monarch would rule out of respect for Yahweh's will (9:7). Isaiah of Jerusalem had the theological resources to cope with the perplexing present and to anticipate a splendid day ahead when his faithful people would in word and deed truly acknowledge Yahweh of hosts as their sovereign Lord.

NOTES

1. Rolland E. Wolfe, "Introduction and Exegesis to Micah," in George A. Buttrick et al., eds., *The Interpreter's Bible* (Nashville: Abingdon Press, 1956), vol. 6, p. 911.
2. Emil G. Kraeling, *Commentary on the Prophets* (New York: Thomas Nelson & Sons, 1966), 2: 210.
3. We are in agreement with Sheldon H. Blank, *Prophetic Faith in Isaiah* (Detroit: Wayne State University Press, 1967), pp. 9–15.
4. Brevard S. Childs, *Isaiah and the Assyrian Crisis*, Studies in Biblical Theology, 2d series, no. 3 (London: SCM Press, 1967), p. 91.
5. For a fuller treatment of Isaiah 13–23, see George W. Anderson, *A Critical Introduction to the Old Testament* (London: Gerald Duckworth, 1959), pp. 108–110.
6. See J. William Whedbee, *Isaiah and Wisdom* (Nashville: Abingdon Press, 1971).
7. See Nahman Avigad, "The Jotham Seal from Elath," *Bulletin of the American Schools of Oriental Research* no. 163 (October 1961): 18–22.
8. For further details, see John Bright, *A History of Israel*, 2d ed. (Philadelphia: Westminster Press, 1972), p. 272.
9. The engineers began working from both ends and met in the middle. Kenyon writes, "The point of junction of the two sections, with frenzied changes of direction hither and thither, gives eloquent illustration to the triumph shown in the inscription." (Kathleen M. Kenyon, *Archaeology in the Holy Land*, 3d ed. [New York: Frederick A. Praeger, 1970], p. 289.)
10. James B. Pritchard, ed., *Ancient Near Eastern Texts Relating to the Old Testament*, 3d ed. (Princeton, N.J.: Princeton University Press, 1969), p. 321. Brackets with ellipses indicate lacunae, and those with words designate textual restorations. The italicized words constitute a conjectured reading, and the words in parentheses are the translator's interpolations to facilitate comprehension of the text. In reference to the measurements given for the tunnel, note that in 1838 the American archaeologist Edward Robinson measured the length of the tunnel. His figure was 1,750 feet, which corresponds rather closely to the length here: 1,200 cubits. (A cubit is approximately 18 inches.)
11. Harry M. Buck, *People of the Lord: The History, Scriptures, and Faith of Ancient Israel* (New York: Macmillan, 1966), p. 226.

12. Sigmund Mowinckel, *The Psalms in Israel's Worship*, trans. D. R. Ap-Thomas (Nashville: Abingdon Press, 1962), 2: 147.
13. Whedbee, *op. cit.*, p. 48.
14. So Johannes Lindblom, *A Study of the Immanuel Section in Isaiah* (Lund, Swed.: C. W. K. Gleerup, 1958), pp. 19–20.
15. Here we fully agree with Kaiser, who claims that the messianic interpretation of Isa. 7:14 "is refuted by v. 17, as well as by the whole content of the passage." (Otto Kaiser, *Isaiah 1–12: A Commentary*, trans. R. A. Wilson, The Old Testament Library [Philadelphia: Westminster Press, 1972], pp. 101–102.)
16. See Pritchard, *op. cit.*, pp. 286–287.
17. *Ibid.*, p. 287.
18. Whether Sennacherib made one or two campaigns into Palestine is much disputed. The theory that he visited Palestine twice holds that the editors of 2 Kings have telescoped two events (the 701 campaign depicted in 2 Kings 18:13–16 and an invasion in about 688 in 2 Kings 18:17–19:37). This interpretation of the biblical evidence is advanced by Bright, *op. cit.*, pp. 296–308. It has been criticized, however, partly because the so-called second invasion is not attested in any extant Assyrian inscription; see Childs, *op. cit.*, pp. 15–18, 118–120. Though the two-campaign theory is not impossible, it cannot be substantiated.
19. For the text, see Pritchard, *op. cit.*, pp. 287–288. The monarch's elaborate account of his attack against Jerusalem reveals more about Assyrian pretension than it does about Jerusalem's state of emergency; so Daniel D. Luckenbill, *The Annals of Sennacherib* (Chicago: University of Chicago Press, 1924), p. 11. In fact, nowhere in the account does Sennacherib declare that he and his contingents actually captured Jerusalem.
20. In 1815 this sudden turn of affairs moved Lord Byron to write his poem "The Destruction of Sennacherib" with its well-known opening line, "The Assyrian came down like the wolf on the fold." See Ernest Hartley Coleridge, ed., *The Works of Lord Byron* (New York: Charles Scribner's Sons, 1900), 3: 404–405.
21. For a more exhaustive study of these issues, see Th. C. Vriezen, "Essentials of the Theology of Isaiah," in Bernhard W. Anderson and Walter Harrelson, eds., *Israel's Prophetic Heritage* (New York: Harper & Row, 1962), pp. 128–146. Our own presentation is indebted to Vriezen. Rendtorff calls Isaiah "the theologian among the prophets." (Rolf Rendtorff, *Men of the Old Testament*, trans. Frank Clarke [Philadelphia: Fortress Press, 1968], pp. 89–90.)
22. B. Davie Napier, *From Faith to Faith: Essays on Old Testament Literature* (New York: Harper & Row, 1955), p. 179.

14

PROPHETIC DISCLOSURE AND THE DEUTERONOMIC REFORM IN JUDAH

For Judah the seventh century B.C. was a time of sudden shifts in the continuing struggle for world power. Assertive Assyrian monarchs, docile vassal kings, calculating court officials, invading hoards of Indo-Aryan peoples, suppressed Yahwists, and outspoken prophets were among the cast of characters who played out history's drama in the ancient Near East at that time. With the death of Hezekiah in 687, Judah had one more century before her own political existence was to be snuffed out.

The major powers took turns dominating Syria-Palestine. In 687, Assyria was still rigorously maintaining her position in western Asia. Periodic defiance by the Egyptians induced Assyria to assert herself all the more. Even so, in the course of the seventh century, Assyria was to undergo a gradual decay that finally led to her death in 609. Although Egypt dominated Syria-Palestine for a few years, in 605 she was forced to acknowledge the superior Babylonian state that now flaunted its own interest in empire.

During this century Judah never enjoyed a commanding position in the ancient Near East. But the gradual demise of Assyria in the second half of the seventh century did permit Judah a few years of self-assertion that furthered the causes of nationalism and Yahwism alike. King Josiah (640–609), whose reform program will soon occupy our attention, was one of the leading figures of that time. In that same half

---

Biblical texts to be read prior to and in conjunction with the present chapter: 2 Kings 21; Zephaniah; 2 Kings 22–23; Deut. 5:1–9:5; 10:12–22; 12:1–13:18; 17:2–20; 20:1–20; 23:15–26:19; 28:1–68; 30:15–20; Nahum; Habakkuk 1–2.

century, four prophets whose works have been preserved in the Hebrew Bible were defending the ancestral faith: Zephaniah, Nahum, Habakkuk, and Jeremiah. Jeremiah was unquestionably the most significant of the four. Because some of Jeremiah's most critical moments involved him in a direct struggle with Jerusalem's inhabitants which began just prior to the city's fall to the Babylonian host in 587, we shall defer our examination of this prophet until Chapter 15. In the present chapter, we shall trace Judah's history to the end of the seventh century, review Josiah's memorable reform program and the related Book of Deuteronomy, and comment on three minor prophets—Zephaniah, Nahum, and Habakkuk—who functioned during the last decades of the southern kingdom.

THE HISTORICAL AND RELIGIOUS CONTEXT OF SEVENTH-CENTURY JUDAH

Hezekiah had never given up hope of restoring political independence to his people, but his dream was not to be realized. When he died in 687, Judah was for all practical purposes Assyria's vassal. When Hezekiah's son and successor, Manasseh (687–642), died forty-five years later, Judah still had to accept Assyrian sovereignty as an inescapable reality. Nor did the situation change during the short tenure of Manasseh's son Amon (642–640). Because the reigns of Esarhaddon (680–669) and Asshurbanapal (668–627) were so effective, Assyria maintained a great deal of international strength. Egypt fell into Esarhaddon's hands in 671. Yet the last of the Twenty-fifth (Ethiopian) Dynasty pharaohs, Tirhakah (ca. 685–664), escaped the brunt of Assyrian pressure and in due course returned home to instigate further trouble for Assyria. Esarhaddon campaigned against Egypt once more, but died en route. His son and successor, Asshurbanapal, was able to quell the Egyptian rebellion, however. In 663 he led a spectacular sack of Thebes.

In the light of Assyria's success in Egypt, it is not surprising that two cuneiform texts from the Nineveh archives attest to Manasseh's willingness to support the Assyrian cause.[1] Manasseh is listed as one of several monarchs along the Mediterranean seacoast who responded to Esarhaddon's call to provide building material of stone and wood. Manasseh is likewise mentioned by Asshurbanapal, who reports that he demanded the services of several kings of western Asia and their armies in his offensive against Egypt.

Manasseh had little choice but to exist as Assyria's vassal. Thus, Judean nationalism and Yahwism both suffered. In fact, the Deuteronomist attributes the time of Judah's greatest apostasy to Manasseh's rule (2 Kings 21:1–18). In rebuilding the high places that Hezekiah had succeeded in crushing (21:3a), Manasseh cancelled the gains of his father's reform. He paid allegiance to the Canaanite deities of Ba͑al and Asherah, who were now worshiped in the Jerusalem Temple, and he also became a·devotee of the Assyrian host of heaven (21:3b). Yahwism was not Manasseh's cause: "And he burned his son as an offering, and practiced soothsaying and augury, and dealt with mediums and with wizards" (21:6).

Religion in Judah became utterly eclectic. Yahweh's heavenly host now included the astral gods of triumphant Assyria. The ancestral faith, with its high regard for Yahweh's deeds in history, was all but obliterated. In 2 Kings 21:10–15 we read that Manasseh encountered some reforming opposition. An anonymous prophet issued the divine warning, "I will wipe Jerusalem as one wipes a dish, wiping it and turning it upside down" (21:13). In contrast to the admittedly flat prose of the Deuteronomist, this invective has an authentic ring. However, Manasseh took decisive measures to silence the prophetic voice of Yahwism, which could only jeopardize his status with the Assyrian monarchy (21:16). What loyal Yahwists there were must have realized that only by speaking in subdued voices would they be permitted to speak at all.

Since Amon carried on his father's policies, he likewise receives a negative assessment from the Deuteronomist (2 Kings 21:20–22). By his day, however, the tenuous quality of Assyria's existence was becoming increasingly evident. Therefore, the scheming (possibly a court intrigue) that resulted in Amon's assassination may have been sparked by rising anti-Assyrian sentiment. Since the rebels themselves were liquidated by "the people of the land" (21:24), many Judeans may still have been unwilling to defy Assyria. Those who knifed Amon's conspirators now ushered Amon's son Josiah (640–609) to the Jerusalem throne at the tender age of eight. During most of the next decade, political decisions were made by court counselors, who acted with only as much independence as they felt the international situation would bear. According to 2 Chron. 34:3, in Josiah's eighth year of rule (632) "he began to seek the God of David his father," and four years later (628) he took on the high places with reforming zeal. Of course, his overt repudiation of Assyrian deities assumes that Nineveh was in no position to intervene, which in fact was probably the case. Like the woods of autumn, Assyria's brilliance in the first half of the seventh century was only the harbinger of bleak days ahead.

But why had Assyria fallen on bad times? Clearly, by the mid-seventh century, she had overextended herself, and her list of enemies was steadily expanding. Elements in Babylon, Elam, Asia Minor, and Egypt were all trying to disrupt Assyrian affairs of state. The death of Asshurbanapal in 627 sealed Assyria's fate. In the nation's last two decades, no leader was strong enough to keep the massive empire together.

ZEPHANIAH AND
HIS MESSAGE

If Hebrew prophecy reached its nadir during Manasseh's reign, it reasserted itself with great force when Zephaniah came to prominence. Specific reference to Josiah in the superscription (1:1); the criticism of pagan religious practices, which Josiah's reform presumably corrected (1:4–6, 9, 12; 3:1–5); and the possible reflection of restless conditions in Mesopotamia (1:2–3, 10) all suggest a date of about 630 for at least some of Zephaniah's pronouncements.[2]

We know very little about Zephaniah. The extraordinary superscription (1:1) that traces the prophet's lineage back four generations is without parallel in the prophetic literature of the Old Testament. Zephaniah's great-great grandfather is said to be Hezekiah. Yet there is no strong evidence that this Hezekiah was Judah's king and that the prophet was of royal blood. Since the name "Hezekiah" was relatively common in Judah, we might reasonably expect specific reference to Hezekiah's royal status if he was the individual intended. Zephaniah's pedigree was presumably sparked by his father's non-Yahwistic name. Perhaps, as Fohrer suggests, "the ancestors of the father were named so as to avoid the embarrassing misconception that Zephaniah's father, Cushi, was an Ethiopian and not a Judean."[3] In any event, Zephaniah was a Jerusalem prophet whose impatience with the religious laxity and indifference of his time led him to comment in unmistakably threatening tones about the future.

The prophet's brief utterances have been gathered into larger literary units. Zephaniah 1:2–2:3 and 3:1–7 contain oracles against Judah; 2:4–15 preserves the prophet's invective against the nations; and 3:8–13 offers hope that all peoples will be converted to Yahwism and that Israel will persist as God's righteous remnant. Only 3:14–20 is clearly not the work of the historical Zephaniah. That passage, which resembles the majestic poetry of Second Isaiah, promises the Jewish exiles in Babylon a joyous homecoming to a restored Jerusalem.

Since Zephaniah's oracles against the nations in 2:4–15 have little originality and few details, we pass over them with brief comment. No doubt Zephaniah's firm conviction about universal judgment required that he speak against the nations. But the offenses of Philistia (2:4–7), Moab, and Ammon (2:8–11) are referred to only vaguely, and Ethiopia's misconduct is not mentioned at all (2:12). Nevertheless, the overthrow of Assyria and its capital (2:13–15) is colorfully expressed. Imposing Nineveh will become an object of scorn for those who pass by her ruins.

So disturbed was Zephaniah by the conduct of his own people, that he insisted that the offended deity would initiate an act of universal destruction. Judah's covenant dereliction would effect the negation of creation itself; man, beast, bird, and fish were all expected to fall into oblivion (1:3). The dreadful day of Yahweh was being brought on by the odious conduct of four groups of Judeans—the "remnant of Baᶜal," which espoused the religion of Canaan (1:4); the rooftop worshipers who paid homage to the Assyrian "host of the heavens" (1:5); those who swore by Milcom, chief deity of the Ammonites (1:5); and the religiously indifferent (1:6) who insisted, "Yahweh will not do good, nor will he do ill" (1:12). Zephaniah was as critical of Jerusalem's leadership as he was of the people as a whole. Jerusalem's officials, judges (3:3), prophets, and priests (3:4) were charged with callously pursuing selfish interests without awareness that Yahweh, the quintessence of righteousness, existed in their midst (3:5).

In Zephaniah's estimation, Yahweh's people were moving toward a perilous future. In order to bring about the chastisement required, the deity intended to "search Jerusalem with lamps" (1:12). In his uniquely detailed pronouncements about the appalling day of Yahweh, Zephaniah radically intensified the earlier view of Amos (5:18–20; 8:9–14):

> The great day of Yahweh is near,
>   near and hastening fast;
> the sound of the day of Yahweh is bitter,
>   the mighty man cries aloud there.
> A day of wrath is that day,
>   a day of distress and anguish,
> a day of ruin and devastation,
>   a day of darkness and gloom,
> a day of clouds and thick darkness,
>   a day of trumpet blast and battle cry
> against the fortified cities
>   and against the lofty battlements. (1:14–16)

Disaster will overtake those who have turned away from Yahweh.

But those who take the deity's commandments seriously are provided with a possible way out:

> Seek Yahweh, all you humble of the land,
>   who do his commands;
> seek righteousness, seek humility;
>   perhaps you may be hidden
>   on the day of the wrath of Yahweh. (2:3)

Though Zephaniah offers no program of easy salvation, he endorses meek human conduct as a means whereby the people of God might be permitted to endure. And even if the remnant is to experience the chastening impact of historical judgment, Yahweh does promise its continued existence (3:12–13).

The words in 3:8–13 reflect Zephaniah's staunch belief that the humble, God-fearing members of the remnant will consist of Israelites and non-Israelites alike. To Jerusalem's native righteous element will be added new arrivals from among the nations who have converted to Yahwism. Zion and its environs will therefore experience light as well as shadow. With individual pride and national arrogance now past, a united, unpretentious people will come into being at Yahweh's pleasure, and his sovereignty will be seen afresh.

Although the teachings of Zephaniah are not wholly original, his pronouncements on the day of Yahweh constitute a classical statement of that theme. Moreover, his candid message may have helped to spur Josiah's rigorous reform movement, which we shall now examine.

JOSIAH'S REFORM: ITS ANTECEDENTS AND ACCOMPLISHMENTS

By the year 630, religious leadership in Jerusalem was continuing its corrupt course. Zephaniah was speaking words of woe and promise in the hope that a few believers would return to the righteous deity, and King Josiah was nearing adulthood. Details of Josiah's far-reaching reform program are preserved in 2 Kings 22:3–23:25 and 2 Chron. 34:3–35:19. While these records agree that this program was Josiah's supreme achievement, they do not concur on when and how it took place. (For example, the Chronicler has assigned too much to Josiah's twelfth year [628], and the Deuteronomist has concentrated all attention on the king's eighteenth year [622]. Josiah's reform must have spanned a considerable period of time.) Since 2 Chron. 34:6–7 suggests that Josiah's reforming efforts in his twelfth year of reign (628) involved operations in Israel and Galilee as well as in Judah, we would assume that the monarch had political as well as religious control of the north.

As an ardent Yahwist and nationalist, Josiah was trying to join northern Assyrian provinces with Judah in order to assert himself in the spirit of David. The prospect that the Assyrians would interfere with Josiah's plans was unlikely, for they were being attacked by the Medes under Cyaxares (ca. 625–585) and the neo-Babylonians under Nabopolassar (626–605). Historical circumstances therefore gave Josiah considerable latitude. No longer was it necessary for the king of Judah to assume the docile posture of a vassal monarch.

Assyria was so close to being finished in 622, the year in which the book of law was discovered in the Jerusalem Temple, that intensive reforming measures were possible near that time. Both 2 Kings 22:8 and 2 Chron. 34:14 agree that the high priest, Hilkiah, came across the book of law in 622, the eighteenth year of Josiah's reign, in the course of Temple restoration. These were no ordinary repairs. They were prompted by the desire to remove traces of foreign influence—notably Assyrian influence —from the holy edifice. Since the reform was in full swing by 622, the book of law discovered at that time reinforced what was already taking place. Strictly speaking, it did not initiate the reform.

Nevertheless, Hilkiah's discovery of the book was an event of considerable magnitude. Because Josiah was fully aware that the laws in this scroll were not being adhered to, he demanded that the authenticity of the document be established (2 Kings 22:13). Therefore, the prophetess Huldah was consulted. Her oracular response thoroughly defended the sanctity and authority of the temple scroll (22:15–20). Because the words of the book of law had been violated, Yahweh would surely inflict disaster on Jerusalem and its inhabitants. But since the king had humbled himself before Yahweh (22:11), Jerusalem's destruction would not occur during his lifetime. Huldah also predicted that Josiah would die in peace (22:20). (Actually the king died in battle against Pharaoh Necho II at Megiddo in 609 [23:29].) Josiah took Huldah's words to heart, assuming responsibility for his people's infidelity to the covenant.

Josiah formally read the law to the people who, at his summons, had assembled in the Jerusalem Temple (2 Kings 23:1–3). The faithful king and then the people as a whole pledged their loyalty to the covenant (23:3). Josiah assumed the role of covenant mediator in the style of Moses (Exod. 24:3–8) and Joshua (Josh. 24). Thereby he implied his willingness to accept the demanding covenant standard first embraced by the sacred league in premonarchical Israel and later upheld by the northern kingdom.[4] The Mosaic covenant with its exacting stipulations was now becoming directly associated with Jerusalem. Previously the court had enjoyed the theological and political benefits of the Davidic covenant, which was based on Yahweh's commitment of eternal support. Now Judah was voluntarily binding herself to a much stricter covenant requirement. In their allegiance to a religious tradition that was both ancient and austere, the people hoped to discover a reliable means of coping with their uncertain existence.

In 2 Kings 23:4–25 the Deuteronomist offers a relatively clear account of how covenant legislation was upheld in the context of Josiah's reform program. Nothing seems to have daunted Josiah. First and foremost, the Jerusalem Temple was further purified. Josiah commanded that any sacral objects connected with foreign deities be put away. In particular, all vestiges of Mesopotamian religion were to be obliterated. With a vengeance, Josiah did away with the pagan cults of Palestine. Indeed, the nucleus of his reform was the notion that the purified sanctuary in Jerusalem should be the only sanctuary. Hence, rival temples in both the north and south were closed down. If the priests of the outlying provincial sanctuaries were to continue to function, they had no choice but to move to Jerusalem and live under the shadow of the one legitimate Temple. Josiah also desecrated the high places in Jerusalem that the indulgent Solomon had established for his foreign wives. Finally, the king's sponsorship of Passover is presented as the fitting climax of the reform

(2 Kings 23:21–23). The claim is made that Passover had not been celebrated since the era of the judges. Presumably, David and his successors had not thought it vital to the religion of Israel. With all this accomplished, it is not surprising that the Deuteronomist thought of Josiah as a reforming king without equal (23:25).

But how did the book of law make its way into the Jerusalem Temple, and who was responsible for its compilation? Several answers have been given. Perhaps the most extreme is that the book was a pious fraud written by Hilkiah and his priestly comrades, who planted it in the sanctuary and passed it off on the unsuspecting Josiah as an ancient scroll. But "if the Jerusalem priestly circles of that day had prepared this Code specifically for the reform, they would hardly have included the provision for the country priests to share their privileges, whose implementation they successfully resisted."[5]

Then was the book of law a foundation volume inserted into the cornerstone of the Solomonic temple at the time of its dedication? This approach is likewise objectionable. The Solomonic traditions in Kings and Chronicles are silent on the matter of such a volume; and it would follow that no legislation in the scroll could be later than the tenth-century Solomonic era. But the Bible plainly discourages our assumption that in Solomonic times there existed only one legitimate sanctuary for the worship of Yahweh in all of Palestine.

Still another hypothesis is that the book was written during Hezekiah's reign (715–687) and indeed was the basis of that king's reform. But nowhere in the Hezekiah tradition do we find mention of a book of law that functioned in that way. Of course, once a reform had been implemented by Hezekiah, its main features might have been recorded by approving priestly witnesses. Such a book might have been hidden by pious Yahwists during the long reign of Manasseh and brought out in the open after it had become clear that Josiah would honor the interests of Yahweh.

The most logical answer, and the one with widest support, is that the book of law was written after Hezekiah's reform and prior to Josiah's. During the syncretic rule of Manasseh, certain dedicated individuals hoped to prepare the way for religious reform that they believed was sorely needed. They set forth in writing what they took to be the significant dimensions of such a program. They recognized, however, that religious reform was out of the question during the reign of Manasseh. Hence, the written guidelines for reform were hidden in the hope that following Manasseh's harsh rule, prospects for full-scale reform might present themselves. Subsequently the book was "found" during Josiah's tenure.

This answer is supported by the commonly held assumption that the book is to be identified with some form of the Code of Deuteronomy (Deut. 12–26). None of the styles reflected in the oracles of the eighth-century Hebrew prophets shows affinities with the Book of Deuteronomy. By contrast, Jeremiah and Ezekiel in the seventh century and Second Isaiah, Haggai, and Zechariah in the sixth century seem to have been influenced by the content and idiom of Deuteronomic legislation. The book of law may therefore have been written relatively early in Manasseh's reign by patient reformers who longed for a future more congenial to the needs of Yahwism.

But why have biblical scholars been willing to establish some kind of equation between the book of law and the Code of Deuteronomy? The answer lies in the fact that many acts of Josiah's reform mentioned in 2 Kings 23 find their legal counterpart in Deuteronomy 12–26. A few of these parallels will be mentioned in passing.[6] First, the suppression of local sanctuaries and the centralization of worship at Jerusalem noted in 2 Kings 23:8, 19 is enjoined by the legislation of Deut. 12:1–7, 13–14. Second, the burning of the vessels of astral worship is cited in 2 Kings 23:4–5, 11; such worship is proscribed in Deut. 17:3. Third, Passover is celebrated in 2 Kings 23:21–23 and legislated in Deut. 16:1–8. Fourth, prostitution is punished in 2 Kings 23:7 and forbidden in Deut. 23:17–18. And last, divination and necromancy are opposed in 2 Kings 23:24 and prohibited in Deut. 18:10–11.

Such affinities need not imply that Josiah was unimaginative in implementing Deuteronomic law. Having committed himself earlier to a complete reform program, Josiah probably felt free to modify the Deuteronomic expectations in some instances. Nevertheless, the parallels between 2 Kings 23 and the Code of Deuteronomy are striking.

Before we move from a consideration of the reform itself to an examination of the canonical Book of Deuteronomy, we should mention what were undoubtedly the two most significant and enduring consequences of Josiah's undertaking.

First, his reform transformed the character of Yahwistic worship. The local shrines were now suppressed. Therefore, the average Israelite worshiper was required to travel to the Jerusalem Temple in order to express formally his devotion to the deity. And corporate worship was hardly practical at harvest time, when he would be most moved to express his gratitude. The reform therefore conferred on cultic worship a seasonal character. Once the faithful Hebrew had arrived in Jerusalem and stood in the environs of the Temple, he would not participate in the act of corporate worship to the degree that he had previously been permitted at the local sanctuary. The distinction between priest and layman was becoming more pronounced, and in the years ahead it would intensify throughout most of Jewish ritual.

Second, Josiah's reform induced his contemporaries to consider the authority of the claim a literary document might legitimately make on the community of faith. By reading aloud "all the words of the book of the covenant" (2 Kings 23:2) in a ceremony of covenant renewal, Josiah was ensuring that this document would function as law within Judah. The formal public reading of that scroll and its official acceptance by the people gave it considerable status. Such firm trust in a written scroll marked a radical departure from the past. Previously, law had rarely assumed a written form. But now a lengthy scroll of legislation had come into being. With such legislation assuming a key position in their religious life, the people of Yahweh would be less motivated to seek prophetic guidance and interpretation. In fact, Deuteronomy may be said to be the beginning of the Hebrew Bible as a written canon. The words inscribed on the scroll therefore began to assume an extraordinary significance.

Although we shall resume our discussion of the canonization of the Old Testament in our treatment of Ezra (see Chapter 18), a definition of the term "canon" may prove useful here. As applied to the cherished literature of the believing community, "canon" may be defined as a "rule, guide, or standard." The word traces back to a common Semitic noun that appears in biblical Hebrew as *qāneh*. Its basic meaning is "reed." The related Greek noun, *kanōn*, designates a carpenter's rule. Thus, *kanōn* came to represent a standard or norm. Soon it was understood in the metaphorical sense as the normative list of biblical books that might be read and cherished by the community of faith. Judaism's most sacred writings were gradually accorded canonical status and consequently claimed an authoritative character.

INSPIRATION FOR JOSIAH'S REFORM: THE BOOK OF DEUTERONOMY

The Intention and Structure of the Book of Deuteronomy

The Book of Deuteronomy consists mainly of three lengthy Mosaic oratories. All three were purportedly delivered to the Israelites as they were encamped in western Moab just prior to Moses' death and the people's crossing of the River Jordan to claim the Land of Promise.

In the first address (1:6–4:40), which is a detailed historical prologue to the law, Moses reviews Israel's experiences from the time she stood at the foot of Mount Sinai until she arrived in Moab. He gives considerable attention to how Yahweh guides his people through the wilderness. As the speech draws to a close, the people are urged to take seriously the various legislation that is forthcoming.

The second address, which is by far the most extensive, is preserved in Deuteronomy 5–26, 28.[7] It offers another, presumably older prologue (Deut. 5–11), which is then followed by a code of legislation (Deut. 12–26). The prologue sets the theological tone for the covenant laws about to be promulgated; it begins with a version of the Decalogue

(5:6–21) that deviates somewhat from the Elohist's recension in Exod. 20:2–17. Moreover, the famous Shema presented in Deut. 6:4–5 has often been regarded as Judaism's greatest commandment: "Hear, O Israel: Yahweh our God is one Lord; and you shall love Yahweh your God with all your heart, and with all your soul, and with all your might." Nothing less than full-scale allegiance to the deity is enjoined. The studied, persuasive style of these chapters urges Israel to avoid attitudes of self-sufficiency (8:17) and self-righteousness (9:4), as well as giving in to easy cultural accommodation (13:12–17).

The legislation of Deuteronomy 12–26 contains much legal material unique to Deuteronomy as well as a number of laws already known from the earlier Covenant Code (Exod. 20:22–23:33).[8] The shifts in style as well as content make clear that here is a collection of quite varied traditional components. Those who exerted the greatest influence on this material were the rural Levites of the north, who for several centuries had been quietly instructing Yahweh's people in the ancient Mosaic faith.[9] The legislation in Deuteronomy 12–26 is not always well arranged, but its strong points are its persistent concern for proper motive and its perceptive theological undercurrents. The experience of reading these chapters is not as arduous or as painful as one might expect.

The third address of Moses in Deut. 29:2–30:20, which is supplemental in character, seeks to "accentuate the covenant aspect of the Deuteronomic law."[10] The attending Israelites are summoned to choose between the two ways: life or death, goodness or evil. Moses admonishes, "I call heaven and earth to witness against you this day, that I have set before you life and death, blessing and curse; therefore choose life, that you and your descendants may live" (30:19). The people must make a commitment in the light of clear-cut alternatives.

The concluding chapters of Deuteronomy (31–34) are a miscellany. They include Moses' final charge to the people and to Joshua (31:1–8), the Song of Moses meditating on Israel's past faithlessness (32:1–43), the Blessing of Moses pronounced on the Israelite tribes (32:2–29), and an account of Moses' death (34:1–8).

A brief comment is in order concerning the style of Deuteronomy. Fluid, skillful oratory pervades this book. Instruction and persuasion often go hand in hand. Ordinarily the law is not succinctly given. Rather, it is preached in the hope that its listeners will be moved to obedience. Consequently, such expressions as the following are characteristic of Deuteronomic prose: "Yahweh, the God of your fathers," "to go after (or serve) other gods," "to hearken to (or obey) the voice of Yahweh," "that you may prolong your days in the land."[11] The book appeals to the conscience of the individual listener primarily through such phraseology. Hence, the Mosaic faith is revived and cast in the language of the seventh century B.C. in the hope that the present generation of Israelites will live up to their great calling as the elect people of Yahweh.

Representative Deuteronomic Legislation

Only the more distinctive emphases in this legislation will be noted here. The importance of the central sanctuary is immediately set forth in Deuteronomy 12. In analogy with the Covenant Code (Exod. 20:24–26) and the Holiness Code (Lev. 17), the opening Deuteronomic law is concerned with appropriate worship of the deity. More specifically, it deals with the kind of altar or sanctuary that is required. According to the Code of Deuteronomy, the Israelites may present their offerings and sacrifices only at the one place that Yahweh will choose (12:5, 13–14). The proper worship of deity cannot tolerate the possibility of many impressionable cults easily influenced by Canaanite religious practices. Hence, Yahweh will select one place, and will make it known by causing his name to dwell there (12:5). While Deuteronomy insists that Yahweh's real home is in the heavens, it also affirms that his name resides in the earthly sanctuary of his own choosing. The name will therefore embody the divine holiness without dissipating it. Whenever the individual Israelite worships Yahweh in the place where the deity has put his name, he has the assurance that Yahweh will hear his prayer. And by saying that it is Yahweh's name that resides at the central sanctuary, Israel was not running the risk of localizing her God.

The injunctions against idolatry in Deuteronomy 13 also invite our attention. Despite the enchanting aspects of his devious craft, the prophet who tries to lure the people away from Yahweh must be scrutinized (13:1–5). In such instances, Yahweh is only testing his people through the cunning of a second-rate individual, and they had better be on guard. Should an individual's blood relative or friend try to entice him from Yahweh, the culprit is to be stoned to death (13:6–11). If an entire city has been lured away from the worship of Yahweh, then it must be destroyed along with its inhabitants (13:12–17).

The Code of Deuteronomy contains admittedly varied legislative elements. It offers both apodictic and casuistic statutes upheld by the Israelite judges at the city gate. Many religious laws have also entered this corpus. These were transmitted through influential Levitical circles in various rural areas and small towns throughout the land. The Code of Deuteronomy, which consciously solicits the obedience of those whom it addresses, often takes into account the motivation of human conduct. For example, Deut. 16:20 declares, "Justice, and only justice, you shall follow, that you may live and inherit the land which Yahweh your God gives you." Yahweh expects righteous behavior from his people. In order to motivate that conduct, an appeal is made to a presumably long life in the Land of Promise, which will be realized when the needs of justice are honored.

The law in Deut. 24:6 is humanitarian: "No man shall take a mill or an upper millstone in pledge; for he would be taking a life in pledge."

Olive Press at Capernaum. This apparatus consists of a round stone trough and a heavy millstone. The trough receives the olives that are to be squeezed in the production of olive oil, and the millstone is rolled along its edge within the trough. Millstones were also used for grinding grain into flour, from which daily bread was made. So essential were they that Deut. 24:6 declares that the creditor shall not demand a millstone from his borrower as collateral. (Photo by Gary Burke.)

The motive clause found in the second half of the verse acknowledges that a millstone is essential for grinding meal, which is turned into daily bread. A limitation is therefore imposed on the creditor; he cannot pursue his interest without regard for fundamental human need. In Deut. 24:17–18 Israel is fervently invited to reflect on her own deliverance from Egyptian bondage. That act itself should sufficiently motivate her to treat kindly the sojourner, orphan, and widow, whom society ordinarily does not favor. In general, the motive clauses of Deuteronomy deftly wed legal rigor with moral passion and sound theological reflection.

Theological Currents in the Book of Deuteronomy

Deuteronomy is something more than a bare code of law. Indeed, in its entirety, this book advances a rather elaborate theological position, which we shall now attempt to outline.

God's Action in History and His Election of Israel. Deuteronomy understands that the love that motivated Yahweh to choose Israel in

Egypt and to lead her from bondage was unmerited. Neither Israel's size (7:7) nor her righteous instincts (9:5–6) prompted the deity to select her as his beloved object. Deuteronomy maintains that Yahweh loved Israel from the first, swearing a promise to the fathers that he would not break, even though Israel was a backsliding people (4:37; 7:7–8; 10:15). Yahweh's love is not indulgent, but it is splendidly supportive (1:31; 32:10–11). This love may be designated an "election love"; it is beyond the reach of human comprehension.

Though Yahweh may be bound to the patriarchs by virtue of a previous oath, the reason that he made that oath in the first place remains a mystery. In celebrating the grandeur of that love, Deut. 4:32 instructs, "For ask now of the days that are past, which were before you, since the day that God created man upon the earth, and ask from one end of heaven to the other, whether such a great thing as this has ever happened or was ever heard of." Indeed, that election love has led one scholar to marvel, "six centuries wasted in sin and constant apostasy are cancelled out and Israel is set once more at Horeb to hear Jahweh's word of salvation, which has not yet lost its power."[12]

Deuteronomy projects a faith that, for all practical purposes, is rigorously monotheistic. The deity's uniqueness is best expressed in the Shema, which begins, "Hear, O Israel: Yahweh our God is one Lord" (6:4). Prohibitions against idolatrous acts and multiple sanctuaries also defend Yahweh's uniqueness. Numerous Deuteronomic passages offer direct statements in support of Yahweh's incomparability (3:24; 4:23–24; 10:17, 21–22). At the conclusion of Deut. 4:37–39, which presents a superb remark about Yahweh's action in history, we read, "Know therefore this day, and lay it to your heart, that Yahweh is God in heaven above and on the earth beneath; there is no other."

As a corollary to the preceding, Deuteronomy speaks about Israel's uniqueness. The book has an exclusivism that stems from the staunch conviction that Yahweh's special concern and favor are directed solely toward Israel. Amos' view that Yahweh cares deeply for other nations (Amos 9:7) is not represented here. Nevertheless, Deuteronomy decrees that the foreigner who places himself under Israelite protection must be treated with gentleness (Deut. 10:19). The solitary traveler is to be valued as a member of the covenant, and he is expected to heed the Torah. Foreign nations, however, are thought of in quite a different way. Whenever an Israelite lent money to outsiders, he was permitted to charge interest, but he was not to press his covenant brother into making interest payments (23:20). Moreover, the Ammonites and Moabites, who had frustrated Israel as she inched her way toward the land of Canaan, are to be excluded from Yahweh's sanctuary (23:3). At times Israel's own greatness is expressed in a less than subtle manner. Thus, Deut. 14:2 proclaims: "For you are a people holy to Yahweh your God, and Yahweh has chosen you to be a people for his own possession, out of all the peoples that are on the face of the earth."

Deuteronomy declares that the sovereign deity has determined to make Israel a gift of the land (1:8, 21; 3:18; 8:7–10; 9:5). He had so promised the fathers. Yahweh is respected as the giver of the land, and he is expected to deliver the gift by being present with Israel as she invades its borders and devotes herself to overtaking its inhabitants. Therefore, Israel is not to fear. The good land will be hers in time (8:7–10). Moreover, Israel's own life in that land is regarded as Yahweh's gift to his people. Here "Israel receives the possibility of a special kind of life— good, undefiled, life in community, life in the worship of Yahweh, life at its fullest and best."[13]

The Israelite institution of holy war frequently informs the theological position of Deuteronomy (2:25, 33–37; 6:19; 7:1–2; 9:1–3; 11:4, 22–25; 20:1–4). Holy war, which finds Yahweh before the Israelite host, is calculated to terrorize the enemy. The people have only to trust in Yahweh, who resides in Israel's midst and takes the initiative in all phases of the war of conquest. Slowly, yet surely they will sweep across the Land of Promise (7:22). Ultimately the people will move freely in the land that Yahweh intends them to have.

Israel's Response to God's Historical Activity and Election. The injunction that Israel love God and obey is the central response Israel is called on to make. Total obedience and fidelity are stressed in terms of love itself (6:4–5; 10:12–13; 13:3–4). The love of Yahweh for Israel requires a corresponding love of Israel for Yahweh. In the Shema, Israel is commanded to love the deity with her entire being (6:5). The inner disposition of the whole man is a matter of profound concern here. That spontaneous love issues from man's obedience to the divine will. It is not too much to say that the command to love Yahweh with all one's heart, soul, and might lies behind every item of Deuteronomic legislation.

At the end of Moses' first discourse, Israel is told that her adherence to Yahweh's statutes will prolong her days in the promised land (Deut. 4:40). Both the present and future generations will prosper. The lively prospect of Israel's material welfare is often asserted as an inducement for obedience (4:40; 5:16, 29; 6:2–3; 11:8–9; 12:25). In the blessings enumerated in Deut. 28:1–14, Israel is promised that if she observes all Yahweh's commandments, she will be elevated above all other nations. "That it may go well with you," "that you may live," "that Yahweh may bless you," "that you may prolong your days," these phrases are all Deuteronomic; they point to the fruits of covenant obedience.

Frequently Deuteronomy asserts that disobedience to Yahweh's statutes will lead to bitterness, oppression, and outright tragedy (4:25– 28; 6:14–15; 7:10; 8:20; 9:6–8, 18–20; 11:16–17; 17:12). With its hyperbole, Deut. 6:14–15 warns that Israelite idolatry will so completely kindle Yahweh's anger that he will destroy the people "from off the face of the earth." Nowhere are rejection and disaster more evident than in the numerous curses in store for Israel if she forsakes Yahweh (Deut. 28:15–68).

In the Deuteronomic theology, Israel is confronted with both the horror of a potential curse and the hope of a future blessing. She is urged to decide for obedience and thereby affirm life itself (30:19). Her future strength depends on her submission to the divine will. Accordingly, Israel is not expected to ponder casually theological issues that may be of interest. She is instead required to make a self-conscious response to Yahweh himself.

On balance, it is clear that Deuteronomy is greatly concerned with the covenant relationship. The love of God for Israel, Israel's lack of worth, and the demand for obedience are among its major themes. The book often reflects a humanitarian bent, which is attractive, yet parts of it do not appeal to contemporary readers. Too often Deuteronomy lacks sophistication. Foreign nations are treated according to a standard different from the one that applies to Yahweh's own people. Certain laws appear to be more firmly grounded in the threat of God's punitive action than in any positive consideration. And there seems to be no understanding of the complexities that plague human life. For example, there is no recognition that the righteous sometimes suffer without reason.

Nevertheless, Deuteronomy did seek to make the traditional Israelite faith central to the life of Hebrew man. In fact, each Israelite generation is addressed by the book's rhetorical disclosures. As Deut. 5:2–3 so deftly expresses the matter, "Yahweh our God made a covenant with us in Horeb. Not with our fathers did Yahweh make this covenant, but with us, who are all of us here alive this day."

THE PROPHECIES OF NAHUM
AND HABAKKUK

Nahum and Habakkuk both prophesied near the end of the seventh century B.C. The Book of Nahum reveals a prophet who was reacting primarily to the vicissitudes of international life. He exulted in the impending overthrow of Nineveh, which he interpreted as Yahweh's revenge against Assyrian cruelty. By contrast, the Book of Habakkuk distills the thinking of a prophet who was responding to the impact of international crisis on Judean faith. He openly challenged the tidy concept of divine justice that had been confidently spawned by recent Deuteronomic reform. It held that adherence to Yahweh's will would lead to material well-being and that defection from his will would inevitably lead to disaster. Habakkuk objected that this doctrine was simplistic. Consequently, he focused on the thorny issue of theodicy—that is, if those who follow the law must suffer adversity, how can the justice of God be upheld?

Nahum

From first to last, the Book of Nahum is concerned with Assyria's impending ruin. The intensity of Nahum's oracle against Nineveh has led most scholars to infer that the prophet was speaking only shortly prior to Nineveh's devastation in 612.[14] As we have already noted, by 625 Assyria was caught in a life-and-death struggle. That she held out as long as she did against the harassments of Nabopolassar and his Babylonian forces was due largely to the support she enjoyed from Psammetichus I and his Egyptian armies. Psammetichus was hopeful that Assyria might serve as a buffer state between Egypt and the increasingly energetic Medes and Babylonians. But very soon Egypt experienced political disappointment and Assyria complete ruination. Assyrian cities gave way to the enemy in rapid succession. In 614 Asshur succumbed to the Medes, and in 612 Nineveh was devastated by the Medes and Babylonians, who also managed to conquer Haran in 610. Many of Judah's inhabitants must have been uncontrollably joyful on hearing that Assyrian power was now completely broken.

It appears that Nahum's role in Hebrew prophecy was to anticipate the imminent fall of Nineveh with as much enthusiasm as he could muster. Predictive descriptions and liturgical responses are played off against each other in an admittedly confusing manner. The alphabetic poem in 1:2–10, which is incomplete, depicts the arrival of the wrathful deity in a theophany designed to crush his proud, violent adversaries. This composition is an introduction; it sets the tone of the book, calling attention to the dimensions of divine vengeance. Moreover, it points to the book's liturgical function, which enabled the Judeans to celebrate Assyria's overthrow in the cult on a recurring basis.[15]

In 1:11–15 and even down through 2:2 invective and promise are juxtaposed. An oracle of assurance intended for Judah appears to include words that signal Nineveh's ruin. Nahum 2 offers the prophet's ode of triumph, which portrays the enemy's assault of Nineveh, the feverish and fruitless defense of its citizens, and its utter ruin. What follows in chapter 3 is a taunt that reinforces the impressions conveyed in the prophet's ode. It insists that on the day of the city's overthrow, Nineveh will receive what it deserves, and the rest of the human family will have reason to rejoice (3:18–19). Convinced that the sack of Nineveh and the victimizing of its inhabitants are in full accord with Yahweh's sovereign will, Nahum pronounces his oracle of gloom: "Desolate! Desolation and ruin! Hearts faint and knees tremble, anguish is on all loins, all faces grow pale!" (2:10).

If the poetry of Nahum makes for literary brilliance, what kind of theology does it offer? Surely it differs from other prophetic books in the Hebrew Bible in focusing on the defeat of a hated tyrant. Nahum seems content to glory in the confusion and horror that will soon engulf the Assyrians. The possibility that Judah might benefit from some correction of her own does not occupy Nahum for even a fleeting moment.

Nevertheless, all is not lost. This prophet speaks as an active member of the international community of the ancient Near East. He is aware of the injuries Assyria has inflicted on others, and he is no less cognizant that it is Yahweh who claims complete mastery over history. His faith in Yahweh as universal sovereign and judge is undaunted. Nahum also offers a hope that with Assyria's destruction, international peace will ensue. This hope was not realized, however, for as the burden of Nineveh was lifted, the burden of Babylon was falling on the lesser nations.

Habakkuk

The Book of Habakkuk is not easy to date. Only one verse (1:6) in the entire book seems reliable in this respect. There Yahweh declares to the prophet, "For lo, I am rousing the Chaldeans, that bitter and hasty nation, who march through the breadth of the earth, to seize habitations not their own."

The term "Chaldeans" may be taken as a reference to the neo-Babylonians, who came to power under Nabopolassar (626–605) and continued to dominate the international scene as Nebuchadnezzar (605–562) succeeded his father to the throne. Since the Book of Habakkuk does not attest that Jerusalem has yet fallen, the prophet's words undoubtedly predate 587 B.C.

If Habakkuk were speaking at the very moment that the neo-Babylonians were rising to power, he would have communicated his message prior to Nineveh's downfall. Yet it is also possible that he prophesied closer to 600, when the international situation had turned in Babylon's favor.

In 609 Necho II (610–594) moved his Egyptian forces to Carchemish to help the Assyrians in their struggle against the Babylonians. The latter had taken Haran in 610, and in the following year the Assyrians sought to reclaim it. On his way north, Necho was met at Megiddo by Josiah, who lost his life in a risky attempt to frustrate the Egyptian-Assyrian alliance. Needless to say, the death of this righteous monarch was regarded by many Judeans as unspeakably tragic. Necho then marched toward Carchemish only to fail with the Assyrians in their attempt to retake nearby Haran. Consequently, he withdrew to the west and began consolidating Syria-Palestine under his own control. He recalled Josiah's son Jehoahaz from the Jerusalem throne after his brief tenure of three months and appointed Jehoahaz' brother Jehoiakim (609–

598) a vassal monarch. Once more Judah was required to hand over substantial tribute to a world power. But soon Judah's vassalage to Egypt was exchanged for vassalage to Babylon.

In 605 the Egyptian forces were badly beaten at Carchemish by Nebuchadnezzar and his contingents. The Egyptians were chased homeward by the Babylonian aggressors, who now had access to western Asia. Again the people of Yahweh became subjects of a Mesopotamian ruler. And it was undoubtedly within this kind of international climate, when Jerusalem's fate hung in delicate balance, that Habakkuk's oracles were collected. Their generally veiled historical allusions suggest that they had been spoken on several different occasions during the preceding years.

In any case, the Book of Habakkuk may be easily outlined. Habakkuk's dialogue with the deity (1:2–2:4) is followed by five woe oracles directed against a plundering, immoral nation (2:5–20)[16] and a psalmic prayer rich in its references to theophany (3:1–19). The Habakkuk Commentary from Qumran only cites and expounds on the book's first two chapters. While this might suggest that Habakkuk 3 postdates the prophet, it does not constitute proof.

The Habakkuk Commentary from Qumran. This significant Hebrew scroll cites and comments on the first two chapters of the Book of Habakkuk. Habakkuk's words are quoted a few at a time and then interpreted in the light of the historical present and the theological disposition of the Qumran sect. The poor condition of the bottom of the scroll is responsible for many gaps in the text. While the numerous historical allusions are not easily deciphered, the scroll seems to have been written in the first century B.C. Above are columns 11–12, which, for the most part, cite and freely interpret Hab. 2:15–18. (Courtesy of the Shrine of the Book, Israel Museum, Jerusalem.)

Because of the complexity of Habakkuk 3 and the obscurity of the woe oracles in 2:5–20, we shall confine our attention to Habakkuk's interview with the deity (1:2–2:4), which offers the prophet's essential message. His dialogue with God consists of two cycles of prophetic complaint and divine response.

Habakkuk opens the first cycle with a vivid protest against the lawlessness rampant in his time (1:2–4). In particular, he expresses anxiety over Yahweh's apparent indifference to the violence that has shown itself. Perhaps both Assyria's oppression of Judah and certain injustices in Judean society itself are reflected here. If God exists and is by nature just, how is the present perversion of justice to be understood? In Hab. 1:5–11 the prophet is invited to observe Yahweh's methods. Presently the deity plans to set judgment in motion by arousing the Chaldean army. Just as Assyria had once been regarded as the rod of Yahweh's anger (Isa. 10:5), Babylonia will now function as God's chosen instrument. True, that "bitter and hasty nation" (Hab. 1:6) venerates its own might (1:11). In no way does it comprehend its international mission as that of fulfilling the will of Yahweh. Nevertheless, in the terror that Babylonia is sure to bring, it will mysteriously function as the instrument of divine justice.

This answer, which defends the reality and efficacy of retribution, does not satisfy the prophet. In his second complaint (1:12–2:1), Habakkuk speaks of his moral anguish. How can the deity seriously consider using the godless Babylonians as the agent of divine judgment? In the havoc that lies ahead, the wicked may indeed suffer. Yet what about the struggling righteous individuals who will surely perish with the wicked? Habakkuk is again appalled that thus far Yahweh has been exceptionally quiet. Does the deity perhaps look silently on the oppressor because he is unable to act in behalf of the righteous (1:12–13)? As his second complaint draws to a close, the prophet resolves to station himself on a watchtower and wait as long as need be for Yahweh's answer (2:1).

That reply comes in 2:2–4. The deity instructs the prophet that the needful vision will appear, though it may be slow in approaching. When it comes, Habakkuk is to write it on tablets with such clarity that "he may run who reads it" (2:2). Here, then, is the assurance that divine justice will finally be realized. Meanwhile, the righteous, God-fearing individual has only to pursue a life of faithfulness: "Behold, he whose soul is not upright in him shall fail, but the righteous shall live by his faith" (2:4).

Humbly awaiting Yahweh, the righteous man will depend solely on divine ability and integrity. Clearly, Habakkuk's theology was one of expectation. It did not respond to the question of theodicy with a pragmatic answer. Nevertheless, the message of Habakkuk contained the declaration that divine justice is inexorable and the assurance that even if satisfying answers to perplexing questions are not always within reach, God is still worthy of man's concern and confidence.

NOTES

1. James B. Pritchard, ed., *Ancient Near Eastern Texts Relating to the Old Testament*, 3d ed. (Princeton, N.J.: Princeton University Press, 1969), pp. 291, 294.

2. Many of Zephaniah's oracles cannot be easily dated. In Zeph. 2:13, however, the prophet foresees, but does not witness, the destruction of Nineveh (612 B.C.). That oracle must predate the historical event itself.

3. Georg Fohrer, *Introduction to the Old Testament*, trans. David E. Green (Nashville: Abingdon Press, 1968), p. 456.

4. See John Gray, *I & II Kings: A Commentary*, rev. ed., The Old Testament Library (Philadelphia: Westminster Press, 1970), p. 729.

5. H. H. Rowley, *The Growth of the Old Testament* (New York: Harper & Row, Harper Torchbooks, 1963), p. 30.

6. For a more comprehensive enumeration, see S. R. Driver, *A Critical and Exegetical Commentary on Deuteronomy*, 3d ed., International Critical Commentary (Edinburgh: T. & T. Clark, 1902), p. xlv.

7. This second oration is interrupted by the third-person account of Deuteronomy 27, with its Shechemite cultic ceremony of covenant renewal.

8. See Gerhard von Rad, *Deuteronomy: A Commentary*, trans. Dorothea Barton, The Old Testament Library (Philadelphia: Westminster Press, 1966), p. 13, for a list of parallels between the legislation of Deuteronomy and that of the Covenant Code.

9. Gerhard von Rad, *Studies in Deuteronomy*, trans. David Stalker, Studies in Biblical Theology, no. 9 (London: SCM Press, 1953), pp. 60–69.

10. G. Ernest Wright, "Introduction and Exegesis to Deuteronomy," in George A. Buttrick et al., eds., *The Interpreter's Bible* (Nashville: Abingdon Press, 1953), vol. 2, p. 502.

11. For a more comprehensive presentation, see Driver, *op. cit.*, pp. lxxviii-lxxxiv.

12. Von Rad, *Studies in Deuteronomy*, *op. cit.*, p. 70.

13. Patrick D. Miller, Jr., "The Gift of God: The Deuteronomic Theology of the Land," *Interpretation* 23 (1969): 458.

14. Though in Nah. 2:1 the prophet speaks of Nineveh's overthrow as having already occurred, this reference is only an indication of Nahum's confidence that such devastation will soon take place.

15. On the liturgical dimensions of the Book of Nahum, see Simon J. de Vries, "The Acrostic of Nahum in the Jerusalem Liturgy," *Vetus Testamentum* 16 (1966): 476–481.

16. In agreement with Fohrer, *op. cit.*, pp. 452–453, we prefer to link problematic Hab. 2:5 with the woes that follow rather than with the dialogue between prophet and deity that precedes.

15

JUDAH'S APPOINTMENT TO THE YOKE

Prior to Jerusalem's destruction by the Babylonians in 587, conflicting views about Judah's best course of action were expressed in the court and the Temple as well as on the street corner. One who was especially vocal on the matter was the prophet Jeremiah, whose career is the subject of the present chapter.

If Jer. 1:2 is correct in its assertion that Jeremiah was summoned to the prophetic office in 627, then Jeremiah was a contemporary of Zephaniah, Nahum, and Habakkuk. Yet Jeremiah led a more active and turbulent existence than his prophet colleagues. The book that bears his name contains a rich store of traditions that allows us to become more intimately acquainted with Jeremiah as a person than is the case with most

---

Biblical texts to be read prior to and in conjunction with the present chapter: (a) Jeremiah 1–6 for Jeremiah's call and early preaching during the reigns of Josiah and Jehoiakim; (b) Jer. 7:1–8:3; 26:1–24 for Jeremiah's Temple sermon during Jehoiakim's reign; (c) Jeremiah 36 for the scroll episode involving Jeremiah, Baruch, and Jehoiakim; (d) 2 Kings 24:1–17 for the Deuteronomist's account of the first Babylonian sack of Jerusalem (597); (e) Jeremiah 27–29 for the prophet's views on the Babylonian yoke during Zedekiah's reign; (f) Jer. 37:1–40:6 for Jeremiah's activity and views just prior to and during the second Babylonian conquest of Jerusalem (587); (g) 2 Kings 24:18–25:21 for the Deuteronomist's account of Zedekiah's reign and Jerusalem's capitulation to the Babylonians (587); (h) 2 Kings 25:22–26 for the Deuteronomist's witness to the governorship of Gedaliah and its termination; (i) Jer. 40:7–44:30 for Jeremiah's experiences in Judah during the governorship of Gedaliah and his time in Egypt following Gedaliah's assassination; (j) Jer. 11:18–12:6; 15:10–21; 17:14–18; 18:18–23; 20:7–18 for the prophet's "confessions"; (k) Jer. 13:1–11; 18:1–12; 19:1–20:6 for Jeremiah's parables and symbolic actions and; (l) Jeremiah 30–31 for portions of the Book of Comfort.

333

biblical prophets. Long sequences of prose narrative and numerous poetic self-disclosures in Jeremiah's so-called confessions offer much useful biographical and autobiographical data.[1]

The Book of Jeremiah portrays a prophet who fathomed the strange ways of God and man with far greater depth than most men. He was firmly convinced that Judah was doomed to the Babylonian yoke. And he accepted this historical inevitability as being in accord with the divine will, for he was certain that following Babylonian exile Yahweh's people would experience renewal. Consequently, he gave fundamental support to his contemporaries through a theological perspective that enabled them to live with the deep wounds of body and spirit that the vicissitudes of contemporary history were to inflict on them. That perspective also led them to a more profound understanding of the deity and his intentions.

THE BOOK OF JEREMIAH
AS LITERATURE

The main divisions of the Book of Jeremiah are clear enough: Jeremiah 1–25 contains prophetic oracles and dramatic actions against Judah and Jerusalem; Jeremiah 26–45 is essentially a biographical narrative about the prophet; Jeremiah 46–51 consists of oracles against foreign nations; and Jeremiah 52 presents a historical appendix drawn from 2 Kings 24: 18–25:30. (Nonetheless, Jer. 52:28–30, with its specific reference to the number of Judeans deported to Babylon, replaces 2 Kings 25:22–26.)

When the contents of the first two divisions are examined, significant problems of arrangement emerge. For example, Jeremiah 1–25 has so many motifs of admonition and doom that one is inclined to suspect that disparate elements have been collected around a single theme of judgment. Yet some passages in this division (for example, 3:11–18; 23:1–8) project an emphatic note of hope. Also the presence of a limited amount of biographical prose in these chapters points to its composite character. Then the dates heading the several biographical episodes in Jeremiah 26–45 reveal a complete disregard for chronological arrangement. Here we confront two different kinds of prose—biographical prose disclosing the prophet's activities and homiletic prose preserving various sermonic utterances attributed to Jeremiah. Moreover, the material in the so-called Book of Comfort (Jer. 30–33) interrupts the narrative flow. In sum, the final ordering of the components in the Book of Jeremiah is less than satisfactory.

An epoch-making contribution toward an intelligent grasp of the composition of the Book of Jeremiah was made by Mowinckel in a monograph that appeared more than a half-century ago.[2] He was convinced that ruptured historical sequences in the Jeremiah narrative, along with obvious disorder in the prophetic pronouncements themselves, betrayed a long editorial process.

Mowinckel identified three different types of material in the book and assigned them the designations A, B, and C. The first type (A) consists of authentic poetic oracles, without prefatory and concluding formulas, preserved in most of Jeremiah 1–25.

The second type (B) offers personal and historical elements in the form of prose narrative. It is found in portions of Jeremiah 19, 20, 29, 39, 40, and 44, and consumes all of Jeremiah 26, 28, 36–38, and 41–43. Mowinckel claimed that the B material was written by a Jew living in Egypt at some point during the first hundred years following Jeremiah's death (ca. 580–480). We digress briefly to note that the designation "Jew" (Yᵉhûdî in Hebrew) was used sparingly during those years when Judah existed independently after Samaria's fall. By the postexilic era, however, it was frequently employed to denote anyone who claimed that his ancestors had been citizens of Judah.

The third type (C) is made up of sermonic prose. Although it has affinities with Jeremiah's authentic oracles, it most closely resembles the prose of Deuteronomy. Mowinckel found this source in ten different chapters of Jeremiah (7, 8, 11, 18, 21, 25, 32, 34, 35, and 44). Two representative examples are 7:1–8:3, containing Jeremiah's famous Temple sermon and appended sayings, and 44:1–14, consisting of an admonition to the Jewish diaspora in Egypt that they not foolishly commit the same apostasy as their fathers. ("Diaspora," which derives from a Greek word meaning "to disperse," refers to the formation of scattered colonies of Jews outside Palestine during and after the Babylonian exile.) Riding herd on the theme of Judah's uninterrupted sinfulness and her deserved chastisement, this C material has a monotonous style and a limited vocabulary. It presents Jeremiah as one whose ideals were in agreement with the religious interests of the Deuteronomic school.

Mowinckel then reconstructed the emergence of the completed Book of Jeremiah. According to his theory, Jeremiah's faithful scribe, Baruch, wrote down at the prophet's dictation certain oracles (A). The biographical material (B) came into being after Jeremiah's death and was later combined with the oracles by an unknown redactor. At various times this literary product (AB) received the sermonic prose (C), which had since been written by the Deuteronomist. Eventually the Book of Comfort (chaps. 30–33), the oracles against the foreign nations (chaps. 46–51), and a historical appendix (chap. 52) were added to this composite (ABC).

Though Mowinckel's classification has been widely embraced, his views have been criticized on several counts. First, his understanding of the date (ca. 580–480) and authorship of the B material is rather arbitrary. The details of Jeremiah's ministry given in the biography suggest an author sympathetic with the prophet's purposes, which Baruch was. Jeremiah 44 reveals that the prophet and the Jewish refugees in Egypt did not see eye to eye. Therefore, Baruch may indeed have had a hand in shaping this supportive treatment of the prophet. Second, the C material of sermonic prose cannot be so readily assessed as being Deuteronomic, and hence, non-Jeremian. While the idiom of the sermonic prose is close to that of Deuteronomy, it remains "a style in its own right with peculiarities and distinctive expressions of its own."[3] It is a rhetorical prose that accords with the speech patterns of seventh- and sixth-century Judah. Therefore, it may be a reliable index of Jeremiah's own viewpoint. And last, Mowinckel's analysis does not provide sufficient clues about the arrangement of the Jeremiah components.

Fortunately Jeremiah 36 gives us several important indications about the book's origin. It states that in Jehoiakim's fourth year (605), Jeremiah was divinely induced to dictate to Baruch oracles stemming from the time of his call (presumably 627) to the present day. While the exact content of the scroll cannot be determined,[4] many of the poetic oracles now preserved in Jeremiah 1–25 were undoubtedly written at that time. The dictated scroll could not have been too long, because it was read aloud three times on a single day with time intervals between (36:10, 15, 21). During its third reading Jehoiakim had the audacity to destroy the scroll. Hence, Jeremiah dictated a second scroll, which contained the oracles of the original scroll plus an undetermined number of new pronouncements (36:28–32). This expanded scroll seems to be the nucleus of our present Book of Jeremiah, and as such it has certain connections with chapters 1–25. Nevertheless, the disorder of these chapters reveals that the expanded scroll was further enlarged by additions of later devotees of the prophet. The Hebrew Masoretic and Greek Septuagint texts vary noticeably in arrangement and length (the Septuagint is one-eighth shorter).[5]

This means that toward the end of the Old Testament era, the Book of Jeremiah was still a fluid work. Yet regardless of which version is read, this book is a valuable anthology of prophetic traditions. Each unit should therefore be confronted for what it has to say. The fact that we do not know all the details about the book's evolution need not limit our quest to acquire a basic understanding of the prophet and his message.

JEREMIAH'S CALL
AND RELATED VISIONS

The superscription at the head of the Book of Jeremiah (1:1–3) leads us to the conclusion that the prophet fulfilled his duties during the reigns of Josiah (640–609), Jehoiakim (609–598), Jehoiachin (598–597), and Zedekiah (597–587).[6] According to Jer. 1:2, Jeremiah was called to the prophetic office during Josiah's thirteenth year as monarch of Judah (627). Since Jeremiah does not allude to Josiah's reform and very few of his pronouncements can be dated to Josiah's tenure, perhaps Jeremiah's prophetic career began significantly later.[7] The projection of an initial period of silence for the prophet has not proved to be a very convincing alternative.[8] Therefore, Hyatt has claimed that the "thirteenth year" (627) designates the year of Jeremiah's birth and that his call came near the year 609, either at the end of Josiah's rule or at the beginning of Jehoiakim's.[9] Although this is an attractive hypothesis, it lacks firm proof.

The issue is not easily settled, and we cannot hide from the fact that many of Jeremiah's pronouncements are undated. Nevertheless, two considerations lead us to the tentative conclusion that the traditional date 627 for Jeremiah's call is not that bad.[10]

First, the two texts (1:2; 25:3) that link Jeremiah's summons to Josiah's thirteenth year as king do not show signs of corruption, and two other passages (3:6; 36:2) attest in a more general way that Jeremiah was active during Josiah's rule. All four texts are in the prose tradition of the book, which appears to have been written only shortly after the prophet's death. It is difficult to think that Jeremiah's career could have been radically distorted at that time.[11]

Second, some of the prophet's oracles are not intelligible if they postdate 609. For example, Jer. 2:18 assumes that both Egypt and Assyria are leading powers in the ancient Near East. Assyria's mention and Babylon's absence urge a date well before 609.

If we have not erred in our discussion of the date of Jeremiah's call, then he was probably born in about 645 in Anathoth. That town lies in Benjaminite territory 2 miles northeast of Jerusalem. When he became a man, Jeremiah was summoned by the deity for a special task. The details of his call to the prophetic office are preserved in Jer. 1:4–19. This summons is a terse, poignant dialogue between Jeremiah and Yahweh. The account consists of three units: Jeremiah's grasp of the divine word (vv. 4–10), his perception of two visions (vv. 11–16), and his confrontation with an additional word of divine charge and promise (vv. 17–19). Both 1:4 and 1:11 declare that "the word of Yahweh came" to Jeremiah. That word impinged on Jeremiah's existence on this occasion and on many others. Even when Jeremiah was overwhelmed by misgivings and depression, he had to surrender to that word (cf. Amos 7:14–15).

Jeremiah's appointment is unique. Yahweh declares that even prior to Jeremiah's conception in the womb, he had appointed him to be a prophet (1:5). Jeremiah's response to this awesome summons is telling (1:6). It reminds us of Moses (cf. Exod. 3:1–4:17). Impressed with his own lack of eloquence, Jeremiah is at first unwilling to heed the divine charge; he believes that he is unable to face up to its responsibilities. The range of these responsibilities is suggested by the phrase, "to the nations" (1:5). In addition to addressing the domestic needs of his own people, Jeremiah is expected to speak on the international situation. He is to become a prophet of a God who is active in the world at large.

The divine word that seeks to allay Jeremiah's fear is crucial: "Be not afraid of them, for I am with you to deliver you, says Yahweh"

(1:8). The future looks difficult indeed, but it will not overwhelm the prophet; Yahweh will be his deliverer. The audience, which criticizes God's spokesman, will not be permitted the last word (see also vv. 17–19). Then in vv. 9–10 Jeremiah's sanctification and readiness are both signaled. As Yahweh touches the prophet's mouth he declares, "Behold, I have put my words in your mouth." It is God's word, not his own, that Jeremiah is called on to express. He becomes aware that he now belongs to Yahweh for a special task. He is commissioned to pluck up, break down, destroy, and overthrow (v. 10bc), but he is also summoned to build and plant (v. 10d).

In 1:11–16, which continues the first-person style of the preceding confrontation, we are informed of two visions that Jeremiah experienced. Though it is difficult to know just how these visions relate to the prophet's call, they offer new data about how he interpreted his prophetic task. Since that understanding must have developed in the course of Jeremiah's daily pursuit of his vocation, the visions probably relate in some way to the earlier years of his career.

The first vision (1:11–12) he has is of an almond branch (shāqēd). A vital play on words indicates that Yahweh is watching (shōqēd) over his word to bring it to fruition. Presumably it was not easily recognizable, as an almond branch sprouting in the spring would be. In fact, it may have been a dry twig.[12] Otherwise why would Yahweh have commended Jeremiah for identifying the branch (v. 12)? Yahweh's expression of determination that his word will be fulfilled would give the prophet needed encouragement as he carried out his mission in a basically unfriendly environment.

The second vision (1:13–16), which may have had a history of its own, involves a boiling pot tilted from the north whose contents might be expected to spill southward. Some enemy will invade Judah from the north, as previous enemies have done. Its identity is not specified, though in time the prophet understood Judah's northern opponent to be Babylon. In any case, the impending invasion accords with the divine will. Yahweh has every intention of holding his people accountable for their idolatry. Jeremiah 1, then, constitutes a thematic whole. Through a momentous and direct conversation with Yahweh the prophet is initially called, and in the subsequent, related visions that calling is clarified.

JEREMIAH'S PROCLAMATIONS AND THEIR RECEPTION

Jeremiah's Early Preaching

Since we understand that Jeremiah was summoned to the prophetic office in 627, his early preaching may be regarded as consisting of those oracles contemporary with Josiah's reign. Many, though not all, are contained in portions of Jeremiah 2–6. We shall concentrate on the leading motifs in chapter 2, which expose the apostasy of the people, and in 4:5–31, which speak of the coming judgment involving a northern invasion. The greater part of chapter 2 has been accepted by most scholars as relating to the earliest phase of Jeremiah's preaching.[13] The poems that comprise 4:5–31 no doubt span several years of Jeremiah's life. Such a vivid prediction of judgment probably had its origins rather early in the prophet's career. Even so, portions of 4:5–31 may date closer to 605, when the Babylonians under Nebuchadnezzar defeated the Egyptians at Carchemish and chased them through Syria-Palestine.

In Jeremiah 2 the prophet denounces the continual infidelity and flagrant apostasy of Yahweh's people. With disarmingly vivid figures of speech, he points out to his listeners their serious error in judgment in leaving Yahweh for the worship of lesser gods. Instead of living up to the standards of the Mosaic covenant, the people have defiantly turned their backs on the deity. The Ba'alim of the land (2:23), trees, and stones (2:27) have won their allegiance.

Jeremiah reflects Hosea's theological position on the history of Yahweh's people. He holds that from the time of her settlement in Canaan, Israel has been unfaithful to Yahweh. As a bride is devoted to her husband (2:2), so Israel had shown her loyalty to Yahweh during the desert sojourn. But shortly thereafter, God's people repudiated him. Jeremiah argues that other nations have not done this badly. They may be worshiping inferior or even unreal gods, but they do not swap these for different deities as Israel has done (2:11). Judah's deficient leadership is emphasized (2:8). Her priests, rulers, and prophets have all failed Yahweh. Moreover, 2:13 testifies that the people have foolishly preferred broken cisterns (the worship of other deities) to the source of living water (Yahweh). In 2:20–28 Jeremiah uses a variety of figures—a stubborn ox, a wild vine, an indelible stain, a camel in heat—to emphasize the appalling character of Judah's apostasy. For her inveterate infidelity, Judah stands condemned. Her future looks forbidding, but it is a fate she assuredly deserves.

In 4:5–31 impending judgment centers on the invasion of the foe from the north. Although the identity of the northern enemy has long been debated, today it is widely held to be the Babylonians. In Jeremiah's vision of the boiling pot (1:13–16), he already had a disquieting premonition about an attack from the north. The poetry in chapter 4 is vivid, yet illusive, and reflects that he spoke on more than one occasion.

Early in this century it was assumed that Jeremiah was referring to Scythian hordes, who, according to Herodotus, had advanced down the Mediterranean coast into Egypt in about 625.[14] But since the Scythians failed to overtake any of Judah's walled cities, we have no grounds for claiming that Jeremiah had these marauders in mind. When the prophet first spoke of the northern foe, he may have been uncertain about its identity. Then as the year 605 approached, he probably came to believe that the Babylonians would be the ones to execute Yahweh's vengeance.

Another dimension in Jeremiah 4 has been exposed by Childs, who maintains that in this book, the tradition of the northern foe was assimilated with a myth of the ancient Near East concerning chaos. Consequently, he writes, "the enemy took on superhuman characteristics and could be depicted with the aid of language drawn from the chaos myth."[15] Certainly the prophet's perception of the ravished land goes beyond historical description: "I looked on the earth, and lo, it was waste and void; and to the heavens, and they had no light" (4:23) and "I looked, and lo, the fruitful land was a desert, and all its cities were laid in ruins before Yahweh, before his fierce anger" (4:26). His pleas for repentance (3:1–4:4) having fallen on deaf ears, Jeremiah had become convinced that a dreadful judgment would be forthcoming.

The prophet's depiction of the foe in 4:5–31 is graphic. The enemy is already on his way, and by the end of the chapter, Zion is groaning as one in the very agonies of death. That this chastisement is instigated by Yahweh is clear from 4:12, with his first-person declaration: "Now it is I who speak in judgment upon them."

From the desert comes the sweeping storm, which is compared to horses "swifter than eagles" (4:13). The sound of the trumpet signals the enemy's arrival, and Jeremiah finds himself in the midst of the turmoil (4:19). The prophet envisages the dreadful effects of the enemy's attack (4:23–26). In the wake of Yahweh's wrath all is desolate. Jeremiah laments over the horrible disaster, which in his own mind has already engulfed Judah.

The judgment motif is further developed in Jeremiah 5–6. While Jeremiah may not have been a prophet of doom during his so-called early years, he was no exponent of easy salvation. He believed that the people's infidelity merited an extreme punishment, and that it would be meted out by Yahweh.

The Temple Sermon

We turn now to words and events that reflect Judah's situation during the reign of Jehoiakim (609–598). Here Jeremiah must be set against the Deuteronomic movement. That reform program sought to refine the Yahwistic religion, promote unswerving fidelity to Yahweh, oppose various high places at which the worship of Yahweh was severely compromised, and urge the full-scale centralization of the cult of Yahweh in Jerusalem.

Jeremiah had no reason to oppose the Deuteronomic emphasis on covenant loyalty, but he did question its excessive reliance on the Jerusalem Temple. Also he could not accept cultic centralization as the panacea for Judah's religious ills. Jeremiah's high regard for Josiah in 22:15–16 suggests that initially he backed the reform. Ultimately, however, he must have become cognizant of its superficiality. Reform worthy of the name, thought he, was internal in character. Consequently Jeremiah had no patience for those who "have healed the wound of my people lightly, saying, 'Peace, peace,' when there is no peace" (6:14).

Jeremiah delivered his unforgettable Temple sermon in 609 at the beginning of Jehoiakim's reign. Jeremiah 7 preserves the key words of that address, and Jeremiah 26 gives an indication of the date, some words of the sermon, and the reaction of the people. The sermon in 26:4–6 is at variance with the one in 7:2–15. In the second passage, the attack on the Jerusalem Temple takes the form of a prophetic pronouncement that is cast in the absolute. Yahweh announces that he intends to destroy the favored cultic edifice. Judah's flagrant violation of the covenant necessitates such extreme action. By contrast, Jeremiah's words in 26:4–6 are conditional; they are informed by the deity's hope that perhaps the people will yet repent and return to him. But the people's response, which is reported in 26:11, is violent. The prophets and priests are in favor of killing Jeremiah for having spoken against their city. Their reaction suggests that the prophet had imparted scathing words of absolute judgment. Hence, the sermon and the reaction to it do not mesh.

In 7:2–15, however, the situation is also clouded by the fact that the sermon begins with a conditional format and ends with a stinging, absolute judgment. Over against the declaration that Yahweh intends to destroy the Temple and cast the people from his sight (7:14–15) stands this word of admonition near the beginning of the sermon: "Amend your ways and your doings, and I will let you dwell in this place" (7:3). The heated response of severely irritated listeners suggests that at its inception, Jeremiah's sermon was cast in the absolute form. The use of the conditional may be attributed to a later redactor who tried to soften the tone of a text that appeared to him inordinately harsh.

In delivering this polemic, Jeremiah still entertained the hope that the people would come to their senses on the matter of a suitable religious orientation. Here he raised the question, "What gives protection?" The answer of his people is evident in the prophet's mocking repetition of the phrase, "the temple of Yahweh" (7:4). Jeremiah countered that security would become a reality only if the divine law was upheld. At present the people's conduct was an outright mockery of the Decalogue (7:9).

As if to jar his listeners out of their complacency, Jeremiah reminded them that possession of the ark of the covenant and a concerted involvement in formal worship had not guaranteed Shiloh's well-being during the era of the judges. Shiloh had been assaulted by the Philistines in about 1050 and had not been reoccupied until Hellenistic times. Therefore, anyone in Jeremiah's audience, if he were inclined, could view the ruins some 20 miles north of Jerusalem and ponder their relevance to present-day Jerusalem. In making this appeal to history, Jeremiah was protesting that authentic security is not to be found in the three popular words of his day—"peace," "covenant," and "temple."

Jeremiah's sermon prompted a vehement reaction from his listeners, who were convinced that his attack against the venerable Temple was nothing less than treason. In the arrest and trial that ensued, the prophet's life was at stake. Nevertheless, Jeremiah was acquitted. There were probably several reasons for this. First, the prophet stated that as Yahweh's messenger, he was offering divine opinion, not his own (26:12). Second, Jeremiah addressed the conscience of those assembled by declaring that they should act on what they considered to be "good and right" (26:14). And among the elders present were some who recalled what had occurred after Micah's harsh judgment against Zion and Jerusalem (see Mic. 3:12). Micah was spared, and Hezekiah, who heard him, repented (Jer. 26:17–19). Maintaining that history had a special relevance in this instance, they recommended moderation. Jeremiah was also assisted by "the hand of Ahikam" (26:24). Therefore, Jeremiah was not molested. Though he won no blessing from his outraged public for his Temple pronouncement, he was permitted to continue in the prophetic office.

The Scroll and Its Burning

It appears that Jeremiah was now barred from the Jerusalem Temple. If that prohibition was not imposed on him immediately after his arrest, it certainly was by Jehoiakim's fourth year (605), the chronological setting of chapter 36, which now concerns us. At Yahweh's bidding, Jeremiah dictated to Baruch a résumé of his past sermons. Baruch was to read the resulting scroll aloud in the Temple in the hope that the people might yet return to the deity (36:3, 7).

For the moment, history followed a tumultuous course. In the summer of 605, Nebuchadnezzar had overwhelmed the Egyptians at Carchemish and sent them retreating homeward. Surely word had already reached Jerusalem that the Babylonians were moving south. In the very month that Baruch publicly read the scroll (December 604; see 36:9), the Babylonian forces overtook Ashkelon on the Philistine plain.

News of this aggression might easily have motivated the people to swarm into the Temple for a day of national fasting. Before the sun had set on this eventful day, the scroll was read by Baruch to those assembled in the Temple; reread by Baruch to members of the court, who curiously had been absent from the Temple services; and read by the prince, Jehudi, to King Jehoiakim. By recommending that Baruch take Jeremiah with him and hide, the court officials showed some respect for the written prophetic word (36:19). By contrast, Jehoiakim consigned the scroll to flames and commanded that Jeremiah and Baruch be seized. But the two were miraculously protected by Yahweh (36:26). The prophet was now instructed to write an expanded version of the scroll that would also contain a judgment against the recalcitrant king (36:30–31). Only Yahweh would have final say in the matter.

Though the content of the scroll cannot be confidently ascertained, the biographical data of chapter 36 suggest that the original scroll contained no narrative reports, only sayings. Moreover, these oracular utterances would have related to the interval between the call of Jeremiah (627) and the dictation of the scroll (605). Most of the words were probably threatening in character and were directed against Judah, Jerusalem, and the foreign nations. Since Jehoiakim was extremely provoked by the scroll, we may infer that it advanced a policy contrary to that of the court. Presumably Jeremiah's words were as much preoccupied with political alternatives as with religious affections, for it was the administrative officials, not the priests, who reported the existence of the scroll to Jehoiakim. As a predominantly judgmental document, it advanced Yahweh's transcendent criticism in a manner that was odious to the state. Jehoiakim understandably took offense. But once more the written word assumed paramount importance in ancient Israel.

JEREMIAH'S MINISTRY AND THE FALL OF JERUSALEM

The Historical Situation

Jerusalem could not hold out indefinitely against the Babylonians. In 597 and again in 587, Nebuchadnezzar and his Babylonian forces plundered the city. Literary documentation of this period is not as complete as we would like. Even so, thanks to the discovery of four more cuneiform tablets of the Babylonian Chronicle in 1956, we now have an extrabiblical text that depicts Nebuchadnezzar's first conquest of Jerusalem. Its description of Nebuchadnezzar's fourth year as king shows that in late November 601, both the Egyptians and Babylonians sustained heavy losses on the Egyptian border. Presumably Nebuchadnezzar's forces suffered a stunning defeat, for during the next year and a half the Babylonians stayed home and rebuilt their militia. This state of affairs provides the motive for Jehoiakim's decision that Judah should now officially renounce its servitude to Babylonia (2 Kings 24:1).

Having heard of the Babylonian defeat, Jehoiakim defiantly withheld tribute. Because Nebuchadnezzar could not engage in an immediate act of reprisal against Judah, he urged professional raiders from among the neighboring peoples to begin his work for him (24:2). But by late 598, Nebuchadnezzar started to move westward. Although he did not take long in coming, Jehoiakim died during this interval,[16] and his

A Cuneiform Account of Jerusalem's Fall. This small clay tablet offers a chronicle of important Babylonian events from Nabopolassar's last year of rule to the eleventh year of Nebuchadnezzar's. Its date for the first Babylonian conquest of Jerusalem is 16 March 597 B.C. (Courtesy of the Trustees of the British Museum.)

eighteen-year-old son Jehoiachin mounted the Jerusalem throne. Three months later, on 16 March 597, Jehoiachin was forced to capitulate to Nebuchadnezzar's powerful assault against the city. This date for the first Babylonian conquest of Jerusalem is determined on the basis of the following cuneiform account of Nebuchadnezzar's seventh year as king:

> Year 7, month Kislimu: The king of Akkad moved his army into Hatti land, laid siege to the city of Judah (*Ia-a-ḫu-du*) [Jerusalem] and the king took the city on the second day of the month Addaru. He appointed in it a (new) king of his liking [Zedekiah], took heavy booty from it and brought it into Babylon.[17]

The biblical depiction of this sack of Jerusalem (2 Kings 24:10–17) indicates that the Temple and royal treasuries were confiscated, and that leading citizens, including Jehoiachin and probably the prophet Ezekiel, were deported to Babylon. As the uncle and successor of Jehoiachin, Zedekiah (597–587) was ushered into the unenviable office of king. With Judah's leading citizens deported, a new, less equipped citizenry held sway.[18] In the years immediately ahead, Judah was often the victim of short-sighted nationalism, and within such a situation Jeremiah found the going difficult. Our immediate task, then, is to consider Jeremiah 27–29, in which the prophet argues that the nation's overthrow by the Babylonian host is imminent.

The Propriety of the Yoke of Babylon

Jeremiah 27 and 28 really depict one event that took place in the year 594 (28:1)—a time when Babylon, especially its army, was experiencing considerable turmoil. Undoubtedly this encouraged many of the deported Jews to assume that their release from Babylonian captivity was imminent. While the rebellion in Babylon did not last long, some Judeans believed that a new day for God's people lay in the offing. Hananiah and other prophets who were not afraid to stand up against Babylon urged their contemporaries to take a hard line against the eastern tyrant. If help were needed, surely it would come from Egypt. According to Jer. 28:2–4, Hananiah proclaimed in the Jerusalem Temple that within two years Babylon would experience a crippling defeat, the exiles would return home, the stolen Temple vessels would be returned, and Jeconiah (that is, Jehoiachin) would be reestablished on the throne of Jerusalem.

Jeremiah entertained another opinion, however. At Yahweh's bidding, he placed a wooden yoke around his neck (27:2). Even at that moment, representatives from Edom, Moab, Ammon, Tyre, and Sidon were meeting with Zedekiah in Jerusalem to settle on an appropriate course of action. Should the coalition of western states join in a concerted act of rebellion, or should it maintain neutrality? With the yoke in full view of his audience, Jeremiah warned against trusting in dreamers and soothsayers who promise that Judah would not have to serve the Babylonian monarch. The divine will dictated that Judah should undergo the humiliating experience of the Babylonian yoke (27:8). Jeremiah admitted that it would be entirely pleasant if Hananiah's optimistic words, which he spoke in Yahweh's name (28:2, 11), were to become a reality, but he doubted that this would happen (28:6). The outstanding prophets of Israel's past were all harbingers of doom. Moreover, Jeremiah countered that the credentials of a prophet who prophesies peace can only be established when peaceful conditions actually come into existence (28:9).

The audience who heard the debate between Jeremiah and Hananiah had reason to feel confused. Hananiah was just as capable of prefacing his pronouncements with, "Thus says Yahweh," as Jeremiah was. How was the true prophet to be distinguished from the false? The legislation in Deut. 18:18–22 did not provide adequate criteria. Surely not all the prophets who spoke had been sent by Yahweh. This was a critical issue in ancient Israel, and one for which no final solution was found.

In any event, Hananiah removed the yoke from Jeremiah's neck, broke it in the presence of the people assembled, and declared that the Babylonian yoke would itself be broken within two years (Jer. 28:10–11). But Hananiah was not to have the last word. Soon Jeremiah was commanded to put on an iron yoke (28:13). Furthermore, a formal Judean conspiracy against Babylon did not materialize in 594. To what extent Jeremiah was responsible we cannot say. Perhaps a few of the political representatives were wise enough to recognize the insanity of such a course.

Jeremiah also defended the propriety of the Babylonian yoke in a letter he wrote to the Jewish exiles (29:4–15, 21–23). This undertaking is not dated, but it was no doubt roughly contemporary with the incident of the yoke. In this letter, Jeremiah urges restless Jewish exiles to settle down in Babylon and maintain their native faith in Yahweh. Even granting that the prophet appeals to Jewish self-interests (29:7), Bright points out that "a command to Jews to pray for the hated heathen power is otherwise unexampled in literature of the period."[19]

Here Jeremiah insists that Yahweh is not going to intervene suddenly and bring the Jews home. The exiles are to put down roots. As cooperative subjects of the Babylonian monarch, they are to pursue as normal a life as possible. Jeremiah was providing a theological justification for the existence of the Jewish diaspora. As the exiles pursued their daily routines, they would discover that they were in fact the recipients of Yahweh's mercy (29:14). If the exiles complied with the divine will by yielding to the Babylonian yoke, they would eventually embark on a better way of life.

The Folly of Judah's Rebellion

Jeremiah 37–44 links the prophet with Jerusalem's destruction and its aftermath. According to chapter 37, Jerusalem's beleaguered citizens experienced some relief when the Babylonian troops withdrew from the city to confront the advancing Egyptians, who were coming to support Zedekiah. Details are scant, but it appears that by 589, excessive patriotism in Judah could no longer be held in check. In his uncertainty, Zedekiah was torn between following the advice of Jeremiah, which he had obtained in secret, and siding with the counsel of his chauvinistic nobles. Early in 588 Jerusalem was feeling pressure from the Babylonian forces, which were claiming various regions of Judah in triumphant succession. Nevertheless, in the summer of 588, Pharaoh Hophra (Apries, 589–570) dispatched his Egyptian troops to relieve the citizenry of Jerusalem. Though the respite was brief, it must have been joyously received by the majority, who thought that once again at the final hour Yahweh was seeking to deliver his own. But Jeremiah insisted that the Babylonians would soon return (37:8).

During the momentary peace, Jeremiah attempted a trip to his home territory in order to "receive his portion" (37:12). The Hebrew is obscure. If Jeremiah was involved in a business transaction concerning the division of property, his action would be symbolic of his faith that the life of Yahweh's people in Judah would continue. In any case, Jeremiah was arrested, charged with desertion, and imprisoned. Again Zedekiah secretly inquired of Jeremiah, "Is there any word from Yahweh?" (37:17).

Candidly the prophet declared that Zedekiah would be delivered over to Nebuchadnezzar. Even so, Zedekiah honored Jeremiah's request that he not be returned to prison. Jeremiah was now placed in "the court of the guard" beside the palace (37:21).

Jeremiah continued to counsel that submission to the Babylonian enemy was Jerusalem's only answer. The Judean princes therefore protested to Zedekiah that the prophet's seditious words were undermining whatever courage the people still possessed (38:4). In their opinion, Jeremiah deserved to die. The uncertain Zedekiah placed Jeremiah in the custody of the princes, and they cast him into a cistern to suffocate or starve. But a certain Ethiopian named Ebed-melech brought Jeremiah's miserable condition to the attention of Zedekiah, who reassigned Jeremiah to the court of the guard. Again Zedekiah interviewed Jeremiah in secret, and once more Jeremiah instructed him to surrender to the Babylonians. But as we might expect, this Judean monarch was not prepared to take the word of Yahweh's prophet seriously.

The towns of Azekah and Lachish both yielded to Babylonian assault, presumably during the first months of 587, and in July of that year the enemy forces broke through Jerusalem's walls (39:2). Zedekiah fled but was soon captured and delivered to Nebuchadnezzar, who showed no mercy. Zedekiah saw the execution of his own sons; he was then blinded, chained, and deported to Babylon, where he died (39:6–7; 52:11). Meanwhile, Jerusalem was leveled. Jeremiah was treated kindly by the Babylonians, who offered him safe conduct to Babylon or an opportunity to go elsewhere. Undoubtedly the aggressors had learned of Jeremiah's pronouncements and accepted them as a sure indication of pro-Babylonian sentiment. Thus the prophet was permitted to move to Mizpah and join Gedaliah, whom Nebuchadnezzar had appointed as governor of the newly created Babylonian province of Judah.

The prose biography in 40:7–44:30 traces Jeremiah's career in Judah during the interim governorship of Gedaliah and reflects on his experience in Egypt following Gedaliah's assassination. As the ruling head of the Jewish population that had not been deported to Babylon, Gedaliah attempted to bring order to a ruined land. For a time he was successful. But some Judeans were convinced that Gedaliah was too obliging to the Babylonians. Gedaliah's friends warned him that anti-Babylonian fanatics might do him in, but he paid little heed. Eventually a certain Ishmael assassinated Gedaliah at Mizpah, and with him Jewish associates and Babylonian soldiers stationed there (41:1–3).

This rash act put the Judeans in a difficult position. The Babylonians, who had appointed Gedaliah governor, would not take the uprising lightly. Many Jews therefore sought refuge in Egypt. Although Jeremiah urged his compatriots to remain in Judah, they refused to heed his advice; in fact, they forced Jeremiah and Baruch to accompany them to Egypt. There they settled in the border fortress of Tahpanhes.

Having arrived in Egypt against his will, Jeremiah did not cease to function as Yahweh's prophet. Through word and symbol, he proclaimed that even in Egypt the people would not be immune from Babylonian treachery. Thus, in Jer. 43:9–13 Yahweh instructs Jeremiah to build a pedestal on which Nebuchadnezzar is expected to erect his throne. (No audience is explicitly referred to, but one is at least assumed.) Nebuchadnezzar did in fact sponsor a third deportation of 745 Judeans in 582 (Jer. 52:30), and in about 568 he invaded Egypt. Jeremiah continued to speak and act with disarming realism.

Further dealings between Jeremiah and the Jews in Egypt are recorded in chapter 44, whose prose admittedly manifests a prolix Deuteronomic style. While it is difficult to determine what is authentic Jeremian oracle, the prophet might well have censured the pagan cultic practices of his contemporaries, who were probably sincere in their belief that disaster could be averted only by the worship of other gods in Egypt.[20] Certainly the heated reply of the people (44:16–18) has an authentic ring. The determined Jeremiah criticized the Jewish women who supported the Babylonian cult of the goddess Ishtar, which had made its way into Egypt. To this "queen of heaven" (44:18) they burned incense, poured out libations, and brought cakes bearing her image.

In Jeremiah's estimation, the ancestral faith of Judah was in jeopardy. The word of Yahweh still penetrated with appalling clarity: "I am watching over them for evil and not for good" (44:27). Until his death in about 580, Jeremiah continued to preach about divine scrutiny and impending judgment against those unable to face the solemn lessons of their history.

THE PERSONALITY
OF JEREMIAH

Jeremiah was so thoroughly involved in Judah's history during the late seventh and early sixth centuries that it has seemed best to permit the momentum of various events to carry us along. Now we propose to move back in time and consider two facets of the Jeremiah tradition that suggest something about the personality of the prophet: Jeremiah's so-called confessions and his parables and symbolic actions.

Introspection

The term "confessions" applies to Jeremiah's intimate, unglossed self-disclosures in which he questions the mission that has been imposed on him by Yahweh. The confessions (11:18–12:6; 15:10–21; 17:14–18; 18:18–23; 20:7–18) contain remarkably intimate thoughts that expose the prophet's painful struggle to function as Yahweh's spokesman. Indeed, here he used legal terminology to be as forceful as possible in arguing his case against the deity, who had thrust him into the prophetic office.[21] The pattern of discourse employed in these lyrics gave Jeremiah the opportunity to make accusations, raise questions, and protest his innocence. These passages reveal that Jeremiah felt a genuine conflict between his natural desires and his deep commitment to his calling. Jeremiah's moods varied. When he was hurt, he wanted Yahweh to know that. He wanted Yahweh to realize that his enemies deserved the worst conceivable forms of punishment. He also complained that he was not at all pleased about his alienation from his fellowmen. He felt excluded from the common joys and satisfactions of life. He was extremely vulnerable to feelings of failure and persecution. The poems also indicate that Jeremiah's brooding met with divine words of rebuke and vindication, which helped him to acquire new purpose and direction. Through it all the prophet matured.

Jeremiah 11:18–12:6 is the first of three confessions that we shall examine briefly. There we learn that Jeremiah's kinsmen from Anathoth would prefer to see him dead. Thoroughly disturbed, he prays for the divine protection promised him at the moment of his call (11:20). Moreover, the prophet asks why the wicked prosper (12:1–4). Those who are ostensibly loyal but actually disloyal often seem to be favored by fortune. The doctrine of divine retribution for human wrongdoing does not seem to be upheld. Conceiving of the deity as a righteous judge, the prophet pleads his case.

Yahweh's answer is scarcely comforting: "If you have raced with men on foot, and they have wearied you, how will you compete with horses? And if in a safe land you fall down, how will you do in the jungle of the Jordan?" (12:5). Jeremiah is destined to face an ominous future. This is plainly part of the prophetic mission.

In another confession (15:10–21) Jeremiah complains about the day of his birth. He also declares that though he has treasured Yahweh's word, he suffers greatly from his close and sustained contact with it. He asks the deity, "Wilt thou be to me like a deceitful brook, like waters that fail?" (15:18b). Yahweh's answer is one of rebuke and comfort. If Jeremiah is to continue in the prophetic office, he must fully repent and return to the deity. Nonetheless, the assurance that came to him at the time of his call is reinforced (15:20).

Finally, as the confession in 20:7–18 opens, Jeremiah again refers to Yahweh's deceit. He has endured much derision. He blames the deity, who has forced him to say things that a normal human being would not have dared to say. Outraged by this apparent injustice, he has tried unsuccessfully to keep the divine word to himself. But the burning word had to be released, and Jeremiah has paid a high price for functioning as Yahweh's spokesman.

Yet this is not the end of the matter. Confession follows complaint, confession that Yahweh is the source of man's power to cope daily with unpleasant situations: "But Yahweh is with me as a dread warrior; therefore my persecutors will stumble, they will not overcome me" (20:11).

As is the case with many of the laments in the Book of Psalms, vengeance is part of the program. Nevertheless, a courageous faith emerges out of a troubled existence. These and other confessions reveal much about Jeremiah's personal make-up. They demonstrate that detachment and objectivity were not characteristic of this prophet. To be sure, the man and his message were one.

Self-Expression

We have already examined chapters 28–29, which involved Jeremiah, Hananiah, and the wooden yoke. Jeremiah wore the yoke to symbolize Judah's impending submission to Babylon, Hananiah removed it to symbolize the near end of the Babylonian threat, and then Jeremiah was divinely instructed to put on an iron yoke to symbolize that matters had gone from bad to worse. This is but one example of the powerful symbolism that pervades the Book of Jeremiah.

Jeremiah shared his people's recognition that Semitic life was permeated with significant gestures and sacramental signs. He often reinforced his spoken word with clear-cut symbols and deeds. With their naïve realism, the various signs and actions of the Hebrew prophets reflect a world of thought admittedly alien to our own. On one level, these actions seem magical; on another, they are closely linked with the very purpose of the deity. Therefore, writes Robinson, "the prophetic act is itself a part of the will of Yahweh, to whose complete fulfillment it points; it brings that will nearer to its completion, not only as declaring it, but in some small degree as effecting it."[22]

The account of the linen waistcloth is highly symbolic. Jeremiah 13:1–11 reports that at Yahweh's request the prophet girded himself with a linen waistcloth. Having worn it for a while, he removed it at Yahweh's instruction, took it to the Euphrates, and hid it in a cleft of the rock. Much later Jeremiah was instructed by Yahweh to return to the rock, where he found a rotten, worthless garment. The symbolism in the narrative is apparent. The cloth that had hugged Jeremiah's loins represented Israel's close relationship with Yahweh. And the spoiled waistcloth stood for the people's profanation of the covenant relationship.

Since the Euphrates was some 400 miles away from Judah, it is improbable that Jeremiah made two trips there, one to insert the cloth and another to remove it. The question can be resolved in several ways. The text can be interpreted as a spoken parable with no basis in fact. It can be understood as a visionary experience that came to Jeremiah but one that was not translated into any other form of experience. The passage can be dismissed as a late prophetic legend that has no connection with the Jeremiah of history. Or finally, the Hebrew text can be modestly emended. Elsewhere in the Hebrew Bible, $p^e r\bar{a}th$ means "Euphrates," but a town with a similar name, "Parah" (Josh. 18:23), lies only a half-dozen miles from Jerusalem. If this had been Jeremiah's destination, his journey would have been reasonably brief.

In any case, this symbolic act can be understood on two levels. On a didactic level, we are shown that Yahweh plans to punish his people in the near future. Yet on the sympathetic level, we witness the authentic suffering of the deity, who must execute that judgment. By wearing the waistcloth, Jeremiah "must learn to feel for himself God's intimate attachment to Israel; he must not only know about it, but experience it from within."[23] The familiar item, the people of Yahweh, will be spoiled, and the deity is disinclined to take the matter lightly.

Once Jeremiah observed a potter reshape a spoiled vessel of clay into a new vessel (18:1–12). This led him to assert the striking applicability of this action to Judah's situation with the deity. Here Yahweh is presented as both a sovereign and a principled being. He determines what does and does not meet his standards. Yet he is not capricious. This text, which is steeped in Deuteronomic terminology, projects the pessimistic note that a worthless people cannot continue indefinitely. The passage indicates that the deity will act favorably toward the renegade nation that "turns from its evil" (18:8). Perhaps Jeremiah first used this symbol to express his confidence that eventually Israel would measure up to Yahweh's expectations.[24]

The prophetic symbol in 19:1–20:6 is an earthenware flask that is shattered outside Jerusalem's Potsherd Gate. Jeremiah is instructed to purchase a potter's flask and smash it in the presence of chosen witnesses (19:1–2). While doing this he is to declare that in like manner Yahweh intends to "break this people and this city" (19:11). Though the text does not state that the prophet carried out Yahweh's instruction, we may assume that he did. From that time on Jeremiah stood in the Temple court and proclaimed that tragedy would befall Jerusalem (19:14–15). In an effort to silence Jeremiah and evade his terrifying words of doom, Pashhur, a priest of the Temple, had him beaten and placed in stocks (20:1–2). This itself is a vivid indication that prophetic symbolism was neither conveyed nor witnessed casually.

THE BOOK OF COMFORT

The so-called Book of Comfort encompasses chapters 30–33: chapters 30–31 consist mainly of poetic oracles, and chapters 32–33 are made up of prose sayings. We shall be concerned with an examination of the former. It is difficult to say just what percentage of chapters 30–31 is the work of the Jeremiah of history. In style and content, such passages as 30:12–15; 31:2–6; and 31:15–22 may be claimed for the prophet. The first portrays Judah's incurable hurt; the second speaks of the joyous rebuilding of Israel; and the third is a poetic meditation on Rachel's lament for her children, who had been hauled off to captivity in 721. Undoubtedly several other units may be attributed to the prophet, who embraced the future with some sense of hope. Nevertheless, the style of such pieces as 30:10; 31:7–9; and 31:10–14 is so close to that of Second Isaiah that we are justified in assuming that they are not Jeremian in origin. Moreover, 30:23–31:1 tells of impending wrath and restoration in a manner that does not resemble other work of Jeremiah. Though Jeremiah himself might have assumed a role in producing a scroll of comfort and hope, others also influenced the shaping of the final product.

The best-known unit in these two chapters is the prose discourse in 31:31–34, which makes the marvelous promise of a new covenant. We do not know whether these verses preserve Jeremiah's actual words. He is probably not to be blamed for the tedious, somewhat awkward phrasing of this unit. Nevertheless, the thought of this classical passage may indeed be attributed to Jeremiah. The prophet's understanding of the new covenant is not based on a promulgation of new legislation. The radically new element is the motivation that makes possible man's fulfillment of existing covenant law. The promised forgiveness and the firsthand knowledge of Yahweh will give mankind a new incentive for obeying the deity. The prophet demonstrates his familiarity with the terminology of the covenant. Speaking for the deity he says, "I will be their God, and they shall be my people" (31:33). What was affirmed at Sinai and denied in Hosea's naming of his second son, "Not my people" (Hos. 1:9), was now reaffirmed by Jeremiah. This projected covenant does not imply that mankind will for the first time experience a continuous state of perfection. Still it points the way to covenant restoration and authentic fellowship between God and people, and it allows for the forgiveness of human wrongdoing. Many readers take this to be Jeremiah's most important teaching.

JEREMIAH'S MESSAGE
IN RETROSPECT

How did Jeremiah conceive of the deity? Obviously this prophet was a functioning monotheist. While he made no statements renouncing the existence of other deities, he denied their power. In his view they were worthless (2:5); they resembled broken cisterns incapable of holding water (2:13) and were poorly equipped to assist man when he was most in need of help (2:28). Jeremiah claimed that the destiny of both Israel and the other nations was in the hands of Yahweh, whose purposive sovereignty and power could not be thwarted. He held that Yahweh related to the world largely through his word. Jeremiah recognized that Yahweh's word had invaded his existence at the time of his call (1:4) and that it often dictated the manner in which he conducted himself in the prophetic office. Jeremiah also fully affirmed that Yahweh acts in history and that principally he does so by electing and relating to a specific people. The nation Israel had been called to live a separate existence—to remain "holy" to Yahweh, to be the "first fruits of his harvest" (2:3). As his beloved (11:15) and first-born (31:9), she was expected to respond obediently to his will. Jeremiah did not often use the word "covenant." Nevertheless, he reflected on the covenant reality, especially in passages where he used the husband-wife and father-son imagery previously employed by Hosea. Jeremiah's God was clearly Lord of the covenant.

Jeremiah also stands close to Hosea in his view of sin and repentance. Jeremiah claimed that the greatest cause of sin was lack of knowledge of Yahweh. Neither the priests (2:8) nor the poor (5:4) knew Yahweh and his ways. At base, Yahweh's people were foolish (4:22); they flagrantly ignored the covenant stipulations.

Jeremiah also spoke of repentance and renewal as experiences involving knowledge: God knows and remembers. He represented Yahweh as saying of Ephraim, "For as often as I speak against him, I do remember him still" (31:20). Jeremiah believed that having violated the covenant relationship, man is incapable of seeing to its repair. His inclination to sin is too firmly rooted in him. Yet it is in Yahweh's power to forgive and to restore the covenant relationship. Ultimately a new covenant will come into being, and the people of God will become what Yahweh has always wanted them to be. Men will know God and want to know him.

What was the nature of Jeremiah's hope? Mainly it rested on his understanding of the new covenant (31:31–34). In contrast with the old covenant, the new one would be engraved on the hearts of the men of Israel and Judah, who would all know Yahweh. Their sin would no longer be remembered. Jeremiah anticipated the return of Yahweh's people to their own land and a renewal of appropriate forms of worship. Yet Jeremiah did not speak for or against the restoration of the Jerusalem Temple. He was too preoccupied with the possibilities of the regeneration of the human heart and the emergence of a new fellowship between God and people.

Jeremiah also held firm convictions about man's individual and communal existence. The prophet's encounter with Yahweh had convinced him that each member of the covenant community was important in Yahweh's sight. Each was called to respond to Yahweh's summons, and each would be held accountable. Jeremiah shared Ezekiel's impatience (Ezek. 18:2) with the popular aphorism, "The fathers have eaten sour grapes, and the children's teeth are set on edge" (Jer. 31:29). That opinion, which undercut the concept of free will, was odious to Jeremiah. But his perception of the new covenant also reveals his respect for communal existence. The covenant to be written on the heart of man is also to be engraved on the heart of the nation. Jeremiah believed that individual salvation is real only when it is closely linked with an authentic renewal of the nation's soul.[25]

During his eventful career, Jeremiah experienced anguish and hope, torture and faith. Throughout his lifetime he testified to the inseparability of God's judgment and grace. Through Jeremiah's eyes we witness Jerusalem's tragic fall in 587 and its significance, and we glimpse part of what the future held in store for Yahweh's chastened people. Jeremiah's own varied responses to the deity were spontaneous, his unrequited love for his people was authentic, and his perception of man and God were equally profound.

NOTES

1. The scope of Jeremiah's "confessions" is difficult to determine. See our delineation on the first page of this chapter (item "j") and Georg Fohrer, *Introduction to the Old Testament,* trans. David E. Green (Nashville: Abingdon Press, 1968), p. 395, for a slightly different listing.
2. Sigmund Mowinckel, *Zur Komposition des Buches Jeremia* (Oslo: J. Dybwad, 1914).
3. John Bright, *Jeremiah: Introduction, Translation, and Notes,* The Anchor Bible, vol. 21 (Garden City, N.Y.: Doubleday, 1965), p. lxxi.
4. For attempted delineations, see Otto Eissfeldt, *The Old Testament: An Introduction,* trans. Peter R. Ackroyd (New York: Harper & Row, 1965), pp. 351–352; and J. Philip Hyatt, "Introduction and Exegesis to Jeremiah," in George A. Buttrick et al., eds., *The Interpreter's Bible* (Nashville: Abingdon Press, 1956), vol. 5, p. 787. But note also the negative judgment of Bright, *op. cit.,* p. lxi, who maintains that any speculation about the precise content of the scroll is futile.
5. For example, the Septuagint offers no counterpart to Jer. 33:14–26. This suggests that the passage was not present in its Hebrew prototype.
6. While Jehoiachin's name is not cited, he ruled for three months prior to Zedekiah's appointment to the throne.
7. For example, this is the approach of Samuel Sandmel, *The Hebrew Scriptures: An Introduction to Their Literature and Religious Ideas* (New York: Alfred A. Knopf, 1963), p. 127.
8. We are in agreement with Norman K. Gottwald, *All the Kingdoms of the Earth: Israelite Prophecy and International Relations in the Ancient Near East* (New York: Harper & Row, 1964), p. 241.
9. Hyatt, *op. cit.,* pp. 779–780, 798; and J. Philip Hyatt, "The Beginning of Jeremiah's Prophecy," *Zeitschrift für die alttestamentliche Wissenschaft* 78 (1966): 204–214.
10. Thomas W. Overholt has recently upheld the traditional view in "Some

Reflections on the Date of Jeremiah's Call," *Catholic Biblical Quarterly* 33 (1971): 165–184.

11. We are in agreement with Bright, *op. cit.*, p. lxxxiv.

12. So Adam C. Welch, *Jeremiah: His Time and His Work* (Oxford: Basil Blackwell, 1955), pp. 46–47.

13. Indeed, the oracle in Jer. 2:14–19 requires such a dating because it speaks of Assyria as a world power. Nevertheless, 2:16, with its apparent reference to Judah's subjection to Egypt in 609, reveals that the chapter could not have been completed until after Jehoiakim had acquired the throne.

14. Herodotus, *Histories*, 1. 105.

15. Brevard S. Childs, "The Enemy from the North and the Chaos Tradition," *Journal of Biblical Literature* 78 (1959): 197.

16. John Bright, *A History of Israel*, 2d ed. (Philadelphia: Westminster Press, 1972), p. 326, maintains that Jehoiakim may have been assassinated by those who hoped to induce the Babylonians to deal more kindly with Judah. Though we cannot rule out that possibility, it cannot be proven.

17. James B. Pritchard, ed., *Ancient Near Eastern Texts Relating to the Old Testament*, 3d ed. (Princeton, N.J.: Princeton University Press, 1969), p. 564. The first pair of parentheses contains a transliteration of the Babylonian word for "Judah" and the second pair contains an interpolation of the translator. The brackets have been added by the author to clarify what is presumably intended by "city of Judah" and "(new) king." According to 2 Kings 24:17, Nebuchadnezzar appointed Mattaniah to be Judah's next monarch and renamed him Zedekiah.

18. The number of Judeans sucked into Babylonian captivity in 597 is given as 10,000 in 2 Kings 24:14; as 8,000 in 2 Kings 24:16; and as 3,023 in Jer. 52:28. Perhaps the last count offers an accurate total of adult males, whereas the other two figures are round numbers intended to include women and children.

19. Bright, *Jeremiah, op. cit.*, p. 211.

20. The logic of their position is clearly set forth in Bright, *ibid.*, pp. 265–266.

21. See William L. Holladay, "Jeremiah's Lawsuit with God," *Interpretation* 17 (1963): 280–287.

22. H. Wheeler Robinson, "Prophetic Symbolism," in D. C. Simpson, ed., *Old Testament Essays* (London: Charles Griffin, 1927), p. 15. Although it is not recent, this essay is quite helpful.

23. Abraham J. Heschel, *The Prophets* (New York: Harper & Row, 1963), p. 117.

24. We are in agreement with Hyatt, "Introduction and Exegesis to Jeremiah," *op. cit.*, p. 960.

25. For a more thorough presentation of Jeremiah's message, see Bright, *Jeremiah, op cit.*, pp. lxxxvi–cxviii.

16
JUDAH'S
BEARING
OF THE YOKE

The Babylonian yoke fell hard upon Yahweh's people. The faithful soberly conceded that in Nebuchadnezzar's conquest of Judah, Yahweh had responded to the nation's conscious neglect of the covenant. The chastening effects of historical adversity could not be averted. We intend now to describe the tenor of the Babylonian exile (587–538) and examine the contribution of Ezekiel, who prophesied in the early decades of the sixth century B.C. Though Ezekiel's bizarre personality tempts us not to linger with the book that bears his name, his provocative insights deserve a fair hearing.

THE PERIOD
OF EXILE

Judah's court officials, priests, and commoners all had reason to assess the Babylonian sack of Jerusalem as a most disruptive episode in the ongoing history of the people of God. We are poorly informed about the fate of Judah's citizens at this hour. Surely some died in their abortive attempt to defend the kingdom, some succumbed to starvation, some were executed by Babylonian officials, some fled to such places of refuge as Egypt and Transjordan, some were forced into Babylonian exile, and some were left to endure within a ravished land. The Jews who settled in Egypt succeeded in establishing a thriving but syncretic colony on the

Biblical texts to be read prior to and in conjunction with the present chapter: Lamentations 2, 4; Psalm 137; Ezekiel 1–24, 33–39.

island of Elephantine at the first cataract of the Nile.[1] Moreover, we have already noted the existence of Tahpanhes, the Jewish outpost on the Egyptian border where Jeremiah and his colleagues settled.

We know practically nothing about what happened in Judah during the half-century that followed Jerusalem's collapse. Even so, the Babylonian rape of the land has been attested through archaeological work conducted at such sites as Beth-shemesh, Lachish, and Debir. Neighboring Ammonite and Edomite inhabitants moved westward into Judah to plunder what they could. Judah was officially reorganized into a Babylonian provincial system. But unlike the Assyrians, the Babylonian officials resettled no foreigners in the newly conquered territory.

There must have been some stability under Gedaliah's governorship, but just how much we cannot say. Certainly his assassination and a third Babylonian deportation in 582 (Jer. 52:30) did not contribute to Judah's well-being. Nevertheless, the Jews persisted in their land. While they must have maintained a low profile, apparently they carried on some kind of cultic observance amid the charred debris of the Jerusalem Temple. With Judah's best days now past and with the props of royalty and Temple now upended, some Palestinian Jews must have completely abandoned the faith. Others, however, accepted the present moment as a justified instance of Yahweh's wrath. Many prophets, after all, had anticipated its arrival. Yet if that wrath were temporal, then perhaps the future would offer a brighter day. Nevertheless, depression was understandably the dominant emotion.

Then what was the Jewish situation in Babylon? If the count of 4,600 persons in Jeremiah 52 is an accurate indication of the number of adult males who had been deported in 597, 587, and 582 B.C., then the Jewish element in Babylon was not especially large. Yet among them were most of Judah's civil and religious leaders. Their physical situation was tolerable enough; they were permitted to live in agricultural communities of their own, build houses, assemble together, and even enter into commercial dealings. Some Jewish exiles who engaged in trade within this foreign land were quite successful. And though Jehoiachin was a prisoner of the Babylonian court, Judah's legitimate king was not dead. The more restless exiles might always hope that internal political chaos or international strife would overtake Babylon and pave the way for their return to Judah.

Undoubtedly the Jews in Babylon suffered more mentally and spiritually than they did physically. Babylon flourished under Nebuchadnezzar's long, successful rule (605–562). Certainly some Jews were led to wonder whether the splendors of Babylon and its patron deity, Marduk, had not eclipsed those of Jerusalem and its deity, Yahweh. The doctrine that Jerusalem enjoyed permanent protection as the eternal seat of Yahweh's residence had now been unmasked as sheer error. The unconditional promises of devine blessing to the Davidic dynasty had been

The Ishtar Gate from Babylon. Dating to the reign of
Nebuchadnezzar (605–562), this magnificent royal gate
received many stately processions as they advanced into the
palace courtyard. Note that one of the animals used in the
decoration of the gate (in the second row from the bottom,
for example) is a composite creature: it has a serpent's head
and a lion's body, and its hind talons are those of an eagle.
The reconstructed gate can be seen at the Staatliche
(Pergamon) Museum in East Berlin. (Courtesy of the
Staatliche Museum.)

rudely broken. Nowhere in the Hebrew Bible is the pain more evident
than in Psalm 137:

> By the waters of Babylon,
>   there we sat down and wept,
>   when we remembered Zion.

> On the willows there
>> we hung up our lyres.
> For there our captors
>> required of us songs,
> and our tormentors, mirth, saying,
>> "Sing us one of the songs of Zion!" (Ps. 137:1–3)

Nevertheless, the present indignities prompted some Jews to affirm their ancestral faith with even greater tenacity. Regular pilgrimages to the blackened ruins of Zion were out of the question. But a devout study of the Torah, weekly observance of the Sabbath, and the practice of circumcision helped God's people to maintain their identity in a foreign land. And perhaps the day was not too distant when Yahweh would honor his name at the expense of arrogant Babylonian power and release the Jews from their confinement. In sum, for many Jews, existence by the waters of Babylon was a theological embarrassment but not an existential impossibility.

THE BOOK OF LAMENTATIONS

The Book of Lamentations offers a lengthy funeral incantation that meditates on the awful tragedy of the fall of Jerusalem. It reflects the sorrow, anguish, and bitterness of those Palestinian Jews left to cope with a severely disrupted existence in their ruined homeland. While the themes in this book lack logical progression, they lay bare the several dimensions of this extreme moment in Judah's history.

Both the city's ruin and Yahweh's departure from his special place of residence are acknowledged:

> Yahweh has scorned his altar,
>> disowned his sanctuary;
> he has delivered into the hand of the enemy
>> the walls of her palaces ... (2:7)

The derision voiced by Judah's enemies is well described:

> All who pass along the way
>> clap their hands at you;
> they hiss and wag their heads
>> at the daughter of Jerusalem;
> "Is this the city which was called
>> the perfection of beauty,
>> the joy of all the earth?" (2:15)

The profound suffering of the people is unmistakably real:

> Remember my affliction and my bitterness,
>> the wormwood and the gall!

My soul continually thinks of it
and is bowed down within me. (3:19–20)

No less real, however, is the stubborn faith of the afflicted:

The steadfast love of Yahweh never ceases,
his mercies never come to an end;
they are new every morning;
great is thy faithfulness. (3:22–23)

Pleas that the defeated Jews examine themselves fully are also recorded:

Let us test and examine our ways,
and return to Yahweh!
Let us lift up our hearts and hands
to God in heaven. (3:40–41)

Each of the book's five chapters is a separate poem about the suffering and self-criticism experienced by Palestinian Judaism at this time. The detailed second and fourth poems are more widely recognized than the others as the work of eyewitnesses to Jerusalem's fall. Nevertheless, all five influenced the thought of exilic and postexilic Jews who annually commemorated the fall of Jerusalem on the ninth day of Ab. Chapters 1, 2, and 4 are funeral chants that reflect on the fall and pillage of Jerusalem. Chapter 3, which begins with the words, "I am the man who has seen affliction under the rod of his wrath," seems to embody the personal suffering of an individual. (Since the Hebrew Bible sometimes depicts communal experiences in individual terms, the case cannot be put more strongly.) By contrast, chapter 5 conveys a style and idiom especially appropriate to communal liturgies that were sometimes used by Yahweh's people in the face of national crisis (cf. Ps. 44, 60, 74, 79, 80, 83).

Chapters 1–4 of the book have two noteworthy features. They take the form of an acrostic in which the first letter of each line is a consonant of the Hebrew alphabet, and they use the Qinah, or lament meter (3+2), which Jeremiah and Ezekiel sometimes employed. While this pedagogic scheme may have been of some help to those who tried to memorize poetic texts, its primary function was probably to present "a literary form corresponding to the [author's] completeness of grief, responsibility and hope."[2] Because all five compositions have a somewhat similar ideology and style, they may be the work of one person. Nevertheless, certain variations in expression, mood, and thought discourage us from becoming dogmatic about the matter.

We may be confident, however, that these sincere, forceful poems are not the work of Jeremiah as ancient tradition would have us believe. The style of Jeremiah's poetic oracles and the idiom we encounter here have little in common. Moreover, Jeremiah never followed an acrostic sequence, which probably impressed him as too artificial. Nor does the anti-Babylonian stance expressed in Lam. 1:21–22 and 3:59–66 square with Jeremiah's position. Also Lam. 4:20 offers a concept of monarchy that does not mesh well with everything else we know about Jeremiah. And finally, the assertion that children suffer from the iniquities of their fathers (Lam. 5:7) is diametrically opposed to the stand Jeremiah took in Jer. 31:29–30.

But whoever its author is, the Book of Lamentations offers us a realistic glimpse of the disappointment that gripped those now condemned to live in their devastated home territory. Despite their precarious situation, this sturdy people did not renounce their faith. Nowhere is this more evident than in 3:19–33, a passage that projects "the indestructible optimism of those who faced history with the secure faith that the future belonged to their God."[3] At least some Judeans were convinced that Yahweh was still sovereign over history. He would somehow resolve the painful ironies of the present within the context of a triumphant future. Though the veil that conceals how Yahweh will bring this to pass is not lifted, a quiet hope in the future is nevertheless expressed.

THE BOOK, PERSON, AND MESSAGE OF EZEKIEL

Literary and Historical Considerations

Psychologically Ezekiel is the Hebrew prophet most distant from our own time. He strikes many readers as an unappealing man who is extraordinarily difficult to interpret. His oracles, which are full of threats and denunciations, can be extremely shrill. However, this austere prophet was able to communicate a penetrating theology of hope. Ultimately his words of comfort were crucial to an exiled people sorely in need of direction and reassurance.

The large blocks of material in the Book of Ezekiel are well organized. Each major section has a specific purpose: chapters 1–24 forecast Jerusalem's imminent destruction, chapters 25–32 speak against the foreign nations, chapters 33–39 expound a theology of hope, and chapters 40–48 disclose the prophet's vision of a restored people, Temple, and land. This orderliness is mainly the outcome of a thorough editing of numerous components as the book took final shape.

Nevertheless, the composition of the Book of Ezekiel has been the subject of remarkably diverse opinion. Judgments by twentieth-century biblical scholars on its unity and date of composition, as well as on the locale of the prophet's career, vary greatly.[4] For example, in 1913 Driver insisted that the book bore "unmistakably the stamp of a single mind."[5] A direct confrontation of the book was enough to convey the impression of unity. But roughly a decade later, Hölscher challenged the book's integrity and unity of authorship.[6] Of the 1,273 verses in Ezekiel, Hölscher

claimed only 170 for the prophet. He did so on the assumption that Ezekiel was a poet of a high order who had nothing to do with the "poor"
prose that dominates the book. Only a few prose units were thought to
be his. Moreover, on metrical grounds, Hölscher held that much of the
poetry was not written by Ezekiel.

Under the influence of such critics as Rowley, Howie, and Muilenburg, the tendency in our time is to attribute much more of the book to
the prophet.[7] Today's critics are likely to contend that the secondary
components in the book are not that numerous. The strong impression of
Ezekiel's personality is given some credence. Further, the hard-and-fast
rule that Ezekiel wrote poetry almost exclusively is rejected by most contemporary critics.

Hölscher has been able to foster an appreciation for Ezekiel's poetic
genius, but on what reasonable grounds may it be asserted that with rare
exception the prophet composed only poetic oracles? The prose in Ezekiel is sometimes pedantic and monotonous, but at its best it is lucid and
instructive. Moreover, on occasion Ezekiel may have offered a prose interpretation of his own poetic oracle. Where that interpretation fails to
understand the poetry in question, its authenticity should, of course, be
suspected. Nevertheless, we had best approach the text with an open
mind.

In sum, the Book of Ezekiel must have been subjected to extensive
editing. Otherwise, jarring transitions, duplicate speeches, and a double
superscription (1:1 and 1:2–3 are not a unit) cannot be explained. Yet
the book that masks the prophet is also the book that tells us who he is.

The question of where the prophet pursued his career has likewise
received many different answers. A simple reading of the text suggests
that along with other Jews, a priest named Ezekiel was deported to Babylon in 597, and that in the fifth year of Jehoiachin's exile (593 [1:2]),
Ezekiel received his call to the prophetic office on Babylonian soil near
the Chebar canal. Accordingly, the prophet addressed his fellow exiles
in Babylon, and so he functioned down to the year 571 (on the basis of
the latest dated oracle in the book [29:17]).

Yet Ezekiel's close contact with Palestine has led some interpreters
to assert that at least part of the prophet's ministry took place in Palestine. The problem is compounded by Ezekiel's extraordinary psychic
talents. This mystic may have had knowledge of events that were taking
place far from where he was. The crux of the problem lies in chapter 11,
where seemingly in the context of vision, Ezekiel, now a Babylonian resident, sees twenty-five men at the east gate of the Jerusalem Temple. (The
visionary aspect of Ezekiel 11 is suggested at the outset by the statement,
"The Spirit lifted me up.") Among the men is Pelatiah (v. 1). Yahweh
commands Ezekiel to prophesy against this iniquitous group (v. 4). Some
verses later Ezekiel states, "And it came to pass, while I was prophesying, that Pelatiah the son of Benaiah died" (v. 13). Does Ezekiel's men-

tion of Pelatiah's death make necessary the conclusion that some, if not all, of the prophet's career was conducted on Palestinian soil?

Critics have proposed three different answers. The first is that Ezekiel worked closely with his Jerusalem contemporaries and only later were his posthumous writings linked with a Babylonian setting. Thus, Herntrich insists that the prophet's oracles addressed to Jerusalem were actually spoken there. In Herntrich's estimation, a disciple of Ezekiel who edited the prophet's sayings expanded chapters 1–39, wrote chapters 40–48, and assigned a Babylonian setting to the total literary product.[8]

The second answer is that Ezekiel's ministry took place partly in Palestine and partly in Babylon. Oesterley and Robinson have emended Ezek. 1:2, and they claim that Ezekiel's career began in Jerusalem in 602 during the fifth year of Jehoiakim's reign. Therefore, the prophet censured Jerusalem's inhabitants prior to the first Babylonian assault on the city in 597.[9] Having committed his denunciations to writing shortly after voicing them, Ezekiel took this literary material with him when he was whisked away into Babylonian captivity in 597. During his Babylonian residence, the prophet added to those writings, and finally one of his disciples gave the entire written work its exilic stamp.[10]

The third answer, which we believe is the most compelling, claims an exclusively Babylonian ministry for the prophet.[11] Several reasons may be given. In the first place, Ezekiel's clairvoyance might well have equipped him to transcend those barriers of time and space that restrict less gifted persons. Perhaps Ezekiel had an awareness of events taking place in Jerusalem without being physically present in that metropolis. And mention of Jeremiah's letter to the Babylonian exiles in Jeremiah 29 confirms that there was some contact between these two centers. Ezekiel may have been partly informed of Jerusalem's situation through letters, and in letters dispatched from Babylon to Jerusalem the opinions of Ezekiel would have reached his homeland. Moreover, oracles directed against a given locale do not necessarily require the physical presence of the one who pronounces them (see Amos 1–2). Even the text in Ezekiel 11, which seems to imply that by virtue of the uncanny power of his prophetic utterance Ezekiel killed an inhabitant of Jerusalem, is not an insurmountable problem. The text does not claim that Pelatiah's death was the direct result of Ezekiel's speech. The phrase "while I was prophesying" (v. 13) might cover a great interval of time. It is also difficult to understand why a disciple-editor would have assigned a Babylonian residence, and only a Babylonian residence, to his mentor if at least part of his career had been spent on Palestinian soil.

We may, therefore, feel somewhat confident that the extant Book of Ezekiel stems mainly from the prophet himself, who ministered to the needs of his fellow exiles in Babylon. Although the text has some glosses and additions, even these reflect Ezekiel's perspective.

In all likelihood, Ezekiel was deported to Babylon in 597. Presumably in 593 he was called to the prophetic office, and in the years that ensued his career unfolded. The first phase (593–587) involved Ezekiel's judgment of the present, and the second (587–571) invited the prophet to be assuring about the future. Before we confront the judgmental element of Ezekiel's pronouncements, however, we must consider the bizarre call of this clairvoyant prophet.

Invitation to the Prophetic Office

The detailed account of Ezekiel's summons to the prophetic office consists of his vision of a throne chariot (1:4–28) and of five commissions (2:1–3:27). Many aspects of the vision are difficult to comprehend. Certainly they are alien to our own experience. Nevertheless, they introduce us to a theological perspective that dominates many of Ezekiel's proclamations: Yahweh is unmistakably transcendent. This vision made it quite clear to the prophet that the deity, who manifests his august presence in the world, exists beyond the reach of men.

The theophany that begins in 1:4 is prefaced by a superscription reporting that Ezekiel lived near the Chebar canal close to the Babylonian city of Nippur. The specification of the "thirtieth year" mentioned at the head of the composite superscription (1:1) has yet to receive a truly compelling interpretation. While it is the latest date offered in the book, presumably it designates the time of the prophet's call. If so, it lies outside the network of other chronological notations in Ezekiel, which refer to various points in the prophet's ministry. The number has been interpreted in many ways: as the thirtieth year after Josiah's reform (592), as the thirtieth year following the founding of the neo-Babylonian empire (596), and as the thirtieth year of the prophet's life. While the last possibility is attractive, the reference to month and day suggests a political dating of some kind. If the thirtieth year refers to the year of Judah's exile, then it might indicate the date for the initial composition of the Ezekiel scroll. A few critics have emended "thirtieth" to read "thirteenth"; they either calculate from the time of Jehoiachin's captivity (deriving the date 585) or accept it as the year of Nebuchadnezzar's reign (592). Most scholars, however, have hesitated to revise the number itself, although mention of the "thirtieth" year in 1:1 is admittedly puzzling.

This singular theophanic experience of Ezekiel seems to have taken place during a thunderstorm.[12] He observes a great cloud from the north (1:4); living creatures resembling flashes of lightning (1:14); the noise of the heavenly beings corresponding to that of many waters (1:24); and the throne of the deity, which looks like a "bow that is in the cloud on the day of rain" (1:28a). God's mobility is emphasized by the wheel imagery. Yahweh is not merely a native of Palestine.

In this complex vision, the four "living creatures" (1:5) are cherubim, the traditional guardians of the deity. As the vision unfolds, the prophet is unable to describe the supernatural. Detail accumulates as he tries to put the ineffable into words. Even so, the transcendent deity impinges on the prophet. Ezekiel is in a foreign land, but he nevertheless claims that Yahweh's hand is on him (1:3). Although Ezekiel fails to provide a coherent account of this episode, we may be certain that it was incredibly real to him.

As the theophany progresses, the deity's throne chariot receives special attention (1:15–28). Above the heads of living creatures and their extended wings is the firmament, which constitutes its platform. The likeness of the firmament resembles the splendid color of sapphires. But as Ezekiel comes closer to describing the deity, he knows that all words will betray him. His reticence in the face of divine mystery reaches its climax in the feeble statement, "Such was the appearance of the likeness of the glory of Yahweh" (1:28b). Ezekiel's response is understandable: "And when I saw it, I fell upon my face" (1:28c). The visual elements of the theophany recede as the prophet hears Yahweh's voice in a series of five commissions.

In the first commission account (2:1–8a), Yahweh commands the prophet to censure the rebellious people of Israel, warns him of the hostile audience he will meet, and tells him not to fear human impudence and stubbornness. Ezekiel is called "son of man," which admirably conveys his sense of remoteness and finitude before transcendent divine being. In this Hebrew idiom, "son" designates a member of a class (cf. Amos 7:14) and "man" (*'ādhām*) is a collective noun referring to mankind. Ezekiel is a man and nothing more. This image of man as a lowly mortal often appears in Yahweh's speeches to Ezekiel. But even as a circumscribed creature, the prophet is required to stand on his feet in order to hear what the deity has to say. Indeed, he is being summoned to no less a task than that of articulating Yahweh's will to his contemporaries. And whatever the people's response to Ezekiel's message will be, they must recognize that one of Yahweh's prophets has made himself known in their midst (2:5).

At Yahweh's direction, Ezekiel eats a papyrus scroll covered on both sides with words of lamentation, mourning, and woe (2:8b–3:3). By eating the scroll, the prophet appropriates its content. Mention of its sweet taste implies that Ezekiel accepts its words as entirely suitable for the occasion (3:3).[13] Jeremiah had himself claimed that his experience of eating Yahweh's words was marked by joy and delight (Jer. 15:16).

In Ezekiel's second commission (3:4–9), the unpleasant side of the prophetic call is elaborated. The people will ignore Ezekiel as he speaks in Yahweh's behalf. At least foreigners would have respected the origin of the divine word and given the prophet a cordial hearing. Even so,

Ezekiel will be fortified for the burdensome task. Yahweh will give him a forehead of adamant (3:9)—that is, an imaginary stone of infinite hardness (cf. Jer. 1:18).

The third commission (3:10–15) reinforces the preceding one. It is a crisp instruction that the prophet receive and proclaim the entire oracle of Yahweh. Ezekiel's listening and speaking are vital to the fulfillment of the divine will. The attention of the people is not.

In the fourth commission (3:16–21), Ezekiel is depicted as Israel's watchman. Due to its close relation with 33:1–20, this commission has often been interpreted as setting in motion a new phase of the prophet's career.[14] It seems to have no genuine connection with the original account of Ezekiel's call. In marked contrast with 3:4–9, which dismisses Israel as a rebellious house incapable of repentance, 3:16–21 entertains the possibility of such a transformation on the part of individual members of the covenant community. Ezekiel 3:16–21 joins 14:12–23; 18:1–32; and 33:1–20 in espousing a doctrine of individual responsibility.[15] In the present editing of the book, that doctrine is directly related to Ezekiel's invitation to the prophetic office. Ezekiel is expected to issue warnings so that the people of God may escape danger. The role of watchman is defined in remarkably precise language in four distinct situations (3:18, 19, 20, 21). As Israel's watchman, Ezekiel bears a special responsibility for the welfare of Yahweh's people.

The last commission (3:22–27) is disturbing, for it focuses on Ezekiel's dumbness. How can a Hebrew prophet function if he is not permitted to speak for seven and a half years? In 24:26–27, which is dated four and a half years later than the commission under examination, Ezekiel is informed that his muteness will disappear on the day he is visited by a fugitive with news of Jerusalem's fall. In 33:21–22, which dates three years after 24:26–27, the fugitive appears and Ezekiel is freed of his affliction. This protracted interval of silence, which appears to come immediately after Ezekiel has been summoned to the prophetic office, is difficult to accept at face value.

Two answers to the problem might be proposed here. First, we might argue that 3:22–27 is a misplaced passage that belongs to the end of the judgmental phase of Ezekiel's career.[16] This would mean that at some time close to Jerusalem's collapse in July 587, the prophet engaged in a symbolic act of dumbness as a vivid way of instructing his fellow exiles that Yahweh had turned his back on his people. Once Ezekiel learned that the city had been taken, he gave up this symbolic behavior. Second, we might argue that early in his career, Ezekiel was struck dumb by the deity in the sense that he could speak on one and only one matter—Jerusalem's impending doom.[17] Until the dreaded fall of Jerusalem had become a historical reality, Ezekiel was required to remain within his own house. To those who visited him the prophet was permitted to speak only on this topic, which was his prophetic obsession.

Proclamations of Doom

If Yahweh's intention in revealing his splendor at the Chebar canal was to press into service someone who would devote himself to pronouncing oracles of impending doom, then he was remarkably successful. As long as Jerusalem stood intact, Ezekiel uttered harsh threats and denunciations (chaps. 4–24).

Moreover, out of the conviction that like produces like, and that the divine will is brought one step closer to fruition through symbolic undertakings, Ezekiel communicated the burden of his message in a number of significant symbolic acts. On a sun-dried brick he drew a portrait of Jerusalem under attack, and then with the help of an iron plate he simulated the siege that its inhabitants would soon experience (4:1–3). To symbolize the number of years that Israel would be punished, Ezekiel was commanded to lie on his left side for 390 days. Then to symbolize the number of years of Judah's punishment, he was instructed to lie on his right side for 40 days (4:4–8). But the text nowhere states that the prophet carried out this instruction. Perhaps Ezekiel did so in some symbolic way, but we really do not know.

As a third act symbolic of Jerusalem's fate, the prophet is instructed to eat meager, defiled rations (4:9–17). Hunger, thirst, and dismay are all to be experienced by Jerusalem's inhabitants at the time of the siege (4:17). In still another symbolic act, the fate of the city's populace is depicted through Ezekiel's hair, which is cut off with a sharp sword (5:1–17). A third of it is burned, another third is struck with a sword, and the last third is scattered to the wind. Yet as the text now stands, some of the prophet's hair is to be fixed to his robe (5:3). A ray of hope is thereby offered in what is surely an expanded version of the original.

Two other symbolic acts deserve mention. In 12:1–16 Ezekiel simulates the experience of an exile who must pack his luggage and leave the doomed city of Jerusalem. As his compatriots look on, he digs a hole in the wall of his mud-brick dwelling and pulls himself through along with his baggage.[18] Then in 24:15–24 Ezekiel responds oddly to the death of his beloved wife. He neither laments her loss nor mourns according to the custom of the time. He instructs the people that the impending loss of their own sons and daughters and the profanation of the Jerusalem Temple will be so horrendous that it will have a numbing effect on them. Their shock will be so severe that they will be unable to express themselves in mourning.

Though many of Ezekiel's symbolic acts were effective, he also had the capacity to express himself in extended prophetic utterances. Here, too, his anticipation of the end of Judah and Jerusalem was poignant. Ezekiel was intent on conveying Yahweh's piercing judgment against Judah for its breach of faith. On occasion Yahweh's case against his people is presented in a tedious prose that tends toward the forensic. However, the motifs of the people's covenant dereliction and the resulting divine judgment are treated with significant variation. In chapter 6 the people's idolatry is denounced, in chapter 7 warranted punishment is forecast, in chapters 8–11 several descriptions of the impending doom are offered, in chapters 12–19 Jerusalem's deplorable record is surveyed, and in chapters 20–24 further oracles of judgment are articulated. In the paragraphs that follow, we shall focus on the major themes in this oracular material.

Denunciation of the People's Idolatry. In chapter 6 the prophet censures the idolatry that exists throughout Palestine. His charge begins, "You mountains of Israel, hear the word of Yahweh" (6:3). As the central hill country, the mountains constitute the geographical backbone of Palestine, but theologically they are the locus of the idolatrous cults Yahweh will no longer tolerate. After Josiah's death, the numerous high places were reopened and their cultic programs reactivated. There Yahwism continued to be confused with various Canaanite forms of worship. Thus, the deity was made the object of impure rites. The cultic hardware of idols, altars, and incense is specifically referred to (6:4–6) as are the severe consequences of pestilence, violence, and famine that such profanation of the deity will bring (6:12). Obviously the people as well as the mountains are criticized.

The deity warns the faithless that at the time of assault, "You shall know that I am Yahweh" (6:7). The declaration that men will one day recognize the deity appears everywhere in the Book of Ezekiel. The knowledge of Yahweh that concerns the prophet is not intellectual familiarity with his various attributes. Rather, it is a recognition in faith of Yahweh's sovereignty and majesty. This knowledge is a willingness on man's part to submit to a deity who is vastly greater than he. In the present instance, the idolators will know Yahweh—first in moments of devastation and severe hardship, and later in confessing the effective lordship of this majestic deity who has entered into a covenant relationship with Israel. For Ezekiel, human history and experience reveal the deity, and in such revelation, which frequently is chastening in character, comes saving knowledge.

The idolatry that Ezekiel castigates in chapter 8 centers on deplorable cultic undertakings in the Jerusalem Temple. Ezekiel is transported by Yahweh's spirit to the Temple's inner court. There he sees an "image of jealousy" (8:5). This reference may refer to a slab on which are depicted mythological scenes that compromised the interests of a purified Yahwism. He also spies a wall with "all kinds of creeping things, and loathsome beasts" (8:10). As if this indication of (Egyptian?) syncretism were not enough, the prophet then witnesses seventy Israelite elders meeting in a darkened chamber to offer incense and participate in obscure cultic rites. Their chant is particularly revealing: "Yahweh does not see us, Yahweh has forsaken the land" (8:12). Ezekiel encounters women weeping over the death of Tammuz, the Akkadian nature god (8:14). Finally Ezekiel is shown twenty-five men who are worshiping the sun (8:16). He is informed (albeit obscurely) that some have provoked the deity because "they put the branch to their nose" (8:17). The Temple tour now completed, the prophet hears the vehement word of divine judgment (8:18). The outraged deity has no intention of yielding to the cries of these insane cultic practitioners on the day of their calamity. Surely Jerusalem's destruction is fated.

Visionary Witness of the Departure of Yahweh's Glory. With one exception (31:18), in Ezekiel the noun "glory" (*kābôdh*) always refers to some manifestation of the deity. And apart from 39:21, mention of Yahweh's glory appears in three different situations: the initial vision and commission of Ezekiel, the departure of the glory from the Jerusalem Temple, and its eventual return to the restored Jerusalem.[19] The glory is so closely identified with Yahweh that its departure from the Temple means that Yahweh has himself abandoned the premises. The glory mounts up from the cherubim and takes its place at the threshold of the Temple (9:3a). Though it returns to the cherubim (10:18), the cherubim themselves lift up their wings and prepare to leave the Temple (10:19). Finally, the glory leaves Jerusalem (11:22–23).

This event was of profound concern to the prophet. Having been reared on the priestly theology of his time, Ezekiel understood that the presence of the divine glory in the Jerusalem Temple guaranteed the cultic presence of the deity. In anticipation of the threatened destruction of the Temple, Yahweh's cultic continuity with Mount Zion is now interrupted. Future prospects are grim.

Perception of the People's Profanation of the Covenant. Yahweh's case against his people is well expressed in Ezekiel 13–14, which meditates on the guilt of Judah's leaders as well as its people. Throughout chapter 13 Yahweh's invective against the false prophets of both sexes is vehement. These individuals see no authentic visions; they are the victims of their own delusions. They say what is pleasing to their audience—words of " 'Peace,' when there is no peace" (13:10). Instead of speaking a word of transcendent criticism, which might have the ultimate effect of protecting their people, they have chosen an easier course and left their people defenseless against the impending day of judgment.

Ezekiel accuses these false prophets of daubing the walls with whitewash to make the cracks invisible (13:10–11). The female prophets in Jerusalem who have yielded to various forms of sorcery and have capitalized upon deceptive visions are likewise exposed (13:17–23). In chapter 14 Ezekiel roundly condemns a group of elders who have worshiped foreign idols. For their infidelity they will be cut off from the covenant people. Moreover, Ezekiel insists that righteousness is not negotiable. Past Israelite worthies such as Noah and Job, along with a righteous Canaanite man of antiquity named Dan'el, might save themselves by virtue of their goodness (14:14). Nevertheless, their upright conduct cannot compensate for Judah's outrageous wrong in repeatedly profaning Yahweh's name and holiness.[20]

Allegorical Expression of the People's Infidelity. Ezekiel has left us two allegories on the harlotry of Jerusalem. In chapter 16 the city is viewed as a foundling who in her adulthood commits harlotry, and in chapter 23 she is regarded as the younger of two sisters who have become harlots. Since Jerusalem had long existed as a Canaanite city, Ezekiel was historically accurate in addressing Jerusalem: "Your origin and your birth are of the land of the Canaanites; your father was an Amorite, and your mother a Hittite" (16:3). His main concern, however, was not to teach ancient history but to give voice to prophetic judgment.

According to the allegory in chapter 16, Jerusalem had been abandoned by her parents, but one day was found by Yahweh who reared her, decked her in elaborate attire, and even took her in marriage. But by placing more confidence in her own beauty than in her husband, Jerusalem settled on a course of harlotry and forgot the days of her youth (16:22). Her deplorable conduct resulted in her failure to remember her covenant duty as Yahweh's bride.[21] For having turned her back on Yahweh and adopting the religion of Ba°al, she now stands condemned.

In chapter 23 the situation is the same; harlotry derives from an original depravity and evokes Yahweh's wrath and judgment. But now two harlot sisters are involved, and the crime is political infidelity. The two cities, Samaria and Jerusalem, are named Oholah (meaning "she who has a tent") and Oholibah (meaning "my tent [is] in her"), respectively. Yahweh married both sisters and to him were born sons and daughters (23:4). Then defection set in. The reference to Oholah's disloyalty (23:5–10) vaguely recalls Samaria's political alliances with Assyria. The outraged deity finally delivered Oholah into Assyrian hands. Oholibah's defection from her husband is presented in 23:11–21, in which she successively chases Assyria, Babylonia, and Egypt. At length Yahweh warns that such infidelity will not go unpunished (23:22–35). Oholibah's lovers will turn against her to her complete undoing. The deity warns, "You have gone the way of your sister; therefore I will give her cup into your hand" (23:31). Such allegories were one vehicle of the prophet's negative pronouncements.

Conviction about Individual Responsibility. Ezekiel was enthusiastic in his belief that each individual in the covenant community is accountable to Yahweh. In chapter 18 the importance of individual human responsibility and the reality of divine righteousness are both persuasively expressed. The entire episode is sparked by the popular maxim, "The fathers have eaten sour grapes, and the children's teeth are set on edge" (18:2). This proverb, which we have already noted in Jer. 31:29, seeks to justify man's natural tendency to blame others for his present plight. This is what the exiles were doing in Babylon. By citing the proverb, they were implying that the sins of their fathers had placed them within an adverse environment.

Ezekiel argues that the blame rests with the exiles themselves. The chapter is full of specifics defending the notion of individual accountability. The injustice of Israel, not God, is at the root of the problem (18:25). While the presentation may strike us as unnecessarily explicit and even tedious, Ezekiel is trying to honor the transcendent deity and to comfort the downhearted. The chapter ends on a strong note of admonition and hope (18:30–32). Since Yahweh is by nature just, the people are invited to repent and return to the deity. While cheap grace is not advertised, the prophet's oracle communicates Yahweh's clear-cut offer of salvation. Ezekiel is inviting his contemporaries to participate in significant decision making and action.

Proclamations of Hope

In Ezekiel 33–48 the prophet is essentially a dedicated spokesman of hope. Significant oracles of restoration are advanced in chapters 33–39, and the vision of the restored Temple and land appears in chapters 40–48. Indeed, the later phase of Ezekiel's career found him speaking primarily of promise and support. Again we shall attempt to highlight the major themes of the biblical text.

News of Jerusalem's Fall. In 33:21–22 a highly crucial event is depicted. A fugitive comes to inform Ezekiel that Jerusalem has fallen to the Babylonians. The vindicated prophet is now freed of his dumbness. Perhaps Judah's history will take a new turn. Nevertheless, the prophet is in no position to dream of urban restoration. The flaws of a delinquent people must still be addressed. Even so, word of Jerusalem's collapse must have encouraged Ezekiel to rethink his course a little.

The People's Rebirth and the Good Shepherd. By means of the shepherd motif in chapter 34, Ezekiel engaged in a frontal attack on the covenant community's impoverished leadership. Presumably he uttered the oracle soon after Jerusalem succumbed to the Babylonian forces. Israel's shepherd-kings no longer occupied the throne; for having shirked their responsibilities, they had been removed. But Ezekiel believed that

Yahweh would establish himself as the good shepherd in their place (34:10).

Though 34:23–24 expresses a messianic hope, Ezekiel does not anticipate a resurrection of the historical David. Nor does he think that Yahweh will establish a king as such. The era of the Judean kingdom is past. Nevertheless, the shepherd prince anticipated by the prophet will function as a divinely appointed leader in the days to come. In a limited sense, the Davidic dynasty will continue. In the new age the people will have a vital knowledge of the God who has delivered them (34:27). They will also be free from enemy harassment (34:28). In sum, chapter 34 projects Ezekiel's confidence that in the time ahead, Israel will be redeemed.

The People's Restoration to the Land. In Ezekiel 36, hope and restoration are further articulated. Yahweh assures his exiled people that they will fare well in their former land, to which they are about to be returned. Moreover, they will no longer betray the God who intends to bring them back.

The promise, however, is couched in an idiom that has irritated some contemporary readers. It insists that Yahweh is acting out of concern for himself rather than out of concern for his people (36:23). Ezekiel fervently desires to represent Yahweh as acting in his own right. He assumes that with the presence of the exiles in Babylonian captivity, Yahweh's reputation among the nations has greatly suffered. Therefore, Yahweh will act so that the nations will again recognize his supremacy. No longer will his holy name be profaned. Nonetheless, in this chapter Ezekiel reflects on Israel's needs. He meditates on the new day that lies in store for the covenant community, and he boldly declares that Israel will enjoy a new heart, one made of flesh (36:26).

The Valley of Dry Bones. The people's rebirth is further signaled in 37:1–14 through the familiar vision of dry bones. Ezekiel is lifted by the spirit and relocated in the middle of a valley that is "full of bones." There the deity instructs him in what he is to say to the lifeless bones that appear before him. An animating breath will enter these bones, which represent "the whole house of Israel" (37:11a). This oracle does not promise the resurrection of the individual from the grave (as does Dan. 12); it focuses on the resurrection of the nation itself. Coming at a time when the people have lost all hope (37:11b), the message is resonant in its declaration that a new life is in the offing for Yahweh's people.

The Symbolic Reunification of Judah and Israel. In 37:15–28 Ezekiel is commanded to take part in an act that will symbolize Yahweh's intention to reunite the splintered kingdoms of Judah and Israel. By writing the name "Judah" on one stick and the name "Joseph" on another and then binding the sticks together, Ezekiel is to assure his exiled contemporaries that Yahweh will do more than simply restore them to their land. He will also reunite them. Over the people Yahweh will appoint a "king" resembling David (vv. 22, 24). The role of the people's leader is ambiguous, but on the whole, the description of the new David buttresses 34:23–24, which lacks the word "king." In any case, under new conditions of reunion, the people will live a faithful, obedient existence. They will enjoy the benefits of an everlasting covenant of peace and Yahweh's presence in their midst.

The Gog and Magog Oracles. Ezekiel's famous prophecy about the king Gog and his nation Magog appears in chapters 38–39. Neither name is identified, although this enemy people and its monarch are said to come from the north. The issue of Yahweh's dominion weighed heavily on Ezekiel. In the light of the people's flagrant violation of the covenant, it was entirely fitting that Yahweh would permit Israel's foes to overtake her. Yet in the process, Yahweh's reputation had been severely damaged. Kraeling cogently refers to the "psychological basis" operative here: "The re-establishment of respect for himself is now his [Yahweh's] main concern. Hence he will send a foe again—this time a real northern one— and will destroy him utterly. That will be proof to the world of his sovereignty."[22]

Gog is to be thought of as the leader of both historical and mythological forces that seek to overthrow Yahweh's people. The deity is portrayed as a triumphant being who conquers the proud powers that would assert their dominion throughout the world. Two versions of the catastrophe are offered. In the first (chap. 38), Yahweh takes the initiative. He leads Gog and all his army into Israel where they are to be defeated. In the second (chap. 39), Gog himself devises the mischievous scheme. He encroaches on the peaceful, open land of Israel, but fails miserably in his attempt to conquer.

Presumably a massive battle on earth's last day with all its apocalyptic imagery did not dominate Ezekiel's thought to the extent that these two chapters imply. The original reflections of the prophet have been expanded in this independent literary unit. Yet to the extent that these events reestablish the good name and esteem of the deity, they represent the thought of the prophet.

The Restored Temple and Land. In chapters 40–48 Ezekiel presents himself as an architect of the future. In some form these chapters undoubtedly originated with Ezekiel. As a priest (1:3), he had a genuine interest in Temple and ritualistic matters. In chapters 34, 36, and 37, he had already portrayed Israel's restoration to her homeland. Now he was to communicate a detailed but historically unrealized blueprint that centered on a restored Temple (40:1–43:12), a renewed cult (43:13–47:12), and a rejuvenated land (47:13–48:35).

Of greatest importance here is the dramatic return of Yahweh's glory to the Temple in 43:1–12. The text is declaring that what once was, now is. Since the glory has come back to its former site in the Jerusalem Temple, Israel may once more approach the future optimistically. Yahweh is again meaningfully present with his people.

The most interesting feature of the restored cult relates to the priorities of the priesthood. The Zadokites will serve as head priests, and under them will be the Levites. The menial status of the latter is said to be a fitting punishment for their participation in improper forms of worship at the high places (44:10–14).

As for the restoration of the land, the prophet's vision boldly ignores geographical realities and ancient tribal boundaries. He accords to each tribe the same amount of land. In the middle of the land will be the Temple. Immediately surrounding that edifice will be territory owned by the princes and priests. The tribe of Judah will have land to the immediate north and Benjamin will claim land to the immediate south. Finally, Jerusalem will be renamed "Yahweh-shammah," meaning "Yahweh is there" (48:35). This itself is an unmistakably dynamic element of prophetic hope.

Here we take leave of the stern, bizzare, and visionary Ezekiel. Although he lacked a winning personality, he helped his people come to terms with their fractured relationship with the covenant deity. He led them to the recognition that Jerusalem's destruction was historically and theologically inevitable. And he was an effective pastor to an exiled flock. In sum, Ezekiel helped ancient Israel to understand herself as the nation still mysteriously foremost in the mind of the deity who had originally called her into existence. The people of God had experienced their undoing. Renewal, however, was already in the making.

NOTES

1. Throughout the fifth century, the Jews on the island of Elephantine successfully accommodated to the political, economic, and religious dimensions of their Egyptian environment. A temple of Yahu (a variant of the name "Yahweh") that was built at Elephantine served as the nucleus of the faith. But Egyptian nationalists destroyed that edifice in 410. In an Elephantine letter dated to the last decade of the fifth century, the Jews requested permission from the Jerusalem authorities to rebuild their temple; for the text, see James B. Pritchard, ed., *Ancient Near Eastern Texts Relating to the Old Testament*, 3d ed. (Princeton, N.J.: Princeton University Press, 1969), pp. 491–492. Despite their unorthodox practice of worshiping Yahweh and a few other deities as well, the Jews of Elephantine wished to maintain contact with Palestinian Judaism. This is but one of a corpus of Aramaic letters depicting the fate of fifth-century Judaism at Elephantine.

2. Norman K. Gottwald, *Studies in the Book of Lamentations*, Studies in

Biblical Theology, no. 14 (London: SCM Press, 1954), p. 32. Hillers states that acrostic compositions were probably used for a number of different reasons. (Delbert R. Hillers, *Lamentations: Introduction, Translation, and Notes,* The Anchor Bible, vol. 7A [Garden City, N.Y.: Doubleday, 1972], p. xxvi.)

3. Gottwald, *op. cit.,* p. 110.

4. For a more detailed presentation, see H. H. Rowley, "The Book of Ezekiel in Modern Study," *Bulletin of the John Rylands Library* 36 (1953–1954): 146–190; and W. A. Irwin, "Ezekiel Research since 1943," *Vetus Testamentum* 3 (1953): 54–66. Your author's comments in this section have been informed by Rowley's article.

5. S. R. Driver, *An Introduction to the Literature of the Old Testament,* 9th ed. (New York: Charles Scribner's Sons, 1913), p. 279.

6. Gustav Hölscher, *Hesekiel, der Dichter und das Buch* (Giessen, Ger.: A. Töpelmann, 1924).

7. Rowley, *op. cit.;* Carl G. Howie, *The Date and Composition of Ezekiel,* Journal of Biblical Literature Monograph Series, vol. 4 (Philadelphia: Society of Biblical Literature, 1950); James Muilenburg, "Ezekiel," in Matthew Black and H. H. Rowley, eds., *Peake's Commentary on the Bible,* rev. ed., (New York: Thomas Nelson & Sons, 1962), pp. 568–590.

8. Volkmar Herntrich, *Ezechielprobleme* (Giessen, Ger.: A. Töpelmann, 1932).

9. W. O. E. Oesterley and Theodore H. Robinson, *An Introduction to the Books of the Old Testament* (New York: Macmillan, 1934), pp. 328–329.

10. For another defense of the prophet's double ministry, see Herbert G. May, "Introduction and Exegesis to Ezekiel," in George A. Buttrick et al., eds., *The Interpreter's Bible* (Nashville: Abingdon Press, 1956), vol. 6, pp. 51–53.

11. For data bearing on the third answer that go far beyond what can be stated here, see Howie, *op. cit.,* pp. 5–26, and Rowley, *op. cit.,* pp. 173–176.

12. Storm theophanies are rather frequent in the Hebrew Bible; see Exod. 19:16, Job 38:1, and especially Ps. 18:7–15.

13. For brief comment on the ecstatic dimensions of this experience and mention of several parallels from biblical and extrabiblical literature, see Johannes Lindblom, *Prophecy in Ancient Israel* (Philadelphia: Fortress Press, 1962), p. 190.

14. So Muilenburg, *op. cit.,* p. 572; and Emil G. Kraeling, *Commentary on the Prophets* (New York: Thomas Nelson & Sons, 1966), 1: 414.

15. For a thorough treatment of this doctrine, see Barnabas Lindars, "Ezekiel and Individual Responsibility," *Vetus Testamentum* 15 (1965): 452–467.

16. This, for example, is the approach of Georg Fohrer, *Die Hauptprobleme des Buches Ezechiel* (Berlin: A. Töpelmann, 1952), p. 30.

17. See Moshe Greenberg, "On Ezekiel's Dumbness," *Journal of Biblical Literature* 77 (1958): 101–105. Especially instructive is the parallel Greenberg adduces from the writings of Josephus; it involves a certain Jesus, son of Ananias, who for seven years and five months uttered his message of woe in Jerusalem.

18. Especially in 12:8–16 the original symbolic act has been reinterpreted to apply to Zedekiah's abortive attempt to escape from the Babylonians.

19. On the initial vision and commission of Ezekiel, see Ezek. 1:28; 3:12, 23; 8:4. On the departure of the glory from the Temple, see Ezek. 9:3; 10:4, 18, 19; 11:22, 23. On the return of the glory to the restored Jerusalem, see Ezek. 43:2, 4, 5; 44:4.

20. The Dan'el reference probably applies to the hero of Ugaritic rather than biblical legend. For further data and bibliography, see Walther Eichrodt, *Ezekiel: A Commentary*, trans. Cosslett Quin, The Old Testament Library (Philadelphia: Westminster Press, 1970), pp. 188–189.

21. For a more detailed presentation of this theme, see Simon J. de Vries, "Remembrance in Ezekiel: A Study of an Old Testament Theme," *Interpretation* 16 (1962): 58–64.

22. Kraeling, *op. cit.*, p. 512.

Part V

THE
RENEWAL
OF THE
PEOPLE

17

SECOND ISAIAH AND THE PROMISE OF IMMINENT RETURN

Despite the physical discomforts and psychological blows that Yahweh's people sustained during the exilic era (587–538), their corporate life remained intact. Of course, the Babylonian destruction of Jerusalem profoundly disturbed those whose Zion-based theology depended on an ongoing cult in the Jerusalem Temple. Forced out of the Land of Promise by a mighty world power, the Jews in Babylon had reason to despair over their present plight. Yet many kept the ancestral faith of Yahwism and fervently hoped that the current purge and testing would be the harbinger of a new day.

It is fitting that this final sequence of chapters opens with a consideration of Second Isaiah and his magnificent oracles of hope. Active in Babylon in about 540, he gave his fellow exiles good reason to believe in a promising future. In contrast with his prophetic predecessors, Second Isaiah declared that at Yahweh's doing Jerusalem had already received "double for all her sins" (Isa. 40:2). The manner of Judah's chastisement and the turn of events in world history led this talented prophet-poet to predict impending salvation for his people. Second Isaiah's optimism was not ill founded. In 539 the chaotic affairs of Babylon were set in order by the conquering monarch, Cyrus of Persia (550–530); by the end of his first year as ruler of Babylon (538), Cyrus issued an edict inviting the exiled Jews to return to their homeland (Ezra 1:2–4; 6:3–5).

Even so, members of the Babylonian diaspora who accepted that invitation were not welcomed with much enthusiasm by the Jewish element that had never left Palestine. Arguments arose as to who constituted the nucleus of Judaism—those who had courageously persisted in

---

Biblical texts to be read prior to and in conjunction with the present chapter: Isaiah 40–55.

the ruined land or those who, having suffered the humiliation of exile, now returned home as Yahweh's chastised and renewed people? As time passed, the returning Jews and their descendants had to cope with problematic public relations, adverse farming conditions, and low morale. Such realities could not help but cast a shadow on Second Isaiah's enthusiastic display of hope.

As we examine the people of ancient Israel during the postexilic era, diverse elements compete for our attention. While they cannot be united under one heading with complete success, we may nevertheless identify this period of Israel's history as the era of renewal. It was characterized by people who strove to remain true to their convictions. Historical circumstances were seldom auspicious, yet the trust of the people remained in Yahweh; for they knew him to be the God of history. They were convinced that the future lay in his sovereign control and that, as the people of Yahweh, they had an inextricable link with the divine plan about to unfold.

SECOND ISAIAH AS
A SEPARATE LITERARY CORPUS

In Second Isaiah we meet a distinguished Israelite prophet with remarkable gifts of self-expression. He had a penchant for embracing both the old and the new. He respected the best of Israel's traditions; in particular, he reflected on Israel's election and her deliverance from Egypt. Still he was intent on relating the past to the present and the future. Unmistakably he stood at a turning point in human history. It was his conviction that very soon Cyrus would carry out Yahweh's judgment against proud, wicked Babylon. Then, having laid low the power that was currently holding the Jews in captivity, Yahweh would lead his own through the wilderness in a new, victorious exodus. Thus, they would be returned to their homeland.

Second Isaiah's writings are eschatological. Though they do not speculate about what shape the remote future will assume, they advance the faith that very soon God will intervene in history in a strikingly new way. Israel's salvation is imminent. Before we say more, however, we must speak for the integrity of Isaiah 40–55 as the work of an exilic Hebrew prophet who lived nearly two centuries after Isaiah of Jerusalem (First Isaiah) had come and gone.

The struggle to establish Second Isaiah's identity and his independence of First Isaiah began in 1775 with the appearance of Döderlein's Isaiah commentary. He was convinced that the oracles in Isaiah 40–66 were written much later than those in Isaiah 1–39. In 1892 Duhm contended that Isaiah 40–55 and Isaiah 56–66 were the efforts of Second and Third Isaiah, respectively.[1] Contemporary biblical critics embrace the view that Isaiah 40 inaugurates the reflections of a new prophet. Moreover, Duhm's stand in separating Isaiah 40–55 from Isaiah 56–66 is often favored. (In Chapter 19, we shall indicate what we believe to be the relation of Third to Second Isaiah.) Duhm also isolated four servant songs (Isa. 42:1–4; 49:1–6; 50:4–9; 52:13–53:12) and assigned them to still another anonymous biblical writer, but here Duhm's work has been more often contested than supported. Nevertheless, the complexities, obscurities, and special interests of these compositions have made them the subject of intensive investigation.

At least four historical considerations argue for the separation of Isaiah 40–55 from Isaiah 1–39. First, in chapters 40–55 the Babylonian exile of the Jews is not prediction but fact. Yet First Isaiah resided in Jerusalem during the second half of the eighth century. Judah and Israel were still independent kingdoms, and their monarchs are referred to by name. Assyria is the noteworthy Mesopotamian power that, under the leadership of Sargon II and Sennacherib, threatens the tranquility of western Asia. Yet in chapters 40–55 Israel is no longer a kingdom. There we find the people of God enduring a period of exile from their Palestinian homeland.

Second, King Cyrus of Persia is specifically referred to in 44:28 and 45:1. He is respected as Yahweh's "shepherd," who will set in motion the rebuilding of Jerusalem and its Temple. Although Cyrus is nowhere mentioned in chapters 1–39, in chapters 40–55 he is directly related to the impending doom of Babylon.

Third, the author of chapters 40–55 seems to have lived in Babylon. He has a knowledge of Babylonian rituals, landscapes, and climate, and assumes the same of his audience. For example, in 46:1–2 his portrait of the procession of Babylonian gods suggests that he has himself witnessed such doings in the streets of Babylon.

And fourth, chapters 40–55 are silent about the kings of Judah, Israel, Phoenicia, and Assyria. This omission would be strange indeed were these chapters a continuation of the prophecies of Isaiah of Jerusalem.

In addition to several Babylonian loan words, which are mainly of interest to the specialists, several literary considerations speak for the independence of chapters 40–55. This literature has a flowing style and warm rhetoric that distinguishes it from chapters 1–39. While the oracles in chapters 1–39 can be moving, the literary units are more terse and less lyrical than those that comprise chapters 40–55.

Moreover, in chapters 1–39 denunciations and threats are prominent. Yet in chapters 40–55 that type of prophetic discourse is infrequent; instead, the oracle of salvation dominates.

One of the most conspicuous rhetorical features of chapters 40–55 is the use of first-person singular statements that identify Yahweh's nature and intent. These present-tense ascriptions center on Yahweh's very being: "I am he who blots out your transgressions for my own sake" (43:25), and "I am he that comforts you" (51:12). The most eloquent example appears in 44:24–28, which celebrates at length Yahweh's deeds in human life.

Two theological considerations also call for the separation of chapters 40–55 from 1–39. The first is that Second Isaiah advances a view of history somewhat different from that assumed in chapters 1–39. Especially pronounced in chapters 40–55 is the notion that nature and history are firmly united under the sovereignty of Yahweh. Chapters 40–55 also establish a close connection between Yahweh the creator and Yahweh the redeemer. The very one who created the world and called Israel into existence will soon deliver his people from Babylonian captivity. In chapters 1–39, however, the connection between Yahweh's creative and redemptive power is not a matter of special interest.

The second consideration is that chapters 1–39 and 40–55 advance two different eschatological perspectives. The former focuses on the hope of a continuing remnant and on a triumphant Davidic ruler; the latter emphasizes the work of a redeeming servant of Yahweh who is destined to suffer.

Finally, the computer-oriented study of Radday speaks for the separation of Isaiah 40–66 from Isaiah 1–39.[2] Radday has examined such matters as word length, sentence length, and transition frequencies of different parts of speech. For various blocks of material in Isaiah 1–66, Radday also has established the percentage of words related to nature, religion, family, and war. He concludes that the probability that one person wrote the entire Book of Isaiah is 1 in 100,000.

THE HISTORICAL SITUATION OF SECOND ISAIAH

Second Isaiah pursued his prophetic career after Jerusalem's destruction in 587 and prior to Persia's invasion of Babylon in 539. A date near the end of this era appears most likely in light of the drama that was to unfold in the ancient Near East after 550, when Cyrus launched the first of his brilliant military campaigns. In the years that followed, the Persian empire had everything to gain and the Babylonian empire much to lose.

The Jewish exiles found themselves in a time of rapid change. After Nebuchadnezzar's death in 562, the Babylonian state followed a steady course toward its ruin. In the short span of seven years, three persons held the throne—Amel-Marduk (562–560), Neriglissar (560–556), and Labashi-Marduk (556)—and of these gentlemen, only Neriglissar appears to have been at all capable. Then in 556 the throne was seized by Nabonidus (556–539). A man of Aramean background, he was supported by Babylonian malcontents who were irritated with the dominant role of the Marduk priesthood in economic and religious matters. Nabonidus himself had a priestly genealogy and was a follower of the moon

VII. THE ERA OF BABYLONIAN EXILE AND JUDEAN RESTORATION (587–398 B.C.)

DATE (B.C.)	EGYPT	JUDAH	BABYLONIA	MEDIA AND PERSIA
600	Apries (589–570)	Fall of Jerusalem (587) Era of Babylonian exile (587–538) 3d deportation of Jews to Babylon (582)	Nebuchadnezzar (605–562)	Astyages, king of Media (585–550)
	Amasis (570–526)		Amel-Marduk (562–560)	
550		Second Isaiah (ca. 540) Edict of Cyrus permitting the Jews to return to Judah (538) Sheshbazzar's return (ca. 538)	Neriglissar (560–556) Labashi-Marduk (556) Nabonidus (556–539) Fall of Babylon to Persia (539)	Cyrus' conquest of Media and establishment of the Persian empire (550) Cyrus (550–530) overtakes Babylon (539) Cambyses (530–522) conquers Egypt (525) Darius I (522–486)
	Persian conquest of Egypt (525) Persian rule (525–401)	Haggai (520) Zechariah (520–518) Rebuilding of the Jerusalem Temple under direction of Zerubbabel (520–515)		
500				Xerxes (486–465)
450		Malachi (ca. 450) Nehemiah as governor (445–?)		Artaxerxes I (465–424)
400	Egypt regains independence (401)	Ezra's mission (398?)		Darius II (423–404) Artaxerxes II (404–358)

deity Sin. As a way of advancing his god, he reconstructed Sin's temple at Haran, much to the displeasure of the priestly devotees of Marduk. In fact, the discontent of Babylon's inhabitants over Nabonidus' religious innovations reached such a level that the king thought it best to spend ten years at the oasis of Tema to the southeast of Edom. His son Belshazzar was given responsibility for affairs of state in Babylon itself. Like his father, he wasted no love on Marduk. Clearly, the Babylonian citizenry was at odds with the court on the matter of Marduk worship, and such tension could not help but subvert the nation's cause.

The international situation also proved threatening for Babylon. Astyages (585–550), king of the Median empire to the north of Babylon, had to confront the defiance of Cyrus, who had been a vassal king. Hoping for the undoing of his Median enemies, Nabonidus supported Cyrus. In 550 Cyrus stormed Ecbatana, the Median capital, ousted Astyages, and absorbed the far-ranging Median state into his own. Because Cyrus scored many military victories in the years to follow, Nabonidus' attitude toward the Persian monarch changed from enthusiasm to fear. Therefore, Nabonidus allied himself with Amasis (570–526), the Egyptian pharaoh, and Croesus (ca. 560–547), the monarch of Lydia. But soon Cyrus took Sardis, the capital of Lydia, and most of Asia Minor. Although Babylon enjoyed a peaceful interval in the 540s, Cyrus' takeover was only a question of time.

In the summer and fall of 539, the Babylonian empire was finally brought to its knees. At Opis on the Tigris River, the Babylonian army was severely beaten by the successful Persian forces. Nabonidus fled and was soon taken prisoner. Led by the Babylonian general Gobryas, who had deserted Nabonidus, the Persian army infiltrated the city of Babylon in October 539. The Cyrus Cylinder reveals that not long thereafter Cyrus himself made his peaceful yet triumphant entry. (We shall examine this important extrabiblical text more closely in Chapter 18.)

Although Second Isaiah does not refer to the Persian takeover of Babylon as an accomplished fact, clearly he was speaking on the eve of that decisive happening. This courageous exilic prophet discerned that under Yahweh's sovereign will, history was shifting dramatically. The liberation of the Jews from their Babylonian captivity appeared to be on the horizon. Such a realization filled the prophet with hope and motivated him to declare in bold, somewhat cryptic terms the nature of Israel's mission in the world at this critical hour.

THE "CALL"
OF SECOND ISAIAH

Isaiah 40:1–11 is often interpreted as relevant to Second Isaiah's call to the prophetic office. While this passage lacks the biographical notations that appear in some prophetic call narratives, it shows the prophet as the herald of good tidings. Here Second Isaiah has an initial theophanic experience that puts him in touch with the heavenly council (cf. 1 Kings 22:19-23, Isa. 6, Jer. 23:18). He shared with others of his day a belief that whatever was determined in the celestial spheres would unfold on earth below.

In this passage Yahweh's imminent return is seen as a resplendent act of self-disclosure: "And the glory of Yahweh shall be revealed, and all flesh shall see it together, for the mouth of Yahweh has spoken" (Isa. 40:5). The prophet boldly states that Yahweh will appear in a self-revelation of unique proportions. Divine glory will fill space and time. Indeed, it will be perceived by "all flesh" (40:5). In this grand eschatological act, darkness will be overcome and all challenges to Yahweh's universal rule annulled. Nature will be radically transformed, and Yahweh will begin his uncontested rule as universal king (40:10).

The power and eternity of God are emphasized through a graphic contrast. Pessimistically, Second Isaiah confesses that the human condition is utterly transient: "surely the people is grass" (40:7). Yet this is not the end of the matter: "The grass withers, the flower fades; but the word of our God will stand for ever" (40:8).

Ultimately the grass, the flower, and man himself must deteriorate. Man is bound by time, but Yahweh is Lord over time, and his word lies beyond the flux and confusion of time and environment. In Hebrew, "word" (dābhār) means both a word that is spoken or written and an action. In fact, "word" and "act" are often accepted as a single reality. Thus, in 40:6-8 we have a dramatic contrast between transient humanity and the eternal God.

The word that Second Isaiah heard in the heavenly council is not the word Isaiah of Jerusalem heard. The latter was charged with announcing a message of judgment before an unresponsive people. By contrast, Second Isaiah is summoned to comfort the despairing Jewish exiles. Israel's servitude lies behind her. The suffering for past sin is now set aside so that a new moment may come into being. That moment will inaugurate Yahweh's universal rule. Second Isaiah's fresh realization of man's mortality, his conception of God's eternity, and his faith in Israel's future are all eloquently expressed in Isa. 40:1-11.

THE MESSAGE
OF SECOND ISAIAH

Second Isaiah communicated his message though the cultic-oriented salvation oracle, the prophetic disputation with its hymnic and wisdom elements, and the juridical speech of the court.[3] In doing so, he elaborated on three themes: Yahweh as creator and redeemer, salvation as imminent reality, and salvation as historical reenactment of the Exodus tradition. Let us look more carefully at each of these themes.

Yahweh as Creator and Redeemer

Through his artistry, this prophet-poet weds the themes of creation and redemption. Second Isaiah recognizes that Israel belongs to the deity and that he chooses to deliver her precisely because he is her creator. Both his creative and redemptive capacities affirm Yahweh's oneness. In fact, Second Isaiah may be considered ancient Israel's greatest monotheist.

> Up to the time of Deutero-Isaiah, one can speak only of a practical monotheism, which binds Israel to Yahweh alone without regard for the existence of other gods. Deutero-Isaiah, following the beginnings made by Jeremiah, represents a theoretical monotheism, which expressly denies the existence of other gods. As a result, all events and all phenomena from the creation of the world through eternity are associated with the one God.[4]

Second Isaiah acknowledges Yahweh as creator of the stars (40:26); the ends of the earth (40:28); the heavens (42:5); light and darkness (45:7); man (45:12); and, in particular, the Israelite people (43:1, 15). As the beginning and the end (41:4; 44:6; 48:12), Yahweh is the doer of first and last things (42:9; 43:18–19).[5] Apart from him there is no creative deity. He originates and fulfills all things. The gods of the nations are only wooden blocks or pieces of metal; they lack authenticity. In 44:9–20 the prophet satirically depicts a man who roasts his food and warms himself by burning the wood of a tree. With the remaining wood he makes an idol. This is his god, and Second Isaiah dismisses the whole procedure as insane. By contrast, the prophet places his confidence in the one creator deity who sustains and redeems the entire cosmos.

As vital as the creation motif is to Second Isaiah, it is not convincingly presented as an independent theme.[6] Rather, the prophet persists in affirming that Yahweh the creator is closely involved in the development of history. The Lord of nature is also Lord of time. Hence, Yahweh the creator is celebrated as Israel's redeemer.

Second Isaiah conveys this belief through several striking contrasts. The Jewish exiles, who are many miles from their homeland, are an unenviable subject people. Yet the sovereignty of Yahweh, God of Israel, extends far beyond Israel's present location and beyond the Land of Promise itself; he is, in fact, the creator of the ends of the earth. Moreover, the exiles are the victims of an arrogant foreign power, but only Yahweh, the uncontested sovereign of nature and history, has the last word on the struggle of the nations. And finally, Babylonian theology and ritual, to which the Jewish exiles had been exposed, soberly held that chaos and order always exist in tension. Although Marduk was able to overwhelm the chaotic powers of the universe, he did not have absolute authority. On the other hand, the omnipotent Yahweh has unconditional initiative. Through such contrasts, Second Isaiah placed the creative power of Israel's God in bold relief.

Hence, creation is a dominant theme in Second Isaiah's oracles precisely because he feels driven to convey his strong belief in Israel's impending redemption. He sets forth Yahweh's original and continuing creation of the world as an indication that he has the resources to upset the present course of history. In sum, Second Isaiah's faith in the creation is based on a lively theology of hope.

Salvation as Imminent Reality

Second Isaiah believed that Israel's redemption was close at hand. Yahweh would soon appear in a glorious world theophany at which time he would lead his people home. In his eschatological reflection, Second Isaiah regarded Cyrus as the human agent who would break Babylonian power and grant Israel her release (44:28; 45:1). Although this Persian ruler is unaware of the role he will play in Israel's history, he is the chosen instrument of divine purpose. That Cyrus is not a convert to Yahwism does not matter particularly.

Isaiah 51:1–16 provides such a stirring expression of what the near future holds for Yahweh's people that it is worth closer inspection. This poem insists that salvation is imminent and that the faithful members of the Israelite community have every reason to look forward to the future. In the first strophe (vv. 1–3) comfort is extended to those who seek Yahweh; in the second (vv. 4–6) the eternal and victorious salvation is declared imminent; in the third (vv. 7–8) the righteous are instructed to forgo fear and dismay; in the fourth (vv. 12–14) Yahweh the creator is presented as Israel's consoler; and in the fifth (vv. 15–16) the creator deity sets forth his purpose—protecting and electing Israel. Between the third and fourth strophes is a historical-eschatological interlude (vv. 9–11) in which an earnest cry is made for Yahweh to continue his work of intervening in human history.

In this brilliant composition Second Isaiah moves forward and backward in time. He focuses on Israel's ancestry. In his picturesque reference to Abraham the rock and Sarah the quarry (vv. 1–2), he affirms Israel's covenant solidarity. Since Israel is at one with her momentous past, there is ground for present optimism. As Yahweh has blessed Abraham, so he will bless Abraham's children, who are Second Isaiah's struggling contemporaries. Moreover, Second Isaiah declares that nature itself will be thoroughly transformed. The wilderness will be changed into the likeness of Eden (v. 3). This implies that eschatological time will resemble primordial time.[7] Sterile land will become habitable. The sovereign Yahweh promises immediate deliverance, and this is well within his power.

The coastlands wait for Yahweh and hope in his strong arm (v. 5). Against the backdrop of man's precarious existence, the eternality of God is boldly portrayed. His triumph and his acts of redemption will endure (vv. 6, 8). Therefore, Israel has no reason to fear. The assuring word that the deity has spoken to the patriarchs of old is spoken anew: "I am Yahweh your God" (v. 15). Yahweh also declares that he has put his words into Israel's mouth (v. 16). Israel is to be the agent of divine revelation. As the new heaven and earth unfold, Israel will be found instructing others, and in this way she will realize her true calling.

Here and in other oracles Second Isaiah consciously relates Yahweh's design for salvation to non-Israelites. Admittedly, the prophet understands that in comparison with Yahweh, the nations are nothing (40:17). He holds the idolatrous worship of the heathen in disdain. Even so, Second Isaiah is a universalist. He refuses to write off the nations as a lost cause. Expanding on the universalism of Amos, he believes that all men derive their life from one God whose name is Yahweh. His God says:

> Turn to me and be saved,
>   all the ends of the earth!
> For I am God, and there is no other. (45:22)

Also, in the second servant song, Yahweh insists that Israel, his chosen, must function in the world as a penetrating light:

> It is too light a thing that you should be my servant
>   to raise up the tribes of Jacob
>   and to restore the preserved of Israel;
> I will give you as a light to the nations,
>   that my salvation may reach to the end of the earth. (49:6)

The prophet looks forward to the time when all nations, in response to Israel's outgoing witness, will acknowledge Yahweh as their God. Perhaps the nations will discern the mighty power of Yahweh in the decisive events that are about to take place. In any case, Yahweh intends to exert his universal sovereignty, and the nations are invited to accept that rule.

Salvation as Historical Reenactment

In Second Isaiah's estimation, Yahweh's intention was to save all mankind. However, Israel's existence was affected most directly. As the prophet meditated on the dimensions of the salvation that lay ahead, he affirmed that the return of Yahweh's people from Babylon to their Palestinian homeland would constitute a splendid new Exodus.[8] Second Isaiah's eschatological reflections often focus on this theme. Isaiah 40:3–5 depicts the highway in the wilderness; 41:17–20 portrays the transformation of the wilderness; 42:16 discloses Yahweh's intention to lead his "blind" people along an unfamiliar path; 49:8–12 projects a dramatic reentry into the Land of Promise; 51:9–11 anticipates a new victory at sea involving Yahweh's reassertion of power over the monsters of chaos; and 55:12–13 describes Israel's arrival in her homeland as an entry into a paradise resembling Eden.

Second Isaiah's eschatology was thoroughly influenced by his conviction that the manner in which the future will unfold depends completely on what has taken place in the past. The end of history is informed by its beginning. The prophet posits a close correspondence between the beginning and the end of time. While the end would be more marvelous in depth and scope, it would correspond dramatically with the primordial reality. The emergence of Cyrus, the impending collapse of Babylon, and the release of the Jewish exiles would all give rise to Israel's new Exodus. Second Isaiah discovers a correspondence between former events and the events soon to take place. He confidently affirms the continuity of history, which unfolds under the creative dictation of Yahweh's purposive will.

Nevertheless, the first Exodus is not merely repeated. It is intensified. The impact of Israel's new Exodus on the world will be far greater than that which Egypt felt when her Hebrew slaves fled into the desert. All nations will somehow witness the new event and Yahweh's might will be manifested to all. Ultimately Israel's salvation will have a direct bearing on the salvation of all nations. Indeed, Second Isaiah believed that the people of Yahweh would be pressed into a unique kind of service that would make redemption and renewal available to all mankind. Nowhere is this article of faith more fully expressed than in the servant songs, which we shall now examine.

THE SERVANT OF YAHWEH

The Servant Songs

One of the greatest contributions of Second Isaiah to the total expression of religious thought in the Hebrew Bible is to be found in the servant songs. Generally these are identified as 42:1–4; 49:1–6; 50:4–9; and 52:13–53:12. Whoever the servant is, we confront a thoroughly individualized entity committed to the task the deity lays upon him. That task involves dealing with Gentile as well as Jewish elements. Intimately related to Yahweh's redemptive concern for the world at large, the servant is obliged to suffer so that others may benefit from that suffering.

While the songs do not in every instance harmonize well with the strophes that immediately precede and follow, they appear in a thoughtful sequence. Not only do all four reflect on the life and mission of the servant, but the first song speaks his divine summons (42:1–4) and the last mentions his death and rescue (52:13–53:12). Nevertheless, the identity and functions of the servant cannot be confidently established.[9] In large measure, the problem is the direct consequence of Second Isaiah's poetic language.

> He is not described in the terms used elsewhere in the Old Testament of a king, a prophet, Israel, or an individual righteous man, although there are reminiscences of each of these. . . . Any interpretation, therefore, of the Servant along any single one of the above lines . . . may be ruled out on principle. The veiled allusions, now to one now to another of these, forbid the adoption of any one to the exclusion of the rest.[10]

Nevertheless, before we concern ourselves with the servant's identity, let us take note of the primary features of each of these lyrics.

In the first servant song (42:1–4), which takes the form of a divine summons, Yahweh is the speaker. The deity's deliberate selection of the servant and his submission to the divine will are both stressed. Unobtrusively the servant is expected to extend "justice" and "law" to the nations. The servant unmistakably belongs to Yahweh (v. 1) and is imbued with the divine spirit.

The second servant song (49:1–6) is the servant's discourse to the nations in which he declares that he has been divinely appointed prior to his birth. Eventually the hour for his mission drew nigh. In pursuit of his task, however, the servant met obstacles and felt despair. Still his confidence in Yahweh and in his universal mission have endured. In this composition the servant's identity is not made clear. In v. 3 the servant discloses that Yahweh said to him, "You are my servant, Israel, in whom I will be glorified." Thus, the nation appears to be the servant. Yet in v. 5 the servant states that he has been designated to relate to Israel as the agent who is capable of returning the covenant people to the deity. The restored Israel and the servant do not seem to be one and the same. Despite such complications, the song reaches its marvelous note of universalism in v. 6. The conversion of Israel alone is too limited an aim. The servant is to be a light that mediates salvation "to the end of the earth" (v. 6).

In the third servant song (50:4–9) the servant speaks again, this time about his teaching ministry. His strength to teach is given to him on a daily basis (v. 4). The divine word must nourish him before he can nourish others. The servant emphasizes the indignities he has endured. Despite these hardships, the servant's dedication to his task and his trust in God are apparent: he is confident that Yahweh will vindicate his efforts.

The fourth servant song (52:13–53:12) incorporates the utterances of two speakers—Yahweh and the nations. It opens with assurances that the servant will be exalted. Astonished kings and nations will look upon this guiltless, humble being as one who has suffered in their stead and offered himself for their sins. The poem concludes by affirming that the servant will be rewarded for having endured the outrageous human actions that have resulted in his death. In this composition the servant suffers deeply. As an unimpressive, despised, and gentle being, he has shown himself willing to suffer for the sins of others:

> Surely he has borne our griefs
>   and carried our sorrows;
> yet we esteemed him stricken,
>   smitten by God, and afflicted.
> But he was wounded for our transgressions,
>   he was bruised for our iniquities;
> upon him was the chastisement that made us whole,
>   and with his stripes we are healed. (53:4–5)

Bearing the full weight of man's iniquity, he has carried out his task without complaint. Indeed, the selfless servant has dedicated his life so that others might live.

The Servant's Identity: Some Tentative Conclusions

Although consensus has not been reached concerning the identity of the servant of Yahweh, various biblical scholars have attempted to equate the servant with individual, corporate, or quasi-corporate existence.

The Servant as an Individual. In these poems the servant is often portrayed as an extremely idealized figure. Perhaps Second Isaiah was alluding to a historical person. Moses, Cyrus, Uzziah, Hezekiah, Josiah, Isaiah of Jerusalem, Jeremiah, Ezekiel, Job, and Second Isaiah himself are among those who have been introduced as possible candidates. But no known person in Israel's history fits the description of the servant in every respect. Second Isaiah may have been influenced by the witness of several of Israel's past leaders. Perhaps the memory of the law-giving Moses and the tormented Jeremiah were often foremost in his mind. But this is not to say that he consciously regarded either of these worthies as the servant. And if Second Isaiah were referring to himself, he would be guilty of immodest praise and he would also be strangely well informed about the details of his own death. Moreover, the equation of the servant with an ideal eschatological monarch is unconvincing because typically Judaism does not consider suffering a vital part of the messianic role. Finally, any identification of the servant with an individual conflicts with the testimony of 49:3, in which it is claimed that the servant is the nation Israel. On balance, the equation of the servant with a person is not a convincing alternative.

The Servant as the Corporate Nation Israel. It has been argued that the servant is Second Isaiah's representation of the presently exiled people Israel. Indeed, elsewhere Second Isaiah depicts Israel as the suffering and witnessing people of Yahweh. Since the word "servant" appears in the discourse of Second Isaiah apart from the servant songs, and in such contexts refers to the nation (42:19; 43:10; 48:20), presumably the servant of the songs must also be Israel. Similarly, in 49:3 the servant-Israel equation is quite explicit. Muilenburg maintains, "Israel, and Israel alone, is able to bear all that is said about the servant of the Lord. For the fundamental fact outweighing all others is the repeated equation of the two in the poems."[11] The humiliation that Yahweh's people suffered during their Babylonian exile might easily have encouraged them to interpret the dispersed nation itself as a suffering servant.

Nevertheless, the matter is not this simple, for some Jews in Babylonian exile were indifferent to their ancestral faith. Presumably only a few of the faithful endured innocent suffering with the willingness sometimes expressed in the servant poetry (50:5–6; 53:7). Perhaps the prophet is referring to a minority within Israel, a select and righteous group that voluntarily puts itself forward in behalf of the entire nation. Yet if one is willing to grant this hypothesis, he might just as well insist that the strong individualistic overtones in the servant songs require us to think of the servant as a single human being. A thoroughgoing collective interpretation also fails to account for a passage such as 49:5, in which the servant's task is to bring the people back to Yahweh.

The Servant as an Individual and a Corporate Entity. This third approach accepts the best of both views. It recognizes that ancient Hebraic modes of thought and logical Western modes need not coincide. Perhaps in Second Isaiah's thinking the servant figure remained deliberately fluid so that at different times it represented the entire nation, an element within that nation, or a single individual. Second Isaiah himself may not have had a precise notion about the servant's identity. Rowley, who notes a fluidity in the prophet's writings, declares, "This view does justice to the links of phraseology with passages outside the songs, and also allows for the fact that in the fourth song, in particular, it is very hard to think that the writer had anything but an individual in mind."[12] As the called people of Yahweh, the nation might be equated with the servant, yet at times the servant might be an individual.

No single, narrowly conceived answer concerning the servant's identity is likely to be satisfying. In the long run, however, the corporate dimension of the servant cannot be overlooked. Indeed, it helps us to understand the servant within the setting of Israel's history. It calls attention to a mission involving the entire body of Yahweh's people in the world. And it recognizes that no one human being living either prior to or during Second Isaiah's time could have met all the demands that this fascinating poetry places on the servant. Through the servant Second Isaiah has undoubtedly given us a brilliant portrayal of the true Israel and the true Israelite.

Second Isaiah was both a prophet and an artist who expressed himself at a critical point in his people's history. He was equally talented in examining Israel's past traditions and in contemplating her future. In his expansive oracles, profound ideas about the restoration of Yahweh's people to their homeland, the reassertion of Yahweh's sovereignty, and the redemption of the Gentile world are advanced in a truly fresh and exciting manner.

NOTES

1. Bernhard Duhm, *Das Buch Jesaia*, 3d ed., Göttinger Handkommentar zum Alten Testament (Göttingen, Ger.: Vandenhoeck & Ruprecht, 1914), pp. xx, 389–390.
2. Y. T. Radday, "Two Computerized Statistical-Linguistic Tests Concerning the Unity of Isaiah," *Journal of Biblical Literature* 89 (1970): 319–324. See also *"Isaiah* and the Computer," *Time*, 13 April 1970, p. 58.
3. For a helpful summary of the major genres employed by Second Isaiah, see H. Eberhard von Waldow, "The Message of Deutero-Isaiah," *Interpretation* 22 (1968): 266–274. On the salvation oracle, see Philip B. Harner, "The Salvation Oracle in Second Isaiah," *Journal of Biblical Literature* 88 (1969): 418–434.
4. Georg Fohrer, *Introduction to the Old Testament*, trans. David E. Green (Nashville: Abingdon Press, 1968), pp. 383–384.
5. See Carroll Stuhlmueller, " 'First and Last' and 'Yahweh-Creator' in Deutero-Isaiah," *Catholic Biblical Quarterly* 29 (1967): 495–511.
6. Here we are in essential agreement with von Rad, "The Theological Problem of the Old Testament Doctrine of Creation," in Gerhard von Rad, *The Problem of the Hexateuch and Other Essays*, trans. E. W. Trueman Dicken (London: Oliver & Boyd, 1966), pp. 134–137. For a contrasting view, see Harner, who claims that "creation faith does have a certain independence of its own as a basis for the prophet's reflection." (Philip B. Harner, "Creation Faith in Deutero-Isaiah," *Vetus Testamentum* 17 [1967]: 305.)
7. We are in agreement with James Muilenburg, "Introduction and Exegesis to Isaiah 40–66," in George A. Buttrick et al., eds., *The Interpreter's Bible* (Nashville: Abingdon Press, 1956), vol. 5, p. 592.
8. See Anderson, "Exodus Typology in Second Isaiah," in Bernhard W. Anderson and Walter Harrelson, eds., *Israel's Prophetic Heritage* (New York: Harper & Row, 1962), pp. 177–195.
9. For a detailed analysis of this crucial issue in Second Isaiah research, see Christopher R. North, *The Suffering Servant in Deutero-Isaiah: An Historical and Critical Study*, 2d ed. (London: Oxford University Press, 1956);

and Sigmund Mowinckel, *He That Cometh*, trans. G. W. Anderson (Nashville: Abingdon Press, 1954), pp. 187–257. An informative but less extensive treatment of the servant songs appears in John L. McKenzie, *Second Isaiah: Introduction, Translation, and Notes*, The Anchor Bible, vol. 20 (Garden City, N.Y.: Doubleday, 1968), pp. xxxviii–lv.

10. Claus Westermann, *Isaiah 40–66: A Commentary*, trans. David M. G. Stalker, The Old Testament Library (Philadelphia: Westminster Press, 1969), pp. 20–21.

11. Muilenburg, *op. cit.*, p. 411.

12. H. H. Rowley, *The Growth of the Old Testament* (New York: Harper & Row, Harper Torchbooks, 1963), p. 97. McKenzie, *op. cit.*, p. lii, basically agrees with Rowley. Yet McKenzie is reluctant to identify the servant as a "fluid" type: "The Servant remains an individual, but an ideal who reflects the general character of all Israel" (p. liv).

18

THE RETURN TO PALESTINE AND THE RESTORATION OF THE JEWISH COMMUNITY

The eagerly awaited moment finally arrived. Late in 539 Cyrus extended his sovereignty to Babylon itself. Only a few months after his peaceful arrival in the city, Cyrus allowed the Jews to return to Palestine and rebuild their Jerusalem sanctuary. In his enthusiasm for Cyrus, Second Isaiah had pinned his hopes on the right man in history. Before we focus directly on the various phases of the Jewish return, however, we should take note of Cyrus' effective penetration of neo-Babylonian territory.

THE CONQUEST OF BABYLON

In the Cyrus Cylinder we have a fascinating account of the Persian take-over of Babylon. This cuneiform inscription, which was found on a clay barrel, appears to have been written by members of the Babylonian priesthood of Marduk, who had long been irritated by King Nabonidus' appalling disrespect for their beloved deity.[1] In an age that cried out for stability, Nabonidus delighted in religious innovation. Such enterprising change included the court's promotion of Sin, the moon god, at Marduk's expense. Naturally the Marduk priests were glad to see in the tolerant Cyrus (550–530) a champion of their own cause.

The Cyrus Cylinder offers a useful portrait of the Persian monarch. Cyrus is depicted as a man of destiny who was deliberately chosen by Marduk for the fulfillment of his will. Constant mention of Marduk

---

Biblical texts to be read prior to and in conjunction with the present chapter: Ezra 1, 3–6; Haggai 1–2; Zechariah 1–8; Malachi 1–4; Nehemiah 1–2, 4:1–7:4, 13:4–31; Ezra 7:1–10:17; Nehemiah 8–10.

The Cyrus Cylinder. This famous cuneiform text refers to Cyrus'
peaceful entry into Babylon in 539 B.C. and his determination to
restore the Babylonian exiles to their former haunts. Moreover, it
declares that the Babylonian deity Marduk deliberately chose the
Persian king for this crucial mission. (Courtesy of the Trustees
of the British Museum.)

implies Cyrus' willingness to support the priestly establishment and promote the worship of this great patron deity of Babylon. In the excerpt
that follows the opening sentences refer to Marduk himself, who is
intent on setting straight the chaotic conditions in Babylon:

> He scanned and looked (through) all the countries, searching for a
> righteous ruler willing to lead him (i.e. Marduk) (in the annual
> procession). (Then) he pronounced the name of Cyrus (*Ku-ra-aš*), king
> of Anshan, declared him (lit.: pronounced [his] name) to be(come) the
> ruler of all the world. . . . Marduk, the great lord, a protector of his
> people/worshipers, beheld with pleasure his (i.e. Cyrus') good deeds
> and his upright mind (lit.: heart) (and therefore) ordered him to
> march against his city Babylon. . . . He made him set out on the road
> to Babylon . . . going at his side like a real friend. His widespread
> troops—their number, like that of the water of a river, could not be
> established—strolled along, their weapons packed away. Without any
> battle, he made him enter his town Babylon . . . sparing Babylon . . .
> any calamity. He delivered into his (i.e. Cyrus') hands Nabonidus,
> the king who did not worship him (i.e. Marduk). All the inhabitants
> of Babylon . . . as well as of the entire country of Sumer and Akkad,
> princes and governors (included), bowed to him (Cyrus) and kissed his
> feet, jubilant that he (had received) the kingship, and with shining
> faces. Happily they greeted him as a master through whose help they
> had come (again) to life from death (and) had all been spared
> damage and disaster, and they worshiped his (very) name.[2]

At this point, the text shifts to the first person, and Cyrus himself speaks throughout the remainder of the inscription. He boasts about his dominion over the world, shows his concern with improving the social conditions of Babylon's populace, and decrees that those who had been restricted to Babylon are now allowed to leave. Cyrus' liberation of the Jews is not mentioned, however.

Clearly, Cyrus' conquest of Babylon was of supreme historical importance. The inscription presents him as the legitimate sovereign of the ancient world, not as an intruding foreign monarch. His peaceful entry into Babylon is also attested throughout this inscription. Cyrus and his army of liberation were actually welcomed by the weary, discontented Babylonian population eager for a shift in government. Both the indigenous inhabitants of Babylon and the captive peoples who lived among them must have been impressed by the peaceable penetration of the Persian forces. Also they had reason to appreciate Cyrus' policy of respecting the social and religious customs of those over whom he was now to rule. The Jews in Babylonian captivity were indeed experiencing something new. In Cyrus they witnessed a monarch who did not feel threatened by cultural pluralism. If the people within his vast empire, which embraced nearly all of the Near East except Egypt, had differing religious predilections, so be it. Their general welfare and loyalty to the Persian crown, which might well be won through enlightened treatment, were of greater importance.

Accordingly, during his first year as ruler of Babylon (538), Cyrus promulgated a decree that allowed for the renewal of the Jewish community and cult in Palestine. Obviously this was a crucial first step. Yet as we shall see, such a restoration of the people of Yahweh to their homeland turned out to be a long, frequently painful ordeal. Unfortunately this important era of Israel's history is not well documented. For the most part, we must work with poorly arranged texts that have been preserved in Ezra and Nehemiah. Extrabiblical sources help a little,[3] as do the infrequent historical allusions in such prophetic works as Haggai, Zechariah, and Malachi. We know almost nothing about the fate of Judaism in Palestine between 515, when the new Temple was dedicated, and 445, when Nehemiah was permitted by the Persian court to go to Jerusalem. Moreover, the dating of Ezra's mission is widely disputed.

Despite such frustrations, the resumption of the Jewish community and cult in Palestine seems to have four major phases. First was the return of some Jews from Babylon in 538, made possible by Cyrus' decree and Sheshbazzar's leadership. These were the people who began to rebuild the Jerusalem Temple only to give up the project when local conditions became unbearable. Second was the return of other Jews from Babylon, apparently not many years later, under the direction of Zerubbabel. While conditions for Temple reconstruction were by no means optimal, the effort was renewed in 520—largely due to the encouragement of Haggai and Zechariah. This led to the completion and dedication of the edifice in 515. A third phase of the Judean restoration program centers on the arrival of Nehemiah in the late 440s. Appointed governor of Judah by the Persian court, Nehemiah first directed the rebuilding of Jerusalem's walls. Then he sponsored various social and cultic reforms designed to offer Palestinian Jews new levels of discipline and a sharper sense of identity. A final phase involved the return of a group of Babylonian Jews under Ezra's direction in about 398. By organizing the reformation community around the Torah, Ezra offered Palestinian Judaism a life style that would dominate for many centuries to follow. We shall devote a section of the present chapter to each of these postexilic phases. Before we examine the first phase, however, we must inquire briefly into the character and intention of the Chronicler's work.

THE HISTORICAL WORK
OF THE CHRONICLER

On the basis of their similarities in style and theological interests, 1 and 2 Chronicles, Ezra, and Nehemiah are commonly attributed to an anonymous postexilic writer known as "the Chronicler." Chronicles-Ezra-Nehemiah can be considered a single expansive historical work. It opens with genealogical data commencing with Adam (1 Chron. 1) and concludes with an account of Nehemiah's second administration (Neh. 13).

In 1 Chron. 1:1–9:34 we have a genealogical survey from Adam to the postexilic era. Then 1 Chron. 9:35–10:14 gives the genealogy of the faithless Saul and an account of his death. The splendid reign of David is the subject of 1 Chron. 11–29, and 2 Chron. 1–9 describes the reign of Solomon. In 2 Chron. 10–36 we have an account of the southern kingdom from Rehoboam to Zedekiah, with 36:22–23 referring to Cyrus' intention to rebuild the Jerusalem Temple. Ezra 1–6 describes the return of the Jews from Babylonian exile and the reconstruction of the Temple, and Ezra 7–10 outlines Ezra's reform program. Nehemiah 1–7 discusses the rebuilding of Jerusalem's walls and other efforts on Nehemiah's part, and Nehemiah 8–13 tells of further reforms undertaken by Ezra and Nehemiah.

In shaping his story, the Chronicler used many different sources. These include the canonical books of Samuel and Kings, the memoirs of Nehemiah and Ezra,[4] Aramaic letters in the non-Hebraic portion of Ezra (4:8–6:18; 7:12–26), genealogies, and Temple documents. Mention of Darius II (423–404) as the most recent Persian king in the Chronicler's work, development of the genealogy of David down to the sixth generation past Zerubbabel (1 Chron. 3:1–24), and the presence of Aramaic expressions contemporaneous with the idiom of the Elephantine papyri (ca. 450–400) suggest 400–350 as a rough date for the Chronicler's history.

If we approach the work of the Chronicler hoping to find a great deal of objective, critical prose, we shall go away keenly disappointed. The premonarchical phases of ancient Israel's history are recounted only in genealogical lists. These are designed to emphasize Israel's election and to defend the superiority of the tribes of Judah and Levi. In the Chronicler's first narrative (1 Chron. 10) we are informed of the death of Saul and his sons on the battlefield. No other phase of Saul's reign is portrayed. The Chronicler is intent on declaring that Saul was unfaithful to Yahweh and therefore died at the hands of the victorious Philistines. This event permitted David to begin his magnificent reign.

The Chronicler's account of David's reign is highly idealized. It reveals as much about what the Chronicler wished had transpired as it does about what actually took place. David's days as an outlaw, his affair with Bathsheba, his involvement in Uriah's death, and the tumultuous character of his later years are not mentioned. Equally telling is the Chronicler's interpretation of David as the patron par excellence of the Jerusalem Temple. Though David is not claimed as its builder, he is credited with having planned the Temple cultus.[5]

Solomon is given a friendly presentation; the Chronicler refrains from depicting the difficulties and bloodshed that accompanied his quest for the throne. As he portrays the various kings of Judah and the sack of Jerusalem the northern kingdom is virtually ignored. The narrative about the restoration community is then offered in Ezra and Nehemiah. In sum, the Chronicler is quite arbitrary. He repeats some passages from Samuel and Kings verbatim, rewrites some, and ignores others as if they were of no consequence.

Despite his limitations as a historian, the Chronicler and his work excel on several counts. First, his selective history focuses on the worship of the people of Yahweh. Presumably the Chronicler was among the personnel employed in the reconstituted Temple; he may have been one of the Levitical singers. In any case, he sought to reflect on the nature of Israel's liturgical response to Yahweh, who had summoned Israel as his chosen people. The Chronicler recognized that at the core of this nation's unique existence lay the act of worship itself. While his preoccupation with the Temple staff and the specific structuring of its priests, Levites, musicians, and custodians may strike us as excessive, no careful study of ancient Israelite worship can ignore the liturgical data presented here.

Moreover, the Chronicler's portrait of David as an enthusiastic patron of Israelite worship is not unfounded. The historical traditions in 1 and 2 Samuel imply as much. David built an altar on the threshing floor of Araunah (2 Sam. 24:18–25); brought the ark of the covenant to his city, Jerusalem (2 Sam. 6:1–15); and expressed a desire to construct a temple in which Yahweh might reside (2 Sam. 7:2). Although David's enthusiasm for right worship may not have been as pervasive as the Chronicler would have us believe, David did not view cultic matters with indifference. The problem is simply one of emphasis.

To a great extent, our understanding of five Judean kings—Jehoshaphat, Joash, Uzziah, Hezekiah, and Josiah—depends on the Chronicler's literary witness. And his use of the Ezra and the Nehemiah memoirs that were available is commendable. Were it not for the Chronicler's work (chronological dislocations and all), our knowledge of the restoration of the Jewish community would be even more scanty than it is.

Finally, the Chronicler remains true to his conviction that Israel restored to her former haunts was far more a religious than a political entity. In the mind of the Chronicler, this was as it should be. The people of Yahweh were not called as a nation into political engagement; they were summoned as a worshiping congregation to reflect on and respond liturgically to Yahweh's presence.

THE JEWISH RETURN
UNDER SHESHBAZZAR

The process of restoration was set in motion by Cyrus' decree of 538, which permitted the captive Jews to return home. While the decree is extant in the Old Testament in both a Hebrew and an Aramaic version, it does not appear in extrabiblical sources. Nevertheless, we see no good reason for denying the basic authenticity of either biblical witness. Variations between the two might simply result from the fact that they served two different purposes.[6]

The Hebrew version of Cyrus' edict of restoration (Ezra 1:2-4) is cast in the form of an oral pronouncement made by a royal herald to a subject people. Here Cyrus claims that "Yahweh, the God of heaven" has put into his hands "all the kingdoms of the earth," and given him the responsibility of building a temple in Jerusalem. Since the lengthy Cyrus Cylinder does not mention Yahweh, biblical scholars suspect that the Chronicler has revised the original royal declaration to suit his own theological preferences. We have no extrabiblical evidence that Cyrus worshiped Yahweh. The Hebrew version of Cyrus' edict also invites the Jewish populace in Babylon to move homeward. Those who would rather not are summoned to lend their financial support. The Aramaic version (Ezra 6:3-5) is a Persian document known as a *dikrona*, or record—in effect, an office memorandum on the oral proclamation. Here specific reference is made to the proportions of the Temple edifice, the style of its construction, and the manner in which the project is to be financed (it is to be underwritten by the Persian royal treasury). Moreover, the

Aramaic decree calls for the restoration of the Temple equipment with which Nebuchadnezzar had previously absconded.

The historical plausibility of Cyrus' edict, which is not referred to elsewhere in the Bible, has been challenged by some interpreters.[7] These two Ezra passages have been discounted as postexilic forgeries founded on the dreams of Second Isaiah, who was dead sure that the Jews would return to their homeland, or on Ezekiel's vision of the new Temple (Ezek. 40–48). It is entirely reasonable, however, that Cyrus would issue a decree that set the restoration in motion. By permitting the Palestinian exiles to return home, Cyrus was not consciously trying to fulfill the rhapsodic expectations of Second Isaiah, who had identified Cyrus as a special instrument of the divine will (Isa. 44:28; 45:1). Cyrus may have been doing nothing more than respecting the customs of a people who, by virtue of his conquest of Babylon, were now his subjects. In taking over what was left of the Babylonian government, he also inherited its problems. Nebuchadnezzar had stolen the Temple vessels from Jerusalem. Now Cyrus wished to have them returned to their rightful place. Since he took responsibility for the construction costs of the Jerusalem Temple, it is reasonable to expect that Cyrus would have had some say in the decision about the dimensions and style of the new edifice. And because Cyrus' massive empire failed to include Egypt, he had much to gain from a content, loyal population along his southwestern frontier. He was addressing his own interests as well as those of the Jewish exiles.

So the Jews began their journey homeward. Nevertheless, the reconstituted Jewish community came nowhere close to measuring up to the impressionistic painting offered by Second Isaiah. His exuberant lyrics anticipated a grand transformation of nature, history, and the human heart. Yahweh's purpose, which had as many implications for the rest of creation as it had for the chosen Israel, was expected to achieve perfect realization. By contrast, the Jews who accepted Cyrus' invitation to return to Palestine found themselves severely hampered by physical hardships, poverty, bad weather, and hostile neighbors.

The restoration project seems to have been placed in the charge of Sheshbazzar, a Judean prince of Davidic ancestry. Since he was one of Jehoiachin's sons,[8] many Jews no doubt hoped that a new, more politically effective Israelite nation might again rear itself on Palestinian soil. Ezra 1:5–11 implies that Sheshbazzar and other venturesome Jews departed for Jerusalem at the first opportunity. Since Palestine was far from Babylon, only the zealous would have accompanied Sheshbazzar on this arduous journey. The list in Ezra 2, which is duplicated in Nehemiah 7, fixes the total at approximately 50,000; but this relates not to the return under Sheshbazzar but to a census of the Judean population a full century later.[9] Many Jews who were financially well off in their businesses in Babylon were little inclined to transplant themselves into

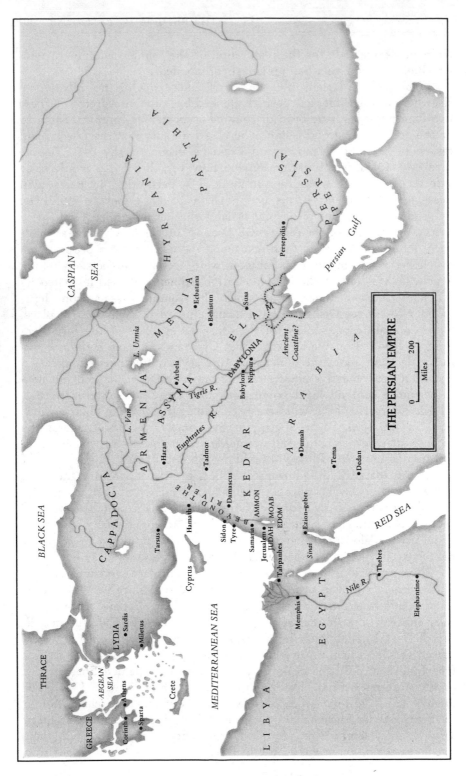

THE PERSIAN EMPIRE

0   200
Miles

CASPIAN SEA

BLACK SEA

THRACE

GREECE
Corinth • Athens
Sparta

AEGEAN SEA

LYDIA
Sardis •
Miletus •

Crete

Cyprus

MEDITERRANEAN SEA

LIBYA

CAPPADOCIA

Tarsus •

Hamath •

Sidon •
Tyre •

Samaria •
Jerusalem •

Haran •

Tadmor •

Damascus •

AMMON
JUDAH MOAB
EDOM

Tahpanhes •

Memphis •

EGYPT

Sinai •

Ezion-geber •

RED SEA

Nile R.

Thebes •

Elephantine •

ARMENIA

L. Van

L. Urmia

ASSYRIA

Arbela •

Tigris R.

Euphrates R.

JORDAN RIVER

KEDAR

A R A B I A

Dumah •

Tema •

Dedan •

MEDIA

Behistun •

Ecbatana •

ELAM

Susa •

BABYLONIA
Babylon •
Nippur •

Ancient
Coastline?

HYRCANIA

PARTHIA

PERSIA (PARS)

Persepolis •

Persian Gulf

an impoverished land that they had left behind long ago.[10] But we doubt that Sheshbazzar returned the Temple vessels without some kind of following. Unfortunately because of the conflation of his work with that of his nephew and successor, Zerubbabel, we cannot determine its extent or success.[11]

In any event, we are informed by Ezra 3 that on their return to Palestine, the Jews immediately tried to erect an altar, appoint Levites, and lay the foundations of the second Temple.[12] Worship of Yahweh again in home territory was of paramount importance. It marked the beginning of a restored Israel. Work on the Temple foundations, however, did not continue for long. A weak, discouraged community soon gave up its efforts. The times did not favor grandiose building projects. Indeed, the task of mere survival must have consumed the physical energy and spirit of most of the stalwart Jews who constituted the first return.

THE RECONSTRUCTION
OF THE JERUSALEM TEMPLE

The Return under Zerubbabel and the Situation prior to 520

At some moment between 538, the year of Cyrus' edict, and 520, the year in which Haggai and Zechariah spoke their prophetic oracles, a second group of Jewish exiles trudged home to Palestine under Zerubbabel's leadership. The struggling postexilic community continued to be plagued by difficulties. Economic problems, partial crop failures, and disagreements about the religious course to be pursued all contributed to the low morale of Judah's citizens.

The hostility of the Samaritans, who had their base of operations at Shechem, had also to be endured. Many years earlier, Shechem had figured in the history of the patriarchs and judges, and with the collapse of Judah the prestige of Shechem and its environs had been noticeably enhanced. At present the northern aristocracy was working hard to subvert Jerusalem's new claim to religious primacy. The Samaritans felt that reconstruction of the Jerusalem Temple required their scrutiny and involvement. When they volunteered to assist in the building project, they were rebuffed by Zerubbabel and his cohorts (Ezra 4:3). The returning exiles regarded the Samaritan brand of Yahwism as a misguided compromise born out of too close an association with neighboring Assyrians. Of course, this stringent attitude made for poor public relations. During the many decades to follow, Jewish-Samaritan dealings did not improve. Thus we can appreciate the radical nature of Jesus' parable concerning a good Samaritan (Luke 10:29–37).

Presently certain problems that plagued the Persian empire were to have a direct impact on Jewish life and thought in Palestine. In 522

King Darius of Persia. This relief of the elaborately attired Darius seated on his carved throne comes from Persepolis. Behind Darius is Xerxes, the crown prince, and facing the king are two incense burners, a respectful Median dignitary, and his two attendants. Directly behind Xerxes are two attendants and behind them are two royal guards. (Courtesy of the Oriental Institute, University of Chicago.)

Cyrus' son Cambyses (530–522) committed suicide. The dynastic conflict and nationalistic revolts that erupted threw Persia into turmoil. Darius, an officer of Cambyses, now sought the throne. Though Darius won the support of the Persian army, it took him nearly two years of hard fighting to achieve peace throughout the empire and to steady his regal position. The political chaos must have encouraged many Jews to infer that Yahweh would soon intervene in history and establish his triumphant rule. And surely Zerubbabel, Judah's governor who had at some point succeeded Sheshbazzar in that position, would rise in significance. The Jewish community again looked hopefully toward the future.

The Witness of Haggai and Zechariah in 520

At this point we must turn to the oracles of two late sixth-century prophets who inspired the Temple reconstruction that was resumed during Darius' second year of rule (520). Since Haggai's oracles extend from August through December 520 and Zechariah's begin in the autumn of 520, we may infer that both prophets responded to the Jewish situation prior to the time Persia was able to recover her political equilibrium. Although Haggai and Zechariah cannot be labeled fiery Jewish nationalists, both drew inspiration from the royal theology central to preexilic kingship. Yahweh's assurances to David and his love for Zion had not been forgotten.

Haggai. In a notably brief span, thirty-eight verses, the Book of Haggai offers an account of Haggai's oracles and the response they sparked within the Jewish community. While we know little about Haggai's background, it is obvious that his chief concern was the rebuilding of the Temple and the fitting resumption of the Jerusalem cult. Haggai's oracles are presented in five short passages, which, in analogy with the priestly-oriented Ezekiel, contain precise dates.

The first oracle (1:1–14, 15b) records the prophet's castigation of the people for their neglect in rebuilding the Temple. Addressing the Davidic prince, Zerubbabel, and the high priest, Joshua, Haggai insisted that the ruined Temple be reconstructed—and the sooner the better. Having declared that the people had thoroughly offended Yahweh by their preoccupation with the condition of their own houses at the expense of Yahweh's house, he forged ahead with an appeal to their self-interest. The present drought and meager harvest were plainly instruments of divine punishment. If only the people reconsidered their priorities, prosperity would surely return. The prophet's oracle did not fall on deaf ears. Work on the Temple was soon renewed.

In the second oracle (2:1–9) Haggai addressed the despondent spirit of those who felt that the new Temple could not possibly measure up to its Solomonic antecedent. The oldest members of the community may indeed have remembered the dimensions and splendor of the first Temple; in retrospect, they may even have exaggerated Solomon's glory. In any event, Haggai declared that Yahweh would soon intervene in behalf of his people by shaking the heavens, earth, and nations. Consequently, the new Jerusalem would enjoy a Temple surpassing its predecessor in splendor, and its citizens would no longer be forced to live in poverty. Presumably Haggai was anticipating the imminent collapse of the Persian empire.

The third oracle (2:10–14) is admittedly difficult to interpret. Apparently Haggai transmitted a priestly judgment to the effect that ritual impurity exceeds ritual holiness in its contagious qualities. Then he applied it to the present situation of his people. What he had to say may be interpreted in two different ways. First, his use of the term "this people" (v. 14) may be pejorative. Haggai may be suggesting that any Samaritan overtures to assist in rebuilding the Temple should be spurned. In other words, the dubious ways of these meddlesome northern neighbors could only contaminate Yahweh's elect in Jerusalem. Second, Haggai may be using a parable to say that evil is more contagious than good and that this truth applies even to man's best-laid plans. This would imply that for the sake of its religious health, the Jerusalem community should not waver in its resolve to rebuild Yahweh's house. Since the Samaritans are not referred to by name in 2:10–14, the second interpretation is the more attractive.

A fourth oracle (2:15–19) refers to the economic well-being that will come to the people once the Temple is rebuilt.[13] Finally, in his last oracle (2:20–23), Haggai has more to say about the upheavals that the nations will experience on the imminent day of Yahweh. In v. 23 Yahweh selects Zerubbabel as his messianic agent. The deity promises to make Zerubbabel "like a signet ring." We doubt, however, that Haggai was recommending a course of political action to his listeners:

> Whatever precise future situation was envisaged, the immediate claim which Haggai is making is that of the sovereignty of God and of his control over all the world. In this, the Temple at Jerusalem is central; alongside it, the establishment of Zerubbabel represents the choice of the agent by whom God effects his rule. The real actor in this is God himself. . . . The real point is the reversal of previous judgment, and hence the reality of the arrival of the new age.[14]

Haggai therefore insisted that if the present foretold ill for Persia, it held a new potential for Yahweh's own people. If they would but overcome their inertia and depression, they would surely experience a better day.

Zechariah. Like Haggai, Zechariah functioned during those critical months when Darius' future as Persia's monarch was anything but secure. Yet unlike Haggai, Zechariah also addressed his people through November or December 518, and thus after Darius had steadied his position (Zech. 7:1). Though Darius presently held sway over a large, secure empire, Zechariah claimed that Yahweh still intended to establish his kingdom over all the earth and to honor Jerusalem as its center. The plan was merely deferred until the time when Zerubbabel and Joshua could fulfill their intended civil and religious functions.

The Book of Zechariah is composite. Whereas chapters 1–8 offer the utterances of Zechariah, who functioned at a relatively late point in the sixth century, chapters 9–14 (Deutero-Zechariah) contain the apocalyptic reflections of perhaps the late fourth century. Chapters 9–11 and 12–14 are the work of one, or perhaps two, disciples of Zechariah. In either case, they postdate Zechariah himself. The Persian setting of the earlier chapters is completely lacking in chapters 9–14. Jerusalem is now the victim of a war that scarcely would be conducive to the Temple reconstruction, and nameless shepherds have replaced Zerubbabel and Joshua as the community's leaders.

Our present task, then, is to come to terms with Zechariah 1–8. The bulk of this material (1:7–6:8) consists of eight nocturnal visions. In the first section of his book (1:1–6), Zechariah invites his people to return to Yahweh. He glances backward to earlier prophetic tradition and observes that the prophets had persistently summoned their audiences to repent. Because the fathers had not heeded their warnings, they became the victims of Yahweh's wrath. Zechariah is in effect admonishing, "Make sure that history does not repeat itself!"

Then 1:7–6:8 contains Zechariah's eight dream visions. Despite their bizarre quality, they form an intelligible sequence. With their portrayal of four horsemen and chariots as harbingers of the earth's final ruin, the first and eighth visions frame the other six, which seem to exist in pairs

(2–3, 4–5, 6–7). Of special interest is the middle pair, which concentrates on Judaism's leaders Joshua and Zerubbabel. At the end of the visions we encounter a crucial though confused passage (6:9–15) that originally must have dealt with the crowning of Zerubbabel as Judah's messianic king. While the tampered text in v. 11 now designates that Joshua will wear the crown, Hag. 2:23 pins its messianic hope on governor Zerubbabel. No doubt after it had become painfully clear that Zerubbabel was not Judaism's awaited messiah, an editor replaced Zerubbabel's name with Joshua's.

Each vision has a dominant motif to advance. In 1:8–17 the vision of the four horsemen announces that the earth is now at peace, the Temple will be rebuilt, and Yahweh will soon return in triumph to Jerusalem. In 1:18–21 four smiths act as Yahweh's agents by striking down four horns, which represent the worldly power that previously had scattered Judah. In 2:1–5 a measuring line is the point of departure for the assurance that the reconstituted Jerusalem will be massive and secure. In 3:1–10 Satan brings charges of defilement against Joshua, who personifies the Jewish community, but Yahweh acquits and sanctifies Joshua so that he might carry out his priestly functions. In 4:1–6a and 10b–14 we confront a lampstand, whose seven candles symbolize the eyes of Yahweh, and two olive trees, which represent Joshua and Zerubbabel. In 5:1–4 a flying scroll symbolizes the purging of those within the Jewish community who steal and bear false witness. In 5:5–11 Judah's cleansing from sin is depicted through a woman named "Wickedness" who flies through the air to Babylon in a basket ("Shinar," v. 11). And in 6:1–8 four patrolling chariots are dispatched to different points on the compass in preparation for Yahweh's final triumph over the world.

The third section of the Book of Zechariah (7:1–8:23) deals with the people's fasting and Yahweh's return to Zion. The fasting issue (7:1–14) focuses on whether the people should continue to fast in the fifth and seventh months as a way of commemorating Jerusalem's fall to the Babylonians. Zechariah replies that the motivation of formal religious observance and upright ethical behavior are of greater import than the fasting per se (7:9–10). Yahweh's return to Zion and the positive consequences that will ensue for his people unify the ten brief oracles in Zech. 8:1–23. These disclosures underscore Yahweh's desire to reinhabit Zion, return the exiled Jews to Jerusalem, and provide the true remnant with a goodly measure of peace and prosperity. Further, Zechariah closes on a resounding note of universalism: "In those days ten men from the nations of every tongue shall take hold of the robe of a Jew, saying, 'Let us go with you, for we have heard that God is with you'" (8:23).

We may be tempted to conclude that the postexilic prophecy of Zechariah was no match for the more stirring pronouncements of such preexilic prophets as Amos and Isaiah. Zechariah's relationship with the deity was not particularly intimate. Also his farfetched symbolism and heavy use of an interpreting angel suggest that prophets were now communicating in a new and not entirely appealing idiom. Sometimes Zechariah gave in too readily to his legalistic and didactic inclinations. Nevertheless, he was truly excited about the prospects of the new day in store for Judaism. Unwilling to view his era as a "day of small things" (4:10), he was certain that Yahweh would soon display his strength, love, and abiding presence.

Zechariah's witness must have had a significant influence on his contemporaries, who completed the construction of the Temple in 515 (Ezra 6:15).[15] To be sure, the final product was not as magnificent as its predecessor. Nevertheless, the second Temple was a dramatic symbol that Yahweh's exiled people had once more established themselves in their

The Wailing Wall of the Jerusalem Temple. Above is part of the western enclosure wall of the Herodian temple. The massive hewn stones are typical of the style of masonry that emerged after Herod began to dismantle the Second Temple in about 20 B.C. so that a more magnificent one might be constructed. At the time of its Roman destruction in A.D. 70, Herod's temple had probably not been completed. This imposing wall has often been referred to as the "Wailing Wall," for it was here that many Jews once lamented the loss of the Jerusalem sanctuary and their national home. (Courtesy of the Israel Government Tourist Office, Chicago.)

homeland. Moreover, with the mysterious disappearance of Zerubbabel, who may have been removed about this time by Persian authorities irritated by messianic predictions that had gathered about him, the priestly dimension of Israel's postexilic existence became all the more significant. Endowed with a completed Temple and an influential high priest, the theocratic Judean community had good reason to believe that even now Yahweh was determined not to abandon his people.

THE RESTORATION OF THE JEWISH COMMUNITY UNDER NEHEMIAH

The Situation prior to Nehemiah: The Witness of Malachi

We are almost entirely ignorant of events in Judah during the seventy years between the dedication of the new Temple (515) and the beginning of Nehemiah's mission (445). The Chronicler offers us merely one misplaced passage in Ezra 4:7–23 which instructs that during the reign of Artaxerxes I (465–424), Samaritan officials induced the Persian monarch to require that Jews stop mending Jerusalem's broken walls. Such opposition must have manifested itself during the first half of Artaxerxes' reign, for in 445 the king granted Nehemiah permission to journey to Jerusalem and oversee the rebuilding of the city (Neh. 2:1–8). Otherwise our knowledge of this period depends on suggestions that emerge from a careful reading of Persian sources, Nehemiah's memoirs, and the Book of Malachi.

Malachi's pronouncements reflect the low ebb of Palestinian Jewish life in about 450. Four considerations speak for such a date. First, references to Judah's existence under a governor (Mal. 1:8) and to the standing Temple (1:10; 3:1, 10) require a date past 515. Second, the phrasing of Malachi's condemnation of mixed marriages (2:10–16) suggests that Nehemiah had not yet confronted the problem, and thus a date prior to 440 is warranted. Third, the lack of a distinction between priests and Levites (2:4–9; 3:3) suggests that the Priestly Code had not as yet been introduced. And fourth, since the priests have grown weary of Temple ritual (1:13) and much of the population was becoming indifferent to the religious tradition, a date appreciably later than 515 commends itself.

Despite the presence of a completed Temple and the gradual return of Diaspora Jews to their homeland, the restoration experiment in Palestine was turning sour. History had not confirmed the expectations of Haggai and Zechariah. The former had rigorously claimed that the rebuilding of the Temple was, among other things, a sound means of overcoming pressing economic problems. But now the Temple was finished, and economic hardship still existed. And what was the depressed community to make of Zechariah's assurance that Yahweh was already preparing to reestablish himself in Zion and favor Jerusalem and Judah with comfort and plenty (Zech. 8:1–15)? The messianic hope that centered on Zerubbabel had come to nothing. Indeed, present realities led some to doubt that Yahweh was watching over the Judean community at all. Resources and protection were both in woefully short supply. The Samaritan aristocracy was still asserting itself from the north, and the Edomites, who had been forced out of former territorial holdings by marauding Nabatean Arabs, were now threatening southern Palestine. Under the guise of self-survival, some Jews were taking their religious heritage rather lightly. The priests were bored with their duties (Mal. 1:13). And many of the laity had no hesitations about cheating one another in everyday dealings (3:5). Mixed marriages and easy divorce were also common (2:10–16). This was not Israel's finest hour.

Nevertheless, in about 450 an anonymous prophet appeared who attempted to set matters right. In the superscription of his book he is called "Malachi" (1:1). But this appellation, meaning "my messenger," seems to have come directly under the influence of 3:1, in which the deity states, "Behold, I send my messenger, to prepare the way before me." Because the statements in this book can be assigned to one period of time and because they express the thought of a single mind, it is convenient to refer to their author as Malachi.

Malachi's distinctive approach reveals something of his personality and his time. He does not favor the oracular style typical of earlier prophets. Instead, he uses dialogue as a form of discourse. The two parties of the dialogue are Yahweh (or the prophet) and the people (or their priests). Yahweh speaks first, and the people respond by raising questions. Yahweh then issues his rejoinder, which may also take the form of a rhetorical question. The three verses that follow will illustrate Malachi's style:

> A son honors his father, and a servant his master. If then I am a father, where is my honor? And if I am a master, where is my fear? says Yahweh of hosts to you, O priests, who despise my name. You say, How have we despised thy name? By offering polluted food upon my altar. And you say, How have we polluted it? By thinking that Yahweh's table may be despised. When you offer blind animals in sacrifice, is that no evil? And when you offer those that are lame or sick, is that no evil? (1:6–8b)

Neil sums up the uniqueness of Malachi's approach when he writes that Malachi "had to argue his case in a way that his predecessors in the heyday of classical prophecy had never been obliged to do."[16]

The Book of Malachi has six sections. In the first (1:2–5) Yahweh's love of Israel is contrasted with his hatred of Edom. Malachi argues that like the descendants of the twin brothers Jacob and Esau, Israel and Edom have experienced very dissimilar fates. Whatever the nature of Israel's plight, it does not compare with the misfortune of the Edomites, who had recently been ousted from their ancestral territory by invading Arabs. The second section (1:6–2:9) is Malachi's sharp attack on the bored priests who have offered Yahweh the blind, lame, and sick animals from the flock, and failed to instruct the laity properly in its religious obligations. Malachi claims that even the Gentiles are purer in their worship of Yahweh than Judah is (1:11; cf. 2:10). The prophet is convinced that professionals who take lightly the law and cult must indeed take lightly the one who called that law and cult into existence. In the third discourse (2:10–16) Malachi inveighs against the dereliction of Judean laymen who have freely divorced their Jewish wives to marry foreign women.

In a fourth section (2:17–3:5) the prophet addresses the future. He refers to the approaching day of judgment that will undo those who speak so skeptically about the reality of divine justice. A fifth discourse (3:6–12) protests against the people's unwillingness to pay their tithes and present their offerings. And a sixth (3:14–4:3) assures that while the wicked appear to have it made, they will suffer in the coming judgment. By contrast, the pious who persist in their service of the deity will ultimately enjoy their reward. Appended to Malachi's words are two short editorial additions. The first (4:4) is probably an attempt to summarize in one sentence the thrust of Malachi's message, and the second (4:5–6) equates Elijah with the nameless "messenger" alluded to in 3:1.

Malachi evokes from most readers both negative and positive reactions. His vindictive attitude toward Edom (1:2–5) is narrow and his opinion that Yahweh is virtually obliged to reward those who pay their tithes (3:10) is crassly expressed. Still, in his day Malachi's efforts were an asset to Judaism. Active at a time when there was little respect for the prophetic office, the reforming Malachi confronted a people who had allowed their corporate life to be tainted by worthless offerings, social abuses, and infidelity to the covenant. We do not know to what extent the prophet was successful. It is reasonable to assume, however, that Malachi proved his worth by paving the way for Nehemiah and Ezra.

Chronological Problems Pertaining to the Work of Nehemiah and Ezra

One of the most formidable problems that Old Testament scholarship must face is the sequence and dating of Ezra and Nehemiah.[17] Did Ezra precede Nehemiah, did Nehemiah precede Ezra, or were the two contemporaries? Though the Persian court dispatched Nehemiah to Jerusalem with political authority and sent Ezra there to engage in religious tasks, the texts of Ezra-Nehemiah reveal that the work of both men was remarkably similar. Thus, the governor Nehemiah regulated the priesthood, promoted a program of tithing in support of the Temple, and sought to implement a suitable pattern of Sabbath observance.

If Ezra served prior to Nehemiah and did so early in the reign of

Artaxerxes I, we must infer that Nehemiah's reforms succeeded whereas most of Ezra's failed. Ezra's impact on later Judaism was so extensive, however, that this sequence does not seem viable. But to place the reforming Ezra entirely after Nehemiah, and thus early in the reign of Artaxerxes II, means that Nehemiah's work is no longer viewed in an especially advantageous light. At least it implies that Nehemiah's reforms had no lasting effect, for Ezra had to address essentially the same problems.

Then perhaps Ezra's mission commenced somewhat late in the reign of Artaxerxes I, while Nehemiah was still in office. This view, which has won advocates in recent years, infers that Ezra reinforced what Nehemiah was already attempting to do. Yet against it stands the fact that the two men are almost never associated in the text.

Our knowledge of Nehemiah's dates is virtually certain. Nehemiah 2:1 and 13:6–7 state that the governor's first administration began in the twentieth year of Artaxerxes and lasted into the thirty-second year, at which point Nehemiah returned to Persia. At some later time, Nehemiah went back to Jerusalem; the precise length of his second administration is impossible to determine. Since the Elephantine papyri report that during the last decade of the fifth century, the two sons of Nehemiah's chief opponent, Sanballat, had assumed positions of leadership, Nehemiah must be placed in the reign of Artaxerxes I (465–424).[18] Hence, we may date Nehemiah's first efforts as governor to 445–433 and posit that his second term in office began in about 432 and lasted for perhaps a decade.

Many scholars maintain that Ezra's mission began in 398, and thus in the seventh year of the reign of Artaxerxes II.[19] There are several reasons. First, within the Ezra story, Ezra 9:9 and 10:1 imply the presence of a walled, populous Jerusalem whose strength may very well attest to Nehemiah's efforts of an earlier day. Second, Ezra's stand against mixed marriages (Ezra 10:3, 11) was more extreme than Nehemiah's (Neh. 13:25), which means that Ezra probably postdates Nehemiah. Third, since Eliashib was high priest in Nehemiah's day (Neh. 3:1) and his grandson, Johanan, seems to have served in that office in Ezra's time (Ezra 10:6; Neh. 12:10–11, 22), Ezra must have arrived in Jerusalem several decades after Nehemiah.[20] And fourth, Nehemiah's memoirs never mention Ezra's name, and the Ezra narrative seldom refers to Nehemiah; therefore we cannot easily accept the two reformers as contemporaries.

Several scholars have linked Ezra with Nehemiah's second administration and have argued that Ezra's mission began in 428 during the thirty-seventh year of the reign of Artaxerxes I.[21] They maintain that the governor, Nehemiah, whose political prerogatives did not give him the advantage he needed to carry through radical religious reform, effected what changes he could prior to 433, whereupon he returned to the Persian court and successfully laid plans for a co-worker with priestly talents to be sent to Jerusalem. Then in 428 Ezra came and worked alongside Nehemiah in an earnest attempt to reorganize the Judean community around the Torah. Ezra therefore joined Nehemiah's struggling cause and brought it to marvelous completion.

Several criticisms of the 428 date may be proposed. First, the textual emendation that changes Ezra 7:7 to refer to Artaxerxes' thirty-seventh year is no more commendable than is the widely embraced proposal to delete Nehemiah's name in Neh. 8:9 where it stands beside Ezra's. Second, the Bible nowhere reports that Ezra and Nehemiah were strongwilled opponents. And finally, the equation of "Hanani" (Nehemiah's brother, who is mentioned in Neh. 7:2) and "Hananiah" (mentioned in the so-called Passover Papyrus discovered at Elephantine) is risky because the name Hananiah (Hanani) was relatively common.

Although conclusive evidence is unavailable, we favor the 398 date for the beginning of Ezra's Jerusalem mission. Surely the sequence Nehemiah-Ezra is historically correct, and for the moment it seems to us that all Nehemiah's efforts predated Ezra.

The Career of Nehemiah

Nehemiah's career as Judah's reforming governor was directly inspired by the arrival of a Jerusalem delegation to the Persian court at Susa in 445 (Neh. 1:1–3). Nehemiah was Artaxerxes' cupbearer at the time. Among the visitors from Jerusalem was Hanani, Nehemiah's brother. Their purpose in coming was to report Jerusalem's destitute situation to the Persian authorities in the hope that help might be forthcoming. In particular, it was called to Nehemiah's attention that Jerusalem's wall and gates lay in ruin. Nehemiah obtained an audience with the king, who acceded to his request that he journey to Jerusalem and rebuild its fortifications (Neh. 2:1–8). Perhaps it was at this moment that Artaxerxes appointed Nehemiah governor of Judah (5:14). By taking such an interest in Judean affairs, Artaxerxes was apparently seeking to build there a strong and loyal buffer state that would protect him from a troublesome Egypt. And if a fortified Jerusalem were governed under Nehemiah, whose loyalty to the Persian court had been well attested, Artaxerxes might have more to gain than to lose.

Nehemiah eventually arrived in Jerusalem (2:11), and after inspecting the city's fallen fortifications by moonlight, he immediately undertook its repair. Nehemiah summoned a labor force, which he organized into various groups. Each was assigned a section of the wall to rebuild (Neh. 3). In a mere fifty-two days (6:15), the basic structure was finished. The builders, who were for the most part unskilled, had worked rapidly and defensively within an extremely hostile environment.

The opposition was headed by Sanballat, who is identified in the Elephantine papyri as Samaria's governor. Undoubtedly he had previously exerted his influence over Judah. Now he had no intention of losing tax revenues and risking the chance that Jerusalem might eclipse his own city in Persian eyes. Sanballat had allies in Tobiah, the governor of the Transjordanian province of Ammon, and Geshem, governor of an Arabian province (Kedar) that extended westward into southern Judah.

The physical and psychological warfare that these three opponents waged against Nehemiah and his following was considerable. To no avail they tried to lower the morale of the wall builders by mocking their efforts (Neh. 4:1–4). They dispatched teams of Arabs, Ammonites, and Ashdodites (Philistines) to victimize Jerusalem and its environs (4:7–9). They tried unsuccessfully to lure Nehemiah away from Jerusalem for an alleged conference (6:1–4). When the enemy threatened to press charges of disloyalty against Nehemiah before the Persian authorities, Nehemiah countered that they lacked the necessary evidence (6:5–8). And when Shemaiah was hired to alarm Nehemiah with news of his impending assassination, Nehemiah did not disgrace himself by fleeing, as was hoped (6:10–11). Such attacks against Nehemiah were incapable of blocking the Judean effort. With the wall built and dedicated (12:27–43), the undaunted Nehemiah could deal with other issues that were already having a devastating impact on the Jewish community.

The governor's reform measures are narrated mainly in Nehemiah 5 and 13. In the former passage, economic problems are dated early in Nehemiah's first term of office, as if to suggest that with the people's preoccupation with wall building, Judah's economic situation had gotten out of hand. In the latter, Nehemiah, now in his second term of office, is portrayed as a staunch religious reformer who dealt with corruption in the Temple, Levitical poverty, Sabbath abuse, and mixed marriages. It is more likely, however, that both the economic and religious health of the restoration community had Nehemiah's attention throughout his career as Judah's governor. Even during his first term of office, Nehemiah probably took some steps to correct what were for him intolerable religious conditions.

In sum, Nehemiah was a forceful administrator who acted in the light of what he believed was right for Judaism. His memoirs reveal that he lacked tact, humility, and flexibility. His devotion to Yahweh was nonetheless intense, and he was convinced that God helps those who help themselves. Nehemiah resolved to make his people worthy specimens of a religious purity that was fast disappearing, and he worked hard, if not always successfully, to make good that resolve.

THE RESTORATION OF THE JEWISH COMMUNITY UNDER EZRA

Presumably Ezra and his delegation appeared in Jerusalem in 398, at which time still another phase of Palestinian Judaism came into being. Ezra had two related goals. First, he tried to spark in the Jewish theocracy a genuine desire to uphold its ancestral law. In Ezra's view, to take the law in anything but a serious manner was to incur Yahweh's wrath. Second, Ezra wished to confer on his comrades a new sense of identity and purpose. As the years passed, it had become painfully evident that the resurrection of the glorious Davidic empire was not a live option. The hopes attached to Zerubbabel had proved false, and the Persian empire still held sway over large segments of the ancient Near East. In addition, bad weather and unfriendly neighbors added a gloomy note to an already tenuous economic and political situation. Nevertheless, Ezra declared that Yahweh's concern for his people had not diminished. Indeed, a new day was now greeting the covenant community. While it was not burgeoning with hopeful prospects as Second Isaiah had anticipated it would, it offered Israel a way to regain a strong sense of purpose. She was now invited to live nobly as a theocratic community firmly rooted in Mosaic law.

The priestly Ezra, whose genealogy reveals that he belonged to the Zadokite order rather than to the Levitical order (Ezra 7:1–5), arrived in Jerusalem superbly equipped for the task of sponsoring comprehensive religious reform. In addition to being well schooled in the law that he brought (7:6, 10), Ezra came to his duties with the backing of a Persian court whose policy of supporting the native cults within its borders had not weakened. Artaxerxes II had appointed Ezra for his mission. Those Jews who opposed Ezra's reform measures by disregarding "the law of God," which he strove to interpret and enforce, were at the same time disregarding "the law of the king" (Ezra 7:26). Hence, Ezra's authority over religious affairs in the Persian satrapy of Abar-nahara (Syria-Palestine) was most impressive.

The Chronicler presents three aspects of Ezra's work within the Judean community: he promulgates the Mosaic Torah (Neh. 8), dissolves mixed marriages (Ezra 9–10), and conducts a significant ceremony of covenant renewal (Neh. 9–10). Ezra viewed proclaiming "the book of the law of Moses" as his first task (Neh. 8:1). Once more literary material was virtually canonized by a public reading. Here Neh. 8:13–18 is of special interest. It states that the people had been ignorant of the proper way of celebrating the Feast of Tabernacles until Ezra had instructed them. Since the celebration reported in Nehemiah 8 accords with Lev. 23:39–43, we may infer that prior to this moment the so-called priestly legislation had been mainly a matter of oral and fragmentary promulgation. Although legislation within the Code of Deuteronomy (Deut. 16:13–15) called for the Feast of Tabernacles, it said nothing about dwelling in freshly constructed booths as a way of commemorating Israel's Exodus from Egypt.[22] Clearly, with Ezra's formal reading of the law, a new ritualistic dimension had been added to the festival.

Ezra's book of law surely contained more than the Priestly Code. In fact, it may have embodied the entire Pentateuch: "It would be a strangely deformed tradition which described for us the solemn acceptance of the Priestly Code but failed to preserve any record of an event so momentous as the canonisation of the Pentateuch as a whole."[23] If not in Ezra's lifetime, then surely soon thereafter, the entire Torah enjoyed widespread recognition and veneration. The law of Moses henceforth became the principal norm within Judaism.

Ezra then moved in other directions. The Chronicler reports that Ezra was profoundly concerned about mixed marriages. Though the energetic Nehemiah had earlier addressed the issue (Neh. 13:23–28), the single men of Judah presumably found the young ladies outside the exilic community extremely appealing despite the governor's proscription against taking foreigners in marriage. Ezra openly displayed his consternation, and in a long prayer to Yahweh he voiced an eloquent confession of the people's sin (Ezra 9:6–15). Moved by it all, the witnessing assembly acknowledged their error and expressed their willingness to make a covenant with the deity and divorce their foreign wives (10:1–5). After a period of three months, which allowed for the investigation of various cases, all mixed marriages were terminated.

The Chronicler likewise reports that Ezra brought the people together in a ceremony of covenant renewal (Neh. 9–10). In that context, the people's promising yet problematic history was reviewed and the ancestral faith was affirmed. The congregation promised to abide by the requirements of the law of Moses. Near the end of this literary unit, such pledges as the following are made: mixed marriages will not be entered into (10:30), the Sabbath Day will be respected in the manner in which it was intended (10:31a), in the seventh year the land will lie at rest and debts will not have to be paid (10:31b), and the Temple cult will be maintained through the collection of an annual tax and the donation of such goods as are required (10:32–39).

Ezra and Nehemiah were intense, rigid individuals who fostered in their people a strong feeling of separatism. Neither was especially inclined to remind Israel that part of her mission might be to bring foreigners to an awareness of Yahweh. Yet their work made it possible for the postexilic community to experience a new burst of life. This period in Israel's history was unmistakably one which demanded that the people of Yahweh engage in a formidable task of self-examination. That this undertaking essentially succeeded was due primarily to the fact that in Nehemiah and Ezra significant resources and direction were available upon which the people might draw.

NOTES

1. The author is in agreement with George G. Cameron, "Ancient Persia," in Robert C. Dentan, ed., *The Idea of History in the Ancient Near East*, American Oriental Series (New Haven, Conn.: Yale University Press, 1955), pp. 83–84.

2. James B. Pritchard, ed., *Ancient Near Eastern Texts Relating to the Old Testament*, 3d ed. (Princeton, N.J.: Princeton University Press, 1969), pp. 315–316; approximately one-fourth of the Pritchard text is cited here. The parentheses contain the translator's interpolations, except for the one instance when they offer a transliteration of the original Akkadian. Ellipses indicate breaks in the text. Note that Anshan is both a district and a city in northeastern Elam. Note also the striking similarity between the sentence, "He made him set out on the road to Babylon . . . going at his side like a real friend," and the wording in Yahweh's speech to Cyrus, "I will go before you" (Isa. 45:2a).

3. Notably Aramaic letters dating to the second half of the fifth century B.C. and emanating from the Jewish military colony at Elephantine in Upper Egypt.

4. It seems Nehemiah's memoirs appear in Neh. 1:1–7:4; 11:1–2; 12:27–43; 13:4–31, and Ezra's in Ezra 7:27–9:15. Perhaps Ezra's memoirs encompass even more of the Ezra story (Ezra 7:1–10:44, Neh. 7:73b–9:38). Albright sees such similarities in style and perspective between the Ezra memoirs and the Chronicler's work as a whole that he sides with the Jewish tradition that the Chronicler is Ezra. (William F. Albright, *The Biblical Period from Abraham to Ezra* [New York: Harper & Row, Harper Torchbooks, 1963], p. 95.)

5. On his deathbed David's main concern in 1 Chron. 28 is to transmit plans for the Jerusalem Temple; this portrayal offers a stark contrast to 1 Kings 2:5–9, in which the dying David calls for the assassination of Joab and Shimei.

6. The authenticity of the Aramaic version, where Cyrus is not set in devout association with Yahweh, has been more widely accepted than its Hebrew counterpart has. The hand of the Chronicler is evident in the Hebrew version.

7. See, for example, Robert H. Pfeiffer, "Books of Ezra and Nehemiah," in George A. Buttrick et al., eds., *The Interpreter's Dictionary of the Bible* (Nashville: Abingdon Press, 1962), E–J, p. 217, who assesses the Hebrew text as "spurious" and the Aramaic version as "historically a dead letter."

8. This assumes that "Shenazzar" mentioned in 1 Chron. 3:18 is one and the same person.

9. See Albright, *op. cit.*, pp. 110–111, n. 180.

10. Writing in the first century of the Christian era, the Jewish historian Josephus declared, "Many remained in Babylon, being unwilling to leave their possessions." *Josephus*, VI (*Jewish Antiquities*, Books IX–XI), Loeb Classical Library, trans. Ralph Marcus (Cambridge, Mass.: Harvard University Press, 1937), p. 317. (XI. 1.3.)

11. Moreover, Sheshbazzar's political status eludes us. See John Bright, *A History of Israel*, 2d ed. (Philadelphia: Westminster Press, 1972), p. 363.

12. Although the Chronicler attributes the laying of the Temple foundations to Zerubbabel (Ezra 3:6–11), in his Aramaic source (Ezra 5:16) Sheshbazzar is given the credit. Perhaps the collective efforts of Sheshbazzar and his colleagues at Temple reconstruction were so minimal that in time Zerubbabel and his following were given full credit for having laid the foundations.

13. This oracle has probably been misplaced, because it seems to have as its introduction the suspended date formula of Hag. 1:15a.

14. Peter R. Ackroyd, *Exile and Restoration: A Study of Hebrew Thought of the Sixth Century B.C.*, The Old Testament Library (Philadelphia: Westminster Press, 1968), pp. 165–166.

15. The Jews who were building the Temple were required to justify their activity to the suspicious Tattenai, satrap of Abar-nahara (meaning "beyond the river," which encompassed all Syria and Palestine). Nevertheless, he did not command them to desist while he conducted his investigation (Ezra 5:3–6:15). Tattenai contacted Darius, who reaffirmed Cyrus' earlier decree and instructed Tattenai in how he should materially assist the Jews. Presumably it was a rumor from Samaritan sources that motivated Tattenai to interfere in Jewish affairs at this point.

16. William Neil, "Malachi," in Buttrick et al., eds., *op. cit.*, K–Q, p. 231.

17. For detailed coverage of the issue, see Bright, *op. cit.*, pp. 392–403, and "The Chronological Order of Ezra and Nehemiah," in H. H. Rowley, *The Servant of the Lord and Other Essays on the Old Testament*, rev. ed. (Oxford: Basil Blackwell, 1965), pp. 137–168.

18. See Pritchard, *op. cit.*, pp. 491–492.

19. This position was first advanced by A. V. van Hoonacker in 1880. Bright, *op. cit.*, pp. 400–402, objects that 398 is probably too late a date for Ezra's arrival. While the 398 date has frequently been challenged, it has not as yet been effectively undercut.

20. Moreover, the papyri from Elephantine indicate that Johanan was Jerusalem's high priest during the final decade of the fifth century B.C.; see Pritchard, *op. cit.*, p. 492.

21. A thorough defense of this date is provided by Bright, *op. cit.*, pp. 401–403. See also Albright, *op. cit.*, p. 93.

22. According to Neh. 8:15, the people must go out into the hill country surrounding Jerusalem in order to gather branches to be used in building the booths. Deuteronomy 16:13–15 makes no such demand of the worshiping congregation, but Lev. 23:39–43 does.

23. George W. Anderson, "The Old Testament: Canonical and Non-Canonical," in P. R. Ackroyd and C. F. Evans, eds., *The Cambridge History of the Bible*, vol. 1 (Cambridge: Cambridge University Press, 1970), p. 123.

19

PROPHETS, PRIESTS, AND POETS IN POSTEXILIC ISRAEL

In the previous chapter we traced the history of the restoration community. Now we intend to examine its religious dimensions more closely. The messages of three units of postexilic prophecy (Third Isaiah [Isa. 56–66], Obadiah, and Joel), the main interests of the priestly narrative and code, and the Book of Psalms will claim our attention. To be sure, the Israelite Psalter is not limited to postexilic expressions of Hebrew piety. Many psalms appear to predate that era. Nevertheless, as the property of the second Temple, the Book of Psalms is especially relevant at this point.[1] Because none of the prophets whom we shall study in this chapter represents Hebrew prophetism at its best, we need not tarry with their proclamations. Still, it would be arbitrary to ignore them completely, for they have earned a place in the Old Testament canon.

The impact of priestly behavior and thought on exilic and postexilic Israel can be appreciated through a consideration of the interests of the P narrative in Genesis 1–11[2] and the Priestly Code as it has been preserved in Exodus, Leviticus, and Numbers.[3] Prophets, priests, and poets all contributed to the religious life and thought of emerging Judaism.

Biblical texts to be read prior to and in conjunction with the present chapter: Isaiah 56–66; Obadiah; Joel 1–3; Leviticus 16, 19; Psalms 8, 20, 21, 80, 51, 116. Also the following passages from Genesis should be read: 1:1–2:4a for the priestly creation account; 6:1–9:29 for the JP flood tradition; 5:1–32 for the P genealogy from Adam to Noah; 10:1–32 for the JP Table of Nations; and 11:10–27, 31–32 for the P genealogy from Shem (Noah's son) to Abraham.

THE PROPHETIC WITNESS
OF THIRD ISAIAH, OBADIAH, AND JOEL

Third Isaiah

Today it is widely held that Isaiah 56–66 is less the distillation of the thoughts and dreams of Second Isaiah near the end of the Babylonian exile than it is the varied reflection of the sober experiences that marked the early decades of the postexilic Judean community. Although Isaiah 40–55 projects a firm hope in Israel's imminent liberation from Babylonian captivity, Isaiah 56–66 reveals that the people of Yahweh are once more entrapped by a dismal existence. Perhaps much of chapters 60–62, with their focus on the glory awaiting Zion and its inhabitants, and 57:14–21, with its moving oracle of comfort, belong to Second Isaiah. Even so, on the basis of style and content, Isaiah 56–66 seems to be a composite product, distinct from what precedes it.

If these chapters (56–66), which are designated Third Isaiah, sometimes sustain a point of view earlier maintained in Isaiah 40–55, they express it with less poetic and theological excellence. Their fundamental lack of literary and thematic unity suggests that Isaiah 56–66 is the work of several individuals who stood in the shadow of their deceased mentor.

At its best, Third Isaiah offers a sensitive portrait of the deity. Such passages as 64:1 and 66:1 emphasize the heavenly residence of a transcendent God who, despite his concern with terrestrial affairs, is not to be confused with the mortal creatures who populate the earth. Though the Jerusalem Temple is a useful rallying point for the corporate worship of Yahweh, the edifice cannot contain the uncontested creator of heaven and earth (cf. 1 Kings 8:27). Nevertheless, the omnipotent deity is not oblivious to the problems and desires of the pious. Only human iniquity creates the hopeless chasm between man and God (Isa. 59:1–3). Moreover, in Third Isaiah the righteous Yahweh is as concerned with genuine brotherhood among the Jews as he is with right worship. This is deftly expressed in the rhetorical questions advanced in Isa. 58:6–7.

There are, however, at least three dimensions to Isaiah 56–66 that coordinate poorly with Second Isaiah's reflections. First, the disciples of Second Isaiah had to relate their religious instruction to a new, often trying Judean environment. Isaiah 58–59 reveals that the restoration community was tainted by their interest in expedience and compromise. The laity fasted solely for pragmatic purposes. When material blessings did not abound, they called Yahweh to account: "Why have we fasted, and thou seest it not? Why have we humbled ourselves, and thou takest no knowledge of it?" (58:3).

This penchant for complaint and the crass definition of the relationship between God and man scarcely remind us of Second Isaiah's lyrics. Also 56:10–12 instructs that the leaders of the community were not setting a good example. Referred to as dumb dogs incapable of barking and as shepherds obsessed with their own gain, the people's leaders are severely rebuked for their corruption. Third Isaiah's poetry instructs us that some preexilic problems in the covenant community had reappeared as postexilic problems.

Second, Israel's destiny and that of the nations were undergoing redefinition. Despite the presence of a servant theme in Isa. 61:1–3, the provocative assertion in Isaiah 40–55 that Israel is called to suffer both for her own sake and for that of the world is wanting in Isaiah 56–66. The nations are no longer viewed so generously. True, foreigners who worship in Yahweh's Temple are accepted as worthy proselytes (56:3, 6–7). Yet Israel's impending salvation is anticipated as unfolding at the expense of other nations, whose wealth will be seized and given to Yahweh's elect (60:5; 61:6; 66:12). Moreover, the oracle of divine vengeance enthusiastically directed against Edom (63:1–6) is alien to Second Isaiah's mentality. In sum, Third Isaiah fosters a separatistic perspective that insists Israel must remain holy by scrupulous observance of the Sabbath (58:13–14) and avoidance of contaminating pagan influences.

Finally, in Isaiah 56–66 eschatological expectations are largely expressed in an apocalyptic idiom that was to become increasingly popular in postexilic Judaism. Yahweh proposes to create "new heavens and a new earth" (65:17), and in the restored Jerusalem a marvelous peace will prevail:

> The wolf and the lamb shall feed together,
>   the lion shall eat straw like the ox;
>   and dust shall be the serpent's food.
> They shall not hurt or destroy
>   in all my holy mountain, says Yahweh. (65:25)

Further, as is normative in the apocalyptic discourse of the Old Testament, a sharp distinction is drawn between the fates of the righteous and the wicked—blessing and eternal damnation, respectively (66:15–17, 24). On the whole, the oracles of Third Isaiah, most of which belong to the fifth century B.C., are not as stirring as those of Second Isaiah. Nevertheless, with some accuracy they record the feelings of the Palestinian Jewish community as it strove to oppose apostasy, engender piety, and anticipate an effective divine deliverance.

Obadiah

We really know nothing about the prophet Obadiah's background. Yet his name is attached to an uncommonly brief book that is striking in the vehemence of its polemic against Edom. While the literary integrity of the Book of Obadiah has sometimes been denied, the text seems to have a fundamental unity.[4] The book is filled with expressions of hate against Edom, and throughout it looks forward to the impending day of Yahweh.

Obadiah's resentment of Edom's past treachery against Yahweh's people probably expressed itself at about the same time that one of Second Isaiah's disciples voiced his hostility toward the hated enemy (Isa. 63:1–6). Therefore, we are inclined to assign the Book of Obadiah a date early in the fifth century B.C.

The movement within Obadiah's message is easy to detect. The prophet first declares that an awful punishment against the proud Edomite nation is imminent (vv. 2–9). She will be humbled, pillaged, and betrayed. Neither the wise nor the mighty in Edom will be able to avert the slaughter that will, to Judah's real satisfaction, overtake the nation. Second, Obadiah bitterly expounds on the treachery of Edom against Judah when Jerusalem was overcome by the Babylonian forces in 587 (vv. 10–14). "Brother" Edom exulted in Jerusalem's fall and stood ready to loot her goods and deliver her refugees to the Babylonians. In a third section (vv. 15–21), Obadiah declares that on the imminent day of Yahweh, circumstances will be splendidly reversed. The divine judgment against Edom will be so sweeping that not one Edomite will survive (v. 18). Judah will then lay claim to Edom's goods and territories, and Yahweh will exercise his sovereignty over a universal kingdom.

Other prophets meditated on Yahweh's impending judgment against the nations. Yet the shrill expressions of nationalism and vengeance in this book tempt us to question the wisdom of those who included Obadiah's words in the Hebrew canon. We should acknowledge, however, that Obadiah was driven by an intense concern for the welfare of his struggling people and was certain of Yahweh's ability to function as sovereign of all things. Although he was not a temperate man, he was a man of faith.

Joel

Presumably the Book of Joel was sparked by an intense swarm of locusts that attacked the Judean countryside. Severe drought and famine undoubtedly followed. Joel detected in this profoundly disturbing visitation a sign of the approaching day of Yahweh with its terrifying judgments. He therefore urged his contemporaries to participate in a solemn fast so that they might publicly repent their misdoings. It is tempting to suggest that Joel may have been directly influenced by Amos, who also had coped with locusts (cf. Amos 7:1–3). Joel was much more forthright in communicating hope, however. He believed that the ominous day of Yahweh would bring to the penitent Israel a blessing as great as the curse it would bring to the pagan world for its past treachery against Yahweh's elect.

Questions about the book's integrity and date go hand in hand. With its famous mention of the outpouring of Yahweh's spirit, Joel 2:28 clearly signals a new and strongly apocalyptic unit (2:28–3:21). Yet the text offers insufficient evidence for asserting, as some scholars have, that 1:1–2:27 and 2:28–3:21 derive from two postexilic prophets who lived at different times.

We shall maintain that the book may be viewed as a whole and probably dates to the second half of the fifth century. Several considerations argue for such a date. First, Israel and Judah are no longer separate kingdoms, and the noun "Israel" is applied to Judah (2:27; 3:2, 16). Second, the restoration of Jerusalem and its Temple seems to have occurred already (1:14; 2:7–9, 17). The Assyrians and Babylonians are nowhere mentioned, and the single reference to the Greeks (3:6) implies that they have not yet severely encroached on Judah's inhabitants. And mention of the cereal and drink offerings (1:9, 13; 2:14) best reflects the postexilic era, as does the prophet's emphasis on the necessity of right worship.

The organization of the Book of Joel is somewhat haphazard, yet the book excels on at least two counts. First, its description of the locust invasion, which comes upon Judah with unprecedented fury, is striking. Its stark realism argues that the prophet was depicting a natural phenomenon that he had personally witnessed. His locusts are locusts, not cryptic symbols of past or future enemy powers that threaten Judah's political status. Second, this book displays a skillful blend of historical and apocalyptic components. Joel artfully integrates the data of an actual plague of locusts with vivid details about the arrival of the day of Yahweh. If the advent of locusts that divested Judah of its vegetation was horrendous, the advent of Yahweh when he comes to conquer and judge his enemies will be equally devastating (3:14–15). Joel asserts that a cosmic reality is in the making: Zion's prosperity and Yahweh's uncontested rule will flourish eternally.

Joel takes his place beside Obadiah and the disciples of Second Isaiah as one who instructed his contemporaries about Yahweh's intentions for the world. This postexilic prophetic literature is most confident about Yahweh's sovereignty and its bearing on the continuation of the struggling remnant of Israel. It refuses to give in to paralyzing feelings of despair about the present. Rather, it looks with hope toward a vastly more promising future.

THE PRIESTLY WITNESS IN NARRATIVE AND LAW

The Narrative of P

Just as the story of Solomon's Israel is incomplete without mention of the literary and theological contribution of the tenth-century Yahwist, the story of exilic and postexilic Israel requires that we acknowledge the

P document, which was the last stratum of the Pentateuch to be completed. We are inclined to agree with Speiser that "P was not an individual, or even a group of like-minded contemporaries, but a school with an unbroken history reaching back to early Israelite times, and continuing until the Exile and beyond."[5]

The modern reader may not feel engaged by the pallid human characterizations typical of P, its heaven-centered orientation, its enthusiasm for genealogies and disinterest in full-scale narrative. Nevertheless, the theological contributions of P are considerable. For example, in the Book of Genesis, P offers four substantial narrative segments, and each is rich in religious overtones: the Creation (Gen. 1:1–2:4a), the Flood (portions of Gen. 6–9), God's self-manifestation and call to Abraham (Gen. 17), and Abraham's purchase of the cave of Machpelah (Gen. 23, which is at least priestly in its framework). While we have already commented on the last two episodes in Chapter 4, we have thus far remained silent about the priestly creation and flood narratives. Since P's thoroughgoing monotheism, concern for divine transcendence, and worldwide perspective are evidenced in the priestly primeval history preserved in portions of Genesis 1–11, we cannot bypass this crucial segment of Pentateuchal tradition. Because the P creation account presupposes a Babylonian cosmology, we must first come to terms with the *Enūma elish*, Babylon's famous creation epic.

The Enūma elish. This detailed epic of creation presents the eventful and recurring contest between cosmic order and chaos that did much to shape the Mesopotamian view of the world. Designated *Enūma elish* after its opening phrase, meaning "when on high," this epic is concerned with how cosmic order was established. From beginning to end, this masterpiece gives expression to the fundamental Babylonian assumption that universal order could only be obtained through periodic struggle.

The Babylonians coveted harmony, but harmonious conditions for human existence were not simply given once and for all at the beginning of time. Harmony depended on an annual combat in which the forces of order overcame the forces of chaos. Each year the creation epic was read aloud and acted out on the fourth day of the Babylonian New Year's festival. Presumably its effective recital provided the worshipers with hope that the year ahead would go well and that life would not unexpectedly lapse into a series of catastrophes. At the center of the cultic reenactment of creation and order was the king of Babylon, who assumed the role of Marduk. As the ritual unfolded, the god Marduk won out over the goddess Tiamat, and order once more dominated chaos. In fact, this patron god of Babylon became the head of the Babylonian pantheon.[6]

While its influence has been exaggerated, this Babylonian text has lent shape to the creation traditions in Genesis.[7] The sequence of textual elements in the *Enūma elish* and in the priestly account of creation is strikingly similar. Moreover, the preexistent watery chaos; the radical division of heaven and earth; the specific mention of the sun, moon, and stars as the heavenly bodies that provide light and determine seasons; the explicit interest in man's creation; and the motif of divine rest are central to both traditions.

Although we need not summarize the entire plot here, several elements in the Babylonian creation epic merit our consideration. The epic opens with mention of the great primordial seas, Apsu (fresh water) and Tiamat (salt water), and the many nature deities generated by them. In time these deities become noisy and disturb their inactive elders, Apsu and Tiamat, who desire sleep. Apsu suggests to Tiamat that they secure peace by killing the troublesome deities. But Tiamat, who has a divine will of her own, refuses to consent to Apsu's proposal. When Apsu resolves to carry out this rash action on his own, he is killed by Ea, the omniscient earth god. Tiamat then decides to avenge her husband's death. She prepares for battle against the major gods of the pantheon. Their only hope for escape lies in the possibility that one of them will overcome Tiamat in physical combat. And this is precisely what Ea's son, Marduk, succeeds in doing. He valiantly divides Tiamat's body in two. He creates the sky out of the upper half and the earth (Esharra) out of the lower, and has the gods Anu (sky), Enlil (air), and Ea (earth) take their places.

Marduk continues his creative acts. He sets up celestial stations for the gods and establishes the constellations to designate time. He creates the moon, sun, clouds, and mountains. From Tiamat's eyes he fashions the Tigris and Euphrates. Later Marduk reveals his desire that a terrestrial temple complex be built and named "Babylon," meaning "the houses of the great gods." The lesser deities, who had stood by Tiamat, are charged with constructing and maintaining the edifice. In addition, they will have to care for and feed the great gods. Because of the magnitude of their tasks, they appeal to Marduk for help. Consequently, from the blood of Tiamat's consort, Kingu, who is slain for the occasion, man is created. It is he who must now attend to the menial temple tasks.

To make this great epic more immediate and vivid for the reader, we shall cite four brief excerpts.

Marduk's initial encounter with Tiamat and Kingu:

> The lord approached to scan the inside of Tiamat,
> (And) of Kingu, her consort, the scheme to perceive.
> As he looks on, his course becomes upset,
> His will is distracted and his doings are confused.
> And when the gods, his helpers, who marched at his side,
> Saw the valiant hero, blurred became their vision.
> Tiamat emitted [a cry], without turning her neck . . .

Physical combat between Marduk and Tiamat:

> Then joined issue Tiamat and Marduk, wisest of gods.
> They strove in single combat, locked in battle.
> The lord spread out his net to enfold her,
> The Evil Wind, which followed behind, he let loose in her face.
> When Tiamat opened her mouth to consume him,
> He drove in the Evil Wind that she close not her lips.
> As the fierce winds charged her belly,
> Her body was distended and her mouth was wide open.
> He released the arrow, it tore her belly,
> It cut through her insides, splitting the heart.
> Having thus subdued her, he extinguished her life.

Marduk's creation of heaven and earth:

> Then the lord paused to view her dead body,
> That he might divide the monster and do artful works.
> He split her like a shellfish into two parts:
> Half of her he set up and ceiled it as sky,
> Pulled down the bar and posted guards.
> He bade them to allow not her waters to escape.
> He crossed the heavens and surveyed the regions.
> He squared Apsu's quarter, the abode of Nudimmud,
> As the lord measured the dimensions of Apsu.
> The Great Abode, its likeness, he fixed as Esharra,
> The Great Abode, Esharra, which he made as the firmament.
> Anu, Enlil, and Ea he made occupy their places.

The creation of man:

> When Marduk hears the words of the gods,
> His heart prompts (him) to fashion artful works.
> Opening his mouth, he addresses Ea
> To impart the plan he had conceived in his heart:
> "Blood I will mass and cause bones to be.
> I will establish a savage, 'man' shall be his name.
> Verily, savage-man I will create.
> He shall be charged with the service of the gods
>   That they might be at ease!..."
> Out of his blood they fashioned mankind.
> He imposed the service and let free the gods.[8]

Thus, man is formally charged with the care of the gods and the temple. While man's life is not without purpose, human nature and destiny are not celebrated here as they are in the priestly creation account of Genesis 1.

   The Priestly Account of Creation. In dealing with Gen. 1:1–2:4a, we shall confine our attention to the basic shape of the material, its affinities with the *Enūma elish,* and the most central features of the priestly creation tradition. This liturgical account projects a strong note of order and dignity. Its depiction of the seven days of creation is balanced. Each day has its own contribution to make to the process of creation. Certain expressions are constantly repeated: "And God said, 'Let there be,' " "And it was so," "And God saw that it was good," "And there was evening and there was morning, a . . . day." At worst, such phrasing is impersonal and studied, yet at times stateliness and grandeur are achieved.

Biblical scholars have found Gen. 1:1–2 especially problematic. Since both the much earlier Babylonian creation epic and the preexilic Yahwist's story of creation open with a temporal clause, it is probable that the first words of the priestly creation account are also intended to convey a temporal reference. Following Speiser's cogent suggestion that v. 2 constitutes a parenthetic clause, we shall translate: "By way of beginning, as God created the heavens and the earth [v. 2 clause], God said, 'Let there be light.' "[9] Hence, v. 1 indicates the subject at hand—namely, the creation of heaven and earth, which set time in motion. The formlessness and darkness in v. 2 are not considered the first phase of the deity's creative work, but instead witness to the chaotic presence of preexistent matter. The Babylonian, Yahwistic, and priestly creation accounts all attest to some preexistent element.

The creation sequence is set forth a day at a time. The emergence of light (day) and darkness (night) is the work of the first day (1:3–5), and on the second day a heavenly firmament is constructed (vv. 6–8). Thought to be a solid vault, the firmament divides the upper and lower waters. The third day involves the creation of the dry earth, which emerges from the seas (vv. 9–10). The terrestrial waters are assigned their place beside the dry land. God also uses the third day to decree that the earth bring forth vegetation (vv. 11–13). The creation of the sun, moon, and stars is the focus of the fourth day (vv. 14–19). The relationship of the creation of these luminous bodies on the fourth day to the creation of light on the first may disturb contemporary readers. But the breakdown in logic appears not to have troubled the Israelite priests, who were mainly concerned with recording the creation of light-giving bodies whose existence is wholly dependent upon the creator God who called them into being. The fifth day witnesses to the beginning of the creation of the animal kingdom (vv. 20–23). The birds and fish are created. Then on the sixth day, the land animals come into being, and man (male and female) is made in the divine image and ordained to have dominion over the earth (vv. 24–31). The work of creation now completed, the seventh day, the Sabbath, is instituted as the day of rest and sanctified by God's own repose (2:1–3).

The order of the events in Gen. 1:1–2:4a corresponds closely with the sequence in the *Enūma elish*. The following list of the eight-step creation sequence in the Babylonian account may prove useful. Beside each entry we include the relevant verse or verses in the priestly narrative of Genesis.

1. The presence of preexistent cosmic matter (1:2a).
2. The existence of primeval chaos and darkness (1:2b).
3. Light issuing from the gods (1:3–4).
4. The making of a firmament (1:6–8).
5. The emergence of dry land (1:9–10).
6. The creation of light-giving bodies (1:14–19).
7. The formation of man (1:26–27).
8. The repose of the gods (2:1–3).[10]

Surely it is not by accident that Gen. 1:1–2:4a is faithful to that same sequence. Again ancient Israel stood in debt to a neighboring culture, and it is entirely understandable that it be Babylon. The formation of this priestly account relates to the years when Yahweh's people suffered exile in Babylon and to the decades immediately thereafter when they returned to their own land. Of course, some of the details in the Babylonian and priestly creation accounts are as dissimilar as their ordering of the creation sequence is similar. For example, Babylonian polytheism with its rival deities, which is so evident in the *Enūma elish,* was unacceptable to Israel's priests. Nevertheless, Israel's conception of the created order was significantly informed by the Babylonian perspective.

Before we go on to consider the priestly account of the flood, let us discuss the most central features of the P creation tradition. First, in the creation liturgy, divine speech is absolutely central. God is depicted as a cosmic organizer who in his speaking has full control over the chaotic primordial situation. Unlike the Babylonian god Marduk, Elohim does not engage in physical combat with another deity. And in contrast with the portrayal in Gen. 2:4b–25 (J), the deity is not depicted as a potter who forms human and animal life by physically working with the ground. Instead, God creates through the active power of his word. Moreover, in faith ancient Israel recognized that God's function of establishing and authenticating was a continuous achievement within nature and history. Throughout, God utters the word and determines that the word spoken will become the word fulfilled.

Second, the practical monotheism of the priestly account presents creation as the work of one deity who has no female consort and does not battle other divine wills. This monotheism is defended in part by implications about what creation is not. For example, in Babylonian tradition, the heavenly luminaries were accepted as independent deities worthy of man's veneration. By contrast, the sun, moon, and stars in Gen. 1:16–18 are divested of divinity. Though the heavenly bodies are permitted to exercise dominion over specific cosmic spheres, they are vassals responsible to the one sovereign deity. The priests who emphatically broke with the Babylonian view were to insist that these celestial objects are merely God's lamps, which provide light and denote the change of seasons.

Admittedly v. 26 contains a statement that at first reading appears to speak against any notion of staunch monotheism: "Then God said, 'Let us make man in our image, after our likeness.'" Closer examination reveals, however, that this expression poses no serious threat. God, who is essentially one in ancient Israelite thought, enjoys many functions, and he exists within a celestial court populated by messengers (angels), cherubim, and Satan, who all serve as his obliging attendants. Genesis 1:26 assumes that as universal king, God addresses his subservient heavenly court.[11] Despite this reference to a celestial plurality, the priestly account is essentially a monotheistic composition. Moreover, the God whom it depicts decidedly stands apart from his creation.

Another significant feature of the P creation tradition has to do with the innate excellence of creation. The formal refrain, "And God saw that it was good" appears frequently, and a climax is reached in v. 31, "And behold, it was very good." This creation tradition does not foster asceticism. Rather, it suggests that man should consider the world good since it was first evaluated that way by the deity himself. Before man was around to praise God for his wondrous accomplishments in creation, the deity contemplated his creative work and delighted in its beauty, purpose, and integrity.

Man's significance, function, and indeed, his very existence are other matters of authentic priestly concern. His place within creation is one of dignity and power (1:26). Made in the divine image, he is to be God's representative on earth. As such, he is to rule all of God's creation. In the Babylonian creation epic, man is far more servile. He is little more than a divine afterthought, an appendage to creation brought into existence to maintain the temple and its gods. By contrast, in Genesis 1 man is viewed as the crown of creation, who will govern the animal and plant world.

Man's relationship to the deity is expressed through two well-chosen Hebrew nouns: ṣelem and dᵉmûth. The former, meaning "image," denotes the concrete similarity between creator and creature, and the latter, meaning "likeness," points to the abstract similarity that is also evident. The word "likeness" tempers the thought that would be expressed had "image" alone been used.

No simple physical relationship between God and man is argued for here. The organic relationship between father and son, which enables the son to resemble his father, is not projected back to the relationship that obtained between God and the first man. Throughout this account, the distance between creator and creature is maintained. Even so, Genesis 1 also implies that the relationship between God and man has a special quality that is lacking in the relationship between God and animals. Essentially that quality involves communication. The priests are witnessing that the created order is such that man may petition God, and God may speak his will to man, who has the ability to understand.

This creation liturgy affirms that man resembles but is not identical with the deity. He is not a god, but like the deity who called him into being he is able to think, speak, and assert himself. He has the capacity for introspection and self-determination. He is lord of the created world. Yet man is creature and servant to the one who himself is universal creator and sovereign.

Finally, the P creation account underscores the seventh day as the day of rest. Indeed, Gen. 2:2–3 seems to disclose the very goal toward which all previous statements in the liturgy strive. The deity himself rests. Blessed and sanctified by God, the Sabbath is an integral part of the drama of creation. The Israelite priesthood, which took this institution very seriously, traced its origin back to the beginning of time. Especially in exilic and postexilic Israel, the Sabbath had become a singularly vital institution that did much to sustain ongoing Israelite existence. On this day Hebrew man could rest from his labors and exalt the one whom he regarded as the giver of life. Sabbath observance, which profoundly shaped the covenant community, is universalized in a cosmic framework.

To be sure, the literary expressions and world views in Gen. 1:1–2:4a are for many in our time more a matter of curiosity than relevance. Ancient Israel's priests believed that the cosmos was created by a sovereign deity within seven 24-hour periods. Today many people react against that notion. Conversations about the emergence of Earth and the development of its plant and animal life ordinarily do not accept the priestly sequential pattern as a useful point of departure. Nevertheless, many who maintain that the process of creation did not unfold precisely in the ways that the Bible claims also affirm as an article of faith that the universe is the creation of one who is to be addressed as God. That there is purpose to creation and history alike is a statement open neither to definitive proof nor disproof. We may infer that the priestly statements on creation preserved in Gen. 1:1–2:4a were meaningful for many ancient Israelites who believed in the existence and purpose of a single sovereign deity. Also there are those in our time who claim that this mythic tradition embraces profound theological truths relevant to contemporary faith as well.

The Priestly Account of the Flood. The P tradition of the great deluge contained in portions of Genesis 6–9 preserves a narrative of high quality. God's response to human violence, his instructions to Noah, the intensity and duration of the universal flood, and God's resulting covenant with all flesh are skillfully depicted. The priests soberly state that the laws of conduct according to which life on earth is to govern itself have been broken. The earth is filled with violence (6:11), and God is unwilling to tolerate this woeful desecration of a created order that was flawless at its inception.

Accordingly, he determines "to make an end of all flesh" (6:13) and reveals his intention to Noah along with specific instructions on building an ark. The exact length of a Hebrew cubit is disputed, but conservatively estimated, the ark would be approximately 450 feet long, 75 feet wide, and 45 feet high—presumably spacious enough to provide room for a pair of every type of animal Noah is expected to bring into it. The account of the flood has inspired a number of readers to come up with a more precise estimate of Noah's craft. Among such endeavors is the model that went on display in Jerusalem in February 1968. It was built by Meir Ben-Uri, a prominent Israeli synagogue designer, who deduced that the ark was a "prismatic rhomboid"—that is, a long bar containing a diamond-shaped cross section.[12] Of course, those who do not share Ben-Uri's belief that the Bible consistently presents a trustworthy account of what actually happened may dismiss such analyses as irrelevant.

The intensity and duration of the flood are thoroughly described in the P account. The flood lasts for a year and ten days. Reference to the gushing forth of "all the fountains of the great deep" and to the opening of "the windows of the heavens" (7:11) indicates that this was nothing short of cosmic catastrophe. Indeed, "creation begins to sink again into chaos."[13] Yet before it is too late, God remembers Noah (8:1) and takes steps to end the destruction. The waters abate, and the ark docks at the mountains of Ararat (in present-day Armenia). At God's command, Noah leads out from his ark all life that has been spared.

A new age is now inaugurated. As is typical of P, it is based not on man's doing but on God's speaking. In Gen. 9:1–17 the deity reaffirms the blessing he had pronounced at creation. Again animal and human life are told to fill the earth. With this opportunity for a fresh start, procreation obviously matters. Family planning will preoccupy a subsequent era. Once more man is ordained to dominate the earth. Two regulations will govern his existence, however. He must not drink the blood of slain animals, and he is forbidden to murder those of his own kind, for in so doing he would be destroying that which had been created in the divine image.

Man's existence in this new era is all the more meaningful because God extends himself in a covenant relationship. In Gen. 9:8–17 the first priestly covenant tradition is given detailed expression. God initiates a covenant with Noah, his family, and indeed, with "every living creature" (v. 10). He promises that the world will never again suffer the ravages of a universal flood. The sign of that covenant is the rainbow, which will remind the deity of his decision. And it will instill in man a confidence that despite whatever else may threaten his existence, he need not fear another flood. This covenant contains no other stipulations. It asks nothing of man. It solemnly reinforces God's command to man that he multiply and sensibly subdue the earth. And with the abatement of divine wrath, man may once more experience blessings that issue from God's mercy.

Incidentally, Tablet XI of the Gilgamesh Epic preserves an ancient Babylonian flood tradition with close affinities to the one present in the Hebrew Bible. This engaging account is narrated by Utnapishtim, the Babylonian flood hero, who willingly responds to Gilgamesh's inquiry about how he, as a mortal, had successfully associated himself with the assembly of the gods and thereby attained immortality. The numerous Babylonian affinities with the Genesis flood tradition include the following: the construction of a boat, the leading of animal species into the craft, the extraordinary proportions of the deluge, the landing of the boat in mountainous country, the dispatching of birds to determine the water level, the sacrifice offered by the flood hero, and the assuring celestial sign (Ishtar's jewels and Yahweh's rainbow) that never again will a flood of such proportions occur.[14]

The Priestly Concern for Primeval Continuity. In a genealogy spanning Adam to Noah, a Table of Nations, and a genealogy spanning Shem to Abraham, Israel's exilic and postexilic priests made further contributions to the primordial history of Genesis 1–11. Through the genealogical constructions of P, God's historical continuity with the world, which began with creation itself, is celebrated in its perfection.

The patriarchal table in Genesis 5 accounts for the generations that immediately followed Adam. The long life that this formal genealogical table attributes to each person has troubled many readers, but for Israel numerical superlatives witnessed to the vitality of earth's first inhabitants. If Methuselah's 969 years seem bizarre (v. 27), we have only to think of the Sumerian King List, which reports that its first eight (antediluvian) kings ruled for a total of 241,000 years.[15] In both the Israelite and Sumerian traditions, the ages and rules of those who existed after the great flood are much less than the ages and rules of those who preceded. Israel's priests were doubtlessly assuming that the most ancient of men lived so long because they were extraordinary people who existed in a time when sin had not yet exerted itself with its customary force.

The priestly genealogy spanning Shem to Abraham (Gen. 11:10–27) need not detain us. While its style closely resembles that of Genesis 5, its contents reveal that it has some basis in history. As we noted previously, such names as Nahor, Terah, and Haran have been identified with sites in northwest Mesopotamia, the very region in which Abraham is thought to have been born.

Finally, Genesis 10 offers the Table of Nations, which is without parallel in ancient literature. This remarkably accurate passage, which is the conflation of J and P with the latter dominating, lists the world's peoples according to three distinct groups. Indo-European peoples with their original political center in Asia Minor are regarded as the descendants of Japheth; African, or Hamidic, peoples are viewed as Ham's descendants; and the Semites are linked with their ancestor Shem. The stylistic formality of P, its interest in precise statement, and its wider geographical horizons have enabled critics to isolate the priestly components in this table with relative confidence. Moreover, the P stratum has provided the framework for Genesis 10.

It is not difficult to conjecture about what motivated the Yahwist and the priests to create such a table. No doubt the Yahwist was elaborating on his earlier assertion (Gen. 9:19) that Noah fathered three sons who were responsible for the repopulation of the earth. And in his manner of viewing Israel simply as a descendant of Shem, J was, without illusion, regarding historical Israel as simply one among many nations. The P stratum contains entries for all three of Noah's sons (in contrast to J who fails to account for the Japheth line) and embraces a vast segment of the earth. Clearly, P's universalism witnesses to the essential unity of the human race. It also attests to the fulfillment of the divine command of Gen. 9:1, "Be fruitful and multiply, and fill the earth."

The Code of P

Despite its pedantic and tedious qualities, the Code of P testifies to the extraordinary impact that the exilic and postexilic priesthood exerted on emerging Judaism. From the remote days of Aaron when the priesthood had been called into being, the priest was accepted as a vital member of the covenant community. As he officiated at the sacrificial altar, delivered blessings and curses, taught the Mosaic Torah to the laity, and assisted in making legal decisions, the priest proved his intrinsic worth to the Yahwistic community. In the exilic and postexilic periods of Israel's history when the monarchy no longer existed and prophecy was pursuing an undistinguished course, leadership of the people increasingly fell into the hands of the priesthood.

Such matters as Sabbath observance, religious festivals and feasts, sacrifice, and circumcision now dominated the religious scene. The covenant community, which had become more and more theocratic in its outlook, expended less energy playing the game of power politics and devoted more of its attention to fulfilling ritualistic expectations. The transcendent deity had to be approached in a manner appropriate to his infinite holiness. Since the forms of Israel's religious expression were thought to bear quite directly on the well-being of the covenant community, it was important that they be spelled out in legislative format. Thus, the Code of P came into existence.

It is difficult to establish a precise date for the codification of the priestly legislation. Its earliest items stem from the preexilic era. The overlap of the concerns of P with those of the priestly oriented Ezekiel suggests that the code was coming into its own during the Babylonian exile. Moreover, some religious ideas in P coalesce with those in several postexilic books of the Hebrew canon. This implies that the code was not completed until the fifth century, after the exiles had again set foot on home territory.

Apart from its interruption in Exodus 32–34, the priestly block spans Exod. 25:1 through Num. 10:28. Exodus 25–31 and 35–40 contain commandments pertaining to the ark of the covenant, the Tabernacle, and the Israelite priesthood. The Book of Leviticus offers detailed legislation about various offerings and sacrifices (chaps. 1–7), the consecration of the priesthood (chaps. 8–10), ritualistic purifications (chaps. 11–15), the Day of Atonement ceremony (chap. 16), the holy life that the deity expects from the covenant community (chaps. 17–26), and religious vows and tithes (chap. 27). Then a miscellany of predominantly cultic matters is taken up in the priestly section that occupies all but the concluding verses of Numbers 1–10.

We cannot undertake a detailed examination of these priestly legislative units. Nevertheless, some focus on two of the units—the Day of Atonement (Lev. 16) and the holiness legislation (Lev. 17–26)—may help us to grasp the main thrust of the restoration community's priestly legislation.

Leviticus 16 enjoins that once a year the people of Yahweh are to observe the Day of Atonement, a day that "seeks to achieve the spiritual health and wholeness, the blessedness of all the community in all its parts for the succeeding year."[16] The ritual itself is set forth in 16:1–28, and in 16:29–34 tangential remarks are made about the fasting and resting appropriate for this occasion. The composite character of the chapter reveals an ancient religious practice that was enlarged through the centuries until it was officially inserted into the Israelite cultic calendar during the postexilic era. The abbreviated version of the ritual in 16:6–10 offers some clue as to what took place. As the people's special representative, the high priest made atonement by casting lots over two goats. One goat was sacrificed as a sin offering before Yahweh, and the other was sent away into the wilderness for Azazel (presumably he was regarded as a desert demon). Released from their sin and sense of guilt, the penitent people could once more approach the deity.

The legislation in Leviticus 17–26 is commonly referred to as the Holiness Code (H). Its cultic and ethical stipulations are profoundly concerned with Israel's conduct as a separate people. This originally independent code, with its sermonic idiom and distinctive theological perspective, was incorporated without official notation into the larger body of priestly legislation.

The issues addressed by Leviticus 17–26 are remarkably heterogeneous. They include restrictions on animal sacrifice, unlawful marriages, sexual offenses, necromancy, blasphemy, the behavior of priests, the sacred calendar, the sabbatical year and year of jubilee (as ways of curbing economic exploitation), and supplies for the proper maintenance of the cult. Nevertheless, "all these differing elements cohere in the conception of a holy people in a holy land, the servants of a holy God."[17]

The holiness enjoined is intended to reflect Yahweh's own glory. Frequently in the code, the deity summons Israel to live in full appreciation of his power and righteousness. The people are repeatedly reminded, "I am Yahweh." This knowledge suffices as the motivation for the ethical and ritual precepts that they are commanded to follow. Holiness as a life style is not interpreted as being inherent in Israel. It is viewed as coming from the transcendent deity himself: "You shall be holy; for I Yahweh your God am holy" (19:2).

Hence, in the Holiness Code and throughout the priestly legislation the people are invited to shoulder specific responsibilities. From beginning to end it is assumed that in their fulfillment of cultic and ethical obligations, the people can acquire a fresh understanding of themselves and their God. The priestly legislation insists that a continuous and meaningful theocratic existence is both possible and mandatory. Quite simply, it is what Yahweh wants for his elect people.

THE WITNESS OF THE POETS:
THE BOOK OF PSALMS

The Book of Psalms is a rich anthology of poetry composed over a period of approximately seven hundred years. Though much of the poetry in the Hebrew Bible lies beyond the scope of the Psalter, some truly remarkable compositions appear on its pages. And while few clues as to its chronology exist, the Psalter preserves compositions that have emerged from many situations and eras in Israelite history.

Before we proceed, we must ask, "What is a psalm?" Mowinckel, who spent much of his life in Psalms research, defined a psalm as:

> a poem which arises from, or is related to, that experience which is
> expressed in worship, a worship which expresses the ideas and sentiments
> of the worshippers and their common attitude to the Godhead; such
> a poem therefore makes a more or less marked use of language which
> has already been shaped by worship.[18]

Mowinckel and many other interpreters believe that the psalms were used primarily in culture contexts and their religious affirmations related closely to the very heart of the worshiping Israelite congregation. Relatively few psalms were written solely for private use. The majority were shaped with the interests and needs of the Yahwistic cult in mind.

The 150 psalms are arranged in five collections or books. Book I (Ps. 1–41), the Davidic Psalter, seems to reflect an early, rather homogeneous assemblage of poems. The designation "to David" was appended to all but four of its poems.[19] Psalm 1, a wisdom composition, serves as a preface to the entire Psalter, and Psalm 2, a royal psalm, may be a Davidic poem that has lost its superscription. In any event, "Yahweh" is the dominant divine name in this collection.

Book II (Ps. 42–72) and Book III (Ps. 73–89) constitute the Elohistic Psalter, so named because the original name "Yahweh" has on most occasions been replaced by "Elohim."[20] When they were read aloud in corporate worship at the restored Jerusalem Temple, the more general designation "Elohim" was no doubt substituted, as an act of reverence, for the special and supremely sacred divine name "Yahweh." The superscriptions of Psalms 42, 44–49, 84–85, and 87–88 are linked with "the sons of Korah," and the superscriptions of Psalms 50 and 73–83 mention Asaph. According to 1 Chron. 6, Korah and Asaph were prominent among the Levitical singers employed in the Temple.

Book IV (Ps. 90–106) and Book V (Ps. 107–150) complete the Psalter. While the two books are heterogeneous in character, "Yahweh" appears as the preferred designation for the deity in both. Book V contains a number of Hallelujah psalms (111–113, 117, 135, 146–150) all beginning "Praise Yahweh!" It also offers a sequence of pilgrimage psalms (120–134) usually referred to as the "Songs of Ascent." Perhaps these were processional hymns sung by the Israelites during their journey to the Jerusalem Temple. The division of the Psalter into five books, which is analogous to the structure of the Torah, probably reflects the efforts of a final editor who also added Psalms 1 and 150, and made sure that each collection ended with a doxology.[21]

The complex origins of the Psalter are also attested by a concluding editorial notation (called a "colophon"), duplicate versions, and frequent psalmic superscriptions. A colophon at the end of Book II (Ps. 72:20), which instructs that David's "prayers" are thereby concluded, is contradicted by the presence of other prayer psalms that are attributed to David (for example, 86, 101, 109). The colophon must therefore have been attached to a poetic collection of unknown scope prior to its incorporation in the Psalter. A few psalms appear as duplicate recensions that have only slight variations. Psalm 14 is equivalent to Psalm 53; Ps. 40:13–17 is equivalent to Psalm 70; and Psalm 108 is equivalent to Ps. 57:7–11 plus Ps. 60:5–12. For the most part, the discrepancies reflect divergent preferences for the divine name. When Psalms 14 and 40:13–17 were first drawn into an Elohistic collection of poems, the name "Yahweh" tended to be replaced by "Elohim."

The superscriptions themselves also reflect the complicated literary history of the Psalter. The two superscriptions that preface Psalms 39, 62 (David and Jeduthun), and 77 (Jeduthun and Asaph) make us doubt their reliability. Moreover, the seventy-three superscriptions in the Psalter that contain David's name cannot be accepted as convincing proof of Davidic authorship. Since such "Davidic" compositions as Psalms 27, 28, and 63 assume that the Jerusalem Temple is standing, they can scarcely be attributed to one who died prior to its construction.

Nor is the precise meaning of the Hebrew *ldwd* clear. In some instances it may mean "by David" and reflect the piety and artistry of the Israelite king who was the patron par excellence of psalmody. Yet on other occasions, the Hebrew may mean "about David" in analogy with *lbʿl* ("about Baʿal") attested in the Ugaritic texts from Ras Shamra. Moreover, "David" might sometimes denote a regal title rather than a personal name. If so, some psalms might have a formal connection with a monarch other than David.

Certainly the superscriptions reflect an era that postdates the compositions to which they are attached. They were affixed by editors who were unaware of that cogent dictum, "What does not add, detracts." Hence, their historical usefulness is minimal. Nor can much be gained from their cryptic musical instructions, which were already misunderstood by the Septuagint translation team in the second century B.C.

Though only one composition (Ps. 137) in the one hundred and fifty may be given a relatively precise date, the origins of even the latest compositions in the Psalter seems to relate to Persian rather than to Maccabean times.[22] Therefore, none of the poems need be dated later than the end of the third century B.C. The Septuagint offers the same sequence of psalms, and the hymns (*hôdhayôth*) from Qumran often quote the Psalter in a manner that suggests that much of the collecting and editing of the canonical Book of Psalms had already been accomplished. Nevertheless, the discovery in 1956 of the Psalms Scroll from Cave 11 at Qumran urges us to be cautious. That text departs significantly from any previously known recension of the Israelite Psalter. Standing beside the canonical compositions in this scroll are eight apocryphal pieces that did not secure a place in the traditional, or Masoretic, Psalter. Certainly the canonization of the Psalms involved a "multi-faceted history."[23] The Psalms Scroll from Qumran attests that in the middle of the first century, not all elements of Judaism were in agreement about what belonged in the Book of Psalms.

The Israelite Psalter is so rich and complex an anthology that no commentator has felt entirely adequate to attempt a detailed clarification of its concerns. Still, the results of form-critical research on the Book of Psalms have been far-reaching. Gunkel, who produced two extensive volumes on Psalms, was the pioneer in these endeavors.[24]

Gunkel classified the psalms according to literary types (*Gattungen*) and posited that each had a characteristic life setting (*Sitz im Leben*).

The Thanksgiving (Hôdhayôth) Scroll from Qumran. At least two scribes of the Qumran sect produced this manuscript. In many instances this hymnic collection duplicates the language of the canonical Psalms. Virtually every composition in the scroll begins, "I thank thee, O Lord," which is typical of the individual songs of thanksgiving preserved in the Israelite Psalter. Despite their deterioration, the sheets of this scroll are unusually long and have from thirty-five to forty-one lines each. Column 2, pictured above, contains the second, third, and most of the fourth hymn of thanksgiving. (Courtesy of the Consulate General of Israel, New York.)

He discovered that five types predominate in the Psalter: the hymn, the royal psalm, the community lament, the individual lament, and the individual song of thanksgiving. Gunkel recognized that in ancient Israelite psalmody formal and recurring elements consistently received greater emphasis than their individualistic counterparts. This led Gunkel to admit that, to a great extent, the psalms are the property of the cult and of the Hebrew people as a whole, and as such they provided the crucial words that accompanied various ritualistic acts. These words took a poetic rather than a prose format, since only the former proved suitable for the self-expression of an assembled body of worshipers.

Nevertheless, Gunkel insisted that numerous psalms that originally had a cultic setting were later loosed from their liturgical connections and established on a more spiritual and individualistic plane. Although sacrificial acts in the cult required the sacred words of the psalms, Gunkel argued that the most profound expressions of piety in the Psalter were independent of the structures of formalistic religion. This was a Protestant bias that was corrected—and doubtless over-corrected—by Mowinckel, who regarded the cult as a much more positive and continuous factor in Israelite religion than Gunkel did. Yet Gunkel did not lose interest in the cultic poetry of the Psalter, and his form-critical categories have been widely accepted by scholars.

With these introductory remarks in mind, we shall now examine the five major categories of poetry to be found in the Israelite Psalter. Each will be described and then illustrated through direct reference to at least one representative psalm. While our selection of illustrative material is necessarily arbitrary, we shall indicate other psalmic texts that may be consulted. If a thorough familiarity with the Book of Psalms cannot be acquired overnight, at least some impression of its style, theology, and multiple religious functions can be gained by sampling its poetry.

The Hymn

The hymn, or psalm, of praise is a crucial type of psalm with very early origins.[25] It was intended for either choral or solo use in the Israelite cult. When its cultic associations are not so evident, we may infer that it was employed to express personal devotion to Yahweh.

The hymn has a definite introduction; it may summon the covenant people, the nations, or the heavenly hosts to an act of divine praise ("O give thanks to Yahweh, call on his name" [Ps. 105:1]), or it may invoke the name of the deity ("O Yahweh, our Lord, how majestic is thy name in all the earth!" [Ps. 8:1a]).

The body, or main section, of the hymn gives poetically stated reasons why Yahweh should thus be praised. Here the deitys attributes and mighty acts are enumerated. On occasion, the elements in the body of the hymn may be distributed antiphonally between two choirs, with one appointed the task of chanting a single refrain ("For his steadfast love [*ḥesed*] endures for ever" [Ps. 136]). Yahweh's self-manifestation (Ps. 29), his creative energy (Ps. 104), his covenant fidelity (Ps. 136), and his saving deeds in history (Ps. 105) are all celebrated.

Usually the conclusion of a hymn repeats the phraseology, or at least the motifs, of its introduction (cf. vv. 1 and 9 of Ps. 8), though sometimes it advances concluding petitions that are new. The hymn praises God with enthusiasm and reverence. While it often extols the deity as the ruler of nature, that theme is typically linked with Yahweh's saving acts in behalf of the Israelite people.

Let us consider Psalm 8 as an example of a hymn. This composition has two main themes: the magnificence of Yahweh as creator and the dignity divinely conferred on man as God's special creation. Various aspects of nature such as the moon, stars, and animal world are also celebrated. Such praise of nature, however, is not the chief end of the poem. Rather, it is the Creator himself who is praised throughout.

The poet also marvels over man as God's creature. Man is no accident; he is seen as the pinnacle of creation. In exuberant tones the poet claims the crown of divinity for man. Yet he is not attempting to shape a theological statement that applies solely to the human animal. Instead, he is calling attention to man as evidence that praise befits the Creator. Although a similarity between God and man is affirmed, man remains fundamentally distinct from his Creator. Yet manifesting an honor and glory of his own, man is said to enjoy a special status as God's appointed deputy. He is lord of the terrestrial part of creation, and for this God is generously praised. (For other representative hymns, see Ps. 19, 29, 33, 103, 104, 136.)

The Royal Psalm

In the royal psalm, Gunkel discovered another category of cultic poetry. Such psalms affirm the king's close relationship with Yahweh, and this was in part symbolized by the prominent position the monarch assumed in Israelite worship. Thus, probably owing to the efforts of the court poets, who were appointed by the king, the royal psalms were created for several different occasions directly involving the monarch. Psalm 2 speaks of the king's coronation; Psalm 20 shows the king praying to Yahweh before he wages war against his opponents; Psalm 21 relates to the festive celebration inspired by the king's victorious return; and Psalm 45 depicts a royal wedding.

With their focus on the various actions of the king, the royal psalms are to be connected with the preexilic Jerusalem Temple, which functioned as a royal or dynastic shrine. It was here that the monarch presented offerings to the deity, received the sacred oracle, and assumed a significant role in the periodic covenant renewal that took place between God and people. The royal psalms are generous in their praise of the reigning monarch and fervent in their hope for his success.

The content of these compositions varies, but typically includes the king's statement that he has observed the divine ordinances, his desire to hear an assuring word from the deity, and his wish that his own reign will be peaceful and prosperous. Of course, the day came when the people of Yahweh no longer existed as a monarchy. Nevertheless, cherished memories of the Davidic kingdom and the developing messianic expectations that took root in the Davidic tradition stimulated the exilic and postexilic community to preserve such poetry.

Psalms 20 and 21 are interesting examples of royal psalms. These two compositions are best understood as a liturgical pair that relate to the "before and after" of a military battle involving the king. Psalm 20 presents the king preparing for war against formidable foes; he offers solemn sacrifices and commits his cause to Yahweh, who alone can grant victory. Prayer offered in the monarch's behalf prior to the ensuing battle is set forth in 20:1–5. The prayer is followed by earnest words of assurance (20:6–8), presumably spoken by a Temple prophet. Yahweh's support is pledged, and the entire assembly then expresses its foremost wish: "Give victory to the king, O Yahweh; answer us when we call" (20:9).

In Psalm 21 the campaign is over, and the king has triumphed. Again people and king assemble in cultic meeting. This psalm offers words of thanksgiving for the blessings that have been granted to the successful monarch (vv. 1–7), an oracle predicting the monarch's triumph over his opponents (vv. 8–12), and a concluding element of divine praise (v. 13). Whereas Psalm 20 opens with an address to the king, Psalm 21 concludes with enthusiastic praise for the deity who has made possible the recent Israelite triumph. Cultic celebration involves more than extolling the king's achievements. Human effort is set within a larger, more theologically satisfying context. (For other examples of the royal psalm, see Ps. 2, 18, 45, 110, 132.[26])

The Community Lament

As another ancient type of liturgical poetry that Gunkel identified in the Psalter, the community lament reveals a worshiping people in the throes of misfortune. Pestilence, crop failure, and oppression by political enemies were the primary circumstances that induced them to go to the sanctuary and voice their lamentation. Fasting, rending garments, and weeping would accompany such cultic occasions as the congregation fervently sought to move the deity toward a merciful course of action. This poetic form thus offered the people an opportunity to state the nature of the misfortune that either threatened them or already existed and to petition Yahweh for immediate assistance.

Gunkel recognized two types of community laments. He called the first "penitential prayers of the community." Here the people confessed their sins and implored Yahweh's forgiveness. In the second, "confessions of innocence of the community," the people sought to convince Yahweh that their adversity was undeserved.

Typical of the style of the community lament are the vocative address to the deity at the beginning of the poem ("O God, why dost thou cast us off for ever?" [Ps. 74:1]) and the use of the first-person plural, which distinguishes the communal from the individual lament. (Of course, since the psalmists acknowledged the corporate aspect of Israelite existence, they sometimes used the first-person singular in framing the community lament [see Ps. 44].) In other respects, the community and individual laments are rather similar. Of note in the lamentation poetry of the Psalter is the assertion that the people's prayer has indeed been heard. This element, which Gunkel referred to as the "certainty of a hearing," derived from an earlier period when the priest spoke in the name of the deity and gave Yahweh's response to the passionate appeal previously voiced by the congregation. Thus, in the community lament, the miserable situation of the people and their confidence in God are both evident.

Psalm 80 is a good example of a community lament. Though the people of Yahweh appear to be harassed by their neighbors, the vague treatment of the problem does not allow us to determine the precise historical occasion. The allusions to Joseph, Ephraim, and Manasseh (vv. 1–2) imply that the psalm originated in the northern kingdom and was written no later than the eighth century. Yet reference to Yahweh's enthronement on the cherubim (v. 1) best suits a Judean perspective.

In any case, the people find themselves the victims of circumstance. They are scorned by their neighbors and are forced to drink their own tears (vv. 5–6). They refer to themselves as a vine that, though deliberately planted by the deity, has been left unprotected.

The composition opens with an initial plea for divine assistance (vv. 1–2). Perhaps the refrain repeated in vv. 3, 7, and 19, which petitions Yahweh to manifest his theophanic presence and deliver his people, was uttered by the entire congregation. The people's current feeling that they are being forsaken is richly portrayed in vv. 8–13.

Complaint, however, is not the last word. The appeal that Yahweh deliver his people is fervently renewed (vv. 14–19). Since the one who has presently forsaken his vineyard Israel is "God of hosts," perhaps he will soon return in triumph and chastise those who have molested his property (v. 16). Personifying itself as the man of God's right hand and as the son of man (v. 17), the congregation solicits divine support and pledges anew its fidelity to Yahweh's cause (v. 18). Their lament is real, but no less so is their faith. (For other examples of the community lament, see Ps. 44, 60, 74, 79, 83, 137.)

The Individual Lament

While the Book of Psalms contains many individual laments, Gunkel observed that this poetic form reflects a rather limited stock of thoughts and images. The individual suppliant typically suffers from both the physical pain of his own illness, which often brings him to the brink of death, and a hostile environment full of persecutors who seek to victimize him. Therefore, he earnestly requests that the deity rescue him from his affliction. Personal suffering is frequently expressed. Its vivid portrayal seems to stem from the assumption that the stark depiction of present cruelties will move Yahweh to take positive action. Often at the heart of the problem are the psalmist's personal opponents, who seek to wear him down. These false accusers utter vicious lies (Ps. 5:6) and are compared to a lion who drags away his prey (7:2). Sometimes the enemies are self-righteous friends who glibly insist that the suppliant's suffering is justifiable divine retribution for past sins. In other instances, they are practitioners of evil who resort to sorcery and magic to intensify the adverse conditions enveloping the one who suffers.

The speaker of the individual lament is motivated by two concerns: he wants Yahweh to enlighten him as to the reasons for his suffering, and he wants him to function as his personal deliverer. If the speaker believes that he has transgressed against the divine commandments, then he is concerned with showing his contrition, confessing his wrongdoing, and throwing himself at the mercy of God. Release from his plight is then anticipated as the sign of Yahweh's forgiveness. On the other hand, if the speaker is certain that he has been wrongly accused by his enemies, then he labors to convince Yahweh that as a God of righteousness, he must intervene in behalf of the innocent. In the hope of securing divine help, the speaker goes to the sanctuary to present his case and offerings, and there he hears an oracle of assurance from one of the sanctuary priests.

Therefore, the typical lamentation opens with words of invocation and complaint, moves into phrases of supplication, and concludes with words of hope and a personal vow of piety. Psalms of individual lament may be divided into three categories: psalms of innocence, which disclose the suppliant's desire to assert his own righteousness; imprecatory psalms, which seek the cursing of the sufferer's enemies; and penitential psalms, which reveal the honest confession of sin and desire for God's forgiveness.[27] In selecting Psalm 51 as an example of an individual's lament, we shall study the last category.

Psalm 51 is best examined after its more suspect elements have been isolated. Though its long superscription identifies David's affair with Bathsheba as the occasion for the composition (see 2 Sam. 11–12), this superscription does not accord well with the psalmist's words to the deity in v. 4: "Against thee, thee only, have I sinned." Moreover, the last two verses of the psalm (18–19) contain a reference to animal sacrifices and a prayer for the restoration of Zion and its cult that disturb the antisacrificial tone immediately preceding (vv. 16–17). We are left, then, with three major sections of unequal length: vv. 1–2 containing a cry for mercy and cleansing, vv. 3–12 setting forth the psalmist's confession and petition, and vv. 13–17 presenting the psalmist's vow.

In the opening section, the psalmist admits his "transgression" (conscious rebellion), his "iniquity" (disregard for the established norm), and his "sin" (missing the mark). Here three overlapping, yet distinct Hebrew nouns are employed. In his request to be restored to wholeness and health, three different imperatives are deliberately used: "blot out," "wash," and "cleanse."

In the continuation of the lament in vv. 3–12, the psalmist reveals that he is keenly aware of his misdoings. He recognizes that he has worked at cross-purposes with the deity. He admits that only a re-creation of self can deliver him, and he fervently prays for such a transformation: "Create in me a clean heart, O God, and put a new and right spirit within me" (v. 10). Not an altar sacrifice, but God's forgiveness, is needed.

The psalmist's vow (vv. 13–17) is also significant. Here the poet resolves to teach others about the saving ways of the deity. But the psalm does not end on this zealous note. Instead, it concludes with a genuine expression of humility, closely resembling its opening lines. (For other examples of the individual lament, see Ps. 3, 7, 22, 31, 88, 130, 143.)

The Individual Song of Thanksgiving

If Hebrew man had cause to lament, he also had cause to give thanks. Thus, the individual song of thanksgiving provided him with a way to express his gratitude for recent acts of deliverance and mercy that he regarded as having come directly from God. Most of these compositions seem to have been linked with cultic proceedings at which time the worshiper asserted his thankfulness through an offering. Having been delivered from grave peril, the psalmist wished to celebrate Yahweh's goodness and power. To state his gratitude as convincingly as possible, the speaker of the individual thanksgiving spends considerable energy narrating his former suffering. He vividly reviews the dangers that threatened his well-being and speaks of the outrageous conduct of his enemies.

In its specific expression and even in its structure this type of psalm closely resembles the individual lament. The speaker in the lament pleads with the deity to consider his present plight and help him. In the song of thanksgiving the speaker gratefully acknowledges, in the presence of both God and people, the nature of his former plight from which he has been divinely delivered and eagerly proclaims his thanks. The expressions of confidence in the individual lament are reasserted here. Moreover, the statement of praise indigenous to the hymn is also part of the individual song of thanksgiving. Despite its affinities with the hymn and the individual lament, however, the individual song of thanksgiving is a distinct category of psalmic composition.

Let us consider Psalm 116 as an individual song of thanksgiving. Although matters pertaining to the strophic structure, date, and personal situation depicted are less than clear, Psalm 116 reveals the sincere piety and gratitude of one who has been delivered from severe illness. As he endured "the snares of death" (v. 3), the sufferer undoubtedly vowed that if Yahweh would assist him, he would visit the Jerusalem Temple (v. 19) to present a suitable sacrifice and give public testimony of God's goodness. The deity had responded positively to his supplication. Now the renewed individual comes to offer thanksgiving in the presence of personal acquaintances. He resolves to "lift up the cup of salvation" (presumably a libation of wine [v. 13]) and to make unspecified vows to Yahweh (vv. 14, 18). The speaker's love for the deity (v. 1), his recollection of anguish (in much of vv. 3–11), his belief in God's innate goodness and desire to uphold those who are humble (vv. 5–6, 15), and his resolve to dedicate his life to Yahweh's service (v. 16) all contribute to the excellence of this composition. (For other examples of individual songs of thanksgiving, see Ps. 18, 30, 92, 138.)

Other types of poetry also appear in the Psalter. These include psalms of Yahweh's enthronement (Ps. 47, 93, 96–99), community songs of thanksgiving (Ps. 67, 107, 124), songs of pilgrimage (Ps. 120–134), liturgies of admission to the Temple (Ps. 15, 24), and wisdom poetry (Ps. 1, 32, 34, 37, 49, 112, 127, 128, 133). Moreover, several specific cultic situations have been proposed for some psalms—notably the covenant renewal festival as advanced by Weiser and a Jerusalem festival focusing on Yahweh's election of Zion and David as set forth by Kraus.[28]

Since we have already discerned in some measure the nature of Israelite piety as it is revealed in the Book of Psalms, we shall end the chapter here. It is little wonder that the Psalter is the favorite biblical book of many readers. In addition to providing a helpful spiritual resource for those within the Jewish and Christian traditions, it is an index of the richness of Israel's reflections about herself and about the deity who had called her into existence.

NOTES

1. Most psalms do not offer even vague historical allusions that might imply their date of composition. Nor do the religious ideas they contain provide a clear indication of date.
2. We attribute the following verses of Genesis 1–11 to the P stratum: 1:1–2:4a; 5:1–28, 30–32; 6:9–22; 7:6, 11, 13–16a, 17a, 18–21, 24; 8:1–2a,

3b–5, 13a, 14–19; 9:1–17, 28–29; 10:1–7, 20, 22–23, 31–32; 11:10–27, 31–32.

3. Of course, in our previous inspection of Pentateuchal traditions, we have come to terms with some components in the P narrative. Relevant portions of Chapters 4–7 may be reviewed if desired. See also Wellhausen's appraisal of P in Chapter 3.

4. We are in agreement with James Muilenburg, "Book of Obadiah," in George A. Buttrick et al., eds., *The Interpreter's Dictionary of the Bible* (Nashville: Abingdon Press, 1962), K–Q, p. 579.

5. E. A. Speiser, *Genesis: Introduction, Translation, and Notes*, The Anchor Bible, vol. 1 (Garden City, N.Y.: Doubleday, 1964), p. xxvi.

6. That the Semitic deity Marduk here enjoys such supremacy implies that the epic originated in oral form during the First Dynasty of Bablyon (ca. 1830–1530 B.C.). Extant texts of the epic do not predate 1000 B.C., however.

7. For a detailed study of the affinities, see Alexander Heidel, *The Babylonian Genesis: The Story of Creation*, 2d ed. (Chicago: University of Chicago Press, Phoenix Books, 1963), pp. 82–140. Also see W. G. Lambert, "A New Look at the Babylonian Background of Genesis," *Journal of Theological Studies* 16 (1965): 287–300, who defines and critically delimits the extent of Babylonian influence on the Genesis creation tradition.

8. James B. Pritchard, ed., *Ancient Near Eastern Texts Relating to the Old Testament*, 3d ed. (Princeton, N.J.: Princeton University Press, 1969), pp. 66–68; the headings are our own. The first three excerpts are drawn from Tablet IV and the last excerpt from Tablet VI of the Babylonian Creation Epic. The brackets indicate the translator's restoration of the text, and the parentheses contain his interpolations so that a clear translation may result.

9. Speiser, *op. cit.*, p. 12. Speiser renders Gen. 1:1, "When God set about to create heaven and earth."

10. For a detailed treatment of this similarity in sequence, see Heidel, *op. cit.*, pp. 128–140.

11. A simple grammatical note also explains Gen. 1:26. "Elohim," with its *-îm* ending, is a masculine plural Hebrew noun. Speiser, *op. cit.*, p. 7, maintains that the point in question is solely linguistic and has no impact whatever on the meaning of the verse. He believes that in this instance the use of the plural may reveal that the deity is referring to himself.

12. "Noah's Liberty Ship," *Time*, 23 February 1968, pp. 76–79.

13. Gerhard von Rad, *Genesis: A Commentary*, rev. ed., trans. John H. Marks, The Old Testament Library (Philadelphia: Westminster Press, 1972), p. 128.

14. For the text of Tablet XI, see Pritchard, *op. cit.*, pp. 93–97. For a detailed comparison of the Babylonian and biblical flood traditions, see Alexander Heidel, *The Gilgamesh Epic and Old Testament Parallels*, 2d ed. (Chicago: University of Chicago Press, Phoenix Books, 1963), pp. 224–269.

15. "The Sumerian King List," in Pritchard, *op. cit.*, p. 265.

16. G. Henton Davies, "Leviticus," in Buttrick et al., eds., *op. cit.*, K–Q, p. 121.

17. Nathaniel Micklem, "Introduction and Exegesis to Leviticus," in George A. Buttrick et al., eds., *The Interpreter's Bible* (Nashville: Abingdon Press, 1953), vol. 2, p. 87.

18. Sigmund Mowinckel, *The Psalms in Israel's Worship*, trans. D. R. Ap-Thomas (Nashville: Abingdon Press, 1962), 1:2.
19. In Book I only Psalms 1, 2, 10, and 33 lack a Davidic superscription. Since Psalm 10 originally belonged to Psalm 9, its lack of superscription is not alarming.
20. Cf. Psalms 14 and 53, which offer a double recension of the same poem. "Elohim" is used in the latter; the former shows a preference for "Yahweh."
21. See Ps. 41:13; 72:18–19; 89:52; 106:48; and all of Psalm 150, which functions as a concluding doxology for both Book V and the entire Psalter.
22. Psalm 137 relates to the initial phase of Babylonian exile in the early sixth century B.C. As for the origins of even the latest compositions, we are in agreement with Frank M. Cross, Jr., *The Ancient Library of Qumran and Modern Biblical Studies*, rev. ed. (Garden City, N.Y.: Doubleday, Anchor Books, 1961), p. 166.
23. J. A. Sanders, *The Dead Sea Psalms Scroll* (Ithaca, N.Y.: Cornell University Press, 1967), p. 13.
24. *Die Psalmen* appeared in 1926, and, with the assistance of Joachim Begrich, *Einleitung in die Psalmen* was published in 1933, a year after Gunkel's death. Gunkel's views are available in English in *The Psalms: A Form-Critical Introduction*, trans. Thomas M. Horner (Philadelphia: Fortress Press, Facet Books, 1967). This short paperback is a translation of Gunkel's Psalms article, which appeared in vol. 4, cols. 1609–1627, of Hermann Gunkel and Leopold Zscharnack, eds., *Die Religion in Geschichte und Gegenwart*, 2d ed. (Tübingen: J. C. B. Mohr, 1930).
25. For example, Psalm 29, which is a hymn, must have been written very early in the history of Israelite religion, for its style and content have clear associations with Canaanite hymnody.
26. Moreover, we recommend Keith R. Crim, *The Royal Psalms* (Richmond: John Knox Press, 1962).
27. Gunkel, *The Psalms*, op. cit., p. 20.
28. Artur Weiser, *The Psalms: A Commentary*, trans. Herbert Hartwell, The Old Testament Library (Philadelphia: Westminster Press, 1962); and Hans-Joachim Kraus, *Worship in Israel: A Cultic History of the Old Testament*, trans. Geoffrey Buswell (Richmond: John Knox Press, 1966). A useful, succinct presentation of the views of Weiser and Kraus on the Israelite cult, and the extent to which their conclusions square with those of Gunkel and Mowinckel appears in Harvey H. Guthrie, Jr., *Israel's Sacred Songs: A Study of Dominant Themes* (New York: Seabury Press, 1966), pp. 17–21.

20

THE GIFT
OF WISDOM

In one of his confessions, Jeremiah reports that his opponents have said, "Come, let us make plots against Jeremiah, for the law shall not perish from the priest, nor counsel from the wise, nor the word from the prophet" (Jer. 18:18). This statement reminds us that three different professional groups influenced the religious and social affairs of ancient Israel. In addition to the priests, who had charge of the authoritative Torah, and the prophets, who claimed direct experience of Yahweh's self-revelation, there were the Israelite sages. Putting to good use their well-developed talents for observation and introspection, the wise men offered helpful counsel on many practical issues and problems. Schooled in the ways of the world, they were equipped to instruct their contemporaries in how the good life should be lived. And because they were convinced that "the fear of Yahweh is the beginning of wisdom" (Prov. 9:10; cf. also Prov. 1:7, Ps. 111:10, and Job 28:28), the sages had something to say about the nature and requirements of authentic religion.

Of course, the wise man delivered his counsel in a manner suited to his training and disposition. He was less passionate than the prophet. Although he did not deny that social change was sometimes needed, he did not wish to rock the boat. In striking contrast to the priest, he showed little interest in institutional religion. Even so, the disciplined and experienced Israelite sage addressed a host of matters, both expedient and existential. He was an active member of Hebrew society and tried to instruct his fellows in how to live a balanced, God-fearing existence.

In addition, he was a member of a world movement that brought

---

Biblical texts to be read prior to and in conjunction with the present chapter: Proverbs 1, 8, 10, 25, 30–31; Ecclesiastes; The Song of Songs; and Job 1–31, 38–42.

him into close contact with the problems and aspirations of all mankind. The wisdom movement in the ancient Near East assumed international proportions. And given Israel's strategic location in the Fertile Crescent, she could not escape the impact of that movement. In fact, the Hebrew Bible confirms that Israel's neighbors were adept in the art of wisdom thinking.[1]

In our time, biblical scholars are tracing the influence of the wisdom movement on ancient Israel's historical, prophetic, and psalmic literature with increased enthusiasm and sophistication.[2] Yet when it comes to isolating books in the Old Testament as "wisdom books," it is often held that there are three—Job, Proverbs, and Ecclesiastes. The Song of Songs is sometimes included in the list, although the justification is somewhat less obvious.[3] Before we direct our attention to these four books, let us examine the emergence, interests, and style of Israelite wisdom within its international setting.

THE WISDOM MOVEMENT AS AN ANCIENT NEAR EASTERN AND ISRAELITE PHENOMENON

Many nations participated in the wisdom movement of the ancient Near East.[4] Although wisdom texts emanating from Canaanite sources are fragmentary, the Tell el-Amarna letters of the fourteenth century reveal two Canaanite proverbs. Numerous words, literary expressions, and themes in Canaanite proverbs are duplicated in verses of the Book of Proverbs.[5]

The most striking parallel between any ancient Near Eastern wisdom text and the Old Testament is found between "The Instruction of Amen-em-Opet" and part of the Book of Proverbs. The former is a moralistic, religious document of thirty chapters that has influenced many of the thirty sayings in Prov. 22:17–24:22—especially those in Prov. 22:17–23:11. (Only seven of the twenty-four verses in Prov. 22:17–23:11 lack a counterpart in the Egyptian source.) Israel probably became aware of this Egyptian text during the cosmopolitan tenth-century rule of Solomon. The Amen-em-Opet text is one of approximately a dozen documents of instruction that stand out prominently in the Egyptian wisdom movement. Each contains the advice of a pharaoh or vital state official, which is addressed (usually in the form of an admonition) to his son and probable successor.

The earliest of these texts, "The Instruction of the Vizier Ptah-hotep," dates to about 2450 B.C. and thus to Egypt's Pyramid Age. In it, an important official seeks on the basis of his own experience to counsel his son concerning the behavior appropriate to public office.[6] He must be modest, completely reliable and upright, and able to get along with peo-

Boundary Inscription at Tell Gezer. This rock is a boundary marker. Photographed in 1968 in its original position, it is one of several that have been discovered at Gezer. The words on its face have been traced in charcoal to make them more visible. The top line, which is inverted Hebrew, means "the boundary of Gezer." The bottom line is in Greek and means "belonging to Alkios," who presumably owned the land long after the marker had been erected. In ancient Egypt and Israel, the removal of such landmarks was considered an offense. (Photo by the author.)

ple. Amen-em-Opet's maxims and "The Instruction of Ani" appeared near the end of the second millennium B.C.[7] The latter was written by an Egyptian temple scribe concerned with both religious and social conduct. A disciplined tongue, a humble manner, and generosity are all recommended by Ani.

Then in the fifth century, perhaps not many decades before the Book of Proverbs was taking shape in Israel, some 550 wisdom sayings were assembled in Egypt as "The Instructions of ʿOnchsheshonqy." In this instance, matters of prudence and morality were addressed to a wide Egyptian audience, not simply to someone about to assume high public office. The Egyptian pessimism reflected in such didactic works as "A Dispute over Suicide" and "The Protests of the Eloquent Peasant," which both date to about 2000 B.C., may have indirectly influenced the writing of the Book of Job.[8]

In the hope that we may develop some feeling for Egyptian wisdom, let us look at a few selections from the Amen-em-Opet instruction:

Give thy ears, hear what is said,
Give thy heart to understand them.
To put them in thy heart is worth while,
(But) it is damaging to him who neglects them. . . . (chap. I)

Guard thyself against robbing the oppressed
And against overbearing the disabled.
Stretch not forth thy hand against the approach of an old man,
Nor steal away the speech of the aged.
Let not thyself be sent on a dangerous errand,
Nor love him who carries it out. . . . (chap. II)

Do not carry off the landmark at the boundaries of the arable land,
Nor disturb the position of the measuring-cord;
Be not greedy after a cubit of land,
Nor encroach upon the boundaries of a widow. . . . (chap. VI)

Do not associate to thyself the heated man,
Nor visit him for conversation.
Preserve thy tongue from answering thy superior,
And guard thyself against reviling him.
Do not make him cast his speech to lasso thee,
Nor make (too) free with thy answer.
Thou shouldst discuss an answer (*only*) *with* a man of thy (own) size,
And guard thyself against plunging headlong into it. . . . (chap. IX)[9]

We can draw several parallels between these brief excerpts from the Amen-em-Opet instruction and the Book of Proverbs. The affinity between the first three lines of the excerpt from chapter I and Prov. 22:17–18a, which opens the Proverbs unit, is especially striking. It was customary for the ancient wisdom teacher to recommend his own instruction. Moreover, the ethical concern for the oppressed and the disabled (chap. II) finds a parallel in Prov. 22:22–23. The admonition against greed in chapter VI recalls the injunctions against the unfair removal of landmarks in Prov. 22:28 and 23:10. And finally, in the excerpt from chapter IX, Amen-em-Opet's admonition against dealing with those who are passionate and easily roused to anger has a parallel in Prov. 22:24.

Amen-em-Opet's reflections reveal how religious and so-called secular interests can be honored in the same document. Man's relationship to his brother and to his God are both of concern here. Of course, the former relationship receives the greater attention through fundamentally pragmatic and optimistic counsel.

Ancient Babylonian and Assyrian sages have also left us a body of representative proverbs, as well as more elaborately framed wisdom texts. Akkadian counsels of wisdom offer advice on such practical matters as maintaining disciplined speech and steering clear of bad company.[10] Religious motivations are also the subject of serious reflection.

Many of the more complex Babylonian wisdom texts reflect a pessimistic, even skeptical, tone that was often nurtured in Babylonian wisdom circles, and this tone is also evident in Ecclesiastes and Job. One such text is often referred to as the "Babylonian Job," though on the basis of its opening line it is titled, "I will Praise the Lord of Wisdom."[11] While this composition takes the form of a hymnic thanksgiving in praise

Tools of the Scribe. This restored set of writing equipment once belonged to an ancient Egyptian scribe. It consists of a writing reed, a palate with two holes for the pigments, and a small container to hold water to be used for thinning purposes. The Egyptian hieroglyph for "scribe" and "writing" depicts the same elements. (Courtesy of the Oriental Institute, University of Chicago.)

of Marduk, who has delivered the sufferer from the clutches of death, it lays bare the sufferer's profound agony and depression. Assessing his behavior toward the gods and mankind as free from offense, the sufferer claims that both heaven and earth have unjustly oppressed him. He insists on his innocence, complains that man in his ignorance does not know what the gods truly desire, and expresses his skepticism about divine justice.

In "The Babylonian Theodicy," we have a vivid example of the skepticism that prevailed during the Cassite period (1500–1200 B.C.). That era has been designated the "Middle Ages of Babylonian history."[12] It was a time of political stagnation. It was also a time when some clerical scholars refuted traditional doctrines and voiced the suspicion that pious men do not always prosper. There was a growing concern with realism. "The Babylonian Theodicy" is a provocative dialogue between the sufferer and his orthodox friend which states quite forcefully that concrete human experience does not always square with the notions of divine justice promoted by the religious establishment. Both the dialogue format and the ideas advanced remind us of the Book of Job. Although Job and "The Babylonian Theodicy" are not directly related, both works may have been influenced by the same intellectual currents in vogue within ancient Near Eastern wisdom circles.

Let us examine a few excerpts from this engaging, occasionally profound dialogue of Babylonian wisdom: The sufferer:

> Where is the counsellor to whom I can relate my trouble?
> I am finished. Anguish has come upon me.
> When I was still a child, fate took my father;
> My mother who bore me went to the Land of No Return.
> My father and mother left me without anyone to be my guardian.

The friend:

> Respected friend, what you say is sad.
> Dear friend, you have let your *mind* dwell on evil.
> You have made your good sense like that of an incompetent person;
> You have changed your beaming face to scowls.
> Our fathers do indeed give up and go the way of death. . . .

The sufferer:

> Those who do not seek the god go the way of prosperity,
> While those who pray to the goddess become destitute and impoverished.
> In my youth I tried to find the will of my god;
> With prostration and prayer I sought my goddess.
> But I was pulling a yoke in a useless corvée.
> My god decreed poverty instead of wealth (for me).
> A cripple does better than I, a dullard keeps ahead of me.
> The rogue has been promoted, but I have been brought low.

The friend:

> My just, knowledgeable friend, your thoughts are perverse.
> You have now forsaken justice and *blaspheme* against your god's plans.
> In your mind you think of disregarding the divine ordinances.
>
> .   .   .   .
>
> Unless you seek the will of the god, what success can you have?
> He that bears his god's yoke never lacks food, even though
>   it be sparse. . . . [13]

The friend's polite response is consistently inadequate to the problems raised by the sufferer's complaints. Nevertheless, the friend does declare that success comes only to those who quest for the divine will. He admits, however, that righteous conduct may not always receive as great a reward as those who pursue it might wish. He goes on to say that while divine wisdom is remote, it is nonetheless real (cf. Job 28:12–28). He also avers that justice is more fully realized than the sufferer thinks.

In the final lines of the text, the sufferer appeals to the gods for help and protection. The ironies and difficulties of his unhappy existence have not been resolved. The honest questioning and realism that were the hallmarks of such Babylonian wisdom poetry carry over into Old Testament wisdom compositions.

Finally, we should allude briefly to "The Words of Ahiqar."[14] This Aramaic papyrus of the fifth century was discovered at the Jewish military colony of Elephantine. Its proverbs, precepts, and fables have affinities not only with Egyptian maxims but with the Book of Proverbs.[15] Framing Ahiqar's teachings is a narrative that links the sage with the court of the Assyrian king Sennacherib. The existence of that narrative plus the fact that Ahiqar is an Assyrian name prompts the conclusion that the Aramaic text traces back to an unknown Assyrian original. In Assyrian the name is "Ahi-yaqar," meaning "the brother is precious."[16]

Throughout the Fertile Crescent, wisdom thinking tended to move in two different directions. First, it produced an impressive quantity of practical instruction. Counsel about the importance of hard work, mastery of one's emotions, and getting along with associates was offered in the belief that success comes to those who apply themselves in an orderly and just universe. The instructional texts of Egypt and the Book of Proverbs are filled with confidently formulated maxims. With their appeal to the experience of good men, these counsels instructed the young in mastering the laws of life.

Second, wisdom thinking of the ancient Near East gave rise to much speculative literature that was reflective, critical, and even skeptical. Many sages recognized that tranquility and material well-being did not always come to those who had worked diligently at living the good life. When the gods appeared to be angry without justification, when the support of friends suddenly vanished, and when political uncertainty and social anarchy held sway, the burden of human existence made optimistic reflection impossible. Hence, prudential wisdom was dismissed as shallow and incapable of preparing man for the dark night of the soul. Such texts as "A Dispute over Suicide," "The Babylonian Theodicy," Ecclesiastes, and Job were created by sages dissatisfied with the glib answers of an easy orthodoxy.

Nevertheless, practical and speculative wisdom did not always work at odds with one another. Both types of wisdom assumed that what was worth stating about life's opportunities and problems should be stated in terms of the individual. Utilitarian and speculative wisdom both viewed man as man. His nationality was unimportant. At base, wisdom thinking was an international quest for the meaning of life. Thus, the wisdom texts of the Hebrew Bible do not meditate on the special historical relationship between Yahweh, the God of Israel, and Israel, the unique people of Yahweh (although this relationship was a central concern of the prophet and the priest). Rather, they instruct the individual in how he should order his existence as a member of the family of mankind. And though the sage sometimes appeals to revelation in his attempt to defend a particular teaching or point of view, more often he simply takes account of human experience, which he accepts as having much to teach the man who is disciplined and intelligent.

Our knowledge about the origins and development of the wisdom movement in Israel is incomplete, but we have some clues on which to draw. Since the effects of the wisdom movement are apparent in four-teenth-century Canaanite sources, Israel presumably was exposed to sapiential reflection when she settled in the Land of Promise. Surely some Israelite elements had earlier observed that the sage played an important role in ancient Egyptian society. The old traditions preserved in Judges offer two early types of wisdom discourse: the fable (9:8–15) and the riddle (14:14). Also the sage was a recognized member of the tenth-century Jerusalem court. The counsel of Ahithophel, a court adviser to David, is praised as being on par with the revelatory word of the prophet (2 Sam. 16:23). Two wise women also figure prominently in portions of the Davidic court narrative (2 Sam. 14:1–20; 20:14–22).

During the rule of Solomon (ca. 961–922), the Israelite wisdom movement made significant strides, and this king was regarded as its greatest patron. (See Chapter 10.) At base, Solomon's quest for wisdom was a quest after that kind of prudence which would most benefit every-day human conduct. It may have concerned itself relatively little with how complicated affairs of state should be handled. Though we cannot take literally the biblical comment that "men came from all peoples to hear the wisdom of Solomon" (I Kings 4:34), the king might have been the author of a few of the aphorisms in Prov. 10:1–22:16, which is the oldest unit of this book.[17] In any event, the tradition that credits Solomon with having written three canonical books (Proverbs, Ecclesiastes, and the Song of Songs) and three noncanonical books (the Wisdom of Solo-mon, the Psalms of Solomon, and the Odes of Solomon), is no more his-torically reliable than are the traditions that Moses wrote the entire Pentateuch and David wrote the entire Psalter. (Psalms 72 and 127 are also ascribed to Solomon. Of course, we are not implying that the asso-ciations of Moses with Torah, David with psalmody, and Solomon with wisdom are inventions entirely lacking historical foundation.)

Still the cosmopolitan interests of the Solomonic court did much to encourage the growth of the wisdom movement in tenth-century Israel. Under Solomon's patronage, a humanistic frame of mind may have read-ily asserted itself in court circles. Regular contacts with foreign represen-tatives must have stimulated Solomon's counselors to see the world in a new light. Perhaps many of Jerusalem's citizens were now joining the in-ternational quest for wisdom.[18]

The portrait of Joseph as the ideal wise man (Gen. 37, 39–50), which must have emerged shortly after Solomon's reign, is further testi-mony that the wisdom movement was making its mark on Israel. Then, under the generally stable rule of Hezekiah (715–687), Israel experienced a new vitality in its political, economic, and cultural life that was favorable to wisdom interests.[19] Indeed, the superscription in Prov. 25:1, "These also are proverbs of Solomon which the men of Hezekiah king of Judah copied," implies the existence of a royal school of sages that sought to preserve the wisdom traditions that had already emerged. And as a contemporary of Hezekiah, Isaiah regularly employed wisdom discourse.[20] Approximately one century later, Jeremiah's confession in Jer. 18:18 attests to the presence of the sages as a "third force" in Israelite culture.

In sum, wisdom currents assuredly existed in preexilic Israel, and with the absence of monarchy and the gradual decline of prophecy in the postexilic era the sage became an important figure in Jewish society. He was entrusted with the education of many Jewish youths. As he became more concerned with the religious motivations of human behavior, his efforts increasingly supported those of the priest. Wisdom and scribal pursuits coalesced, and the sage took his place beside the priest as a staunch defender and zealous interpreter of the law.

Therefore, the wisdom movement in Israel had many sides and assumed diverse forms of expression.[21] It first asserted itself as "folk wisdom" in the form of terse, metaphoric sayings that sought to describe and assess one aspect or another of human conduct. Thus, the proverb, maxim, or aphorism came into being:

> Out of the wicked comes forth wickedness. (1 Sam. 24:13)
> Let not him that girds on his armor boast himself as he
>   that puts it off. (1 Kings 20:11)

Having its roots in folk wisdom, the literary proverb (*māshāl*) emerged as a two-part verse; the second part was usually antithetical to the first:

> Hatred stirs up strife,
>   but love covers all offenses. (Prov. 10:12)

Sometimes the second part of the proverb paralleled the first:

> To get wisdom is better than gold;
>   to get understanding is to be chosen rather than silver. (Prov. 16:16)

And that parallelism could be synthetic, making use of a vivid simile:

> Like a dog that returns to his vomit
>   is a fool that repeats his folly. (Prov. 26:11)

In time, the literary proverb came to have four or even more parts in order that a particular theme might be elaborated.

Other forms of wisdom discourse were created. One wit attempted to compete with another by way of the riddle (Judg. 14:14, 1 Kings 10:1–3). A moralistic comment about human relationships might be cast in the form of a fable; for example, trees and animals might be credited with human speech (Judg. 9:8–15, 2 Kings 14:9). Rhetorical questions became a favored device of the wise as they sought the consent of logical minds:

> Why should a fool have a price in his hand to buy wisdom,
>   when he has no mind? (Prov. 17:16)

The antithetical thrust of contrasting life situations was sometimes emphasized by means of "better sayings." This method of the Israelite sage was frequently used in Proverbs and Ecclesiastes:

> It is better to live in a corner of the housetop
>   than in a house shared with a contentious woman. (Prov. 25:24)

Graduated-numbers sayings allowed the wisdom teacher to comment on various aspects of the phenomenal world:

> Under three things the earth trembles;
>   under four it cannot bear up:
> a slave when he becomes king,
>   and a fool when he is filled with food;
> an unloved woman when she gets a husband,
>   and a maid when she succeeds her mistress. (Prov. 30:21–23)

The Israelite sage also made frequent use of assertions and admonitions. The former consisted of helpful observations about life put in the indicative mood:

> He who guards his mouth preserves his life;
>   he who opens wide his lips comes to ruin. (Prov. 13:3)

By contrast, admonitions offered direct counsel cast in the imperative mood:

> Answer not a fool according to his folly,
>   lest you be like him yourself. (Prov. 26:4)

Just as the forms of wisdom speech were multiple, so were the settings that they reflected. On the whole, it is difficult to establish the life setting of a given wisdom piece except to say that it involved a teaching situation. Israelite parents, clan elders, court advisers, and religious teachers tended to offer their instructions along similar stylistic lines.[22] The home, the street, the city gate, the court, the synagogue, the scribal school, and the cult all became settings in which teaching might take place.

But whatever the forms and settings of sapiential discourse were, they reflected an honest search for "wisdom" (*ḥokhmāh*) in its several manifestations. If at one extreme *ḥokhmāh* was understood as embracing highly utilitarian considerations, at the other it was thoroughly integrated into the religious thought of ancient Israel and equated with the divine will. Therefore, Yahweh was to be feared, and his commandments were to be kept (Prov. 1:7). In several texts, wisdom and law appear as virtually synonymous entities. (See Ezra 7:25; Ps. 37:30–31; 119:97–104; Prov. 1:7; and Job 28:28.) Human wisdom was thought to derive from a respectful knowledge of Yahweh's revealed law. Such knowledge was regarded as a supreme endowment that gave man sound direction in his day-to-day thought, speech, and action.[23]

THE BOOK OF PROVERBS
AND ITS OPTIMISM

In the Book of Proverbs we have a useful index of the varied concerns and styles of Israel's leading sages. Proverbs, which consists of succinct two-part aphorisms and more elaborate wisdom discourse, seems to have been edited in near-final form in the fourth century B.C.[24] Some of its contents, however, may easily trace back to the tenth century and to the Solomonic court. In the study of this highly diverse book, we therefore grasp something of the history of the wisdom movement in ancient Israel.

Because of the conspicuous lack of logical development in many of its sections, the Book of Proverbs does not make for easy reading. Moreover, contemporary readers who have little use for those who speak glibly about the power of positive thinking are likely to weary of the book's predominantly optimistic tenor. Here it is simply assumed that man is so constituted that he may learn the ropes to successful living. It is likewise assumed that order and dependability prevail in the deity's government of the world and that the man who tries to conform to the instruction of the wise will meet little or no opposition. Nevertheless, Proverbs offers a welcome contrast to the heavy tones of human anguish and despair in Ecclesiastes and Job.

The use of varied poetic forms, the seven distinct headings, and the repetition of several aphorisms all speak for the composite character of the Book of Proverbs. It would be unusual indeed for one sage to have expressed himself in such diverse ways. The presence of rather extensive discourses (in reality, poetic essays) in Proverbs 1–9, the preponderance of antithetical couplets in Proverbs 10–15 and 28–29, the predilection for vivid similes in Proverbs 25–26, the explicit use of numerical wisdom sayings in Prov. 6:16–19 and 30:15–31, and the acrostic composition in praise of the ideal wife in Prov. 31:10–31 suggest that Proverbs is an assemblage of earlier wisdom collections. This impression is further supported by the presence of seven headings (1:1; 10:1; 22:17; 24:23; 25:1; 30:1; and 31:1) that credit the contents of the Book of Proverbs to several distinct sources. Also the existence of identical or very similar maxims can be explained most readily as the result of "committee" effort. Within the massive unit of Prov. 10:1–22:16, 16:25 repeats 14:12 while 10:1 and 19:5 closely resemble 15:20 and 19:9, respectively. Then some aphorisms appear in more than one collection. For example, 18:8; 20:16;

and 22:3, which stand in one body of so-called Solomonic proverbs, are duplicated exactly in another: 26:22; 27:13; and 27:12. In sum, the Book of Proverbs is a full-fledged anthology of wisdom thinking that acquired its final literary expression over a span of several centuries.

The first collection (Prov. 1–9) begins with a superscription (1:1) intended to relate to the whole of Proverbs. As a royal genre, wisdom compositions blossomed under court patronage. Thus, mention of Solomon's name was a fitting way of claiming that the wisdom movement prospered in Israel with the king's assistance. Proverbs 1:2–7 then presents a formal statement acknowledging the instructional intention of the book. Proverbs seeks to school the callow and the mature in "wisdom" (ḥokhmāh). That noun is used early in v. 2 and is immediately reinforced by seven synonymous terms: "instruction," "insight," "prudence," "knowledge," "discretion," "learning," and "understanding." Then as a climax, 1:7 communicates the key slogan of the Israelite wisdom movement: "The fear of Yahweh is the beginning of wisdom." Proverbs 1–9 reflects a far greater integration of thought than the second collection does (Prov. 10:1–22:16), and mainly for that reason, it has been widely regarded as the latest section in the book.[25] Extended poetic discourses of admonition are intended to assist the reader in acquiring wisdom and virtue. The fool, the sluggard, and the sexually promiscuous are to be studiously avoided. Instead, a life style that embraces discretion, hard work, and reverence for God is to be cultivated.

The second collection (Prov. 10:1–22:16) and the fourth (Prov. 25–29) may be treated together. Both consist entirely of maxims that ordinarily take the form of aphoristic couplets. Along with 24:23–34 they are classified by McKane as "sentence literature."[26] These two atomistic collections lack logical progression. Yet both reflect a concern for the health of the individual and the welfare of a well-oiled society. Indeed, the proverbs in these two collections frequently contrast the behavior of the wise with that of the foolish. Many of these couplets may trace back to Solomonic times.

The third collection (Prov. 22:17–24:22) contains thirty sayings (22:20) to which has been added a short appendix of aphorisms denouncing partiality and sloth (24:23–34). The close similarity between the opening verses of this collection (22:17–23:11) and the Egyptian maxims of Amen-em-Opet speak for a preexilic date. The aphoristic couplet is infrequent in this collection. Instead, the quatrain and even longer literary units prevail. The tendency toward elaboration, the presence of an introductory statement of purpose (22:17–21), and the recurring use of the vocative ("my son") remind us of several features that are conspicuous in Proverbs 1–9.

Bearing superscriptions with the names of Agur (30:1) and Lemuel (31:1), the last two chapters of Proverbs contain four appendices whose form and content reflect the postexilic phase of Israelite wisdom. The components in Proverbs 30 present a confusing situation that makes it impossible for us to determine the extent of Agur's sayings. While vv. 1–9 have sometimes been accepted as a unit of dialogue between skeptic and believer, this is not certain.[27] Yet vv. 1–4 present a despairing confession by one who is painfully aware that he lacks wisdom. And a sequence of five rhetorical questions (v. 4) dramatically protests that the deity himself is unknowable. While the noun *massā'* in 30:1 may be understood as a reference to a place in the Arabian peninsula, it is perhaps better translated "oracle," in which case the superscription would read, "The words of Agur son of Jakeh, the oracle." In vivid contrast to vv. 1–4 are vv. 5–9, which reflect the thinking of the sage grasped by the concerns of Jewish piety. Here the deity is thought to be accessible to a man who does not bemoan his lack of wisdom. Rather, he lives in the fear that he might transgress against the Torah.

A second appendix of numbers sayings (30:15–33) offers a provocative enumeration of what is insatiable (vv. 15–16), awesome (vv. 18–19), socially intolerable (vv. 21–23), small yet wise (vv. 24–28), and regally proud (vv. 29–31). Another appendix (Prov. 31:1–9) is ascribed to an unknown king Lemuel and his presumably influential mother. It speaks in behalf of a righteous rule that must not be jeopardized by the dangerous side effects of strong drink and injudicious relationships with women.

A final appendix (Prov. 31:10–31) contains an acrostic poem praising the ideal housewife, ready and able to assume considerable responsibility and work hard. All in all, Proverbs has much counsel to offer sons and cultivates a generally negative attitude toward women. Yet by implication, daughters are addressed here, and the outstanding traits of a good wife are generously celebrated. This poem, writes Sandmel, "has been greatly influential in determining the role of Jewish wives and mothers."[28] No doubt its somewhat labored use in Christian worship on Mother's Day has also been for the good.

But what are some of the basic theological perspectives advanced by Proverbs? Certainly this anthology is not in the mainstream of the law and the prophets, where so much emphasis falls on Yahweh's historical election of Israel as his special people and the consequences of that election for concrete human behavior. With its prevailing optimism, Proverbs maintains that the ways of God are accessible to man, but it makes that claim from the human side. The book assumes that man is capable of bringing intelligence and reason to concrete human experience. He will therefore know how to conduct himself in the world of men and how to relate to a transcendent deity. On occasion, Proverbs seems inclined to celebrate human secularity. Many of the 375 maxims in Prov. 10:1–22:16 express no overt religious interest. The needs of Israelite worship and sacrifice are peripheral, and throughout there is a striking lack of interest in Israel's covenant relationship with Yahweh.

Canaanite, Egyptian, and Babylonian sources have all contributed to the literary expressions and themes in Proverbs. Even so, this book does more than mirror the intellectual currents that dominated the Fertile Crescent. It has its own Hebraic tenor. Sometimes its doctrine of reward and punishment sounds Deuteronomic. Moreover, the manner in which it contrasts the righteous with the wicked and the wise with the foolish recalls the Book of Psalms.

To a greater extent than is true for ancient Near Eastern wisdom as a whole, Proverbs belongs to the entire people of Israel. Its wisdom applies to a circle that extends far beyond the Jerusalem court. Since Proverbs consistently defends a high ethical standard, it reinforces the efforts of the priest and prophet. Of course, on the matter of what motivates a man's actions, Proverbs has not always endeared itself to its readers. Such an aphorism as "A good man obtains favor from Yahweh, but a man of evil devices he condemns" (Prov. 12:2) is one of many that claims that prudent behavior pays rich dividends and implies that man should get all he can. Nevertheless, Proverbs recognizes that such prudence is typically manifested among the wise and further maintains that wisdom itself comes from a sovereign deity who is the source of all wisdom. Here the underlying premise of the Israelite wisdom movement must be recalled: "The fear of Yahweh is the beginning of wisdom, and the knowledge of the Holy One is insight" (Prov. 9:10).

Undoubtedly the most striking theological perspective in the book lies in its personification of wisdom in Prov. 1:20–33 and 8:1–9:6. An abstract divine quality is here accorded human powers of mobility and speech. The figure personified is Lady Wisdom who, with the fervor of a street-corner prophet, summons men to her in the hope that they will acquire prudence. Proverbs 8:22–36 offers a significant first-person utterance by Wisdom in which she advertises her primordial existence and intimate association with the deity. She speaks of herself as a constructive principle who was active in the world's creation. She also claims a part in the ongoing maintenance of creation, especially as this relates to the life of men (8:34–35). Then, in 9:1–6, Wisdom is portrayed in the third person as a hostess who invites the simple to come and partake of insight from her table.

At first reading, these passages seem to jeopardize the monotheism that is either expressed or implied in so much of the Hebrew Bible. It is doubtful, however, that these personifications constitute such a threat, for they do not go so far as to grant wisdom complete independence (hypostatization) from the deity. She seems not to be a divine being who stands apart from Yahweh. Rather, the creative process depicted here involves the one deity whom Israel worships. To put the matter in less mythic language, Proverbs 8 affirms that "in his wisdom God made the world and its every aspect displays the rightness of the creative design."[29] Hence, personified wisdom is to be identified either as a divine messenger, or as Yahweh himself. In the intertestamental literature, Wisdom achieved a distinct status as an emanation of the deity (see Wisd. of Sol. 7:25–27), but this is not the case in the canonical Book of Proverbs. Still Proverbs did pave the way for developments in Judaism.

THE BOOK OF ECCLESIASTES AND ITS SKEPTICISM

The confidence and optimism of the Israelite sage are reflected everywhere in the Book of Proverbs. By contrast, Ecclesiastes is famous for its thoroughgoing skepticism. It advances the reflections of an Israelite sage whose theoretical training and life experience induced him to question traditional values. Though he had no intention of denying God's sovereignty, he painted an exceedingly bleak picture of the human condition. Perverted justice, chance happenings, unfulfilled yearnings of the human spirit, and arbitrary death are all depicted with such astounding realism in Ecclesiastes that at first one is tempted to infer that its author was a nihilist.

In fact, it is a marvel that Ecclesiastes actually won its way into the Old Testament canon. Its heterodox attitude and internal contradictions might have seriously threatened its admission. But its superscription (1:1) claimed Solomon as its author, and its concluding editorial notation piously advanced an admonition intended to summarize all that had gone before: "Fear God, and keep his commandments; for this is the whole duty of man" (12:13). And by the time the question of whether Ecclesiastes should be included among the canonical works had become a lively issue among the rabbis at the end of the first century of the Christian era, its open-minded reflections may have already become popular in many Jewish circles.

No doubt, the superscription in Eccles. 1:1 was inspired by 1:12–2:26, in which the author refers to himself as "king over Israel in Jerusalem" (1:12). What Jerusalem monarch would have been considered wiser than Solomon, who had reigned over a great nation centuries earlier? Yet critical scholarship refuses to accept the tradition that Solomon wrote Ecclesiastes. Solomon would scarcely have referred to "all who were over Jerusalem before me" (1:16; cf. 2:7, 9), for only one Israelite monarch (David) had preceded him on the Jerusalem throne. The weakness of monarchy implied in 4:13 and 10:5, the criticism leveled against the law court or Temple in 3:16, and the mention of unrelieved suffering among the oppressed in 4:1 mirror the thinking of someone who does not occupy a position of authority. Also the book's numerous Aramaisms, its late form of Hebrew, and its occasional reflection of Hellenistic thinking all point to a postexilic date. Because Ecclesiastes has influenced the thinking of ben Sira (ca. 180) and appears among the manuscript fragments found at Qumran, it can scarcely be dated past 200. The book nowhere alludes to known historical events. It probably was written in the third century B.C.

Then who was its author? In Eccles. 1:12 the author refers to himself as "Koheleth" in a passage in which he attempts to impersonate Solomon. He neither calls himself Solomon nor states that he is one of David's sons. (Such sonship is claimed in Eccles. 1:1, but this is the work of an editor.) In an effort to bolster his own theological position, however, he presents himself as the renowned royal patron of wisdom. The biographical note in the first editorial postscript in 12:9–10 discloses that Koheleth was a wisdom teacher who scrutinized the proverbs that he gathered and instructed students. His casual attitude toward religious observance (5:1–7) implies that he may have lived in Jerusalem and thus in close proximity to the Temple, whose existence he took for granted. Ecclesiastes 12:1 suggests that its author wrote mainly in his autumn years, after he had acquired much experience and spent countless hours pondering the confident platitudes of the orthodox and the counterclaims of those whose views were much closer to his own. In any case, he chose the pen name "Koheleth," which derives from the Hebrew root *qhl* and means "to gather." Perhaps the author wished to present himself as one who assembles a group of listeners for the purpose of instructing them. As the Greek equivalent, the Septuagint offers *Ecclesiastes*, a noun denoting one who is a member of an assembly. "The Preacher," the commonly used English designation, traces back to the Latin commentary of Jerome. But this is a deceptive translation, for it sparks notions in the minds of most readers that have little to do with Koheleth's skeptical temperament.

Today the majority of scholars accept most, if not all, of the book as the work of Koheleth. When assertions in different parts of the book contradict one another, this is ordinarily thought to reveal Koheleth's own deliberations about human existence. These are the reflections of a rugged individual who had the courage to change over the years. The total revision of Koheleth's work probably involved more than the obvious editorial touches in 1:1 and 12:9–14, but the glosses are few.[30]

This biblical book therefore preserves the random musings about life and religion of one of Israel's more disillusioned sages. Although Koheleth's so-called notebook has greater coherence than the sentence literature preserved in Proverbs, the former does not pretend to offer a systematic, tightly woven argument. Nor does it reflect a steady progression in thought. Nevertheless, it reveals a uniformity of language and mood that many find appealing.

The author was, of course, influenced by his intellectual environment. He appears to have been well acquainted with the pessimistic and skeptical aspects of Egyptian and Mesopotamian wisdom. And if, as seems likely, he lived in the third century B.C., he was undoubtedly attracted by the philosophical tenor of Hellenic thought. For example, Koheleth's propensity to face facts and to accept with grim resignation what cannot be changed resembles Greek Stoicism (1:9). Nevertheless, the text does not yield sufficient evidence to warrant the conclusion that Koheleth came into direct contact with any one school of Greek philosophy. He was an independent spirit who probably felt no compulsion to affiliate closely with any particular movement. To be sure, he knew that he was a Jew, and he recognized that his religious tradition was both an asset and a liability. Much of the conventional Jewish thinking of his day probably impressed him as idealistic and alarmingly superficial. His fondness for empiricism instructed him that the data of revealed religion should not be embraced blindly. Koheleth had no use for the easy solutions sometimes advanced by the orthodox. He was not waging a war against Jewish religion and ethics, however.

Rather, he was constantly striving for intellectual honesty. Personally he found life weary and monotonous. Though a wise man and a fool can be distinguished in life, in death they meet the same hopeless fate (2:15–16; 3:20–21). Man is regarded as the victim of events that have been predetermined by the all-knowing deity. Striking forth with his famous phrase, "vanity of vanities" (1:2; 12:8), Koheleth complained that life is utterly empty (2:11, 17, 22–23). The Hebrew noun *hebel*, which is ordinarily rendered here as "vanity," refers not to man's pride but to the tenuous quality of human existence. Thus, in this book of somber wisdom, knowledge, wealth, love, and even life itself are considered illusory. Like the animals, man is only a concrete embodiment of the fact that the natural world teems with incessant motion that has no significant effect (1:4–11). Yet as a creature of promise, man's plight exceeds that of any other creature: "I have seen the business that God has given to the sons of men to be busy with. He has made everything beautiful in its time; also he has put eternity into man's mind, yet so that he cannot find out what God has done from the beginning to the end" (3:10–11). Man is therefore doomed to misery. His mind and spirit are large enough to recognize that God exists, yet too limited to grasp the divine purpose.

Despite his skepticism, Koheleth affirmed God's transcendence and sovereignty. He viewed human existence as a gift of the deity, though he recognized that the gift was given with strings. For all his certainty that life was permeated by vanity, he had sufficient faith to affirm that life's frustrations are in some way resolved in God's own design. But so intent was he on reacting to the world from the perspective of a rugged empiricist that he failed to disclose how the great resolution would take place. Probably he did not know. Ultimately he found theological speculation to be fruitless, but this did not lead him to self-destruction. On the practical level, he was capable of embracing an existence woefully lacking in ultimate meaning. And here Koheleth had a few affirmations to make. He submitted that in spite of his tenuous existence, man could find satisfaction in daily work (3:22); restrained pleasure in social intercourse (2:24; 3:12–13; 5:18; 9:7); and joy in discreet worship (5:1–2), friendship (4:9–12), and marriage (9:9).[31]

In sum, the predominantly pessimistic Book of Ecclesiastes betrays the vacillations of an author who remained unsuccessful in his attempt to solve the riddle of life. Yet Koheleth believed that man could come closer to the truth by accepting harsh facts and pondering concrete human experience with its attendant pain than he could by accepting the pallid assertions of complacent orthodoxy. He was singularly honest in his approach to life, and the skepticism he fostered was at base religious. Above all, he knew that man in his finite wisdom cannot really comprehend the infinite wisdom of God. Hence, he moved beyond the weak optimism of Proverbs to a far more realistic perspective.

THE SONG OF SONGS AND ITS SENSUAL LYRICISM

From start to finish, the Song of Songs contains approximately two dozen lyrical compositions on the propriety and delight of romantic love. Through its use of bold metaphors, this sensuous folk literature acknowledges that human sexuality is a healthy instinct that accords with the divine will that man exist as a fully integrated being. Though these lyrics are not in the mainstream of Israel's wisdom movement, the sages probably played an appreciable role in their arrangement and transmission. Indeed, the beauties of nature that the songs celebrate were of great interest to many of the wise.

Although this book did not have an easy time making its way into the Hebrew canon, the presence of Solomon's name in its title (1:1) certainly helped.[32] Solomon's fame as a composer of songs (1 Kings 4:32) and references to this king in the lyrics themselves (1:5; 3:7–11; 8:11–12) must have prompted the inclusion of his name in the title.

Rabbi Akiba's dramatic statement made at Jamnia in ca. A.D. 90 that "no day outweighed in glory the one on which Israel received the Song of Solomon" must have also been of assistance. Pious realists of his day were offended by the extraordinarily sensual and secular tones of this poetry. But Akiba believed that the Song of Songs was an allegory that offered vital truths about the historical relationship between God and his people. More than eight centuries earlier, Hosea had spoken metaphorically of Israel as Yahweh's bride (Hos. 2:16–20). Similarly, in Christian circles the allegorical approach was widely embraced by those who insisted that the real subject of these lyrics was the love that existed between Jesus Christ and his bride, the church. Nevertheless, the allegorical interpretation of this poetry has often moved beyond all reasonable bounds:

> The greatest extravagances of exegesis have been indulged in, such as Hengstenberg's interpretation of the Shulammite's navel (7:2) as the chalice from which the Church revives those thirsting for salvation, and Wordsworth's conclusion from the relative number of the concubines and the queens (5:8), that the sectarians should outnumber the true Church. On such principles anything may mean anything.[33]

Consequently, many other interpretations of these erotic lyrics have been advanced.[34] One view sees them as a drama involving either two actors

The Spring of Ein Gedi. The Ein Gedi oasis, first mentioned in the Old Testament in connection with David's flight from Saul (1 Sam. 23:29), has a refreshing spring, which is shown here. Located directly west of the Dead Sea, this oasis is also noted for its vineyards, which are referred to in Song of Songs 1:14. (Photo by the author.)

(Solomon and a Shulammite maiden) or three (Solomon, a Shulammite maiden, and a shepherd). In the former, Solomon wins the heart of the Shulammite; in the latter, he loses her to her shepherd lover. But the absence of clear traces of dramatic progression in the text as well as the vague identity of its speakers make this interpretation doubtful.

Another approach sees these poems as originating in the fertility cult of Adonis. A sacred marriage that set loose nature's powers of fertility was thought to have taken place between a goddess (the Shulammite) and the king. In time the songs were reassessed as symbols of the love that existed between Yahweh and his bride, Israel, and absorbed into the faith of Judaism. While this interpretation has all the markings of scholarly ingenuity, it seems contrived. Its refusal to relate the songs to human love seems little more than another instance of unwarranted allegorization. This is not to deny, however, that the songs may in their own way reflect ancient Near Eastern fertility customs.

Still other interpreters have drawn a parallel between the wedding customs of twentieth-century Syrian Arabs and the practices of ancient Palestinians. The Song of Songs is thus regarded as a cycle of wedding songs that were chanted during a week-long wedding ceremony at which time the bride and groom were addressed as king and queen. While such a parallel bridges too much time and geography to be credible, it is possible that some of the lyrics in the Song of Songs were sung at ancient Jewish weddings. Even so, not all these poetic compositions, which take such delight in the rites of springtime lovemaking, appear to be set in the context of the marriage ceremony.

It is probably best to accept the Song of Songs as a collection of lyrics that are similar in style and that celebrate the splendor of human love. That love is viewed in both its nuptial and prenuptial phases. The many Aramaisms in the text, as well as the presence of Persian and Greek loan words, suggest that portions of the anthology were written as late as the third century B.C. Some of the poems may derive from a much earlier period, however. These lyrics reflect expressions and concerns that also appear in extrabiblical literature.[35] No less impressively they reflect the thinking of the down-to-earth covenant people, who viewed the mystery of human love with complete awe.

THE BOOK OF JOB
AND ITS STUBBORN FAITH

The haunting question, "What is the real purpose of God-given human existence?" dominated the thinking of another outstanding Israelite sage, whose words are preserved in the Book of Job. Though this book probably predates Ecclesiastes by at least two centuries, we treat it last in recognition of its widely acclaimed status as the most masterful product of the wisdom movement of ancient Israel.

The Book of Job is a series of reflections on life itself. It is manifestly concerned with the suffering of the innocent. Although it provides no thorough, convincing explanation, it may well improve the reader's perception of the problem.

Even more, the book is a testimonial in behalf of the intrinsic worth of stubborn faith. It reveals what can happen when the easy word of orthodox piety fails to grasp significant dimensions of the human predicament. Unfounded accusations and misguided counsels are given to one who is unprepared to accept either. Yet the sufferer is willing to endure the outrageous cruelties that presently assail him, and in the long run, the Promethean struggle proves worth the effort. At the end of the book, thorough answers to life's perplexities still remain beyond man's easy reach. Nevertheless, the night of despair is over, and the day of faith is at hand. In his direct confrontation with deity, Job encounters truths vastly larger than those that his orthodox associates were capable of supplying. In short, he is permitted to view the relationship between God and man in a new, positive light. We shall therefore maintain from the outset of our discussion that the Book of Job is not devoted solely to an examination of human suffering. Although that topic greatly interested the poet-sage who authored this literary masterpiece, he was equally, if not more, concerned with the entire question of man's faith.

Title, Composition, and Date

The title of this anonymous book is provided by the name of its hero, 'iyyôbh, which in its Latin form is Job. While a precise meaning is unavailable, both "enmity" and "hostility" are suggested. The noun is probably related to the verb root 'yb, meaning "to be hostile, to treat as an enemy." Hence, it may denote one who is the object of hostility and persecution. This reading makes sense in the light of both the prologue, where Job is the victim of Satan's cruel wager with Yahweh, and the poetry, which portrays Job as the target of harsh criticism from orthodox colleagues.

Job is immediately identified with "the land of Uz" (1:1), which is presumably a part of Edom. This judgment is supported by 2:11, with its mention of the homes of Job's associates. Also the divine name "Eloah," which is rare in the Old Testament but common in the Book of Job, appears in Edomite literature. If the characters are Edomite, then the ensuing action and discussion unfold on neutral ground. Consequently, the knotty problems of suffering and faith are deliberately isolated from any Palestinian surroundings that might unduly influence the theological case.

The vast majority of chapters (3:1–42:6) take the form of protracted, sometimes tense poetic dialogue between Job, his "comforters," and the deity. These chapters are framed by a prose prologue (1:1–2:13) that describes the afflictions that suddenly overtake the unsuspecting Job and a prose epilogue (42:7–17) that tells of the ultimate victory and reward that come to the suffering hero.

The movement within the text is complicated by three sections commonly accepted as secondary elements. First is chapter 28, a poem in praise of wisdom. Man's technology in reaching earth's depths and exposing its wealth is acknowledged in vv. 1–11, which introduces the fundamental truth that the poem seeks to assert: "But where shall wisdom be found? And where is the place of understanding? Man does not know the way to it, and it is not found in the land of the living" (28:12–13). Human perception of wisdom is thought to be fragmentary at best. By contrast, the deity knows wisdom in its fullness and has even ordained that wisdom be charged with the task of assisting him in the creation process. Wisdom truly belongs to God, not man.

We doubt that chapter 28 was composed by the Joban poet. It has no logical connection with its immediate context. Job's declaration that wisdom is inaccessible to man is curious for it is made by someone who is fervent in his determination to discover what divine wisdom is about. Moreover, Job 28 anticipates Yahweh's word in 38:2–40:2.

The Elihu speeches in chapters 32–37 constitute the second and longest intrusion in the book. Their secondary status may be argued on several counts. Elihu appears nowhere in the book save in chapters 32–37, and his views are never referred to elsewhere. And though Job's three friends are rebuked in the epilogue, Elihu is not. Yet his approach and opinions are not very different from theirs. Theologically and dramatically, Job's oath of clearance in chapter 31 demands Yahweh's immediate response (38:2–40:2), not the tedious remarks of Elihu. And finally, Yahweh's opening address in 38:2, "Who is this that darkens counsel by words without knowledge?" is aimed at Job, not at Elihu, who has just finished speaking. In sum, the Elihu speeches reflect the thought of a later sage. Though they repeat much of what has been said by Job's friends, they do not lack substance.

Finally, the words of the deity, which appear in two speeches, seem to come from different sources. While the authenticity of the first speech (38:2–40:2) is seldom doubted, the second (40:7–41:34) is regarded as somewhat irrelevant. The long descriptions of Behemoth (the hippopotamus) and Leviathan (the crocodile) in 40:15–41:34 scarcely measure up to the disclosures in Yahweh's first speech. And when we consider Job's submission in 40:4–5, the second speech appears to be the word of an overly insistent, nagging deity. It has been argued, however, that whereas the first speech of Yahweh wins only Job's silence (40:4–5), the second elicits his assent (42:2–6). But this may imply too strong a contrast between Job's two responses. Certainly Job's challenge in 31:35 requires that Yahweh answer in some manner. But as they now stand, chapters 38–41 seem to have undergone later embellishment. The extent of the spurious material is difficult to determine, however.

Nor is it easy to establish a date for the Book of Job. The prose framework contains several archaic elements that remind us of the patriarchal traditions in Genesis. For example, a central shrine is lacking, and in the absence of an established priesthood Job himself offers sacrifices to the deity (Job 1:5). As was true for Abraham (Gen. 12:16) and Jacob (Gen. 32:5), wealth is measured in terms of slaves and cattle (Job 1:3; 42:12). Job's many years (42:16–17) remind us of Isaac's (Gen. 35:28–29). The mention in Ezek. 14:14, 20 of three righteous men— Noah, Daniel (Dan'el), and Job—implies that a Job story existed in ancient Semitic legend. Noah's antiquity is scarcely subject to question, and thanks to the Ugaritic texts from Ras Shamra, we know that Dan'el was an outstanding figure in the Canaanite epic tradition dating to about 1500 B.C. Also as early as about 2000 B.C. the Sumerians possessed a story with a so-called Job motif.[36] Because Israel's hostility toward Edom intensified after the Babylonian conquest of Jerusalem in 587, in which the Edomites assisted, this folk tale about an upright Edomite hero would certainly have been absorbed into Israelite tradition by the early seventh century B.C. In its oral form it was surely known in ancient Israel several centuries earlier.

Evidence for the date of the poetic dialogues is also inconclusive. Job's curse of his birth (3:3–26) and Jeremiah's (20:14–18) are similar enough to warrant the judgment that one has been influenced by the other, and here Jeremiah's soliloquy is probably the more original. This would suggest that the Joban poet did not live earlier than the sixth century. Many affinities of thought and style exist between the poetry of Job and that of Second Isaiah. Both texts advance the theme of innocent suffering, yet the notion of vicarious suffering is upheld only in Second Isaiah. Since the Joban poet examines human suffering from so many angles but ignores completely the possibility of vicarious suffering, presumably he was ignorant of Second Isaiah.[37] This consideration suggests the possibility of a date prior to 540. Still, dogmatism on the matter is unwarranted, for these parallels do not constitute facts.[38] Since segments of a Targum of Job are numbered among the finds at Qumran, the Book of Job must have been well known by 100 B.C.[39] It is most likely, however, that it assumed final form long before the end of the third century.

The Prose Framework

Job 1:1–2:13 and 42:7–17 preserve an engaging folk narrative about the righteous, wealthy Job whose children presumably followed his example. Lest they had sinned without his knowing, Job rendered the necessary burnt offerings to make atonement. Therefore, the disasters about to unfold could not be justified as divine vindication. Instead, they were the outcome of a conversation and wager that took place in the divine council between Yahweh and Satan, whose Hebrew designation means "the adversary."

Satan's function was to spy on the world in order to bring instances of sordid human conduct to the attention of the deity (cf. Zech. 3:1–10). In response to Yahweh's gracious praise of Job's piety, Satan asks, "Does Job fear God for nought?" (1:9). Satan, who appears to be better informed than Yahweh about human motivation, reminds him that it is easy for Job to serve God when all goes well. But is Job capable of manifesting his god-fearing qualities in the face of adversity?

Satan secures Yahweh's permission to test Job's piety by touching his possessions—including his children—but not his person. Though Job wins, Satan is not at all sure that he himself has lost. As the result of a second audience with Yahweh, Satan is allowed to strike Job's person. Job is now afflicted with a skin ailment of such severity that his wife advises, "Curse God, and die" (2:9). Job, however, is determined to remain absolutely faithful (2:10). Eventually Job's three Edomite friends come to comfort him. They are so appalled by his physical condition that they engage in a mourning ritual for the dead (2:12).

The epilogue offers the remainder of the folk narrative. Yahweh's severe words against the friends (42:7–8) suggest that the Joban poet has not utilized all portions of the Job story that were available. But because Job intercedes, the friends who have spoken out of folly are spared Yahweh's wrath, and Job receives twice as much as he previously possessed. Also the upright Job, who had thus demonstrated that his was a disinterested religion, is granted many years of uninterrupted happiness by a pleased, righteous deity.

There are several inconsistencies between the framework of prose narrative and the poetic dialogues. In the folk tale, Job is patient, tranquil, and submissive; in the poetry, he is impatient, stormy, and blasphemous. In the epilogue (42:7–8), Job's friends are treated in an arbitrary manner; in the poetry, they are allowed to have their say. And while they are insensitive to Job's condition, they affirm nothing that warrants such a display of divine wrath. Moreover, the epilogue flatly testifies to the double restitution of Job's original fortune. These passages are scarcely on the same level as the subtle, complex poetry in which the character of Job's relationship to the deity is presented. The prologue and epilogue are narrated by the storyteller, whose description is interested yet relatively detached. By contrast, the poetic dialogue preserves the reflections of a poet who in no small measure is writing his own autobiography. He, too, has experienced the hell of human anguish.

Despite such inconsistencies between the prose and the poetry, the narrative framework offers some valuable psychological insights and establishes a setting for the poetry. Without it, the Joban poetry would lose much of its power and meaning. Although we may wish that the Joban poet had omitted the epilogue, he may have had little choice. There is a high probability that his audience was familiar with the Job folk tale and would have demanded its well-known conclusion.

Job's Dialogue with His Orthodox Companions

The dialogue between Job and his three Edomite friends who have come to comfort and advise him (Job 3–31) unfolds within a formal structure. Job opens the discussion with a poignant lament cursing the day of his birth (chap. 3). Eliphaz reacts with counsel that Job declares unacceptable (chaps. 4–7). Bildad now expresses his opinion, and Job offers his retort (chaps. 8–10). Then to complete the first cycle of dialogue, Zophar speaks and Job responds (chaps. 11–14).

A second and third cycle appear in chapters 15–21 and 22–27, respectively. The text of the third cycle, however, shows signs of subsequent editing, apparently in an attempt to play down Job's heretical declarations. Zophar says nothing, Bildad very little (25:1–6), and Job makes statements that conform to the orthodoxy of his friends (24:18–24; 27:13–23; 26:5–14).[40]

Then immediately following the intrusive hymn in praise of wisdom (chap. 28) comes Job's stirring monologue in which he reasserts his innocence, reviews his past, and laments the anguish of his present situation (chaps. 29–31). In spite of all that his friends have said, Job pleads his cause as fervently as ever.

Job's moving lament (chap. 3) breaks the week-long silence between the three friends and himself. With great intensity Job curses the day of his birth:

> Let the day perish wherein I was born,
>   and the night which said,
>   "A man-child is conceived."
> Let that day be darkness!
>   May God above not seek it,
>   nor light shine upon it. (3:3–4)

Since Job did in fact exit the womb, he is convinced that it would have been better had he gone immediately into the grave. Instead, he has become the victim of a meaningless life. Wistfully he expresses his surprise that those who desire death must live so long (3:20–22). Finally, he admits that even in his previous condition, which seemed so prosperous and enviable, he had not been at peace. Now he knows that his former worries were justified (3:25). By speaking in this way, Job has neither cursed God nor doubted his sovereignty and power. Nevertheless, this chapter exposes a man virtually without hope.

Presently the voice of orthodoxy asserts itself. At base, all three of

Job's colleagues express the same viewpoint. They insist that God blesses the good man with health and material well-being, but punishes the culprit who has transgressed against his will with illness and material want. Throughout their history the Deuteronomists maintained that this had been Yahweh's manner in dealing with his chosen people, and here within the Israelite wisdom movement this premise was directly related to individual existence. To be sure, many of the sentences preserved in Proverbs convey such a theological understanding of divine government.

The argument of Job's companions has been usefully compressed in the following syllogism:

1. Everyone who suffers is guilty of sinfulness.
2. Job suffers.
3. Therefore, Job is guilty of sinfulness.[41]

Job should repent. His suffering is clear evidence that he has sinned. He must renounce his past conduct and change his rebellious attitude, which is wrong and even dangerous. Yet Job's friends discover that it is easy to write the prescription, but well nigh impossible to force the patient to take the medicine.

Eliphaz, the eldest and most gentle of the colleagues, speaks first (chaps. 4–5). He comments on the universality of sin (4:17). No man is perfect in God's sight. Thus, suffering befalls all men as the sure consequence of sin. Without charging Job with particular sins, Eliphaz says that he must acknowledge God's just retribution for human behavior. He admonishes Job to return to the sovereign deity, who will then restore the penitent sufferer to a more promising existence. Eliphaz is concerned with defending divine goodness. God's determination to chastise man is a clear indication that he has man's ultimate welfare at heart (5:17–18).

In the second cycle (chap. 15), Eliphaz reveals his impatience with Job's "windy knowledge" (15:2), which threatens to upset the smooth course that orthodoxy expects. Job convicts himself by refusing to accept his circumscribed existence and acknowledge that suffering always visits the wicked.

In the third cycle (chap. 22), Eliphaz accuses Job of specific crimes. Because Job has oppressed the poor man, the widow, and the orphan, he is now being chastised by a God whose righteousness is perfect. Yet Eliphaz still recommends, "Return to the Almighty and humble yourself" (22:23). The hope that the proud, defiant Job can again experience the light of day and the good life is not abandoned.

Bildad also speaks enthusiastically for God's perfect justice and implies that in death Job's children suffered a deserved fate (chap. 8). The experience of generations has instructed that sure retribution awaits the sinful. Therefore, Job must turn immediately to God and implore his mercy. Because God's method of rewarding and punishing is consistently fair, Job may be sure that God will treat him justly. In the second cycle, Bildad paints an extraordinarily grim portrait of the disaster that awaits the wicked (chap. 18). Perhaps by scare tactics Job can be forced to affirm an orthodox position. In his third speech, Bildad points to God's splendor in order to emphasize human uncleanness (chap. 25) and emphasizes the deity's inscrutable omnipotence in order to expose man's finitude (assuming that 26:5–14 originally belonged to Bildad).

From the outset (chap. 11) Zophar reveals his lack of tact. He harshly declares that Job's rhetoric must be stopped and contends that Job's punishment is even less than he merits (11:6). Zophar argues that God in his infinite wisdom discerns sins of which man is oblivious. The right course for Job lies in a submissive return to the deity. In the second cycle (chap. 20), Zophar contrasts the fleeting triumph of the wicked with the inevitable destruction that awaits them. If 24:18–24 and 27:13–23 may be accepted as Zophar's contribution in the third cycle, it is apparent that his morbid preoccupation with the destiny in store for the wicked remains. Clearly, the doctrine of individual retribution finds an enthusiastic friend in Zophar.

All three counselors wish to impress Job with God's supreme justice. According to their logic, Job must make no further attempts at arrogant self-defense. Instead, he is to make an unrestrained confession. If Job submits to divine correction, God will hear his prayer and restore his membership in the good life. If he persists in his struggle against God, he will end a broken man. But the smugly orthodox counselors are victims of their own inadequacy. Their ability to enter fully into Job's situation and to extend their own understanding of the nature of suffering and faith is virtually nonexistent.

Then what does the dialogue reveal about Job? As our hero replies to each friend, two of his attitudes become clear.

First, Job often voices keen despair over his outrageous physical torment and mental anguish. The inscrutable deity appears to have ignored Job's past righteousness in favor of a cruel, meaningless course. And his friends have offered him no comfort. He feels betrayed by God and man alike. Thus, the despondent Job is tempted to long for death as a solution to his present plight (6:8–13).

Second and more pervasive is Job's protest against the circumstances that presently assail him and his emphatic assertion of his essential goodness. But Job's insistence that he is a good man is not a reflection of unrestrained human pride. Rather, it exposes his compulsion to fathom the underlying causes of his meaningless situation. Job's friends seem entirely too defensive about the safety of their own theological position. To Eliphaz he says, "You see my calamity, and are afraid" (6:21). In Job's view, his comforters have not demonstrated that he deserves the misfortune that has overtaken him. Like Eliphaz (4:17),

Job declares that sin touches the life of every human being (14:1–6). Yet unlike Eliphaz and his colleagues, Job denies that the punishment is commensurate with the wrongs he has committed.

Instead Job asserts that God has overreacted and shown himself to be his enemy. He is annoyed that God has focused attention on him. In words usually regarded as an intentional play on Psalm 8, Job inquires of the deity: "What is man, that thou dost make so much of him, and that thou dost set thy mind upon him, dost visit him every morning, and test him every moment?" (7:17–18).[42] In these lines Job communicates his confusion and displeasure that God is concerned at all about human conduct. If man sins, what is that to God, who exists in remote seclusion from the world below?

Job also protests that the omnipotent deity has unfairly exerted his power against him and that in no respect is this a contest between equals (9:17–19a; 16:9, 12–17). The deity is his enemy par excellence. Commenting on Job's moving statements in chapter 16, von Rad states:

> No one in Israel had ever depicted the action of God towards men in this way before. . . . God as the direct enemy of men, delighting in torturing them, hovering over them like what we might call the caricature of a devil, gnashing his teeth, "sharpening" his eyes. . . . and splitting open Job's intestines.[43]

If God's strength is evident, his righteousness is not. With bland indifference God "destroys both the blameless and the wicked" (9:22).

Job speaks out as the tormented, blasphemous rebel certain that his God is unfit for the divine office. He longs for a direct audience with the deity so that he may confidently defend his own cause (31:37; cf. 23:2–7) and cross-examine God about the manner in which he is running the universe. At the same time, Job is mindful that God is thoroughly inaccessible (9:11). Convinced that he has not been insensitive to God or to mankind, Job cannot repent. He refuses to affirm the orthodox premise that all who suffer have sinned.

How, then, can Job hope to receive the benefits of disinterested justice and resolve his plight? Refusing to give up every shred of faith, Job courageously articulates his confidence in the existence of a personal vindicator (gô'ēl) who will deliver him from his present affliction and make possible his reconciliation with the deity:

> For I know that my Redeemer lives,
>   and at last he will stand upon the earth;
> and after my skin has been thus destroyed,
>   then from my flesh I shall see God,
> whom I shall see on my side,
>   and my eyes shall behold, and not another. (19:25–27b)

The corrupt Hebrew text here is most problematic to interpret. Even so, we must attempt to determine who Job's vindicator is and when he is expected to take action.⁴⁴ The Hebrew phrase in 19:26 may be rendered either "from my flesh" or "without my flesh." While the former translation suggests that vindication will occur in this life, the latter points to a time after death. If the latter is correct, the Joban poet is offering what is perhaps the earliest biblical affirmation of bodily resurrection. Elsewhere Job does not articulate any belief in a personal resurrection. Like Koheleth, he perceives the finality of death. Then if Job should be calling attention to a vindication after death, perhaps he is merely giving expression to what he would like to believe. Still Job is insisting that the cause of justice will triumph—and in his behalf.

The identity of Job's redeemer is also baffling. Is he a human being who is closely related to Job, a heavenly mediator, or God himself? Since Job's sons have died and his relatives have forsaken him, the first possibility is unlikely. If the redeemer is God, perhaps we are to assume that "Yahweh will vindicate Job's cause before the 'God' of traditional religion."⁴⁵ Job seems to be declaring war on the God of easy orthodoxy in the hope of discovering God as he really is. Job's previous thoughts about an umpire (9:33) and a heavenly witness (16:19), both of whom are clearly conceived to be other than God, are strong support for the view that the vindicator in 19:25 is not God himself. Once more Job is placing his hope in the existence of a heavenly advocate who will bring to an end his present estrangement from God. And to the very conclusion of the dialogue, Job proudly insists that he is a good man who has been supremely wronged.

The Voice from the Whirlwind

Finally Yahweh speaks to Job out of the whirlwind (chaps. 38–41) and expresses his disdain for Job's vulgar protests of innocence. Rather than answering the inquiries Job has already put to him, Yahweh becomes the supreme questioner. By posing one rhetorical question after another, Yahweh forces Job to recognize his own mortality in the face of divine magnificence. Through this divine rebuke, Job is shown that he has no basis whatever for criticizing the Creator.

Yahweh's technique is neither to charge Job with moral impoverishment nor to beat him into submission. Instead, he seeks to unmask Job's ignorance through "the rhetoric of allusion and analogy."⁴⁶ What does Job really know about the creation of the world? Did he take part in the founding of the earth and the confinement of the sea? Does he have charge of storm and rain? Is it his wisdom that determines the behavior of the animal world? The humbled Job responds to this interrogation with a simple declaration that invalidates his earlier pretension. He confesses that in the presence of such creative wonder he feels impotent. He can speak no further (40:4–5). Then at the end of a second speech in which

Yahweh further advertises his wisdom and power over creation, Job confesses his ignorance and humbly repents:

> Therefore I have uttered what I did not understand,
>   things too wonderful for me, which I did not know. . . .
> I had heard of thee by the hearing of the ear,
>   but now my eye sees thee;
> therefore I despise myself,
>   and repent in dust and ashes. (42:3, 5–6)

Thus, the broken hero discerned God afresh. The shock treatment that Job received from the deity required that he move beyond the confining orbit of self. As an overwhelmed yet liberated creature, Job could finally free himself of the obsessive quest for self-justification. Accordingly, he was favored with an enlarged perception of God and his positive relationship with him was restored.

The problem of human suffering, however, is not resolved. Even after Yahweh has spoken, Job is not really better informed as to why some men suffer and others do not. The notions that suffering helps man in his quest for self-discipline, that it serves the cause of retribution, and that it is fundamentally inexplicable are all left in a state of suspension. Still, the dogma that sin is the sole reason for human suffering is given an emphatic burial.

Yahweh's words offered Job an intelligible though incomplete answer. He was led to see that just as harmony, beauty, and goodness are properties of the natural world, they also belong to the moral order in which men find themselves. More impressive, however, is the fact that the transcendent Creator had in effect taken time off from governing the universe to concern himself with the defiant and troubled Job. Like the suffering Jeremiah, Job was to learn that ultimately deliverance depends on divine immediacy, not on the rights and privileges that men like to think are theirs.

No doubt, the Job of the poetry and the Joban poet himself had both coped with human suffering in its many outrageous forms, and in the process they gained fresh insights about the relationship between God and man. The sheer mystery of human existence is not explained away. But the possibility that man may persist in his faith in a wise, sovereign, and loving deity is persuasively presented by a truly skillful wisdom poet.

NOTES

1. Genesis 41:8, Exod. 7:11, 1 Kings 4:30, and Isa. 19:11–12 refer to Egyptian wisdom; Isa. 44:25, Jer. 50:35, and 51:57 mention the wisdom of Babylon; Jer. 49:7, Obadiah 8, and Job 2:11 allude to Edomite wisdom; 1 Kings 7:14 and Ezekiel 28 reflect the wisdom of Tyre.

2. For the intersection of wisdom with historical, prophetic, and psalmic Old Testament literature, see J. L. Crenshaw, "Method in Determining Wisdom Influence upon 'Historical' Literature," *Journal of Biblical Literature* 88 (1969): 129–142; Samuel L. Terrien, "Amos and Wisdom," in Bernhard W. Anderson and Walter Harrelson, eds., *Israel's Prophetic Heritage* (New York: Harper & Row, 1962), pp. 108–115; and Roland E. Murphy, "A Consideration of the Classification, 'Wisdom Psalms,'" *Congress Volume: Bonn, 1962*, Vetus Testamentum Supplement, vol. 9 (Leiden, Neth.: E. J. Brill, 1963), pp. 156–167, respectively.

3. In recent years, the Book of Esther has also been defended as a wisdom text. See Shemaryahu Talmon, "'Wisdom' in the Book of Esther," *Vetus Testamentum* 13 (1963): 419–455. Though Talmon constructs a strong case, we prefer to treat Esther as one of three crucial postexilic short stories that have been preserved in the Old Testament canon; see Chapter 21.

4. For a more thorough presentation, see R. B. Y. Scott, *The Way of Wisdom in the Old Testament* (New York: Macmillan, 1971), pp. 23–47. Many of the pertinent ancient Near Eastern texts are scrutinized by William McKane, *Proverbs: A New Approach*, The Old Testament Library (Philadelphia: Westminster Press, 1970), pp. 51–208.

5. William F. Albright, "Some Canaanite-Phoenician Sources of Hebrew Wisdom," in Martin Noth and D. Winton Thomas, eds., *Wisdom in Israel and in the Ancient Near East*, Vetus Testamentum Supplement, vol. 3 (Leiden, Neth.: E. J. Brill, 1960), pp. 1–15.

6. See James B. Pritchard, ed., *Ancient Near Eastern Texts Relating to the Old Testament*, 3d ed. (Princeton, N.J.: Princeton University Press, 1969), pp. 412–414.

7. *Ibid.*, pp. 420–424.

8. *Ibid.*, pp. 405–410.

9. *Ibid.*, pp. 421–423. The parentheses contain the translator's interpolations, and the italicized words denote conjectured readings.

10. *Ibid.*, pp. 425–427, 593–596. These texts date between 1500 and 1200 B.C.

11. *Ibid.*, pp. 434–437.

12. W. G. Lambert, *Babylonian Wisdom Literature* (Oxford: Clarendon Press, 1960), p. 13. On stylistic grounds, Lambert dates the composition of the extant text of "The Babylonian Theodicy" to about 1000 B.C. (p. 67).

13. Pritchard, *op. cit.*, pp. 601–604. The parentheses contain the translator's interpolation and the italicized words denote conjectured readings.

14. *Ibid.*, pp. 427–430.

15. For example, Ahiqar's sayings resemble such instructions as the following in the Book of Proverbs: 4:23–24; 13:3, 24; 16:1, 9, 14; 23:13–14; 27:7.

16. For a brief, helpful discussion on the Assyrian origins of the Ahiqar text, see E. G. Kraeling, "Book of Ahikar," in George A. Buttrick et al., eds., *The Interpreter's Dictionary of the Bible* (Nashville: Abingdon Press, 1962), A–D, p. 69.

17. The fact that many of these proverbs advocate a humble way of life, which seems so antithetical to Solomon's personal example, does not prove that Solomon had no part in their origin. Perhaps Solomon advised

his subjects, "Do what I say, not what I do." Even so, we cannot attribute this entire literary block to Solomon.

18. This is the view of Norman W. Porteous, "Royal Wisdom," in Noth and Thomas, *op. cit.*, p. 250.

19. See R. B. Y. Scott, "Solomon and the Beginnings of Wisdom in Israel," *ibid.*, pp. 262–279, who insists that only in Hezekiah's time did Hebrew wisdom emerge as a vital literary phenomenon.

20. See J. William Whedbee, *Isaiah and Wisdom* (Nashville: Abingdon Press, 1971), and our previous comments in Chapter 13.

21. For a most helpful form-critical presentation of wisdom discourse, see Gerhard von Rad, *Wisdom in Israel*, trans. James D. Martin (Nashville: Abingdon Press, 1972), pp. 24–50.

22. Roland E. Murphy, "Form Criticism and Wisdom Literature," *Catholic Biblical Quarterly* 31 (1969): 481.

23. For a superb presentation of the concerns of wisdom, especially their connection with the rest of Israelite faith, see von Rad, *op. cit.*

24. It is difficult to establish a precise date for the completed Book of Proverbs. For a helpful discussion, see S. H. Blank, "Book of Proverbs," in Buttrick et al., eds., *op. cit.*, K–Q, pp. 939–940. Because four brief sections of the book (30:1–14; 30:15–33; 31:1–9, 10–31) appear in a different sequence in the Septuagint than in the Hebrew Bible, they are frequently judged to be appendices attached after all of Proverbs 1–29 had been compiled.

25. But McKane, *op. cit.*, pp. 6–7, cogently argues that it is the widespread use of the international instruction genre that gives these chapters their integrative character and that this cannot be used as an argument for a late date. He also claims that instruction genre for Prov. 22:17–24:22 and 31:1–9.

26. *Ibid.*, pp. 10–22.

27. *Ibid.*, p. 643.

28. Samuel Sandmel, *The Hebrew Scriptures: An Introduction to Their Literature and Religious Ideas* (New York: Alfred A. Knopf, 1963), p. 262.

29. Norman K. Gottwald, *A Light to the Nations: An Introduction to the Old Testament* (New York: Harper & Row, 1959), p. 471.

30. See the convincing presentation by S. H. Blank, "Book of Ecclesiastes," in Buttrick et al., eds., *op. cit.*, E–J, p. 10. On doctrinal grounds, he accepts 3:17; 7:18b; 8:5, 12–13; 11:9b; and 12:13b-14 as glosses.

31. Gordis claims that in Koheleth's understanding, "joy is God's categorical imperative for man." (Robert Gordis, *Koheleth—The Man and His World: A Study of Ecclesiastes*, 3d ed. [New York: Schocken Books, 1968], p. 129.)

32. Although English versions offer the title "The Song of Solomon," the Hebrew designation is a superlative to be rendered, "The Best of Songs."

33. H. H. Rowley, *The Growth of the Old Testament* (New York: Harper & Row, Harper Torchbooks, 1963), p. 148.

34. For a much more thorough treatment, see "The Interpretation of the Song of Songs," in H. H. Rowley, *The Servant of the Lord and Other Essays on the Old Testament*, rev. ed. (Oxford: Basil Blackwell, 1965), pp. 197–245.

35. For specimens of Egyptian love poetry dating from about 1300 to 1100 B.C., see Pritchard, *op. cit.*, pp. 467–469. The sheer delight in doves, gazelles, flowers, vineyards, and springtime itself, as well as references to the bride as "my sister" (4:9–10, 12; 5:1–2), show that the Song of Songs was subject to Egyptian influence. See also Jerrold S. Cooper, "New Cuneiform Parallels to the Song of Songs," *Journal of Biblical Literature* 90 (1971): 157–162, who calls attention to useful Sumerian data.

36. S. N. Kramer, " 'Man and His God': A Sumerian Variation on the 'Job' Motif," in Noth and Thomas, *op. cit.*, pp. 170–182.

37. So Samuel L. Terrien, "Introduction and Exegesis to Job," in George A. Buttrick et al., eds., *The Interpreter's Bible* (Nashville: Abingdon Press, 1954), vol. 3, p. 890.

38. For a thorough discussion of the date of Job, see Marvin H. Pope, *Job: Introduction, Translation, and Notes*, 3d ed., The Anchor Bible, vol. 15 (Garden City, N.Y.: Doubleday, 1973), pp. xxxii–xl. Pope accepts the seventh-century date as a "best guess."

39. *Ibid.*, p. xl.

40. We are following Terrien, "Introduction and Exegesis to Job," *op. cit.*, p. 888, who attributes the first two of these units to Zophar and the last to Bildad.

41. H. Joel Laks, "The Enigma of Job: Maimonides and the Moderns," *Journal of Biblical Literature* 83 (1964): 351.

42. Job's sentiments also have a close affinity with Ps. 144:3–4.

43. Von Rad, *op. cit.*, p. 217.

44. The discussion by Terrien, "Introduction and Exegesis to Job," *op. cit.*, pp. 1051–1057, is especially recommended.

45. Walter Harrelson, *Interpreting the Old Testament* (New York: Holt, Rinehart and Winston, 1964), p. 435.

46. These words constitute the title of a most interesting chapter in Robert Gordis, *The Book of God and Man: A Study of Job* (Chicago: University of Chicago Press, 1965), pp. 190–208. Gordis' volume is an unusually fresh, penetrating study of the Book of Job.

21

ISRAEL
AND THE WORLD
AT THE CLOSE
OF THE
OLD TESTAMENT
ERA

A new phase of ancient Near Eastern history began when the Greeks under the gifted and energetic leadership of Alexander of Macedon (336–323 B.C.) marched eastward and brought all of the Fertile Crescent under their control. Tolerant Persian rule of Palestine (539–332 B.C.) gave way to Greek dominion (332–63 B.C.), which was not always as sensitive to Jewish interests. Judah had earlier felt the influence of Persian Zoroastrianism within her borders, and now she would surely be unable to resist things Greek. Nevertheless, in the face of new opportunity and danger, Judaism persisted in its course.

Due to the scarcity of sources, this phase of biblical history is difficult to reconstruct. The Chronicler's story breaks off early in the fourth century B.C. after its account of Ezra's reforms, and no other historical work in the Old Testament deals with a later period. Only in 1 and 2 Maccabees does the narrative about Yahweh's people resume, and there we are suddenly introduced to events that date to the second century B.C.

Nevertheless, some suggestion of the religious tenor of the decades succeeding the reform era of Nehemiah and Ezra is made by three biblical short stories: Esther, Ruth, and Jonah. While it is impossible to claim that all three pieces of religious fiction postdate Ezra's time, each reflects the tensions that Judah's citizens felt in an era increasingly forced to acknowledge the political supremacy of the Hellenists. The Gentile world could not be ignored. But what attitudes should the faithful cultivate in their relationships with the Gentiles? Esther, Ruth, and Jonah present their respective answers to this critical issue.

Biblical texts to be read prior to and in conjunction with the present chapter: Esther, Ruth, Jonah, and Daniel.

Once we have examined these brief narratives, we shall follow the history of Judaism down to the middle of the second century, which provides the setting for the apocalyptic Book of Daniel. Since we shall confine our inquiry to the Hebrew Bible, our examination of the Book of of Daniel will bring this study of the people of ancient Israel to a close.

THE SHORT STORY
AND THE PROBLEM OF
JEWISH-GENTILE RELATIONS

The books of Esther, Ruth, and Jonah all focus on the problem of Jewish-Gentile relations. Reflecting the ways of a sinister world that seemed unrelenting in its threat to Jewish tranquillity, the story of Esther reveals Judaism's distrust and hatred of the outsider. The book's defensive spirit reminded the people of Yahweh that the possibility of continued existence depended on banding together against the enemy. By contrast, the artfully constructed narratives about Ruth and Jonah claim that Yahweh's concerns extend far beyond Israel's borders. If the deity had acted providentially in Israel's behalf in Esther's threatening situation, his providence was no less evident in the life of a Moabite woman named Ruth and in the repentance of that loathsome Assyrian city, Nineveh. In his wondrous universality, Yahweh could appreciably influence the existence and good fortune of those who were not Jews. An attitude of indiscriminate exclusivism was therefore dramatically challenged. Many modern readers claim that a study of these literary masterpieces has done more than simply sharpen their awareness of the dynamics of postexilic Judaism. It has also forced them to reconsider their attitudes toward those they accept and do not accept as "their kind of people."

Keeping on Guard: The Witness of Esther

The suspenseful narrative about Esther and her cousin Mordecai, who bravely defended Judaism's cause, is the work of an anonymous author with an admittedly nationalistic bent. As he wrote, he seemed to have three goals in mind. First, he wished to emphasize Judaism's ability to survive in the face of severe oppression. Second, he wanted to account for the origins of the popular religious festival of Purim, whose celebration was not enjoined by the Torah. Finally, he sought to delight his audience with a truly absorbing story.

A straightforward reading of the text discloses that Esther better qualifies as fiction than as history. The author shows some knowledge of Persian court practices, but many elements in his narrative are implausible in historical terms. Although it may seem encouraging that the name "Ahasuerus" is the Hebrew equivalent of "Xerxes," the king who ruled Persia between 486 and 465 B.C., this observation puts the notation of 2:5–6 in a ludicrous light. There it is claimed that Mordecai was among the Jews deported from Jerusalem to Babylon in 597. Thus, Mordecai would have been at least one hundred and ten when Xerxes began his reign, and it was some twelve years later that he was assigned a significant political office as Haman's successor. It is unlikely that Xerxes had a Jewish queen and unthinkable that he would have allowed the Jews to wipe out 75,000 of his Persian subjects (9:16). Nor do banquets lasting for six months (1:4), royal edicts legislating that "every man be lord in his own house" (1:22), or gallows 75 feet in height (7:9) impress us as the stuff of history.

They do constitute appropriate fictional touches, however, as does the delightful turn of events that occurs when Haman is tricked into recommending lavish honors for Mordecai, whom he hates (6:6–10). Not long afterward, the king falsely accuses Haman of having assaulted the queen; that charge ushers Haman to the gallows, since Esther deliberately says nothing to correct her husband's mistaken impression (7:8–10). This entertaining story portrays the beautiful, courageous Esther; the resourceful Mordecai; and the unscrupulous Haman, who are all duly rewarded for their attitudes and behavior. The narrative was meant to be enjoyed, as indeed it must have been at the annual festival of Purim when it was read aloud. Moreover, the name of that festival is directly connected with Haman's use of "lots" (*pûrîm* [3:7; 9:24–26]) in his eager attempt to determine the date for the Jewish massacre, which, thanks to the heroic efforts of Esther and Mordecai, never materialized.

Several factors encourage a second-century B.C. date for the book. Its language is late. No fragments of Esther have as yet been uncovered at Qumran. The earliest reference to Purim in Jewish sources apart from Esther appears in 2 Maccabees, presumably a document of the first century B.C., which alludes to "Mordecai's day" (15:36). And ben Sira's famous list of Israelite heroes (Ecclus. 44:1–50:24) does not include Mordecai and Esther. The matter-of-fact reference to Jewish dispersion (Esther 3:8) and the strong nationalistic tone of the narrative further suggest that this is one of the latest books in the Hebrew canon.

The Book of Esther presents the origin and purpose of the festival of Purim via well-told narrative. Haman's plot to persecute all Jews living within the Persian empire was frustrated by his own execution and a retaliatory bloodbath that gave the Jews opportunity to take vengeance. The massacre, which lasted only one day, was carried out on the thirteenth of Adar and commemorated with joyous, unrestrained celebration on the following day.[1]

Esther is often said to be the Bible's least religious book.[2] It propounds no turn-the-other-cheek ethic and takes pains not to make any direct mention of religious considerations. God is not even referred to when his benevolent care of his people is implied; in 4:14 Mordecai speaks of divine deliverance as coming "from another quarter." Yet such passages as 4:14 and 6:1 assume that divine providence is at work. Further, the issue of Judaism's survival is not without religious ramifications. A monarch is told:

> There is a certain people scattered abroad and dispersed among the peoples in all the provinces of your kingdom; their laws are different from those of every other people, and they do not keep the king's laws, so that it is not for the king's profit to tolerate them. (3:8)

Of course, the possible consequences of such an interview for the continuing existence of the Yahwistic faith are of considerable significance.

Still the delight that the Jews take in annihilating their enemies reinforces the vindicative Nahum more adequately than it does Second Isaiah. Esther preaches that the covenant people must guard against outsiders, who will do them in. But since the history of Yahweh's people is full of villains like Haman who worked overtime to jeopardize the very existence of the faithful, it is understandable that such a book as Esther was written, cherished, and incorporated into the canon.

Opening the Door: The Witness of Ruth and Jonah

Ruth. Ruth is one biblical short story that indirectly declares that the ranks of the faithful should not close too tightly. It highlights the life of a humble Moabite woman whose devotion and generosity were cherished by those Israelites whose lives she touched most intimately.

Once more we confront fiction rather than history. Several of the characters have symbolic names: Mahlon means "weakness," Chilion "wasting," Orpah "stiff-necked," Naomi "my sweetness," and Ruth "companion." Moreover, Ruth, Naomi, and Boaz are set forth as models of gentle conduct. Ruth is devoted to her mother-in-law, who in turn has Ruth's welfare at heart; and Boaz in his dealings shows a genuine respect for both individual human beings and the laws governing Israelite society. The customs of this ancient era are also recalled in a consistently idyllic fashion. The poor are permitted to glean in fields not their own (2:2), and the end of the barley harvest is celebrated with a generous amount of food and drink (3:7). Throughout, the main characters give no thought to personal gain as they labor to meet the demands of a simple family existence within the context of an agrarian society. If the premonarchical period seems treacherous in the Book of Judges, it is portrayed with nostalgia by the author of Ruth.

The Book of Ruth probably dates to either the fifth or fourth century B.C. The reference to time with which it opens implies its author's acquaintance with the sixth-century Deuteronomic edition of Judges. Moreover, in 4:7–10 the author of Ruth feels obligated to explain the custom of levirate marriage, which had presumably become obsolete in his own day.[3] No doubt the predominating classical Hebrew style reflects the writer's studied attempt to narrate events of bygone days in a fashion he believed best suited to the interests of the narrative.

But what might have stimulated the writing of this short story, which came to be read annually at the festival of Weeks (Pentecost) when the conclusion of the wheat harvest called for celebration? The book's imprecise allusion to the law of levirate marriage makes it unlikely that it was written to revive an interest in an ancient sociological custom. Since the story is full of examples of upright conduct, it may have been used to instruct youth in the values of human kindness that go beyond the requirements of either law or custom. Even so, its author may have thought of himself primarily as an artist who sought only to give shape to an entertaining story. Certainly the Book of Ruth can be enjoyed apart from thought about its social and moral implications.

In any event, the book can scarcely be considered a vehement political tract directed against the position Nehemiah and Ezra had taken against mixed marriages in the postexilic community. True, Ruth was a foreigner, not a native Israelite. Presumably someone other than the author of the narrative, who felt this consideration merited further emphasis, attached a genealogical notation (4:17b–22) in support of a tradition, long current in some circles, that David had descended from Moabite ancestors. Nevertheless, the narrative does not have the quality of political propaganda, and in Ruth's adoption of Israelite customs and religion (1:16–17) her continuing status as a foreigner is considerably weakened, if not annulled. In fact, Ruth is the kind of proselyte Nehemiah and Ezra would have accepted with open arms. Still the author was undoubtedly inviting his Jewish contemporaries to reexamine their attitudes toward non-Israelites. He was asking them to reflect a moment on Yahweh's way with the individual foreigner whose innate goodness made him precious in the divine sight. A firm believer that Israel should deal graciously with foreigners who expressed a willingness to embrace Yahwism, the author produced a simple yet effective portrayal of human generosity that transcends geographical boundaries and affiliations. Indeed, his liberating universalism has won over many readers.

Jonah. Again we confront a lucid, engaging narrative with several noteworthy characteristics. While Jonah is considered one of the twelve minor prophets, the style and central character of the Book of Jonah differ sharply from what is typical of Old Testament prophetic literature. Jonah's prophetic message is not cast in the customary poetic format of extended prophetic oracle directed against Israel and her neighbors.[4] It is a succinct declaration to the inhabitants of a foreign city, and it is compressed into less than one verse: "Yet forty days, and Nineveh shall be overthrown!" (3:4b).

The narrative focuses on the career of the prophet. Moreover, Jonah is presented as reacting strangely to his listeners, who actually heed his warning. The prophet is greatly disturbed by their formal expression of remorse, which means that his prediction of Nineveh's downfall will not be verified by impending history. In stark contrast to Jeremiah, who was profoundly disappointed that his audience ignored his words and did not return to Yahweh, Jonah sulks because his divinely inspired mission is successful. Horror of horrors! The enemy has converted to Yahwism.

The author of the Book of Jonah probably drew on a previous Jonah legend. In 2 Kings 14:25 "Jonah the son of Amittai," is said to have foretold the impressive territorial expansion achieved by the northern kingdom under Jeroboam II (786–746). The actual connection between that prophet and the character portrayed in the Book of Jonah is surely nothing more than a convenient literary attempt by the narrator to link his tale with an individual whose reputation had grown across the centuries. In fact, the notation of 2 Kings 14:25 can be misleading. It has led some readers to think that the author of the Book of Jonah, who may have lived in the fourth century B.C., was reporting an actual historical event.[5]

The Port of Jaffa (Ancient Joppa). Today this ancient port on the Mediterranean coast of central Palestine is linked with Tel Aviv, its sister city to the north. According to the Jonah story (1:3), the reluctant prophet's ill-fated journey originated at Joppa. (Courtesy of the Israel Government Tourist Office, Chicago.)

The following considerations, however, indicate that the Jonah story is fiction. First, excavations at Nineveh have uncovered an impressive ancient city whose circumference measures roughly 8 miles, yet we learn in 3:3 that it would have taken Jonah three days simply to walk from one end of the metropolis to the other. Second, Nineveh's exaggerated size is matched by an overstatement as to its population (4:11), where it is claimed that the city's children alone numbered 120,000 persons. Third, the overnight conversion of an entire pagan city to the faith of a foreign people is most unlikely. And fourth, Jonah's stay in the belly of the great fish is peculiar, to say the least. Even so, this humorous short story is a significant piece of religious literature. Indeed, its author has an unmistakably prophetic message to convey.

The Jonah author warns that Judah's penchant for reform can be carried too far—to the detriment of all concerned. His parable depicts the intolerant member of the faith whose rigidity and dogmatism make it impossible for him to share his religious heritage with the threatening foreigner, who may be far more worthy of the gift than he thinks. The writer objects to a narrow frame of mind incapable of fathoming the sweep of God's sovereignty. He calls on his audience to turn away from thoughts of self-preservation and entrenchment to consider a human compassion that transcends national boundaries.

Yahweh's concern for all mankind wins out over Jonah's provincialism. The narrative reveals that Jonah erred both in his determination not to address the inhabitants of Nineveh and in his anger over their repentance. While Jonah would prefer to have the entire city destroyed than to have his word proved false, Yahweh is eager to lay claim to a Gentile metropolis that is amenable to his correction. This universalistic author shares Second Isaiah's attitude that Israel is to be a light to the nations. The outsider must be sought. The sharp message in this narrative must have jolted those of the author's contemporaries who believed that postexilic Israel had an exclusive claim on Yahweh and should spend all her efforts at home cultivating a beautiful relationship with him. To no less a degree, anyone who insists that God is on his side, and on his side alone, may discover after his scrutiny of the Jonah parable that his rash declaration must be tempered by a serious reexamination of the issue.

THE IMPINGEMENT OF HELLENISM
ON THE POSTEXILIC JUDEAN COMMUNITY

Major Events and Obstacles

Though the details need not detain us, certain weaknesses in the Persian empire appeared during the reigns of Artaxerxes II (404–358) and Artaxerxes III (358–338). Consequently, when Darius III (336–331) ascended the throne, the Persian state was to enter its last half-decade of existence. During those years when Artaxerxes III governed the affairs of Persia, various Greek states were uniting under Philip II of Macedon (359–336).

At Philip's death, his twenty-year-old son Alexander (336–323) took the throne and soon succeeded in a magnificent series of triumphant, wide-ranging campaigns. In 334 he crossed the Hellespont and rapidly laid claim to Asia Minor. In 333–332 he swept southward to dominate most of Phoenicia, Palestine, and Egypt. While in Egypt, he founded the city of Alexandria. In 331 his eastern campaign into Mesopotamia gave him control over Babylon, Susa, and Persepolis. In that same year, a Persian official assassinated the defeated Darius, who was once more fleeing from Alexander's fury. By 326 Alexander had visited the Indus valley, and according to legend, he wept because there was no more land to take. As he was returning to the West, Alexander became ill and died prematurely in Babylon in 323. Wherever he went, this talented warrior and former student of Aristotle made sure that Greek ideals, customs, and language were given ample opportunity to take root. The ancient Near East was truly confronting a new day.

After his death, Alexander's vast empire fell into the hands of four of his competing generals. Two of them, Ptolemy and Seleucus, were the founders of dynasties that concern us here. Ptolemy I (323–285) took Egypt and claimed Alexandria as his capital. Seleucus I (312–280) mastered Syria and Mesopotamia and made his capital in Antioch. For approximately a century (301–198) the house of Ptolemy claimed political supremacy over Palestine.

We know next to nothing about how things fared with the Jews at this time. Jewish existence may not have been appreciably different than it was under Persian dominion. Presumably the Jews were content to cooperate, maintain a low political profile, and submit to whatever the Ptolemies expected in the way of taxation. Internal matters were left to the discretion of the Jerusalem high priest, whose status was considerable.

Throughout the third century, Palestine had been coveted by the Seleucid monarchs in Antioch. But lacking political strength, they saw no means of wresting Palestine from the Ptolemies. Under the rule of Antiochus III (223–187), however, the Seleucid state showed signs of resurgence and finally in 198 seized Palestine from Ptolemy V (203–181), incorporating it within its own territorial domain. Following the example of both the Persians and the Ptolemies, the house of Seleucid first left the Jews to manage their own domestic affairs. Judah's situation soon declined, however, in direct correlation with the loss of prestige and power the Seleucid kings were now experiencing because of Rome's increasing prominence. By 190 Antiochus had to agree to demanding terms of peace from Rome. In the years that followed, the Seleucid kingdom

Alexander the Great Presents an Offering to the Egyptian God Amon. The relief above, which is from a wall of the temple of Karnak, attests to the mixing of different cultures in the late fourth century B.C. It is framed by Egyptian hieroglyphics and a Greek inscription. The ancient Egyptian notion that a king is the son of a god would have served Alexander's purpose. (Courtesy of the Oriental Institute, University of Chicago.)

was in desperate need of funds to buy off Rome, which was periodically turning its attention to the east. During the rule of Seleucus IV (187–175), it was evident that the Seleucid state was losing ground.

Antiochus IV Epiphanes (175–163), who succeeded his assassinated brother to the throne, defended the Seleucid cause with new vigor. He resolved to find fresh sources of revenue and press for a more intensive cultural unification of his subjects. He believed that the systematic plunder of existing temples in his domain would help meet obvious financial

VIII. THE ERA FROM EZRA TO THE FIRST OF THE MACCABEES (398–160 B.C.)

DATE (B.C.)	EGYPT	PALESTINE	PERSIA
400		Ezra's mission (398?)	Artaxerxes II (404–358)
350	Persian reconquest of Egypt (343) Alexander takes Egypt (332) Ptolemaic kingdom Ptolemy I (323–285)	Alexander the Great (336–323) Hellenistic Age (ca. 330–63)* Ptolemaic rule of Palestine (301–198)	Artaxerxes III (358–338) Arses (338–336) Darius III (336–331) Seleucid kingdom (Mesopotamia and Syria)
300	Ptolemy II (285–246)		Seleucus I (312–280) Antiochus I (280–261)
250	Ptolemy III (246–221) Ptolemy IV (221–203)		Antiochus II (261–246) Seleucus II (246–226) Seleucus III (226–223)
200	Ptolemy V (203–181) Ptolemy VI (181–146)	The Seleucids seize Palestine from the Ptolemies (198); accordingly the Jews live under Seleucid rule. Profanation of the Jerusalem Temple (167) Maccabean rule in Palestine (167–63) Judas Maccabeus (166–160) Cleansing of the Temple (164)	Antiochus III (223–187) Seleucus IV (187–175) Antiochus IV (Epiphanes) (175–163) Antiochus V (163–162) Demetrius I (162–150)

*When the Roman forces under Pompey occupied Jerusalem and asserted control of Syria-Palestine in 63 B.C., the Roman age was inaugurated.

needs and that the promotion of Greek customs would unify his subjects. Antiochus was particularly zealous in advancing the worship of Greek deities, and this offended Judah's more loyal Yahwists.[6] Moreover, Antiochus had a gymnasium set up in Jerusalem that attracted a considerable number of young Jewish males. Membership presupposed their willingness to acknowledge the Greek cult under whose patronage the gymnasium existed.[7]

Antiochus also took sides in the unfortunate contest of various rivals in Judah for the office of high priest. A certain Jason sought to displace his more conservative brother, Onias III, who was then high priest. Jason promised the Seleucid king substantial funds and support in Hellenizing Jerusalem in return for the appointment, and Antiochus consented (2 Macc. 4:7–10). Yet only three years later Antiochus expelled Jason and installed Menelaus, who offered him more lavish gifts for the position (2 Macc. 4:23–26). (Both Jason and Menelaus went by Greek names that accorded well with their Hellenizing tendencies.) Then in 169 Jason was deceived by a rumor that Antiochus had died in Egypt. Jason advanced on Jerusalem with the support of 1,000 men, expelled Menelaus, unmercifully slaughtered many of his countrymen, and once more assumed the role of high priest. Antiochus therefore declared war on the strife-torn Jerusalem, which he believed was acting in defiance of his wishes (2 Macc. 5:5–14). Jason escaped to Transjordan, where he was forced to live as a fugitive. Having secured the cooperation of Menelaus, whom he had returned to the post of high priest, Antiochus entered the Jerusalem Temple and hauled off much of its wealth (2 Macc. 5:15–21, 1 Macc. 1:20–24).

As if this were not enough, the tactless Antiochus outraged loyal Jews by his conduct two years later. The Seleucid monarch had recently been intimidated; he had been ordered to leave Egypt by the Roman Senate and was further disturbed by reports that some Jewish elements in Jerusalem were resisting his program of enforced Hellenization. Consequently, he sent a sizable army against the city (1 Macc. 1:29–35). Many Jewish inhabitants were killed, and others were enslaved. Part of the city was destroyed, and a citadel known as "the Acra" was built and equipped with Syrian military forces. To crush Jewish resistance completely, Antiochus soon issued an edict that prohibited major festivals, Sabbath observance, and Temple rituals of sacrifice; the edict also made it a crime for Jewish families to practice circumcision or to own a copy of the Torah (1 Macc. 1:41–64). Under pain of death, the Jews were forced to eat ritually impure food and to sacrifice unclean animals on pagan altars. Finally, as "the abomination that makes desolate" (Dan. 11:31; 12:11; cf. 1 Macc. 1:54), an altar of Zeus was installed in the Jerusalem Temple in December 167, and on it a pig was sacrificed. Threats against Judaism appeared to be legion.

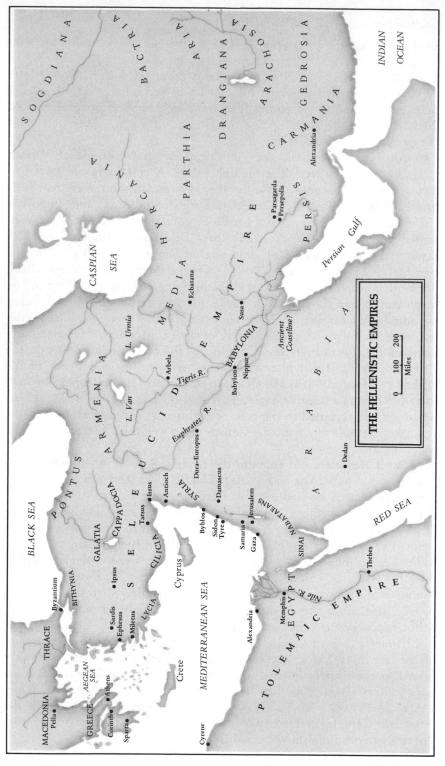

THE HELLENISTIC EMPIRES

0   100   200
Miles

INDIAN OCEAN

SOGDIANA

BACTRIA

ARIA

DRANGIANA

ARACHOSIA

GEDROSIA

CARMANIA

PARTHIA

HYRCANIA

Alexandria

PERSIS

Parsagarda
Persepolis

Persian Gulf

CASPIAN SEA

MEDIA

Ecbatana

Susa

BABYLONIA

Babylon
Nippur

Ancient
Coastline?

L. Urmia

L. Van

Arbela

Tigris R.

ARMENIA

Euphrates R.

Dura-Europus

S E L E U C I D   E M P I R E

A R A B I A

Dedan

PONTUS

BLACK SEA

BITHYNIA

GALATIA

CAPPADOCIA

Issus

Antioch

Tarsus

CILICIA

SYRIA

Damascus

Byblos

Sidon
Tyre

Jerusalem

Samaria

Gaza

NABATAEANS

SINAI

RED SEA

Thebes

Byzantium

THRACE

Sardis

Ipsus

Ephesus
Miletus

LYCIA

Cyprus

MEDITERRANEAN SEA

Memphis

Nile R.

P T O L E M A I C   E M P I R E

E G Y P T

MACEDONIA

Pella

GREECE

Corinth

Sparta

Athens

AEGEAN SEA

Crete

Cyrene

Alexandria

Jewish Response to the Hellenic Option

Before we consider the Maccabean rebellion against repressive Hellenism, we must briefly reflect on earlier Jewish reactions to Greek influence. During the fifth and fourth centuries B.C., Hellenic culture had gently pressed in on Palestinian Jews as a result of trade contacts. In Alexander's reign, however, Greek influence intensified. Convinced of the superiority of Hellenic learning and culture, Alexander was eager to expose his subject peoples to things Greek. Though his massive kingdom did not hold together after his death, Alexander's successors displayed the same enthusiasm for spreading the gifts of Greek culture. The more liberal Jews, most of whom lived in the urban areas of Palestine, came to believe in the intrinsic worth of Hellenic ideas and customs. Wealthy Jews took delight in Greek dress. Presumably the more radical Jews felt that Greek philosophy, art, and customs had much to offer a less accomplished and sophisticated world.

More conservative Jews, however, were incensed by the behavior of their liberal brothers. By the time of Antiochus IV Epiphanes, they had become profoundly disturbed that competing priests had conferred on a Seleucid monarch the prerogative of appointing Judaism's high priest. They were appalled that compromising young priests were willing to take "study breaks" from the Torah to enter nude athletic competitions at the Greek gymnasium. That some Jewish youths underwent surgery in the hope of disguising their circumcision scarcely set well with more pious Jews, for whom circumcision was a symbol of their covenant relationship with Yahweh. When Antiochus issued his proscription against long-standing Jewish practices and ushered the cult of Zeus into the Jerusalem Temple, the pious realized that an effective stand against Hellenism was necessary if Judaism were not to lose out altogether.

Some Jews lacked the courage to defy Antiochus' edict (1 Macc. 1:43), but this was by no means true of all of them. The Hasidim, who claimed Judaism's most loyal members, refused to compromise their ancestral faith. These staunch people, from whom the later Pharisees and Essenes probably descended, were willing to lay down their lives for the Torah. And they were fully aware that the time for war had come.

Open conflict formally broke out in the village of Modein, some 20 miles northwest of Jerusalem (1 Macc. 2:15–28). There a Syrian officer ordered the priest Mattathias to offer a sacrifice to the Greek deities in the presence of his neighbors. Mattathias refused. When another Jew expressed his willingness to comply with the order, the furious Mattathias assassinated him on the spot and also slew the Syrian officer who had made the request. After tearing down the altar, Mattathias called out to his fellow Jews, "Let every one who is zealous for the law and supports the covenant come out with me!" (1 Macc. 2:27). Fleeing with his five sons to the hills, he was joined by like-minded companions. Mattathias and his zealous followers now waged an impressive guerilla war against the Seleucid oppressors and the Jews who had slipped over to the Greek side (1 Macc. 2:44–48).

When Mattathias died a few months later, his role as leader of the rebellion was assumed by his son Judas whose outstanding courage earned for him the nickname "Maccabeus" (the hammerer). Since the early phases of the war so thoroughly involved Judas, the revolt came to be called the "Maccabean rebellion." Thanks to the valor of the recruits who followed Judas and to the Parthian pressure on Antiochus from the east, the Maccabean forces were frequently victorious. Antiochus dispatched what troops he could spare, but they proved quite insufficient. Eventually Judas and his men were able to return to Jerusalem in triumph. In December 164, exactly three years after its profanation, Judas sponsored a thorough cleansing and joyous rededication of the Jerusalem Temple and thereby instituted the feast of Hanukkah, which Judaism has observed ever since.

The wars of the Maccabees were not over, but an auspicious beginning had been made. In their turn, three of Mattathias' sons—Judas, Jonathan, and Simon—successfully led their zealous brethren against the Seleucid oppressors. The Maccabean era lasted until 63 B.C., when Pompey arrived and Rome began to assert itself in Jerusalem. Though the Jews of that era had to cope with further military defeat and internal corruption, the era from Antiochus IV to Pompey did provide a time in which they could again govern themselves with a significant measure of independence.

THE DANIEL APOCALYPSE

The Theological and Rhetorical Orientation of Apocalyptic Literature

In the thick of Hellenistic harassment, the Book of Daniel came into being. This apocalyptic book attempted to address the situation that plagued Jerusalem as Antiochus Epiphanes sought in every way possible to proscribe the Jewish religion. Before examining the Book of Daniel, however, we should take account of the chief interests and modes of expression that characterize apocalyptic thought.

The late phases of Israelite prophecy and the provocations from the political oppressor paved the way for another distinctive genre of the Old Testament: apocalyptic literature. The noun "apocalypse" means "revelation." It is linked with the writings of ancient Israel that purport to be a detailed disclosure of the deity intended to inform and comfort the faithful. Because apocalyptic literature takes history so seriously, it has been identified as the child of prophecy. (This, of course, is not to deny that apocalyptic literature also has something in common with wisdom literature.)

Nevertheless, prophetic and apocalyptic discourse do not reflect on God's intention in like manner. The Israelite prophet was a speaker first and a writer second. He came forward in public and said, "Hear this word of Yahweh!" By contrast, the apocalyptic writer expressed himself through the written word and consistently founded his point of view on earlier written prophecy (see Dan. 9:2, which meditates on Jer. 25:11–12).

Moreover, the prophet was active socially and could not conceal his identity. But the apocalyptist maintained his anonymity by using a pseudonym. Thus, he laid hold of the image of an ancient worthy such as Adam, Noah, Enoch, or Daniel and claimed it for himself. By using this device, he linked the insecure present with a more stable and exemplary past. He appropriated ancient wisdom to buttress present needs and shape future expectations.

In their overlapping, yet different views of history, apocalyptic and prophetic texts contrast in a third way. The apocalyptic writer and the biblical prophet both claimed that the complex affairs of the world were directly influenced by Yahweh's will. Both believed that the deity would impinge on history as judge and redeemer to realize his purposes for both Israel and the world at large. Nevertheless, the apocalyptist was unimpressed by the prophet's assumption that, with God's help, man might bring about positive change in times of crisis. The apocalyptic writer emphasized that the forces of evil have such a firm hold on the world that God himself must intervene if any transformation is to take place. Hence, the apocalyptist centered his attention on the end of time, when God's kingdom would arrive in undiminished splendor.

The apocalyptic writer had a style of his own that drew heavily on bizarre imagery. This stylistic predilection is also evident in Ezekiel and Zechariah. Indeed, the later phases of prophecy were laying the groundwork for a fully developed apocalyptic discourse. The lion sprouting the wings of an eagle, the four-headed leopard with wings, and the monster with iron teeth and ten horns (Dan. 7) scarcely accords with the natural world of roaring lions, wild bears, and biting adders reflected in the oracles of Amos. The eccentric imagery and cryptic numerology of apocalyptic literature seek to rekindle the belief of the pious that God is unmistakably in control of history. They constitute a special language to be used with the initiated. Therefore, the symbolic references to animals, horns, and the sea are intended to lead the initiated to reflect on certain worldly kingdoms and mighty leaders, and on the force of evil itself. The initiated are thereby reminded that all is determined according to the master plan of the deity.

Finally, the prophet and the apocalyptic writer differ in the amount of detail with which they describe the future. Though the prophet refused to be locked in by the present, he was unwilling to commit himself to many specifics concerning the future. He did not presume to know the precise hour when Yahweh would intervene in human affairs. By contrast, the apocalyptic writer freely speculated about a final moment that would call time on history's present course. Also his habit of grasping time in clearly delineated blocks led him to write confidently and concretely about the future. Of course, the apocalyptic writer had an advantage because he placed himself within the chronological framework of the ancient personage with whom his book purported to deal. Consequently, in the guise of prediction he presented certain events that had already taken place. But where a survey of clearly differentiated ages is offered in apocalyptic writing, as it is in Daniel, the author's capacity to foretell events accurately runs out at that point in time in which he actually stands as a flesh and blood mortal. This, of course, helps us to date the writing in question.

Although history is bound to expose the ignorance of the apocalyptic writer concerning the future, his efforts were appreciated by many of his countrymen, who felt thoroughly encouraged by his message. The apocalyptic writer maintained that when the well-defined ages had run their predetermined span of years, Yahweh would demolish the powers of this world and establish his eternal kingly rule. Consequently, the suffering Hasidim are challenged to persist in their belief in God's determination and capacity to create a new order and to bless those who rightly claim membership among his elect.

The Witness of Daniel

While such texts as Isaiah 24–27, Ezekiel 38–39, and Joel 3:9–21 bear the markings of apocalyptic literature, Daniel is the only book in the Old Testament canon that is overtly an apocalypse. This highly symbolic book speculates on the consummation of history, which will mark the advent of a splendid new age. Accordingly, the reader of Daniel is led to take heart in meditations about the glorious future that will unfold in that divinely ordained moment when God and his saints triumph over the powers of darkness. This is certainly the message of the four apocalyptic visions in the second half of the book (chaps. 7–12). The preceding chapters (1–6) offer six fascinating narratives about the vicissitudes of Daniel and his friends in the Babylonian court. These legends are presented in the hope that the reader will be righteous and brave during the treacherous present.

Date. Ostensibly the Book of Daniel dates from the sixth-century era of Jewish exile in Babylon, but several factors speak for a much later date of composition. First, Daniel appears not in the prophetic section of the Hebrew canon but in the Writings, whose canonical status was determined last. Yet if Daniel had been written in the sixth century, it would predate several of the prophetic books with which it surely would have been reckoned. And while ben Sira's recollection of famous men (Ecclus. 44:1–50:24) mentions Isaiah (48:22), Jeremiah (49:6), Ezekiel (49:8), and "the bones of the twelve prophets" (49:10), it has nothing to say about the stalwart Daniel. Nevertheless, 1 Maccabees, which dates to early in the first century B.C., reflects its author's familiarity with the Daniel narrative (1 Macc. 2:59–60). Moreover, the Book of Daniel displays a Hebrew that is late, an Aramaic that is certainly not early, and a tendency to incorporate Persian and Greek loan words.

The author of Daniel demonstrates a poor grasp of sixth-century history. For example, in Dan. 1:1 Jerusalem's capture by Nebuchadnezzar and his Babylonian forces is related to Jehoiakim's third year (606), but this is confirmed in no other extant source. And though in the absence of his father, Belshazzar functioned as regent of Babylon, he never served as king (5:1; 7:1); and his father was Nabonidus, not Nebuchadnezzar (5:11). Media did not succeed Babylon as an energetic world empire in the Near East (5:28) and never had a ruler named Darius (5:31). And whereas other sources report that a Persian monarch named Cyrus took the Babylonian kingdom from Nabonidus, here we are erroneously informed that Darius the Mede, son of Xerxes ("Ahasuerus" [9:1]), ruled Babylon after Belshazzar's death (5:30–31).

The author's reflections in 11:2–39 also have a direct bearing on the problem of dating Daniel. There we are given a "predictive" sketch of the Greek era that is more accurate and elaborate than anything that either precedes or follows it. The powerful monarch who is expected to "rule with great dominion and do according to his will" (11:3) is surely none other than Alexander of Macedon. The seizure and splintering of Alexander's massive kingdom immediately after his death (323) is mentioned (11:4) as is the contest between "the king of the south" (the house of Ptolemy) and "the king of the north" (the house of Seleucid [11:5–6]). After further reference to the power and ambition of the Greeks in the third and early second centuries B.C. (11:7–20), a lengthy segment offers a carefully veiled depiction of the rule of Antiochus Epiphanes (11:21–45). The disclosure that Antiochus will conquer Libya and Ethiopia only to die shortly thereafter along the coastal route of Palestine (11:40–45) amounts to wishful thinking on the part of the apocalyptic author, who has now moved from purported to genuine prediction. The facts turned out to be otherwise. By contrast, the preceding verses (11:21–39) offer a sober reflection on the oppressive rule of "a contemptible person" (11:21) as it has existed up to the apocalyptic writer's own day. Antiochus' campaigns against Egypt are recalled (11:25–31). Also reference is made to his vicious tactics against the Jews, which involved the appointing of the Hellenizing Jason to the office of high priest (11:23) and the pollution of the Jerusalem Temple in 167 with "the abomination that makes desolate" (11:31). And cryptic mention of "a little help" for the Jews (11:34) suggests that the first stages of the Maccabean rebellion were now under way.

Most significant for the establishment of an accurate date for the Book of Daniel, however, is this final factor: the apocalyptist alludes to Antiochus' desecration of the Temple (167) but makes no reference to its cleansing under Judas' direction three years later. Nor does he refer to the circumstances of Antiochus' death (163), which took place in Persia (1 Macc. 6:1–16) and not near the coast of Palestine as forecast in Dan. 11:45. Thus, we may infer that the book was written between 167 and 164 B.C.

The Language of Daniel. The Book of Daniel is bilingual. The Hebrew (1:1–2:4a; 8:1–12:13) and Aramaic (2:4b–7:28) portions of the book do not accord with the shift in 7:1 from third-person legend to first-person vision, however. Rather, the transition from Hebrew to Aramaic occurs at the beginning of the Chaldeans' speech to Nebuchadnezzar in 2:4b, and only with the second vision does Aramaic give way to Hebrew.

No explanation of this peculiar state of affairs is entirely satisfactory. The notion that some of the originally Aramaic portions of Daniel were translated into Hebrew as a way of ensuring the book's place in the canon is conjecture at best, as is the view that the Aramaic passages constitute a later translation of a substantial portion of the Hebrew original that was lost.

Rowley's approach is one of the most cogent. He holds that all visions but the first (chap. 7) were deliberately written in Hebrew. They were not intended for widespread consumption by a second-century Jewish reading public, whose vernacular language was Aramaic. Rather they were written for the student of Hebrew. Rowley also submits that all the Daniel legends were originally in Aramaic and that when they were subsequently joined, the first narrative was rewritten in Hebrew so that Daniel and his companions might receive the benefit of a more carefully framed introduction.[8]

In any event, the bilingual quality of Daniel does not demand that we view the book as the work of several authors. Chapters 2 and 7 have certain affinities in style and content, and the narratives and visions as a whole are based on the same theological premise—that the succession of well-defined ages is strictly ordained by a transcendent and sovereign deity.[9]

To be sure, the apocalyptic writer may have drawn on earlier traditions. He may have been aware of certain legends about Jews who had distinguished themselves in the service of the Persian court. What he may have known of the Daniel legend is difficult to determine. The personage of Daniel that he creates has little in common with the Dan'el of

Ugaritic tradition, who devotes his attention to judging the cases of widows and orphans. Nor are the verses about Daniel in Ezekiel (14:14, 20; 28:3) of much help, although the last mentioned attests to Daniel's wisdom.

Two important pieces of evidence suggest that the various legendary tales on which the author of Daniel relied had an independent existence: chapter 3 narrates the adventures of Daniel's companions, but has nothing to report about Daniel himself; and the chronological notations (1:1, 5; 2:1) project a confusing picture.

The Narratives. Despite their individuality, the six narratives (Dan. 1–6) all support the Hasidic premise that the second-century Jew who lives a blameless existence and trusts only in Yahweh has nothing to fear. The stories instruct that just as God did not allow Nebuchadnezzar to prevail over Daniel and his friends, so he will not allow Antiochus Epiphanes to obliterate Judaism. Nor will he forget those who diligently fulfill the law.

The narrative about Daniel and his companions in chapter 1 teaches that fidelity to the law is its own reward. As residents of Nebuchadnezzar's court, they refuse to defile themselves by eating the king's food, which is not prepared according to Jewish dietary regulations. Yet their diet of vegetables and water sees them through so successfully that in ten days they appear to be healthier than the other trainees for Nebuchadnezzar's service. Moreover, the wisdom that God confers on Daniel and his colleages outshines the wisdom of Nebuchadnezzar's magicians and enchanters. The second-century reader is led to believe that if he refuses to eat the unclean food that Antiochus' officers are forcing on him, God will sustain him.

The narrative in chapter 2 instructs that divine wisdom surpasses human wisdom. Nebuchadnezzar makes an impossible request of his Babylonian sages. They are to tell as well as interpret his dream. With God's help Daniel describes and interprets the dream. He discloses that the God of Israel has willed that one kingdom will emerge on the ruins of another (2:36–45). The gold, silver, bronze, and iron components of the great image in Nebuchadnezzar's dream symbolize the Babylonian, Median, Persian, and Greek empires, which in turn are each to dominate. Yet even the last of these is doomed to destruction when God's own kingdom establishes itself. A stone not cut by human hand will strike and destroy the great image. The successful inauguration of God's kingdom will therefore depend on the power of deity, not on the might of armed men. Nebuchadnezzar confesses that Daniel's God is truly supreme and makes Daniel ruler of the province of Babylon and head of his wise men. The king's positive response to Daniel might easily spark in the reader new hope that the oppression Yahweh's people had to endure would soon come to an end as Gentile rulers became cognizant of

Yahweh's greatness. Further, the eternality of God's triumphant rule that is forecast (2:44) would likewise sustain the suffering faithful.

The story in chapter 3 involves Daniel's companions, who prefer to be thrust into a furnace rather than worship Nebuchadnezzar's golden image. It speaks with uncanny directness to second-century Jews who were being intimidated into worshiping Zeus. Nebuchadnezzar is so astounded that the flames have not overtaken the divinely protected youths that he orders them out of the furnace, legitimizes their religion, and promotes them to a higher office. The faith that underlies the reply of Daniel's three friends to the king is especially striking:

> If it be so, our God whom we serve is able to deliver us from the burning fiery furnace; and he will deliver us out of your hand, O king. But if not, be it known to you, O king, that we will not serve your gods or worship the golden image which you have set up. (3:17–18)

That brand of courage, implies the writer of Daniel, is requisite in the present moment as well.

The remaining three Daniel legends also insist that a bold faith is a necessary and precious possession. In chapter 4 the arrogant Nebuchadnezzar falls in the face of divine power. One day as he strolls proudly on the roof of his palace, the king goes insane. And as Daniel had predicted in an earlier interpretation of his dream, Nebuchadnezzar is condemned to live for seven years as a grass-eating beast. Once his sanity returns, he fervently acknowledges the sovereignty of Daniel's God.

Daniel 5 declares that the God of Israel will not permit sacrilegious acts to go unpunished. At a lavish banquet, Belshazzar and his merry company presumptuously drink out of the sacred vessels that Nebuchadnezzar had stolen from the Jerusalem Temple and pay their respects to idol gods. The festive tone subsides, however, when the guests are unexpectedly confronted by the cryptic message written on the palace wall by the fingers of a human hand. No sage save Daniel is able to interpret the message. To Belshazzar he says, "You have been weighed in the balances and found wanting" (5:27). Daniel is handsomely rewarded for his wisdom, and Belshazzar is slain that same night.

In chapter 6 Daniel's fidelity to his religion necessitates his being thrown into a lion's den. But his life is miraculously spared through the visiting presence of an angel, and Darius decrees that all his subjects shall revere Daniel's God.

The Daniel legends emphasize that in times of oppression, the Hasidim must be exceedingly faithful to Yahweh. Though their zeal for the law may thrust even further discomfort (and possibly death) on them, this holy cause is worth the price. For Judaism is allied with a God whose dominion over all things is sure and eternal. Moreover, even now the faithful may live in complete confidence that their God will not forsake them.

The Visions. This stubborn faith is equally apparent in the second half of the Book of Daniel, but the message is now communicated in elaborate visions that proclaim that the end of time is near. Godless worldly power is doomed, and the deity's triumph, in which his faithful people will participate, is assured.

In Daniel's first vision (chap. 7) four fearful beasts are seen emerging from the watery deep. The last creature, with its great iron teeth and ten horns, is by far the worst. An interpreting angel informs Daniel that these beasts symbolize four world empires (7:16–17). The lion is understood to be Babylon, the bear Media, the leopard Persia, and the ten-horned monster Greece. The ten horns symbolize Alexander's successors, and the sprouting little horn "speaking great things" (7:8) is none other than the arrogant Antiochus Epiphanes. The deity is portrayed as "the Ancient of Days" (7:13, 22) who comes to sit in judgment on the evil affairs that are destroying the earth. Then "one like a son of man" (7:13) appears and is presented to the Ancient of Days so that he may receive a universal and everlasting kingdom. Because this human figure is identified by the interpreting angel as "the saints of the Most High" (7:18), he seems to be deliberately equated with the pious Jews who truly constitute the covenant community of Israel.

In Enoch, a later apocalyptic book, the son of man is portrayed as a figure of primordial history who appears at the end of time in his splendid otherworldliness to introduce a new aeon. In Daniel, however, the son of man symbolizes the Hasidim, who are soon to share in God's triumphant rule. The messianic kingdom is not to be founded, however, until Antiochus has oppressed God's people for three and a half years (7:25). The destruction of the loathsome Greek power is nonetheless assured, as is the establishment of God's kingdom.

Daniel's second vision (chap. 8) focuses on a vigorous two-horned ram (Media-Persia), which is destroyed by a he-goat with a prominent horn between its eyes (Alexander). While it is still strong, the goat's horn is broken (Alexander's death) and in its place four horns sprout (symbolizing the division of Alexander's massive empire into four kingdoms). A "little horn" (Antiochus Epiphanes) then appears out of one of the four. That horn dares to challenge the Prince of the host (God himself) by depriving him of his daily burnt offering, defiling the Temple, and casting truth "down to the ground" (a veiled allusion to Antiochus' attempt to destroy copies of the Torah). Daniel is further informed that the Temple's continual burnt offering will be suspended for 2,300 "evenings and mornings" (roughly three years), at which time it will be restored. Antiochus is expected to persist in his harassment of Judaism, yet the assurance resounds that "by no human hand, he shall be broken" (8:25). All hostility to Yahweh and his people will finally end.

In Daniel's third vision (chap. 9), the apocalyptic writer reinterprets the prophetic words of Jeremiah that Jerusalem will be desolated for seventy years (Jer. 25:11–12; 29:10). This refashioning of the prophet's earlier message illustrates "the tendency characteristic of that age to seek to make earlier prophecy contemporary in its relevance."[10] Although the author erred in his novel mathematical calculation, he succeeded in bolstering his belief that Antiochus' vicious assault on Judaism would soon be arrested by God's own intervention. Perplexed as to what Jeremiah's word might mean, Daniel prays for assistance. The angel Gabriel now instructs Daniel that the seventy years actually refer to seventy weeks of years—that is, 490 years (9:24–27). These are divided into three epochs that span seven, sixty-two, and one week of years, respectively. The actual time sequences to which they seem to refer are 587–539, 539–170, and 170–164 (in 539 Babylon fell; in 170 the high priest, Onias III, was assassinated; and in 164 the Jerusalem Temple was cleansed and rededicated). The last week of years, which symbolizes the reign of Antiochus Epiphanes, is divided into two halves, with the latter half (three and one half years) denoting the period when Antiochus defiled the Temple. As sixty-two weeks of years, the second epoch is too long for the actual time covered. Nevertheless, this scheme conveys the apocalyptic writer's conviction that the length of historical epochs is predetermined by the divine will and that the end time is near.

Daniel 10–12 contains one lengthy disclosure that a celestial being (perhaps Gabriel) is said to have made to Daniel in Cyrus' third year (535). As we have observed previously, only in 11:40 does the author make genuine predictions. What appears in the many preceding verses is a sketch of Seleucid history that is carried into the present reign of Antiochus. Throughout it is assumed that the affairs of men unfold precisely according to divine plan. Even Antiochus' attacks on the Jews are accepted as part of what God has foreordained (11:36). No less a part of the divine blueprint is the king's steady march to his own destruction. Since the ultimate triumph belongs to the God of Israel, the Hasidim may rejoice that they are allied with the divine cause.

At history's divinely appointed final moment, Michael, the patron angel of Israel, will arise in defense of God's people (12:1). The faithful, whose names are inscribed in the book of life, will be delivered from the tribulations that will ensue. The apocalyptist also articulates his belief in a general resurrection (12:2). Although he was not seeking to lay the theological groundwork for a refined doctrine of life beyond the grave, he did wish to instill in his Hasidic readers confidence that Judaism's apostles and martyrs would receive their due. Death itself would not annul the participation of the faithful in God's triumphant kingdom.

The Book of Daniel often evokes mixed feelings in today's readers. The doctrine of divine determination is so pervasive that we may first be tempted to conclude that human initiative would be severely undercut by such thinking. Yet we doubt that a people encouraged by Daniel's example would have been likely to pursue a spineless course.

The apocalyptic writer boasted that he knew God's plan, and in claiming to know it so well he exposed his own deficiencies. History did not confirm all his expectations. Nevertheless, the author of Daniel kept hope alive among a people who were forced to live in an extremely trying environment. Thus, for many of his countrymen, the daily pursuit of the faith must have remained a compelling, wholly worthwhile option.

After Daniel

In spite of the stirring hope projected in the Book of Daniel, the consummation of history did not come speedily. One year followed another in sometimes uneventful sequence. No doubt many of the faithful must have viewed the early successes of the Maccabean rebellion as extremely heartening. Yet before the century of Maccabean rule had run its course, the office of high priest was once more being coveted by persons of questionable reputation. It had also become clear that the years of independent rule for Palestinian Judaism were running out. With the arrival of Pompey in Jerusalem in 63 B.C., Rome made its appearance as another worldly kingdom that would impose its will on the Jews. The author of Daniel had promised that with the end of Greek oppression God's kingdom would establish itself, but history was now inviting Rome to dominate Palestine.

The world that enveloped Judaism therefore remained hostile. Yet as the possessors of a historically centered heritage, the Jews continued to affirm the world. True, the apocalyptic mode of writing became quite popular in the uncertain era between the Old and New Testaments. In their struggle, the Jews still persisted in the hope that God's eternal kingdom would soon make its triumphant appearance. Meanwhile, they had to go on existing in imperfect, often frustrating circumstances. To put the matter simply, the challenge of the present moment was to continue existing as the "people of God" in the best sense of the term. Through such opportunities as could be provided by a systematic study of the Torah, regular sacrificial worship, and recurring religious festivals, the Jews persisted in their affirmation of meaningful uniqueness.

As decade followed decade, the people of Yahweh moved closer to consensus on the question, "In addition to the books of Moses, what else belongs in our Scriptures?" In our treatments of Josiah and Ezra in Chapters 14 and 18, we have commented briefly on the authoritative status of the Torah, which was tantamount to its canonization. Moreover, Judaism's veneration of the law did much to unite the people in a common cause.

But what about the Prophets and the Writings, which make up the remaining divisions of the Hebrew canon? We know very little about the canonical history of the Prophets. Nevertheless, such a passage as Jeremiah 36, with its witness to the existence of a provocative prophetic

The Synagogue at Masada. Atop the rock of Masada at the eastern edge of the Judean wilderness is a fascinating complex of Roman and Zealot ruins. Among them is the Jewish synagogue pictured above. This rectangular hall, which is oriented toward Jerusalem, has two rows of columns and numerous mud benches. It dates to the first century of the Christian era and is the most ancient synagogue known. (Photo by the author.)

scroll, suggests that if the spoken word of the prophet was authoritative, the same must have been true of the prophet's written word. Moreover, when the gift of prophecy appeared to be on the verge of extinction, available specimens of the written prophetic message probably acquired even greater significance. Even a few decades prior to the writing of the Book of Daniel, the prophetic corpus appears to have come into being. In ben Sira's eulogy to famous men (Ecclus. 44:1–50:24), key happenings in Joshua, Judges, Samuel, and Kings are reviewed; Isaiah, Jeremiah, Ezekiel, and "the twelve prophets" are also mentioned. (Specific reference to "the twelve prophets" [Ecclus. 49:10] implies that by about 180 B.C., even the collected writings of the minor prophets had achieved authoritative status.) Judaism could therefore rally around these cherished writings, too.

The earliest witness to the Writings as the third main division of the Hebrew canon appears in the Greek prologue to Ecclesiasticus, which was composed in about 130 B.C. Its author was ben Sira's grandson, who refers to "the law and the prophets and the other books of our fathers." While that designation betrays the loosely defined quality of this third division of the canon, it confirms its existence.

Three factors helped to confer dignity and status on the Writings. First, there was the simple fact of survival. Since Judaism's scrolls had to be laboriously copied by hand, undoubtedly only those scrolls were copied and circulated for which there was a clear-cut demand.

Second, the anonymous authorship of several of the Writings made possible their attribution to well-known ancient personalities. For example, the claim that David composed the Psalms and that Solomon wrote Proverbs, the Song of Songs, and Ecclesiastes did much to enhance the worth of these books.

A third influence on canonization was public opinion. Thus, the Book of Esther, which contains very few religious elements, was a good candidate for the canon because it was a superbly written short story that stood in close connection with the popular festival of Purim. Final settlement on the contents of the Writings was not achieved, and con-

Excavations at Masada. The rock of Masada, which lies more than 1,300 feet above the western shore of the Dead Sea, was thoroughly excavated under the direction of Yigael Yadin of Hebrew University. It had been selected as a stronghold by the Hasmonean priest-king Alexander Jannaeus; transformed into an impressive fort by Herod; and taken in a surprise attack by the Zealots in A.D. 66. The latter defied the Roman forces by living there until A.D. 73. At the end of the three-year Roman siege, the Zealot defenders died by their own hand rather than be captured by the enemy. (Courtesy of the Consulate General of Israel, New York.)

Cave Four at Qumran. This cave, which was first discovered by Judean Bedouins in 1952, contained the most extensive cache of Qumran scrolls and fragments yet encountered. It yielded portions of every Old Testament book except Esther and many nonbiblical writings as well. The cave overlooks the Wadi Qumran and lies directly west of Khirbet Qumran, the ancient site of the Essene sectarians that was excavated under the direction of de Vaux and Harding from 1951 to 1956. (Photo by the author.)

cluding deliberations on the Hebrew canon as a whole were not made formally until about A.D. 90, when debate in the rabbinic school at Jamnia intensified. Undoubtedly the discussions of the rabbis at Jamnia helped Judaism give the Hebrew Bible its final shape.[11]

As men of faith, the Jews would diligently study the Scriptures. They would try to obey God's demands and to be courageous in expressing their religion. Yet as men of flesh, whose vision was sometimes necessarily limited, the Jews had many differences of opinion about Jewish life and worship. Addressing a Roman audience, the first-century Jewish historian Flavius Josephus claimed that in Judaism four philosophies had come into existence. But the Pharisees, Sadducees, Zealots, and Essenes who are referred to in this context are more appropriately regarded as leading Jewish parties.

These factions did not see eye to eye on some fundamental issues. For example, the belief of the Pharisees in the resurrection of the body was repudiated by the Sadducees. The latter claimed that there was no such teaching in the written Torah. And unlike the Pharisees, the Sadducees were unwilling to embrace the growing body of oral law that sought to update the Torah. The Pharasaic party of Judaism, which consisted mainly of middle-class members, was convinced that the conservative, well-to-do Sadducees were too prone to collaborate with the political powers that be. The Pharisees, however, were not as concerned with revolution as were the Zealots who provoked a Jewish rebellion against Rome in an abortive struggle for independence (A.D. 66–70). The Essenes, in turn, appear to have been the most exclusivist in their ways. Though they inhabited urban as well as rural areas, their stringent customs have become far better known through the discovery of the Dead Sea Scrolls near Wadi Qumran. Regarding themselves as the true Israel, these sectarians at Qumran were preparing for the glorious coming of the messianic kingdom through diligent work, study, and prayer. Finally, there were many Jews who were not affiliated with any one of these groups.

Despite the many factions within first-century Judaism, this vigorous religion had won the allegiance of a number of deeply committed adherents. In time Pharisaic Judaism prevailed, and a so-called normative Judaism came into being. Some Jews, however, were convinced that one among them, Jesus of Nazareth, was the Christ—that is, the hoped-for Messiah who fulfilled the expectations of the Torah and the Prophets. Therefore, a Jewish Christianity was born.

The Qumran Refectory. Here near the Dead Sea lie the excavated foundations of the Essene Refectory, or Assembly Hall, at Khirbet Qumran. Common meals, prayers, and sacred assemblies all appear to have been held in this ample rectangular area, which measures approximately 74 by 15 feet. The discovery of much dining equipment (plates, bowls, cups) in an adjacent room attests to this hall's function as a refectory. (Photo by the author.)

To this day, Judaism and Christianity have both maintained themselves as sturdy world religions. Those in our time who are members of either tradition have a right to take pride in the rich Israelite heritage that exists within the Old Testament as well as an obligation to know it better.

NOTES

1. In mentioning that the Jews of Susa took part in a second day's massacre on the fourteenth day of Adar and celebrated it on the fifteenth day (Esther 9:15–19), the author was apparently trying to harmonize conflicting customs in Purim observance.

2. The name of God does not appear at all in the Book of Esther. Nevertheless, with the incorporation of six additional passages, the Septuagint version displays an overtly religious dimension. Prayer and use of the divine name are both prominent. In the fourth century of the Christian era Jerome assigned all these additions to the end of the book. They appear in the Protestant Apocrypha as "The Additions to the Book of Esther." For further remarks on the so-called absence of religious dimensions in a book he classifies as wisdom literature, see Carey A. Moore, *Esther: Introduction, Translation, and Notes,* The Anchor Bible, vol. 7B (Garden City, N.Y.: Doubleday, 1971), pp. xxxii–xxxiv.

3. But the manner in which this is carried through is not congruent with the legislation of Deut. 25:5–10. As we have already mentioned, according to the law of levirate marriage, the brother of a man who died without male progeny had to marry his widowed sister-in-law to perpetuate the deceased's name and inheritance. The Deuteronomic legislation states that the man who refuses to fulfill such a crucial duty shall be publicly humiliated by having his sandal removed by the widow in question. In Ruth 4:7–10 the sandal is pulled off by the next of kin himself to symbolize his desire that Boaz take Naomi's land as well as Ruth. Perhaps the variation between Ruth 4:7–10 and Deut. 25:5–10 results from the fact that in this instance the next of kin was not a very close relation. Neither Boaz nor the unnamed kinsman was Mahlon's brother.

4. The only poetic unit in the book is 2:2–9, and it does not seem to be the work of the Jonah narrator. First, as a psalm of thanksgiving for past deliverance, it is inappropriate to Jonah's present emergency. Moreover, the Jonah psalm nowhere refers to the great fish that has swallowed Jonah. And once the psalm is deleted, we are left with a smooth narrative. Probably a late editor to whom this poem was available understood it as reflecting a deliverance at sea and consequently inserted it into the Jonah narrative.

5. Since the author of Jonah employs a late form of Hebrew and renounces the religious provincialism of the Nehemiah-Ezra era in favor of the universalism of Second Isaiah, a date near the end of the Persian period seems warranted. His portrayal of Nineveh could have issued only long after her fall to the Babylonians in 612 B.C.

6. In fact, Antiochus even expected his subjects to worship him as a

manifestation of Zeus. The name "Epiphanes," which he took for himself, means "the god revealed." The noun *theos* (god) was inscribed on coins bearing Antiochus' image.

7. John Bright, *A History of Israel*, 2d ed. (Philadelphia: Westminster Press, 1972), p. 422.

8. H. H. Rowley, *The Growth of the Old Testament* (New York: Harper & Row, Harper Torchbooks, 1963), p. 160.

9. Discussions in behalf of the unity of the Book of Daniel must bear in mind that 12:11 and 12:12 are two subsequent interpolations. These presumably attempted to recalculate the moment of history's consummation after the projected estimate of three and one half years (7:25; 12:7) had proved false.

10. Norman W. Porteous, *Daniel: A Commentary*, The Old Testament Library (Philadelphia: Westminster Press, 1965), p. 134. Such application to contemporary circumstances is also achieved in the Habakkuk Commentary from Qumran, which reinterprets the words of Habakkuk that were first uttered late in the seventh century B.C.

11. For a more extensive discussion of the canonization of the Old Testament, see George W. Anderson, "The Old Testament: Canonical and Non-Canonical," in P. R. Ackroyd and C. F. Evans, eds., *The Cambridge History of the Bible*, vol. 1 (Cambridge: Cambridge University Press, 1970), pp. 113–159. Anderson offers a useful yet briefer presentation in George W. Anderson, *A Critical Introduction to the Old Testament* (London: Gerald Duckworth, 1959), pp. 10–18.

BIBLIOGRAPHY

Although this list of readings refers to many studies not mentioned in the notes, it is nevertheless selective. Moreover, several items appearing in the notes are not repeated here. Very few works written in a language other than English are cited. The abbreviation "Pb." indicates a paperback edition.

GENERAL READINGS

A. Recent Translations of the Bible

Albright, William F., and David N. Freedman, eds. *The Anchor Bible.* Garden City, N.Y.: Doubleday, 1964–. An interfaith venture by American and some European scholars. It offers original translations, introductory commentary, and brief notes. About twenty volumes have appeared to date; at least that many more are anticipated.

Catholic Biblical Association of America. *The New American Bible.* New York: P. J. Kenedy & Sons, 1970. Pb. A vigorous translation with helpful critical notes.

Joint Committee on the New Translation of the Bible. *The New English Bible with the Apocrypha.* Oxford: Oxford University Press, 1970. Pb. An attractive, up-to-date translation with much poetic sensitivity.

Jones, Alexander, ed. *The Jerusalem Bible.* Garden City, N.Y.: Doubleday, 1966. Pb. A translation of a recent French version produced by the Dominican Biblical School in Jerusalem. The highly readable text is accompanied by useful notes.

May, Herbert G., and Bruce M. Metzger, eds. *The New Oxford Annotated Bible with the Apocrypha,* Revised Standard Version, containing 2d ed. of the New Testament. New York: Oxford University Press, 1973. Succinct articles and notes along with outstanding maps and useful chronological tables make this the best student Bible available.

Orlinsky, Harry M., Harold L. Ginsberg, and Ephraim A. Speiser, eds. *The Torah: The Five Books of Moses.* Philadelphia: Jewish Publication Society of

America, 1962. This initial volume of The New Jewish Bible is the work of highly qualified biblical scholars. Until its completion, its predecessor remains significant: *The Holy Scriptures According to the Masoretic Text.* Philadelphia: Jewish Publication Society, 1917.

B. Bible Dictionaries

Buttrick, George A., et al. *The Interpreter's Dictionary of the Bible.* 4 vols. Nashville: Abingdon Press, 1962. Noted for its high quality and comprehensive coverage. A most useful tool. A supplementary volume is in preparation.

Grant, F. C., and H. H. Rowley, eds. *Hastings Dictionary of the Bible.* 2d ed. New York: Charles Scribner's Sons, 1963. A solid one-volume Bible dictionary; it contains no photographs, however.

McKenzie, John L. *Dictionary of the Bible.* Milwaukee: Bruce Publishing Co., 1965. Pb. A remarkable effort by a well-known Roman Catholic scholar. Quite readable.

Miller, Madeleine S., J. Lane Miller, et al. *Harper's Bible Dictionary.* New York: Harper & Row, 1952. The best one-volume Bible dictionary available.

C. One-Volume Commentaries

Black, Matthew, and H. H. Rowley, eds. *Peake's Commentary on the Bible.* Rev. ed. New York: Thomas Nelson & Sons, 1962. This updated liberal Protestant work is one of the most helpful one-volume commentaries available.

Brown, Raymond E., Joseph A. Fitzmyer, and Roland E. Murphy, eds. *The Jerome Biblical Commentary.* Englewood Cliffs, N.J.: Prentice-Hall, 1968. A superb one-volume commentary by modern Roman Catholic scholars.

Laymon, Charles M., ed. *The Interpreter's One-Volume Commentary on the Bible.* Nashville: Abingdon Press, 1971. The product of Jewish, Catholic, and Protestant critical scholarship. Contains helpful introductory articles and photos as well as instructive Bible commentary.

D. Multivolume Commentaries

Albright, William F., and David N. Freedman, eds. *The Anchor Bible.* Garden City, N.Y.: Doubleday, 1964–.

Buttrick, George A., et al., eds. *The Interpreter's Bible.* Nashville: Abingdon Press, 1952–1957. A tool that is as valuable to the general reader as it is to the scholar. Widely used as a reference work.

Cohen, Abraham, ed. *Soncino Books of the Bible.* 14 vols. London: Soncino Press, 1945–1952. Contains the Hebrew text, its English translation, and succinct critical notes.

Marsh, John, and C. A. Richardson, eds. *Torch Bible Commentaries.* London: SCM Press. Primarily intended for the general reader.

Plummer, Alfred, et al., eds. *The International Critical Commentary.* New York: Charles Scribner's Sons. In production between 1895 and 1951, this thorough and technical exegetical series continues to be useful.

Tucker, Gene M., and Rolf P. Knierim, eds. *The Interpreter's Handbook of Old Testament Form Criticism.* 2 vols. Nashville: Abingdon Press. Expected to appear in the late 1970s, this commentary will divide the Bible into small literary units which will be foremost examined for their genre, structure, intention, and setting.

E. *Atlases*

Aharoni, Yohanan, and Michael Avi-Yonah. *The Macmillan Bible Atlas*. New York: Macmillan, 1968. Apart from its general usefulness, it is invaluable in its presentation of the geographical context for specific biblical events.

Grollenberg, L. H. *Atlas of the Bible*. Translated and edited by Joyce M. H. Reid and H. H. Rowley. New York: Thomas Nelson & Sons, 1956. Lavish photographs and informative commentary accompany detailed maps.

May, Herbert G., ed. *Oxford Bible Atlas*. New York: Oxford University Press, 1962. Pb. Many excellent full-page maps and an informative text.

Wright, G. Ernest, and Floyd V. Filson. *The Westminster Historical Atlas to the Bible*. Rev. ed. Philadelphia: Westminster Press, 1956. This carefully prepared volume has highly readable maps and an instructive text.

F. *Extrabiblical Source Materials*

Pritchard, James B., ed. *The Ancient Near East: An Anthology of Texts and Pictures*. Princeton, N.J.: Princeton University Press, 1965. Pb. A selection from the more important items in the first two Pritchard volumes listed below. Most useful in introducing the student to the world of the Old Testament.

————, ed. *Ancient Near Eastern Texts Relating to the Old Testament*. 3d ed. Princeton, N.J.: Princeton University Press, 1969. This volume illumines the wider environment of ancient Israel in many ways.

————, ed. *The Ancient Near East in Pictures Relating to the Old Testament*. 2d ed. Princeton, N.J.: Princeton University Press, 1969.

————, ed. *The Ancient Near East: Supplementary Texts and Pictures Relating to the Old Testament*. Princeton, N.J.: Princeton University Press, 1969. Supplementary materials for earlier editions of Pritchard's two books listed immediately above.

Thomas, D. Winton, ed. *Documents from Old Testament Times*. 1958. Reprint. New York: Harper & Row, Harper Torchbooks, 1961. Pb. While this volume contains fewer texts and photos than the paperbound Pritchard anthology, it offers many helpful editorial notes.

G. *Journals*

The advance of biblical scholarship may often be detected within the available professional periodicals. While some of their articles are quite technical, others are within the grasp and interest of the general reader. The journals listed below contribute significantly to the field of biblical studies.

The Bible Today. A nontechnical Roman Catholic publication appearing six times annually.

Biblica. Published quarterly by the Jesuits of the Pontifical Biblical Institute (Rome) with significant technical articles on the Old and New Testaments.

The Biblical Archaeologist. Issued quarterly by the American Schools of Oriental Research to inform the general reader about archaeological discoveries of greatest interest to biblical studies.

Bulletin of the American Schools of Oriental Research. Issued quarterly to present the more technical facets of Syro-Palestinian archaeology.

The Catholic Biblical Quarterly. This journal, which is by no means confined to the efforts of Roman-Catholic biblical scholars, has grown significantly in the past decade. Articles tend to be technical.

The Expository Times. Published monthly by T. & T. Clark, Edinburgh, this periodical contains a number of nontechnical essays on the Bible.

Hebrew Union College Annual. Several of its articles directly relate to the Hebrew Bible.

Interpretation: A Journal of Bible and Theology. Hermeneutical and not overly technical in its approach.

Israel Exploration Journal. Archaeological discoveries in Israel are covered by articles in Hebrew and English.

Journal of the American Academy of Religion. A number of its articles deal with biblical studies. Until 1967 published under the title, *The Journal of Bible and Religion.*

Journal of Biblical Literature. Issued quarterly by the Society of Biblical Literature, this is the most important technical journal devoted to biblical research on the American scene.

Journal of Near Eastern Studies. Its technical articles deal mainly with ancient Near Eastern texts, history, art, and religion.

Revue Biblique. This outstanding French journal in biblical studies offers a few articles in English.

Revue de Qumran. Research in the Dead Sea Scrolls and related matters is covered by articles written in several languages.

Vetus Testamentum. Issued quarterly by the International Organization for the Study of the Old Testament, this journal contains essays in English, French, and German.

Zeitschrift für die alttestamentliche Wissenschaft. A leading German journal that publishes some of its technical articles in English and French.

H. The History of Biblical Research

Alonso-Schökel, Luis. *Understanding Biblical Research.* New York: Herder & Herder, 1963. A study of the emergence and development of modern biblical criticism by a Roman Catholic scholar.

Hahn, Herbert F. *The Old Testament in Modern Research,* with a survey of recent literature by Horace D. Hummel. Expanded ed. Philadelphia: Fortress Press, 1966. Pb. Various facets of biblical criticism are clearly and interestingly presented.

Hyatt, J. Philip, ed. *The Bible in Modern Scholarship.* Nashville: Abingdon Press, 1965. Contains papers read at the hundredth meeting of the Society of Biblical Literature in New York City, December 1964.

Kraeling, Emil G. *The Old Testament since the Reformation.* 1955. Reprint. New York: Schocken Books, 1969. Pb. A skillful, informative presentation.

Levie, Jean. *The Bible, Word of God in Words of Men.* New York: P. J. Kenedy & Sons, 1961. A valuable examination of the inception of the modern biblical movement by a Roman Catholic scholar.

Rowley, H. H., ed. *The Old Testament and Modern Study.* New York:

Oxford University Press, 1951. Pb. Extremely useful chapters written by eminent scholars.

Terrien, Samuel L. "History of the Interpretation of the Bible: Modern Period." In *The Interpreter's Bible*, edited by George A. Buttrick et al., vol. 1, pp. 127–141. Nashville: Abingdon Press, 1952. Begins with the emergence of biblical criticism (ca. 1650–1800).

I. Canon and Text of the Old Testament

Anderson, George W. "The Old Testament: Canonical and Non-Canonical." In *The Cambridge History of the Bible*, vol. 1: *From the Beginnings to Jerome*, edited by P. R. Ackroyd and C. F. Evans, pp. 113–159. Cambridge, Eng.: Cambridge University Press, 1970. An instructive, judicious, and very readable presentation.

Jeffery, Arthur. "The Canon of the Old Testament." "Text and Ancient Versions of the Old Testament." In *The Interpreter's Bible*, edited by George A. Buttrick et al., vol. 1, pp. 32–45, 46–62. Nashville: Abingdon Press, 1952. Both essays are packed with helpful data.

Kenyon, Frederic. *Our Bible and the Ancient Manuscripts*. 5th ed., revised by A. W. Adams. New York: Harper & Row, 1958.

Murphy, Roland E., Albert C. Sundberg, Jr., and Samuel Sandmel. "A Symposium on the Canon of Scripture." *The Catholic Biblical Quarterly* 28 (1966): 189–207. A vigorous and informative presentation.

Orlinsky, Harry M. "The Textual Criticism of the Old Testament." In *The Bible and the Ancient Near East*, edited by G. Ernest Wright, pp. 140–169. Garden City, N.Y.: Doubleday, Anchor Books, 1965. Pb. A cogent presentation by an authority in the field.

Roberts, Bleddyn J. *The Old Testament Text and Versions: The Hebrew Texts in Transmission and the History of the Ancient Versions*. Cardiff: University of Wales Press, 1951.

Skehan, Patrick W. "The Scrolls and the Old Testament Text." In *New Directions in Biblical Archaeology*, edited by David N. Freedman and Jonas C. Greenfield, pp. 99–112. Garden City, N.Y.: Doubleday, Anchor Books, 1971. Pb. A consideration of the Old Testament textual tradition as preserved in the ancient Qumran manuscripts.

Sundberg, Albert C., Jr. *The Old Testament of the Early Church*. Harvard Theological Series, no. 20. Cambridge, Mass.: Harvard University Press, 1964. An original, provocative treatment.

Wright, G. Ernest. "The Canon as Theological Problem." In Wright, *The Old Testament and Theology*, pp. 166–185. New York: Harper & Row, 1969.

Würthwein, Ernst. *The Text of the Old Testament*. Translated by Peter R. Ackroyd. Oxford: Basil Blackwell, 1957.

J. Introductions to the Old Testament

Anderson, Bernhard W. *Understanding the Old Testament*. 2d ed. Englewood Cliffs, N.J.: Prentice-Hall, 1966. A first-rate introduction that anchors Old Testament literature and faith in the historical emergence of ancient Israel.

Beebe, H. Keith. *The Old Testament: An Introduction to Its Literary, Histori-cal, and Religious Traditions.* Belmont, Calif.: Dickenson Publishing Co., 1970. A work that has an attractive format, shows a keen interest in literary forms, and draws many parallels from Western literature.

Buck, Harry M. *People of the Lord: The History, Scriptures, and Faith of Ancient Israel.* New York: Macmillan, 1966. Frequently focusing on specific biblical readings, this carefully written text has a distinctive format.

Fromm, Erich. *You Shall Be As Gods: A Radical Interpretation of the Old Testament and Its Tradition.* New York: Holt, Rinehart and Winston, 1966. An insightful, if unconventional, approach to the Hebrew Bible that focuses mainly on postbiblical Judaism.

Harrelson, Walter. *Interpreting the Old Testament.* New York: Holt, Rinehart and Winston, 1964. An introduction that adheres to the sequence of the Hebrew canon and resembles a one-volume commentary. Packed with insights and informed judgments.

Jensen, Joseph. *God's Word to Israel.* Boston: Allyn and Bacon, 1968. Pb. The Old Testament is succinctly presented by a Roman Catholic scholar.

Napier, B. Davie. *Song of the Vineyard: A Theological Introduction to the Old Testament.* New York: Harper & Row, 1962. Contains an astute analy-sis of ancient Israel's literature and a vivid presentation of its dominant theological motifs.

Rowley, H. H. *The Growth of the Old Testament.* 1950. Reprint. New York: Harper & Row, Harper Torchbooks, 1963. Pb. A concise, helpful introduc-tion by a brilliant British biblical scholar.

Sandmel, Samuel. *The Hebrew Scriptures: An Introduction to Their Literature and Religious Ideas.* New York: Alfred A. Knopf, 1963. This critical study by an outstanding Jewish scholar treats the biblical books according to the sequence of their final editing, thus creating an unusual format. Accessible to the general reader.

West, James King. *Introduction to the Old Testament.* New York: Macmillan, 1971. A concise, well-written examination of the canonical and apocryphal books of the Hebrew Bible that takes account of historical and theological matters as well.

K. Technical Introductions to the Literature of the Old Testament

Anderson, George W. *A Critical Introduction to the Old Testament.* London: Gerald Duckworth, 1959. A terse, competent survey that examines the biblical books in canonical sequence.

Bentzen, Aage. *Introduction to the Old Testament.* 2 vols. in 1. 2d ed. Copen-hagen: G. E. C. Gad, 1952. An excellent technical introduction by a Scandi-navian biblical scholar whose interpretation of the role of oral tradition is particularly useful.

Bewer, Julius A. *The Literature of the Old Testament.* Revised by Emil G. Kraeling. 3d ed. New York: Columbia University Press, 1962. This lucid presentation of the biblical text, which was widely used a generation ago, is available in a revised and expanded edition.

Eissfeldt, Otto. *The Old Testament: An Introduction.* Translated by Peter R. Ackroyd. New York: Harper & Row, 1965. An outstanding technical treat-ment by a distinguished German scholar, based on the third German edition.

Fohrer, Georg. *Introduction to the Old Testament*. Translated by David E. Green. Nashville: Abingdon Press, 1968. Initiated by Ernst Sellin in 1910, this completely rewritten edition excels in its technical insights into literary and form-critical matters. Its straightforward presentation is within the grasp of the general reader.

Pfeiffer, Robert H. *Introduction to the Old Testament*. Rev. ed. New York: Harper & Row, 1948. The literary-critical problems of the Old Testament are handled in great detail in this encyclopedic volume, which has worn well over the years. But it is scanty in form-critical observations.

Robert, André, and André Feuillet, eds. *Introduction to the Old Testament*. Translated by Patrick W. Skehan et al. 2 vols. Garden City, N.Y.: Doubleday, Anchor Books, 1970. Pb. Contains the technical contributions of several competent Roman Catholic scholars.

Weiser, Artur. *The Old Testament: Its Formation and Development*. Translated by Dorothea M. Barton. New York: Association Press, 1961. A readable yet technical work by a leading German scholar. Full of judicious interpretations and form-critical insights.

Young, Edward J. *An Introduction to the Old Testament*. Rev. ed. Grand Rapids, Mich.: Wm. B. Eerdmans, 1960. Undoubtedly the favorite Old Testament introduction in conservative Protestant circles.

L. The History of Ancient Israel

Ackroyd, Peter R. *Israel under Babylon and Persia*. New Clarendon Bible. New York: Oxford University Press, 1970. A brief, informative treatment of the historical and intellectual developments of this era.

Albright, William F. *The Biblical Period from Abraham to Ezra*. 1950. Reprint. New York: Harper & Row, Harper Torchbooks, 1963. Pb. A concisely written, perceptive history of ancient Israel.

Bright, John. *A History of Israel*. 2d ed. Philadelphia: Westminster Press, 1972. A very readable, instructive presentation, this major work has been strongly influenced by the approach of William F. Albright.

Bruce, F. F. *Israel and the Nations: From the Exodus to the Fall of the Second Temple*. Grand Rapids, Mich.: Wm. B. Eerdmans, 1963. Pb.

Ehrlich, Ernst L. *A Concise History of Israel*. Translated by James Barr. 1962. Reprint. New York: Harper & Row, Harper Torchbooks, 1965. Pb.

Noth, Martin. *The History of Israel*. 2d ed. Revised translation by Peter R. Ackroyd. New York: Harper & Row, 1960. A major study by a German historian who proposes many brilliant solutions to historical problems on the basis of his critical assessment of various biblical traditions. More difficult reading than Bright's *History of Israel* listed above, but extremely worthwhile.

Orlinsky, Harry M. *Ancient Israel*. Ithaca, N.Y.: Cornell University Press, 1954. Pb. A succinct, useful study of ancient Israelite history.

*M. Biblical Archaeology and Israel's Geographical
and Cultural Setting in the Ancient Near East*

Albright, William F. *Archaeology and the Religion of Israel*. 1946. Reprint. 2d ed. Garden City, N.Y.: Doubleday, Anchor Books, 1969. Pb.

———. *The Archaeology of Palestine*. Rev. ed. Baltimore: Penguin Books, 1961. Pb. A standard work by a profoundly significant American archaeologist.

———. "The Old Testament World." In *The Interpreter's Bible*, edited by George A. Buttrick et al., vol. 1, pp. 233–271. Nashville: Abingdon Press, 1952. An excellent summary.

Frank, Harry T. *Bible, Archaeology, and Faith*. Nashville: Abingdon Press, 1971. A very readable presentation of archaeological methodology and discoveries as these throw light on the biblical record.

Frankfort, Henri. *Kingship and the Gods*. Chicago: University of Chicago Press, 1948. The distinctive nature of Israelite kingship is viewed in the light of the surrounding culture of the ancient Near East.

Frankfort, Henri, H. A. Frankfort, et al. *Before Philosophy*. 1946. Reprint. Baltimore: Penguin Books, 1949. Pb. A superb discussion of aspects of Egyptian and Mesopotamian culture that exerted an appreciable influence on emerging Israelite thought. Previously published as *The Intellectual Adventure of Ancient Man* (with a section on Hebrew culture).

Freedman, David N., and Jonas C. Greenfield, eds. *New Directions in Biblical Archaeology*. 1969. Reprint. Garden City, N.Y.: Doubleday, Anchor Books, 1971.

Gaster, Theodor H. *Myth, Legend, and Custom in the Old Testament*. New York: Harper & Row, 1969. This expansion of James G. Frazer's *Folklore in the Old Testament* links a remarkable number of aspects of ancient Near Eastern folklore to specific biblical chapters.

———. *Thespis: Ritual, Myth, and Drama in the Ancient Near East*. 1950. Reprint. New York: Harper & Row, Harper Torchbooks, 1961. Pb. The nature and centrality of myth and ritual for the ancient Near Eastern world are deftly presented.

Gray, John. *Archaeology and the Old Testament World*. 1962. Reprint. New York: Harper & Row, Harper Torchbooks, 1965. Pb.

Hooke, S. H. *Middle Eastern Mythology*. Baltimore: Penguin Books, 1963. Pb. An instructive study of the mythological features of ancient Mesopotamian, Egyptian, Canaanite, Hittite, and Hebraic culture.

Kenyon, Kathleen M. *Archaeology in the Holy Land*. 3d ed. New York: Frederick A. Praeger, 1970. Pb. A competent survey by an eminent British archaeologist. Gives special consideration to the prehistorical phases of Canaanite settlement.

Kramer, Samuel Noah, ed. *Mythologies of the Ancient World*. Garden City, N.Y.: Doubleday, Anchor Books, 1961. Pb.

Moscati, Sabatino. *The Face of the Ancient Orient*. 1960. Reprint. Garden City, N.Y.: Doubleday, Anchor Books, 1962. Pb. A useful presentation of the history, literature, religion, and art of ancient Israel and her several neighbors.

Noth, Martin. *The Old Testament World*. Translated by Victor I. Gruhn. Philadelphia: Fortress Press, 1966. The first three parts of this basic work deal most instructively with the geography of Palestine, archaeological undertakings in Palestine, and selected topics on the history of the ancient Orient.

Ringgren, Helmer. *Religions of the Ancient Near East.* Translated by John
    Sturdy. Philadelphia: Westminster Press, 1973. A selective yet instructive
    presentation of Sumerian, Babylonian, Assyrian, and West Semitic religion.
Sanders, James A., ed. *Near Eastern Archaeology in the Twentieth Century.*
    Garden City, N.Y.: Doubleday, 1970. A valuable collection of relatively
    technical essays on archaeology.
Thomas, D. Winton, ed. *Archaeology and Old Testament Study.* New York:
    Oxford University Press, 1967. Various European, Israeli, and American
    scholars have contributed to this comprehensive Jubilee Volume of the
    Society for Old Testament Study; it describes the archaeological work
    accomplished at some twenty-five Near Eastern sites. A wealth of useful
    information.
Wright, G. Ernest, ed. *The Bible and the Ancient Near East.* 1961. Reprint.
    Garden City, N.Y.: Doubleday, Anchor Books, 1965. Pb. Instructive essays
    by eminent scholars define the bearing of recent archaeological discoveries
    on biblical research.
————. *Biblical Archaeology.* Rev. ed. Philadelphia: Westminster Press,
    1962. This lucid, nontechnical work by a leading American archaeologist
    and biblical scholar shows how archaeological findings enhance our grasp
    of biblical history.
————, and David N. Freedman, eds. *The Biblical Archaeologist Reader.*
    Garden City, N.Y.: Doubleday, Anchor Books, 1961. Pb. Contains articles
    reprinted from *The Biblical Archaeologist;* a second (1964) and third (1970)
    Reader, edited by Freedman and Edward F. Campbell, Jr., are also available.
Yadin, Yigael. *The Art of Warfare in Biblical Lands in the Light of Archaeo-
    logical Study.* 2 vols. New York: McGraw-Hill, 1963. A definitive study with
    lavish illustrations.

N. *The Religion, Theology, and Culture of Ancient Israel*
Albright, William F. *From the Stone Age to Christianity: Monotheism and the
    Historical Process.* 2d ed. 1946. Reprint. Garden City, N.Y.: Doubleday,
    Anchor Books, 1957. Pb. Argues in detail about the role that monotheism
    played in ancient Israel's historical development.
Alt, Albrecht. *Essays on Old Testament History and Religion.* Translated by
    R. A. Wilson. Garden City, N.Y.: Doubleday, Anchor Books, 1966. Pb.
Anderson, George W. *The History and Religion of Israel.* New Clarendon
    Bible. New York: Oxford University Press, 1966. Among the briefer treat-
    ments available, this is superb.
Boman, Thorleif. *Hebrew Thought Compared with Greek.* Translated by
    Jules L. Moreau. Philadelphia: Westminster Press, 1960. This volume has
    been thoroughly criticized by Barr. (James Barr. *The Semantics of Biblical
    Language.* New York: Oxford University Press, 1961.) Both studies have
    evoked considerable interest and discussion among biblical theologians.
Childs, Brevard S. *Memory and Tradition in Israel.* Studies in Biblical The-
    ology, no. 37. London: SCM Press, 1962. Pb. Discusses psychological
    aspects of Hebrew memory and assesses its centrality for Israelite worship
    and history.
De Vaux, Roland. *Ancient Israel: Its Life and Institutions.* Translated by John

McHugh. 1961. Reprint. New York: McGraw-Hill, 1965. Pb. A comprehensive, thoroughly competent treatment of the social, political, and religious institutions of ancient Israel.

Eichrodt, Walther. *Man in the Old Testament.* Translated by K. and R. Gregor Smith. Studies in Biblical Theology, no. 4. London: SCM Press, 1951. Pb.

———. *Theology of the Old Testament.* Translated by John A. Baker. 2 vols. The Old Testament Library. Philadelphia: Westminster Press, 1961–1967. A significant work that acknowledges the covenant concept as the center of Old Testament theology.

Fohrer, Georg. *History of Israelite Religion.* Translated by David E. Green. Nashville: Abingdon Press, 1972. An incisive and comprehensive study of the religion of ancient Israel in its historical and cultural context.

Jacob, Edmond. *Theology of the Old Testament.* Translated by Arthur W. Heathcote and Philip J. Allcock. New York: Harper & Row, 1958. An instructive work by a French Protestant theologian who uses the reality of God for ancient Israel as his organizing principle.

Johnson, Aubrey R. *The One and the Many in the Israelite Conception of God.* 2d ed. Cardiff: University of Wales Press, 1961.

———. *The Vitality of the Individual in the Thought of Ancient Israel.* Cardiff: University of Wales Press, 1949. Contains many insights into ancient Hebrew psychology.

Kaufmann, Yehezkel. *The Religion of Israel.* Translated and abridged by Moshe Greenberg. Chicago: University of Chicago Press, 1960. The provocative work of an eminent Jewish scholar who is unwilling to accept many of the conclusions of contemporary biblical scholarship.

Köhler, Ludwig. *Old Testament Theology.* Translated by A. S. Todd. Philadelphia: Westminster Press, 1958. A useful volume that defends the sovereignty of God as the leading theological motif in the Old Testament.

Kuntz, J. Kenneth. *The Self-revelation of God.* Philadelphia: Westminster Press, 1967. A form-critical, exegetical study of selected Old Testament theophanies.

McKenzie, John L. *The Two-Edged Sword: An Interpretation of the Old Testament.* 1956. Reprint. Garden City, N.Y.: Image Books, 1966. Pb. An introduction to Old Testament theology by a leading Catholic scholar. Intended for a general audience.

Muilenburg, James. "The History of the Religion of Israel." In *The Interpreter's Bible,* edited by George A. Buttrick et al., vol. 1, pp. 292–348. Nashville: Abingdon Press, 1952. An excellent summary.

———. *The Way of Israel: Biblical Faith and Ethics.* 1961. Reprint. New York: Harper & Row, Harper Torchbooks, 1965. Pb.

Pedersen, Johannes. *Israel: Its Life and Culture.* 4 vols. in 2. New York: Oxford University Press, 1926–1940. An extremely thorough presentation of ancient Hebrew psychology.

von Rad, Gerhard. *Old Testament Theology.* Translated by D. M. G. Stalker. 2 vols. New York: Harper & Row, 1962–1965. A truly significant work that acknowledges the multiplicity of theological currents in ancient Israelite thinking. Volume 1 deals with historical and volume 2 with prophetic traditions. Harper & Row has made most of volume 2 available under the title *The Message of the Prophets* (pb.).

Ringgren, Helmer. *Israelite Religion.* Translated by David E. Green. Philadelphia: Fortress Press, 1966. A readable, instructive, and judicious treatment.

Robinson, H. Wheeler. *Corporate Personality in Ancient Israel.* Philadelphia: Fortress Press, Facet Books, 1964. Pb. A brief yet extremely valuable study showing how Hebrew man understood the interconnection between individual and communal existence.

————. "Hebrew Psychology." In *The People and the Book: Essays on the Old Testament,* edited by A. S. Peake, pp. 353–382. Oxford: Clarendon Press, 1925.

————. *Inspiration and Revelation in the Old Testament.* 1946. Reprint. New York: Oxford University Press, 1962. Pb. An illuminating study of Hebrew thought.

Rowley, H. H. *The Biblical Doctrine of Election.* London: Lutterworth Press, 1950. A lucid, convincing expression of a basic biblical theme.

————. *The Faith of Israel: Aspects of Old Testament Thought.* Philadelphia: Westminster Press, 1956. A persuasive treatment of seven topics including revelation, man, and the good life.

Vriezen, Th. C. *An Outline of Old Testament Theology.* Translated by S. Neuijen. Oxford: Basil Blackwell, 1958. A helpful study by a Dutch theologian.

Wright, G. Ernest. "The Faith of Israel." In *The Interpreter's Bible,* edited by George A. Buttrick et al., vol. 1, pp. 349–389. Nashville: Abingdon Press, 1952.

————. *God Who Acts: Biblical Theology as Recital.* Studies in Biblical Theology, no. 8. London: SCM Press, 1952. Pb. The historical center of ancient Israelite faith is superbly defended.

————. *The Old Testament and Theology.* New York: Harper & Row, 1969.

Zimmerli, Walther. *The Law and the Prophets: A Study of the Meaning of the Old Testament.* Translated by Ronald E. Clements. Oxford: Basil Blackwell, 1965. Pb.

READINGS BY CHAPTER

Chapter 1. The Old Testament Today: Ancient Traditions Intersect with a Modern World

Many of the works listed in sections H through N of the General Readings address themselves to questions of relevance and methodology. In addition, the works below may be consulted.

Textual, Literary, and Form Criticism

Ap-Thomas, D. R. *A Primer of Old Testament Text Criticism.* 2d ed. Oxford: Basil Blackwell, 1964. Pb.

Good, Edwin M. *Irony in the Old Testament.* Philadelphia: Westminster Press, 1965. A fresh, masterful analysis of the ironic presentations found in Genesis, 1 Samuel, Isaiah, Jonah, Ecclesiastes, and Job.

Habel, Norman C. *Literary Criticism of the Old Testament.* Guides to Biblical Scholarship. Philadelphia: Fortress Press, 1971. Pb.

Koch, Klaus. *The Growth of the Biblical Tradition: The Form-Critical Method.* Translated by S. M. Cupitt. New York: Charles Scribner's Sons, 1969. Pb.

Muilenburg, James. "The Gains of Form Criticism in Old Testament Studies."
    The Expository Times 71 (1960): 229–233.
Nielsen, Eduard. *Oral Tradition*. Studies in Biblical Theology, no. 11. London:
    SCM Press, 1954. Pb. This leading Scandinavian scholar maintains that an-
    cient Semitic traditions enjoyed a widespread and accurate oral transmission.
Rast, Walter E. *Tradition History and the Old Testament*. Guides to Biblical
    Scholarship. Philadelphia: Fortress Press, 1972. Pb.
Tucker, Gene M. *Form Criticism of the Old Testament*. Guides to Biblical
    Scholarship. Philadelphia: Fortress Press, 1971. Pb. An excellent introduction.

Historical Criticism

Bright, John. *Early Israel in Recent History Writing*. Studies in Biblical The-
    ology, no. 19. London: SCM Press, 1956. Pb. Confronts fundamental issues
    in historical methodology, and in the process criticizes the procedures of
    Noth.
Dentan, Robert C., ed. *The Idea of History in the Ancient Near East*. American
    Oriental Series. New Haven, Conn.: Yale University Press, 1955. Pb.
De Vaux, Roland, et al. "Method in the Study of Early Hebrew History." In
    The Bible in Modern Scholarship, edited by J. Philip Hyatt, pp. 15–43.
    Nashville: Abingdon Press, 1965.
Lapp, Paul W. *Biblical Archaeology and History*. New York: World Publishing
    Co., 1969.
Mendenhall, George E. "Biblical History in Transition." In *The Bible and the
    Ancient Near East*, edited by G. Ernest Wright, pp. 27–58. Garden City,
    N.Y.: Doubleday, Anchor Books, 1965. Pb.
Williams, Walter G. *Archaeology in Biblical Research*. Nashville: Abingdon
    Press, 1965.

Biblical Theology and Hermeneutics

Anderson, Bernhard W., ed. *The Old Testament and Christian Faith*. New
    York: Harper & Row, 1963. A volume resulting from an international sym-
    posium on biblical hermeneutics.
Bright, John. *The Authority of the Old Testament*. Nashville: Abingdon Press,
    1967.
Childs, Brevard S. *Biblical Theology in Crisis*. Philadelphia: Westminster Press,
    1970. A penetrating methodological study proposing that biblical theology
    should engage in a disciplined reflection on the Bible in the context of the
    canon.
Dentan, Robert C. *Preface to Old Testament Theology*. Rev. ed. New York:
    Seabury Press, 1963.
Farmer, Herbert H. "The Bible: Its Significance and Authority." In *The Inter-
    preter's Bible*, edited by George A. Buttrick et al., vol. 1, pp. 3–31. Nash-
    ville: Abingdon Press, 1952.
Hasel, Gerhard F. *Old Testament Theology: Basic Issues in the Current Debate*.
    Grand Rapids, Mich.: Wm. B. Eerdmans, 1972. Pb. A succinct and balanced
    treatment.
McKenzie, John L., ed. *The Bible in Current Catholic Thought*. New York:
    Herder & Herder, 1962.

Mowinckel, Sigmund. *The Old Testament as Word of God.* Translated by R. B. Bjornard. Nashville: Abingdon Press, 1959.

Smart, James D. *The Interpretation of Scripture.* Philadelphia: Westminster Press, 1961. A solid presentation of biblical hermeneutics.

Stendahl, Krister. "Method in the Study of Biblical Theology," and response by Avery Dulles. In *The Bible in Modern Scholarship,* edited by J. Philip Hyatt, pp. 196–216. Nashville: Abingdon Press, 1965.

Westermann, Claus, ed. *Essays on Old Testament Hermeneutics.* English translation edited by James L. Mays. Richmond: John Knox Press, 1963. Contains several crucial essays by leading German thinkers.

Chapter 2. The Lay of the Land: The Geographical Context of the Old Testament

See section E of the General Readings for a list of recommended Bible atlases. In addition, the studies below are helpful.

Aharoni, Yohanan. *The Land of the Bible: A Historical Geography.* Translated by A. F. Rainey. Philadelphia: Westminster Press, 1967.

Baly, Denis. *Geographical Companion to the Bible.* London: Lutterworth Press, 1963.

————. *The Geography of the Bible: A Study in Historical Geography.* Rev. ed. New York: Harper & Row, 1974. This recent study and the preceding are entirely readable presentations by a scholar with first-hand knowledge of his subject.

Noth, Martin. "Geography of Palestine." In Noth, *The Old Testament World,* pp. 2–104. Translated by Victor I. Gruhn. Philadelphia: Fortress Press, 1966.

Chapter 3. The Torah: Its Origin and Structure

A good orientation in Pentateuchal criticism may be obtained from reading relevant portions of most of the entries in sections J and K of the General Readings. The following studies are also recommended.

Anderson, George W. "Some Aspects of the Uppsala School of Old Testament Study." *Harvard Theological Review* 43 (1950): 239–256. In particular, the so-called Scandinavian approach to Pentateuchal criticism is clearly set forth.

Bright, John. "Modern Study of Old Testament Literature." In *The Bible and the Ancient Near East,* edited by G. Ernest Wright, pp. 1–26. Garden City, N.Y.: Doubleday, Anchor Books, 1965. Pb.

Cassuto, Umberto. *The Documentary Hypothesis and the Composition of the Pentateuch.* Translated by Israel Abrahams. Jerusalem: Magnes Press, 1961. This Jewish scholar, while admitting the existence of pre-Torah traditions, seeks to disprove the documentary hypothesis.

Engnell, Ivan. "The Pentateuch." In Engnell, *A Rigid Scrutiny: Critical Essays on the Old Testament,* pp. 50–67. Translated by John T. Willis. Nashville: Vanderbilt University Press, 1969. A provocative presentation of the traditio-historical position by an eminent Scandinavian scholar.

Freedman, David N. "Pentateuch." In *The Interpreter's Dictionary of the Bible,* edited by George A. Buttrick et al., K–Q, pp. 711–727. Nashville: Abingdon Press, 1962. An outstanding introduction to the composition and form of the Pentateuch as well as a survey of Pentateuchal criticism, more broadly conceived than the essay by North below.

Montgomery, Robert M. *An Introduction to Source Analysis of the Pentateuch.* Auxiliary Studies in the Bible. Nashville: Abingdon Press, 1971. Pb. The chief concerns of Pentateuchal source criticism are conveyed through a programmed-learning approach consisting of fifty frames.

North, C. R. "Pentateuchal Criticism." In *The Old Testament and Modern Study,* edited by H. H. Rowley, pp. 48–83. New York: Oxford University Press, 1951. Pb. A helpful survey of the dominant approaches to the Pentateuch espoused in the twentieth century.

Noth, Martin. *A History of Pentateuchal Traditions.* Translated by Bernhard W. Anderson. Englewood Cliffs, N.J.: Prentice-Hall, 1972. A leading work on Pentateuchal form criticism and tradition history.

————. *Überlieferungsgeschichtliche Studien.* I, Halle, East Germany: Niemeyer, 1943. While this volume focuses on the historical works of the Deuteronomist and Chronicler, its findings are also important for Pentateuchal criticism.

von Rad, Gerhard. "The Form-Critical Problem of the Hexateuch." In von Rad, *The Problem of the Hexateuch and Other Essays,* pp. 1–78. Translated by E. W. Trueman Dicken. London: Oliver & Boyd, 1966. A masterful analysis.

Thompson, R. J. *Moses and the Law in a Century of Criticism since Graf.* Vetus Testamentum Supplement, vol. 19. Leiden, Neth.: E. J. Brill, 1970.

Wellhausen, Julius. *Prolegomena to the History of Ancient Israel.* 1885. Reprint of English translation of the German (1883). Translated by Allan Menzies and J. Sutherland Black. New York: Meridian Books, 1957. Pb. A monumental study.

Chapter 4. Origins Anticipated: The Patriarchal Traditions

Historical Considerations

Albright, William F. "Abram the Hebrew: A New Archaeological Interpretation." *Bulletin of the American Schools of Oriental Research,* no. 163 (October 1961): 36–54.

Gordon, Cyrus H. "Biblical Customs and the Nuzu Tablets." In *The Biblical Archaeologist Reader,* vol. 2, edited by David N. Freedman and Edward F. Campbell, Jr., pp. 21–33. Garden City, N.Y.: Doubleday, Anchor Books, 1964. Pb.

————. "The Patriarchal Age." *Journal of Bible and Religion* 21 (1953): 238–243.

Greenberg, Moshe. *The Ḥab/piru.* New Haven, Conn.: American Oriental Society, 1955.

Gurney, O. R. *The Hittites.* 2d ed. Baltimore: Penguin Books, 1954. Pb. A definitive treatment.

Holt, John M. *The Patriarchs of Israel.* Nashville: Vanderbilt University Press, 1964. A very helpful work on patriarchal backgrounds that often alludes to archaeological findings.

Kramer, Samuel Noah. *History Begins at Sumer.* Garden City, N.Y.: Doubleday, Anchor Books, 1959. Pb. A presentation of twenty-seven firsts in the recorded history of ancient man that are anchored in early Sumerian culture.

————. *The Sumerians: Their History, Culture, and Character.* 1963. Reprint. Chicago: University of Chicago Press, Phoenix Books, 1971. Pb. A leading work.

Oppenheim, A. Leo. *Ancient Mesopotamia: Portrait of a Dead Civilization.* 1964. Reprint. Chicago: University of Chicago Press, Phoenix Books, 1968. Pb.

Van Seters, John. *The Hyksos: A New Investigation.* New Haven, Conn.: Yale University Press, 1966.

Zigmond, Maurice L. "Archaeology and the 'Patriarchal Age' of the Old Testament." In *Explorations in Cultural Anthropology,* edited by Ward W. Goodenough, pp. 571–598. New York: McGraw-Hill, 1964. This essay insists that those who would juxtapose biblical traditions with the archaeological data of the Middle Bronze era must exercise extreme caution.

Commentaries on the Genesis Text

Gunkel, Hermann. *The Legends of Genesis: The Biblical Saga and History.* Translated by W. H. Carruth. 1901. Reprint. New York: Schocken Books, 1964. Pb. An English translation of the detailed introduction in Gunkel's epoch-making Genesis commentary.

Hooke, S. H. *In the Beginning.* The Clarendon Bible. New York: Oxford University Press, 1947. Though somewhat limited in scope, quite helpful as a commentary on Genesis.

von Rad, Gerhard. *Genesis: A Commentary.* Rev. ed. Translated by John H. Marks. The Old Testament Library. Philadelphia: Westminster Press, 1972. The standard commentary on Genesis with superb form-critical and exegetical insights.

——————. "The Joseph Narrative and Ancient Wisdom." In von Rad, *The Problem of the Hexateuch and Other Essays,* pp. 292–300. Translated by E. W. Trueman Dicken. London: Oliver & Boyd, 1966. Sheds much light on Genesis 37–50.

Redford, Donald B. *A Study of the Biblical Story of Joseph.* Vetus Testamentum Supplement, vol. 20. Leiden, Neth.: E. J. Brill, 1970. A thorough, perceptive study of Genesis 37–50.

Speiser, E. A. *Genesis: Introduction, Translation, and Notes.* The Anchor Bible, vol. 1. Garden City, N.Y.: Doubleday, 1964. A valuable contribution by an eminent Jewish scholar.

Patriarchal Religion

Alt, Albrecht. "The God of the Fathers." In Alt, *Essays on Old Testament History and Religion,* pp. 1–100. Translated by R. A. Wilson. Garden City, N.Y.: Doubleday, Anchor Books, 1966. Pb.

Cross, Frank M., Jr. "Yahweh and the God of the Patriarchs." *Harvard Theological Review* 55 (1962): 225–259.

Chapter 5. Origins Actualized: The Exodus Event

Historical Considerations

Hay, Lewis S. "What Really Happened at the Sea of Reeds?" *Journal of Biblical Literature* 83 (1964): 397–403.

Pfeiffer, Charles F. *Tell el Amarna and the Bible.* Baker Studies in Biblical Archaeology. Grand Rapids, Mich.: Baker Book House, 1963. Pb.

Rowley, H. H. *From Joseph to Joshua: Biblical Traditions in the Light of Archaeology.* London: Oxford University Press, 1950. A detailed study which, among other things, criticizes the views of Meek in *Hebrew Origins* listed below.

Steindorff, George, and Keith C. Seele. *When Egypt Ruled the East.* 1957. Reprint. Rev. ed. Chicago: University of Chicago Press, Phoenix Books, 1963. Pb. A well-written, instructive presentation that focuses on the Eighteenth Dynasty.

Wilson, John A. *The Culture of Ancient Egypt.* Chicago: University of Chicago Press, Phoenix Books, 1951. Pb. Effectively covers a vast sweep of Egyptian history and achievement.

Commentaries on the Exodus Text

Buber, Martin. *Moses: The Revelation and the Covenant.* 1946. Reprint. New York: Harper & Row, Harper Torchbooks, 1958. Pb. An excellent study.

Finegan, Jack. *Let My People Go: A Journey Through Exodus.* New York: Harper & Row, 1963.

Noth, Martin. *Exodus: A Commentary.* Translated by J. S. Bowden. The Old Testament Library. Philadelphia: Westminster Press, 1962.

Rylaarsdam, J. Coert. "Introduction and Exegesis to Exodus." In *The Interpreter's Bible*, edited by George A. Buttrick et al., vol. 1, pp. 833–1099. Nashville: Abingdon Press, 1952. A first-rate contribution.

Other Studies

Coats, George W. *Rebellion in the Wilderness: The Murmuring Motif in the Wilderness Traditions of the Old Testament.* Nashville: Abingdon Press, 1968.

Gaster, Theodor H. *Passover: Its History and Traditions.* 1949. Reprint. Boston: Beacon Press, 1962. Pb.

Meek, Theophile J. *Hebrew Origins.* Rev. ed. 1950. Reprint. New York: Harper & Row, Harper Torchbooks, 1960. Pb. A provocative study of the emergence of the Hebrew people, law, deity, priesthood, prophecy, and monotheism.

von Rad, Gerhard. *Moses.* World Christian Books. London: Lutterworth Press, 1960. Pb. A brief, readable, and insightful treatment.

Chapter 6. Origins Clarified: The Theophany and Covenant at Sinai

In addition to the works listed below, several entries listed in Chapter 5 (especially the Exodus commentaries) apply here.

Alt, Albrecht. "The Origins of Israelite Law." In Alt, *Essays on Old Testament History and Religion*, pp. 101–171. Translated by R. A. Wilson. Garden City, N.Y.: Doubleday, Anchor Books, 1966. Pb.

Baltzer, Klaus. *The Covenant Formulary in Old Testament, Jewish, and Early Christian Writings.* Translated by David E. Green. Philadelphia: Fortress Press, 1971. A thorough investigation into the structure and language of covenant treaties.

Beyerlin, Walter. *Origins and History of the Oldest Sinaitic Traditions.* Translated by S. Rudman. Oxford: Basil Blackwell, 1965. This perceptive study attacks the position of Noth and others who maintain that originally the Exodus and Sinai traditions were separate.

Harrelson, Walter. "Law in the Old Testament." In *The Interpreter's Dictionary of the Bible,* edited by George A. Buttrick et al., K–Q, pp. 77–89. Nashville: Abingdon Press, 1962.

Hillers, Delbert R. *Covenant: The History of a Biblical Idea.* Baltimore: Johns Hopkins Press, 1969. Pb.

McCarthy, Dennis J. *Old Testament Covenant: A Survey of Current Opinions.* Richmond: John Knox Press, 1972. Pb.

Mendenhall, George E. *Law and Covenant in Israel and the Ancient Near East.* Pittsburgh: The Biblical Colloquium, 1955. Pb. An investigation into ancient treaty formulation and its influence on legal forms in Old Testament literature; an influential essay that has recently attracted trenchant criticism from McCarthy (in the work listed immediately above) and other scholars.

Newman, Murray L., Jr. *The People of the Covenant: A Study of Israel from Moses to the Monarchy.* Nashville: Abingdon Press, 1962. A thorough, perceptive study of the nature and historical impact of two prominent covenant traditions in ancient Israel.

Nielsen, Eduard. *The Ten Commandments in New Perspective.* Translated by D. J. Bourke. Studies in Biblical Theology, 2d series, no. 7. London: SCM Press, 1968. Pb. A traditio-historical investigation.

Noth, Martin. *The Laws in the Pentateuch and Other Essays,* pp. 1–107. Translated by D. R. Ap-Thomas. Philadelphia: Fortress Press, 1967.

Rowley, H. H. "Moses and the Decalogue." *Bulletin of the John Rylands Library* 34 (1951–1952): 81–118.

Stamm, Johann J., and Maurice E. Andrew. *The Ten Commandments in Recent Research.* Studies in Biblical Theology, 2d series, no. 2. London: SCM Press, 1967. Pb. An exegetical study prefaced by form-critical considerations.

Chapter 7. Wilderness Wandering and the Conquest of the Land

Israel's Wilderness Wandering

Engnell, Ivan. "The Wilderness Wandering." In Engnell, *A Rigid Scrutiny: Critical Essays on the Old Testament,* pp. 207–214. Translated by John T. Willis. Nashville: Vanderbilt University Press, 1969. A thoughtful analysis of the cultic context in which the narrative of ancient Israel's wilderness wandering is seated.

Marsh, John. "Introduction and Exegesis to Numbers." In *The Interpreter's Bible,* edited by George A. Buttrick et al., vol. 2, pp. 137–308. Nashville: Abingdon Press, 1953.

Noth, Martin. *Numbers: A Commentary.* Translated by James D. Martin. The Old Testament Library. Philadelphia: Westminster Press, 1968.

Israel's Conquest of Canaan

Bright, John. "Introduction and Exegesis to Joshua." In *The Interpreter's Bible,* edited by George A. Buttrick et al., vol. 2, pp. 541–673. Nashville: Abingdon Press, 1953. A discussion that excels both in its literary analysis and in its treatment of the archaeological data.

Kaufmann, Yehezkel. *The Biblical Account of the Conquest of Palestine.* Translated by M. Dagut. Jerusalem: Magnes Press, 1955.

Kenyon, Kathleen M. *Digging Up Jericho.* New York: Frederick A. Praeger, 1957.

Mendenhall, George E. "The Hebrew Conquest of Palestine." In *The Biblical Archaeologist Reader*, vol. 3, edited by Edward F. Campbell, Jr., and David N. Freedman, pp. 100–120. Garden City, N.Y.: Doubleday, Anchor Books, 1970. Pb. A provocative study challenging the view that the ancient Israelite tribes experienced an ethnic emergence in the desert that was the direct cause of their eastern assault against Canaan.

Noth, Martin. *Das Buch Joshua*. Handbuch zum Alten Testament, I, 7. 2d ed. Tübingen: J. C. B. Mohr, 1953. A more skeptical approach than that reflected in Bright's work listed above.

Pritchard, James B. *Gibeon Where the Sun Stood Still*. Princeton, N.J.: Princeton University Press, 1962. A fascinating account of the excavations at El-Jib (biblical Gibeon).

von Rad, Gerhard. *Der Heilige Krieg im alten Israel*. 1951. Reprint. 5th ed. Göttingen, Ger.: Vandenhoeck & Ruprecht, 1969. Pb.

Soggin, J. Alberto. *Joshua: A Commentary*. Translated by R. A. Wilson. The Old Testament Library. Philadelphia: Westminster Press, 1972.

Weippert, Manfred. *The Settlement of the Israelite Tribes in Palestine*. Translated by James D. Martin. Studies in Biblical Theology, 2d series, no. 21. London: SCM Press, 1971. Pb.

Wright, G. Ernest. *Shechem: The Biography of a Biblical City*. New York: McGraw-Hill, 1965.

Chapter 8. Israel's Settlement in Canaan

Historical and Literary Studies

Anderson, George W. "Israel: Amphictyony." In *Translating and Understanding the Old Testament*, edited by H. T. Frank and W. L. Reed, pp. 135–151. Nashville: Abingdon Press, 1970.

McKenzie, John L. *The World of the Judges*. Englewood Cliffs, N.J.: Prentice-Hall, 1966.

Mayes, A. D. H. "The Historical Context of the Battle Against Sisera." *Vetus Testamentum* 19 (1969): 353–360.

Myers, Jacob M. "Introduction and Exegesis to Judges." In *The Interpreter's Bible*, edited by George A. Buttrick et al., vol. 2, pp. 677–826. Nashville: Abingdon Press, 1953.

Orlinsky, Harry M. "The Tribal System of Israel and Related Groups in the Period of the Judges." In *Studies and Essays in Honor of Abraham A. Neuman*, edited by Meir Ben-Horin et al., pp. 375–387. Leiden, Neth.: E. J. Brill, 1962. Offers trenchant criticism of Noth's thesis that the tribes of ancient Israel organized themselves as an amphictyony.

Israelite-Canaanite Culture Contact

Ahlström, G. W. *Aspects of Syncretism in Israelite Religion*. Translated by Eric J. Sharpe. Lund, Swed.: C. W. K. Gleerup, 1963. Pb.

Albrektson, Bertil. *History and the Gods: An Essay on the Idea of Historical Events as Divine Manifestations in the Ancient Near East and in Israel*. Lund, Swed.: C. W. K. Gleerup, 1967. Pb. Persuasively maintains that the notion of God acting in history is not uniquely Israelite.

Albright, William F. *Yahweh and the Gods of Canaan: A Historical Analysis of Two Contrasting Faiths.* 1968. Reprint. Garden City, N.Y.: Doubleday, Anchor Books, 1969. Pb.

Ginsberg, H. L. "Ugaritic Studies and the Bible." In *The Biblical Archaeologist Reader,* vol. 2, edited by David N. Freedman and Edward F. Campbell, Jr., pp. 34–50. Garden City, N.Y.: Doubleday, Anchor Books, 1964. Pb.

Gray, John. *The Canaanites.* London: Thames & Hudson, 1964. A useful but less technical analysis than the work by Gray that follows.

————. *The Legacy of Canaan.* 2d ed. Vetus Testamentum Supplement, vol. 5. Leiden, Neth.: E. J. Brill, 1965. An investigation into the texts from ancient Ugarit and their impact on ancient Israelite culture.

Habel, Norman C. *Yahweh Versus Baal: A Conflict of Religious Cultures.* New York: Bookman Associates, 1964.

Pedersen, Johannes. "Canaanite and Israelite Cultus." *Acta Orientalia* 18 (1940): 1–14.

Rainey, A. F. "The Kingdom of Ugarit." *The Biblical Archaeologist* 28 (1965): 102–125. A helpful introduction to Canaanite culture.

Wright, G. Ernest. *The Old Testament Against Its Environment.* Studies in Biblical Theology, no. 2. London: SCM Press, 1950. Pb. A defense of the uniqueness of ancient Israelite faith even in its earliest and most basic forms.

Chapter 9. The United Monarchy under Saul and David

Albright, William F. *Samuel and the Beginnings of the Prophetic Movement.* Cincinnati: Hebrew Union College Press, 1961. Pb.

Caird, George B. "Introduction and Exegesis to I–II Samuel." In *The Interpreter's Bible,* edited by George A. Buttrick et al., vol. 2, pp. 855–1176. Nashville: Abingdon Press, 1953.

Hertzberg, Hans W. *I & II Samuel: A Commentary.* Translated by J. S. Bowden. The Old Testament Library. Philadelphia: Westminster Press, 1964. A thorough, insightful exegetical treatment.

Kenyon, Kathleen M. *Jerusalem: Excavating 3000 Years of History.* New York: McGraw-Hill, 1967.

Maly, Eugene H. *The World of David and Solomon.* Englewood Cliffs, N.J.: Prentice-Hall, 1966.

Mendelsohn, Isaac. "Samuel's Denunciation of Kingship in the Light of the Akkadian Documents from Ugarit." *Bulletin of the American Schools of Oriental Research,* no. 143 (October 1956): 17–22. An illuminating examination of 1 Samuel 8.

Newman, Murray. "The Prophetic Call of Samuel." In *Israel's Prophetic Heritage,* edited by Bernhard W. Anderson and Walter Harrelson, pp. 86–97. New York: Harper & Row, 1962.

Rost, Leonhard. *Die Überlieferung von der Thronnachfolge Davids.* Beiträge zur Wissenschaft vom Alten und Neuen Testament, vol. 42. Stuttgart: Kohlhammer, 1926. A penetrating analysis of the court history of David as a "succession document" with limited historical objectivity. Rost's findings are summarized in the study of Whybray that follows.

Whybray, R. N. *The Succession Narrative: A Study of II Samuel 9–20; I Kings 1 and 2.* Studies in Biblical Theology, 2d series, no. 9. London: SCM Press, 1968. Pb.

Wright, G. Ernest. "Fresh Evidence for the Philistine Story." *The Biblical Archaeologist* 29 (1966): 70–86.

Chapter 10. Solomonic Rule and the Ensuing Schism

The Solomonic Monarchy

Aharoni, Yohanan. "The Israelite Sanctuary at Arad." In *New Directions in Biblical Archaeology*, edited by David N. Freedman and Jonas C. Greenfield, pp. 28–44. Garden City, N.Y.: Doubleday, Anchor Books, 1971. Pb. An account of the recently discovered Arad sanctuary and its relevance to Solomon's temple in Jerusalem.

Gray, John. *I & II Kings: A Commentary*. Rev. ed. The Old Testament Library. Philadelphia: Westminster Press, 1970.

von Rad, Gerhard. "The Deuteronomic Theology of History in I and II Kings." In von Rad, *The Problem of the Hexateuch and Other Essays*, pp. 205–221. Translated by E. W. Trueman Dicken. London: Oliver & Boyd, 1966.

Snaith, Norman H. "Introduction and Exegesis to I–II Kings." In *The Interpreter's Bible*, edited by George A. Buttrick et al., vol. 3, pp. 3–338. Nashville: Abingdon Press, 1954.

Wright, G. Ernest, et al. "The Significance of the Temple in the Ancient Near East." In *The Biblical Archaeologist Reader*, vol. 1, edited by Wright and David N. Freedman, pp. 145–200. Garden City, N.Y.: Doubleday, Anchor Books, 1961. Pb.

Yadin, Yigael. "New Light on Solomon's Megiddo." In *The Biblical Archaeologist Reader*, vol. 2, edited by David N. Freedman and Edward F. Campbell, Jr., pp. 240–247. Garden City, N.Y.: Doubleday, Anchor Books, 1964. Pb.

The Yahwist's Mythological Reflections

For help in understanding the contributions of the Yahwist in Genesis 2–11, see the following works and, in addition, the Genesis commentaries recommended for Chapter 4.

Barr, James. "The Meaning of 'Mythology' in Relation to the Old Testament." *Vetus Testamentum* 9 (1959): 1–10.

Childs, Brevard S. *Myth and Reality in the Old Testament*. Studies in Biblical Theology, no. 27. London: SCM Press, 1960. Pb. A superb analysis of the nature of Israelite myth in the light of the ancient Near Eastern environment.

McKenzie, John L. "Myth and the Old Testament." *The Catholic Biblical Quarterly* 21 (1959): 265–282.

Napier, B. Davie. *Come Sweet Death: A Quintet from Genesis*. Philadelphia: United Church Press, 1967. Pb. Stimulating reflections in free verse on Genesis 2–12.

Westermann, Claus. *The Genesis Accounts of Creation*. Translated by Norman E. Wagner. Philadelphia: Fortress Press, Facet Books, 1964. Pb. A deft treatment of Genesis 1–3 accessible to the general reader.

Chapter 11. The Dialogue Between Established
Monarchy and Emerging Prophetism

The commentaries of Gray and Snaith on Kings listed in Chapter 10 are relevant to the present chapter and to Chapters 12 through 15 as well. The general and specific studies in Israelite prophecy listed below augment not only the present chapter but also Chapters 12 through 19.

General Studies in Old Testament Prophetism

Buber, Martin. *The Prophetic Faith*. 1949. Reprint. New York: Harper & Row, Harper Torchbooks, 1960. Pb. A superb, theologically sensitive presentation by a leading Jewish scholar.

Heschel, Abraham J. *The Prophets*. New York: Harper & Row, 1962. A penetrating treatment of both the theological and psychological dimensions of Old Testament prophetism.

Hyatt, J. Philip. *Prophetic Religion*. Nashville: Abingdon Press, 1947. A helpful topical presentation.

Lindblom, Johannes. *Prophecy in Ancient Israel*. Philadelphia: Fortress Press, 1962. An illuminating study of many important facets of Hebrew prophecy by an eminent Swedish biblical scholar.

Napier, B. Davie. *Prophets in Perspective*. Nashville: Abingdon Press, 1963. A brief, lucid presentation of the office, nonecstatic function, and fundamental message of the Israelite prophet.

Orlinsky, Harry M., ed. *Interpreting the Prophetic Tradition*. Cincinnati: Hebrew Union College Press, 1969.

von Rad, Gerhard. *Old Testament Theology*. Vol. 2. Translated by D. M. G. Stalker. New York: Harper & Row, 1965. Most of this definitive study of ancient Israel's prophetic traditions appears in paperback under the title *The Message of the Prophets*.

Scott, R. B. Y. *The Relevance of the Prophets*. Rev. ed. New York: Macmillan, 1968. Pb. An extremely helpful study that takes various literary, sociological, and theological features into account.

Specific Studies in Old Testament Prophetism

Ahlström, G. W. "Some Remarks on Prophets and Cult." In *Transitions in Biblical Scholarship*, edited by J. Coert Rylaarsdam, pp. 113–129. Chicago: University of Chicago Press, 1968.

Anderson, Bernhard W., and Walter Harrelson, eds. *Israel's Prophetic Heritage*. New York: Harper & Row, 1962. Several of the essays in this useful volume are listed elsewhere in this bibliography.

Clements, Ronald E. *Prophecy and Covenant*. Studies in Biblical Theology, no. 43. London: SCM Press, 1965. Pb. A perceptive assessment of the impact of prophetic preaching on Israelite-Jewish religion.

Crenshaw, James L. *Prophetic Conflict: Its Effect upon Israelite Religion*. Beihefte zur Zeitschrift für die alttestamentliche Wissenschaft, vol. 124. Berlin: Walter de Gruyter, 1971. A concise yet thorough study of so-called true and false dimensions in Hebrew prophecy.

Gottwald, Norman K. *All the Kingdoms of the Earth: Israelite Prophecy and International Relations in the Ancient Near East*. New York: Harper & Row, 1964. An excellent treatment.

Huffmon, Herbert B. "Prophecy in the Mari Letters." *The Biblical Archaeologist* 31 (1968): 101–124. An examination of prophecy in the Mari texts and its relevance for the study of Israelite prophecy.

Johnson, Aubrey R. *The Cultic Prophet in Ancient Israel.* 2d ed. Cardiff: University of Wales Press, 1962. The cult is viewed as a significant force even in the early stages of Hebrew prophecy.

McKane, William. *Prophets and Wise Men.* Studies in Biblical Theology, no. 44. London: SCM Press, 1965. Pb.

Mowinckel, Sigmund. *Prophecy and Tradition.* Oslo: Jacob Dybwad, 1946. Deals incisively with the emergence of fragmentary prophetic sayings in their oral and, finally, written context.

Muilenburg, James. "The 'Office' of the Prophet in Ancient Israel." In *The Bible in Modern Scholarship,* edited by J. Philip Hyatt, pp. 74–97. Nashville: Abingdon Press, 1965.

Robinson, H. Wheeler. "Prophetic Symbolism." In *Old Testament Essays,* edited by D. C. Simpson, pp. 1–17. London: Charles Griffin, 1927.

Rowley, H. H. "Elijah on Mount Carmel." *Bulletin of the John Rylands Library* 43 (1960–1961): 190–210. An illuminating treatment of 1 Kings 18.

————, ed. *Studies in Old Testament Prophecy.* Edinburgh: T. & T. Clark, 1950.

Westermann, Claus. *Basic Forms of Prophetic Speech.* Translated by Hugh C. White. Philadelphia: Westminster Press, 1967. A penetrating form-critical inspection of the judgment speeches issued by the prophets against individuals as well as Israel and the foreign nations.

Chapter 12. Amos, Hosea, and the End of the Northern Kingdom

In addition to the following, the general studies in Old Testament prophetism recommended for Chapter 11 may be consulted.

Amos

Crenshaw, James L. "The Influence of the Wise upon Amos." *Zeitschrift für die alttestamentliche Wissenschaft* 79 (1967): 42–52. In part, a critical response to Terrien's essay, which is listed below.

Fosbroke, Hughell E. W. "Introduction and Exegesis to Amos." In *The Interpreter's Bible,* edited by George A. Buttrick et al., vol. 6, pp. 763–853. Nashville: Abingdon Press, 1956.

Kapelrud, Arvid S. *Central Ideas in Amos.* 1956. Reprint. Oslo: Oslo University Press, 1961.

Mays, James L. *Amos: A Commentary.* The Old Testament Library. Philadelphia: Westminster Press, 1969.

Terrien, Samuel L. "Amos and Wisdom." In *Israel's Prophetic Heritage,* edited by Bernhard W. Anderson and Walter Harrelson, pp. 108–115. New York: Harper & Row, 1962. Establishes a close link between Amos and the wisdom movement.

Hosea

Brueggemann, Walter. *Tradition for Crisis: A Study in Hosea.* Richmond: John Knox Press, 1968. An illuminating study of Hosea in the light of ancient Israelite covenant traditions.

Buss, Martin J. *The Prophetic Word of Hosea: A Morphological Study.* Beihefte zur Zeitschrift für die alttestamentliche Wissenschaft, vol. 111.

Berlin: A. Töpelmann, 1969. A technical study with fresh form-critical and anthropological insights.

Mauchline, John. "Introduction and Exegesis to Hosea." In *The Interpreter's Bible*, edited by George A. Buttrick et al., vol. 6, pp. 553–725. Nashville: Abingdon Press, 1956.

Mays, James L. *Hosea: A Commentary*. The Old Testament Library. Philadelphia: Westminster Press, 1969.

Rowley, H. H. "The Marriage of Hosea." *Bulletin of the John Rylands Library* 39 (1956–1957): 200–233. An excellent survey of many divergent approaches.

Wolff, Hans Walter. *Hosea*. Translated by Gary Stansell. Hermeneia Series. Philadelphia: Fortress Press, 1974. A monumental study of the Book of Hosea.

Chapter 13. Micah, Isaiah, and the Struggle of the Southern Kingdom

Blank, Sheldon H. *Prophetic Faith in Isaiah*. 1958. Reprint. Detroit: Wayne State University Press, 1967. Pb. A study that attempts to isolate the Isaiah of history from the legend that has engulfed him.

Childs, Brevard S. *Isaiah and the Assyrian Crisis*. Studies in Biblical Theology, 2d series, no. 3. London: SCM Press, 1967. Pb.

Kaiser, Otto. *Isaiah 1–12: A Commentary*. Translated by R. A. Wilson. The Old Testament Library. Philadelphia: Westminster Press, 1972.

Scott, R. B. Y. "Introduction and Exegesis to Isaiah 1–39." In *The Interpreter's Bible*, edited by George A. Buttrick et al., vol. 5, pp. 151–381. Nashville: Abingdon Press, 1956. An excellent presentation.

Vriezen, Th. C. "Essentials of the Theology of Isaiah." In *Israel's Prophetic Heritage*, edited by Bernhard W. Anderson and Walter Harrelson, pp. 128–146. New York: Harper & Row, 1962.

Whedbee, J. William. *Isaiah and Wisdom*. Nashville: Abingdon Press, 1971.

Wolfe, Rolland E. "Introduction and Exegesis to Micah." In *The Interpreter's Bible*, edited by George A. Buttrick et al., vol. 6, pp. 897–949. Nashville: Abingdon Press, 1956.

Chapter 14. Prophetic Disclosure and the Deuteronomic Reform in Judah

Deuteronomy

von Rad, Gerhard. *Deuteronomy: A Commentary*. Translated by Dorothea Barton. The Old Testament Library. Philadelphia: Westminster Press, 1966. An extremely helpful commentary.

————. *Studies in Deuteronomy*. Translated by David Stalker. Studies in Biblical Theology, no. 9. London: SCM Press, 1953. Pb. Excellent presentation of the sacred traditions that undergird the Book of Deuteronomy.

Weinfeld, Moshe. *Deuteronomy and the Deuteronomic School*. New York: Oxford University Press, 1972. Especially illuminating in relating the Deuteronomic literature with the wisdom movement.

Wright, G. Ernest. "Introduction and Exegesis to Deuteronomy." In *The Interpreter's Bible*, edited by George A. Buttrick et al., vol. 2, pp. 311–537. Nashville: Abingdon Press, 1953. A first-rate treatment.

Zephaniah, Nahum, and Habakkuk

Haldar, Alfred. *Studies in the Book of Nahum.* Uppsala, Swed.: A. B. Lundequistska, 1947.

Taylor, Charles L., Jr. "Introduction and Exegesis to Nahum." In *The Interpreter's Bible,* edited by George A. Buttrick et al., vol. 6, pp. 953–969. Nashville: Abingdon Press, 1956.

————. "Introduction and Exegesis to Habakkuk." In *The Interpreter's Bible,* edited by George A. Buttrick et al., vol. 6, pp. 973–1003. Nashville: Abingdon Press, 1956.

————. "Introduction and Exegesis to Zephaniah." In *The Interpreter's Bible,* edited by George A. Buttrick et al., vol. 6, pp. 1007–1034. Nashville: Abingdon Press, 1956.

Chapter 15. Judah's Appointment to the Yoke

Bright, John. *Jeremiah: Introduction, Translation, and Notes.* The Anchor Bible, vol. 21. Garden City, N. Y.: Doubleday, 1965. The introduction is especially rich in useful data and insights.

Hyatt, J. Philip. *Jeremiah: Prophet of Courage and Hope.* Nashville: Abingdon Press, 1958.

————. "Introduction and Exegesis to Jeremiah." In *The Interpreter's Bible,* edited by George A. Buttrick et al., vol. 5, pp. 777–1142. Nashville: Abingdon Press, 1956. In many respects, a very good treatment.

Leslie, Elmer A. *Jeremiah.* Nashville: Abingdon Press, 1954. Pb.

Overholt, Thomas W. *The Threat of Falsehood: A Study in the Theology of the Book of Jeremiah.* Studies in Biblical Theology, 2d series, no. 16. London: SCM Press, 1970. Pb.

Rowley, H. H. "The Prophet Jeremiah and the Book of Deuteronomy." In *Studies in Old Testament Prophecy,* edited by H. H. Rowley, pp. 157–174. Edinburgh: T. & T. Clark, 1950.

Skinner, John. *Prophecy and Religion: Studies in the Life of Jeremiah.* 1922. Reprint. New York: Cambridge University Press, 1961. Pb. An established work on Jeremiah.

Welch, Adam C. *Jeremiah: His Time and His Work.* 1928. Reprint. Oxford: Basil Blackwell, 1955.

Chapter 16. Judah's Bearing of the Yoke

Historical Background

Ackroyd, Peter R. *Exile and Restoration: A Study of Hebrew Thought of the Sixth Century B.C.* The Old Testament Library. Philadelphia: Westminster Press, 1968.

Lamentations

Gottwald, Norman K. *Studies in the Book of Lamentations.* Studies in Biblical Theology, no. 14. London: SCM Press, 1954. Pb. A monograph indispensable for an understanding of the literary and theological dimensions of this poetry.

Hillers, Delbert R. *Lamentations: Introduction, Translation, and Notes.* The Anchor Bible, vol. 7A. Garden City, N.Y.: Doubleday, 1972.

Meek, Theophile J. "Introduction and Exegesis to Lamentations." In *The Interpreter's Bible*, edited by George A. Buttrick et al., vol. 6, pp. 3–38. Nashville: Abingdon Press, 1956.

Ezekiel

Eichrodt, Walther. *Ezekiel: A Commentary*. Translated by Cosslett Quin. The Old Testament Library. Philadelphia: Westminster Press, 1970.

Howie, Carl G. *The Date and Composition of Ezekiel*. Journal of Biblical Literature Monograph Series, vol. 4. Philadelphia: Society of Biblical Literature, 1950. Pb.

May, Herbert G. "Introduction and Exegesis to Ezekiel." In *The Interpreter's Bible*, edited by George A. Buttrick et al., vol. 6, pp. 41–338. Nashville: Abingdon Press, 1956. One of the best treatments available.

Rowley, H. H. "The Book of Ezekiel in Modern Study." *Bulletin of the John Rylands Library* 36 (1953–1954): 146–190.

Zimmerli, Walther. *Ezechiel*. Biblischer Kommentar. 2 vols. Neukirchen, Ger.: Neukirchener Verlag, 1959. A monumental work by a prominent German scholar. An English translation is planned by Fortress Press in its Hermeneia Series.

Chapter 17. Second Isaiah and the Promise of Imminent Return

Ackroyd, Peter R. *Exile and Restoration: A Study of Hebrew Thought of the Sixth Century B.C.* The Old Testament Library. Philadelphia: Westminster Press, 1968.

Anderson, Bernhard W. "Exodus Typology in Second Isaiah." In *Israel's Prophetic Heritage*, edited by Anderson and Walter Harrelson, pp. 177–195. New York: Harper & Row, 1962.

McKenzie, John L. *Second Isaiah: Introduction, Translation, and Notes*. The Anchor Bible, vol. 20. Garden City, N.Y.: Doubleday, 1968.

Muilenburg, James. "Introduction and Exegesis to Isaiah 40–66." In *The Interpreter's Bible*, edited by George A. Buttrick et al., vol. 5, pp. 381–773. Nashville: Abingdon Press, 1956. An outstanding presentation.

North, Christopher R. *The Suffering Servant in Deutero-Isaiah: An Historical and Critical Study*. 2d ed. London: Oxford University Press, 1956. An excellent survey of numerous interpretations of the servant songs.

Radday, Y. T. "Two Computerized Statistical-Linguistic Tests Concerning the Unity of Isaiah." *Journal of Biblical Literature* 89 (1970): 319–324. Within the grasp of the general reader interested in computer-oriented biblical research.

Rowley, H. H. *The Servant of the Lord and Other Essays on the Old Testament*, pp. 3–60. Rev. ed. Oxford: Basil Blackwell, 1965.

Smart, James D. *History and Theology in Second Isaiah: A Commentary on Isaiah 35, 40–66*. Philadelphia: Westminster Press, 1965.

Westermann, Claus. *Isaiah 40–66: A Commentary*. Translated by David M. G. Stalker. The Old Testament Library. Philadelphia: Westminster Press, 1969. Provides an illuminating exegesis and sometimes a novel arrangement of the biblical text.

Chapter 18. The Return to Palestine and the Restoration of the Jewish Community

Historical Background

Ackroyd, Peter R. *Exile and Restoration: A Study of Hebrew Thought of the Sixth Century B.C.* The Old Testament Library. Philadelphia: Westminster Press, 1968.

Bickerman, Elias. *From Ezra to the Last of the Maccabees: Foundations of Post-biblical Judaism.* New York: Schocken Books, 1962. Pb.

Myers, Jacob M. *The World of the Restoration.* Englewood Cliffs, N.J.: Prentice-Hall, 1968. An especially useful study.

Rowley, H. H. "The Chronological Order of Ezra and Nehemiah." In Rowley, *The Servant of the Lord and Other Essays on the Old Testament*, pp. 137–168. Rev. ed. Oxford: Basil Blackwell, 1965.

———. "Nehemiah's Mission and Its Background." *Bulletin of the John Rylands Library* 37 (1954–1955): 528–561.

The Work of the Chronicler

Bowman, Raymond A. "Introduction and Exegesis to Ezra and Nehemiah." In *The Interpreter's Bible*, edited by George A. Buttrick et al., vol. 3, pp. 551–819. Nashville: Abingdon Press, 1954.

Elmslie, W. A. L. "Introduction and Exegesis to I–II Chronicles." In *The Interpreter's Bible*, edited by George A. Buttrick et al., vol. 3, pp. 341–548. Nashville: Abingdon Press, 1954.

Myers, Jacob M. *I Chronicles: Introduction, Translation, and Notes.* The Anchor Bible, vol. 12. Garden City, N.Y.: Doubleday, 1965.

———. *II Chronicles: Introduction, Translation, and Notes.* The Anchor Bible, vol. 13. Garden City, N.Y.: Doubleday, 1965.

———. *Ezra, Nehemiah: Introduction, Translation, and Notes.* The Anchor Bible, vol. 14. Garden City, N.Y.: Doubleday, 1965. The introduction provides many helpful comments on difficult literary and historical matters.

North, Robert. "Theology of the Chronicler." *Journal of Biblical Literature* 82 (1963): 361–381.

Haggai, Zechariah, and Malachi

Dentan, Robert C. "Introduction and Exegesis to Malachi." In *The Interpreter's Bible*, edited by George A. Buttrick et al., vol. 6, pp. 1117–1144. Nashville: Abingdon Press, 1956.

———. "Introduction and Exegesis to Zechariah 9–14." In *The Interpreter's Bible*, edited by George A. Buttrick et al., vol. 6, pp. 1089–1114. Nashville: Abingdon Press, 1956.

Thomas, D. Winton. "Introduction and Exegesis to Haggai." In *The Interpreter's Bible*, edited by George A. Buttrick et al., vol. 6, pp. 1037–1049. Nashville: Abingdon Press, 1956.

———. "Introduction and Exegesis to Zechariah 1–8." In *The Interpreter's Bible*, edited by George A. Buttrick et al., vol. 6, pp. 1053–1088. Nashville: Abingdon Press, 1956.

Chapter 19. Prophets, Priests, and Poets in Postexilic Israel

The Prophetic Witness

Kapelrud, Arvid S. *Joel Studies.* Uppsala, Swed.: Almquist & Wiksells, 1948.

Muilenburg, James. "Introduction and Exegesis to Isaiah 40–66." In *The Interpreter's Bible,* edited by George A. Buttrick et al., vol. 5, pp. 381–773. Nashville: Abingdon Press, 1956. Includes an excellent study of Third Isaiah (Isa. 56–66).

Thompson, John A. "Introduction and Exegesis to Joel." In *The Interpreter's Bible,* edited by George A. Buttrick et al., vol. 6, pp. 729–760. Nashville: Abingdon Press, 1956.

————. "Introduction and Exegesis to Obadiah." In *The Interpreter's Bible,* edited by George A. Buttrick et al., vol. 6, pp. 857–867. Nashville: Abingdon Press, 1956.

The Priestly Witness in Narrative and Law

In addition to the following works, see the study by Westermann on Creation in Chapter 10 and the Genesis commentaries in Chapter 4.

Harrelson, Walter. "The Significance of Cosmology in the Ancient Near East." In *Translating and Understanding the Old Testament,* edited by H. T. Frank and W. L. Reed, pp. 237–252. Nashville: Abingdon Press, 1970.

Heidel, Alexander. *The Babylonian Genesis: The Story of Creation.* 1951. Reprint. 2d ed. Chicago: University of Chicago Press, Phoenix Books, 1963. Pb. Contains a careful comparative analysis of the Babylonian and Hebrew creation accounts.

————. *The Gilgamesh Epic and Old Testament Parallels.* 1946. Reprint. 2d ed. Chicago: University of Chicago Press, Phoenix Books, 1963. Pb. The Babylonian and Hebrew flood stories are judiciously compared.

Micklem, Nathaniel. "Introduction and Exegesis to Leviticus." In *The Interpreter's Bible,* edited by George A. Buttrick et al., vol. 2, pp. 3–134. Nashville: Abingdon Press, 1953. A perceptive analysis.

Noth, Martin. *Leviticus.* Translated by J. E. Anderson. The Old Testament Library. Philadelphia: Westminster Press, 1965.

Israelite Cult and Worship

Clements, Ronald E. *God and Temple.* Philadelphia: Fortress Press, 1965. An investigation into the meaning and theological significance of the Jerusalem Temple as a witness to Yahweh's presence in ancient Israel.

De Vaux, Roland. *Studies in Old Testament Sacrifice.* Cardiff: University of Wales Press, 1964.

Harrelson, Walter. *From Fertility Cult to Worship.* 1969. Reprint. Garden City, N.Y.: Doubleday, Anchor Books, 1970. Pb. A fresh consideration of ancient Israelite worship.

Hooke, S. H., ed. *The Labyrinth.* London: SPCK, 1935. Maintains that Hebrew thought and its cultic expressions were significantly influenced by ancient Near Eastern mythology.

————. *Myth, Ritual, and Kingship.* New York: Oxford University Press, 1958. Less extreme in its position than the immediately preceding work.

Johnson, Aubrey R. *Sacral Kingship in Ancient Israel.* 2d ed. Cardiff: University of Wales Press, 1967.

Kapelrud, Arvid S., et al. "The Role of the Cult in Old Israel." In *The Bible in Modern Scholarship,* edited by J. Philip Hyatt, pp. 44–73. Nashville: Abingdon Press, 1965.

Kraus, Hans-Joachim. *Worship in Israel: A Cultic History of the Old Testament.* Translated by Geoffrey Buswell. Richmond: John Knox Press, 1966. An excellent survey.

Rowley, H. H. *Worship in Ancient Israel: Its Forms and Meaning.* Philadelphia: Fortress Press, 1967.

The Psalms

Barth, Christoph F. *Introduction to the Psalms.* Translated by R. A. Wilson. New York: Charles Scribner's Sons, 1966. Pb. Briefly examines questions of origin, authorship, and purpose, and sketches the various types of psalms.

Crim, Keith R. *The Royal Psalms.* Richmond: John Knox Press, 1962. A discussion of Israelite kingship is followed by commentary on various royal psalm compositions.

Dahood, Mitchell. *Psalms: Introduction, Translation, and Notes.* The Anchor Bible, vols. 16, 17, 17A. Garden City, N.Y.: Doubleday, 1966–1970. A provocative, predominantly technical analysis of the Psalter with an emphasis on related Canaanite literature.

Engnell, Ivan. "The Book of Psalms." In Engnell, *A Rigid Scrutiny: Critical Essays on the Old Testament,* pp. 68–122. Translated by John T. Willis. Nashville: Vanderbilt University Press, 1969.

Gunkel, Hermann. *Die Psalmen.* Göttinger Handkommentar zum Alten Testament. Göttingen, Ger.: Vandenhoeck & Ruprecht, 1926.

————. *The Psalms: A Form-Critical Introduction.* Translated by Thomas M. Horner. Philadelphia: Fortress Press, Facet Books, 1967. Pb. An extremely useful presentation.

Guthrie, Harvey H., Jr. *Israel's Sacred Songs: A Study of Dominant Themes.* New York: Seabury Press, 1966.

Johnson, A. R. "The Psalms." In *The Old Testament and Modern Study,* edited by H. H. Rowley, pp. 162–209. New York: Oxford University Press, 1951. Pb. Especially useful in outlining the various psalm types and in summarizing the contributions of Gunkel and Mowinckel.

Kraus, Hans-Joachim. *Psalmen.* 2d ed. Biblischer Kommentar. 2 vols. Neukirchen, Ger.: Neukirchener Verlag, 1961. A definitive work.

Mowinckel, Sigmund. *The Psalms in Israel's Worship.* Translated by D. R. Ap-Thomas. 2 vols. Nashville: Abingdon Press, 1962. A comprehensive, technical study by a leading Scandinavian scholar whose influence on Psalms studies has been considerable. Not a Psalms commentary as such.

Ringgren, Helmer. *The Faith of the Psalmists.* Philadelphia: Fortress Press, 1963. The religious dimensions of the psalms in the light of their cultic context are deftly presented.

Terrien, Samuel L. *The Psalms and Their Meaning for Today.* Indianapolis: Bobbs-Merrill, 1952. An outstanding introduction to the Psalter. Within the grasp of the general reader.

Weiser, Artur. *The Psalms: A Commentary*. Translated by Herbert Hartwell. The Old Testament Library. Philadelphia: Westminster Press, 1962. Offers a pertinent introduction to the Psalter as a whole that links many psalms to the covenant renewal festival. Also provides a thorough exegesis of each psalm.

Westermann, Claus. *The Praise of God in the Psalms*. Translated by Keith R. Crim. Richmond: John Knox Press, 1965. An excellent study of Israelite psalmody as a manifestation of praise and thanksgiving.

Chapter 20. The Gift of Wisdom

The Israelite Wisdom Movement

Brueggemann, Walter A. *In Man We Trust: The Neglected Side of Biblical Faith*. Richmond: John Knox Press, 1972. A helpful study of selected wisdom traditions in the Bible and their relevance for contemporary theology.

Murphy, Roland E. "A Consideration of the Classification 'Wisdom Psalms.'" *Congress Volume: Bonn, 1962*. Vetus Testamentum Supplement, vol. 9. Leiden, Neth.: E. J. Brill, 1963, pp. 156–167.

Noth, Martin, and D. Winton Thomas, eds. *Wisdom in Israel and in the Ancient Near East*. Vetus Testamentum Supplement, vol. 3. Leiden, Neth.: E. J. Brill, 1960. Contains many valuable essays which, among other things, sketch the universal context within which ancient Israel's wisdom movement emerged and matured.

von Rad, Gerhard. *Wisdom in Israel*. Translated by James D. Martin. Nashville: Abingdon Press, 1972. A definitive and comprehensive examination of Hebrew wisdom and its relationship to ancient Israel's faith as a whole.

Rankin, O. S. *Israel's Wisdom Literature: Its Bearing on Theology and the History of Religion*. Edinburgh: T. & T. Clark, 1936. Old but still useful in its presentation of important wisdom motifs (for example, providence, reward and retribution, the future life).

Scott, R. B. Y. *The Way of Wisdom in the Old Testament*. New York: Macmillan, 1971. Pb. An illuminating survey intended primarily for the general reader.

Proverbs

Fritsch, Charles T. "Introduction and Exegesis to Proverbs." In *The Interpreter's Bible*, edited by George A. Buttrick et al., vol. 4, pp. 767–957. Nashville: Abingdon Press, 1955.

McKane, William. *Proverbs: A New Approach*. The Old Testament Library. Philadelphia: Westminster Press, 1970. Part I contains a comprehensive study of the wisdom movement in ancient Egypt, Babylon, and Assyria; part II offers a definitive commentary on Proverbs.

Scott, R. B. Y. *Proverbs, Ecclesiastes: Introduction, Translation, and Notes*. The Anchor Bible, vol. 18. Garden City, N.Y.: Doubleday, 1965. Its brief treatment of ancient Near Eastern wisdom is outstanding and its commentary on Proverbs and Ecclesiastes cogent.

Whybray, R. N. *Wisdom in Proverbs: The Concept of Wisdom in Proverbs 1–9*. Studies in Biblical Theology, no. 45. London: SCM Press, 1965. Pb. Takes account of the influential prototypes in Egyptian wisdom.

Ecclesiastes

Gordis, Robert. *Koheleth—The Man and His World: A Study of Ecclesiastes.* 1951. Reprint. 3d ed. New York: Schocken Books, 1968. Pb. A brilliant commentary with a vigorous translation of the biblical text.

Rankin, O. S. "Introduction and Exegesis to Ecclesiastes." In *The Interpreter's Bible,* edited by George A. Buttrick et al., vol. 5, pp. 3–88. Nashville: Abingdon Press, 1956. A first-rate treatment.

Scott, R. B. Y. *Proverbs, Ecclesiastes: Introduction, Translation, and Notes.* The Anchor Bible, vol. 18. Garden City, N.Y.: Doubleday, 1965.

The Song of Songs

Gordis, Robert. *The Song of Songs: A Study, Modern Translation and Commentary.* New York: Jewish Theological Seminary of America, 1954.

Meek, Theophile J. "Introduction and Exegesis to the Song of Songs." In *The Interpreter's Bible,* edited by George A. Buttrick et al., vol. 5, pp. 91–148. Nashville: Abingdon Press, 1956. A very able treatment.

Rowley, H. H. "The Interpretation of the Song of Songs." In Rowley, *The Servant of the Lord and Other Essays on the Old Testament,* pp. 197–245. Rev. ed. Oxford: Basil Blackwell, 1965.

Job

Crook, Margaret B. *The Cruel God: Job's Search for the Meaning of Suffering.* Boston: Beacon Press, 1959. A penetrating literary analysis of the Book of Job.

Gordis, Robert. *The Book of God and Man: A Study of Job.* Chicago: University of Chicago Press, 1965. Its great sensitivity to the message of the Book of Job and its literary expression make this one of the best Job studies available.

Hone, Ralph E., ed. *The Voice out of the Whirlwind: The Book of Job.* San Francisco: Chandler Publishing Co., 1960. Pb. An excellent anthology of sermons, essays, and contemporary adaptations of the biblical classic.

Pope, Marvin H. *Job: Introduction, Translation, and Notes,* 3d ed. The Anchor Bible, vol. 15. Garden City, N.Y.: Doubleday, 1973. The translation and notes offer many valuable insights.

Snaith, Norman H. *The Book of Job: Its Origin and Purpose.* Studies in Biblical Theology, 2d series, no. 11. London: SCM Press, 1968. Pb.

Terrien, Samuel L. "Introduction and Exegesis to Job." In *The Interpreter's Bible,* edited by George A. Buttrick et al., vol. 3, pp. 877–1198. Nashville: Abingdon Press, 1954. A superb study.

————. *Job: Poet of Existence.* Indianapolis: Bobbs-Merrill, 1958. A helpful treatment for the general reader.

Chapter 21. Israel and the World at the Close of the Old Testament Era

Esther, Ruth, and Jonah

Anderson, Bernhard W. "Introduction and Exegesis to Esther." In *The Interpreter's Bible,* edited by George A. Buttrick et al., vol. 3, pp. 823–874. Nashville: Abingdon Press, 1954.

Burrows, Millar. "The Literary Category of the Book of Jonah." In *Translating and Understanding the Old Testament,* edited by H. T. Frank and W. L. Reed, pp. 80–107. Nashville: Abingdon Press, 1970.

Hals, Ronald M. *The Theology of the Book of Ruth.* Philadelphia: Fortress Press, Facet Books, 1969. Pb.

Moore, Carey A. *Esther: Introduction, Translation, and Notes.* The Anchor Bible, vol. 7B. Garden City, N.Y.: Doubleday, 1971.

Rowley, H. H. "The Marriage of Ruth." In Rowley, *The Servant of the Lord and Other Essays on the Old Testament,* pp. 171–194. Rev. ed. Oxford: Basil Blackwell, 1965.

Smart, James D. "Introduction and Exegesis to Jonah." In *The Interpreter's Bible,* edited by George A. Buttrick et al., vol. 6, pp. 871–894. Nashville: Abingdon Press, 1956.

Smith, Louise P. "Introduction and Exegesis to Ruth." In *The Interpreter's Bible,* edited by George A. Buttrick et al., vol. 2, pp. 829–852. Nashville: Abingdon Press, 1953.

Apocalyptic Literature and Daniel

Frost, Stanley B. "Apocalyptic and History." In *The Bible in Modern Scholarship,* edited by J. Philip Hyatt, pp. 98–113. Nashville: Abingdon Press, 1965.
————. *Old Testament Apocalyptic.* London: Epworth Press, 1952.

Funk, Robert W., ed. *Apocalypticism.* New York: Herder & Herder, 1969. Pb. A series of nine articles by leading contemporary scholars in the field.

Hanson, Paul D. "Old Testament Apocalyptic Reexamined." *Interpretation* 25 (1971): 454–479.

Jeffery, Arthur. "Introduction and Exegesis to Daniel." In *The Interpreter's Bible,* edited by George A. Buttrick et al., vol. 6, pp. 341–549. Nashville: Abingdon Press, 1956.

Mowinckel, Sigmund. *He That Cometh.* Translated by G. W. Anderson. Nashville: Abingdon Press, 1954. A masterful treatment of Hebrew eschatology and messianism.

Porteous, Norman W. *Daniel: A Commentary.* The Old Testament Library. Philadelphia: Westminster Press, 1965.

Rowley, H. H. *The Relevance of Apocalyptic: A Study of Jewish and Christian Apocalypses from Daniel to the Revelation.* Rev. ed. New York: Association Press, 1963.

Russell, D. S. *The Method and Message of Jewish Apocalyptic.* The Old Testament Library. Philadelphia: Westminster Press, 1964. A clear and comprehensive treatment of apocalyptic texts from 200 B.C. to A.D. 100.

Intertestamental Studies and the Qumran Scrolls

Brockington, L. H. *A Critical Introduction to the Apocrypha.* London: Duckworth Press, 1961.

Burrows, Millar. *The Dead Sea Scrolls.* New York: Viking Press, 1955. An extremely careful, detailed presentation accompanied by responsible translations of select Qumran texts.
————. *More Light on the Dead Sea Scrolls.* New York: Viking Press, 1958. A rich supplement to the preceding work.

Charles, Robert H., ed. *The Apocrypha and Pseudepigrapha of the Old Testament in English.* 2 vols. New York: Oxford University Press, 1913. An old but standard edition of the text with introduction and notes.

Cross, Frank M., Jr. *The Ancient Library of Qumran and Modern Biblical Studies.* 1958. Reprint. Rev. ed. Garden City, N.Y.: Doubleday, Anchor Books, 1961. Pb. An extraordinarily good study of the Dead Sea Scrolls and the sectarian commmunity that wrote and preserved them.

Foerster, Werner. *From the Exile to Christ: A Historical Introduction to Palestinian Judaism.* Translated by Gordon E. Harris. Philadelphia: Fortress Press, 1964.

Gaster, Theodor H. *The Dead Sea Scriptures.* Rev. ed. Garden City, N.Y.: Doubleday, Anchor Books, 1964. Pb. An idiomatic translation accompanied by a helpful introduction and critical notes.

Milik, Jósef T. *Ten Years of Discovery in the Wilderness of Judaea.* Translated by John Strugnell. Studies in Biblical Theology, no. 26. London: SCM Press, 1959. Pb. An extremely useful introduction to the Dead Sea Scrolls.

Pfeiffer, Robert H. *History of New Testament Times, with an Introduction to the Apocrypha.* New York: Harper & Row, 1949.

Ringgren, Helmer. *The Faith of Qumran: Theology of the Dead Sea Scrolls.* Translated by Emilie T. Sander. Philadelphia: Fortress Press, 1963. Pb.

Sanders, James A. "The Dead Sea Scrolls—A Quarter Century of Study." *The Biblical Archaeologist* 36 (1973): 110–148.

Vermès, Geza. *The Dead Sea Scrolls in English.* Baltimore: Penguin Books, 1962. Pb. An outstanding introduction to the history, structure, beliefs, and practices of the Qumran sectarians, accompanied by quite readable translations.

AUTHOR
INDEX

SUBJECT INDEX